Fragile Resistance

Fragile Resistance

Social Transformation in Iran from 1500 to the Revolution

John Foran

Westview Press

BOULDER • SAN FRANCISCO • OXFORD

Published in 1993 in the United States of America by Westview Press, Inc., 5500 Central Avenue, Boulder, Colorado 80301-2877, and in the United Kingdom by Westview Press, 36 Lonsdale Road, Summertown, Oxford OX2 7EW

Library of Congress Cataloging-in-Publication Data
Foran, John.
   Fragile Resistance : social transformation in Iran from 1500 to
the Revolution / John Foran.
      p.   cm.
   Includes bibliographical references and index.
   ISBN 0-8133-8478-8
   1. Iran—Social conditions.   2. Social change.   I. Title.
HN670.2.A8F67   1993
306'.0955—dc20

92-36456
CIP

Printed and bound in the United States of America

10   9   8   7   6   5   4   3   2   1

The system is bad, and those who suffer from it naturally hate the persons who administer it; and to this feeling, destructive of all the social ties between the governors and the governed, we may, in a great degree, attribute the recurrence of those internal troubles, which have for so long a period exposed Persia to a succession of civil wars and revolutions.

—John Malcolm, *The History of Persia*
(1829)

* * *

And hold fast, all of you together, to the cable of God, and do not separate. And remember Allah's favor unto you: how ye were enemies and He made friendship between your hearts so that ye became as brothers by His grace; and how ye were upon the brink of an abyss of fire, and He did save you from it.

—the Qur'an, surah 111, verse 103, in
Mohammed Marmaduke Pickthall, *The Meaning of the Glorious Koran*

Contents

Social Structure and Social Change in Iran:
    Substantive Results, *410*
Comparative Dimensions and Methodological
    Considerations, *414*
Theories: Findings, Refinements, *416*
Notes, *419*

Tables and Diagrams

Acknowledgments

It is a pleasure to thank the many people who contributed to the writing and producing of this book, my first. The list begins with important intellectual advisors and mentors of my graduate student days at UC Santa Barbara and Berkeley, where this work first took shape: Richard Appelbaum, Dick Flacks, Ira Lapidus, Tom Gold, and Vicki Bonnell. All shaped my thinking about issues of history, sociology, theory, method, and craftspersonship. I should also like to thank several teachers of Persian, especially Jaleh Pirnazar, Faridun Badre'i, Hamid Algar, and Javad Rassaf, who helped me master to some degree this beautiful and challenging tongue. At a later point in the revision process, I sought the feedback of a number of outstanding scholars in the field of Iranian studies, each of whom commented on one or more chapters. They are Janet Afary, Reza Afshari, Mangol Bayat, Farideh Farhi, Willem Floor, Amir Hassanpour, Leonard Helfgott, Homa Katouzian, Nikki Keddie, Rudi Matthee, Mansoor Moaddel, Val Moghadam, Misagh Parsa, and James Reid. Their generous readings helped me avoid a number of errors and added numerous provocative insights and (in some cases!) needed encouragement. To all of them I am grateful, as I am to the many "teachers" whose works grace the notes of this book. Despite all our disagreements, it is a pleasure to be part of such a community of scholars and individuals.

Other thanks are due to various institutions and journals. Research was supported by the University of California at Berkeley and at Santa Barbara for trips to archives and living expenses at various points between 1980 and 1992. The *International Journal of Middle East Studies, Review, Iranian Studies, Theory and Society* and *Humanity and Society* have all agreed to the use of versions of parts of articles that appeared in their pages. These include: "An Historical-Sociological Framework for the Study of Long-Term Transformations in the Third World," pp. 330-349 in *Humanity and Society*, volume 16, number 3 (August 1992), which forms the basis for some of the ideas developed in chapter one; "The Modes of Production Approach to Seventeenth-Century Iran," pp. 345-363 in *International Journal of Middle East Studies*, volume 20, number 3 (August 1988), part of which is used in chapter two; "The Making of an External Arena: Iran's Place in the World-System, 1500-1722," pp. 71-119 in *Review* (Journal of the Fernand Braudel Center for the Study of Economies, Historical Systems, and Civilizations), volume 12, number 1 (Winter 1989), parts of which have found their way into chapters two and three; "The Long Fall of the Safavid Dynasty: Moving Beyond the Standard Views," pp. 281-304 in *International Journal of Middle East Studies*, volume 24, number 2 (May 1992), parts of which are incorporated in chapter three; "The Concept of Dependent Development as a Key to the Political Economy of Qajar Iran (1800-1925)," pp. 5-56 in *Iranian Studies*, volume 22, numbers 2-3 (1989), which is an earlier version of chapter four; and "The Strengths and Weaknesses of Iran's Populist Alliance: A Class Analysis of the Constitutional Revolution of 1905-1911," pp. 795-823 in *Theory and Society*, volume 20, number 6 (December 1991), which informs the interpretation of part of chapter five.

Other thanks are due to Princeton University Press, which permitted the use of quotations and a map from Ervand Abrahamian, *Iran Between Two Revolutions* (1982); Cambridge University Press, for quotations from Edward G. Browne, *The Persian Revolution of 1906-1909* (1910), as well as two tables, one from Bert Fragner's contribution to *The Cambridge History of Iran*, volume 6, *The Timurid and Safavid Periods* (1986), and one from Moojan Momen, "The Social Basis of the Babi Upheavals in Iran (1848-53)," which appeared in the *International Journal of Middle East Studies*, volume 15, number 2 (May 1983); and the University of Texas Press, for permission to use a table from Eric J. Hooglund, *Land and Revolution in Iran, 1960-1980* (1982).

This book could not have been produced without the editorial encouragement of Amos Zubrow and Barbara Ellington of Westview Press, the typesetting expertise and skills of Eric Dahlin of the Humanities Computing Facility at UCSB, Julie Seko at Westview, and Bob Nideffer, my research assistant, who did much of the actual typesetting, including the tables and diagrams (if you're reading this, he succeeded!).

A final debt, of a different nature, is owed to friends and family who have supported me along the way: my sister and parents, Bruce Bortin, Alex Green, Little Man, Chris Appy, Nina Sharif, Lois West, Anita Weiss, Karla Hackstaff, Leigh Kienker, Greg Turner, and most recently, Kum-Kum Bhavnani. This book is collectively dedicated to you all.

John Foran

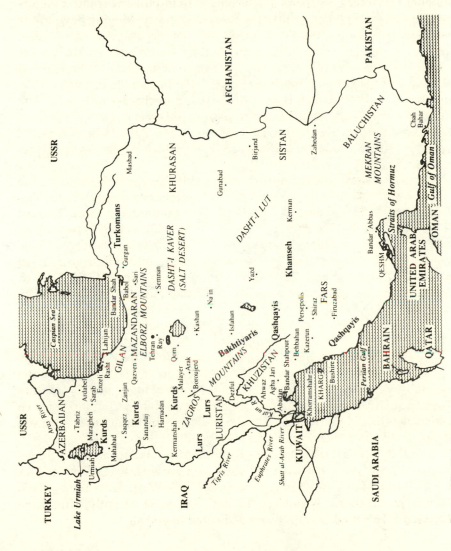

Iran and Its Neighbors

Introduction

This book analyzes the processes of social transformation in Iran from the height of the country's power in the sixteenth and seventeenth centuries under the Safavid dynasty to the aftermath of the startling revolution that overthrew the Pahlavi monarchy in 1979. It addresses two intertwined central issues: how to conceptualize a changing social structure and how to account for the periodic social explosions that have marked the process of change with a record of social movements unmatched in the modern era. Social structure is approached through the prisms of class, ethnicity, and gender, with an emphasis on the first of these dimensions but attention to the salience of the others as well. A key problem that must be carefully explored hinges on the degree to which Iran's relations with the West (in the broad sense of the more industrialized nations) have, over a period of several centuries, shaped state, society, and economy in a distinct direction of *dependence* on the world economy and on politics in the most powerful countries. The interaction of these external pressures with the pre-existing and ongoing structure of Iranian society has yielded ever more complex social relations over time. The resulting tensions have been reflected in a series of protests, rebellions, revolutions, separatist movements, and coups that originated in the *resistance* of multiple sectors of the population to the realities of foreign control and state autocracy. The puzzle is to explain under what conditions such opposition has been possible and why its liberating potential has been so repeatedly frustrated. The roots of an answer, I shall argue, lie in the complexity of Iranian social structure, the political cultures of opposition articulated by the groups involved, and the internal and external balances of power. The story is one of frequently courageous efforts to change the unequal structures of power, and just as frequent collapses of these fragile projects. It is an enormously inspiring, if ultimately tragic, tale.

I attempt to go beyond the current state of the literature in several ways, aiming to find two somewhat different audiences in addition to the generally interested reader. For Iran specialists in all the disciplines, and especially historians, this study offers a synthesis of many sources over a longer period of time than is usually attempted, and it does this in the spirit of a theoretical reinterpretation of Iranian society and its experience of social change. Controversies in the literature over the nature of long-term changes in that society and the composition of recurrent social movements are engaged, sifted through, and recast in light of the sociologies of development and social change. For social scientists with an interest in theoretical issues, I hope to establish the relevance of a particular form of dependency theory for a non-Latin American case and to put Iran on the "theoretical map" in terms of both Wallersteinian world-systems theory and neo-Marxist modes of production analysis. I also propose a model of Third World social revolutions and suggest the utility of a dialectical approach to social change, one that brings together economic, political, and cultural levels of analysis. My overarching intent then is dual: to gain insight into the subject of social change in an enormously important single case on the one hand and to suggest, on the other, approaches to a range of unresolved theoretical problems in the study of development and social movements. I leave it to the reader to judge the value of this enterprise.

1

A Framework for the Study of Social Change in Iran

La théorie c'est bon, mais ça n'empêche pas d'exister. . . . theory is all very well, but that does not prevent the facts from existing.
—A saying of Jean Martin Charcot, repeated by Sigmund
Freud, in Peter Gay, *Freud. A Life for Our Time*

Introduction

The vast social movements that swept across Iran in 1978-79 and toppled the shah from power through an unprecedented combination of massive unarmed street demonstrations, a determined general strike lasting several months, and a brief guerrilla uprising in February 1979 have by now generated a considerable body of social science literature. Both long-time researchers and a growing group of younger scholars have been struggling to come to terms with the causes, form, and timing of the revolution, as well as its subsequent, rather tortuous course and uncertain long-term prospects. Controversies have arisen as to whether (or to what degree) the upheaval has been an "Islamic" or a "social" revolution (or even merely a political change of elites); the nature of the roles played by workers, the urban poor, students, ulama (Muslim scholars and preachers), "old" and "new" middle classes of bazaar merchants and professionals, and long-suffering rural groups; the weight to be accorded outside factors such as the dependent aspects of Iran's relations with the West; and finally, the relative importance of political and economic versus religious and ideological variables as central explanatory dimensions. Yet the dramatic events on which these questions are focused constitute only the most recent instance in a very long and rich history of Iranian social change, political and economic development and underdevelopment, and social movements. And an understanding of the events and resolution of the debates they have touched off is best not dissociated from a careful analysis of earlier cases of social transformation from the sixteenth century onward. This is because the social forces that emerged to make the revolution, and the various religious and political cultures and experiences that sustained them, cannot be adequately understood without extensive historical and sociological knowledge of the patterning of social change that has occurred and re-curred in Iran.

This study focuses on the changing nature of Iran's society, state, and economy over a time-frame of almost five centuries and is intended to shed light on the principal features of the process of social change in Iran during this period, which has taken the general shape of a long transformation from pre-capitalist forms of social and economic organization to a more capitalist (though underdeveloped) system of production, punctuated along the way by social and political movements of several kinds, including tribal civil wars, urban rebellions, attempted social revolutions, and successful coups d'état. The term "social change" in this study thus covers both gradual social structural transformations and sudden, shorter-term social movements aimed at changing the distribution of power in society, as well as the complex relations between these processes and movements.

There is a widespread belief within Iran that foreigners have influenced and indeed brought about every major change that has occurred in the country's modern history. Some Western historians and social scientists reject the dependency argument in part because it can be so easily tied to this seemingly "crude" popular mythology. The present study does not argue that "the West caused everything" but rather that a complex and changing set of relations between internal and external actors and struc-tures accounts in large part for the particular forms that social change has historically assumed in Iran. One goal is to set this record straight through a realistic assessment of the major role that the West has played in Iran, properly balanced by a full appreciation of the equally leading roles played by Iranian actors, who were by no means simple victims of or passive witnesses to their own history. On the whole, the result is to suggest the rational kernel underlying the popular perception, however distorted and exaggerated it may seem apart from this larger context. A second goal is to show how and why this process of dependency has generated such deter-mined movements of resistance, by specifying the contradictions inherent in the Iranian mixture of dependent development and state autocracy, and the material and ideal resources available to various sectors of society that enabled rebellion. The fragile bases of these social movements, and the factors accounting for their transformational limits, constitute a final analytic puzzle. To clarify these propositions theoretically, various strands in the sociologies of development and social change must be critically fashioned into a broad and flexible framework of analysis.

Theories of Underdevelopment

Developed primarily by Latin American social scientists in the mid- and late-1960s, dependency theory constituted a powerful critique of the then prevailing North American modernization perspective. Its most sophisticated practitioners are F. H. Cardoso and Enzo Faletto in *Dependency and Development in Latin America*.[1] The preliminary definition they offer of dependency stresses the limits to development: "From the economic point of view a system is dependent when the accumulation and expansion of capital cannot find its essential dynamic component inside the system."[2] This formulation points to an international economic system within which the various nations occupy positions of qualitatively different levels of power and influence. At the *center* the advanced industrial nations control the key sectors of technology and finance, an advantage that shapes the special forms taken by industrialization in the *periphery*. It should be stressed that "development" under these circumstances is not impossible: Economic growth, as measured by increased trade, rise in GNP, and industrialization, may occur in some Third World countries at certain points in time. However, these gains are generally accompanied by significant negative consequences, such as inflation, unemployment, health problems, inadequate housing and education, and the like. It is thus a *dependent development*, meaning growth within limits, advances for a minority of the population, and suffering for the majority. This seminal idea, with its coequal attention to a form of "progress" and its disadvantages, should be contrasted with earlier, simplistic versions of the dependency thesis such as that of André Gunder Frank, who felt that no development could occur under conditions of dependency on the advanced industrial capitalist powers, unless the links were disrupted during exceptional periods of worldwide economic crisis or war. Cardoso and Faletto's interpretation of the dependency paradigm, with its attention to the interaction between external structures and patterns of internal development, constitutes a major breakthrough in the sociological literature and provides the overarching framework within which to locate the historical experiences of development and social change in Iran. Its explanatory power is considerably enhanced, however, by consideration of two related bodies of literature—world-system theory and modes of production analysis.

World-system theory, associated above all with the work of historical sociologist Immanuel Wallerstein on the emergence of a capitalist world economy in sixteenth-century Europe,[3] moves the analytic focus to the level of a global framework, within which a dependent or underdeveloped capitalism is the lot of most Third World nations. The modern world-system, dominated in Wallerstein's view by a capitalist mode of production (within which to be sure various "modes of labor control"—debt bondage, share-cropping, tenancy, and eventually mostly wage labor—were and are found), can be divided into a *core* of strong states taking the greatest part of the international economic surplus, a *periphery* of weak states that is super-exploited, and a *semiperiphery* consisting of a stratum of states exploited by the core yet able to profit vis-à-vis the periphery. In the sixteenth and seventeenth centuries, there was also a relatively independent *external arena* of countries and regions that were not yet an integral part of the European world-economy and which subsequently were incorporated into the pe-riphery.[4] Wallerstein's assessment of the Third World's development pros-pects is pessimistic: Some changes can occur between the core and the semiperiphery (such as the decline of Spain in the seventeenth century) or between the semiperiphery and the periphery (consider the rise of South Korea and Taiwan by the 1980s). This is especially possible during periods of world-wide economic crisis and change. The system as a whole, how-ever—divided into core, semiperiphery, and periphery—does not change much, at least under capitalism.

The world-system model has provoked a number of important criticisms since its original formulation in 1974.[5] The most telling of these have to do with the definition of capitalism as an economic system only in terms of its exchange side, that is, markets and trade between countries; there is no equivalent importance attached to production relations and national inter-nal class structures. A second, related problem is the characterization of the entire world-economy today as capitalist, with no theoretical space for pre-capitalist or socialist modes of production within individual societies. These criticisms are justified but may be remedied by consideration of modes of production analysis. The irrefutable strengths of the world-system perspective, however, include the need to take the world-economy as the essential background framework for the study of Third World social change and its demonstration of the utility of examining long historical periods and the various economic phases and cycles in the history of the capitalist world-economy as the framework in which dependency and development take place. In the present case study, the emerging world-system will be treated as the broadest parameter out of which emanated the external forces to which the Iranian state, economy, and society increasingly had to re-spond after the sixteenth century. One of the tasks of the analysis will be to map Iran's developmental process in terms of quantitative and qualitative integration into the world-system, first as part of the external arena in the seventeenth and eighteenth centuries, then as a peripheral supplier of raw materials in the nineteenth to mid-twentieth centuries, and, finally, its wavering status between the periphery and semiperiphery in the post-World War II period.

Another solution to some of the difficulties of employing the dependency paradigm, this time moving the analytic focus down to the inner workings of the Third World society and economy, has come in the form of modes of production analysis, also introduced in the 1970s.[6] Useful definitions of the key terms "social formation" and "mode of production" can be found in the work of English sociologist John Taylor. He points out that "social formation" is the Marxist equivalent of "society as a whole," that is, actual historical societies in their political, economic, and socio-cultural aspects. The second key term, "mode of production," is a somewhat more abstract structure, consisting of the combination of two elements: (1) a labor process (or several), referring to the way(s) in which raw materials and other inputs are worked up into products for consumption and/or exchange (that is, the setting and manner in which human beings produce their goods, for example in a factory or a small shop, on a plantation or a plot of their own, and the techniques they use to do this), and (2) a system of relations of production, denoting the social arrangement (usually in distinct social classes) through which the various labor processes are structured to yield an economic surplus (this refers to the patterns of ownership and control of the key means of production—such things as land, tools, raw materials, and machinery). Each different mode of production—self-sufficient village communes, nomadic pastoralism, slavery, feudalism, capitalism, socialism, and others—is characterized by its own combination of labor process and relations of production.[7]

The most important insight of modes of production analysis for our purposes is its conceptualization of fundamental societal transitions such as that from feudalism to capitalism in the West, or the introduction of capitalism into pre-capitalist Third World social formations, in terms of "the articulation of two modes of production, one of which establishes its dominance over the other . . . not as a static given, but as a *process*, that is to say a combat between the two modes of production, with the confrontations and alliances essentially between the *classes* which these modes of production define."[8] The present study will argue that the Iranian social formation in the sixteenth century already consisted of a combination of more than one mode of production and that from the seventeenth century onwards, through contact with the expanding European capitalist mode of production, can be usefully analyzed as a transitional social formation in which *several* modes of production combined to produce a complex and changing class structure. Mapping the gradual changes in this social structure over time will help us account for the types of development and social change that have occurred, both as a measure of structural transformation and a basis for assessing class coalitions on either side of social movements.

It is important to note that class is not the only organizing principle of stratification systems. The impact of a decade or more of recent scholarship in the fields of feminist and ethnic studies has challenged neo- and post-Marxist analyses by drawing attention to the coequal significance of race/ethnicity and gender in understanding social structure. This study explores some of the interactions among ethnicity, gender, and class in Iranian social structure and social movements, both conceptually (more so for class, which is a disputed concept in Middle East studies) and empirically (to try to integrate the best insights of secondary scholarship on Iranian women and ethnic groups). It has only been possible to scratch the surface here, and much further work needs to be done in these respects.

A central theoretical contribution of the present study is to indicate a solution to the problem of integrating the world-system and modes of production perspectives on underdevelopment into the dependency paradigm.[9] Diagram 1.1 indicates the contribution of each of the major perspectives to a synthetic framework of analysis. This diagram suggests that the dependency paradigm provides the overarching framework for the consideration of the relation between the most encompassing external and the basic internal units of analysis—that is, the relation of the world economy to the social classes of a given Third World country. World-system theory is necessary to explain the external impulses that emanate downward from the core to the social formations of the periphery, while modes of production analysis is needed for an account of how these external pressures are mediated within the social formation itself. *None* of these perspectives taken alone can adequately account for the causes of long-term social transformation. Rather, all three levels of analysis must be investigated and related to provide an adequate account of Third World social change and develop-

DIAGRAM 1.1 Levels of Articulation

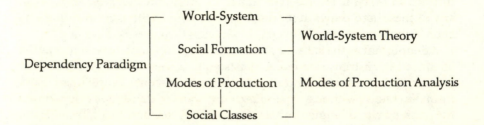

ment over long periods of time. My essential point in all of this is to show that the three approaches complement one another, and secondly, that the modes of production and world-system perspectives are of great help for the problem of how to concretely *apply* the dependency paradigm.

State and Culture in Social Change

In moving from the sociology of development's emphasis on long-term processes of social transformation to the concerns of the literature on social movements with more explosive processes of change, we must consider two more key concepts—the state and cultures of opposition. Theda Skocpol has attempted to bring the state to center stage in the study of social revolutions by treating it as an autonomous structure, i.e., "a structure with a logic and interests of its own not necessarily equivalent to, or fused with, the interests of the dominant class in society or the full set of member groups in the polity."[10] For Skocpol, the state is not just an arena of struggle among classes, it is a macro-structure, whose basis is a "set of administrative, policing, and military organizations headed, and more or less well coordinated by, an executive authority."[11] Thus it has the latitude to occasionally act against, or at cross purposes with, dominant classes in competing for society's resources (taxes), keeping internal order, and competing internationally with other states. It is this attention to the specifically political level of domination exercised by the state (and party system if there is one) that makes Skocpol's analysis so instructive, as she makes the point that Marxists would do well to supplement analyses of class relations and economic development with a look at "the strength and structure of old-regime states and the relations of state organizations to class structures."[12] This is not to deny the existence of a long-standing and rich Marxist debate on the nature of the state, among, for example, Ralph Miliband, Nicos Poulantzas, Fred Block, and perhaps especially Göran Therborn, whose distinction between state apparatus and state power mirrors Skocpol's combination of an institutional and class relational approach to the state. But she goes further than any of these, and draws more resolutely on a non-Marxist tradition going back to de Tocqueville, Weber, and Hintze.

As important as the state has been in the development experiences of the advanced industrial economies, it has proven even more central to the process of dependent development in the periphery. In twentieth-century Iran, the state's position as recipient and disburser of vast oil revenues and the shah's role as originator of economic policies and virtually the sole political arbiter, added to the characteristic weakness of the industrial capitalist class, combined to give the state a preeminent role in all economic, social, and political development. We shall see that this has been the case historically too, as the Iranian state from the Safavid dynasty's height in the seventeenth century onward has aspired (sometimes more successfully, often less) to be a centralizing monarchy with a great concentration of political, military, and economic power. This role has involved the state intimately in most cases of social change in Iran, whether as initiator of socio-economic transformations or the target of political and social movements aimed at reform and revolution. Here too the interplay of state and ethnicity can be traced by examining the central tribal dimension of state formation and dissolution from 1500 to 1800, and the gradual severing of this connection by the Qajars and especially the Pahlavis thereafter. In the Iranian case—and probably in other monarchies—the state was exceptionally conflated with the king and court, and thus forms part of the ruling class. This may explain how the state could be such a solid target of social movements: It was easily identified with the shah (who may be hated), and it had a clear class content *without* implicating all the rest of the dominant classes, who were therefore not obliged to rush to defend it. This makes its overthrow easier, but leaves serious unresolved problems of power for after the change of regime.

Although recent theoretical perspectives have refined the sensitivity with which the dependency paradigm can analyze the economic processes involved in Third World transitions to dependent capitalism, they have had very little to offer for the study of the political and especially the cultural dimensions of these social formations. Phenomena such as religion, nationalism, pre-capitalist and non-capitalist cultural forms and the orientations of social movements remain undertheorized by both world-system theory and modes of production analysis, as well as in Skocpol's work on the state and social revolutions.[13] In part, this was a negative reaction by the advocates of the political economy approaches of the 1970s to the great emphasis placed on cultural values sometimes taken out of context by the modernization perspective in the 1950s and 1960s. Today, more sophisticated approaches to culture, offered in the work of such diverse thinkers as Clifford Geertz, Raymond Williams, Marshall Sahlins, Michel Foucault, Pierre Bourdieu, James Scott, and Stuart Hall need to be reintegrated into discussions of social change. It is beyond the scope of the present study to assess each of these writers' contributions, but one way forward might be to work with a notion of *political cultures* of resistance and legitimation in the Third World.

Dependence on foreign capital and internal state domination of society impinge on and are in turn shaped by the material and spiritual well-being of the various groups and social classes who must "live" them within the everyday context of their own cultural and political orientations. "Political culture" is a complex amalgam of explicit ideological formulations, folk

DIAGRAM 1.2   Levels of Analysis

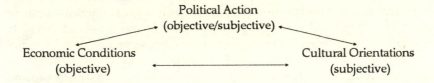

Political Action
(objective/subjective)

Economic Conditions
(objective)

Cultural Orientations
(subjective)

culture and traditions, and practical orientations to actual circumstances and situations. Each aspect must be analyzed (where data exist) and taken into account to explain how and why specific groups conclude that opposition to authority is feasible. Such political cultures of resistance may be a crucial intervening moment between "objective" relations of exploitation and oppression, and political action (see Diagram 1.2). Cultural resources, along with the important organizational, material, and other capacities identified by resource mobilization theory, thereby claim our attention as relevant to the making of history by social actors. Not only cultures of opposition and resistance embodied in social movements, but the cultures of legitimation deployed by ruling groups, need to be considered potentially autonomous areas of investigation with causal significance in their own right. In the Iranian case, we will examine the various political cultures present in each of the major periods, as meaningful elements both of social stability and for change.[14]

A Synthetic Framework

Rather than a general theory of world-wide development and social change, then, we have a paradigm, or framework, that requires the researcher to pursue the historically specific processes of class formation and articulation of modes of production in a given social formation under the pressures of particular conjunctures of the world economy. One way to picture the overall model of social change advanced in this chapter is suggested in Diagram 1.3. Here the original diagram of long-term social transformation (social change 1) is expanded to include a second route to social transformation that may follow from it. Once a dependent pattern of development is generated by the encounter of the world-system and the internal modes of production in a Third World society, a repressive state is often (though not always) needed to contain the social forces unleashed by this process. Such a state (and the foreign powers that sustain it) will almost

DIAGRAM 1.3   A Model of Social Change

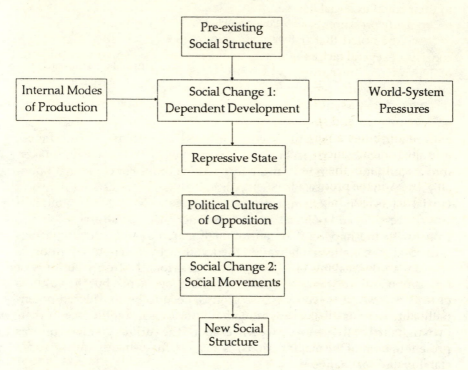

inevitably generate oppositions that draw on the available political cultures of society. Under certain conditions (which must be historically specified, and are examined for the case of Iran in several periods later in this study) social movements for change will then arise. If these are vigorous enough, even when defeated, a new social structure may eventually be consolidated. This provides a second path to social structural transformation.

Two important findings of this study may be prefigured here. First, *all* major national-level social movements in Iran in the period studied here have reposed on broad social bases, which I have termed *populist* alliances.[15] Dependent development has generated diverse sets of grievances among social classes, which have articulated distinctive cultures of resistance. Multi-class and typically urban (for reasons noted later), populist coalitions have stood the best chance for success in touching off vigorous movements for change. The outcomes of such movements present a second key empirical insight: Most have encountered tremendous difficulty in bringing about social transformation on a wide scale. Once a measure of power has been won, such populist coalitions have tended to fragment into their constituent elements, as sharp disputes have arisen over the shape of the new order. The ultimate *fragility* of these movements is traced in each case to their complex social bases, differing ideological visions, and the persistent outside pressures exacerbating these.

It will be noted that this is a complex, conjunctural causal model.[16] It consists of several factors—world-system, modes of production, situations of dependency, the nature of the state, and political cultures—which must evolve in particular combinations for social movements to get under way. It is arrived at by a synthesis of existing theories in the fields of the sociology of development and social change, each of which, though insufficient in itself, contributes a part to the overall model. Theoretical work must be informed and advanced by solid case studies that are not imprisoned inside one or another of the several perspectives, but rather draw intelligently on all of them, in the process providing a basis for the evaluation of their merits and deficiencies. Only in this way can our knowledge of the Third World be improved, and it is only through such case studies that a better integration of the theories can be effected.

In the present study the logic of comparative-historical method will be used in two ways, both of which will help evaluate the manner in which key theoretical variables affected the social structures and processes of change in each of several historical periods. First, for each period to be studied, the relevant comparisons of Iran with other countries will be briefly considered. Second, and most important, the logic of comparative-historical method will be turned upon a single historically and culturally significant country, Iran, which experienced social change in several historical epoches. Thus, although the greater portion of the study is devoted to instances of social transformation from the late nineteenth century to the present, the early chapters on social change in the sixteenth to eighteenth centuries will help us grasp the degree to which the key variables indeed set the parameters of change in Iran in a particular manner by the twentieth century. And careful comparisons of various periods within the twentieth century will highlight the importance of a nuanced and detailed consideration of the changing forms and circumstances of such concepts as dependency, cultures of opposition, and the state, and their impact on the types of social movements that Iranians have engaged in. The result is a sort of qualitative time-series analysis comparing instances of social change in a single case with itself at different points in time.[17]

The chapters that follow take up this abstract framework on Third World social change and seek to bring it to life in the concrete case of a vitally important Middle Eastern country. The aim is to challenge Iran specialists to enter into theoretical debates on the patterns and causes of social change in the country that interests them, and simultaneously to spur sociologists of development and social change to rethink the connections among isolated and/or competing paradigms by focussing on a richly complex case study. Though the risks of satisfying neither constituency are many, the promise of a better integration of theory and data than is usually attained in these literatures may justify the attempt.

Notes

1. Fernando Henrique Cardoso and Enzo Faletto, *Dependency and Development in Latin America*, translated by Marjory Mattingly Urquidi (Berkeley: University of California Press, 1979). The book was originally written between 1965 and 1967, and published as *Dependencia y desarrollo en America Latina* (Siglo Veintiuno Editores, SA, 1971). The English edition is an expanded and amended version of the 1971 text. Possibly because of this publishing history, many English-language discussions of dependency theory in the 1970s did not assess this work, which provides cogent answers to a number of the criticisms posed at that time (and since).

2. Ibid., xx.

3. The key works are the three published volumes of a projected four-volume history of the modern world-system, and a collection of essays on current theoretical and political problems. See Immanuel Wallerstein, *The Modern World-System I, II* and *III* (Cambridge: Cambridge University Press, 1974, 1980, and 1989), and *The Capitalist World Economy. Selected Essays* (Cambridge: Cambridge University Press, 1979).

4. Iran under the Safavid dynasty belongs precisely in this external arena and I shall explore the utility of this concept in chapters two and three.

5. Insightful critiques include Theda Skocpol, "Wallerstein's World Capitalist System: A Theoretical and Historical Critique," pp. 1075-1090 in *The American Journal of Sociology*, volume 82, number 5 (1977); Robert Brenner, "The Origins of Capitalist Development: a Critique of Neo-Smithian Marxism," pp. 25-92 in *New Left Review*, number 104 (July-August 1977); Maurice Zeitlin, *The Civil Wars in Chile (or the bourgeois revolutions that never were)* (Princeton: Princeton University Press, 1984), 217-37; Aidan Foster-Carter, "The Modes of Production Controversy," pp. 47-77 in *New Left Review*, number 107 (January-February 1978); and Daniel Garst, "Wallerstein and his Critics," pp. 469-495 in *Theory and Society*, volume 14 (1985). A summary of the various criticisms is offered by Daniel Chirot and Thomas D. Hall, "World-System Theory," pp. 81-106 in *The Annual Review of Sociology*, volume 8 (1982).

6. The *locus classicus* of modes of production analysis lies in the "new economic anthropology" of French Marxists such as Maurice Godelier, Emmanuel Terray, and most notably, Pierre-Philippe Rey, according to Foster-Carter, "The Modes of Production Controversy." These writers developed the insights of French structuralist philosophers and social scientists of the 1960s such as Etienne Balibar, Louis Althusser, and Nicos Poulantzas.

7. John G. Taylor, *From Modernization to Modes of Production. A Critique of the Sociologies of Development and Underdevelopment* (London: Macmillan, 1979), 106.

8. Pierre-Philippe Rey, *Les Alliances de classes: Sur l'articulation des modes de production*, followed by *Materialisme historique et luttes de classes* (Paris: François Maspero, 1973), 15, translated and cited by Foster-Carter, "The Modes of Production Controversy," 56.

9. That this integration still needs to be effected is illustrated by the lack of explicit recognition accorded by the major writers in the principal perspectives to the other bodies of literature. Thus Cardoso and Faletto, even in their 1979 edition, have no references to modes of production analysis or Wallerstein's world-system, while Wallerstein, even in the 1989 third volume of *The Modern World-System* makes no mention of dependency or multiple modes of

production. Taylor's *From Modernization to Modes of Production* devotes a whole chapter to a critique of "the sociology of underdevelopment" which singles out texts by Paul Baran, Paul Sweezy, and André Gunder Frank but has nothing to say about the further elaboration of underdevelopment theory, nor about its close relations, the dependency and world-system perspectives. I have worked out this synthesis in "An Historical-Sociological Framework for the Study of Long-Term Transformations in the Third World," pp. 330-349 in *Humanity and Society*, volume 16, number 3 (August 1992).

10. Theda Skocpol, *States and Social Revolutions. A Comparative Analysis of France, Russia, and China* (Cambridge: Cambridge University Press, 1979), 27.

11. Ibid., 29.

12. Ibid., 34-35.

13. Emphasis on the "objective relationships" at the expense of the "interests, outlooks and ideologies of particular actors" is perhaps the major weakness of Skocpol's approach for understanding social change in the Third World today and in historical perspective, for it seems plausible that specific political and religious cultures may play a decisive role in influencing the causes, processes, and outcomes of social revolutions. Skocpol has recognized this to a certain degree, in her own discussion of, interestingly enough, Iran: "Rentier State and Shi'a Islam in the Iranian Revolution," pp. 265-284 in *Theory and Society*, volume 11, number 3 (May 1982).

14. These remarks draw on a diverse body of literature, including A. Sivanandan, "Imperialism in the Silicon Age," pp. 24-42 in *Monthly Review* (July-August 1980), 25; James C. Scott, *Domination and the Arts of Resistance. Hidden Transcripts* (New Haven and London: Yale University Press, 1990); Craig Jackson Calhoun, "The Radicalism of Tradition: Community Strength or Venerable Disguise and Borrowed Language?" pp. 886-914 in *American Journal of Sociology*, volume 88, number 5 (March 1983); Farideh Farhi, *States and Urban-Based Revolutions: Iran and Nicaragua* (Urbana and Chicago: University of Illinois Press, 1990), chapter 4; William H. Sewell, Jr., "Ideologies and Social Revolutions: Reflections on the French Case," pp. 57-85 in *Journal of Modern History*, volume 57, number 1 (March 1985); and Theda Skocpol, "Cultural Idioms and Political Ideologies in the Revolutionary Reconstruction of State Power: A Rejoinder to Sewell," pp. 86-96 in *Journal of Modern History*, volume 57, number 1 (March 1985).

15. I am not here using the term populist in its more restricted Latin American sense/context, where it tends to denote mass *authoritarian* movements. I am instead appropriating it more positively to indicate the widely popular bases of Iranian social movements, and to try to capture the flavor of the political aspirations unleashed—always against internal tyranny and external influence, often democratic and participatory, involving the people as a whole. That such movements have particular limitations will be an important part of the argument.

16. The best historical macrosociology searches for such causal complexity. See the discussion by Charles D. Ragin, *The Comparative Method. Moving Beyond Qualitative and Quantitative Strategies* (Berkeley and Los Angeles: University of California Press, 1987), 23-25.

17. See ibid., 23, 72.

Social Structure and Social Change in Pre-Capitalist Iran, 1500-1800

"What Iran was, in terms of fundamental social structure, before the West intruded, and what Iranian society has become today—these are questions for which even a careful student may not find satisfactory answers."[1] These words, only slightly less true today than when they were written in 1955, pose the question which will preoccupy us in part one of this study. The researcher today has the very real advantage of more than thirty years of efforts by historians working on this or that aspect of Iranian society in the sixteenth to eighteenth centuries, but the task remains one of trying to assemble a vast puzzle with some pieces missing and others that do not quite fit. The goal of this first part is to uncover the basic configurations of the Iranian social formation in the period of the Safavid dynasty, which ruled Iran from 1501 to 1722, and then to relate this social structure to the social changes that occurred during and after its reign, through the tumultuous changes of dynasty that punctuated the eighteenth century, until another durable and yet fundamentally weaker dynasty—the Qajars—seized power on the threshold of the nineteenth century.

Chapter two is devoted to a careful empirical and theoretical analysis of Safavid social structure at the height of the dynasty's power, circa 1630, just after the death of Iran's most illustrious ruler, Shah 'Abbas. After a brief introduction on the history of the Safavids' rise to power around 1500 and the most important developments through the 1620s, the heart of the chapter examines the nature of the Safavid state and the three interrelated economic sectors of the Iranian social formation—tribal pastoralists, sedentary agriculturalists, and urban guild producers. I argue here that pre-capitalist Iran cannot be understood in terms of any single mode of production, whether feudal or Asiatic, but was much more complex than this. Nor can Iran's newly emerging links with the nascent European capitalist world-economy from 1500 to 1630 be seen as constituting a dependent relationship:

Iran in this period was a powerful world-empire in its own right. The empirical picture is rounded out with a look at some key ideological and political aspects of the seventeenth-century Iranian social formation, focusing in particular on the legitimation efforts of the monarchy and its relations with the religious specialists of the ulama, but also introducing such cultural and value orientations of the social orders below as can be discerned.

Chapter three then turns our attention to the contours of social change in Iran from 1500 to 1800. Here the varieties of social change under the Safavids are first identified, and then the dynastic revolutions of the eighteenth century are assessed in terms of the internal dynamics of the social formation and the role played by the growth in commercial relations with the West during the Safavid period. A second axis of explanation revolves around the weight to be accorded to all of these structural factors vis-à-vis the notoriously inadequate personal characteristics of the later Safavid shahs. Only by raising such questions in light of careful examination of Iranian society on its own terms during this early period of Iran's relations with the West can a baseline be established against which later instances of social change will disclose a richer significance.

Note

1. Nikki Keddie, "The Impact of the West on Iranian Social History," Ph.D. dissertation, Department of History, University of California, Berkeley (1955), 1. Nikki Keddie would subsequently go on to become one of the foremost historians of Iran writing in the English language.

2

The Iranian Social Formation,
circa 1630

Comment peut-on être Persan?

—Montesquieu, *Lettres Persanes*, 1721

"How can one be Persian?" The present chapter attempts to sketch the broad outlines of a basis for answering Montesquieu's question through a look at the social structure of Iran in the first half of the seventeenth century. The date, "circa 1630," derives its significance from the fact that the Safavid empire is generally acknowledged to have reached its peak under Shah 'Abbas, who ruled Iran from 1587 to 1629. This society, like any other, possessed tendencies for change, such that it was not the same as the Safavid Iran of the early sixteenth or early eighteenth centuries. Thus a preliminary task is to briefly trace its evolution to the 1620s, the period that concerns us here.

Though its continuity with earlier dynasties that ruled Iran has been remarked by historians, the rise of the Safavid dynasty to power can also be considered the opening moment in the modern history of Iran for two important reasons. First, before 1501, and since the seventh-century Arab conquest, "Iran" had generally either been part of some larger empire or had been splintered into a number of smaller dynasties; second, the proclamation of Shi'ism as the new state religion came over the next century to sharply demarcate Iran from its Sunni neighbors, the Ottoman, Mughal, and Uzbek empires in Turkey and the Arab world, India, and Central Asia.

The Safavids' name and origin have been traced to an early fourteenth-century Sufi *shaykh* (holy man) named Safi, who established a base in the northwestern town of Ardabil. His successors gradually attracted significant numbers of devoted followers, especially from among the Turkoman tribes of the Anatolian plateau to the west. Around 1450 the Safavid order was transformed into a militant social movement based on the semidivinization of its leader, Junaid, who mobilized his tribal disciples for religious conquest (*ghaza*) against Christians in Trabzon on the Black Sea and in Georgia. When Junaid fell in battle, this policy was continued by his son Haidar who died fighting in the Caucasus in 1488. Haidar's troops became known as the *qizilbash* (Ottoman Turkish for "red head") because of the scarlet headgear they wore, with twelve triangular pieces representing the twelve Shi'i imams. Haidar's young son Isma'il went into hiding, waiting for a propitious moment to make his bid for political power in northwest Iran.[1]

The 1490s were marked by severe succession struggles in the Aq Quyunlu dynasty, the Turkoman tribal confederation which had held much of Iran since 1468. The contemporary chronicler Qazvini describes the deterioration of the political situation: "when the Aq-qoyunlu state became weak, confusion reigned in the Iranian lands . . . and plunder and raids became prominent, and the affairs of the world lost order and organization."[2] Isma'il's tribal army defeated the Aq Quyunlu several times in 1500 and 1501. This opened the way for Isma'il's coronation at Tabriz, the capital, and the declaration of Ithna 'Ashari (Twelver) Shi'ism as state religion in the summer of 1501. Conversion of most of the Iranian population from Sunnism to Shi'ism would take place over the coming decades.[3]

Between 1503 and 1510 the Safavid tribal army scored a series of victories that consolidated its territorial hold over virtually all of Iran, from the Caspian provinces in the north to the Persian Gulf in the south, and from Baghdad in the west to Khurasan in the east. This phenomenal expansion was checked only by the power of the Ottoman army in 1514. This defeat undermined Isma'il's claims to invincibility, but neither could the Ottomans build upon it to annex Iran or roll back Shi'ism, and thus the setback paradoxically consolidated Iran as Safavid and Shi'i. Isma'il never personally took the field again until his death in 1524 and the bases of Safavid legitimacy shifted perceptibly away from theocracy to ordinary bureaucratic-monarchic conceptions.[4]

When Isma'il's son Tahmasp became shah in 1524 he was only ten years old. The qizilbash chiefs of the Turkoman clans engaged in what amounted to a civil war from 1524 to 1533, during which several attempts were made to seize control of the state. This internal chaos was compounded by invasions in the east by the Uzbeks and then by the Ottomans in the west in 1534-35.[5] Tahmasp assumed effective control of the state about this time and consolidated the Safavid empire by ruling altogether for over fifty years until 1576. He attempted to balance the powerful tribes, dividing key provincial governorships among them and also using native Iranian bureaucratic families in his administration, as well as introducing Georgian prisoners into a few state positions. His foreign policy was basically defensive: He moved the capital from Tabriz to Qazvin to make it less accessible to Ottoman encroachments and signed a peace treaty with the Ottomans at Amasya in 1555.

Tahmasp's death in 1576 touched off another period of instability, with the qizilbash chiefs lining up behind different contenders for the throne. After twelve years of internal intrigues and foreign invasions, Tahmasp's seventeen-year-old grandson 'Abbas came to the throne in October 1588. With the help of a new standing army of 40,000 men, 'Abbas embarked on a reconquest of Iran. By 1597 most of the provinces under Safavid authority were secured from internal strife and unruly provincial governors had been removed from office. Turning next to the external enemy, 'Abbas retook Khurasan from the Uzbeks in 1598 and regained Tabriz and Georgia in campaigns against the Ottomans between 1605 and 1607. Thus, by 1607 he had established his sovereignty over virtually all of Iran as defined by the 1555 treaty of Amasya.[6]

'Abbas had a profound impact on the major institutions of Iranian society. In the administration, as well as the army, a new and delicate balance was sought among Turkoman tribal qizilbash, Persian bureaucrats, and the new military and civilian personnel drawn from the Caucasus. Tribal power was systematically reduced in a variety of ways, all of which contributed to the absolutist power of the monarchy. In 1597/98 the capital was moved from Qazvin to Isfahan and massive public works were undertaken there. Diplomatic and commercial contacts with Europe were steadily expanded during the course of 'Abbas's reign and a functional peace was eventually established on all frontiers and remained intact for the rest of the seventeenth century, greatly stimulating internal and external trade and security and enriching the state. On the eve of 'Abbas's death in 1629, the Iranian social formation had reached a zenith of power and solidity.

The Nature of the State

The Safavid state can be analyzed in terms of three key institutions—the central bureaucracy, the provincial government, and the army.[7] The shah and his court constituted the apex of a substantial bureaucracy centered in Isfahan, the capital. The highest officials of the court included the Grand Vazir (chief minister), the senior military officers, the state treasurer, and the chief religious official (*sadr*). Behind this topmost stratum came numerous other posts and offices—court physicians, astrologers, palace eunuchs, aides-de-camp, pages, artists, and skilled artisans. The administrative bureaucracy included clerks and financial agents attached to each of the several branches and departments of the government—court, workshops, tax collection, military units. Eskandar Beg Monshi estimates that in 1576 there were some 1,500 officials at the court, each with five to fifty attendants and subordinates, making more than 20,000 people (not including their families) in all. The personnel of the central bureaucracy were paid partly in cash and fees for their services, but mostly in drafts against some portion of the land taxes paid to the state by the peasantry.[8]

Shah 'Abbas presided over a state administration consisting of three major ethnic groups—long-standing Persian notable families who occupied many of the civilian posts in the bureaucracy, the Safavids' original Turkoman tribal base which provided military commanders and provincial governors, and a new elite consisting of Christian Georgians, Armenians, and Circassians. The latter had been taken prisoner on campaigns in the Caucasus and brought up at court as Muslims who in the early seventeenth century came increasingly to furnish top civilian and military personnel. Comparisons of the lists of high-ranking amirs (military commanders) in 1576 and 1629 show a dramatic change from primarily Turkoman qizilbash chiefs to about 40 percent qizilbash, 40 percent non-qizilbash tribal chiefs (mostly Kurds and Lurs), and 20 percent *ghulams* (royal slaves) from the Caucasus.[9] There are a number of instances recorded of people rising from obscure or lower class origins to positions of influence, as well as sudden declines in fortune for those who incurred the shah's wrath, and this was probably the main form of social mobility in the Safavid period. Chardin notes that the shah made appointments without regard to birth, asserting there was no hereditary nobility in Iran and going so far as to claim that consideration was given only to one's office, merit, and wealth.[10]

The provincial government also came to be shared out among the several components of the elite. The governors "sent to the capital only limited sums of cash, but considerable stocks (*barkhana*) of local products for the King's table and raw materials for the royal workshops."[11] In addition, each governor was required to provide a stipulated number of troops to the royal army in time of war. In return, "the governors enjoyed great freedom. They collected local revenue and used local resources for assignments to their subordinates among whom there were considerable contingents of armed attendants."[12] Chardin tells us that the provincial governors were appointed for life and their sons could succeed them, but data from both the sixteenth and later seventeenth centuries suggest that the shahs exercised their prerogative to remove these "hereditary" governors with some regularity.[13] Chardin writes too that each governor was assisted and observed by administrators who reported to and depended on the shah.[14] Falling from grace often entailed not just dismissal from one's post, but the confiscation of much of one's wealth. Under a strong monarch such as 'Abbas, then, the central authority held the upper hand vis-à-vis its erstwhile provincial representatives, though at other times both before and after his reign, the governors ruled far more autonomously.

The third great institution of the Safavid state—the army—was also by the seventeenth century an amalgam of the older tribal elite from the provinces and a newer state-controlled force created by 'Abbas. The tribal army that brought the Safavids to power had shown its limitations in the 1514 defeat by the Ottomans at Chaldiran and its disadvantages from the viewpoint of the monarchy in the civil war periods of 1524-33 and 1576-88. The key reforms—bringing in peasants, Iranian tribesmen, and convert soldiers and equipping them with modern fire-arms on a large scale—took place in 1598-1600, and were one of the cornerstones of 'Abbas's successful centralization policies aimed at containing tribal power. The actual number of troops varied, but was on the order of 70,000 to 100,000 men, over half of them tribal cavalry. Like the civilian bureaucracy, both officers and rank and file soldiers were paid with drafts on the land revenue; an ordinary trooper would receive between five and twelve *tuman*s a year (the tuman was a unit of account, worth 10,000 dinars or 3.3 pounds sterling in the seventeenth century).[15]

The total revenues and expenditures of the Iranian state for an average year in the seventeenth century are very difficult (and indeed perhaps impossible) to estimate accurately. The *Tadhkirat al-muluk* suggests cash revenues of 783,862 tumans against expenditures of 625,320 tumans for the 1720s. This does not include the vast amounts of goods that came in kind to the court, nor does it include labor service, especially in construction, that the shah could demand free of charge from certain guilds. Nevertheless these figures tally remarkably well with Chardin's estimate of the 1670s that the shah's income came to 700,000 tumans (32 million French livres) and expenditures came to about 744,000 tumans (34 million livres). The overwhelming majority—roughly 83 percent—of the Safavid state's income derived from various forms of the land tax. On the expenditures side, the military soaked up some 66.5 percent according to Minorsky (including governors' salaries), or 38.2 percent according to Chardin. Much of the rest was spent on the upkeep of the court (50 percent, according to Chardin), leaving only 11.8 percent to be spent rather more productively on the royal workshops.[16]

The net annual balance of revenues and expenditures in the 1722 data was positive to the amount of some 160,000 tumans (about 20 percent of total income), worth over 500,000 pounds sterling in the seventeenth century. This money would be hoarded in the royal treasury, which contained immense amounts of wealth for the times. Chardin judged the Safavid shah the "richest monarch in the universe," as rich himself as "all the rest of his kingdom."[17] A very rough comparison of Safavid Iran with the great European kingdoms of the period is made in Table 2.1. The Iranian state income compares very evenly with England's, though not too well with the heavy taxing machinery of absolutist France (the amount of the shah's income in

TABLE 2.1   England, France, and Iran, circa 1700

Country	Population	State Income
Iran	6-10 million	goods in kind + 800,000 tumans
England	6 million	3.8 million pounds sterling = 930,000 tumans
France	19 million	577 million francs = 12,800,000 tumans

Source: based on Minorsky, *Tadhkirat al-muluk,* 186.
Note: figures for Iran's population are very approximate, as for England's net income. Chardin observes that the shah's income consisted more in goods than in cash (*Voyages,* V, 415).

goods in kind would however redress part of the balance).[18] It is interesting that only one-third of English revenue came from the land tax in 1700; much more derived from customs and trade duties. England invested this income wisely in a vast fleet which would later bring it rich dividends. If the table could be projected back to the 1620s, Iran at its peak under Shah 'Abbas would probably have compared even more favorably with the European kingdoms; conversely, the latter may be supposed to have made greater gains in the course of the seventeenth century than did Iran, whose relative (and perhaps absolute) stagnation will be examined in chapter three.

By virtue of its control over the key state institutions—central bureaucracy, provincial government, and army—the seventeenth-century Iranian ruling class of shah, high bureaucrats, military commanders, and provincial governors *was* the state. Taken as a whole this state had a powerful grip on the rest of society and commanded much of the country's overall surplus, but equally importantly this ruling class was internally much divided into the multiple interests which composed it. In the sixteenth century tribal military leaders had twice fought among themselves for paramount positions in Iranian society and there was a more or less constant tension between largely Persian-speaking bureaucratic families and the Turkoman qizilbash tribal elite over control of the state. After 1590 'Abbas redistributed the balance of power away from the tribes by bringing in a counterweight of Georgians and other Caucasian captives and their descendants as high civil and military personnel. By creating a standing army directly under royal control 'Abbas exercised firm mastery over the provincial governors, none of whom could henceforth presume to challenge the central authority. The Safavid state, then, evolved under 'Abbas toward a more fully-fledged absolutism which worked most smoothly when its fractious internal elements were kept in check by a powerful monarchy. It was then well placed to tax the surplus production of the economic bases on which it rested.

The Economic Structure of Iran in the 1620s

The total population of seventeenth-century Iran is rather difficult to know, as estimates (which for this period are really guesses) vary from about five or six million to a high of ten million, a figure equal to the population as recently as about 1900.[19] These six to ten million inhabitants were distributed among three interrelated economic sectors as tribal pastoralists, rural peasants, and urban craft producers. Again, estimates of the proportions in each sector range widely. The tribal population has for example been estimated at anywhere from one-quarter to one-half the total population.[20] (Note too that some tribes, such as most of the Kurds, were sedentary and in economic terms, classifiable as peasants.) Taking averages of both total inhabitants and these proportions—say 33 to 40 percent of eight million people—the tribal population may be very roughly guessed to have encompassed some three million people in the seventeenth century (other combinations of these figures range from a possible low of one and a half million to a possible high of five million). It is to this large group in the population that we turn first in an empirical analysis of the Safavid economy.

The Pastoral Nomadic Sector

From about 1000 A.D. onward, the Iranian social formation witnessed periodic co-existence and conflict between two political economies—that of settled Iranian villagers and townspeople, and that of successive migrations into Iran of Turkic pastoralists from Central Asia. The Turkoman tribes who brought the Safavids to power are traditionally held to have been seven in number—the Ustajlu, Shamlu, Takkalu, Rumlu, Zul-qadar, Afshar, and Qajar. The term qizilbash was later extended to certain non-Turkoman supporters of the Safavids, including Central Asian, Iranian, and Kurdish elements. The entire list of tribal pastoralists living in seventeenth-century Iran would be even longer, as Helfgott observes, "Forming over two hundred separate tribal units divided into five major ethnic groupings (Turkoman, Iranian, Kurdish, Arab, and Baluch)."[21] These tribal entities were composed of groups of various sizes, with a number of families making up a clan, a number of clans forming a tribe, and in some cases at the top of the system a number of tribes joining into a tribal confederation. In Safavid times this largest unit was most commonly referred to as an *uymaq*—a fluid grouping of tribal military supporters, each ranked with respect to its relative prestige and influence within the Safavid state.

Pastoralism constituted the economic basis of nomadic tribal life. As nomads, originally from Central Asia and later Anatolia and the Caucasus, gradually settled into niches in the Iranian ecosystems (whose mountains and plains differed from the steppes), they adapted distinct semi-annual migration paths between secure campgrounds in the mountains and winter sites on the plains, entering into more predictable and less warlike relations with the settled population.[22] The main economic activities of pastoralists were aimed, as in all natural economies, at satisfying basic needs, through grazing herds, engaging in handicraft production, and sometimes in limited amounts of cultivation: "Most generally, the basic means of production of nomad society consist of various kinds of herd animals and the land on which these herds pasture. Herds provide the society with its most important needs: food (meat, cheese, butter, yogurt), drink (milk), clothing (wool, hides), fuel (dung), means of transport (horses, camels, oxen, donkeys) and paraphernalia."[23] The pasture land that supported these herds was held collectively by the tribe and not "owned" in terms of legally established boundaries, but allocated by chieftains who might give the usufruct rights to a campsite to the same or a different family in each successive year. Herds were privately held by individual extended families, as were their produce, tools, implements, dwellings, and precious items such as jewelry. Production for use within the tribe was supplemented by production for exchange with the village peasants or townspeople along the migration routes; this generally involved simple bartering of animals and their by-products for agricultural and handicraft goods. For this reason many historians and anthropologists speak of "interdependence" between tribespeople and the settled population and this is one good example of how different modes of production may coexist, yet interact. The extent of these interactions was necessarily limited by the natural economy of pastoralism and the limits to accumulation posed by the need for mobility.

In terms of internal stratification and appropriation of the surplus, tribes relied on a hierarchic structure.[24] The qizilbash chieftains (or amirs) at the top of the tribal system—undoubtedly few in number—were the greatest flockowners and employed most of the dependent laborers at the bottom, who served as shepherds and prepared the various animal products—food, clothing, and shelter—for them. At the highest levels a handful of them participated in non-pastoral economic systems by virtue of holding posts in the military and provincial government. The many independent flockowners who constituted the core of the tribal economy would acknowledge lower-level chiefs or elders (*rish safids*, literally "white beards") as mediators of such crucial issues as allocation of specific pasture lands along the migration routes to each family in the camp group. Below these came tribespeople who owned either too few flocks to support themselves, or none at all, and who lived by tending the flocks of others. Keddie notes the key economic roles performed by women: "Tribal women, like most peasant women, are not veiled, and they usually do more physical labor then the men, including spinning, weaving, cooking, agriculture, and animal husbandry."[25] It is difficult to know much about the conditions of life of the ordinary tribesperson. On the one hand the limits of a natural economy must have asserted themselves to keep most people at a virtual subsistence level, and this was compounded by the extraction of surplus upwards to the chiefs and state. The major form of surplus extraction occurred through a tax on animals, apparently ranging from one-seventh (or even lower) to one-third. On the other hand, at either rate, a smaller percentage of surplus was extracted from the armed tribesperson than from the peasant, and in Bausani's judgment, "Few nomads, and then only the most wretched, ever settled on the land, and the condition of the settled peasant farmer was definitely worse than that of the nomad."[26]

In almost another world altogether were the tribal elite who occupied high military and provincial posts, and, to a lesser extent, those tribesmen who served in the army. When appointed by the state to a governorship or other administrative position, chiefs of tribes came into control over non-tribal sources of wealth, particularly in their capacity as the fiscal taxing agents and legitimate military power of the provincial bureaucracy. The tribal domination of the larger economy had however reached its peak by the end of the sixteenth century, when tribal chiefs lost much of their hegemony to Shah 'Abbas.[27] The tribal troops who served in the provincial armies and on the major campaigns of the shah may in some senses have had a higher standard of living than the average pastoralist. Tribal troops were far more likely to be involved in a money economy and likely had rather different chances of social mobility than the ordinary shepherd. Of course, only a fairly small proportion of all tribesmen could have served in the army (up to 60,000 out of our estimated three million tribespeople), while most of the booty taken went to the chiefs.

The tribal political economy of seventeenth-century Iran thus exhibited tensions between its traditional egalitarianism and growing stratification at several levels. At the economic base, tribal members were connected to one another and to their immediate chiefs through the necessary self-reliance and "rough democracy" of pastoral life.[28] Taxes were perhaps not extortionate and tribeswomen participated fully in economic life and were more equal with their male counterparts than elsewhere in Iranian society. These communal characteristics were nevertheless overlaid by the vast gap separating the high-level chieftains from the mass of ordinary tribespeople, a gap that spanned nearly the entire spectrum of the social structure, from the elite handful of provincial governors to the near subsistence-level existence of the basic producers. A further significant split arose at the base between tribesmen living as pastoralists and those who served in the cavalry units of the Safavid army. There was thus objectively much inequality between chiefs and tribespeople, but cutting across this were the customary relations that permitted the extraction of some surplus from the pastoralists and the ties of tribal loyalty that made the troops a reliable instrument for extracting an even greater surplus from the peasantry.

The Peasant Sector

As with the tribal population, the proportion and absolute numbers of Iran's settled peasantry in the Safavid era can only be very roughly estimated. Accepting the previous estimate of the tribal sector as 35 to 40 percent of the total and putting the urban population at 10 to 15 percent, the peasantry would then be the largest single component of the population, with 45 to 55 percent of the total. Out of a population ranging from six to ten million people, then, high and low estimates yield 2,700,000 to 5,000,000 peasants, with the figure of four million being perhaps a reasonable guess.

The basic agricultural unit was the village, of which there were thousands scattered and clustered around the country. Lambton and other scholars infer that the original village settlements were communal, but landlords had come to be superimposed on them from very early times.[29] Minorsky, following Chardin, notes four categories of land in Safavid Iran: the shah's own domains, the state lands, religious endowments, and private holdings.[30] The crown lands (*khassa*) were the personal estates of the ruler and his family.[31] In Safavid times, as before, the somewhat ambiguous concept of the shah as theoretical owner of all land was maintained, with various internal contradictions and compromises in reality. In practice the extent of crown lands fluctuated in the Safavid period: Most of the very valuable land around Isfahan belonged to the shahs, and the silk-producing regions of Gilan and Mazandaran passed to 'Abbas in 1595-96. A second major category of land was state land (*mamalik* or *divani*), whose taxes and rent were due to the public treasury, not to the shah's own account (though the distinction was often rather blurred).[32] Shortage of cash in the underlying natural economy forced all dynasties from the Abbasids in the tenth century onwards to use state lands for the payment of the bureaucracy and military. The key form that state land assumed in Safavid times was the *tiyul*: the revenue on large grants of state land to the provincial governors (often tribal chieftains) in their own outlying areas, and revenues on lands designated to pay the salaries of specific offices in the army and bureaucracy. Tiyuls were not (in theory) hereditary; though a tiyul might pass from father to son, this was contingent on the shah's decision. The tiyul-holder possessed considerable authority over the peasants on the property, such as the right to assess fines, but this too derived, at least in theory, from the shah. State lands, according to Chardin, "contain the greatest part of the kingdom."[33]

The third major category of land in Safavid Iran after the royal domain and state lands was vaqf land. Vaqf was an endowment of land for some charitable or religious purpose. It thus supported some specified group of beneficiaries—often judges, high-ranking ulama, or sayyids (descendants of the Prophet Muhammad), and also an administrator (*mutavalli*) who took a tithe from the income. It could not be sold or transferred and generally paid no taxes to the state. Private landowners, including Shah 'Abbas, often converted their property into a vaqf to avoid the ill effects of taxes, Islamic inheritance laws, and confiscation, appointing their families as administrators. Ulama, too, were often appointed as administrators of vaqf land, thus increasing their economic leverage in the rural sector. As a result of these processes, by the end of 'Abbas's reign, vaqf land had come to be quite extensive, second probably only to tiyul grants.[34]

The final type of land-holding in the seventeenth century was private estates. Though it is impossible to know the extent to which individuals owned land unconditionally, there is ample evidence in the contemporary sources that they in fact did so.[35] The fact that many individuals constituted "their" land into vaqf endowments implies that they had the right to so alienate their possessions but also that they felt insecure in the first place. A recurrent pattern in Iranian dynastic history is the gradual growth of private holdings out of land grants; Banani notes that "In the Safavid era the gamut was run once again."[36] In later Safavid times this privatization process seems to have overtaken both land held as tiyul and vaqf lands. Two general conclusions may be drawn: The line between "usufruct" and "possession" was blurred, and the tendency to cross it probably increased in the later seventeenth century as the strong central control of 'Abbas gradually weakened. For the period focussed on here—the 1620s—the principal categories of land-holding were first, state lands assigned as tiyuls, followed by the royal domains and vaqfs, with private property probably last in extent.

Turning to the issue of surplus appropriation, it can be observed that most lands, whether the shah's, private property, or vaqf, were rented to peasants according to a crop-sharing arrangement of some kind. Paying a certain sum per amount of land used was usually only done around large towns and even so was not particularly common.[37] In practice, the proportion actually paid as rent varied to a considerable degree. Chardin writes of the shareholding contract (whether with the shah or a private landlord) that water and fertilizer may be provided by either party; after the harvest seed for the next year is removed, then usually the owner takes one-third, though sometimes one-fourth to one-half of the crop. The landlord, whether the shah or a private individual, thus took the bulk of the agricultural produce of Iran; if the harvest was poor, the peasantry would face the prospect of starvation (though the chronicles record cases of tax relief, successful protests, and means of recourse against excessive taxation). Peasants were also subjected to other taxes and some labor services, but these almost certainly did not equal, qualitatively or quantitatively, the regular unpaid labor service on the feudal estates of Europe.[38]

In assessing the overall condition of Iran's peasantry in the seventeenth century, one is confronted by an evident sparseness of data. The most celebrated contemporary judgment on the peasants' lot is offered by Chardin, given here in full:

> They live well enough, and I can assure you that there are incomparably more wretched peasants in the most fertile regions of Europe. I have seen Persian peasant women everywhere with silver necklaces, and great silver rings on their hands and feet, with chains from neck to navel, laced with silver pieces and sometimes gold. One sees children likewise adorned, with coral necklaces. Both men and women are well dressed, with shoes; they are well furnished with utensils and furniture; but on the other hand (*en échange de ces aises*), they are exposed to the insults (*injures*), and sometimes the blows, of the king's men and vazirs, when they do not give quickly enough what is demanded, which holds for the men only; as for the women, they are respected throughout the Orient and they are never touched.[39]

To fill in the picture of women offered here, Keddie notes that peasant women, like tribal women, also participated in hard physical work and often went unveiled and that they had important roles in the making of carpets and textiles.[40] Chardin had travelled in both the northwest and from Isfahan south to the Gulf more than once and he says in general: "Those [of the lowest rank] of Persia, either in the countryside, or in the cities, are well-nourished and well-clothed, having all the necessary utensils, even though they work not half as hard as our [poorest subjects in France]."[41] B. G. Martin discusses a document from 1592 that refers to the "scattered peasants" of Kasaj in Khalkhal, who

> may well have fled their homes to escape the extortion of officials, or heavy taxation. . . . The existence of a horde of officials whose chief duty was to press the multifarious taxes, dues, tolls and other exactions out of the miserable peasants and crop-sharers must have signified widespread poverty and subsistence-level existence in the countryside.[42]

The peasantry undoubtedly did live on the margins of subsistence, providing as they did the bulk of the state's revenues and supporting the army, much of the ulama, and private landowners. It is difficult to disagree with Bausani's conclusion: "the condition of the settled peasant farmer was definitely worse than that of the nomad."[43] On the other hand, general economic prosperity in the seventeenth century and strong central control most likely made the period one of relatively less exploitation for the peasantry as a whole, which Chardin's eyewitness accounts tend to substantiate.

The Urban Sector

As with the tribal and peasant sectors, the extent of the Iranian urban population in the seventeenth century can be estimated only very crudely. According to Minorsky, the English traveller Sir Thomas Herbert, "who probably echoes some official tradition of 'Abbas I's time, [estimates] there were in Persia 90 walled towns and about 40,000 villages."[44] Available contemporary European estimates indicate the population of most of the chief urban places totalled perhaps one million people, with anywhere from a quarter to a half of them concentrated in Isfahan, the capital.[45] This gives an urban population of at least 10 to 15 percent in the seventeenth century.

The primary locus and real underpinning of the seventeenth-century urban economy were the guilds. Craft producers engaged in the manufacture of metalwork, textiles, hardware, and the like, as well as trades ranging from building, baking, and transport to entertainments of all sorts. They varied enormously in size, status, and wealth, but possessed a degree of self-administration within the broader context of firm Safavid control of urban government as a whole.[46] The important issue of the tax assessment was a matter of negotiation between the headmen of the guilds and the official representing the government. The headman then apportioned the total tax among the members of his guild, each paying according to his amount of business. Certain guilds performed unpaid labor services for the court. The overall picture that emerges suggests a tension between an unusually strong central government whose mechanisms of control included some influence over prices and quality with an ability to tax and demand significant labor services, and guilds with a measure of internal autonomy, against a general background of economic expansion that probably allowed all parties to benefit.[47]

Internally, there were three levels or grades of workers in a guild: apprentice (*shagird*), journeyman or pre-master (*khalifa*), and master (*ustad*). Often a craft remained in the family, with father taking on son as an apprentice, though obviously there were cases where masters took on others, or their sons were apprenticed to another craft.[48] Though the evidence is somewhat fragmentary, it can nevertheless be perceived that a graded hierarchy of petty craft producers and workers existed in Safavid Iran, from the guild masters in their own shops at the top, to skilled artisans working for wealthy patrons, to journeymen/*khalifas* who had skills but lacked the means to set up a shop and thus rented shops or space in the royal square, or worked for masters, or sold their products to artisans and traders with shops, to itinerant ambulatory skilled and unskilled labor ("street artisans") who served the poorer urban classes and perhaps outlying villages, with apprentices hoping to eventually rise as high on this scale as their acquired skills and capital resources permitted.[49]

The most important of the several types of commodity produced in Safavid times was textiles, with a great variety of raw materials and techniques. Merchants, urban and rural artisans, and the shah all seem to have had a share in the production and marketing of the many textile products which constituted the core of Iranian "manufactures" in the seventeenth century and despite the encroachment of merchants and the shah, the weavers were probably the most powerful guild in Safavid times, strong in Isfahan, Tabriz, Yazd, and Kashan, where they were able to protest unfair tax increases.[50] Other major manufactures included porcelain objects and faience tiles, high quality arms and armor, leather goods, glasswork, jewelry, dyes, paper, and soap. In the seventeenth century Iranian artisans adequately met the vast majority of the country's varied needs, excelled in a number of products on an international level (from carpets and other textiles to pottery and metalwork), lagged far behind Europe in some emerging advanced technologies (watches, armaments, printing) and were holding their own in a spirited competition with the rest of the world in the most prized mass manufactures—hand-made textiles of all types.[51]

A second major sector of the urban economy centered on the productive activities organized by the shah in the royal household. Chief among these were the thirty-odd royal workshops employing some 5,000 workers in activities ranging from the kitchen and palace services to artisanal work, with a total budget for the workshops on the order of 4-5 million livres (over 100,000 tumans), i.e. one-seventh to one-eighth of total state expenditures.[52] Artisans in the royal workshops had relatively good working conditions, wages, and benefits. There were also separate royal "manufactories" of one sort or another, involving thousands more workers in the production of textiles, carpets, and porcelain, in all making the shah by far the biggest employer of labor in Iran (even leaving out the court, bureaucracy, and army). Some of the products, especially high-quality silks and carpets, were both used at court and exported abroad to Europe and India.

A number of sources imply that the volume of commerce in Safavid Iran was relatively small, hindered by an undermonetarized economy (and conversely the large role of the agricultural sector), the difficulty of transportation, royal economic policy, and other factors.[53] Merchants nevertheless played a key role in the urban economy. They did not form permanent organizations similar to the guilds, but instead divided into more loosely affiliated groups based on their city of origin, nationality, and religion, or line of business, thus somewhat weakening their influence. Unlike the guilds, too, they paid no shop taxes, but they were subject to customs dues levied on imported goods. Iranian merchants generally dominated the internal trade of Iran and had a far more limited role in the external trade. The key intermediaries in both import and export trade in Safavid Iran proved to be members of the Armenian merchant community, formed by forced migration to Isfahan after Shah 'Abbas's 1604 campaign in the Caucasus. Working with Armenians established in the Ottoman Empire, India, and Europe, they served as privileged agents of the shah in exporting Iran's raw silk and as independent merchants in their own right.[54] Despite the wealth accumulated by individual Iranian and Armenian merchants, there do seem to have been limits to their potential for capital investment as a class. Some of these have to do with the preponderance of the royal production and commercial sector and Safavid economic policy. Beyond a certain point, merchants tended to hoard capital or invest in land. They profited by the existence of price differentials in various areas and by wholesaling; certainly there were as yet no real capitalist production units based on wage labor.[55]

The principal remaining urban groups in Safavid Iran included the ulama, the urban lower classes, women, and religious minorities. As Keddie observes, the term *ulama* is "a word inadequately rendered by 'clergy,' as their role is not to intercede between people and God, but to carry out Muslim law, education, charity, and so forth—a broader role than that of the Western clergy."[56] There are several ways to conceptualize internal differentiation among the ulama in Safavid Iran. The standard distinction is a political one between official government appointees, and popular teachers and jurists. More recently, Said Amir Arjomand has revised the split in an interesting manner, at once cultural and political-economic, discerning an estate of clerical notables from Iranian, mostly land-owning families who converted to Shi'ism under the Safavids and maintained control over clerical institutions, and a new group of Shi'i scholars imported from Arab lands, some of whom were appointed to high office while others subsisted as independent scholars.[57] The complex pattern of cooperation and competition between the two groups ended with the ascendency of the religious professionals, and the role of this struggle in the fall of the Safavid dynasty will be examined in chapter three. Finally, one can note the varied material bases of different groups within the ulama. These include the role of some as landowners and high officials (part of the ruling class); the more independent, middle to upper class position of the many ulama connected by marriage, residence, and economic function to the bazaar as well as the sayyid strata who were often petty landowners or middle-class urban groups; and finally the markedly lower-class groups of darvishes and some more economically marginal sayyids, both rural and urban.[58]

The existence of a destitute urban underclass below the poorer artisans is hinted at in the sources. Olearius says that the lower classes in Isfahan— "the Scum of the Town"—frequented the taverns (while the upper classes patronized coffee and tea houses where poets and historians held forth). There is much evidence of a demi-monde of gambling houses, opium dens, and brothels in Safavid cities. An acquaintance of Chardin's, when they passed a beggar, replied to Chardin's question of why he gave him no alms: "It's because there are no poor in our kingdom, truly reduced to begging; and this dog who shouts at us is a scoundrel who begs from laziness; look at him, he's bursting from eating."[59] Chardin judged that the poorest subjects of Iran, in the countryside or in the cities, were well enough off, well-nourished, and clothed, and worked less hard than the poor of Europe. Eskandar Beg Monshi, however, makes reference to "the poor and needy, both men and women" who lived "in most of the large cities."[60]

Of urban women generally, who crossed all class strata, the sources do not say a great deal. Most women of course engaged in productive activity in the household—cooking, cleaning, raising children, making clothing (weaving and spinning). Upper-class women on the other hand were idle and urban women were to a great extent veiled and secluded generally.[61] Writing on the nineteenth century, Keddie observes that some women obtained an education, serving others in religious, medical, and commercial capacities.[62] According to Islamic law women received one-half the inheritance that men did, although Keddie notes that this, "plus the fact that a married woman continues to hold her own property, is more favorable to women than were most Western laws before this century."[63]

A final urban group that crossed class lines comprised the main religious minorities. The merchant activities of the Christian Armenians have been discussed above; there were also numerous skilled artisans in the community. Keyvani gives a comprehensive list of the economic activities of the estimated 30-35,000 Jews of Iran, including women: "Large numbers of them were silk weavers, dyers, goldsmiths, jewellers, druggists, wine makers and wine sellers, brokers, second hand dealers, ambulatory vendors, musicians, dancers, and singers. A definite preponderance of Jews was observed in midwifery and in certain highly remunerated female occupations, e.g. brokeresses (*dallala-ha*) who carried messages and negotiated between Muslim *harim* ladies, suppliers of recipes for love potions and magic concoctions, and story-tellers."[64] On the other hand, Emerson suggests that many were poor, while others prudently gave the impression of being so; according to the early nineteenth-century historian John Malcolm, they were often poor.[65] Chardin says that the Zoroastrian community, totalling perhaps 80,000 people, lived throughout Iran, but especially at Kirman and Yazd. They were industrious and worked as agricultural laborers or textile workers, but rarely if ever as artisans or merchants. Few received an education and most were very poor.[66]

International Trade and Relations with the West through 1630

Iran has had a long history of economic, political, cultural, military, and diplomatic relations with the West going back at least to the Greek and Persian wars of the fifth century B.C., but the Dark and early Middle Ages in Europe, coupled with the rise of Islam and later the Ottoman Empire to a great extent cut off contact between Iran and the West. The kingdom's principal relations then shifted to its neighbors to the immediate west—the Ottomans—and east—the dynasties of India. The thirteenth century saw the beginning of commercial relations between Iran and the Italian city-states of Genoa and Venice, and in the fourteenth and fifteenth centuries Iranians increasingly crossed Anatolia to meet European traders in Otto-man Bursa and the ports of the eastern Mediterranean. In the fifteenth century the European silk industry underwent a great expansion, making Bursa the international market for raw silk and Iran the main source of Middle Eastern silk cultivation.[67]

The rise of a Shi'i dynasty in Iran in 1501 changed the equation dramat-ically by inaugurating a long period of hostilities or outright warfare between the Ottomans and the Safavids, especially from 1512 to 1555 and the 1580s to 1616, that severely disrupted the trade patterns of the past. The high volume "peddling trade" of small merchants managed to continue in the sixteenth century, but the wars and high peace-time tariffs cut heavily into the overland silk routes and Bursa's prominence. With the reign of 'Abbas and the beginning of the seventeenth century a new interest arose both in Iran and Europe for commercial and military alliances designed to circumvent and undermine the intervening Ottoman power. The keys to 'Abbas's project both economically and politically were the establishment in 1619 of a Safavid monopoly on Iran's valuable raw silk exports and attempts to open up alternative water routes through Russia or the Persian Gulf in addition to the longstanding overland route through Ottoman territory. 'Abbas took one-third of all silk produced in Iran as the royal share and paid the producers for the rest at fixed rates. Anyone seeking to export silk from Iran through any source but the state was required to pay high customs. The most often quoted estimate of Iran's total silk harvest is Olearius's 20,000 bales (roughly 2,000 tons); Inalcik feels that 1,000 tons would probably be a more realistic figure for the annual production of raw silk in the 1620s, of which perhaps two-thirds was exported to Europe.[68]

From Iran's point of view, raw silk was the key commodity exported, followed at a great distance by finished silk and carpets, wool, some precious stones such as turquoise, dried fruits, and tobacco. From a world-wide point of view, it was merely one commodity that fit into a much larger pattern of trade that was just emerging in the seventeenth century and whose two main products were spices from the Far East and gold and silver bullion from the Americas. To some extent these currents met in Iran, as Olearius points out: "There is not any nation in all Asia, nor indeed almost of Europe, who sends not its Merchants to Isfahan, whereof some sell by Whole-sale, and others by Retail.... [These include over 12,000 Indians and] Tartars, Turks, Jews, Armenians, Georgians, English, Dutch, French, Italians and Spaniards."[69] A more detailed look at the emergence and development of Iran's international trade with both Europe and Asia, from 1500 up to about 1630, would show the rise of new, more extensive relations with the West, ones built on reciprocity and rough equality within the embryonic European-centered world-system. Italian trade peaked by 1600 and declined thereafter due to recession and competition. The Portuguese, who tried to dominate much of Asia militarily, fell by the sword in the Gulf when Safavid troops took their island forts of Qishm and Hurmuz with English naval assistance in 1622, moving the trade to the mainland town of Gombrun, renamed Bandar 'Abbas.

The English, Dutch, and later in the seventeenth century, the French, all came to Iran primarily as traders, not belligerents. The English East India Company (EIC) entered the ambit of the Iranian economy after 1615 for two reasons: to purchase silk directly at its source and to export as many European (and Asian) commodities as possible to avoid paying in cash.[70] On both counts its success through 1630 was limited, although its accomplishment in opening up the trade should not be underestimated, for it heralded the emergence in embryo of a world-system of markets. Spanish silver came from the Americas to Europe, where the English purchased it for trade in the East and used the spices and other products (among them Iranian silk) obtained in the East to finance their silver purchases in France, Spain, and the Netherlands. The EIC profited at several points in the chain of transactions—Europe, Iran, and India. Nevertheless, this emerging new system was both fragile and still somewhat inchoate in 1629, the year of 'Abbas's death. The EIC's position in Iran was far from overwhelming—it lacked cash, its cloth was often of poor quality, the trade routes were long and uncertain. Finally, just when the English star appeared to be rising most rapidly in the mid-1620s after the victory at Hurmuz, a well-organized competitor appeared on the horizon.

The Dutch United East India Company (hereafter VOC, from its Dutch initials) fashioned a powerful combination of the Portuguese military model and the English merchant capital one. The overall project of Dutch

Asiatic trade is classically captured in a letter of 1619 from Jan Coen to the directors:

> Piece goods from Gujarat we can barter for pepper and gold on the coast of Sumatra, rials and cottons from the coast for pepper in Bantam, sandalwood, pepper and rials we can barter for Chinese goods and Chinese gold; we can extract silver from Japan with Chinese goods, piece goods from the Coromandel coast in exchange for spices, other goods and rials, rials from Arabia for spices and various other trifles—one thing leads to the other. And all of it can be done without any money from the Netherlands and with ships alone. We have the most important spices already. What is missing then? Nothing else but ships and a little water to prime the pump. Is there any other country in the world with more ships than the Netherlands? Is there a shortage of water with which to prime the pump? (By this I mean sufficient money so that the rich Asian trade may be established). Hence, gentlemen and good administrators, there is nothing to prevent the Company from acquiring the richest trade in the world.[71]

To a great extent this project was successfully carried out: By 1629 the VOC is acknowledged to have caught and surpassed the English in the new trade of the Persian Gulf. Braudel attributes Dutch success to its superior access to Spanish silver, the motor of the Asian trade.[72] To this must be added the capture of the bulk of the world spice market, which unlocked the supply of Iranian raw silk. The Dutch worked more closely with Shah 'Abbas and the local Armenian merchants than did the English, but for all this they were not one-sided victors in the new trade. In the first place the English were far from eclipsed decisively at this point. In the second, the Dutch had their problems with the Iranian authorities, while other difficulties included the inelasticity of the spice market, compounded by Dutch overproduction of pepper and competition from Indian merchants, as well as the logistical challenge of transporting raw silk from Isfahan to the Gulf and then to the Netherlands via Surat in India, a trip of one to one and a half years. The Dutch-Safavid trade was (more or less) a trade between equals; as the Dutch themselves acknowledged in 1650 it was not based on conquest as in the Banda Islands and Taiwan, or on monopoly-contracts as in the Moluccas, but in a class

> "with several other Oriental kings and princes, whether by formal agreements, or by free admission as merchants on the same footing as those of all other nations who are allowed to trade in their lands, at the pleasure of the ruler concerned." Or, as they noted elsewhere: "in neutral places with free peoples, where we find the laws and cannot impose our own."[73]

The trade was nevertheless very profitable and important to the Dutch, already in the 1620s.

In addition to these new ties with Europe, Safavid Iran conducted important international relations with powers closer to home—India, the Ottomans, Russia, and the Central Asian Uzbek khanates. Of these, the friendliest contacts were between Iran and Mughal India, which engaged in a fairly extensive trade and diplomacy. Iranian imports from India included silk and cotton goods, sugar, rice, coffee, spices, perfumes, precious stones, dyestuffs, and steel. In exchange, Iran sent India its agricultural products (fresh fruit, dried fruit, nuts, rose-water, and dyestuffs), fine silk textiles and carpets, manufactures such as porcelain and leather goods, and horses (on which large profits were made though few were sent). Though this trade was to a certain degree complementary, the balance was definitely not in Iran's favor.[74] The Ottoman Empire was even closer to Iran, both prosperous in itself and the land gateway to Europe, but the natural tendency for a large trade with and through the Ottoman territories was to a significant degree offset by the shifting conditions of war and peace between the two Islamic empires. The overall context was much less that of an extensive Ottoman-Iranian exchange of products, than a transit trade to the Mediterranean ports and European markets.[75] Direct Russian contact with Iran became possible around the mid-sixteenth century. The principal Russian export was a state monopoly in furs, while from the Iranian side came fine silk and some cotton textiles, raw silk, leather, and precious stones. It would probably be most accurate to conclude that in this period a modest and somewhat irregular trade with Russia was established through both royal and private channels.[76]

In assessing the overall pattern of Iran's relations with the international economy, 1615 is the key moment from which sustained commercial contact with Europe should be dated. In the 1620s, a direct trade was started up between the Safavid state and the Dutch and English East India companies, a trade which, taken as a whole, was one between more or less equal parties. Favorable to Iran was the fact that the terms and partners in the trade of silk, the key commodity, were determined by Shah 'Abbas in free negotiations with the Europeans. As Ralph Davis has written with regard to the Armenian merchants' dealings with the European companies: "the English were not foreign traders using economic power to exploit a poor and backward people; they were tolerated foreigners living in a highly civilised community with local merchants, as rich, as well-informed, and as sharp as themselves."[77] The types of products exchanged involved manufactures and raw materials on both sides, as well as a favorable balance for Iran in terms of an inflow of silver bullion. On the less auspicious side was the fact that transport was in the hands of the Europeans by virtue of their direct sea-routes to the Middle and Far East. The revolution in long-distance shipping after 1500 meant that the apportionment of total profits would favor the party which brought the products to their final markets and this meant the Europeans, not the shah. So here a gap was opening in technology that would widen into a whole new pattern of trade, though only in the coming two centuries. An assessment of the overall extent of Iran's relations with the West as of circa 1630 must conclude therefore that despite the real significance of the opening of trade relations for the Europeans, *there is no possibility of dependence* at this early stage in the emergence of a capitalist world-economy.

In Wallerstein's world-systemic terms, seventeenth-century Iran would be classified as "a world-empire in the external arena." World-empires were world-systems (i.e., "a unit with a single division of labor and multiple cultural systems"), with a common political system: "World-empires were basically redistributive in economic form. No doubt they bred clusters of merchants who engaged in economic exchange (primarily long-distance trade), but such clusters, however large, were a minor part of the total economy and not fundamentally determinative of its fate."[78] The pattern of trade and commerce in Safavid Iran certainly fits this characterization. On the relationship of the emerging European to the non-European world-systems in the sixteenth century, Wallerstein writes: "Once the Hapsburg dream of world-empire was over—and in 1557 it was over forever—the capitalist world-economy was an established system that became almost impossible to unbalance. It quickly reached an equilibrium point in its relations with other world-systems: the Ottoman and Russian world-empires, the Indian Ocean proto-world-economy."[79] Iran was rather marginal to and thus not part of the "Indian Ocean proto-world-economy" (which encompassed Java, Ceylon, and East Africa); rather, though Wallerstein nowhere attempts to explicitly so classify it, the Safavid social formation clearly belongs with the Ottoman and Russian ones, as a world-empire in its own right.

By 1640, vis-à-vis the European capitalist world-economy, Iran should be considered part of the "external arena." Again, Wallerstein:

We shall denote this distinction as one between the periphery of a world-economy and its external arena. The periphery of a world-economy is that geographical sector of it wherein production is primarily of lower-ranking goods (that is, goods whose labor is less well rewarded) but which is an integral part of the overall system of the division of labor, because the commodities involved are essential for daily use. The external arena of a world-economy consists of those other world-systems with which a given world-economy has some kind of trade relationship, based primarily on the exchange of preciosities, what was sometimes called the "rich trades."[80]

The Ottoman Empire to Iran's west and Asia to its east, both belong, for Wallerstein, in the external arena in the sixteenth century.[81] In the seventeenth century both may have begun to move closer to the periphery of the European world-system, the Ottomans on a basis of political-military equality, parts of the Far East increasingly as proto-colonies. Neither, however, really entered into peripheral status, as had all of "Latin" America by the sixteenth and seventeenth centuries.[82] Safavid Iran was even further from such incorporation than the Ottomans and the rest of Asia in the period up to 1630—at once economically and politically more difficult to penetrate and control. The Europeans were forced to come there with cash if they wanted Iranian silk and imposed no terms on the seller (unlike their position in the Asian spice trade). The results of the above analysis clearly situate the Iranian social formation of circa 1630 as a *world-empire* in the *external arena* of the emerging capitalist world-system. Indeed, as much as any non-European world-empire, Iran could consider Europe as part of *its* external arena. That is, both the Iranian and European economies, though now in contact with one another, were relatively self-sufficient and when seeking the products of the other, did so as equals. This important base-line finding for the seventeenth century should be held in mind as we contemplate the significant changes to come.

The Social Structure of Pre-Capitalist Iran

It is now time to draw this emerging picture of social structure together. Various scholars have attempted to characterize seventeenth-century Iran as a whole. Minorsky, for example, terms the early Safavid system "tribal feudalism" and speaks of the "great transformation" by the reign of Shah 'Abbas to "patrimonial absolutism," a lead which has been followed by Keddie, Bausani, and Banani.[83] Such terms are useful in that they hint at the *mixed* economic bases of the Iranian social formation, an approach which has been absent in the Marxist literature on Iran. A majority of the Marxist historians have simply characterized pre-capitalist Iran as feudal, sometimes with a qualifier such as "specifically Iranian feudalism," "Asiatic feudalism," or "feudal-nomad formation."[84] This strategy is vitiated by the obvious importance of both the tribal sector and urban craft production, while even in the agrarian sector of the economy one finds few characteristics of feudalism: no hereditary nobility, no juridical serfs, few labor services, no manorial system.

A few Marxist scholars have tentatively proposed the Asiatic mode of production as an alternative to these difficulties.[85] Key elements of this concept include the absence of private property in land, with a strong state claiming sole possession and collecting tax or tribute from numerous, small, self-sufficient villages. This is an improvement over feudalism *if* a single mode of production must be posited, but again, the large pastoral nomadic component of society and the vigorous non-state directed urban sector fall largely outside the model, while the agrarian economy included private landowners, vaqf properties, and individual peasant cultivators in addition to extensive crown holdings.

A better approach to the problem is provided by the modes of production perspective. This views the whole system as a social formation made up of three distinct but interacting modes of production corresponding to the three major economic sectors already identified by empirical analysis—a pastoral nomadic mode of production in the rural tribal sector, a peasant crop-sharing mode of production in the agricultural economy, and a petty-commodity mode of production in urban areas. Diagram 2.1 identifies the classes and social groups found in seventeenth-century Iran in light of a modes of production approach (percentages indicate the proportion of the population in each sector). The result is a conceptualization that acknowledges the complexity of social structure in pre-capitalist Iran and provides

DIAGRAM 2.1 The Seventeenth-Century Iranian Social Formation

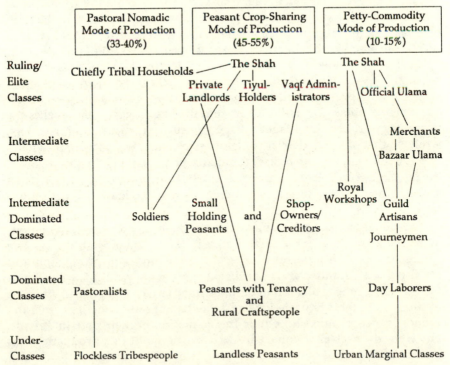

a basis for grasping the nature and dominant position of the Safavid state in this period.

The pastoral-nomadic mode of production was controlled by a ruling class of tribal chiefs, supported by a dominated class of pastoralists and an underclass of flockless tribespeople. An intermediate dominated class of tribesmen served in the military as soldiers and lived (at least when campaigning) somewhat better than the ordinary pastoralist. In the urban economy, the basic labor process centered on petty-commodity craft production by artisans working with their own tools in their own shops. Above them were found the wealthier merchants, and at the top of the social structure, the shah, who taxed them all and operated his own royal workshops. The variety of journeymen and day laborers constituted a dominated social class, while below them were the poor and unemployed of the urban marginal underclass. The ulama, as a social group with a range of class situations, can be divided into the official clerics appointed by the shah at the top of the social structure and the more popular ulama of the bazaar, ranked alongside the guild masters with whom they had ties.

While both pastoral nomadism and petty commodity production are found in the works of Marx and his successors, the "peasant crop-sharing" mode of production is a new coinage, conceived as an alternative to an unsatisfactory feudalism in the agrarian sector of the economy. As empirical analysis indicated, the agrarian sector surplus was appropriated in the form of a share of the crop produced by peasants with security of tenure. This holds true whether the dominant class involved consisted of private landlords, the shah on his crown lands, tiyul-holders on state lands assigned by the shah, or vaqf administrators. There was also a less numerous group of small-holding peasants and in some larger villages a relatively better off stratum of shopkeepers, mill-owners, and the like. On the same level as the peasantry were certain village craftspeople such as smiths and carpenters, while on that of the underclass of landless peasants below were providers of services including bath house attendants, barbers, and field guards. Since the peasantry controlled its labor process, but surrendered the surplus as a share of the crop, the term peasant crop-sharing mode of production has been used here.

The modes of production approach illuminates the reasons for the dominant overall position of the Safavid state in the period of Shah 'Abbas. The ruling class of Iran was spread over the three modes of production and consisted of a disunified array of tribal khans and governors, landlords and *tiyul*-holders, official ulama and perhaps some large merchants, in addition to the shah and his household. The Safavids not only benefited from the economic, geographic, and ethnic fragmentation of their potential rivals, but were themselves involved in each of the modes of production—as leaders of the tribal and standing army, possessors of crown lands and distributors of *tiyuls*, owners of the royal workshops, collectors of guild taxes and customs and tolls from the merchants, and monopolizers of the lucrative trade in raw silk and a few other items. No other elite group was in a position to capture more than a fraction of Iran's overall surplus, due both to location in a sole mode of production and the need to divide it among themselves, whereas the Safavids took a proportion of almost all of it.[86] This power was reinforced ideologically: The only groups with legitimating authority that crossed modes of production were the Safavids themselves as monarchs and the ulama as the bearers of Islam, and in the main the Safavids succeeded in imposing their claims in this arena. Such a situation goes a long way toward explaining the overwhelming hegemony of the Safavid state in the reign of 'Abbas.

Finally, Banani, Keddie, and Reid among others have argued that precapitalist Iran should be conceptualized in "vertical" estate-type divisions as much as "horizontal," class ones.[87] There is certainly an element of truth to such claims, in the sense that contemporaries, especially the elites who left the records, so saw the world and acted accordingly in intra-group rivalries, mobilizing supporters among their subordinates. When tribal pastoralists, for example, came into contact more frequently with their own chiefs than with urban artisans or even sedentary villagers, it should not be surprising that they were bound by various ties to the elite that dominated them and were separated in many ways from the other dominated classes of Iran. That there was no cohesive dominated class, class consciousness or class action across the modes of production (just as there was no unified ruling class) does not diminish the reality of classes within each mode of production. In fact, the difficulties of alliance between dominated classes located in different modes of production become more intelligible in the light of the present analysis: In Lukacsian terms, classes-in-themselves (with definite objective positions in a system of unequal social relations) did exist in seventeenth-century Iran. What Reid and others suggest by an accent on vertical groupings is the difficulty of the formation of classes-for-themselves, that is, with consciousness of their objective situation and collective organization and action based on this.

Ideological and Political Conceptions in Safavid Iran

The sources of legitimacy form part of any consideration of social structure and social power. In seventeenth-century Iran, these centered on the religious and political claims of the Safavid shahs, the embryonic oppositional element in the Shi'a political culture of the time, and the other manifestations of popular consciousness that can be discerned in the population. Key ideas about the duties of kingship in general include notions of the king as bringer of order, dispenser of justice, wager of war, and furtherer of prosperity. Both Islam and the earlier ethic (and political economy) of kingly patrimonialism influenced ideas about justice and are reflected in the literature known as "mirrors for princes," edifying manuals of rule for the leaders of the medieval Islamic world. Ghazali, for example, wrote that the ruler should avoid the extremes of tyranny and weakness and cites the saying of the wise that "religion depends upon kingship, kingship upon the army, the army upon material possessions and material possessions and material prosperity upon justice."[88]

Related to these conceptions is the ideal of a hierarchical social order based on the maintenance of definite groups, or classes, of people. A seventeenth-century work, the *Jami'i Mufidi*, suggests this arrangement of the social order: "The first class consists of the chief military and civil officials and the court; the second comprises the religious classes; the third class is composed of landowners, merchants, craftsmen, such as architects and goldsmiths; and the fourth class of artisans, other craftsmen, the people of the bazaar, and workmen."[89] The shah's role is to see that each of the classes carries out its duties and that the harmonious social order is preserved. The claims of the shahs to be "Shadow of God on Earth" (*zilla allah fi'l-arzi*), "King of Kings" (*shahanshah*), possessors of *dawla* ("turn of fortune," i.e. the right to rule) and "kingly glory" (*Farr*), tapped both Islamic and pre-Islamic sources to legitimate their position atop this hierarchy.[90]

The Safavids drew naturally on this centuries-old tradition of sacral kingship and patrimonialism, but they also created a new, complex synthesis evoking several (primarily religious) bases of authority, particularly in the reign of the founder of the dynasty, Isma'il. Isma'il made extravagant claims in his poetry variously associating himself with or suggesting he was either 'Ali, the Hidden Imam (the *mahdi*) or sometimes Allah himself, and derived great charisma and devoted followers from among the tribes that brought him to power. Beginning with Tahmasp, the extreme mahdistic tenet fell by the wayside, but the Safavids retained three basic sources of legitimacy: as representatives of the *mahdi* through alleged descent from the seventh Shi'i Imam, Musa al-Kazim, which led to the claim of possessing *'isma* (infallibility); as spiritual directors (*murshid*) of the Safavid order of Sufis, from whom they could command absolute obedience (this appealed in particular to their tribal supporters); and by claiming royal descent from Yazdigird III, the last Sasanian (pre-Islamic) monarch (whose daughter, moreover, was supposed to have married 'Ali's younger son, Husayn). Under 'Abbas the theocratic basis of rule shifted further in the direction of a more secular absolutism. Chardin's view from the 1670s that "there is surely no sovereign in the world as absolute as the king of Persia" is echoed in the 1720s by Père Krusinski: "there is not, perhaps, in the Universe, a King that is more Master of the Life and Fortune of his subjects, than was Shah Abbas and his Successors."[91]

Though Shah 'Abbas retained certain religious claims to authority which were doubtless effective among the peasantry, tribes, and many townspeople, the ulama in the seventeenth century posed challenges to the unmitigated powers of the monarchy. To do this, they tapped the radical ambiguity inherent in Shi'a Islam's treatment of the central questions of authority and legitimation. Arjomand identifies three possible attitudes toward secular authority in any religious belief system: compliance with authority, opposition to it, or indifference. Following from these are a variety of modes of religiosity: World-rejecting tendencies in a religion generally lead to indifference to nonreligious social action and independence or separation of religion and politics, while world-embracing attitudes are more ambiguous.[92] When the infant twelfth Imam disappeared without a trace in 873/874, the group which would evolve into the Twelver Shi'is in the next century or so elaborated a theory of occultation (*ghaybat*): that he was in hiding and would appear only at the end of time as the *mahdi* to restore justice to the world. This provided a basis for the separation of religion and politics— good Shi'is were piously *indifferent* to secular power, their focus being other-worldly. This apparent separation of the theological and political spheres allowed some Shi'is from the tenth century onward to participate in governments with the goal of making them more ethical and to prevent abuses, while others dissimulated their faith before the state and avoided it as usurped and evil. But paradoxically, a third position beyond compliance or indifference was derivable from the theory of occultation: Politics and religion may be separate spheres while the Imam is in hiding, but the Hidden Imam may appear at any moment to take charge of both spheres, righting injustice and banishing oppression.[93] Alongside the attitudes deriving from quietistic mystical piety another mode of religiosity was thus possible—charismatic, millenarian, activist. Shi'ism might induce, in fact, two related, but opposite tendencies in its adherents: normally other-worldly and quietistic, but at times (and the rise to power of the Safavids around 1500 was an example) messianic, revolutionary, and utopian. Absolute legitimacy belonged only to the Hidden Imam, but in his absence, in both revolutionary and stable times, functional or derivative authority might be claimed by both the government and the ulama.[94]

These problems were reproduced in ulama-state relations during the Safavid period. The ulama generally could support some of the elements of Safavid religious policy as the sixteenth century wore on, most notably the basic establishment of Shi'ism as the religion of Iran and Tahmasp's moves to eliminate the extremist beliefs associated by his qizilbash followers with Isma'il. In a sense a kind of compromise was put in place: The divine right

of kings as Shadow of God appears in theological works of the period and
the right of the shah to obedience was acknowledged at the same time as
his obligation to be just (Arjomand considers this legitimating, but not
sacralizing, kingship as political, temporal rule).[95] Thus a number of the
ulama, who may be called the "official ulama," had connections with the
court and Iranian elite through office-holding, tax exemptions, and mar-
riages.[96]

But the underlying legitimation issue of who represented the Imams
remained. Already in the sixteenth century the shahs' claims to be the
Hidden Imam's deputy had been challenged. By the later seventeenth
century, the existence of conflicting claims is recorded in an interesting
passage in Chardin:

> The Iranians thus are divided among themselves, concerning who should
> represent [the Hidden Imam] and be sovereign in both spiritual and temporal
> matters. The ulama [*gens d'église*], and with them all the devout, and all those
> who profess a strict observance of religion, claim that in the absence of the
> imam, the royal throne should be filled by a sinless *mujtahid* . . . but the most
> common opinion, which has prevailed, is that in truth this right belongs to a
> direct descendant of the imams; but that it is not absolutely necessary that this
> descendant be pure nor learned to such a degree of perfection, being none-
> theless the true lieutenant of God and vicar of the prophet and imams. As I
> just said, this is the dominant view, because it establishes and affirms the right
> of the ruling king.[97]

Chardin goes on to report the considerable underlying antipathy of some
of the ulama toward the Safavids:

> "How is it possible," say the ulama, "that these impious kings, drinkers of wine,
> carried away by passion, could be the *vicars of God* and communicate with
> heaven, receiving the light necessary to guide the faithful? How can they
> resolve cases of conscience and doubts of faith, as a true *lieutenant of God* must,
> these men who sometimes can hardly read? Our kings being iniquitous and
> unjust, their domination is a tyranny, to which God has subjected us to punish
> us, after taking from the world the legitimate *successor of his prophet*. The
> supreme throne of the universe should belong only to a *mujtahid*, a man who
> possesses sanctity and learning beyond the ordinary. It is true that since the
> *mujtahid* is holy and thus a peaceful man, there must be a king to carry the
> sword for the exercise of justice; but this should be only as his minister and
> dependent upon him."[98]

These attitudes found expression in the views that the shahs' confiscations
of property were illegal, that the civil courts and urban government were

tyrannical and founded on force, and the reluctance on the part of some ulama to accept office and their preference instead to be ranked with the taxable subject population.[99]

Whether such negative evaluations were widespread or not is difficult to discern. There is little doubt that the Safavids tended to impose their hegemony on the rest of society. The strongest legitimating combination was a powerful *and* pious shah, such as Tahmasp and perhaps 'Abbas could claim to be; in any case, 'Abbas was famous for his degree of control over the religious establishment. The result was, in Arjomand's view, the sometimes uneasy coexistence of two sets of legitimating principles of authority, one religious, the other patrimonial, monarchic, and tribal.[100] One might conclude, however, *contra* the overall thrust of Arjomand's argument, that on the whole religion was simply not the decisive factor in the politics of the Safavid period. It was clearly important, but reasons of historical contingency—its role in the Safavids' rise and its use by both the state and ulama for legitimation purposes, as well as the splits between clerical notables and religious professionals, and Safavid royal prestige—all combined to soften its impact in any single direction. This is not to say that the ulama did not possess significant power and prestige in this period, as well as lay some of the groundwork for more successful challenges to later, less imposing dynasties.

The religious authority of the ulama among the people, and in particular, among the urban population, gradually grew in the course of the institutionalization of Shi'ism during the sixteenth and seventeenth centuries. Sixteenth-century texts mention *taqlid*—the desirability of "imitating" or following a leading mujtahid, and *ijtihad*—the scholar's competence to determine legal norms—both rather innovative in light of earlier Shi'i jurisprudence. In Nasr's view, "The *mujtahids* were often a protection for the people against the tyranny of various government officials and fulfilled a major function of both a religious and social nature."[101] Such ulama, for the most part unconnected with the state, may be termed the "popular" or "bazaar" ulama, by virtue of their closeness to the population.

Shi'ism also fostered the development of a variety of key values, practices, and ethics on the part of the individual believer. Faith (*iman*), brotherly love, and assistance to others within the community came to be seen as important virtues for salvation. With the spread of Shi'ism too was activated in the mass of the population "a theodicy of suffering centered on the tragedy of Husayn's martyrdom in Karbala and, more importantly, of an other-worldly soteriology."[102] Under the political ethics of Islam, Arjomand notes *jihad* (both in the sense of a holy war to defend the faith and an inner struggle to preserve it), enjoining what is good while forbidding evil, and the "authority verse" of the Qur'an: "O believers, obey God, and obey the Messenger and those in authority among you."[103] Finally, conceptions of justice and combatting its opposite, oppression, were potent values for believing Shi'is and rulers could be held to uphold the former or lose legitimacy before God in the eyes of the people. All of these attitudes, beliefs, and practices must be factored into the growing impact of Shi'a Islam on the Iranian population in the seventeenth, and subsequent, centuries.

In addition to the religious components outlined above, a few other aspects of popular culture and attitudes can be inferred from the available sources. In the tribal sector, for example, the phenomena termed *'asabiyya, uymaqiyyat*, and *intisab* all acted as principles of unity within the tribe. *'Asabiyya* carries meanings ranging from "zealous partisanship, party spirit" to "tribal solidarity, clannishness"; Reid defines it as "the obligations of individuals or family groups in any one uymaq to support one another according to the priorities of uymaq solidarity."[104] *Uymaqiyyat* conveyed the sense of tribal loyalty or tribal ties, and contributed to the great fighting spirit of the qizilbash tribesmen. Reid also argues that kinship relations were of less importance than power relations in the authority structure of the Turkic tribes; that various unrelated families tended to cluster around a talented or successful leader (military or otherwise). Out of this arose a set of relationships called *intisab*, meaning "membership, affiliation," whether in a political, religious or genealogical group: "The weaker member attempted to further his master's position and wealth, while his master, in turn, treated the weaker member as his client or protégé."[105] Interestingly, too, based on the oral traditions of Central Asia, Reid discerns various oppositional tendencies among rural groups, as well as urban craftsmen, religious orders, and bandit organizations. The folk epic embodied in the Koroglu stories and its widespread evocation in Safavid literature of the seventeenth century "implies that a good deal of latent hostility toward the controlling uymaqs existed among the local populations, pastoral and agricultural."[106]

In the urban sector, the guilds possessed long-standing secret ties with Sufi brotherhoods and fraternal or protective associations. Banani writes that these "posed the danger of possible 'proletarian' dissent and unruliness. 'Abbas I was apparently cognizant of this danger, since by means of the urban police he kept a close watch over the activities of the *asnaf* [guilds]."[107] Under the later Safavid onslaught against the Sufi mystical orders, the guilds were gradually forced toward the Haydari, Ni'mati, and other factions, originally Sufi orders which had degenerated into hostile groups, sometimes manipulated and encouraged by the state "in order to deprive the bazaars of political unity and strength."[108] Guild imperatives to act honestly were shared by the larger urban culture and value system of the *futuvva* orders, which have existed in Iran since the ninth or tenth century, extolling loyalty toward one's friends, support for the weak and oppressed, truthfulness, bravery, patience, and purity of motive. Ideals of this type were carried earlier in Islamic history by the *'ayyaran*—"groups of urban youths who in times of anarchy and oppression acted as an unofficial police in defense of the common people"[109]—and in nineteenth-century Iran by the *lutis*, local associations of men who would protect their district, make levies on the rich in the name of the poor, and provide for the education of poor and orphaned children. In the Safavid period, futuvva groups included not only guild members but also dervishes and poor people, usually under the guidance of a Sufi shaykh.

Finally, some evidence exists on attitudes in Iranian society toward authority. Chardin provides the following insights into the nuances involved:

> notwithstanding what I have just said [about the popularity of a mulla Qasim who preached against the government], the Persians have a sincere submissiveness which comes from the heart for the orders of their king, greater perhaps than any other people on earth. They believe that kings are naturally violent and unjust, that one must consider them thus; and nevertheless, however unjust and violent their orders may be, one is obliged to obey them, except in cases of religion or conscience, as if it were a royal prerogative to commit any manner of injustice. One of their expressions of speech is "to play the king," to say "oppress someone and violate justice.". . . However, as I have said, they are the most submissive people in the world and one hasn't heard talk of uprisings or revolts in Persia for two hundred years.[110]

There are undoubtedly opposing currents at work here, a natural recognition of injustice and abuse of power on the part of the population, coupled with an acceptance of the overwhelming power on the side of the court (though we shall soon see that uprisings and revolts were not negligible in Safavid Iran). Lambton feels that in "medieval Persia" there existed two contrasting social tendencies: equality, deriving both from Islam and Turkish tribal custom, alongside hierarchy, represented in the ethos of pre-Islamic monarchy and the longstanding elite families of Iran. The issue is certainly complex, with tendencies and counter-tendencies at all levels. For example, "Within the *umma* [community of believers] all were on an equal footing. There were no distinctions of rank, but there were distinctions of function."[111] Reid's discussion of the evolution of Persian miniature painting reveals some of these conflicting attitudes at the court as well: By the time of Shah 'Abbas and after in the seventeenth century, contemporary miniatures portray a contradictory complex of less deference than in earlier Safavid times, more individuality, lackadaisical body-guards, lack of discipline and "a vicious resentment for authority."[112] Seventeenth-century art, in Richard Ettinghausen's view, became in general more realistic, attentive to the lives of ordinary people, at work and in relaxation.[113] Poetry in the Safavid period, among many other features, included more of the "language of the streets," according to Savory.[114] Though much more analysis could be done in each of these areas, the picture emerges of a constellation of mixed emotions toward authority in Safavid Iran: The view that the government was evil, its officials unjust and their wealth usurped, *and* acquiescence to authority, or even cooperation and participation, existed side by side, most manifestly in the urban setting. The result would be a situation fraught with considerable tension, to be activated from time to time in opposition.

Notes

1. On these events see Michel M. Mazzaoui, *The Origins of the Safawids. Shi'ism, Sufism and the Gulat*, 42, 72ff., and Said Amir Arjomand, *The Shadow of God and the Hidden Imam. Religion, Political Order, and Societal Change in Shi'ite Iran from the Beginning to 1890* (Chicago and London: The University of Chicago Press, 1984), 77ff.

2. Yahya Qazvini, *Lubb at-tawarikh* (Tehran, 1932), 240, quoted in Mazzaoui, *The Origins of the Safawids*, 80.

3. These events are recounted in Mazzaoui, *The Origins of the Safawids*, 81-82, and in Roger Savory, *Iran under the Safavids* (Cambridge: Cambridge University Press, 1980), 24-26.

4. See Hafez F. Farmayan, *The Beginnings of Modernization in Iran. The Policies and Reforms of Shah Abbas I (1587-1629)*, Middle East Center research monograph number 1 (Salt Lake City: University of Utah, 1969), 5; Mazzaoui, *The Origins of the Safawids*, 15; and Savory, *Iran under the Safavids*, 45-46.

5. These events are discussed in some detail in Martin B. Dickson, "Sháh Tahmásb and the Uzbeks (The Duel for Khurásán with 'Ubayd Khán: 930-946/1524-1540)," Ph.D. dissertation, Department of Oriental Studies, Princeton University (1958), 51-295.

6. For the events of 1576-1607 see the outstanding chronicle of the Safavid period by Eskandar Beg Monshi, *History of Shah 'Abbas the Great (Tarik-e 'Alam ara-ye 'Abbasi)*, translated by Roger M. Savory in two volumes (Boulder: Westview Press, 1978), 203-494, 515-947. I have also drawn on Savory, *Iran under the Safavids*, 67-91, and Farmayan, *The Beginnings of Modernization in Iran*, 9-14. Note that some Iranian dates, such as "1597/98" in the next paragraph, are split by the symbol "/" because the Iranian year begins on March 21, spreading each Iranian calendar year over two Christian-style years.

7. Relevant aspects of the state's economic activities (especially the royal workshops and the silk trade), urban government, and questions of legitimation will be considered later in this chapter.

8. On the court and bureaucracy, see V. Minorsky, *Tadhkirat al-muluk. A Manual of Safavid Administration (circa 1137/1725)* (London: Luzac, 1943), 44-52, 85-91, 112-25, 132 (hereafter this work is cited as *TM*); Jean Chardin, *Voyages du Chevalier Chardin, en Perse, et autres lieux de l'orient* (Paris: Le Normant, 1811), volume V, 237-39, 429-30, 449; Guy le Strange, translator and editor, *Don Juan of Persia, a Shi'ah Catholic (1560-1604)* (London: Broadway Travellers, 1927), 45; and Monshi, *History of Shah 'Abbas*, 228.

9. These lists are compiled by Monshi, *History of Shah 'Abbas*, 222-28 (for 1576) and 1309-17 (for 1629). They are broken down and analyzed by Minorsky, *TM*, 15-18. My percentages are based on the further decomposition of the tribal chiefs provided by Alessandro Bausani, *The*

Persians. From the earliest days to the twentieth century, translated from the Italian by J. B. Donne (London: Elek Books, 1971), 147-48. The percentages here are rough indicators indeed and like most statistical data from this period, should be treated with considerable skepticism.

10. Chardin, *Voyages,* V, 290, 333.

11. Minorsky, *TM,* 25.

12. Ibid.

13. Dickson gives evidence to this effect: "Sháh Tahmásb and the Uzbeks," 13, 18, 19, 66, 351-52, 365. See also Minorsky, *TM,* 166, and Le Strange, *Don Juan of Persia,* 46-47.

14. Chardin, *Voyages,* V, 258. See also V, 285-86, VII, 430; Minorsky, *TM,* 181 note 4; and Monshi, *History of Shah 'Abbas,* 533.

15. On the numbers and payscale in the army, see Minorsky, *TM,* 32-35, 161; Chardin, *Voyages,* V, 299-330; and Farmayan, *The Beginnings of Modernization in Iran,* 18. On the new social basis of the Safavid army, see Monshi, *History of Shah 'Abbas,* 527. For an astute glimpse into the complexities of ethnic politics in the army and other high posts, see Masashi Haneda, "The Evolution of the Safavid Royal Guard," translated by Rudi Matthee, pp. 57-86 in *Iranian Studies,* volume XXII, numbers 2-3 (1989).

16. The relevant data can be found in Minorsky, *TM,* 105-109, 175, 177, and Chardin, *Voyages,* V, 412-13, 497-98. In general, Chardin is only making educated guesses, while the *Tadhkirat al-muluk* gives detailed figures based on the state's accounts (in 1720).

17. Chardin, *Voyages,* V, 414-15. See also ibid., 491, and Minorsky, *TM,* 185.

18. The income of the French state moreover rose enormously, from 17 million livres (or francs) in 1610 to 44 million in 1644 to the 577 million noted in table 2.1 for circa 1700. Thus at the Safavids' height circa 1630 the Iranian state's income was roughly on a par with that of France at the time. By 1700 this would no longer be true. For figures, see Perry Anderson, *Lineages of the Absolutist State* (London: New Left Books, 1974), 98.

19. See estimates by Laurence Lockhart, *The Fall of the Safavi Dynasty and the Afghan Occupation of Persia* (Cambridge: At the University Press, 1958), 11; Minorsky, *TM,* 186; John Emerson, "Ex Occidente Lux. Some European Sources on the Economic Structure of Persia Between About 1630 and 1690," Ph.D. dissertation, Department of Oriental Studies, University of Cambridge (1969), 229; and Charles Issawi, "Population and Resources in the Ottoman Empire and Iran," pp. 152-164 in Thomas Naff and Roger Owen, editors, *Studies in Eighteenth Century Islamic History* (Carbondale and Edwardsville: Southern Illinois University Press, 1977), 162.

20. These estimates are made respectively in Leonard M. Helfgott, "Tribalism as a Socioeconomic Formation in Iranian History," pp. 36-61 in *Iranian Studies,* volume X, numbers 1-2 (Winter-Spring 1977), 36; Bausani, *The Persians,* 150; and Charles Issawi, editor, *The Economic History of Iran: 1800-1914* (Chicago and London: The University of Chicago Press, 1971), 20 (hereafter cited as *EHI*).

21. Helfgott, "Tribalism as a Socioeconomic Formation," 36. For lists and discussions of the various tribes and clans see Minorsky, *TM,* 16-17, 187-88, 193-95; le Strange, *Don Juan of Persia,* 45-46; James J. Reid, *Tribalism and Society in Islamic Iran, 1500-1629* (Malibu: Undena Publications, 1983), 29, 43-47; and Richard Tapper, "Black Sheep, White Sheep and Red Heads. A Historical Sketch of the Shahsavan of Azarbaijan," pp. 61-84 in *Iran* (Journal of the British Institute of Persian Studies), volume IV (1966), 77-78. This paragraph draws also on Reid, *Tribalism and Society,* 108; Mazzaoui, *The Origins of the Safawids,* 59 note 1; Nikki Keddie, *Roots of Revolution. An Interpretive History of Modern Iran* (New Haven and London: Yale University Press, 1981), 26; and R. D. McChesney, "Comments on "The Qajar Uymaq in The Safavid Period, 1500-1722"," pp. 87-105 in *Iranian Studies,* volume XIV, numbers 1-2 (Winter-Spring 1981), 88.

22. Reid, *Tribalism and Society,* 42.

23. Jahangir Saleh, "Social Formations in Iran, 750-1914," Ph.D. dissertation, Department of Economics, University of Massachusetts, Amherst (1978), 59. Saleh refers to L. Krader, *Social Organization of the Mongol-Turkic Pastoral Nomads* (The Hague: Mouton and Co., 1963), 317. This

paragraph draws also on Reid, *Tribalism and Society*, 1, and Perry Anderson, *Passages from Antiquity to Feudalism* (London: New Left Books, 1978 [1974]), 222.

24. This discussion is based on Reid, *Tribalism and Society*, 76-77; Helfgott, "Tribalism as a Socioeconomic Formation," 49; and Petrushevsky, *Ocherki po istorii feodal'nykh otnoshenii v Azerbaidzhane i Armenii v XVI- nachale XIX vekov* (Leningrad, 1949), cited by McChesney, "Comments on "The Qajar Uymaq in The Safavid Period"," 95.

25. Keddie, *Roots of Revolution*, 26. Though she is writing of nineteenth-century Iran, I see no reason to doubt the applicability of her statement to the seventeenth-century tribal economy. This is not to deny the problematic nature of extrapolating backward from later accounts and periods, which plagues much of the work on tribal society in Iran.

26. Bausani, *The Persians*, 150. On tribal taxes see also ibid., 149; Monshi, *History of Shah 'Abbas*, 774; Chardin, *Voyages*, V, 392, 397; Adam Olearius, *The Ambassadors from the Duke of Holstein's Travels into Muscovy . . .*, pp. 1-112 in John Harris, *Navigantium atque Itinerantium Biblioteca* (London: Thomas Bennet, 1705), volume II, 65; and I. P. Petrushevsky, "The Socio-economic Condition of Iran under the Il-khans," pp. 483-537 in J. A. Boyle, editor, *The Cambridge History of Iran*, volume 3, *The Saljuq and Mongol Periods* (Cambridge: Cambridge University Press, 1968), 530 (hereafter cited as "Iran under the Il-khans").

27. There is a major debate in the literature on the extent of their control over the Iranian economy, with Reid taking the position that at least in the sixteenth century it was virtually all-encompassing, a view challenged by Helfgott and McChesney, who raise questions about some of the evidence. See James J. Reid, "Rebellion and Social Change in Astarabad, 1537-1744," pp. 35-53 in *International Journal of Middle East Studies*, volume 13 (1981), 3; James J. Reid, "The Qajar Uymaq in The Safavid Period, 1500-1722," pp. 117-143 in *Iranian Studies*, volume XI (1978), 120; Helfgott, "Tribalism as a Socioeconomic Formation," 74; and McChesney, "Comments on "The Qajar Uymaq in the Safavid Period"," 92, 93, 96, 100-102. Rather than intervening directly in the production process, it seems that the main role performed by tribal chiefs was to extract a surplus in the name of the state from the urban and agricultural communities they provisionally administered.

28. The phrase "rough democracy" is Keddie's: "Iran, 1797-1941," pp. 137-157 in *Iran: Religion, Politics and Society. Collected Essays* (London: Frank Cass, 1980), 140-42. Fredrik Barth explains the egalitarian basis of (twentieth-century) camp life: "Every day the members of the camp must agree in their decision on the vital question of whether to move on, or to stay camped, and if they move, by which route and how far they should move. These decisions are the very stuff of a pastoral nomad existence; they spell the difference between growth and prosperity of the herds, or loss and poverty. . . . The maintenance of a camp as a social unit thus requires the daily unanimous agreement by all members on economically vital questions": *Nomads of South Persia. The Basseri Tribe of the Khamseh Confederacy* (Boston: Little, Brown and Company, 1961), 25-26.

29. Ann K. S. Lambton, *Landlord and Peasant in Persia. A Study of Land Tenure and Land Revenue Administration* (London: Oxford University Press, 1953), 5-6. Private landownership dates from at least Sasanid times, i.e. by the fifth or sixth century A.D. Petrushevsky reports that the ancient village commune seems to have disappeared by the Mongol period (thirteenth/fourteenth centuries): "Iran under the Il-khans," 523.

30. Minorsky, *TM*, 195. Chardin's discussion is found in volume V of his *Voyages*, 380ff. Petrushevsky discerns the same four categories of land for the fourteenth century: "Iran under the Il-Khans," 515.

31. On crown lands, see Amin Banani, "Reflections on The Social and Economic Structure of Safavid Persia at Its Zenith," pp. 83-116 in *Iranian Studies*, volume XI (1978), 94; Lambton, *Landlord and Peasant*, 11, 25, 59-61; and Chardin, *Voyages*, V, 382-83.

32. For the history of state land in Iran, see Petrushevsky, "Iran under the Il-khans," 519-20; B. G. Martin, "Seven Safawid Documents from Azarbayjan," pp. 171-206 in S. M. Stern, editor, *Documents from Islamic Chanceries*, First Series, Oriental Studies, III (Oxford: Bruno Cassirer,

1965), 192; Ann K. S. Lambton, "The Evolution of the *Iqta'* in Medieval Iran," pp. 41-50 in *Iran* (Journal of the British Institute of Persian Studies), volume V (1967), 45; Klaus-Michael Rohr-born, *Provinzen und Zentralgewalt Persiens im. 16. und 17. Jahrhundert* (Berlin: Walter de Gruyter & Co., 1966); Lambton, *Landlord and Peasant*, 66; Minorsky, *TM*, 28; Farhad Nomani, "The Origin and Development of Feudalism in Iran: 300-1600 A.D.," Ph.D. dissertation, Department of Economics, University of Illinois at Urbana-Champaign (1972), 61 note 106; Vladimir Minorsky, "A Soyurghal of Qasim b. Jahangir Aq-qoyunlu (903/1498)," pp. 927-960 in *Bulletin of the School of Oriental and African Studies*, volume XI (1937-1939), 956; and Ann K. S. Lambton, "Two Safavid Soyurghals," pp. 44-54 in *Bulletin of the School of Oriental and African Studies*, volume XIV (1952).

33. Chardin, *Voyages*, V, 380. The quote by Minorsky is from *TM*, 28. On the tiyul see Lambton, "The Evolution of the Iqta'," 49; *A Chronicle of the Carmelites in Persia and the Papal Mission of the XVIIth and XVIIIth centuries*, (London: Eyre and Spottiswoode, 1939), volume 1, 53 note 1; and V. Minorsky, article on "Tiyul," pp. 799-801 in *The Encyclopedia of Islam*, first edition (London: Luzac, 1934), 800.

34. On vaqfs in the Safavid period, see Nomani, "The Origin and Development of Feudalism in Iran," 33-35; Chardin, *Voyages*, V, 381; Monshi, *History of Shah 'Abbas*, 535, 954; Emerson, "Ex Occidente Lux," 247; Lambton, *Landlord and Peasant*, 113; Banani, "Reflections," 96; and Savory, *Iran under the Safavids*, 185.

35. See Raphaël Du Mans, *Estat de la Perse en 1660*, edited by Ch. Schefer (Paris: Ernest Leroux, 1890), 226-27, and Tavernier, *Voyages*, Book 5, chapter xi (1930 edition), 237 (both cited by Emerson, "Ex Occidente Lux," 247); Chardin, *Voyages*, V, 381-82; Monshi, *History of Shah 'Abbas*, 1016, 1262; Minorsky, *TM*; and Savory, *Iran under the Safavids*, 156.

36. Banani, "Reflections," 94. See also Minorsky, *TM*, 19; Lambton, *Landlord and Peasant*, 105-6, 113, 126; and Bausani, *The Persians*, 142. Chardin writes: "the lands which are assigned as salary are not under the king's inspection; they are like the property of the one to whom they are given. He arranges the revenues as he wishes with the inhabitants of the place and it is like our European *benefice*": *Voyages*, V, 418. On the other hand, he notes: "as offices are a hereditary institution in the [Persian] empire, everyone considers his assigned land as his own property forever, because one hopes to remain in one's post till the end of one's life and to perform so well in it that one's children will succeed to it": V, 419-420.

37. Minorsky, *TM*, 22. Evidence in this paragraph is drawn from ibid., 22; Chardin, *Voyages*, V, 384, 392, 396; Lambton, *Landlord and Peasant*, 113, 123; Monshi, *History of Shah 'Abbas*, 774, 1073, 1103, 1158; and M. Ravandi, *Tarikh-i Ijtima'i-yi Iran* [Social History of Iran], second edition (Tehran, 1977), volume 3, 159, cited by Arjomand, *The Shadow of God and the Hidden Imam*, 194.

38. See the relevant documents and instances of labor service and taxes in Lambton, *Landlord and Peasant*, 116-17; Minorsky, "A Soyurghal of Qasim b. Jahangir Aq-Qoyunlu," 950-51; Minorsky, *TM*, 84; Chardin, *Voyages*, V, 386-87, 390, 419; Nomani, "The Origin and Development of Feudalism in Iran," 76; and Monshi, *History of Shah 'Abbas*, 1211-12.

39. Chardin, *Voyages*, V, 391-392.

40. Keddie, *Roots of Revolution*, 34, here referring to the nineteenth century.

41. Chardin, *Voyages*, V, 465-466.

42. Martin, "Seven Safawid Documents," 199.

43. Bausani, *The Persians*, 150.

44. Minorsky, *TM*, 162, citing Sir Thomas Herbert, *Some Yeares Travels*, third edition (1665), n.p.

45. These estimates are gathered and presented in John Foran, "Social Structure and Social Change in Iran from 1500 to 1979," Ph.D. dissertation, Department of Sociology, University of California, Berkeley (1988), 75 table 2.7.

46. Bausani observes that the guilds in Safavid times had more influence in running their cities than in the Seljuq or Il-khanid periods, but that cities were not generally self-governing: *The Persians*, 151-152. Lambton speaks of "a considerable measure of self-government" in the

towns in Iranian history generally: *Islamic Society in Persia*, An Inaugural Lecture delivered on 9 March 1954 at the University of London School of Oriental and African Studies (Oxford: Oxford University Press, 1954). Petrushevsky notes that towns had no "overall self-government" before or after the Mongols—"There was however self-administration within the limits of the quarter ... and the guild or corporation—either merchant, craft, or religious": "Iran under the Il-khans," 509.

47. On the urban government and guild organizations of Safavid Iran, see Lambton, *Islamic Society in Persia*, 11-12, 14-15, 21-22; Minorsky, *TM*, 81-83, 148-149, 181-82; Savory, *Iran under the Safavids*, 182; Chardin, *Voyages*, V, 399; Willem Floor, "The Guilds in Iran—an Overview from the Earliest Beginnings till 1972," pp. 99-116 in *Zeitschrift der Deutschen Morgenländischen Gesellschaft*, volume 125, number 1 (1975); and Mehdi Keyvani, *Artisans and Guild Life in the later Safavid period. Contribution to the socio-economic history of Persia*, Islamkundliche Untersuchungen, volume 65 (Berlin: Klaus Schwarz Verlag, 1982), 67-71, 82-87, 106-7, 115-18, 142-47.

48. Keyvani, *Artisans and Guild Life*, 88-89, based on Tavernier, *The six voyages* ([1678] 1930), 34.

49. On the guild stratification system, see Keyvani, *Artisans and Guild Life*, 88-93; Olearius, *The Ambassadors*, 80; Chardin, *Voyages*, IV, 91-93, VII, 339-40; Du Mans, *Estat de la Perse*, 194-95. The situation of apprentices may be appreciated from N. A. Kuznetsova's data on the city of Erivan, circa 1800, where in 7 of 11 guilds there were two to three times as many apprentices as masters, implying that over half of all apprentices would not end up as masters, but in one of the other categories above: "Urban industry in Persia during the 18th and early 19th centuries," pp. 308-321 in *Central Asian Review*, volume 11, number 3 (1963), 316.

50. On textile production and the weavers, see Emerson, "Ex Occidente Lux," 248-52, and Keyvani, *Artisans and Guild Life*, 39, 49. Saleh emphasizes merchants' control of textile manufacturing, as compared with metalworks, ceramics, and leather products which were generally controlled by the craft producers: "Social Formations in Iran," 104-105.

51. On these manufactures and their workers, see Emerson, "Ex Occidente Lux," 253, 255-57; Savory, *Iran under the Safavids*, 144, 147, 153; Chardin, *Voyages*, VII, 403; Olearius, *The Ambassadors*, 70; Marshall G. S. Hodgson, *The Venture of Islam. Conscience and History in a World Civilization*, volume 3: *The Gunpowder Empires and Modern Times* (Chicago: University of Chicago Press, 1974), 40; Keyvani, *Artisans and Guild Life*, 130, 183; Margaret Medley, "Islam, Chinese Porcelain and Ardabil," pp. 31-45 in *Iran* (Journal of the British Institute of Persian Studies), volume XIII (1975); and Bausani, *The Persians*, 152.

52. The number of about 5,000 workers is derived from Chardin's statement that each workshop (he says there were 32) had on average 150 workers, some more (180 tailors), some less (72 painters, attached to the library): *Voyages*, VII, 329, V, 499. For other data here, see ibid., V, 422, 498, VII, 329-34.

53. See for example Banani, "Reflections," 97-98; Minorsky, *TM*, 20; and Chardin, *Voyages*, V, 416.

54. On the Armenian contribution to the Iranian and world economy, see John Fryer, *A New Account of East India and Persia being Nine Years' Travels*, volume II (London: The Hakluyt Society, 1912), 249; Emerson, "Ex Occidente Lux," 258 note 1, 260-62; Chardin, *Voyages*, VIII, 106; Vartan Gregorian, "Minorities of Isfahan: The Armenian community of Isfahan, 1587-1722," pp. 652-680 in *Iranian Studies*, volume VII, numbers 3-4 (1974), 665, 669, 680; Keyvani, *Artisans and Guild Life*, 179-80, 217, 228; Monshi, *History of Shah 'Abbas*, 859-60; R. W. Ferrier, "The Armenians and the East India Company in Persia in the Seventeenth and Early Eighteenth Centuries," pp. 38-62 in *Economic History Review*, Second Series, volume XXVI, number 1 (February 1973), 44; Fernand Braudel, *The Mediterranean and the Mediterranean World in the Age of Philip II*, translated by Sian Reynolds (New York: Harper and Row, 1976), volume II, 1167, and volume I, 50-51; and Minorsky, *TM*, 20.

55. This paragraph draws on Banani, "Reflections," 93-94; Emerson, "Ex Occidente Lux," 273-75; Chardin, *Voyages*, VII, 296; and Saleh, "Social Formations in Iran," 112.

56. Keddie, *Roots of Revolution*, 4.

57. Arjomand, *The Shadow of God and the Hidden Imam*, 122; also 107, and passim. See also Keddie, *Roots of Revolution*, 17, and Hossein Nasr, "Religion in Safavid Persia," pp. 271-286 in *Iranian Studies*, volume VII, numbers 1-2 (1974), 275-277.

58. This discussion draws on Arjomand, *The Shadow of God and the Hidden Imam*, 107, 122-23, 127-32; Minorsky, *TM*, 15-16; and Keyvani, *Artisans and Guild Life*, 152.

59. Chardin, *Voyages*, VII, 392.

60. Monshi, *History of Shah 'Abbas*, 204. This paragraph draws on Olearius, *The Ambassadors*, 80-81; Arjomand, *The Shadow of God and the Hidden Imam*, 189; Monshi, *History of Shah 'Abbas*, 203; Chardin, *Voyages*, V, 371; Emerson, "Ex Occidente Lux," 284; and Keyvani, *Artisans and Guild Life*, 109.

61. Chardin writes that "it is known that women don't leave the house": *Voyages*, V, 270. See also Keddie, *Roots of Revolution*, 14.

62. Keddie, *Roots of Revolution*, 32, 34.

63. Ibid., 33.

64. Keyvani, *Artisans and Guild Life*, 177-178, citing Chardin, *Voyages*, II, 55-56.

65. Emerson, "Ex Occidente Lux," 270-271. Malcolm is cited by Gregorian, "Minorities of Isfahan," 657.

66. Chardin, *Voyages*, VIII, 355-362, 380. Pre-Islamic Zoroastrian culture had a high regard for cultivation in general and planting of trees and reclaiming land in particular: Lambton, *Landlord and Peasant*, xviii-xix.

67. Halil Inalcik, "The Ottoman Economic Mind and Aspects of the Ottoman Economy," pp. 207-218 in M. A. Cook, editor, *Studies in the Economic History of the Middle East: from the rise of Islam to the present day* (London and New York: Oxford University Press, 1970), 210. For a more detailed treatment of the whole topic in this section, see my article, "The Making of an External Arena: Iran's Place in the World-System, 1500-1722," pp. 71-119 in *Review* (Journal of the Fernand Braudel Center), volume XII, number 1 (Winter 1989).

68. This paragraph draws on Niels Steensgaard, *The Asian Trade Revolution of the Seventeenth Century. The East India Companies and the Decline of the Caravan Trade* (Chicago and London: The University of Chicago Press, 1974), 28, 33ff, 381; Halil Inalcik and Niels Steensgaard, article on "Harir," (silk) pp. 209-221 in *The Encyclopedia of Islam*, New Edition (Leiden: E. J. Brill, and London: Luzac & Co., 1979), volume 3, 210, 213; Savory, *Iran under the Safavids*, 196; Chardin, *Voyages*, V, 398; Ferrier, "The Armenians and the EIC," 46; M. A. P. Meilink-Roelofsz, "The Earliest Relations between Persia and the Netherlands," pp. 1-50 in *Persica* (Jaarboek van het Genootschap Nederland-Iran Stichting voor Culturele Betrekkingen), number VI (1972-1974), 40; and Issawi, *EHI*, 12.

69. Olearius, *The Voyages and Travels* (London, 1662), 299, cited by Issawi, *EHI*, 11. On the products traded, see Minorsky, *TM*, 20. On the world-system, see Braudel, *The Mediterranean*, 551, 568-69; and Inalcik, "The Ottoman Economic Mind," 211-12.

70. Details of the trade are found in Ferrier, "The Armenians and the EIC," 41 note 1, 45; Steensgaard, *The Asian Trade Revolution*, 334-35, 395 table 19; Emerson, "Ex Occidente Lux," 154-55; Bal Krishna, *Commercial Relations between India and England (1601-1657)* (London: George Routledge & Sons, Ltd., 1924), 73 note 1; Issawi, *EHI*, 11-12; K. N. Chaudhuri, "The East India Company and the Export of Treasure in the Early Seventeenth Century," pp. 23-38 in *Economic History Review*, 2nd series, volume XVI (1963), 25-28; and Savory, *Iran under the Safavids*, 199.

71. Coen to the Heeren XVII, 8 May 1619, cited by Steensgaard, *The Asian Trade Revolution*, 407.

72. Braudel, *The Mediterranean*, 635.

73. From the VOC's points and articles in the form of a general instruction for the governor-general and his council at Batavia, as cited by C. R. Boxer, *Jan Compagnie in War and Peace 1602-1799. A Short History of the Dutch East-India Company* (Hong Kong: Heinemann Asia, 1979), 21. See also Savory, *Iran under the Safavids,* 198-99; Ferrier, "The Armenians and the EIC," 47; Emerson, "Ex Occidente Lux," 156; Steensgaard, *The Asian Trade Revolution,* 374; and Meilink-Roelofsz, "The Earliest Relations between Persia and the Netherlands," 22-23, 34-36, 41-42, 44.

74. On India and Iran, see Emerson, "Ex Occidente Lux," 151-52, 159, 161-65, 248-49, 264-65; Krishna, *Commercial Relations,* 10; Khanbaba Bayani, *Les Relations de l'Iran avec l'Europe occidentale à l'époque Safavide (Portugal, Espagne, Angleterre, Hollande et France),* published doctoral thesis, University of Paris (Paris: Les Presses modernes, 1937), 48; Ferrier, "The Armenians and the EIC," 56 note 1; Keyvani, *Artisans and Guild Life,* 229-30; and Riazul Islam, *Indo-Persian Relations. A Study of the Political and Diplomatic Relations between the Mughal Empire and Iran* (Lahore: Ripon Printing Press, 1970).

75. On the Ottoman-Safavid relationship, see Inalcik, "The Ottoman Economic Mind," 213-14; Steensgaard and Inalcik, "Harir," 213-14; Braudel, *The Mediterranean,* 549ff, 1172; Emerson, "Ex Occidente Lux," 119-20; and Ferrier, "The Armenians and the EIC," 39 note 1, 161-62 note 8.

76. Data on Iran's relations with Russia are found in Muriel Atkin, *Russia and Iran 1780-1828* (Minneapolis: University of Minnesota Press, 1980), 3-4; Savory, *Iran under the Safavids,* 112, 196; Monshi, *History of Shah 'Abbas,* 679, 681; Bayani, *Les Relations de l'Iran avec l'Europe,* 60; Emerson, "Ex Occidente Lux," 174-90; and Braudel, *The Mediterranean,* 193, 195.

77. Ralph Davis, *Aleppo and Devonshire Square: English Traders in the Levant in the Eighteenth Century* (London: Macmillan, [1963] 1967), 146, cited by Ferrier, "The Armenians and the EIC," 61-62 note 8.

78. Wallerstein, *The Capitalist World Economy,* 6.

79. Wallerstein, *The Modern World-System I,* 26.

80. Ibid., 301-302.

81. Ibid., 325, 332.

82. According to Wallerstein, Europe only *begins* to incorporate parts of Asia after 1700 or so: ibid., 343-344.

83. Minorsky, *TM,* 13-14; Keddie, *Roots of Revolution,* 12-13, 20-21; Bausani, *The Persians,* 124, 125, 143; and Banani, "Reflections," 101, 105. My argument on social structure in this section is amplified in John Foran, "The Modes of Production Approach to Seventeenth-Century Iran," pp. 345-363 in *International Journal of Middle East Studies,* volume 20, number 3 (August 1988).

84. Representatives of this approach include Nomani, "Origin and Development of Feudalism in Iran," 67, 70-72, 117; Petrushevsky, "Iran under the Il-khans," 514, 515; Saleh, "Social Formations in Iran," 88; and Thomas M. Ricks, "Politics and Trade in Southern Iran and the Gulf, 1745-1765," Ph.D. dissertation, Department of History, Indiana University (1975), 6, 9, 12. For the critique of feudalism, see Lambton, "The Evolution of the *Iqta'*"; Hodgson, *The Venture of Islam,* II, 49, 80-81; and Anderson, *Lineages of the Absolutist State,* 401-408, 424.

85. See Fattaneh Mehrain, "Emergence of Capitalist Authoritarian States in Periphery Formations: A Case Study of Iran," Ph.D. dissertation, Department of Sociology, University of Wisconsin-Madison (1979), 58-59, 73-74, 112; and Ervand Abrahamian, "European Feudalism and Middle Eastern Despotisms," pp. 129-156 in *Science & Society,* volume XXXIX, number 2 (Summer 1975), especially 155-156.

86. This idea is suggested by Mehrain, "Emergence of Capitalist Authoritarian States," 75, and Homa Katouzian, "The Aridisolatic Society: A Model of Long-Term Social and Economic Development in Iran," pp. 259-282 in *The International Journal of Middle East Studies,* volume 15, number 2 (May 1983), 270. Tribal khans, especially as governors, did sometimes control other economic activities, but only in their local areas, however extensive.

87. Banani, "Reflections," 105, and more to the point, Reid, *Tribalism and Society*, 6, 66-67, and Keddie, *Roots of Revolution*, 36, and "Iran, 1797-1941," 137.

88. This and other examples are discussed by Lambton, *Landlord and Peasant*, xxi-xxv. More pre-Safavid syllogisms of rule can be found in Arjomand, *The Shadow of God and the Hidden Imam*, 95, and Petrushevsky, "Iran under the Il-khans," 493.

89. Lambton, *Islamic Society in Persia*, 4. The work is by Muhammad Mufid, the quote from British Museum Oriental ms. 210, f.332b, now published in three volumes.

90. Arjomand, *The Shadow of God and the Hidden Imam*, 93, 98, 99; Roger Savory, "The Safavid State and Polity," pp. 179-212 in *Iranian Studies*, volume VII, numbers 1-2 (1974), 184.

91. Chardin, *Voyages*, V, 229; Father Judasz Tadeusz Krusinski, *The History of the Late Revolutions of Persia*, translated to English with a short History of the Sophies, by Father Du Cerceau (London: J. Osborne, 1740 [Reprint Edition 1973 by Arno Press]), 41. The quote is actually from Du Cerceau's prefixed material. This paragraph draws also on Arjomand, *The Shadow of God and the Hidden Imam*, 179, and Savory, *Iran under the Safavids*, 27, and "The Safavid State and Polity," 184.

92. Arjomand, *The Shadow of God and the Hidden Imam*, 11, 18.

93. See Ibn Babuya, in A. A. Fyzee, *A Shi'ite Creed* (London, 1942), 96, cited by Ann K. S. Lambton, *State and Government in Medieval Islam. An Introduction to Islamic Political Theory: The Jurists* (London: Oxford University Press, 1981), 232, or Arjomand, *The Shadow of God and the Hidden Imam*, 39.

94. These terms are taken from Lambton's resolution of the "just" vs. "usurped" government conundrum: *State and Government*, 254-255 note 45.

95. Arjomand, *The Shadow of God and the Hidden Imam*, 177; see also Banani, "Reflections," 86-87, and Lambton, *State and Government*, 282-283.

96. Ibid., 285. See also Ann K. S. Lambton, "Quis Custodiet Custodes? Some Reflections on the Persian Theory of Government (Conclusion)," pp. 125-146 in *Studia Islamica*, volume VI (1956), 131.

97. Chardin, *Voyages*, V, 208-212.

98. Ibid., V, 216.

99. This paragraph makes use of Lambton, *State and Government*, 268, 276-77; Arjomand, *The Shadow of God and the Hidden Imam*, 141-42, 206; Hodgson, *The Venture of Islam*, III, 35; Chardin, *Voyages*, VI, 70-71, VII, 319; and Emerson, "Ex Occidente Lux," 247. Also relevant to this discussion is du Mans, *Estat de la Perse*, 162.

100. Arjomand, *The Shadow of God and the Hidden Imam*, 9. See also ibid., 186. Lambton concludes: "From the evidence available, it would seem that the position of the shah, so far as it concerned his claim to rule on behalf of the *imam*, when not actually disputed, remained ambiguous": *State and Government*, 282. See also ibid., 280-81; Chardin, *Voyages*, V, 467, VI, 47-48, 75; and Savory, *Iran under the Safavids*, 233.

101. Nasr, "Religion in Safavid Persia," 276. See also Arjomand, *The Shadow of God and the Hidden Imam*, 138-41, 211; and Lambton, "Quis Custodiet Custodes? . . . (Conclusion)," 131.

102. Arjomand, *The Shadow of God and the Hidden Imam*, 164, also 28, 165-66. Bausani mentions the new popular and semi-popular religious poetry of the Safavid period, expressing the passion of the early Shi'i martyrs: *The Persians*, 141.

103. Arjomand, *The Shadow of God and the Hidden Imam*, 33. See too Keddie, *Roots of Revolution*, 20.

104. Reid, *Tribalism and Society*, 70, 31. See also Savory, *Iran under the Safavids*, 50; and Dickson, "Sháh Tahmásb and the Uzbeks," 215.

105. Reid, *Tribalism and Society*, 32, also 8.

106. Ibid., 143, based on Nora Chadwick and Victor Zhirmunsky, *The Oral Epics of Central Asia* (London: Oxford University Press, 1968).

107. Banani, "Reflections," 98-99.

108. Keyvani, *Artisans and Guild Life*, 210.

109. Ibid., 25; see also on urban ideals, Ravandi, *Tarikh-i Ijtima'i-yi Iran*, volume 3, 576-582; Lambton, *Islamic Society in Persia*, 17-19; and Savory, *Iran under the Safavids*, 182.

110. Chardin, *Voyages*, V, 219-220.

111. Lambton, *State and Government*, 13, and "The Evolution of the *Iqta'*," 47.

112. Reid, *Tribalism and Society*, 147-148.

113. Richard Ettinghausen, "Stylistic Tendencies at the Time of Shah 'Abbas," in *Iranian Studies*, volume VII (1974), 600-603, 610, cited by Savory, *Iran under the Safavids*, 135-136.

114. Savory, *Iran under the Safavids*, 213. Some important perspectives on the nature of the literature of the period are sketched by Ehsan Yar-Shater, "Safavid Literature: Progress or Decline?" pp. 217-270 in *Iranian Studies*, volume VII, numbers 1-2 (1974).

3

Social Change in Iran
from 1500 to 1800

If the Revolution of Persia has been so astonishing, when taken only in a general View, and according to the very imperfect Ideas we can form of it from the Gazettes and other publick News Papers, we may affirm, it will appear still more amazing, when we come to give a particular Account of the remote Causes and Events that prepar'd the Way to it for above twenty Years.

—Judasz Tadeusz Krusinski, *The History of the Late Revolutions of Persia*

The centerpiece of social change in the "long" Safavid period from the sixteenth to the eighteenth centuries is the fall of the dynasty itself to a fairly small invading party of Afghan tribesmen at Isfahan in 1722, the event to which the Polish Jesuit Krusinski alludes in such perceptive terms above. The present chapter devotes itself in large measure to the "remote Causes" that prepared this event, starting with an inventory of the types of social change that occurred in Iran from 1500 to 1722, including those both internal and external to the social formation and its constituent parts—tribal nomads, urban groups, peasants, and the court. This establishes a context to evaluate the various theories that have been put forward to explain the dramatic fall of the dynasty and to contribute to this debate by drawing attention to the role played by fiscal crisis tendencies, on the one hand, and political and ideological problems of the Safavid state, on the other (the fiscal crisis, in particular, has never been properly identified and brought to bear). A briefer examination follows of the successive tribal families that sought dominion in the course of an eighteenth century marked by fairly frequent changes of "dynasty"—the Afghans from 1722 to 1729, Nadir Shah and the Afshars from 1729 to 1746, Karim Khan Zand in Shiraz from 1750 to 1779, and finally the rise of the Qajars to a more permanent position of power after 1785. The conclusion points to the negative developmental consequences of the fall of the Safavids and the centrality of the eighteenth-century tribal civil wars as a watershed separating the independent and relatively dynamic political economy of the seventeenth century from the dependent and increasingly thwarted development of the nineteenth-century Qajar social formation, the subject of part two of this study.

Types of Social Change under the Safavids, 1500-1722

Internal Conflicts

Two basic types of conflict emerged in Safavid Iran—social movements with a popular base, particularly urban-led uprisings but also involving tribal and peasant groups, and inter- and intra-elite conflicts over political power, such as the sixteenth-century tribal civil wars, 'Abbas I's centralization effort, and the rise of the harem and ulama to influence over the later Safavid shahs. Popular social movements can be in part conceptualized as incipient class conflicts based on often fragile alliances among dominated groups, whereas elite struggles might be seen as "mode of production" or "sectoral" conflicts since these were waged at the top of the social structure between elites seeking control over the social surplus. The proto-class urban and peasant uprisings of the period failed because they could be contained within their modes of production and isolated in their geographical areas by a state that possessed overwhelming power vis-à-vis any single uprising. Elite struggles, however, would eventually play a role in undermining the Safavid state, along with other factors. Finally, it should be noted that many of the movements discussed spill over analytic boundaries and involved elements of both popular and elite participation, or urban, peasant, and tribal actors.

Incipient class conflict can be discerned in several popular social movements of the Safavid period whose primary locus was in an urban setting. The events in eastern Khurasan known as the Harat revolution of 1535-37 had roots in the repeated extortions of the local population by qizilbash governors, especially when the city was under siege by the Uzbeks, but also even in peacetime. In late 1535 a "mob" of the poor of Harat murdered the extortionate governor in the baths. Resistance to qizilbash control was led by landowners and notables of the agricultural suburbs around the city, who had been severely oppressed by the qizilbash. When a plot was discovered and all the notables of Harat proper were imprisoned, a "popular army" of suburb-based revolutionaries besieged the city and called on the Uzbek leader Ubayd Khan for help. Dickson has analyzed the social composition of the movement and its aims: "The nameless miller who advanced with sword in hand against the walls of Harát, the looting of the homes in

Harát at its entry, the references to the *dahátí* and the *rustáyí* (the 'villagers' or 'peasants') in the movement, would indicate that an element of 'class warfare' and jacquerie were involved."[1] Harat was abandoned by the Uzbeks in early 1537 and a compromise joint notable-qizilbash interim government was set up until the Safavid army liberating Khurasan from the Uzbeks entered the city and a general amnesty was issued. More acute class-based conflict occurred at Tabriz and Astarabad in the sixteenth century. The second largest city in Iran, Tabriz, witnessed a revolt by artisans and shopkeepers against an unpopular governor and other local notables between 1571 and 1573, requiring state military intervention to quell.[2] The rebellions in Astarabad between 1537 and 1600 were an instance of a multi-faceted popular movement including artisans, peasants, and tribespeople, inspired by a secret egalitarian ideology, and led by elites who too frequently capitulated or changed course once in power. By 1600 the royal army had ended the revolt, with tribes and local people submitting their problems to Shah 'Abbas and returning to their tasks.[3]

Peasant involvement in popular social movements was more extensive, or at least better documented, than that of tribespeople. Reid has argued that "The peasants of Iran in the Safavid period were the furthest thing possible from a 'nonrevolutionary' peasantry. The record of rebellion as found in the various chronicles of the Safavid period is immense."[4] Peasants supported the urban revolts at both Harat and Astarabad; their movements may have often involved secret associations with apocalyptic, egalitarian overtones. Eskandar Beg Monshi's chronicle records a revolt in the densely settled silk, tea, and rice-growing region of Gilan from 1593 to 1595 and articulates the court's rather hostile view of the people of that province:

> The common people are seditious to such a degree that, even when they are ruled by an independent sultan, some farmer's son has only to take to the forests in revolt for everyone to flock to his standard. On the first day, an enormous group gathers round him, but, on the very same day, either because there is some simple matter to be attended to, or because they hear a rumor from some ignorant fellow who does not even know what he is supposed to be doing himself, they disperse and pay the penalty for their folly. The next day, they are capable of repeating the whole performance. . . . For the sake of being king for a day, they are ready to destroy themselves. . . . There are innumerable instances of this sort of behavior in the history of Gilan—perhaps it is something to do with the climate![5]

In April 1629 a serious uprising broke out when a group of local Iranian ruling families led by a certain Kalinjar Sultan revolted against qizilbash control.[6] These notables played on discontent due to excessive taxes to mobilize some 30,000 poor and common people "without name or position" and defeated those officials who remained loyal to the shah, gaining control of the whole province. They seized royal warehouses and distributed goods among the people before meeting with final defeat in the summer.

The numerousness of rebellions of several kinds, especially in the period from the 1520s to the 1630s, is as striking as the fact that virtually all of them failed to achieve significant gains for the majority of the population. Alliances of oppressed groups *across* modes of production lines were difficult to effect and sustain in Safavid Iran, and rarely occurred. Internal divisions and conflicts of interest also arose, such as the disputes in Gilan in 1629 over whether to protect or distribute merchants' goods that were seized. When disadvantaged groups did somehow manage to make contact, such as the peasants and townspeople of Harat in 1535, or the peasants, artisans, and tribespeople in the millenarian movements of Astarabad, a strong tendency can be discerned for their leaders to compromise and be coopted once in power. Where this failed to occur, provincial or central authorities stepped in to crush real resistance—on occasion with some difficulty—an almost inevitable outcome given the primarily local character of the rebellions that took place. Reid's pessimistic conclusion about social movements in Astarabad is that "The only effect the rebellions had was to make the lot of the peasants and urban laborers harsher and more unbearable."[7] While this is true especially for the sixteenth century, when qizilbash governors often imposed heavy taxes on the population and warfare was endemic in the life of each generation, the more centralized absolutism of Shah 'Abbas after 1600 and the long period of external peace after the Treaty of Zuhab with the Ottoman Empire in 1639 found an internal reflection in a far more quiescent seventeenth century, about which Krusinski could write with only some exaggeration, that "there was not one Town that discovered so much as a Thought of revolting."[8]

Struggles for power at the top of the social structure were common throughout the Safavid period. One way to conceptualize these changes is in terms of the degree of centralization of the Safavid state, the key to which was the shah's relation to the qizilbash tribes. The form and degree of resistance of tribal chiefs to royal authority gradually changed as the balance of power shifted. By 1600, due to 'Abbas's centralization efforts, the great amirs declined in wealth, territory, and military manpower and their ambitions shrank from political control of provincial governorships to a desperate attempt to hold onto their social bases in the local pastoral units. 'Abbas's reform measures sealed the fate of the sixteenth-century uymaq/tribal state system and heralded a new Safavid absolutism that lasted well into the seventeenth century. Table 3.1 offers a periodization of this process in the Safavid period. 'Abbas's absolutist project endured for several generations after his death in 1629, until a constellation of factors led to a decline in Safavid hegemony by the early eighteenth century.

TABLE 3.1 Central vs. Decentralized State Power in Iran, 1500-1800

Strong Central Control/Absolutism	*Decentralized Power/Tribal State*
1500-1524/6	
	1526-1533
1530s-1576	
	1576-1590s
1600-1690s	
	Eighteenth Century

One of the key elements in the centralization process of the seventeenth century was the conversion of state provinces (*mamalik*) administered by qizilbash chieftains who retained the bulk of the tax revenues generated in exchange for providing the shah with a contingent of troops on demand, into crown provinces (*khassa*) administered directly by an official of the central bureaucracy. This reduced qizilbash power in two important ways—economic and military, and thus as viable *political* rivals of the state as well. The traveller Chardin suggested that the consequences of converting state to crown lands were quite negative for the Iranian people, the economy, and the state's military preparedness: Royal administrators increased taxation to please the king and keep their appointments, transferred the surplus out of the provincial economies, and undermined the military preparedness of the state by replacing tribal commanders who controlled local troops.[9] Tribal amirs who used to serve as provincial governors lost ground politically and economically to the Safavid state, but this would disclose its negative side when no provincial army rallied to the Safavids during the siege of Isfahan in 1722. Though hard to discern, it is quite probable that local tribal power increasingly reasserted itself in outlying areas of the empire by 1700. Certainly local protection broke down and freebooting increased. Meanwhile the decline in numbers, pay, and training of the standing army, corruption and neglect in high places, and the long peace with the Ottomans all combined to seriously erode the regular army's morale and preparedness.[10]

Intra-elite conflict also increasingly plagued the court itself. The personal capacities of the Safavid shahs declined and the influence of the harem rose as a result of Shah 'Abbas's practice of bringing up his children not to rule provinces but in the confines of the harem, where they learned little of statecraft or military science. The last four Safavid shahs—Safi (ruled 1629-1642), 'Abbas II (1642-1666), Sulayman (1666-1694), and Sultan Husayn (1694-1722)—are variously described by observers as incompetent, neglectful rulers, given to overindulgence and drink.[11] As the shahs degenerated in capabilities, a private harem council of leading eunuchs, princesses, and mistresses became "the Arbiters of Affairs, the Dispensers of Employments and Favors, and Absolute Masters of the Government,"[12] deciding issues of war and peace, conducting foreign relations, and making appointments to all offices. Harem infighting and provincial bureaucratic abuses were linked, as alliances formed and positions were bought and sold, with intra-elite rivalries at court leading to frequent changes in both military and provincial appointments. Another elite which attained a new degree of power at the shah's expense in the latter stages of the seventeenth century was the highest-ranking ulama. There was not just a struggle to evolve a power base independent of the state; the ulama also achieved notable successes in directly controlling the last two shahs from 1666 to 1722. This attempt to influence the government *from within* intensified with the appointment of the eminent mujtahid Muhammad Baqir Majlisi as shaykh al-islam of Isfahan in 1687. One of Majlisi's most historically consequential actions was the initiation of campaigns of persecution against not only the non-Muslim religious minorities, but also against Sunnis, thus alienating both the Afghans who eventually toppled the dynasty and potential supporters in the Caucasus, Kurdistan and Khurasan.[13]

In the long run, elite conflicts would prove more devastating to the Safavid state than internal social movements. Despite the numerousness of the popular movements that occurred, particularly in the sixteenth century, all were unsuccessful in altering the basic terms of power. Instead, under Shah 'Abbas, an absolutist state had triumphed by 1630, but one which required a strong, independent, active shah to direct the bureaucracy, conduct foreign relations, command the army, enforce justice, and foster trade. The crown land conversion project and the immuring of the royal princes in the harem revealed their limitations in the next generations, allowing a several-sided and fractious struggle for influence among the ulama, led by Majlisi, the harem, itself internally divided, and an excluded, discontented old-line qizilbash tribal and Iranian bureaucratic court and provincial administration. More than the popular mass-based social movements, these inter- and intra-elite conflicts at the top of the social formation gradually undermined the absolutist Safavid state by the turn of the eighteenth century.

External Relations of Iran, 1630-1722

Another form which development and social change took in Safavid Iran derived from external relations with Europe (especially Holland and England) and the neighboring Russian, Ottoman, and Mughal empires.[14] In chapter two, Iran was characterized from 1500 to 1630 as part of the external arena of the emerging capitalist world-economy, engaged in roughly egalitarian patterns of trade with the European core countries that centered on luxury items such as silk rather than large-scale bulk commodities. The Dutch East India Company—the VOC—was Iran's pre-eminent trading partner for the balance of the seventeenth century. In the mid-1630s the VOC tried to achieve a monopoly on Iranian silk exports by cutting out both the English and the overland Levant trade but the project soon failed due to continued use of the other routes and sources, and a fall in prices in Europe that left a gross profit rate of only 25 percent. The key to Dutch commercial supremacy in the seventeenth century was not its silk exports but rather its lucrative monopoly of the Asian spice trade *into* Iran. At Bandar'Abbas in the 1670s John Fryer observed: "the greatest Traffick, next *Indian* Cloth, comes from the Spice Trade; which the *Dutch* engross, beside Sugar and Copper formerly, for which they carry off Fifty thousand *Thomands* worth of Velvets, Silk, Raw and Wrought, with Rich Carpets, besides many Tunn of Gold and Silver, Yearly."[15] The Dutch, then, by selling spices (and some of the Indian cloth referred to) in Iran and purchasing a limited amount of silk, had a quite favorable balance of trade with Iran, a development which added to the Safavids' tendency toward fiscal crisis. The English EIC admitted their rival's predominance in a letter of 1664 from Bandar'Abbas: "The Dutch walk away with all, and (to our sorrow) are now the sole actors."[16] There is nevertheless some uncertainty as to whether or not Dutch commercial power may have peaked by the turn of the eighteenth century. Lockhart feels there was no decline before 1730, Boxer dates the beginnings of decline between 1700 and 1740.[17] Dutch shipping fell as Holland became embroiled in European wars. It would seem that while certain products experienced a decline in popularity or were eliminated from the trade altogether, others were found to take their place. The period after 1700 or so most likely witnessed less any absolute decline for the Dutch as a relative closing of the considerable gap that had separated them from their main rivals in Safavid Iran, the English.

The English East India Company (EIC) attempted to build on its promising beginnings in the silk trade after 'Abbas's death in 1629. Shortly after 1640 however the English silk purchases stopped altogether, as prices fell in Europe and rose in Iran and supplies became difficult to obtain since Armenian merchants were apparently carrying the bulk of the crop overland to the Levant ports on the Mediterranean. While a letter from Surat to the EIC of 1650/51 declares that "Persia is the most certain trade of all,"[18] serious problems were undermining the EIC both at home and in Asia. These included competition from the Dutch and other English traders, continued Armenian control of the overland routes, and the poor quality of English cloth. A new product, Kirmani goats' hair wool, was used in the

English hat and button industries after 1659; by 1698 exports had reached 300 bales a year and large profits of 100 percent or more were made on its sale in England. The demand however stimulated the local wool-weaving sector in Kirman, which slowed exports to Europe. The best conclusion overall would probably be that by the first quarter of the eighteenth century, the Dutch were being commercially challenged by the EIC but less from any conspicuous English success in Iran than due to the EIC's rising fortunes in the world-system as a whole, particularly in the trade with China and India. Though the VOC remained first in Iran's foreign trade, the relationship with its main European competitor was no longer hegemonic, as in the period from 1650 to the 1680s.[19] None of Iran's other European trading partners could come close to the volume and presence of England and Holland in the period under consideration here.

A final, important set of countries in contact with Iran in the seventeenth century includes its immediate neighbors, mostly world-empires like Iran itself. Russia fits better into this group than it does among the European nations, due both to its relative isolation from Europe until this very period and to the fact that its proximity to Safavid Iran after 1600 made contact easier and entailed a "security" dimension which would explode into invasion and occupation in the 1720s. After turning inwards during the Time of Troubles (1603-13), the Russian economy began a recovery in the 1640s. In 1673 Chardin reported that the Russian ambassador was given precedence over the French and English, the Iranians stating that "The Muscovite is our neighbor and our friend, and trade has been established between us without interruption and for a long time (*d'ancienneté*)."[20] Notwithstanding this warm avowal, the amounts on the whole were probably fairly modest without being negligible, as customs records show some forty Iranian merchants leaving Astrakhan in 1676 with Russian goods, thirty in 1680, twenty-five in 1681, fifty in 1686, twenty or more in 1687 and 1688. Peter the Great, who ruled Russia from 1682 to 1725, sought more extensive commercial relations and though trade seems to have picked up, it cannot be judged great or continuous. He also harbored expansionary designs in the Caspian area, held in check until about 1720 by long wars with Sweden and conflicts with the Ottomans.[21]

Hostilities with the powerful Ottoman Empire to the west came to an end in 1639 and the resulting lengthy period of peace until the 1720s revitalized the overland routes from Iran to the Levant ports. Though the Asian spice trade was definitively diverted to sea-routes around Africa by the Europeans in the seventeenth century, this was not true of Iran's silk trade. The balance of this trade was greatly in Iran's favor, which had the positive effect of increasing the amount of money in circulation in Iran, but also exposed the economy to Ottoman inflation. The size of this transit trade is very difficult to estimate: Ferrier makes an "inspired guess" of a little less than

700,000 pounds sterling worth of imports from Turkey in the mid-seventeenth century; in 1801 Malcolm thought it accounted for over one-quarter of Iran's total foreign trade.[22]

Iran's diplomatic and commercial relations with India in the seventeenth century were basically friendly, aside from a dispute over the city of Qandahar. Trade in the Gulf with India was stimulated by the expulsion of the Portuguese, and the English report it had quadrupled in the 1630s. Fryer said that at Bandar 'Abbas in the 1670s the largest trade was that of Indian cloth; as much as one-third of total Indian production may have gone to or through Iran. The amount of Iran's trade with India is rather difficult to quantify; to use Malcolm's figures for a century after the period which interests us here, it represented some 22.5 percent of Iran's foreign trade. This is close to the Ottoman Empire's 26 percent, though two important differences existed: the trade was much more for consumption than further transit elsewhere and a decided trade imbalance obtained in India's favor, though again, by how much is hard to say.[23]

To sum up, in chapter two we saw that sustained commercial contact with Europe had just begun in the 1620s. Both Lockhart and Ferrier conclude that the patterns of trade and foreign relations established then were maintained intact through 1722. Iran's average annual exports in the seventeenth century, based mainly on silk, have been estimated at 1-2 million pounds sterling. Putting this into global perspective, England (and Wales) with a total population roughly equal to Iran's, had exports of 5,000,000 pounds sterling in 1688, and France, with two to three times the population, had exports of 4,800,000 pounds sterling in 1715.[24] The key changes which occurred between 1630 and 1720 had mainly to do with the silk trade. The collapse of the royal monopoly in 1630 undoubtedly shifted the profit shares in favor of Armenian middlemen at the Safavids' expense. Silk production seems to have risen from 1620 to 1670: An English estimate of 1620 is that 1,350,000 lbs. were exported to Europe, while Olearius put the total crop in the mid-1630s at 4,300,000 lbs. and Chardin in 1670 put it at 6,072,000 lbs.[25] These are all guesses, however, and a plausible counter-guess would be that by 1670 the export of silk reached a peak and may thereafter have declined through 1720.[26] The East India companies found a cheaper source of silk in Bengal by 1650; this led to a drop in demand in the Persian Gulf. Though the Armenians continued to ply the overland routes, the price in Europe generally fell (with exceptions in the early and mid-1690s), which must have had an impact on their abilities to sell Iran's silk in the Levant. Another disquieting trend to which these developments contributed was Iran's balance of payments, which turned increasingly unfavorable: As less silk was sold and wool failed to make up the difference, it became necessary to spend more and more cash for the spices the Dutch brought from Asia.

The overall qualitative impact of these relations on the Iranian social structure was probably fairly slight. The expansion of Kirman wool production did lead to local increases in the domestic weaving industry. With much or most of the country's silk production going abroad, there would logically have been some loss in potential silk manufactures for internal use. However, there was no major re-orientation of the economy for exports and no significant dependence on any imports, except for pepper and sugar, which were consumed by some urban classes but not yet the mass of the population. The conclusion drawn here is that Iran in the seventeenth century remained a world-empire in the external arena of the world-economy. The internal economy and social structure possessed its own strong dynamic, with limited (if growing) external relations with both neighboring world-empires (Russia, the Ottomans, and Mughals) and emerging European core countries (Holland and England) that did not much disrupt it. There was certainly no *dependency* of Iran on the West in the seventeenth century. But the long period in the external arena did herald the beginnings of a gradual, relative decline vis-à-vis an expanding Europe. In the seventeenth century the Middle Eastern states of the Safavids and Ottomans were far too strong to be colonized and dominated by the core, *and yet* too weak to compete with Europe in the new peripheries of Asia, southeast Asia, and Africa, not to mention Latin America. Thus the Middle East merely held its ground (which in Western eyes has since been invariably labelled a "decline"), unable to function as either core or periphery of the emerging world-economy.

Secular Trends in the Seventeenth-Century Safavid Political Economy

The fall of the Safavid dynasty becomes more intelligible in light of the principal long-term economic trends in seventeenth-century Iran—balance of payments deficits, inflationary dynamics, and the growing fiscal problems of the Safavid state.[27] The question of Iran's overall balance of trade should be seen against an international backdrop. Beginning in the sixteenth century and continuing into the seventeenth, there was a steady flow of silver and to a lesser degree gold, from Latin America into Spain, whence it was diffused throughout Europe and then carried by the East India fleets into Asia. From Asia to the West, the reverse trade routes tended to carry valuable commodities—silk and spices above all. The export of Iran's vast silk production drew gold and silver into the country, though how much remained inside is difficult to say. Ferrier estimates the value of an average year's silk production at perhaps 1,750,000 pounds sterling, with wide fluctuations.[28] In the sixteenth century most of this silk may have been paid for with cash, but with the growth of English cloth and Dutch spice exports into Iran in the seventeenth, much less would have been paid for in this manner. The other major source of inflow was the Levant, both from the Ottomans themselves and the European companies there. The amounts most likely increased after the Ottoman wars and prohibitions of the sixteenth century gave way to more peaceful relations in the seventeenth, but again the figures are simply unknown.

The money obtained by a favorable balance in the silk trade with the West then flowed to the East, as spices, drugs, and cotton goods were imported and had to be paid for in part with cash. The main sources which drained specie away from Iran were the Dutch and the Indians. The Dutch, in Fryer's famous words, "carry off . . . many Tunn of Gold and Silver, Yearly."[29] This they did by supplying Iran with expensive spices from their Asian trade. And since Mughal India had no need for the raw silk of Iran, the cotton and other textile goods it exported had to be paid for with cash. Thus could du Mans in 1660 compare Iran to a caravanserai with two gates passing coins from Turkey to India, and conclude that "the wealth of Persia is only like the humidity of water which attaches itself to the channels it passes through into its basin . . . little remains in the country."[30] Judging from such evidence we may cautiously infer that the balance of trade was on the whole negative by the latter decades of the seventeenth century. In the overall pattern of world trade, then, Iran fit neither the classic European core or Asian periphery role—it bought Asian products (like the Europeans) and sold its own silk (like the Asians), but it was the European companies who profited twice on these transactions for they brought the silk to market in Europe and the spices to market in Iran, adding costs to the latter and deducting profits from the former. Iran was as much a short-circuit as a conduit in this trade, from the European point of view.

While large-scale commerce with the Dutch and India drained currency away from Iran, the continued overland silk trade exposed Iran to the Ottoman Empire's inflation problems. The latter were part of another world-wide trend. In Europe, the last quarter of the sixteenth century had seen a three- to fourfold increase in prices for goods and services compared with 1500. Originating in western Europe, inflation spread to Italy and central Europe and then, by the 1580s, to the Ottoman Empire. How much inflation did Iran, midway geographically and commercially between the Ottoman and Mughal empires, in fact experience? Emerson notes that due to the scarcity of coins the prices of foreign goods were falling, which would imply a strengthening of Iran's currency. Other evidence from *A Chronicle of the Carmelites in Persia* and Krusinski suggests that the tuman was stable relative to Italian, French, English, and Spanish currencies till the 1670s, then appreciated by about 33 percent by the 1690s or 1700s.[31] Nevertheless, there is ample evidence of a certain amount of internal inflation. By 1684, most of the coins in circulation were seriously debased; the bazaars at

TABLE 3.2   Value of the Tuman, 1510-1718

Year	Gold Value of One Tuman Expressed in German Gold Marks of 1913
1510	270.0
1522	195.0
1530	165.0
1550	133.0
1577	162.0
1580	129.0
1593	100.0
1622	83.0
1660	77.0
1680	69.0
1711	63.5
1718	63.5

Source: Fragner, "Social and Economic Affairs," 566, based on the work of Walther Hinz.

Isfahan were closed and new money was ordered minted. Fragner has constructed a table showing the approximate gold value of one tuman in the Safavid period (see Table 3.2). This table would appear to show the effects of the Ottoman inflation from 1550 to 1622, as well as a steady later internal inflation after 'Abbas's death (the decline from 1510 to 1550 is harder to account for; it continued a sharp drop from the pre-Safavid fifteenth century). Prices on the few commodities for which even roughly comparable information exists suggest a generally rising pattern of prices in the later seventeenth century. Table 3.3 provides a rough index of the long-term trends, which, it must be stressed, are far from clear, given our lack of knowledge about real prices and problems of seasonal fluctuations. It should be noted that the price of bread at Isfahan in 1668 is anomalous; there had been a bad harvest in 1666 followed by an outbreak of famine and disease.[32] The table, incomplete as it is, hints at a rise in prices of major foodstuffs and wood in the course of the seventeenth century, confirmed by various European observers.[33]

To reconcile these two major negative trends—a drain of currency from the imbalance of foreign trade and an apparent rise in internal prices—is not a simple matter. Logically the first should have caused prices to fall by increasing the demand for coins. The only hint of a mutual resolution of

TABLE 3.3   Prices in Safavid Iran, 1581-1716

Year/Place	Bread	Rice	Hen	Wood
1581/Isfahan	1.52 dinars/lb	10.6 dinars/lb		1.52 dinars/lb
1588-1629/Sultaniyeh			62.5 dinars	
1629-1642/Isfahan '	3.70 dinars/lb			
1636-1638/Isfahan				.95 dinars/lb
1668/Isfahan	15.75 dinars/lb			
1667-1694/Isfahan		25.0 dinars/lb	75.0 dinars	4.17-5.21 dinars/lb
1716/Isfahan				5.36 dinars/lb

Source: Keyvani, Artisans and Guild Life, 119-20. Calculations, with corrections, mine.

these counteracting trends is the fact that Indian moneylenders, Armenian merchants, and the Safavid state itself took the best coins either out of the country or out of circulation, leaving the least fine and thus debasing the currency that circulated internally. Other explanations may be necessary. What seems to be the case empirically is both that good currency was hard to find, resulting in an undermonetarized economy that limited overall trade, and that prices rose, with inevitably negative consequences for the urban poor and those living on fixed incomes, a group which included some, perhaps many, who worked for the Safavid state, among them holders of tax benefits and those paid in lump sums rather than a percentage of the land revenues. In a society with little wage labor, inflation most likely harmed those who had no product to sell or those whose income could not be raised to compensate; thus the urban poor and marginal populations undoubtedly suffered more than merchants, artisans or state officials. Peasants paying a fixed portion of their crop and living in a subsistence economy were presumably not too badly affected, and tribespeople even less.

Whatever their ultimate explanation, both these trends contributed to what may be characterized as the fiscal crisis of the Safavid political economy. The conversion of state land to crown land was certainly designed to raise revenues for the Safavid state. First recorded under Tahmasp in the sixteenth century and practised on a wider scale by 'Abbas during his reign, the process accelerated from 1642 to 1666. Could it have been a response to incipient fiscal crisis rather than a mere stratagem to increase the vast income of an absolutist state? In the 1670s, Chardin, who was admittedly only guessing, posited revenues of 700,000 tumans (32 million livres) against expenditures of 744,000 (34 million livres); he, certainly, had some sense that there was a deficit to be taken into account. Could a fiscal crisis then have emerged between 1630 and the 1670s? Two probable causes were the large outlays on the army and harem. Chardin felt that the army accounted for 38.2 percent of total state spending in the 1670s, while the *Tadhkirat al-muluk* indicates that the army and provincial military governors consumed 66.5 percent of the budget. Chardin's 1670 estimates on the cost of the harem were 11.8 percent, with the royal family and its attendants at another 29.4 percent. Sultan Husayn's pilgrimage to Mashhad in 1706-08 included the entire harem and some 60,000 men, "which not only compleatly drein'd his Exchequer, but also ruin'd all the Provinces through which he pass'd."[34] Given these fiscal pressures, the last two Safavid shahs resorted to the sale of offices and a limited amount of tax-farming (though not on the scale of the absolutist states of Europe). Krusinski observes that under Sulayman and Sultan Husayn, "Offices were disposed of, not to the most deserving, but to the highest bidder." Though their offices were expensive to acquire, the provincial "appointees" used the pretext of having to provide "presents" to the court to raise "ten Times as much upon the People."[35]

The inevitable result of such state responses to fiscal crisis was economic hardship for the population. Chardin notes that by 1677, "The impoverished great men everywhere scorched the people, to keep up their standard of living."[36] Krusinski writes of provincial extortion a generation later:

> every Governor . . . hasten'd to fill his Purse, that he might have wherewithal to purchase a new Palace, or to defend himself against any Prosecution he had to apprehend for his Oppressions, the whole at the Expence of the poor People, who were fleeced in all Respects by those too frequent Alterations.

> . . . the People had a great deal to suffer under Governors who regarded their Post no more than a Place to bait at, made it more their Study to pillage the Cities and Provinces, than to keep up good Order; and this they did with the less Caution and Reserve, because they were very sensible that they might do it with Impunity.[37]

Famines broke out in Isfahan itself in 1666/7 and 1707 (the latter leading to a revolt) and the situation was such in 1717 that a German soldier described widespread poverty there: "Bread was so scarce that the poor people used to devour dead camels, horses and mules. Once, when a horse died in the Dutch compound, its body was thrown into the street; within an hour, all the flesh had been picked from its bones."[38] Such conditions may not have been the rule at all times in all parts of Safavid Iran, but that they were acute at least three times in the capital over fifty years gives some idea of the impact of the changes discussed here.

The sum of these diverse trends is one of definite economic deterioration at all levels of society. The drain of currency and decline in the terms of trade for silk hurt the merchant classes (and the ulama who depended on

their contributions). Military and harem expenditures led to fiscal crisis at
the apex of the state and undermined the Safavid family and the vast
numbers of courtiers and others it supported. In turn this unleashed new
abuses such as sale of offices, corruption, and higher taxes. These hurt the
whole population, especially the peasantry and urban laboring classes, who
were further hard-pressed by the rise in prices which impacted most on the
urban poor. By the turn of the eighteenth century the flourishing political
economy of Shah 'Abbas and his immediate successors appears to have been
lurching into a crisis whose strands were woven into the entire social
formation.

The Long Fall of the Safavids

The fall of the Safavids was not a single event, for the actual taking of
Isfahan by a smallish invading army of Afghan tribesmen in 1722 was
preceded by a *process* of decline and crisis extending over half a century or
more. Vladimir Minorsky's classic theses on "the more conspicuous factors"
among the causes of decline are worth quoting in full, since they have to
date proved largely unsurpassable by subsequent historians of the period.
He notes:

> (a) The complete disappearance of the basic theocratic nucleus round which
> Shah Isma'il had built up his state, without the substitution of some other
> dynamic ideology.

> (b) Great opposition between the old and the new elements in the Persian
> military class.

> (c) The disturbance of the equilibrium between the *mamalik* and *khassa*, the
> expansion of the latter having diminished the interest of the service classes in
> the cause which they were supporting.

> (d) The irresponsible character of the 'shadow government' represented by
> the harem, the Queen Mother and the eunuchs.

> (e) The degeneration of the dynasty whose scions were brought up in the
> atmosphere of the harem, in complete ignorance of the outside world.[39]

Laurence Lockhart similarly stresses the conversion of state to crown provinces and the personal shortcomings of the last two shahs. Only a few
scholars have tried to pinpoint structural, political-economic factors. Thus
Hodgson notes the concentration of wealth at the court and capital, Keddie

mentions economic decline, and Helfgott hypothesizes the "trade revolu-tion" as a probable factor in Safavid decline, responsible for inflation, loss of commercial power, and an increased tax burden.[40] A coherent, unified account would build on the insights of Minorsky and hints in later works to conceptualize the fall of the dynasty in terms of simultaneous and interrelated economic, political, military, and ideological crises. These crises are linked by the one which has till now been least explored—an eco-nomic/fiscal crisis that had military, political, and ideological effects. This economic crisis had largely internal causes—there is no argument to be made for the category of dependency in the seventeenth and early eigh-teenth centuries—but there were two exogenous, world-system factors at work, namely, trade deficits and inflation. There were also regional military pressures by 1715-20 emanating from the Ottoman Empire, Russia, and especially the Afghan tribes. The present explanation therefore draws partly on world-system analysis within the main framework of an internal political economy in crisis, and on a synthesis of economic, political, and ideological levels of analysis.

The economic crisis has been detailed above. Far more than the oft-noted negative consequences of state land conversion, it involved a tale of infla-tion, balance of payments deficit, fiscal crisis of the state, tax-farming of the customs and sale of offices, corruption and growing tax exploitation of the population. A military impact came with the alienation of the tribal armies through the replacement of qizilbash provincial governors by state-ap-pointed intendants, often Georgians, which led to the dismantling of the old-style tribal cavalries. If this had been compensated with increased spending by the state on the standing army there would have been little problem. But caught in a budget deficit and at peace with their powerful Ottoman neighbors, the later Safavid shahs allowed themselves to be convinced by the private harem council to save money by not spending it on the central army. The only competent Safavid military forces after 1700 were Georgian-led contingents, and neither they, nor any tribal provincial forces would rally to the side of the dynasty in its hour of need.

Political deterioration too played a role. The rise of faction-ridden new groups to power at court—the eunuchs, shah's harem, and the ulama—proved a disaster for the making of coherent state policy when coupled with the bringing up of the royal princes in the highly artificial and sheltered atmosphere of the harem. Among the ill-consequences of fractious council-lors and divided counsels were the unpreparedness of the army, the under-mining due to jealous rivalries of Georgian military and civil officers in the state, the frequent replacement by bribery and personal animosity of pro-vincial governors which exacerbated economic exploitation, and general self-seeking on the part of the highest and most influential Safavid courtiers at the country's expense.

On the ideological plane, the rise to influence of the ulama over Sultan Husayn likewise had grave repercussions. Persecution of Armenian and Hindu merchants harmed the economy, and compelling Jews and Zoroastrians to convert to Islam caused many of the latter to flee to Kirman where in 1719 they looked upon the Afghan invaders as liberators. Most fatefully, the anti-Sunni hostility of militant Shi'i clerics like Majlisi contributed to the alienation of the Afghans who would eventually topple the dynasty, while from 1719 on uprisings occurred in numerous border regions with non-Shi'i populations, such as Shirvan, Kurdistan, Khuzistan, and Baluchistan. Though the Iranian masses were largely Shi'i by the early 1700s and there was no organized anti-Safavid position among them, they too failed conspicuously to rally to the Safavids under siege. So while Shi'ism had taken firm root, it was not in the eighteenth century strong enough to hold together a disintegrating state, especially one whose leading ulama promoted so exclusive a form of it.

There were, finally, as in any historical process, some more or less conjunctural or contingent reasons for the Afghans' success in 1722, most notably the failure of the Georgians to assist Isfahan, the critical defeat at the Battle of Gulnabad outside the city, and various bad decisions taken during the siege. These emerge from consideration of the course of events between 1698 and 1722. Starting in 1698 a series of provincial disturbances sounded distant warnings of the coming collapse. Giorgi XI, a Georgian prince, rose to prominence when he quelled these with his own contingents rather than a qizilbash force or the Safavid standing army. Meanwhile, a more serious situation was developing among the Sunni Afghan tribes of Qandahar and Harat. The Afghan leader Mir Vais was arrested for leading an uprising against Georgian rule, but while in Isfahan exploited the factional hostility he found there against the Georgians and avowed his allegiance to the Safavids. Later, on pilgrimage to Mecca, he obtained a *fatva* (legal opinion) from Sunni ulama authorizing him to undertake a holy war against the infidel Georgians and their Shi'i supporters (i.e. the Safavids). Back in Qandahar, Mir Vais killed Giorgi and took control of the city. Three Safavid expeditions against him failed; when Mir Vais died in 1715 his son Mahmud assumed the tribal leadership and soon both Qandahar and Harat were independent of Iran.[41]

By 1717-19 there were multiple signs of revolt, especially among the Sunni tribes in the more distant provinces. Meanwhile, there were disturbances in Isfahan during Shah Sultan Husayn's absence in 1718. The court moved first to Qazvin and then Tehran to raise troops, but the shah's ministers intrigued against the two leading military commanders, who were Sunnis from Daghistan in the Caucasus. Their armies promptly broke up, leaving Iran with few seasoned troops or competent leaders. Yet another military force was removed from the scene when the same ministers suspended the local operations of Wakhtang VI in Georgia, who vowed never to lift his sword in defense of the Safavids again. This opened the door for Russian intervention in Iran when rebellious tribes looted Russian merchants in the Caucasus in the autumn of 1721, providing Peter the Great with his long-sought pretext to invade.[42]

The dénouement came from a different quarter, beginning in the fall and winter of 1721, when the Afghan leader Mahmud of Qandahar once more entered Iran. With him he had perhaps 10,000 Ghalzais and several thousand Hazaras, being joined en route by Baluchi tribesmen for a total force of about 18,000. Besieging Kirman from late October 1721 till January 1722, Mahmud lost 1,500 men in a direct assault, then marched away in return for a sum of money. In February 1722 he failed to take Yazd, after which he immediately began an advance on Isfahan. An Iranian army of perhaps 40,000 men, some experienced but many hastily assembled from among the peasants and townsmen of the area, marched out to meet the Afghans at Gulnabad, about nineteen miles from Isfahan. There, on March 8, 1722, owing to their lack of training coupled with the indecision and perhaps treachery of certain of their officers, they were routed with the loss of 5,000 soldiers to the Afghans' 500.[43]

Though Isfahan was not completely encircled by the rather limited Afghan forces until the end of April, the shah was advised to stay in the city by his incompetent (and in at least one case, traitorous) ministers. Appeals for aid went out to Wakhtang in Georgia, 'Ali Mardan Khan in Luristan, the Bakhtiari and Shahsavan tribes, and others. Wakhtang, true to his vow, refused to come and also prevented his son from setting out. 'Ali Mardan Khan, the *vali* of Luristan, reached Golpaygan, 140 miles to the northwest, on May 13; when his demand to be made commander-in-chief was refused, he withdrew his forces. The Shahsavan tribes of Azarbaijan failed to muster. One relieving force was routed by the Afghans in early May; another under Malik Mahmud, governor of Tun, was bought off by Mahmud. On the night of June 7/8, Tahmasp Mirza, the shah's third son and heir apparent, managed to get out of the city and reached Kashan, then Qazvin, where he did nothing to raise any troops. By and large, the disinterest of the provinces in rallying to the Safavids was conspicuous in its uniformity.[44]

Already in April the price of bread had undergone a "marked increase" as the Afghans surrounded the city, which was swelled beyond its normally huge population by villagers seeking refuge. Famine broke out in mid-June, Mahmud burned the crops around Isfahan at the end of the month and prices soared in July. Friar Alexander of Malabar, who lived through the siege, has described the last stages of it in graphic detail:

> all streets and gardens were covered with dead bodies, so that it was not
> possible to put down your feet without coming to a place where piles of two

or three human bodies lay rotting. For at the end of September . . . horses, donkeys, dogs, cats, rats, mice and all that seemed eatable were sold at very high prices, but when all this had been consumed nothing but human flesh remained which could be purchased at the market, although it was not openly called by that name. Yea, the sword of hunger was sharpened so much, that not only when a person died, two or three men at once came who cut off pieces of the warm flesh, eating it without any pepper with great relish, but even young men and girls were enticed into houses and killed there to appease hunger. This sad banquet lasted to October, accompanied by such terrible circumstances that they cannot be described without shedding tears. . . . Camel-hides, bark of trees, leaves, rotten wood pounded and boiled in water tasted as sweet as honey, and oh! this unheard-of horror I saw with my own eyes, that people had to satisfy their hunger with dried human excrement.[45]

Famine, disease, vain efforts to escape through the Afghan lines, and a very limited amount of actual combat reduced the population by as many as 100,000 people.[46] Isfahan was utterly decimated by the siege; when James Morier visited almost a century later, he wrote: "Houses, bazaars, mosques, palaces, whole streets, are to be seen in total abandonment; and I have rode for miles among its ruins, without meeting any living creature."[47] Finally, on October 23, 1722, Shah Sultan Husayn left Isfahan and went to Mahmud's camp, where he placed his crown on the Afghan's head, saying "The Absolute King, God most High, is just; and to whom do they say, 'He makes him head'? At one time to me, now to you. At last, my son, I also submit to you. God alone be blessed."[48] With these pious words the long fall of the Safavid monarchy came abruptly to its end.

Iran under the Afghans, 1722–1729

The Afghan conquerors, first under Mahmud until 1725 and then led by his cousin Ashraf till 1729, ruled in Iran for only seven years, but their impact, politically, socially, and economically, and in terms of external relations, was quite devastating, setting in motion eight decades of internal strife before a stable new dynasty emerged on the eve of the nineteenth century. In referring to the 1720s, the contemporary chronicler Shaykh Muhammad 'Ali Hazin lamented: "the whole empire was in a state of ruin, and the royal ordinances and statutes during these few years of interregnum had been broken and scattered to the four winds."[49] Modern historians have generally concurred with this assessment. If the political institutional framework and administrative class as a whole weathered the storm reasonably intact, economically and in human terms, however, "decline" is too mild a word for what happened. Lockhart characterizes the state of the

Iranian people during Ashraf's reign as "terrible," due to wars, rebellions, famine, pestilence, and the destruction of their homes and means of livelihood. Malcolm, writing in 1815, estimated that almost one million people had died as a result of the Afghan invasion (out of a population we have estimated at 6-10 million).[50] The urban sector seems to have borne the brunt of the economic dislocations that followed. The main cities of Iran may have lost two-thirds or even more of their inhabitants (in the whole of the eighteenth century). Regional and long distance trade were drastically reduced. Towndwellers of all classes were hit by high prices and periodic shortages that led to famine. Prices of rice at Isfahan in 1724 were five times those of 30 to 50 years earlier, and bread was two to three times higher. In 1729, the Turkish ambassador reported that "many people were dying of starvation in the streets of Isfahan, where the citizens lived in fear of being expelled from their houses and put to death."[51] The ulama too were a particular group that suffered disproportionately, as hundreds were displaced along with their families to the Shi'i shrine cities of Najaf and Karbala in Ottoman Iraq by the Sunni Afghans, who also confiscated vaqf properties, killed clerics, and destroyed their educational institutions. The overall result was the start of a collapse unprecedented in the two hundred years of development so far traced, comparable only to the even more devastating Mongol invasions of the thirteenth century in their ruinous impact on the Iranian political economy.

The extensive diplomatic and commercial relations that Iran had enjoyed with its neighbors and the European world under the Safavids deteriorated and crumbled as decisively as did the internal economy under the Afghans. When the nearby empires of the Ottomans and Russians invaded an Iran divided between Ashraf and the Safavid claimant Tahmasp a complex, four-sided struggle was touched off that added greatly to the economic and political dislocations of the period. This in turn forced a drastic reduction in commercial contact with the West, particularly England and Holland, further exacerbating the downward spiral. Since at least 1715 Peter the Great had harbored ambitions of extending the Russian presence on the Caspian Sea in order to obtain a share of Iran's silk trade and to lay the basis for trade with India through Iran or Khiva. By the summer of 1722 Russia had moved about 130 miles into Iran along the Caspian coast, but lost 33,000 men to the diseases of the region and raiding tribesmen. This intervention was diplomatically confirmed and extended on July 8, 1724, when Russia and the Ottoman Empire, after barely averting a war with each other over Iran, signed a treaty partitioning Iran among themselves and Tahmasp. Russia was to administer the territories it had already claimed, the Ottomans were to receive Tabriz and most of Azerbaijan, Kurdistan, Georgia, and parts of Shirvan. The final article of the treaty was an ultimatum to Tahmasp that he must accept the loss of these provinces or he would be deposed and the

Russians and Ottomans would mutually designate another Iranian to rule what was left of the country. The powerful impetus behind Russian intervention was seriously undermined when Peter the Great died in 1725, after which the initiative passed to the Ottomans in Iran. The original aim of gaining control over the silk produced in Gilan probably brought little profit to Russia in the 1720s owing to the warfare and instability of the region in that decade.[52] Ottoman incursions came primarily to forestall Russian advances in the Caucasus toward the Black Sea, although their longstanding religious and political rivalries with the Safavids undoubtedly also played a role and magnified the violence of the encounter. By 1725 Ottoman forces had advanced beyond the terms of the partition to Ardabil, Luristan, and the Kirmanshah area. In 1726 they declared war on Ashraf; the latter offset his inferior numbers by appealing to their common Sunni beliefs and calling for an alliance against the "heretical" Shi'i Safavids. This caused 20,000 Kurds to defect to his side and the demoralized Ottoman army lost 12,000 men in the ensuing battle. In late 1727 Ashraf crowned this success by agreeing to a treaty whereby the Ottoman sultan was acknowledged as "head of the Muslim world" and granted sovereignty over large parts of western and northwestern Iran, while Ashraf was recognized as shah of an Iran now reduced to Persian Iraq, Fars, Sistan, Kirman, and western Khurasan. During the period of belligerency, in late autumn 1726, Ashraf had ex-Shah Sultan Husayn executed, as the Ottomans declared they were fighting to reinstate him. The Ottomans thus shifted from opportunistic support of Tahmasp's claims to Safavid legitimacy to partition of Iran with the Afghans and Russians, whom they uneasily continued to accept as allies through 1729.[53]

European trade with Iran in the 1720s fell off drastically due to the Afghan invasion and occupation, and the ensuing external and internal warfare and disturbances. The representatives of the various East India companies suffered economic losses through looting and extortion at the hands of the Afghans and were not immune to the general hardships of famine and even loss of life in the period from 1722 to 1725. Despite Ashraf's desire to restore trade with the Europeans, the adverse conditions persisted and trade remained at a virtual standstill.[54] The Dutch saw money extorted from them, trading posts destroyed, and agents killed; the English fared no better in the 1720s. The period of the Afghan occupation thus witnessed a near total cessation of trade abroad.

The main forces responsible for bringing the Afghan occupation to an end were internal. In April 1725, as Mahmud became increasingly ill and mentally unbalanced, his cousin Ashraf was released from prison by leading Afghans and proclaimed shah after Mahmud was murdered. Ashraf's effective jurisdiction was limited to such central Iranian cities as Isfahan and Shiraz, and he could get no reinforcements from Qandahar because

Mahmud's elder brother opposed him there. In 1726, Tahmasp, the Safavid claimant to the throne, joined forces with a military adventurer named Nadir from the Afshar tribe in Khurasan. Over the next two years this newcomer emerged as the real military and political leader of the anti-Afghan movement, with Tahmasp a necessary and useful rallying symbol for the Iranian people who gave the cause enthusiastic support. Ashraf's army was defeated for the final time outside Shiraz in late December 1729 and Ashraf himself was killed while fleeing eastward a week later. The Afghan conquest of Iran was over, leaving Tahmasp a figurehead Safavid shah and his general Nadir the de facto ruler of Iran.[55]

Iran under Nadir Shah, 1729-1747

Nadir, the military leader who proclaimed himself shah in 1736 and ruled until his death in 1747, can be credited with restoring the national sovereignty of Iran by driving out the Afghans in 1729 and forcing the departures of the Russians and the Ottomans in the 1730s. From 1738 on he carried the military exploits of Iran beyond its own borders, into Mughal India, Uzbek Central Asia, and the Persian Gulf. In the process he wore the country out, financially and in terms of human lives, to supply his enormous armies. After deposing the incompetent Tahmasp II in 1732 in favor of his infant son 'Abbas III (both were killed by order of Nadir's son in 1740), Nadir dropped all pretense of serving the Safavid dynasty in 1736 when he assumed the throne himself.

After 1729, the old Safavid political structures were reinvested and renewed as Afshar, Bayat, Zanganah, and Shamlu tribal families returned to high positions and the bureaucracy was restored. Nadir sought to reestablish central authority over the provinces, often appointing his own relatives and successful generals as governors and frequently changing his personnel. To distinguish his imperial project from that of the Safavids, Nadir presented himself as a military leader on the model of Timur (Tamerlane), campaigning far beyond the borders of Iran throughout Central Asia, Afghanistan, and India. Politically, this expansionist tendency entailed less of an emphasis on the bureaucracy as the central ruling institution than on the army as the basis of imperial power. This aggressive military policy proved to be a considerable expense for the state and played a major role in the economic impoverishment of the population.[56]

The widespread hardship of the period, and its principal cause, are attested in the EIC's *Gombroon Diary* for July 21/August 1, 1743: "Nothing but Misery, Tyranny and Oppression are to be seen or heard in these Parts, the People being daily tax'd (so) that before Time is given for collecting one

Another is laid on."[57] Overtaxation of the merchant class distorted the local and regional trade of the internal Iranian economy; the effects on the import/export trade were also serious. Though at times Nadir arbitrarily intervened in the markets to lower the prices of goods (as at Isfahan in 1747), there is ample evidence of inflationary tendencies for the period overall. On the production side, a certain amount of "industry" and building activity was organized by the state, but this went primarily for military purposes and involved forced, rather than paid labor, thus benefitting local people very little. Nadir's capital, Mashhad, grew into a thriving commercial city with two or three hundred thousand inhabitants. The evidence from the rest of the country, however, is uniformly negative. The tax-collectors claimed: "Money, money, . . . the Shah wants it, whether justly or unjustly: say that another man owes you so much, and you and we shall be quits."[58] The EIC reported that Nadir, in the final stages of his growing madness, was killing 40-50 people a day to extort money. The rest of the country suffered equal disasters, from natural famines and plague to state-caused taxes and wars. A traveller from India to Basra through the Persian Gulf in 1750 wrote that since Nadir's "Tyranny and Depredations . . . the whole Country had assumed a new face, for there was not above one House in ten but was deserted of Inhabitants, at least if we may judge of other Places by what appeared at Gombroon."[59] Judging from the available data, Gombroon (Bandar 'Abbas) *was* indicative of the state of most of Iran in this period.

The peasantry faced a double burden on their crops and their labor. They continued to pay their usual quarter to a half of the crop to the state and/or landlord, and in addition often had their crops requisitioned to feed the massive army on its campaigns. A goodly number too must have been drafted into military service, while others did forced labor on the state's military and construction projects.[60] The condition of the tribal sector of the economy presents a more mixed picture. Of the eighteenth century generally, Lambton discerns "an increase in the numbers and influence of the tribal groups" at the expense of the settled population.[61] Two distinct groups of tribes must be considered however. For those who served in Nadir's army—a heterogeneous ethnic and religious mix of Turkomans, Afghans, Uzbeks, Baluch, Kurds, and Bakhtiaris—there was a gain in political and economic status through military service and the booty this brought, but this expansion slowed down after 1741 and ceased altogether upon Nadir's death and the dispersal of his army in 1747. The military amirs were discouraged from acquiring vast estates, and even if they heeded this prohibition, their tenure was rather precarious, tied to Nadir's rise and fall. For other, primarily non-eastern tribal groups, including both Iranian tribespeople and mountaineers, and many of the pro-Safavid Turkoman qizilbash tribes, Nadir's reign witnessed the hardships of forced migration and resettlement.[62] Other tribes may have been relatively well-off in their local areas but the constant warfare worked against anyone being left alone for long. The overall tribal share of national wealth probably did increase; this was however unevenly divided among these several groups and differentially distributed within any given tribe between simple pastoralists and chiefs. Whether these gains outpaced the overall decline in the economy is difficult to assess in the absence of more specific data on tribal conditions. In the end, rather than a "resurgence" of tribal power, as Lambton discerns, the period evidences more a fragmentation of many competing tribal forces, thus setting the stage for the continued struggles for national preeminence and local influence which raged after Nadir's death.

The ulama were unfavorably affected by Nadir's policies. Beginning with his self-elevation to the throne in 1736 Nadir attempted to establish a kind of "truncated" Shi'ism or "synthetic" Islam, based on the teachings of the Imam Ja'far ibn Muhammad as-Sadiq. He demanded that this be recognized as a fifth orthodox school (*mazhab*) of Islam both within Iran and by the Ottomans. The underlying motives involved both internal and external *raisons d'état*: to undercut support for the Shi'i Safavid dynasty, to gain the allegiance of his many Afghan, Uzbek, and other Sunni soldiers, and to bolster his claim for leadership of the Islamic world against the adjacent Ottoman and Mughal empires. The project died with Nadir in 1747 as his successors quickly abandoned it for a return to Shi'ism. The developments of this period nevertheless entailed significant ideological, political, and material consequences for the ulama who had to live through them. Great amounts of vaqf land, especially around Isfahan, were confiscated and claimed by the crown; though Nadir's successor revoked the decree, the lands were still not fully restored by the nineteenth century. Paradoxically, this trend, along with emigration to Iraq beyond the reach of the Iranian state, greatly augmented the independent authority of the ulama.[63]

Turning to external developments between 1729 and 1747, Nadir's most extensive "foreign relations" were basically adversarial conflicts with the neighboring world-empires—the reconquest of Iranian territory from the Ottomans, the return of territory more diplomatically from the Russians, and more aggressive wars of conquest fought with the Mughals and Uzbeks. Thus he went beyond the popular demand for national territorial liberation to what amounted in effect to a policy of military expansionism with ruinous consequences. Wars were fought with the Ottomans from 1732 to 1746, broken by intermittent lulls to try to negotiate peace. The Treaty of Kurdan, finally agreed to on September 4, 1746, acknowledged the borders set by the 1639 Treaty of Zuhab. The withdrawal of Russian forces from Iran was accomplished with far less human and economic destruction. Peter the Great's death in 1725 fortuitously removed the architect of Russian expansion into Iran from the scene. A further impetus was the deaths of some 130,000 Russian soldiers in Gilan and adjoining areas, mostly from disease. On February 1, 1732 the Empress Anna Ivanovna agreed to return the Caspian coastline to Iran in return for a promise of peace and friendship, and commercial concessions to the effect that Russian merchants might trade freely throughout Iran, paying no customs or duties on exports and imports. Although such terms afforded a considerable advantage to Russian merchants in Iran over those of other nations, actual trade does not seem to have amounted to much.[64] The long period of friendly relations between Iran and Mughal India came to an end with Nadir's first major expansionist thrust, the invasion of 1739. Military conquest was followed by spectacular extortions: Lockhart estimates that Nadir took 60-70 million pounds sterling in money, jewels, and objects of value out of India, of which one-fourth was lost en route back to Iran. Most of this wealth was used by Nadir to pay his army and finance further campaigns against the Ottomans, or else was hoarded in his treasure-house, so the net benefits to the Iranian economy from this massive plunder of India were minimal at best.[65]

Divergent opinions exist on the impact of Nadir's reign on relations with the European powers. Lockhart concludes that the period from 1729 to 1746 "was, on the whole, a most unfortunate time for trading in Persia."[66] In this view he is supported by Thomas Dorill, the English East India Company's resident at Basra, who wrote London in December 1745 that "the Name of Trade is forgot . . . in Persia."[67] Ricks, in a discussion of the period from 1745 to 1750, states that "caravan-trade continued and transfer of treasure, foodstuffs and piece goods were carried on with little decrease in volume while the EIC and the OIC remained resolute in continuing their business in Southern Iran and the Gulf."[68] He also detects some shift in Iran's exports away from wool, foodstuffs, and textiles to gold, silver, copper, and pearls to pay for an increasing number of European woolen textiles. If we consider regional variations some light may be shed on this controversy. Centered in the north, the silk production of Iran was said by English observers to have been a royal monopoly around 1739-40. It is not clear, but seems unlikely, that this monopoly remained for long in the state's hands. In any case, its advantages were effectively limited by a great decrease in production: In Gilan, which usually had produced almost half of Iran's silk, production fell precipitously from Chardin's estimated 1,380 tons in the 1670s to Hanway's estimate of 160-180 tons in the 1740s, an almost total collapse, while the breeding of silkworms came to a complete stop in nearby Shirvan.[69] In the Gulf, meanwhile, the British increased their exports of Kirmani goats' hair wool through 1736, but thereafter trade suffered due to the intertwined scourges of government extortion and famine. The Dutch VOC had, by the 1730s, entered a period of decline on the world scene. Inside Iran their commerce made a partial comeback from the cessation of trade in the 1720s but to a very modest level much below the peak Safavid years. Overall, in Lockhart's view, the Dutch "fared no better than their British rivals during these troubled times."[70]

In the last years of his reign, Nadir became increasingly unbalanced mentally. Excessive tax demands were followed by executions of leading citizens and civil and military officers at Isfahan, Kirman, and Mashhad. 'Ali Quli Khan, Nadir's nephew who was sent to Sistan to suppress yet another rebellion, instead joined with the rebels there and gained Sistani, Baluchi, and Afghan tribal support, marching on Harat, closer to Nadir's own forces. Finally, on June 19, 1747, Nadir assembled his Afghan elite and ordered the arrests of his Iranian generals. Hearing of this, Muhammad Khan Qajar and other conspirators forestalled Nadir, killing him in his tent. This put an end to a reign which had become increasingly bloody and wearisome for the Iranian people, but it inaugurated yet another period of tribal infighting for control of Iran, before Karim Khan Zand would emerge at Shiraz in the 1760s, leaving Khurasan in the northeast to Shahrukh, Nadir's grandson.

Iran under Karim Khan Zand, 1750-1779

After Nadir's death in 1747 his grandiose empire fragmented along ethnic and tribal lines. Political power decentralized rapidly as his variegated armed forces melted away to their homes or tried to impose themselves in suitable niches around the former kingdom. Independent areas were consolidated on the fringes of Iran (where some regions had been quasi-autonomous since the 1670s), notably in the Afshari region to the east and the Qajar tribal area around the Caspian in the north, as well as among the Kurds, Arabs, and Baluchis. In turbulent Khurasan, where Nadir's capital had been, the victorious rebel 'Ali Quli (Nadir's nephew) ruled for one year as 'Adel Shah before being deposed and blinded by his brother Ibrahim who was himself soon executed by supporters of Nadir's grandson Shahrukh. Shahrukh would rule as an Afghan vassal until the rise of the Qajars in 1796.[71]

The real struggle for power was occurring elsewhere, however, and was even more complex. At Isfahan in 1750 a coalition of Iranian tribes (Bakhtiaris, Kurds, and Lurs, including the Zands, a small sub-group associated with either of the latter two) proclaimed a minor Safavid prince as Shah Isma'il III. The power behind this facade lay in a triumvirate consisting of two rival Bakhtiari chiefs, 'Ali Mardan Khan and Abu'l Fath Khan, and Karim Khan Zand, who had served in Nadir's army. By 1751, Karim Khan alone exercised a tenuous control over most of central and southern Iran, as 'Ali Mardan Khan eliminated Abu'l Fath Khan and was in turn killed by one of his own followers. The period from 1751 to 1758 witnessed a bloody contest for all of Iran among Karim Khan, Muhammad Hasan Khan Qajar in the Caspian area, and Azad Khan Afghan in Azarbaijan. When the Qajars took Gilan and Mazandaran from Azad Khan in 1756 the defeated commander entered Karim's service and the Zand-Qajar confrontation began. In 1758 Muhammad Hasan Khan was defeated and killed by a Zand army in Mazandaran. By 1764 Karim Khan held all of Iran, except Khurasan under Shahrukh and in the northwest, parts of northern Azarbaijan and Shirvan under Turkoman and Lezghi chiefs, eastern Armenia, and Georgia under its king Erekle. From 1765 to his death in 1779 followed a welcome period of stable rule under Karim Khan based at Shiraz, who devoted himself to "repairing the broken circle of justice," with positive consequences for development, which would, however, prove temporary.[72]

Karim Khan ruled Iran as "an intermediary between the people and a purely symbolic monarchy," first assuming the title *vakil al-dawla* ("representative of the government") while the nominal shah, the Safavid Isma'il III was kept in prison until his death in 1773. Already in 1765 Karim had changed his own title to *vakil al-ra'aya* ("representative of the people") quietly letting both the Safavid absolute monarchy and Nadir's imperial tyranny fade into the background. While he ostensibly never called himself shah, he was *de facto* king of Iran after 1773. Still, his reluctance to appoint a successor would open the door to another debilitating round of tribal civil wars after his death in 1779.[73]

Karim ruled with a less elaborate institutional framework than had his predecessors. The bureaucracy was streamlined and the standing army was reduced in size. Provincial governors tended to be drawn from among Karim's relatives and the local elites. Given the limitations of communications and tribal independence, this decentralized administration proved comparatively efficient and just at the provincial and urban level. Impressive also, in that it was achieved without the use of crushing "extraordinary" taxes or widespread deployment of the army, was the total state tax revenue, at about 535,000 tumans, perhaps two-thirds of the late Safavids' income. Characteristically, Karim is said to have left only 7,000 tumans unspent in his treasury at death, implying a fiscal policy of returning state income to the economy rather than unproductively hoarding it (by contrast Nadir left 7.5 million tumans in his treasury). Such policies account for Karim's remarkable popularity in the public imagination, as the traveller William Francklin found in 1786: "nor is his name ever mentioned by them, especially the middling and lower classes of people, but in terms expressive of the highest gratitude and esteem."[74]

With the renewed civil wars the 1750s had brought very great hardship once again to the population, particularly in the urban sector, and its adjacent village peasantry. Each time a town fell to one side or another, a set sum would be exacted by the victors.[75] A natural reaction to this by those who could manage it was migration, to India, Ottoman Iraq, and Yemen. In the 1760s and 1770s an economic recovery began to reverse these trends in central, western, and southern Iran. Karim endeavored to re-establish trade and agriculture by efforts to maintain safety on the roads, invitations to merchants to return, public building and infrastructural projects, and, most importantly, moderate levels of taxation. State granaries were constructed in the provinces for military campaigns, but in times of crop failure as in the middle and late 1770s the granary at Isfahan was thrown open to relieve the hunger of the poor and additional grain was brought to Shiraz and sold below cost. Karim Khan is supposed to have said: "We have a common duty [*vazifa-i 'ammi*] towards all the people of Iran. This we have fulfilled by ordering foodstuffs, clothing and the necessities of the people to be bought and sold at very low prices so that every hired man ... will have enough."[76] Though the value of the tuman continued to drop, from 2.5 pounds sterling in the 1740s to 1.875 in the 1760s, the new Bishop of Isfahan verified in 1763 that "living is cheap."[77] Trade and manufacturing likewise revived and cities and regions resumed production of their specialties. This upswing was marked, but must not be exaggerated; it was relative to the collapse that lasted from 1722 to 1760. It was also localized at the new capital in Shiraz where Karim engaged in extensive building projects. New bazaars, caravanserais, public baths, palaces, and mosques were erected; important shrines were embellished and restored. Underground water reservoirs were built and streets in the bazaar and residential neighborhoods were paved, with wells and a central drainage channel. There continued to be royal workshops in the manufacturing sector; though these were far less extensive than in Safavid times, there were significant textile and glass-making workshops, presumably in both the royal and private sectors.[78] The Armenian and Jewish minorities were well-treated. According to the traveller Waring, the city was politically calm as a result of Karim's good government: "During his whole reign, I have been informed by several natives of Shirauz, that by his excellent police and management there was not a single tumult or riot productive of bloodshed."[79]

The agrarian sector would seem to have shared in the general return to better times. Tax levels were reduced and the especially burdensome "extraordinary" taxes and requisitions were eliminated to a great degree. Irrigation works were restored and expanded in Fars and the south. But were the degree of landlord oppression and large share of the surplus really affected? Lambton and Perry both imply that private property ownership increased in terms of both numbers of landlords and size of estates. Leading Zand family members, such as Mirza Muhammad, the kalantar of Shiraz, acquired property. One can infer that the lot of the peasantry was at best one of improvement over the uncertain conditions and prevalent extortion of the preceding four decades to something approaching the "ordinary" low standard of living it had enjoyed under the Safavids.[80] Tribal conditions were similar to what they had been under Nadir and the Afghans, with a shift mainly in the particular tribes favored by the state. Karim's original Iranian and Kurdish supporters were used in his standing army and allowed to administer their own regions. Other, less fortunate tribes were scattered to reduce their power, while still others retained independence locally due to the indifference or inadequate coercive means of the central government.[81]

A final internal development of note occurred in the realm of political culture. The ulama were gradually recovering in the 1760s and 1770s from the ravages against their lives and property in Nadir's time. The transition from state patronage and control of vaqf land to reliance on kinship networks and bazaar ties for livelihood continued. Despite low levels of state support, many ulama migrated back to Iran in the 1770s, pushed by the plague and an economic downturn in Iraq. This strengthened the position of the adherents of the *usuli* movement in Iran at the expense of the *akhbari* school. Usulis insisted that believers submit to the guidance of a learned mujtahid in religious matters, Akhbaris denied the authority of mujtahids to render judgments in the absence of the Hidden Imam. The triumph of the usuli movement under Aqa Muhammad Baqir Bihbihani in the late eighteenth century laid the foundation for the enhanced authority and prestige of the highest-ranking ulama—the mujtahids—independent of the state, a development whose political repercussions would become evident in the social movements of the late nineteenth century. Popular religiosity was also deepened by the emergence in the Zand period of *ta'ziya* productions—the passion play enacted during the month of Muharram that depicts the martyrdom of Husayn at Karbala in the seventh century. This too would inculcate a political culture with far-reaching emotional undercurrents of self-sacrifice and resistance to oppression.[82]

Iran's External Relations, 1747-1800

By the late eighteenth century a significant shift in Iran's external relations appeared to be taking place: The European East India companies were abandoning the Gulf trade to concentrate on exploiting their colonial possessions in India and the Far East, leaving the bulk of Iran's foreign trade with its immediate neighbors—the Ottoman Empire, India, Russia, and the Arab tribes and states of the Gulf. As much as 85-90 percent of Iran's trade in 1801 was estimated by Malcolm to be with these partners and one may assume that in Karim Khan's time from 1765 to 1779 this shift was well under way, if not yet quite so dramatic. This did not necessarily mean a lesser role for European commerce in Iran, since Iran's trade with India and the Ottomans was largely a transit trade for European products and imports, while Russia was making a transition of its own into a more significant actor in the European setting.

Karim made diplomatic contact with the Ottoman Empire only in 1775, at the latter's initiative, and no agreement was reached before he died. In fact from 1774 to 1784 there were hostilities between the two countries over the Iraqi port city of Basra and relations remained unstable until the end of the Zand period in the 1790s. Nevertheless, when trade was possible, it amounted to as much as 26 to 35 percent of Iran's total trade, or some 62,221 pounds sterling according to Malcolm in 1801. Although respectable, this was far below the late Safavid amounts of perhaps 700,000 pounds sterling worth of imports alone from the Ottoman Empire. The trade was moreover to a great extent a transit trade between Europe and India (by 1801). The balance was in Iran's favor, although Ricks feels this was more true of the 1765-75 period than later.[83] Commercial and diplomatic relations with India were likewise in a state of flux, as the Mughal Empire continued to disintegrate before external and internal challenges. The Indian commercial presence in Iran revived from its low point earlier in the century and reached 20 to 30 percent of Iran's foreign commerce by 1801, largely in India's favor. A report from the 1780s estimates that four-fifths of Iran's imports must be paid for in cash, since silk was not in demand in India.[84] In the Persian Gulf, meanwhile, up to 75 percent of the trade in the latter stages of the century was carried on by Arab traders working with Armenians, Iranians, Turks, and Indians. The volume, however, was presumably much lower than a century before.[85]

Of more long-lasting import from the standpoint of the nineteenth century, Iran's relations with Russia underwent expansion and change after 1750. No direct Russian contact was made with the Zands until 1784, after Karim's death, but Russian diplomats and importers of raw silk dealt with the Qajars and other local elites in the north. Trade suffered after 1743 and remained somewhat stagnant through the 1770s. Despite the vicissitudes of these decades a gradually rising commercial position for Russia in Iran may be glimpsed. Scattered data show Russian exports worth 81,151 rubles (equal to 8,115 tumans) annually in 1758-60, which increased fourfold by 1792 to 325,310 rubles (equal to 32,531 tumans), still a relatively small amount. Imports in 1758-60 averaged 107,000 rubles (no figures for 1792), so the balance of trade was in Iran's favor. Russia may have accounted for 15 to 20 percent of Iran's total trade by 1801. The directors of the EIC complained in the late 1780s: "In the north, Russia is making rapid strides towards commercial pre-eminence; and at Moscow, Persian silk is sold in large quantities, whilst it is seldom, if ever, seen in London."[86] A proto-imperialism was developing politically and militarily as well as economically. In 1781 Count Voinovich attempted to garrison a force in the Bay of Astarabad, bringing him into conflict with the emerging Qajar state, while in 1783 Russia assumed a higher profile in Georgian affairs, alarmed by growing Qajar power. This clash would develop into several wars in the first third of the nineteenth century.

Relations with the European powers likewise evolved in this transitional period. Karim Khan was generally "pro-trade," and as the opening of his grant to the English EIC in 1763 described him, "desirous that the said Kingdoms [of Persia] should flourish and re-obtain their ancient grandeur by the increase of trade and commerce, as well as by a due execution of justice."[87] But, interested as he was in the economic well-being of his realm, Karim was concerned that Iran's commerce in the Gulf entailed a negative balance of trade which drained specie out of the country, and these two tendencies—the desire to promote commerce, the need to prevent a short-age of money—made for far from smooth relations with the English, Dutch, and French in this period. A second major trade issue was the great down-turn in silk production and exports, now a confirmed trend since the 1720s and one which led directly to the negative balance of trade. This put pressure on both Karim Khan and the Europeans to find some other pattern of trade; the failure to accomplish this ended in the temporary eclipse of a European commercial presence in the Gulf on the eve of the nineteenth century. The Dutch position collapsed completely when Gulf pirates cap-tured their outpost on Kharg Island in 1766; the VOC itself was dissolved in 1798.[88] English imports of Kirmani wool persisted in the 1750s and 1760s, but thereafter difficulties arose over English recalcitrance in assisting Iran-ian operations against Gulf pirates and a perception that Karim opposed all export of specie from Iran (thus putting an effective limit on British imports). The result was a tenfold decline in trade from 1770 to 1775. A report on commerce from the early 1790s indicated net losses on the slim volume of sales the EIC conducted. The late eighteenth century thus proved to be the lull before a storm of increased commercial relations would break in the nineteenth.[89]

The Rise of the Qajar Dynasty

A number of factors combined to bring a new dynasty, the Qajars, to a position of what would prove to be long-lasting political power in Iran by the turn of the nineteenth century. Political, ideological, and economic causes were at work, mostly internal in origin, though to a lesser degree external as well. The Zands revealed considerable disunity after Karim's death in 1779. His reticence to clearly claim the monarchy from the now defunct Safavids and to designate a successor, coupled with a merciful nature that left several of his family members alive and with their sight intact, created a situation where the Zands consumed each other in deadly infighting for the throne. The Qajars, though historically divided into two branches, were forcefully united by a single claimant for power, Aqa Muhammad. Located in the more populous north and situated near to Iran's growing commercial partner, Russia, the Qajars were eventually able to mobilize a more dynamic economic and human resource base, while the Zands found themselves in the less populous south, with a more fractious tribal situation and vastly diminished ties to the world economy, partly the result of Karim's ultimate spurning of the East India companies and the decline of trade in the Gulf. The sum of these advantages was a more efficient Qajar military machine, which was aided at several junctures by fortuitous outcomes in key encounters. The course of events was influenced and determined by the momentum generated by these several trends.

Aqa Muhammad Qajar was the son of Muhammad Hasan Qajar whom Karim's army had defeated and eliminated in 1758. After this, Aqa Muhammad and his brother fled and lived among the Yamut Turkomans until they gave themselves up to Karim in 1771. Aqa Muhammad resided at Karim's court where he was able to observe the family infighting and the military state of the empire, and upon Karim's death he immediately fled north to the Qajar homeland of Astarabad. From 1779 to 1783 he consolidated his hold as leader of the Qajars, expanding his territorial jurisdiction to include the neighboring Caspian province of Mazandaran.[90]

During this same period the Zands were fighting among themselves at Shiraz. By 1781 four different men had held the throne, decimating the family with their internecine quarrels. Three years later the situation was one of dual competing tribal states in Iran, the Qajars in the north and the Zands in the south. The Zand ruler 'Ali Murad died in early spring 1785; his half-brother Ja'far Khan claimed the throne at Isfahan. A number of Zand tribal supporters declared their independence, weakening the Zands militarily. Ja'far needed the aid of Hajji Ibrahim, a leading merchant, to secure Shiraz from 'Ali Murad's nephew, Sayyid Murad Khan. Hajji Ibrahim was made kalantar of Shiraz and Fars for his efforts. From 1786 to 1789 both sides consolidated their forces in anticipation of the coming showdown. The Qajars continued to make progress, occupying Isfahan permanently in 1788, while on the other side Ja'far Khan Zand was poisoned in 1789 in a conspiracy led by Sayyid Murad Khan. Lutf 'Ali Khan, Ja'far's son, assembled a mostly Arab army at Bushire, and aided by forces at Shiraz again led by Hajji Ibrahim, deposed and killed Sayyid Murad Khan, making himself shah.[91]

Lutf 'Ali's jurisdiction in 1789 was limited to Fars, parts of Khuzistan, and the area north of Bushire. His army numbered about 20,000 men. Shiraz, economically in good shape, was his main base. The Qajar territories in 1789 included Astarabad, Mazandaran, Tehran, Isfahan, and eastwards to Hamadan, and an alliance with the ruler of Kurdistan. Aqa Muhammad's army was "well in excess" of 20,000. By 1790 he had taken control of Azarbaijan, none of whose tribal leaders nor the merchants who administered Tabriz could successfully oppose him. At Shiraz, meanwhile, dissension erupted between Lutf 'Ali and his influential kalantar, Hajji Ibrahim. When Lutf 'Ali went to meet the Qajar army near Isfahan in 1791, Hajji Ibrahim's supporters in the Zand army deserted and Lutf 'Ali had to flee to Bushire after Hajji Ibrahim denied him entry into Shiraz. Helfgott points out that Hajji Ibrahim acted both to save himself and out of a class-conscious motive: As a merchant he wanted stable rule in Iran, and by 1791 he could see that the Qajars were more likely to provide this than the Zands. A decade later he told Malcolm: "None except some plundering soldiers, cared whether a Zund or a Kujur was upon the throne; but all desired that Persia should be great and powerful, and enjoy internal tranquillity."[92] Thus Hajji Ibrahim, who would go on to serve as Aqa Muhammad's chief minister, was a pivotal participant from the merchant/bureaucratic class in the otherwise tribal civil war between Qajars and Zands.

The final encounter lasted from 1791 to 1794. For three years Lutf 'Ali fought a hopeless rearguard action, until in November 1794 he was betrayed and captured at Bam, then taken to Tehran and executed. The remaining Zand family members were hunted down and mutilated or killed by Aqa Muhammad; by the early nineteenth century little trace of the tribe remained.[93] Aqa Muhammad was now ready to proclaim himself shah. This he did in early 1796. After pacifying Khurasan, Aqa Muhammad had to hurry back to the Caucasus which the Russians had entered. In May 1797 he was killed in camp by two servants whom he had sentenced to death for a minor offence (reminiscent of Nadir, Malcolm says that Aqa Muhammad bordered on insanity at the time of his death).[94] But Iran was territorially intact—except for the Caucasus and Afghanistan it was at its Safavid borders—and when Aqa Muhammad's nephew took the throne as Fath 'Ali Shah, ruling till 1834, the Qajars had established their dynasty.

Notes

1. Dickson, "Sháh Tahmásb and the Uzbeks," 323. My account of this rebellion follows Dickson, passim; the events are also mentioned in Monshi, *History of Shah 'Abbas*, 101-102.

2. See Keyvani, *Artisans and Guild Life*, 155, and Hasan Rumlu, *Ahsan al-tavarikh*, edited and translated by Charles Norman Seddon, *A Chronicle of the early Safawis*, in two volumes: I (Persian text), II (translation) (Baroda: Gaekwad's Oriental Series, 1931, 1934).

3. See Reid, "Rebellion and Social Change in Astarabad," 38, 41, 45-46; Dickson, "Sháh Tahmásb and the Uzbeks," 381-84; and Monshi, *History of Shah 'Abbas*, 765-72.

4. Reid, "Rebellion and Social Change in Astarabad," 52 note 8. The allusion is to Farhad Kazemi and Ervand Abrahamian, "The Nonrevolutionary Peasantry of Modern Iran," pp. 259-304 in *Iranian Studies*, volume XI (1978). Tribal warriors were more active in certain elite conflicts discussed later, such as civil wars and local independence movements, rather than in popular social movements of their own.

5. Monshi, *History of Shah 'Abbas*, 668.

6. This account is based on N. V. Pigulevskaya, A. V. Yakubovsky, I. P. Petrushevsky, A. M. Belenitsky, and L. V. Stoeva, *Tarikh-i Iran az Dauran-i Bastan ta Payan-i Sadeh-i Hijdahumin-i Miladi* [History of Iran from Ancient Times till the End of the Eighteenth Century], translated from Russian to Persian by Karim Kishavarz (Tehran: Payam Press, 1354/1975), 554-56.

7. Reid, "Rebellion and Social Change in Astarabad," 51.

8. Krusinski, *The History of the Late Revolutions*, 94.

9. On these consequences of the conversion process, see Chardin, *Voyages*, V, 251-54, 276-79, VIII, 446; Krusinski, *The History of the Late Revolutions*, 84, 85, 100, 104; R. M. Savory, "The Safavid Administrative System," pp. 351-372 in Jackson and Lockhart, editors, *The Cambridge History of Iran*, volume 6, 367; Minorsky, *TM*, 25-26; Lambton, *Landlord and Peasant*, 105-109; and Lockhart, *The Fall*, 23-24. On court appointments, see Rohrborn, *Provinzen und Zentralgewalt Persiens*, 33.

10. On the army, see Roemer, "The Safavid Period," 291; Savory, "The Safavid Administrative System," 367; Chardin, *Voyages*, V, 315, 317, 325-26; and A. K. S. Lambton, "The Tribal Resurgence and the Decline of the Bureaucracy in the Eighteenth Century," pp. 108-129 in Naff and Owen, editors, *Studies in Eighteenth Century Islamic History*, 115.

11. On the new upbringing, ironically motivated by 'Abbas's fear of intrigues against him, see Savory, *Iran under the Safavids*, 94-95, and Chardin, *Voyages*, V, 246-47, VI, 30. On the qualities of the last four shahs, see Krusinski, *The History of the Late Revolutions*, 47, 51-52; Lockhart, *The Fall*, 28, 31, 114; Fryer, *A New Account of East India and Persia*, volume III, 51, cited by Laurence Lockhart, "European Contacts with Persia, 1350-1736," pp. 373-409 in Jackson and Lockhart, editors, *The Cambridge History of Iran*, volume 6, 403; and Minorsky, *TM*, 24.

12. Krusinski, *The History of the Late Revolutions*, 83. On these developments, see also ibid., 76-84, 98-100; Roemer, "The Safavid Period," 307; Lockhart, *The Fall*, 29-30; Chardin, *Voyages*, V, 240; and Leonard Michael Helfgott, "The Rise of the Qajar Dynasty," Ph.D. dissertation, Department of History, University of Maryland (1973), 61-67.

13. This paragraph draws on Jean Aubin, "La politique religieuse des safavides," pp. 235-244 in *Le Shi'isme Imâmite*, Colloque de Strasbourg (6-9 mai 1968) (Paris: Presses Universitaires de France, 1970), 61-67; Arjomand, *The Shadow of God*, 122, 211; Savory, *Iran under the Safavids*, 234; Banani, "Reflections"; Minorsky, *TM*, 24; Lockhart, *The Fall*, 119-122; Roemer, "The Safavid Period," 313; and Jean Aubin, "Les Sunnites du Larestan et la chute des safavides," pp. 151-171 in *Revue des études islamiques*, volume 33 (1965), 151.

14. This section is a condensed version of part of my article, "The Making of an External Arena."

15. Fryer, *A New Account of East India and Persia*, II, 163. See also Kristoff Glamann, *Dutch-Asiatic Trade 1620-1740* (Copenhagen: Danish Science Press, and The Hague: Martinus Nijhoff, 1958), 116-22, and Steensgaard, *The Asian Trade Revolution*, 376.

16. Gombroon to Surat, April 23, 1664, *India Office* G/36/104, p. 76, cited by Ferrier, "The Armenians and the EIC," 48 note 4. See also Boxer, *Jan Compagnie*, 51.

17. Lockhart, *The Fall*, 427, 434 note 2, based on C. H. Wilson, *Anglo-Dutch Commerce and Finance in the XVIIIth Century* (Cambridge, 1941); Boxer, *Jan Compagnie*, 71-72.

18. Ferrier, "The Armenians and the EIC," 48, citing *India Office*, E/3/21/2204, Surat to E.I.Co., 31 January 1650/51. Data on silk is drawn from ibid., 42; Ronald Ferrier, "Trade from the mid-14th Century to the End of the Safavid Period," pp. 412-490 in Jackson and Lockhart, editors, *The*

Cambridge History of Iran, volume 6, 459, 469-71, 479; Steensgaard, *The Asian Trade Revolution*, 395 table 19; and Emerson, "Ex Occidente Lux," 154-55.

19. This paragraph draws on Boxer, *Jan Compagnie*, 47, 55; Emerson, "Ex Occidente Lux," 125-26, 156; Ferrier, "Trade from the mid-14th Century," 461, 479, 480; Keyvani, *Artisans and Guild Life*, 220; Robert Dillon, "Carpet Capitalism and craft involution in Kirman, Iran: A study in economic anthropology," Ph.D. dissertation, Department of Anthropology, Columbia University (1976), 206-7; Ferrier, "The Armenians and the EIC," 49-62; Lockhart, *The Fall*, 384, 385, 388-90; Krishna, *Commercial Relations*, 142; and K. N. Chaudhuri, *Trade and Civilisation in the Indian Ocean. An Economic History from the Rise of Islam to 1750* (Cambridge: Cambridge University Press, 1985), 483 figure 1, 486, 489, 497-98 table 1. Though Lockhart claims "Both the English and Dutch Companies exported [from Iran] large quantities of gold and silver in bullion or in coin" (*The Fall*, 386 note 6), I see no evidence of this in the case of the English, whose cloth exports fell far short of the Dutch spice exports, leaving an undoubted net trade deficit with Iran.

20. Chardin, *Voyages*, III, 171, cited by Ferrier, "Trade from the mid-14th Century," 472. See also Emerson, "Ex Occidente Lux," 178-79.

21. On Russia and Iran, see Emerson, "Ex Occidente Lux," 173-83, 193-94; Ferrier, "Trade from the mid-14th Century," 472-74; Lockhart, *The Fall*, 59, 61, 62, 106, 176; and Roemer, "The Safavid Period," 306.

22. On Iran and the Ottomans, see Hurewitz, *Diplomacy*, I, 21; *A Chronicle of the Carmelites in Persia*, 495-97; Boxer, *Jan Compagnie*, 28; Steensgaard, *The Asian Trade Revolution*, 170; Lockhart, *The Fall*, 368 note 1; Ferrier, "Trade from the mid-14th Century," 472, 489; Emerson, "Ex Occidente Lux," 121; Savory, *Iran under the Safavids*, 202; and John Malcolm, *The Melville Papers*, "Commercial State of Persia," pp. 262-267 in Issawi, *EHI*. Given the disruption of the eighteenth century, Malcolm's figures for 1801 must be taken as of questionable utility for the period under study here.

23. On India, see Ferrier, "Trade from the mid-14th Century," 448-49, 470, 475, 483; Fryer, *A New Account*, II, 163; and Malcolm, *The Melville Papers*, in Issawi, *EHI*, 263-64.

24. Lockhart, "European Contacts," 197; Ferrier, "Trade from the mid-14th Century," 489-90; Issawi, *EHI*, 12.

25. Figures compiled by Issawi, *EHI*, 12.

26. Lockhart, citing a Russian source, notes a possible drop by half in the silk exports of Gilan from 1670 to 1720, though he puzzlingly concludes that total production may have stayed the same: *The Fall*, 238 note 2.

27. This argument is made in my article, "The Long Fall of the Safavid Dynasty: Moving Beyond the Standard Views," pp. 281-304 in *International Journal of Middle East Studies*, volume 24, number 2 (May 1992), which informs the next sections as well. Appearing too late to be properly incorporated into the present study is the excellent research of Rudi Matthee, which both confirms and nuances the argument here by providing a wealth of data and insight on topics from currency, bullion, and prices to foreign trade: see Rudolph P. Matthee, "Politics and Trade in Late Safavid Iran: Commercial Crisis and Government Reaction under Shah Solayman (1666-1694)," Ph.D. dissertation, Department of Islamic Studies, University of California, Los Angeles (1991).

28. Ferrier, "Trade from the mid-14th Century," 489.

29. Fryer, *A New Account of East India and Persia*, II, 163.

30. Du Mans, *Estat de la Perse*, 192-93.

31. Emerson, "Ex Occidente Lux," 279; *A Chronicle of the Carmelites in Persia*, 775-76; Krusinski, *The History of the Late Revolutions*, xvii-xix. To calculate the true value of the tuman vis-à-vis these currencies one would want to know the rate of inflation in Europe, which had been fairly high a century earlier.

32. Emerson, "Ex Occidente Lux," 281, based on Chardin, *Voyages*, X, 1-8; Roemer, "The Safavid Period," 305-6.

33. See *A Chronicle of the Carmelites in Persia*, 445; Lockhart, *The Fall*, 125; and Keyvani, *Artisans and Guild Life*, 120-21.

34. Krusinski, *The History of the Late Revolutions*, 127. On the army and harem expenses, see Minorsky, *TM*, 155, 105-09, and Chardin, *Voyages*, V, 498.

35. Krusinski, *The History of the Late Revolutions*, 84-88.

36. Chardin, *Voyages*, III, 292.

37. Krusinski, *The History of the Late Revolutions*, 100, 104. On worsened conditions for the peasantry in the late seventeenth century, see the sources cited by Keddie, "The Impact of the West," 35 note 22.

38. Cited by Lockhart, *The Fall*, 107 note 2.

39. Minorsky, *TM*, 23.

40. Lockhart, *The Fall*, 17-33; Roger Savory, "Safavid Persia," pp. 394-429 in Holt et al., eds., *The Cambridge History of Islam*, volume 1: 423-25; Savory, "The Safavid Administrative System," 367, 368, 371; Savory, *Iran under the Safavids*, 226; Hodgson, *The Venture of Islam*, III, 50, 55, 56; Keddie, "The Impact of the West," 35-37; Keddie, *Roots of Revolution*, 13; Martin B. Dickson, "The Fall of the Safavi Dynasty" (a review article on *The Fall of the Safavi Dynasty*), pp. 503-517 in *Journal of the American Oriental Society*, volume 82 (1962), 514; and Helfgott, "The Rise of the Qajar Dynasty," 47, 59-65.

41. These events are detailed in Lockhart, *The Fall*, 46-99; D. M. Lang, "Georgia and the Fall of the Safavi Dynasty," pp. 523-539 in *Bulletin of the School of Oriental and African Studies*, volume XIV, part 3 (1952), 527-31; Krusinski, *The History of the Late Revolutions*, 156-58; Minorsky, *TM*, 9-10; and Hamid Algar, "Shi'ism and Iran in the Eighteenth Century," pp. 288-302 in Naff and Owen, editors, *Studies in Eighteenth Century Islamic History*, 290.

42. These events are chronicled in Lockhart, *The Fall*, 99-129; Roemer, "The Safavid Period," 318-20; Lang, "Georgia and the Fall," 535-39; *A Chronicle of the Carmelites in Persia*, 542; and Krusinski, *The History of the Late Revolutions*, 198.

43. Lockhart, *The Fall*, 130-43; T. H. Weir, "The Revolution in Persia at the Beginning of the 18th Century (from a Turkish MS in the University of Glasgow)," pp. 480-490 in T. W. Arnold and Reynold A. Nicholson, editors, '*Ajabnameh. A Volume of Oriental Studies presented to Edward G. Browne* (Cambridge: At the University Press, 1922), 488.

44. On Wakhtang, see Lang, "Georgia and the Fall," 538. On 'Ali Mardan Khan, see Lockhart, *The Fall*, 159; Savory says he got within forty miles of Isfahan in June and demanded the shah's abdication in favor of his brother, which was refused: "Safavid Persia," 426. Krusinski attributes the failure of the Luris and Bakhtiaris to come to Isfahan's rescue to factional divisions within each tribe: *The History of the Late Revolutions*, 97. On the Shahsavan, see Tapper, "Black Sheep, White Sheep and Red Heads," 67. See also Lockhart, *The Fall*, 159, 161, 167, and Friar Alexander of Malabar, "The Story of the Sack of Ispahan by the Afghans in 1722," pp. 643-653 in *Journal of the Royal Central Asian Society*, volume XXIII, part IV (October 1936), 648.

45. Friar Alexander, "The Story of the Sack of Ispahan," 648-49.

46. Lockhart, *The Fall*, 169.

47. James Morier, *A Second Journey through Persia, Armenia and Asia Minor* (London, 1818), 134, cited by Lockhart, *The Fall*, 169.

48. Sultan Husayn is quoted in Apisalaimian's manuscript—Weir, "The Revolution in Persia," 489. This is an echo of the kingship verse in the Quran: "God gives kingship to whom he will": Minorsky, "Persia," 250.

49. Muhammad 'Ali Hazin, *Tadhkirat al-Ahwal*, translated by F. C. Belfour, *The Life of Shaikh Mohammed Ali Hazin* (London, 1830), cited by Lockhart, *The Fall*, 299.

50. Lockhart, *The Fall*, 298, 349-50; Malcolm, *The History of Persia*, volume II, 42. On political continuities, see Ricks, "Politics and Trade," 56.

51. Cited by Lockhart, *The Fall*, 294. This paragraph draws on ibid., 192, 298, 349-50; Malcolm, *The History of Persia*, II, 42; Issawi, "Population and Resources," 162; Pigulevskaya et al., *Tarikh-i Iran*, 598; *A Chronicle of the Carmelites*, 579, 586; Friar Alexander, "The Story of the Sack of Ispahan," 650; Keyvani, *Artisans and Guild Life*, 231-32; Laurence Lockhart, *Nadir Shah. A Critical Study Based Mainly Upon Contemporary Sources* (London: Luzac & Co., 1938), 17-24; Juan Cole, "Shi'i Clerics in Iraq and Iran, 1722-1780: The Akhbari-Usuli Conflict Reconsidered," pp. 3-34 in *Iranian Studies*, volume XVIII, number 1 (Winter 1985), 5; and Algar, "Shi'ism and Iran," 290.

52. Lockhart, *The Fall*, 177-89, 233-35, 242-50, 296-97, 358. The text of the "Russo-Ottoman Treaty for the Partition of Persia's Northwest Provinces," dated June 13/24, 1724, is found in Hurewitz, *Diplomacy*, I, 44-45.

53. Lockhart, *The Fall*, 261-72, 289-92; *A Chronicle of the Carmelites in Persia*, 578; Savory, "Safavid Persia," 428; Rouhollah K. Ramazani, *The Foreign Policy of Iran. A Developing Nation in World Affairs, 1500-1941* (Charlottesville, Virginia: University Press of Virginia, 1966), 20-22.

54. Lockhart, *The Fall*, 417-19.

55. Lockhart, *The Fall*, 330-39; Lockhart, *Nadir Shah*, 17-24, 36-39; Pigulevskaya et al., *Tarikh-i Iran*, 593-94; Aubin, "Les sunnites du Larestan," 163 note 2.

56. On these institutions and policies, see J. R. Perry, "The Last Safavids, 1722-1773," pp. 59-69 in *Iran* (Journal of the British Institute of Persian Studies), volume IX (1971), 64; Roemer, "The Safavid Period," 328; Lockhart, *Nadir Shah*, 113, 197 note 1, 201 note 2, 214-16, 221-22; Helfgott, "The Rise of the Qajar Dynasty," 56; and Lambton, *Landlord and Peasant*, 130-31.

57. Cited in Lockhart, *Nadir Shah*, 218. This paragraph is based on ibid., 42, 112, 170, 181, 197, 214-15, 241-43, 257, 259, 270, 285-86; Ricks, "Politics and Trade," 126; *A Chronicle of the Carmelites in Persia*, 654; Muhammad Hashim Asaf (Rustam al-Hukama), *Rustam al-tavarikh* [Rustam's History], edited by Muhammad Mushiri (Tehran: Shirkat-i Sahami-yi Kitabha-yi Jibi, 1348/1969), 211; and H. L. Rabino di Borgomale, *Coins, Medals and Seals of the Shahs of Iran, 1500-1941* (Hertford, England: S. Austin and Sons, Ltd., 1945), table IV, between pp. 18 and 19.

58. *A Chronicle of the Carmelites in Persia*, 649-51.

59. John Perry, *Karim Khan Zand. A History of Iran, 1747-1779* (Chicago: University of Chicago Press, 1979), 226, citing B. Plaisted, *A Journey from Calcutta, in Bengal, by Sea, to Busserah . . . in the Year 1750* (London, 1758), 10.

60. On the peasantry, see Lockhart, *Nadir Shah*, 180-81, and *A Chronicle of the Carmelites in Persia*, 360.

61. Ann K. S. Lambton, "Persia: The Breakdown of Society," pp. 430-467 in P. M. Holt et al., editors, *The Cambridge History of Islam*, volume 1, *The Central Islamic Lands* (Cambridge: Cambridge University Press, 1970), 433-34.

62. Lambton, *Landlord and Peasant*, 131; Lockhart, *Nadir Shah*, 51-54, 110; Aubin, "Les sunnites du Larestan," 168-69.

63. On the ulama and religious developments, see Algar, "Shi'ism and Iran," 291-93, 298-99; Lambton, "Persia," 431; Arjomand, *The Shadow of God and the Hidden Imam*, 216-17; Lambton, *Landlord and Peasant*, 132; and Cole, "Shi'i Clerics," 9, 12-13.

64. Hurewitz, "Treaty of Peace, Amity and Commerce: Persia and Russia," pp. 45-46 in *Diplomacy*, I; V. Minorsky, "Nadir Shah," pp. 810-814 in M. Th. Houtsma et al., editors, *The Encyclopedia of Islam* (Leyden: E. J. Brill, 1927), 811; Lockhart, *Nadir Shah*, 58, 84, 84 note 1, 86, 282. Ferrier feels that "The impetus to trade given by Peter the Great survived his ill-fated campaign in 1722" ("Trade from the mid-14th Century," 474), but in the absence of any data on this trade it seems best to be skeptical as to its volume.

65. On these events, see Lockhart, *Nadir Shah*, 122-24, 128-53, 161, and Minorsky, "Nadir Shah," 811.

66. Lockhart, *Nadir Shah*, 282.

67. Cited in ibid., 286 note 1.

68. Ricks, "Politics and Trade," 102.

69. Lockhart, *Nadir Shah*, 175-76; Issawi, *EHI*, 13; Inalcik and Steensgaard, "Harir," 211; Ferrier, "Trade from the mid-14th Century," 478.

70. Lockhart, *Nadir Shah*, 286.

71. Helfgott, "The Rise of the Qajar Dynasty," 105-7; Perry, "The Last Safavids, 1722-1773," 65; Lockhart, *Nadir Shah*, 264-65.

72. On these events see Helfgott, "The Rise of the Qajar Dynasty," 108-21; Perry, *Karim Khan Zand*, 13-96 (and 227 for the phrase on "the broken circle of justice"); and Minorsky, *TM*, 137 note 2.

73. Perry, *Karim Khan Zand*, 215-20, 294; Perry, "The Last Safavids, 1722-1773," 67-68.

74. William Francklin, *Observations made on a tour from Bengal to Persia in the years 1786-7* (London, 1790), 108, cited by Lambton, "The Tribal Resurgence," 120. See also ibid., 124-26; Perry, *Karim Khan Zand*, 213, 218-19, 229, 235, 241, 279-80, 293; and *A Chronicle of the Carmelites in Persia*, 672.

75. Data in this paragraph is drawn from *A Chronicle of the Carmelites in Persia*, 660, 662, 669, 671, and Perry, *Karim Khan Zand*, 226, 230, 238, 240-42.

76. Asaf, *Rustam al-tavarikh*, 309, cited and translated by Lambton, "The Tribal Resurgence," 122. See also Asaf, 421-22, in ibid., 128-29.

77. Mgr. Cornelius of St. Joseph, letter from Basra dated July 5, 1763, in *A Chronicle of the Carmelites in Persia*, 663. On the tuman, see Rabino di Borgomale, *Coins, Medals and Seals*, table IV between pp. 18 and 19; and Perry *Karim Khan Zand*, xi.

78. Perry, *Karim Khan Zand*, 243; Pigulevskaya et al., *Tarikh-i Iran*, 615.

79. Waring, *A Tour to Sheeraz*, 302, cited by Perry, *Karim Khan Zand*, 283. See also Perry, *Karim Khan Zand*, 240, 243, 272-74, 277-78, 287; Cl. Huart, "Karim Khan Zand," p. 762 in M. Th. Houtsma et al., editors, *The Encyclopedia of Islam* (Leyden: E. J. Brill, 1927), 762; Pigulevskaya et al., *Tarikh-i Iran*, 615; and Helfgott, "The Rise of the Qajar Dynasty," 122.

80. On the agrarian sector see Perry, *Karim Khan Zand*, 228-29, 235-36; Pigulevskaya et al., *Tarikh-i Iran*, 615; and Lambton, "The Tribal Resurgence," 121.

81. Tapper, "Black Sheep, White Sheep and Red Heads," 67; Perry, *Karim Khan Zand*, 225.

82. On the ulama, see Lambton, "The Tribal Resurgence," 122; Cole, "Shi'i Clerics," 21; Algar, "Shi'ism and Iran," 300, 301; and Perry, *Karim Khan Zand*, 222.

83. On the Ottomans, see Perry, *Karim Khan Zand*, 249, 253, 256; Malcolm, *The Melville Papers*, in Issawi, *EHI*, 264; Ferrier, "Trade from the mid-14th Century," 489; and Ricks, "Politics and Trade," 397. Conversion rates here are based on Minorsky's rate of 30 rupees to the tuman for the seventeenth century (*TM*, 154), and Perry's rate of 1.875 pounds sterling to the tuman (*Karim Khan Zand*, xi).

84. *Three Reports of the Select Committee Appointed by the Court of Directors* (London: n.d. [circa 1792]), pp. 85-89 in Issawi, *EHI*, 88. See also Perry, *Karim Khan Zand*, 271; Malcolm, *The Melville Papers*, in Issawi, *EHI*, 263.

85. On the situation in the Gulf, see Ricks, "Politics and Trade," 232-33, 269-71, 323, 388; *A Chronicle of the Carmelites*, 670 note 1; and Perry, *Karim Khan Zand*, 256, 263.

86. *Three Reports*, 89. Data above is derived from comparing Malcolm, *The Melville Papers*, in Issawi, *EHI*, 264, with Malcolm cited by Perry, *Karim Khan Zand*, 249, and from G. I. Ter-Gukasov, *Politicheskie i ekonomicheskie interesy Rossii v Persii* [Political and Economic Interests of Russia in Persia] (Petrograd, 1916), extracts translated pp. 144-146 in Issawi, *EHI*, 145-46. The rate of ten rubles to the tuman (for 1743-48) is found in Rabino di Borgomale, *Coins, Medals and Seals*, table IV, between pp. 18 and 19. See also Perry, *Karim Khan Zand*, 207-8, 250-52.

87. "Grant of Special Privileges at Bushire to the (British) East India Company," pp. 52-54 in Hurewitz, *Diplomacy*, I, for the text; Perry, *Karim Khan Zand*, 248, for the tariff differentials of three percent for Europeans versus seven to ten percent for Middle Easterners.

88. Ricks, "Politics and Trade," 273. See also Boxer, *Jan Compagnie*, 76-102.

89. On relations with England, see Lord G. Curzon, *Persia and the Persian Question* (London: Longman, Green and Co., 1892), two volumes, II, 550-51; Dillon, "Carpet Capitalism," 210, 222; Perry, *Karim Khan Zand*, 227, 256, 258, 260; Ricks, "Politics and Trade," 293, 339, 417 Appendix G, 418 Appendix H; *Three Reports*, 87; *A Chronicle of the Carmelites in Persia*, 663 note 2; and Hurewitz, *Diplomacy*, I, 53-54.

90. Helfgott, "The Rise of the Qajar Dynasty," 167-80. On the origins and earlier history of the Qajar tribe, see ibid., 126-67, and Reid, "The Qajar Uymaq," 124-30.

91. These events are chronicled by Helfgott, "The Rise of the Qajar Dynasty," 179-85, and Perry, *Karim Khan Zand*, 296-98.

92. Malcolm, *History of Persia* (London: Longman and Co., 1825 edition), volume II, 183 note. Malcolm adds "there can be no doubt his real motive was that of self-preservation." See also Helfgott, "The Rise of the Qajar Dynasty," 193-98.

93. Ibid., 200-03; Perry, *Karim Khan Zand*, 300-01.

94. Helfgott, "The Rise of the Qajar Dynasty," 204-12; he cites Malcolm, *History of Persia* (1825 edition), volume II, 300.

The Significance of the Safavid Period and the Eighteenth Century

It will be useful to stand back now from the empirical detail of our historical narrative and attempt to draw together the theoretical and sociological threads of the underlying analysis, so that the relationship between the two orders of explanation can be once again made clear. The ground covered so far has focused on three principal moments in the history of social change in Iran from 1500 to 1800—the seventeenth-century peak, the fall of the Safavids in 1722, and the eighteenth-century watershed.

An undisputed economic peak was attained in the seventeenth century under Shah 'Abbas and his immediate successors. Chapter two argued that the entire social formation was best conceptualized in Marxian terms not as a unitary feudal or Asiatic mode of production but as a hybrid articulation of three interrelated modes of production—pastoral nomadism in the tribal sector, a peasant crop-sharing system under several overlords (the state, tiyul holders, vaqf administrators, and private owners) in the agrarian sector, and a petty-commodity mode of production organized by both the state and a private sector in the urban economy. The complexity of this social structure meant that Iran possessed several ruling classes in the seventeenth century—tribal chiefs, controllers of land revenue, and merchants and official ulama—over all of whom the Safavid ruling family loomed hegemonic, by virtue of its location at the top of all three modes of production, drawing on the surplus produced in each. The dominance of the Safavid state had other determinants as well: Its successful absolutism reposed on multiple legitimations—the pre-Islamic divine right of kings and the prestige accorded the founders of the dynasty as heads of a sufi order, claimed descent from the Shi'i imams, and credit for the establishment of Shi'ism as the new state religion in Iran. All these earned respect and authority for the ruling family among tribespeople, peasantry, and towndwellers. The Safavids' 222-year reign was the longest in a millennium in Iran (and the longest since) and this durability constitutes further testimony to the political stability they enjoyed.

In assessing Iran's external relations in the seventeenth century, we found them characterized qualitatively as above all relations of parity vis-à-vis both the rising commercial powers of the West (Holland, England, and France) and Iran's neighboring Islamic empires (the Ottomans, Mughals, and Uzbeks). In terms of the mix of raw materials and "manufactures," balance of trade, and apportionment of profits, there was no possibility of finding Iran dependent on Europe at this early stage in their relations. Rather, in world-systemic terms, Iran was a world-empire in the external arena, or, seen from the Iranian point of view, Europe was part of *Iran's* external arena. Both sides were fairly self-sufficient and structurally independent of each other, and thus, when they interacted, they did so as relative equals. This relationship was yet another factor in the stability of the Iranian political economy and the paramount position of the shahs, who were among the main internal beneficiaries of the world trade.

For all its longevity and material and cultural accomplishments, this social structure, and its underlying political economy, were anything but static. The existence of several modes of production exacerbated tendencies to conflict and shaped these in certain directions. Popular movements of peasants, tribespeople, and bazaar classes did occur in the sixteenth and seventeenth centuries, but the obstacles to organizing resistance across economic and geographic sectors rendered success at the level of national political power or achieving local independence illusory. Rather, inter- and intra-elite struggles proved more salient in the Safavid period. After several tribal civil wars in the sixteenth century, the Safavid state temporarily succeeded in imposing its absolutist claim over the unruly tribal elite in the early seventeenth century. Two generations later, an intra-elite conflict within the ruling household involving the harem factions and leading ulama undermined the ability of the shahs to control this fractious system, and 'Abbas's successors were incapable of furthering his policies. At the same time, signs of fiscal crisis appeared—an unfavorable balance of trade drained specie out of Iran and prices rose internally, while the state's expenditures on the army, court, and harem grew inordinately. Thus external economic relations were a contributing factor to a political and economic deterioration that had largely *internal* determinants.

The Safavid dynasty lurched into an intertwined economic, political, and ideological crisis by the turn of the eighteenth century. Budgetary problems, intra-elite squabbling, and a long period of peace with the Ottomans undermined its military capabilities. Persecution of non-Shi'i minorities rent the social fabric, alienating Georgian military commanders and bureaucrats, Armenian merchants, Zoroastrian and Hindu communities, and most fatefully, the Sunni tribal groups on the periphery of the empire in the

Caucasus, Baluchistan, Khuzistan, and the Afghan provinces. A small army of Afghan tribesmen easily brought down the whole edifice in 1722 when no provincial army rallied to the aid of the Safavids besieged at Isfahan, and high level betrayals and dissension precluded any effective military response from an army that had been neglected for several decades. When the state faltered, the empire quickly collapsed. Iran's more powerful and aggressive neighbors, the Ottomans and Russians, promptly made incursions in the west and north, and by 1724 the country was divided at least four ways by the Afghans, Ottomans, Russians, and remaining Safavid forces under Tahmasp and his soon-to-be master, Nadir.

The depth of the disastrous circumstances which the Iranian people lived through for the remainder of the eighteenth century—almost eight decades—was recognized as early as the 1780s when an EIC report noted "the comparison between the past and present state of Persia, in every respect, will be found truly deplorable."[1] A modern historian, Jean Aubin, has characterized the century as "catastrophic . . . by far the blackest period in the whole history of Islamic Iran."[2] And our analysis of conditions during the successive reigns of the Afghans, Nadir Shah, Karim Khan Zand, and the rise of the Qajars has borne this out in a tale of economic collapse and societal dislocation, of wars, civil and foreign, famine, disease, and emigration, adding up to destruction of the economy and depopulation of the country.

The consequences of this experience, in light of the achievements of the Safavid period, went very deep. The reversal of the internal dynamic of economic development in Iran is the most striking. Jahangir Saleh and Alessandro Bausani have suggested that the breakdown entailed the loss of a historic opportunity to develop an indigenous capitalism, whether by state direction from above or by merchant capital in the urban sector.[3] While this may seem exaggerated, it is intriguing to speculate how an intact Safavid political economy, after another century of stable growth and prosperity, would have fared in the nineteenth century. There can be no doubt that the urban economy's development was set back enormously, and the eighteenth century *did* in effect seal off any incipient evolution toward capitalism, *if* one was in motion at the Safavid zenith in the seventeenth century. In a related development, the state was weakened as the central single economic actor in the social formation—the Afghans, Afshars, and Zands lacked the extensive royal domains of the Safavids, did far less building and commercial infrastructural work, controlled the lucrative silk monopoly less determinedly (and more significantly, saw the volume of silk exported plummet quite drastically), and for the most part commanded far fewer resources. This weakened the state politically as well, with effects extending through the next century. The role of the tribes was likewise transformed in the seventeenth and eighteenth centuries—while the prominence of Afghans, Afshars, Zands, and finally Qajars in the successive tribal wars would seem to verify Lambton's thesis of a "tribal resurgence," none of these could maintain itself for long except the Qajars. The Afghans were rejected as alien interlopers, the Afshars rose and fell with Nadir's imperial delusions, the Zands failed to found a dynasty for all Karim's popularity. Many tribes still managed to thrive in their local areas within the limits of the pastoral nomadic mode of production, but their chiefly leaders, as contenders for hegemony among the several ruling classes of Iran, never recovered the preeminent position they had fought for in the sixteenth century. Finally, peasants undoubtedly suffered more than tribespeople in the eighteenth century as irrigation systems deteriorated, troop movements bankrupted them, military commanders drafted them, and the state squeezed them for taxes.

In conclusion, internally, though each mode of production remained intact from the sixteenth to the late eighteenth centuries, *all* were significantly weakened, as was the state as an economic entity, and the sum of their parts as a social formation was rather less by 1800 than it had been under 'Abbas in the 1620s. The eighteenth century was a developmental reversal of huge proportions and its consequences, in terms of an unmeasurable lost opportunity, continued to adversely affect the country into the nineteenth and twentieth centuries.

Externally, the century saw an erosion of the developing contacts with the West of 'Abbas's day, not in the qualitative direction of any tendency toward an incipient dependency but in absolute terms as a lack of any contacts at all by the 1780s and 1790s. If the Europeans were not major actors in the turbulent eighteenth century, they were in a sense yet another missing ingredient in the political economy of the Afghans, Nadir Shah, and Karim Khan alike. This too represented a decline in state power vis-à-vis late Safavid times. As the European-centered world system of capitalism emerged along the new maritime routes to India, southeast Asia, and the Americas, the loss of Middle Eastern centrality as a link between East and West increasingly made itself felt. While Iran suffered neither the hyperinflation and military pressure that the Ottomans did nor the growing colonial incursions that the Mughals felt, its long stay in the external arena of this world economy meant an inability to emerge definitively as either a powerful core or a dominated periphery. Loss of contact with the West thus contributed to a gradual, relative decline commercially, militarily, and politically which would be a heavy legacy for the Qajars in the nineteenth century. Thus, due to isolation from opportunities and stimulus, we have a case of decline in the world system without dependency or peripheralization, a distinctive path in comparative international perspective, roughly true also of China and Japan.

In terms of political culture, finally, the century was also a watershed in some crucial ways. The Safavid absolutist project did not die suddenly. It required the ruthlessness of the Afghan occupation, the syncretic religion and military expansionism of Nadir's false starts, and Karim's successorless experiment with just government and moderation at Shiraz before a viable new dynasty superseded 'Abbas the Great's descendants. Each of the three intervening "dynasties"—Afghans, Afshars, and Zands—weakened the Safavid hold on the popular and elite imaginations, but each lacked one or more of the material or ideological resources that had made the Safavids hegemonic. The failure of Karim Khan in particular to perpetuate his reign of efficiency and justice was a historical missed opportunity for Iran, but one which was in a sense inevitable without a wider internal and external base or far-reaching claim to monarchical legitimation. The successive failures to establish firm central control had the cumulative effect of weakening the institution of the monarchy as a whole, and lessened the prospects for any future absolutism as unquestioned as had been the Safavids'.

A parallel development of import was the decoupling of the state-ulama connection that flourished under the Safavids. The Sunni Afghans and Nadir attempted to lodge Shi'ism from its position as state and national religion; Karim restored it only nominally. While Iran retained for the most part a Shi'i religious culture, the ulama lost economic power in the form of state patronage and vast vaqf landholdings and in the course of the century developed a greater reliance on economic, kinship, and ideological ties with the urban bazaar classes. As Algar observes, "Religious loyalty was no longer synonymous with loyalty to the monarch, and Shi'ism was established as an autonomous force."[4] This trend was reinforced by the emergence of the high ulama as a pole of cultural and political influence with the usulis' insistence that mujtahids were needed to interpret the faith. Despite all the political and economic dislocations of the century, Shi'ism proved durable and socially cementing in Iran, but saw a shift in its locus of legitimation away from the monarchy and downward into the popular milieu.

It took the greater part of the eighteenth century to effect the transition from Safavids to Qajars—via Afghan invasion, Nadir's reconquest and Asian campaigns, renewed civil wars, Karim Khan's smaller Iran, another round of civil wars, and finally, the bloody rise of the new Qajar dynasty. In multiple respects the century provided a disastrous link between the promising political economy of the seventeenth and the social formation of the nineteenth, which would be stable but at a far more precarious level of development. The suffering of the Iranian people was great in this period, and the shadows it cast would prove to be long. A study of the contours of the resulting system will make clear the terms of the new dispensation, whose limits are best considered against the achievements of an earlier time, now lost to view.

Notes

1. *Three Reports*, 86.

2. Aubin, "La politique religieuse des safavides," 241. This would seem to overlook the even greater devastation wrought by the Mongols in the thirteenth century.

3. Bausani, *The Persians*, 152-53; Saleh, "Social Formations in Iran," 107.

4. Algar, "Shi'ism and Iran," 300. See also Arjomand, *The Shadow of God and the Hidden Imam*, 215: "temporal rule was deliberately shorn of all hierocratic trappings."

PART TWO

Social Structure and Social Change in Qajar Iran, 1800-1925

From 1905 to 1925 Iran was plunged into a whirlwind of social dislocation and change. The years 1905 to 1911 witnessed a tumultuous upheaval known as the Constitutional revolution, involving mass participation, particularly in the urban sector, directed primarily against the autocratic domination of society by the Qajar state and its helplessness in the face of foreign powers. In 1906 Muzaffar al-Din Shah was forced to grant a constitution; in 1908 his successor Muhammad 'Ali staged a coup against the first parliament (the *majlis*); and in 1909 the anti-constitutional shah was compelled to abdicate in favor of his eleven-year old son. The revolution finally ended in late 1911 when Russian troops entered Iran to dissolve the second majlis and prop up the shaky Qajar monarchy. World War I brought severe economic hardship exacerbated by Turkish and Russian armies fighting on Iranian soil and culminating in a tragic famine in 1918-19 that took an enormous toll in human lives. While the Russian revolution removed the tsar's strong hand from Iranian affairs, the British proposed a protectorate-like status for Iran in 1919, and when this proved unpopular and politically unacceptable, backed the coup of a rising military commander named Reza Khan Pahlavi in February 1921 to restore the state's authority. Reza Khan maneuvered steadily into a position of unquestioned power until the majlis dissolved the Qajar dynasty late in 1925 and he crowned himself as the founder of a new Pahlavi dynasty.

This dramatic sequence of events reposed on a prior transition in the Iranian political economy brought about largely by the growing dependence of Iran on the Russian and British governments and economies in the course of the nineteenth century. The alternately defiant and hopeful attitudes of the early Qajar shahs toward the two European powers had been dashed decisively by the turn of the twentieth century, as the Qajar state found itself in growing debt, with little control over its own customs revenues and tariffs, roads, communications, banks, or army. Internal economic development had slowly taken place over the hundred year period, as evidenced by the available data on foreign trade, agricultural production, and population growth. But much of its pace and form was likewise determined from abroad and its benefits were limited to a few groups, notably the court, a new class of landlords, and a section of merchants. The great bulk of peasants, tribespeople, artisans, small traders, and urban poor were living through an experience of either stagnation or deterioration in their changing conditions of life. Only now, especially in the cities, they were finding articulate voices among the ulama and other educated groups to criticize the political system that subjected them to foreign control.

Chapter four of this study analyzes these major political, economic, and ideological developments in the Iranian social formation by bringing into play the key concept of *dependent development*. We shall thus trace the impact of Iran's insertion into the nineteenth-century world capitalist system as a peripheral area to the European core and semiperiphery, exploring the consequences of a deepening dependency upon Russia and Great Britain for the principal social classes and significant groups in Iranian society in empirical detail. And in light of this process, the major movements for social change discussed in chapter five—reform efforts by the state, urban and tribal rebellions, the Constitutional revolution, and the separatist movements and Pahlavi coup of the post-World War I period—can be seen as complex responses by the groups and classes living through the turmoil of transition to a dependent relationship with outside forces. Taken together, the two chapters of this part demonstrate the dialectic of political economy and culture discussed in chapter one and reveal the interplay of the internal and external logics of social change in a concrete historical setting.

4

Crossing the Threshold of Dependence: The Iranian Social Formation from 1800 to 1914

The shah is sovereign of his country, and as such he desires to be independent. There are two great powers with whom Persia is in more or less direct contact—Russia and the English power in India. The first has more military means than the second: on the other hand, England has more money than Russia. The two powers can thus do Persia good and evil; in order above all to avoid the evil, the shah is desirous of keeping himself, with respect to them, within the relations of good friendship and free from all contestation. If, on the contrary, he finds himself threatened on one side, he will betake himself to the other in search of the support which he shall stand in need of. That is not what he desires, but to what he may be driven, for he is not more the friend of one than of the other of those powers: he desires to be with them on a footing of equal friendship. What he cherishes above all is his independence, and the maintenance of good relations with foreign powers.

—Husayn Khan, Iranian diplomat during the reign of Muhammad Shah (1834-1848)[1]

* * *

[T]he antagonism existing between Russia and England has become such that should I wish to go out for an excursion or a shooting expedition in the north, east and west of my country, I must consult the English, and should I intend to go south I must consult the Russians.

—remarks attributed to Nasir al-Din Shah in 1888 by the English chargé d'affaires Wolff[2]

A central controversy in the economic history of Iran revolves around the nature of the changes that occurred in the nineteenth century: Was there an economic "decline" or can one see the "beginnings of moderniza-tion" in the long reign of the Qajar dynasty from 1800 to 1925?[3] Did livings standards rise or fall? Did the level and type of consumption improve or deteriorate for the majority of the population, and within the subsectors of peasant agriculture, tribal pastoralism, and urban production and trade? In the view of Julian Bharier, "In 1900 Iran was . . . a fairly primitive, almost isolated state, barely distinguishable as an economic entity. . . . There were signs that the economy was developing but at the turn of the century it still remained one of the most backward countries in the world."[4] Other impor-tant works lay stress on the benefits of commercialized agriculture, rising per capita incomes, and more Western-style ("modern") political institu-tions.[5]

"How much" development took place in Qajar Iran, then? In contrast to Bharier and others who are either looking forward into the petroleum-led industrialization of the post-World War I period or are comparing early twentieth-century Iran unfavorably with its Ottoman, Egyptian, and Brit-ish Indian neighbors, it will be demonstrated here that considerable devel-opment took place in the course of the nineteenth century and that Iran in 1914 was transformed significantly from the situation prevailing in 1800. But in contrast to analyses that optimistically assess the changes as progres-sive and the seeds of modernization, it will be argued that Iran's develop-ment was dependent because it was shaped from abroad and severely limited in both form and extent. Thus the key concept of *dependent develop-ment* now comes into play, as a process of change involving internal and external actors and causes, with political, economic, and social effects.

In exploring the nature of dependence in Qajar Iran, this chapter moves from the external political and economic relations of Iran with Britain, Russia, and other countries to internal economic developments in Iran's three (and later four) modes of production. This procedure, the inverse of that followed in chapters two and three, is now invoked because a theory of growing dependence of Iran on the West is operative. This is not to say that all (or perhaps even most) of the internal economy was determined by the external relations but rather that a critical threshold was crossed in this period such that increasingly large numbers of people were affected to a greater extent than ever before in their daily lives by forces emanating from outside Iran. This process extended to the Qajar state as well, whose institutions were recast and weakened by their new relations to the West and civil society. Along the way, data on secular trends in the Qajar political economy assess such realities as the composition and balance of foreign trade, inflation and wage data, and the fiscal crises faced by the state—all key indicators of the impact and nature of dependent development.

External Political and Economic Relations

The Napoleonic wars in the first decade of the nineteenth century re-stimulated European contact with Iran as both England and France sought friendly relations while Russia invaded the country again.[6] After the long disruptions of the eighteenth century, the English East India Company signed treaties of alliance and commerce with the Qajars in 1801 but failed to come to Iran's aid when Russia occupied the Caucasus in 1804. After a disappointing alliance with the French, Iran turned to the English again and in late 1814 the two signed a "(Definitive) Treaty of Defensive Alliance." The British failed to come to the shah's aid when war broke out between Russia and Iran from 1826 to 1828, alleging (falsely) that Iran had been the aggressor. A growing consensus emerged in England by the early 1830s however that Russia posed a threat of further expansion in Asia at the expense of Iran, the Ottoman Empire, and Central Asia. Thus was born the outlines of what came to be known as the "Eastern Question," or "the Great Game," in which Iran assumed increasing strategic importance as a buffer against Russian advances toward India. From 1837 to 1857, England used force or the threat of it on several occasions to thwart Iran's own ambitions in Afghanistan, which was also emerging as a new buffer state supported by Britain. The use of military power to achieve diplomatic and strategic advantage thus confirmed the commercial preeminence of Great Britain in Iran by mid-century.[7] Actual British trade with Iran saw a sharp rise in the first half of the nineteenth century, both in the Persian Gulf and along new routes to the more populous northern markets. As the EIC established its political hegemony in India, it began to replace Indian textiles with its own piece goods in the Gulf trade with Iran. A more substantial trade also began to reach northern Iran by ship to the Black Sea Ottoman port of Trabzon, then overland to Tabriz, which became Iran's largest emporium. By the 1850s, Britain was well-entrenched as Iran's leading trade partner, accounting for up to or over 50 percent of exports and even more of Iran's imports.[8]

The half-century from 1863 to 1914 witnessed a series of "concessions" to exploit or monopolize raw materials and infrastructural development in Iran, granted to both English and Russian subjects and their governments.[9] In 1872 the shah entered into an agreement with British subject Baron Paul Julius de Reuter for a seventy-year concession to lay railroads, install telegraph lines, regulate river navigation, exploit mines and state forests, and construct irrigation works, with first option on future concessions to open a bank, build streets and roads, mills and factories—all this in return for a 40,000 pound sterling deposit to the shah. The British viceroy to India, Lord Curzon, called the Reuter concession "the most complete and extraordinary surrender of the entire industrial resources of a kingdom into foreign hands that has probably ever been dreamed of, much less accomplished, in history."[10] Public opinion soon forced its cancellation, but in compensation, Reuter was authorized to establish the Bank of Reuter (later the British-owned Imperial Bank of Persia) and a mining corporation that prospected unsuccessfully for oil in the 1890s. The bank however had a monopoly on the issue of bank notes and cut significantly into the local money-lending markets, making loans of 500,000 pounds to the government in 1892, 200,000 in 1903, and 100,000 in 1904.[11]

Two final concessions of note were for the exploitation of tobacco and oil. In 1890 the shah granted a monopoly on tobacco sales to a British company; a massive social movement forced its cancellation, but not without an indemnity of 500,000 pounds sterling which he had to borrow from the English Imperial Bank. A less controversial but equally fateful concession was the "special and exclusive privilege" granted to William Knox D'Arcy in May 1901 "to search for, obtain, exploit, develop, render suitable for trade, carry away and sell natural gas petroleum, asphalt and ozokerite throughout the whole extent of the Persian Empire for a term of sixty years." The Iranian state was to receive in return a one-time payment of 20,000 pounds sterling in cash and an equal amount in shares in the company, plus 16 percent of the annual net profits.[12] Oil was discovered in the southwest on May 26, 1908 and the Anglo-Persian Oil Company (APOC), under complete British ownership, was created. The British Admiralty under Winston Churchill acquired controlling financial interest in the APOC in May 1914 by buying 2,001,000 pounds sterling out of 4,000,000 in shares, making Iran's 20,000 pound interest a very small one indeed. In 1923, Churchill claimed that the investment had earned his government forty million pounds sterling, while Iran's share of the revenues had come to two million pounds.[13]

In addition to the profits generated by these concessions, British trade with Iran continued to increase in the period up to World War I. Total trade climbed from 1.7 million pounds sterling in 1875 to 3 million in 1895 and 4.5 million by 1914. The balance was in England's favor by as much as 20 percent. Due to Russia's rapid rise in the overall trade of Iran, this absolute increase for British trade still entailed a decline in its share, down from the 50 percent or more of the 1850s to 33 percent in 1903 and 20 percent by 1914, about one-half of which was with British India. The British empire's share of the export trade to Iran was higher, at about 25 percent. Litten's rough estimate of British capital investment in Iran from 1860 to 1913 totals almost ten million pounds sterling in oil, loans, transport, telegraphs, and carpet companies.[14]

If the overarching aim of English policy in Iran was to use the country as a buffer in defense of its greater interests in India and to contain undue Russian expansion into Asia, to fully assess the British position in Iran it is necessary to examine the position of her main nineteenth-century competitor, Tsarist Russia, which by 1914 had become the dominant foreign power in Iran. Russia fought and won two major wars with Iran between 1801 and 1828. The first gave Russia large amounts of Iranian territory, including Baku, and set trade duties at five percent. A second war, instigated by Russian treaty violations in 1826, saw initial Iranian victories followed by defeat and further loss of territories, an indemnity of three million pounds sterling, and confirmation of the favorable commercial rights.[15] Economic gains followed military victories. Exports to Iran, according to one set of estimates, rose tenfold from 1758-60 to the time of the second war in 1826. By the mid-nineteenth century 5.3 million rubles of goods were imported from Iran against only 900,000 rubles of exports. This represents under one-tenth of the imports and about one-third of the exports of Iran, no great increase perhaps over Malcolm's estimate in 1800 that gave Russia roughly 15 percent of Iran's total trade, but significant in view of England's phenomenal rise.[16]

After 1850 Russia began a rise to commercial and political hegemony in Iran, in part encouraged by its own industrialization and expansion into Central Asia toward Iran. This generated demands for labor and agricultural staples and greatly increased access to Iran's markets for the fledgling Russian manufactures. Russian methods shifted to a more peaceful emphasis on economic penetration—what Marvin Entner has called "ruble imperialism." Like the English, the Russians sought concessions, influence over institutions, and increased trade. The most important concessions they obtained were in fisheries on the Caspian, road-building, telegraphs, railroads, and banking. The series of agreements *not* to build railways between 1890 and World War I is instructive in showing how Britain and especially Russia acted to preserve their own interests and thwart each other's at Iran's expense. A key institution of economic penetration was the Russian Bank established in 1891, which soon acquired vast mortgage properties, operated mercantile transactions, and made large loans to the Qajar state. By 1914 the bank's 127 million rubles exceeded that of all capital investments by the British government and its citizens in Iran on the eve of World War I.[17] The turning point in the rise of Russian hegemony came in the 1880s and 1890s. As Table 4.1 shows, Russia had drawn even to if not surpassed England as Iran's leading trading partner by 1895; the gap continued to widen through the next decade. By 1914 it was indisputable: Russia provided 56 percent of Iran's imports and took 72 percent of exports, to Britain's 28 and 13 percent, respectively. The balance of trade also slowly shifted into Russia's favor, reaching one million pounds sterling by 1910-14. The extraordinary degree of Russian control over Iran in the economic sphere by the outbreak of the First World War has been eloquently stated by Entner:

TABLE 4.1   Total Trade of Iran with Russia and Britain, 1875-1914
(in pounds sterling)

Year	With Russia	With Britain
1875	circa 1.0 million	1.7 million
1895	3.4-3.5 million	3.0 million
1904	3.75-5.5 million	2.5-3.0 million
1914	12.0 million	4.5 million

Sources: Ashraf and Hekmat, "Merchants and Artisans," 734; Platt, *Finance, Trade and Politics*, 228; Bausani, *The Persians*, 168; Keddie, "The Impact of the West," 93; Rabino, "An Economist's Notes on Persia," 267; MacLean, "Report on Conditions and Prospects," in Issawi, *EHI*, 137; Entner, *Russo-Persian Commercial Relations*, 8-9; Issawi, *EHI*, 142.

"To a remarkable extent, Persia had been drawn into Russia's economic orbit and was a functioning part of her economy."[18]

This control was mirrored on the political plane. In 1904, the instructions of the Russian Foreign Ministry to a new minister in Tehran read:

> The main object that has been pursued by us . . . in the course of a long contact with Persia, may be defined in the following manner: To preserve the integrity and inviolability of the Shah's domains, not seeking territorial increases for ourselves and not permitting the dominance of a third power, gradually to subject Persia to our domination without the violation, however, of either the external signs of Persia's independence or her internal structure. In other words, our task is: politically to make Persia obedient and useful; that is sufficiently strong to be a tool in our hands—economically, to preserve for ourselves the major share of the Persian market for free and exclusive exploitation by Russian efforts and capital. This close relationship and its consequent economic and political results, when attained by us, will result in a substantial foundation upon which we can carry on fruitful activity.[19]

The specific classes among which Russia expanded its hold from economic to political influence extended from the merchants with whom it had dealings, and to a lesser extent northern peasants and tribespeople, all the way to the court. Another key state institution where Russia came to have preponderant influence was the weak Qajar army, whose most reliable unit by the 1890s was the Russian-trained and officered "Cossack Brigade"; three times a day the soldiers were ordered to shout in Turki "Hurrah Emperor, chok saghol Shah!" (Hurrah to the [Russian] Emperor, long life to the Shah!).[20]

In the 1890s, then, Russia began to pull away in the peaceful, gradual economic competition for control in Iran, but on a world scale still lagged behind other imperialist powers and possessed internal military and industrial weaknesses. The attempted revolution of 1905 and the external defeat by a rising Japan in their 1904-5 war brought these to light and slowed down absolute Russian hegemony in Iran. The existing balance of forces between Russia and England was accurately reflected and formalized in the "Anglo-Russian Convention on Persia, Afghanistan and Tibet" of August 1907. The preamble to this document claims that Great Britain and Russia are "mutually engaged to respect the integrity and independence of Persia," but goes on to state that "each of them has, for geographical and economic reasons, a special interest in the maintenance of peace and order in certain provinces of Persia." According to the agreement's terms Russia "received" as its sphere of influence the wealthiest and most populous provinces of Iran, along with the capital and other key political centers, while Britain's area in the south was quite limited. The oil fields (discovered a year later) lay in the neutral zone between them.[21] The "Great Game" came to a quiet end with this peaceful division of interests in Iran and the rise of a mutual threat to Russia and England in the form of a belligerent German empire in the years from the Agreement to the First World War. Russia dominated Iranian affairs even more thoroughly with a military occupation that ended the Constitutional revolution in 1911 and Britain acquiesced in this, content to have a stable, pliant government and secure in its access to Iran's oil and India's hinterland. Thus Russia enjoyed unchallenged hegemony in Iran on the eve of 1914, having overcome both internal and external opposition to do so.

As Table 4.2 makes clear, no other country challenged the predominance of Russia or the distant but solid second place of England in Iran's foreign trade by the eve of World War I. The Ottoman Empire was in third place overall, with roughly four times less than the trade of Great Britain. Germany had more of the imports but far fewer of Iran's exports than the Ottomans. Especially active in the export of carpets, there was also a surge of German investments in early modern factories from 1910 to 1914 and hopes for a link to the German-built Baghdad railroad. France enjoyed considerable cultural influence through its religious missions and schools, but France, Italy, Belgium, Austria-Hungary, and Afghanistan combined provided only 8-9 percent of Iran's imports and took only 5-6 percent of her exports. The situation had changed drastically since the start of the Qajars' reign in 1800. Then, according to Malcolm's report, Iran's main trading partners were Afghanistan and Central Asia (33.75 percent), the Ottoman empire (26 percent), and India (19.5 percent), followed by Russia with 15

TABLE 4.2 Trade of Iran, by Country, 1913/14
(in thousands of rubles)

Trading Partner	Imports to Iran	Percent	Exports from Iran	Percent
Russia	64,000	55.53	54,371	71.57
Great Britain/India	32,032	27.76	10,280	13.53
Ottoman Empire	4,021	3.49	6,637	8.74
Germany	5,468	4.74	531	.69
France	3,533	3.06	826	1.09
Italy	1,008	.87	2,614	3.44
Belgium	2,740	2.38	41	.05
Austria-Hungary	1,606	1.39	130	.17
Afghanistan	899	.78	534	.70

Source: Entner, Russo-Persian Commercial Relations, 64 table 9, calculations mine.

percent, while the English EIC had only 3 percent, barely ahead of the Gulf and Red Sea principalities (2.25 percent).[22] A major change, then, was the rise of the Europeans as trading partners, from under 19 percent (to include a backward Russia) to about 94 percent (transferring British India to the European column), between 1800 and 1914.

In looking at the overall trends in the foreign trade we can see growth, certainly, but of a problematic kind. Total trade seems to have doubled from 1800 to 1860, then quadrupled from 1860 to 1914. If prices are adjusted for, the volume of products traded may have risen by three times from 1800 to 1860 and four times from 1860 to 1914, or twelve-fold in the 114 years. Since figures for 1800 included a large amount of goods in transit both ways, the rise in "real" imports and exports was even larger, perhaps on the order of 15-20 times.[23] Large as the increase was in terms of the internal Iranian economy, it should also be seen in international perspective as on the low side for the region in this period: World trade as a whole grew 50 times from 1800 to 1914, including Egypt at 50-60 times, India (50 times), and Turkey (15-20 times). According to Issawi, "The available figures for Iraq and Syria also show a much higher rate of growth."[24] As imports outstripped exports after mid-century a trade deficit arose, reaching three million pounds sterling by 1913. This led to foreign loans, depreciation of the currency, and further business concessions. All of these indicated growing dependence of Iran on the West, most had negative consequences.

The composition of Iran's trade also changed dramatically in this period toward a classic "colonial" pattern by the early twentieth century. The trends in textiles tell much of the story. In 1857 27 percent of Iran's exports consisted of hand-made cotton, wool, and silk textiles but by the early twentieth century this had fallen to little more than one percent, replaced on the one hand by a "traditional" manufacture—carpets (12 percent in 1911-13)—and on the other by an increase of raw material exports of silk, wool, and especially cotton (26 percent or more in 1911-13). Iran's major exports moved decisively in the direction of raw materials such as rice, dried fruits and nuts, and opium (these were 4 percent in 1857, 32 percent in 1911-13). On the import side the preponderance of two kinds of products is striking: Machine-made textiles of all kinds represented 63 percent of imports in the 1850s and still over 30-40 percent a half century later, while tea and sugar rose from 11 percent to 30 percent of the total. The remaining imports in both eras were largely manufactures—metals, hardware, glassware. Iran's imports in the 1850s were 76 percent manufactures against 32 percent for her exports; in 1904 imports were over 60 percent manufactures but manufactured exports were down under 25 percent (with carpets alone accounting for 10 percent); in 1911-13 imports were more than 73 percent manufactures (counting refined sugar), while Iran's manufactured exports were something over 13 percent, with carpets at 12 percent.[25]

As might be expected, the composition of Iran's trade had a serious impact on its terms of trade and this too was negative. 'Abbas Chamseddine Kia has estimated that in the late nineteenth century Iran's volume of raw material exports was five times greater than the volume of its imported manufactures, yet the imports cost three times as much.[26] A depreciating currency made Iran's exports cheaper on the international market; this combined with a general drop in world prices for raw materials beginning in the 1870s and lasting a quarter of a century.[27] The price of wheat, for example, fell from $1.50 a bushel in 1871 to $0.23 in 1894; for opium, from almost 18 shillings a pound in 1867-69 to about 8 in 1901-03; for raw silk, from 1 pound sterling per kilogram before 1864 to 0.25 pounds sterling thirty years later. Iran had to export twice as much rice to the north to pay for the rice it imported from India in the south.[28] The export "boom" then was in *volume*, rather than *value*, a dubious advantage for the economy. On the import side, the prices for tea and sugar dropped by factors of three and two as well, while textiles fluctuated less, so some of Iran's losses were made good,[29] although on the whole it would seem that the terms of trade deteriorated more for exports than imports, to Iran's ultimate detriment.

The inescapable conclusion to be drawn out of the evidence is the ineluctable rise of foreign control and power vis-à-vis Iran. In the terms of world-system theory, Iran moved from the *external arena* of the sixteenth, seventeenth and eighteenth centuries—and from its own point of view it was part of a non-European *core* at the height of Safavid splendor in the seventeenth—to the *periphery* of the world capitalist system in the course of the nineteenth century. Late Qajar Iran clearly fits Wallerstein's definition of the periphery: "The periphery of a world-economy is that geographical sector of it wherein production is primarily of lower-ranking goods (that is, goods whose labor is less well rewarded) but which is an integral part of the overall system of the division of labor, because the commodities involved are essential for everyday use."[30] The increasing exchange of Iran's raw materials—opium, cotton, rice, wheat, tobacco, dried fruits, nuts, silk, and wool—for Europe's manufactures, and European control of the terms of trade, tariffs, shipping, and transport, are all powerful indicators of this new pattern of peripheralization and dependence.

But due to the intensity of Russian-British rivalry in Iran, Iran was a periphery of a particular kind. Unlike those countries and regions that were directly colonized (India, Egypt, much of Africa, southeast Asia, and elsewhere), or were formally independent but subject to a single strong outside power (most of Latin America, first to England and then to the United States), Iran was a battleground for two strong imperialisms—England, *the* core power, and Russia, a semiperipheral giant on its northern border. In this, Iran was comparable to Afghanistan and in a more complex way, due to the greater number of competitors, to China and the Ottoman Empire. As Bausani notes, "Iran thus had all the disadvantages of being a colony without any of the few advantages, such as the creation of industries either to the direct benefit of the colonizers or for their military purposes, improvements in the juridical system, and so forth."[31] The clearest examples of this are in the lack of infrastructural development, especially the agreements *not* to build railroads, and the "most favored nation" commercial status that had to be won by Russian armies, extended under the overbearing pressure of English force and eventually granted to most of the industrialized world, to the detriment of Iran's urban handicraft sector. On the positive side, of course, political independence was nominally maintained, but within very circumscribed limits whose contours have been suggested. The mixed and uneven blessings of dependent development will come more sharply into focus as we turn to internal economic developments in the Qajar period.

Internal Social and Economic Development

Given the state of the available estimates, the demographic picture of Qajar Iran is at first as bewildering as the sheer "guesstimates" looked at in chapter two for the seventeenth century. Estimates of total population for the early nineteenth century are far from in agreement, leaving us with anywhere from five million to ten million people (roughly the same range as for the seventeenth-century Safavid peak, it should be noted). The difficulties of estimating Iran's sizable tribal population account for much of the variation; it should also be borne in mind that when Georgia and other areas in the Caucasus were lost to Russia in 1813 and 1828, this took as many as one million people out of Iran's population. The available estimates of contemporaries and present-day economic historians allow us to conclude that Iran's population grew, but not at a uniform rate. There were spurts due to prosperity and peace and setbacks due to famines, epidemics, and loss of territories, adding up to a very mixed record of overall, but neither constant nor rapid, improvement. Gilbar suggests that annual births ran at 45-50 per thousand and deaths at 40-45 per thousand, for an annual net growth rate of 0.5 percent. Hambly, based on Cipolla's estimate for agrarian societies, feels that Iran's rate was "normal" at 0.5 to 1.0 percent per year. Hill, Katouzian, and Gilbar agree on a steady and sizable increase of two to three million people from roughly 1873 to 1910.[32] A heavy toll was periodically exacted by epidemics and famines. By late century, epidemics subsided somewhat as quarantine methods improved and medical clinics, often British, were opened. Famines likewise occurred at all too frequent intervals, as for example, in 1860-61, 1869-72, 1880, and in the 1890s and early 1900s. The cataclysm known as the "Great Famine" of 1869-72 caused anywhere from 500,000 to 1,500,000 deaths in a total population of not more than nine or ten million.[33] Though later famines were less severe, they continued to take a toll. One further demographic trend can be noted here. From the again somewhat bewildering variety of available estimates as to the proportion of the population engaged in each of the major economic activities, it may be concluded that the proportion of people living in cities more than doubled from about 10 to 25 percent between 1800 and 1914, while the proportion of nomadic pastoralists would seem to have fallen from *perhaps* as high as 50 percent in 1800 to 33 percent by 1850 and to 25 percent by 1914. The sedentary agricultural sector appears to have roughly held its own as a simple proportion of the population. The reasons for these shifts and the absolute numbers in each sector will be clarified in the sections that follow.

The Agricultural Sector

It is instructive to examine briefly the vicissitudes of the major crops as an index to the gradual rise of export agriculture and the advantages and disadvantages of the process known as "the commercialization of agriculture." The major subsistence crop, as it had been since before Safavid times, was wheat, along with other cereals. In the mid-nineteenth century, domestic production met all of Iran's needs and in 1858 wheat and barley were

Iran's second-largest agricultural export, at about 10 percent of total exports. An eight-fold increase in wheat exports from the Gulf between 1869 and 1894 was about matched by the seven-fold *decline* in its price over the same period. Over-exporting at low prices gradually undermined Iran's self-sufficiency in the production of this basic staple so that by the early 1900s imports of wheat flour surpassed exports of wheat.[34]

A series of other products exhibit variations on this boom and bust pattern. Raw silk was Iran's largest export item in 1850, accounting for 31 to 38 percent of the total. Output reached a peak in 1864 at over 1.4 million pounds sterling. The spread of a silkworm disease from Europe decimated the crop shortly thereafter, as did a 400 percent fall in prices on the world market, so that output in 1902 was worth only 256,000 pounds sterling.[35] About the same time that silk production was collapsing in the north, opium began a meteoric rise as a southern export. By the early 1880s it was Iran's leading export at over 25 percent of the total and a value of 600-800,000 pounds sterling. With little control over competing supplies in Bengal and Japan, or the markets in China, South Africa, and England, Iran's exports rose and fell erratically after 1900, a trend exacerbated by drought, over-cultivation, adulteration, and unfavorable tariffs. While McDaniel observes that "The peasant who grew opium did better all around than those who stuck to wheat," and Gilbar argues that all classes involved in its production—from agricultural laborers to sharecroppers, peasant proprietors, landlords, and merchants—could profit from it, it seems nevertheless clear that the bulk of the profits accrued to merchants, while subsistence farmers were increasingly drawn into a cash economy that exposed them to indebtedness at the hands of moneylenders, landlords, and tax collectors.[36] Added to this was the more general threat to the population of higher prices and famines as wheat acreage was reduced, as well as the addiction of growing numbers of Iranians in both city and countryside.[37] The same mixed blessings attended the rise of other cash crops like cotton, rice, and dried fruits, all exported in considerable quantities to Russia. Landlords, merchants, and Russian speculators profited at the peasants' expense, while subsistence crops shrank in extent for the local markets.[38]

Taking all these crops together, a rough estimate of the total agricultural GDP around 1860 may be 19-20 million pounds sterling.[39] Gilbar concludes that the whole period from 1865 to 1906 saw "fairly rapid growth in the agricultural sector. . . . there was a substantial increase in real terms in the *per caput* agricultural output."[40] The issue is not so clear-cut, given the two major shocks that were suffered with the collapse of silk in 1864 and the drought and great famine of 1869-72; the large population increase of 1870-1914 raises doubts about any real per capita gain overall as well. The 1870s to 1900 also witnessed a shift toward cash crops for export, such that, in Nowshirvani's view, by 1900-1910 "we can no longer characterize Iranian agriculture as subsistence farming. By then it was well integrated into the national economy and commercial relations were widespread."[41] He himself notes however that "Many features of subsistence farming persisted," and Issawi that cash agriculture was less extensive in Iran than elsewhere in the Middle East. But even more important than its extent was its pervasive negative side. Among the crops just examined, we saw the collapse of silk, upon which the economy was quite dependent in mid-century; its replacement by opium, which went into serious decline by 1905 (it would later boom again); that cotton benefited merchants, landlords, and the Russians more than peasants; and that rice exports grew at the expense of internal consumption. Wheat suffered a decline as cash crops became more popular and intruded on it, so that by 1914 it was in net deficit, casting doubts on whether subsistence farming kept up with population. The subsistence sector in general showed no substantial gains in productivity or technique, and irrigation systems, the most crucial infrastructure, deteriorated. The shift to cash crops played a role in compounding the hardship of drought years, in an economy where there had been minimal surplus food production to begin with. Seyf in fact discerns a pattern of "constant disequilibrium": Growing too many cash crops led to the threat of famine, causing cutbacks in export crops; then more subsistence crops led to price falls and a shift to export crops once again, and another possibility of famine. Thus the terrible famine of 1869-72 was followed by the shift to cash crops in the 1870s, another food shortage at Bushire in 1887, then more cash cropping and another reduction in cotton in the Gulf in 1893-94.[42] From this it emerges that both subsistence and cash crops had their limits and limited each other. Incorporation into world markets brought very mixed results for the economy as a whole and for the various classes comprising the agricultural sector.

Underlying the impetus to growing cash crops for export, the land tenure system itself was undergoing profound shifts. Though the basic types of landowner remained the same—the state, tiyul-holders, private individuals, vaqf administrators, and small-holding peasants—the proportion of land controlled by each changed. The early Qajars continued to grant revenue rights to their officials, favorites, and military leaders from the crown lands, Eastwick estimating the extent of these at one-third to one-half the total cultivated area of Iran in 1861. Though Lambton confirms that state and crown land was considerable at mid-century, "it was for the most part in a state of decay and made little contribution to the revenue."[43] Other forms of land tenure, including a certain amount of peasant small-holdings and a more extensive area held as religiously endowed vaqf land, also persisted throughout the Qajar period.

The most marked development, however, was the rise of land held by large-scale private individuals. Minorsky observes that "The *tiyul* often led to the transformation of its holder into a landed proprietor."[44] Pavlovitch, writing in 1910, suggested that sometime after 1850 and certainly by 1880, land ownership passed increasingly out of the hands of the crown and tiyul-holders into the hands of merchants, ulama, and officials.[45] The result of these somewhat obscure processes was the rise of a new, more stable class of landowners (*mulkdar*), whose holdings were not just private, but large.[46] Bureaucrats and urban notables, provincial governors and tribal chiefs all came to acquire such large-scale holdings, which normally started as theoretically revocable tiyuls. A second major constituent element of the new landed class was urban merchants investing in agricultural property, a trend which increased after the 1870s when the boom in export crops coincided with state sales of the crown lands. They also acquired estates by making loans to bureaucrats, governors, and other notables in need of cash who had put up their land as collateral. The largest among them, who owned many villages, lived in the cities as absentee landlords, appointing overseers. Landed power was enhanced by keeping a body of armed retainers, made possible by possession of land, and in turn increasing one's power, prestige, and sometimes holdings.[47]

In the course of the nineteenth century, then, land came to be regarded as an ever more prized source of wealth and prestige. This, it may be concluded, was due to the combination of rising land taxes and Iran's closer integration into world markets, which simultaneously increased the needs of the upper and upper-middle classes for sources of income and made land the best generator of this through cash crops for export. The new landlords—whether of merchant, bureaucratic or tribal background—came to wield considerable political-economic power, as Lambton observes: "Throughout the Qajar period the landowning classes (which included the tribal *khans*) were the most powerful element in the kingdom."[48] On the other hand, their diverse sectoral and ethnic origins undercut the unity which this potential class power might have engendered.

Sharecropping remained the usual method of apportioning the output between peasant and landowner. Gilbar puts the landlord's share at one-third to one-half of the crop in general; Pavlovitch estimated the basic rate at 20 percent in 1910, but this could rise as high as 85 percent if the landlord provided seed, draft animals, and tools.[49] On the more high-value export cash crops, rent came to be taken more commonly in cash as the century wore on. Paying in cash was not a radical departure in itself, since it could still involve simple calculation of the cash value of the stipulated share of the crop. But as commercialization of agriculture spread with export crops and had already existed in the case of market gardening near towns, there was a trend to pay a fixed sum as rent. Landlords liked this because they could pay their tenants a set amount and then sell the whole crop for a large profit, thus effectively increasing their share. This procedure also imbricated peasants more deeply in the vicissitudes of a cash economy, furthering their dependence on landlords and moneylenders. The depth of this incipient transition to capitalist market relations is hard to measure; it is clear that sharecropping continued to predominate on the whole even in late Qajar Iran. Although the rise in agricultural exports must have led to a somewhat more cash-oriented agrarian sector, we are still a long way from capitalist production relations on any wide scale.[50]

The situation of the peasantry was circumscribed by the mode of production, the shifting patterns of land tenure, and the rise of cash cropping for exports in the course of the nineteenth century. Though landlords did increase their power at villagers' expense, the labor process seems to have remained substantially under the control of peasant work teams or cooperatives, known as *bunehs*.[51] Some internal stratification within and between villages certainly existed. Villages varied widely in size, nearness to markets, fertility of soil, and other favorable production factors. Within villages too, despite the egalitarian nature of the buneh system, one might find well-to-do peasants with more than a subsistence-size plot, sharecroppers with less than enough land to live on, and laborers with either fixed work or seasonal employment on a daily basis, as well as the majority of peasants who had buneh rights and subsistence-size holdings. In addition to landlords, small-holding peasants might hire landless laborers, whose existence in various places and at different times in Qajar Iran is well-documented.[52]

The situation of women in general was difficult. Pavlovitch reported in 1910 that landlords had or took the right of temporarily marrying their peasants' daughters, a practice sanctioned by Shi'i law, if entered into freely.[53] Despite this evil, whose prevalence is hard to know, village women certainly lived less gender-restricted lives than their veiled counterparts in urban settings; Fraser said "the wives and daughters of the peasantry pursue their occupations like those of the same class of Europe."[54] As craft activities such as making clothing were somewhat undermined in villages over the course of the century, Gilbar argues that women abandoned domestic industries to some extent and "joined the men in their field work."[55] Craft production in general, which involved men as well as women, must have persisted to a considerable degree nevertheless. This was true not only of handmade textiles and shoes, but especially of carpets, originally for home use and local markets, which burgeoned into a major handicraft industry in the late nineteenth century, much of whose production took place in village settings.[56]

A major debate has raged in the literature over whether Iran's peasantry experienced a decline or improvement in their living standards in the course of the nineteenth century. Nowshirvani and especially Gilbar have argued that as agriculture was commercialized and trade expanded, the peasants registered improved consumption patterns, while Keddie and Seyf, backed up by Lambton, Issawi, and Olson, have argued that on the contrary, a deterioration occurred. Let us begin to sift through this debate by reviewing a representative sample of eyewitness accounts taken in chronological order.[57] John Malcolm, assessing the standard of living in the first decade of the nineteenth century, commented that "among the other classes [including the peasantry], though few are rich, hardly any are in actual want."[58] Fraser, writing in the 1820s, gives a rather mixed set of judgments reminiscent of those offered by Chardin 150 years earlier:

> The cultivators of the soil . . . are those on whom the tyranny of their rulers falls the most heavily. Yet their houses are comfortable and neat, and are seldom found without a supply of good wheaten cakes, some mas or sour milk, and cheese—often fruit makes its appearance, and sometimes a preparation of meat, in soup or in pillau. Their wives and children, as well as themselves, are sufficiently though coarsely clad; and if a guest arrives, there are few who cannot display a numed or felt carpet in a room for his reception. In fact, the high rate of wages proves that the profits of agriculture are high, while food is cheap; and we may be satisfied, that in spite of rapacity, enforced by torture [!], no small share of the gain is hoarded by the farmer.[59]

At least in all that touches on living standards this is quite favorable. According to Eastwick, the peasants of Mazandaran in 1861 were badly clothed, housed, and fed: "the bare walls of the mud huts and scanty clothing and thin faces of the inhabitants, confirmed their distress."[60] As to diet, George Jenner of the British Legation reported in 1870 that in periods of *no scarcity*: "the winter diet . . . consists almost entirely of bread, rice, and bad cheese, with a small quantity of tea . . . the summer diet of bread and 'sayfi', or summer produce, *i.e.*, melons, cucumbers, vegetable marrows, eggplants, and various forms of edible gourds."[61] There is no mention here of meat, eggs, or milk. In 1878 the British consul at Rasht found the local peasantry earning "no less than" five to nine pounds sterling a year (compared to two pounds in India); they ate rice, and "meat is cheap."[62] Two accounts from the 1890s present similarly conflicting data. The British consul Lascelles, travelling in the south in 1892-93 found the situation in Fars "quite indescribable": "the people say that never in their recollection have they been so badly treated, so utterly thrust down by oppression,"[63] while Thomas Gordon wrote in 1896 that "In the course of my journeying in Persia, I generally found excellent quarters in the village houses. The rather mean outer appearance of the dwellings conveys the idea of poor accommodation within, but the reality is a pleasing disclosure of plain but well-carpeted rooms."[64] The record, then, is highly variegated, with favorable reports from the early nineteenth century and again at the turn of the twentieth, framing a skein of more depressed descriptions. In part these observations reflect the differences in regions visited and the specific conjunctures (of famine or drought, for example). In part too they reflect the different strata and situations that existed within the peasantry in this period of change. Gilbar observes that the better-off peasants tended to be those who owned their own land or worked on the estates of landlords who lived there and took an interest in their development, but both of these groups were in a distinct minority.[65] His broader, more radical argument is that while there had been only marginal change in the peasantry's difficult circumstances from 1800 to 1850, later "a certain improvement in the standard of living of the peasants took place." Evidence of this is held to be increased peasant consumption of "Sugar, tea, tobacco and opium," and local and foreign industrial goods, especially textiles.[66] Nowshirvani makes a similar argument about consumption "beyond the bare minimum of food and clothing," again based on the same items, and evidently finding participation in a cash economy indicative of improved material standards.[67] Keddie quite correctly finds consumption of "goods" such as sugar and tea, tobacco and opium dubious proof of improved standards of nutrition.[68] Moreover, the commercialization of agriculture meant less production of basic foodstuffs, higher rents and prices, and increasing indebtedness. Having meager savings and cash on hand was of little help in a drought or famine, especially when transport was as poor as in Qajar Iran. The large numbers of peasants who joined the urban lower classes in migrating to Russia to search for work is further indication of a crisis of underemployment in the rural sector; peasants also migrated to other agricultural areas, cities, and the southern oil fields. Though the travellers accounts are somewhat more mixed than Keddie suggests, I agree with her main contention that conditions worsened rather than improved in the course of the nineteenth century.[69] As Issawi concludes, "even in normal times, the mass of Iranians lived at a very low level."[70] The subsistence-level existence of Iran's peasantry, difficult as it had been in the first half of the nineteenth century, would seem on balance to have worsened after 1850 until the end of this period in 1914 or 1925, due in large measure to the commercialization of agriculture in the broader context of Iran's increasingly dependent and peripheral position in the world system.

The Urban Sector

The urban population is said to have grown from 10-14 percent of the total population of Iran in 1800 to 20-25 percent by 1914. In numbers of people this would be an increase from perhaps 500-800,000 in 1800 to about 2-2,500,000 in 1914. Growth seems to have been slow through 1868, but fairly rapid thereafter. It was uneven by city and region, again responding to the rhythms of a changing economy.

Merchants constituted the most powerful urban class in the Qajar period. In addition to selling domestic agricultural, handicraft, and tribal products throughout Iran and engaging in the foreign import and export trade, they were also the bankers and creditors of the country, part of the new landed class, and active in the first attempts to establish industry. Two trends governed the situation of Iran's largest merchants from 1800 to 1914: a growth in the wealth of some and diversification into new activities. A great concentration of wealth, due mostly to increases in foreign imports and export crops, has been noted from the 1870s onward. Atrpet comments: "Until 1880 there were few millionaires and rich property owners but in 1900 one could count them in hundreds."[71] Another source of wealth and risk crystalized in the 1880s and 1890s with the formation of a cluster of large banking and trading companies uniting several large merchants in a single enterprise. Some of these great companies, such as the Fars Trading Company, were successful for "many years"; a number of others failed to survive major problems of capital shortages and in some cases, embezzlement of funds.[72] A much more numerous group than the handful of large merchants was Iran's small and medium-sized traders and moneylenders. They paid more in taxes and road tolls owing to their inability to make "special arrangements" with the authorities. While many of them constituted the mainstay of the bazaar, at the bottom end of the scale they shaded off into the petty venders, peddlers, and hawkers who were part of the marginal and urban lower classes.[73]

Despite their solid position in urban society as a whole, considerable tension developed in merchants' relations with the state and foreign capital in Iran. Economically as wealthy as the landowning and tribal elements who governed society, politically they found themselves on the same subordinate level as the rest of urban society.[74] While a few of the largest could compete directly in foreign markets and turn substantial profits, others were reduced to the status of middlemen and employees of foreign firms. In some accounts, Iranian merchants were referred to as *padu-yi dukkan* ("errand boy"). By the turn of the century, foreign firms had control of all the key export sectors, except for opium and dried fruits and nuts. The flooding of Iran's markets by foreign imports and the failure of attempts to establish modern factories hurt others.[75] Contact with the West, then, benefitted mainly a minority of large merchants with foreign ties and deepened the distance between them and smaller merchants, creating substantial grievances with the Qajar state and foreign powers in Iran.

Urban productive activity continued to be the province of Iran's numerous artisan class. The principal trend in the handicraft sector is the decline of Iran's manufactures in the course of the nineteenth century. Issawi cautions against exaggerating the extent of decline, arguing that it started later and went less far than elsewhere in the Middle East.[76] Nevertheless, if we analyze specific products and cities both the centrality of textiles and their decline undeniably emerge. While some cities found new economic bases such as the production of carpets and shawls (now increasingly outside the guild structure), most saw their handmade textile sector suffer erosion verging on decimation. As British piece goods took over the southern textile market by 1860-70, Shiraz's weaving establishments fell in number from 500 in 1800 to ten (producing coarse fabrics) by 1857.[77] Cities like Kashan, which had depended primarily on silk and cotton weaving for generations, were thoroughly depressed: "Flandin, who visited Kashan in 1840, reports that the import of British materials had destroyed the large factories of Kashan."[78] Isfahan suffered a particularly precipitous drop in its handicraft production. In the silk weavers guild, the number of workshops declined steadily from 1,250 in the 1820s, to 486 in the 1840s, 240 in the early 1850s, and 12 in the late 1870s. Curzon in the 1890s said that Isfahan had become a consumer of "manufactured cotton goods, almost wholly from Manchester and Glasgow."[79] The collapse of hand-crafted textiles in turn affected the many widows who lived by spinning thread and other guilds, notably dyers, carders, and workers in the bleaching houses sectors which "have mostly disappeared." As the economic base contracted, the demand for hat-making, boot-making, and engraving went slack and artisans and merchants left the city. The chronicler Mirza Husayn found in 1877 that "most of the turners of Isfahan are now working in Tehran" and half the city's moneylenders now lived in Tehran, Tabriz, and other cities.[80] While a number of indispensable activities held their own, for a majority of Iran's urban artisans and especially the large numbers who had engaged in textiles in the first half of the century, the impact either reduced their markets and incomes or pushed them out of work altogether, making them candidates for new craft and factory industries, migration to Russia, or descent into the urban marginal classes.

One response to the decline of artisanal production was an incipient transition to larger-scale factory-type worksites that yet remained in many ways artisanal in their labor process. Units of 10-50 workers were established after 1900 in leather-working, opium-, henna-, and tobacco-processing, dyeing, brick-making, soap-making, pottery, and other occupations.[81] Towering above these activities was the carpet industry, which affords the best example of changes in the organization of production under the Western impact. Until the nineteenth century carpet-making had generally been a tribal or village craft for domestic use (and as a form of personal savings against hard times), or a male, urban craft destined for consumption by the Iranian elite. As European and American firms took much of the market in hand by 1900, putting-out systems on a contract basis were extended from the countryside to urban sites, absorbing some of the unemployed silk and cotton weavers. After 1900, large workshops began to bring workers under the same roof; one in Tabriz employed as many as 1,500 people. Carpet exports rose swiftly as a result of these changes in production and demand from 75,000 pounds sterling in the early 1870s to one million in 1914. By then carpets composed one-eighth of Iran's total trade and its single largest export item (soon to be surpassed by oil).[82] The number of workers involved in carpet making was estimated in 1910 at 65,000, far more than in any other craft or industrial type of production. Working conditions seem to have ranged from bad to atrocious, characterized by long hours, low pay, and unhealthful workplaces.[83]

Industrial production with mechanized equipment also emerged in Iran in this period. After isolated earlier attempts, both the government and private individuals constructed small factories for paper, glass, gunpowder, sugar-refining, and cotton-spinning in the 1850s and 1860s. All but the munitions factories soon proved unprofitable.[84] At a meeting between the shah and a group of merchants in 1893, Amin al-Zarb pointed out the lack of industry in Iran and the country's dependence on the West's manufactures: "what do we have for manufacturies and industries that we can say: we don't want the European commodities?"[85] In the next two decades a second wave of mostly privately-owned Iranian and foreign factories would be set up and struggle to survive.[86] In the Iranian sector, some twenty factories employing 524 workers could be found, in textiles, paper, glass, soap, bricks, cartridges, public utilities, and brewing. Though Amin al-Zarb's silk-cord factory proved fairly profitable and the electric power plants were maintained in operation, most of these ventures failed, in some cases due to direct competition from cheap foreign imports. Other obstacles were posed by the expense and formidable difficulties of transporting equipment and finished products, the cost of fuel and scarcity of energy resources, a lack of skilled personnel, the small size of the internal market, and the failure of the state to protect local industry against often fierce foreign competition. A 1909 list of clients of the Russian Bank showed 1,060 Iranians engaged in trade or finance versus only nine in industry.[87]

More striking successes in modern-type factories were registered by foreigners. The largest "industrial" concerns in Iran by far were the British oil industry with 7-8,000 workers and the Russian Caspian fisheries, with 4-5,000. In addition, foreigners established some forty-one modern factories and large workshops, employing 1,132 workers.[88] Russian cotton-ginning plants were more numerous and better equipped with oil-run motors than their Iranian counterparts. Russians also monopolized oil-refining (with Baku crude) and dominated northern forestry and road-building. Germans were active too, with a brickworks, steam mill, sawmill, cartridge factory, carpet factory, and construction facility. As in foreign trade, by 1914, Euro-

TABLE 4.3 The Iranian Working Class, circa 1914

Sector	Number of Workers
Modern Industry	
Oil Industry (APOC)	6,000
Fisheries (Russian)	3,000
Factories	1,650
Mining	200
Total	10,850
Service Sector	
Servants	5,000
Porters and Dockers	4,000
Railroad/Road Construction	3,300
Printers	300
Electrical Workers	100
Total	12,700
Traditional Industry/Crafts	
Carpet-weaving	65,000
Weaving	20,000
Metal-working Crafts	20,000
Leather Production and Crafts	3,900
Other Handicrafts	10-15,000
Total	118,900-123,900
Grand Total	142,450-147,450

Sources: Floor, *Industrialization in Iran*, 5 table 3, 29 table 10; Issawi, *EHI*, 261; Ashraf, *Mavane'-i Tarikhi*, 98 table 2, 99 table 3; Floor, *Labour Unions*, 43 table 3.

peans were in a fairly commanding position in the modern industrial sector, small as it was in comparison with the rest of the economy.

Table 4.3 helps us survey the composition of the Iranian working class in the broad sense—including its now-changing "traditional" sectors such as carpet weavers and artisans as well as the modern factory, industrial, and construction settings—in the period up to about 1914. The preponderance of traditional industry is underlined by this table—some 120,000 out of 145,000 workers, roughly 83 percent of the total, fall into this category. Carpet weaving alone accounts for almost one-half of the total and only a fraction of Iran's 65,000 carpet weavers labored in factory settings or can be considered urban working class. Only about eight percent of the total worked in "modern" industry—some 10,850 workers, of whom the vast majority were in the British-owned oil sector or the Russian-owned Caspian fisheries. Only 1,650 workers are found in factories, almost all of them in small to medium units of five to thirty workers, with two-thirds (1,132 workers) in foreign-owned factories, as opposed to one-third (524) in Iranian-owned establishments. The "service sector" accounts for 12,000 people (about nine percent of the total), but of these 5,000 were servants. Sizable contingents also worked as porters and dockers, and in road construction, both mostly in the north. Another 300 Iranians did mostly skilled work in printing. The table shows above all the very modest size of the modern, industrial working class at this time and the domination of foreign capital within this sector.

The origins of this early working class lie in various places. The hard-hit artisanal sector provided some—perhaps most—of Iran's first skilled industrial workers. Unskilled workers, who constituted a majority of all workers, came from two sources—the urban poor and unemployed (including unemployed artisans), and peasants who migrated in search of work, not only as seasonal agricultural labor, but also in construction and on road projects.[89] A final vector in the formation of the Iranian working class leads to Russia and back. Hakimian, who has done the most detailed study, estimates that 100,000 Iranians lived in Russia in 1900 and by 1913 between 450,000 and 500,000 were permanent residents. Another 100-200,000 temporary workers came each year.[90] Most of those who went seem to have been peasants in Iran, but evidence exists of unemployed craftspeople, merchants, and unskilled laborers migrating as well. Most of the migrants were Azari Turkish speakers from Azarbaijan. While some did agricultural work, others labored in Baku and elsewhere as masons, porters, construction workers, oil workers, and miners. Despite the hard work and low wages, many remitted or brought considerable sums back home to their families in Iran.

In Iran itself, working conditions were not good. Floor's study of labor conditions in this period concludes overall that "it is a bleak picture of the lot of the worker with regard to hours, health conditions, wages, and social conditions." A ten to twelve hour work day was usual, with up to sixteen hours possible. In terms of occupational safety and health, "Normal working conditions in Iranian industry were very bad. This was true for children as well as adults."[91] Workers might be paid a fixed wage or on a piece rate basis. Textile workers earned 1 1/2 - 3 krans (15-30 cents) a day for men, 1/2 - 1 kran for women, and 1/2 kran for children. In the foreign-owned sector wages were higher, but wage differentials existed between Iranian and Russian fishery workers with the former making two krans a day, the latter five; a four-tiered wage system prevailed in the British oil industry—unskilled and skilled Iranians, Indians and English.[92] These conditions formed the backdrop for numerous attempts to organize unions and conduct strikes when political circumstances proved favorable, such as from 1906 to 1909 during the Constitutional revolution and in the unsettled climate prevailing after WWI. Given foreign control of much of Iran's industrial sector, it can be said that Iran's working class, however small in this period, was formed before its capitalist class, or at least, that it had developed to a far greater degree than the internal capitalist class by 1914. Much of it, however, remained tied to the larger agricultural sector—the early oil workers, the seasonal agro-industrial workers, and the migrants who constantly journeyed back from Russia. This kept many of its members in two modes of production, at least mentally, and while it may have radicalized the villages somewhat, in converse fashion it also may have conservatized the working class, or some portion of it.

There were also groups who lived closer to—or below—the margin of subsistence in urban society. Their existence is attested to by Abdullaev: "Travellers' accounts abound in material showing that the streets and bazaars of Iranian towns, especially the large commercial centers, were overcrowded with poor and unemployed persons, ready to sell their labor for a piece of bread."[93] Specific subgroups of the urban poor included petty vendors, peddlers, and haulers. Certain day laborers, including poorly-paid and infrequently employed ditch diggers, water sellers, porters, and others may be included. There were also large numbers of unemployed people—artisans out of work, older laborers, the injured, ill, and others who had given up hope of finding work. The *lutis* were a group which drew on several urban classes including the poor and marginal, whose activities ranged from charitable to venal forms of extortion and neighborhood "protection."[94] Amanat has suggested that the "poorer classes" and the "average woman in Tabriz or even in Isfahan" could purchase European-made clothing more cheaply than Iranian-made products. One recalls also Malcolm's remark from the early 1800s: "among the other classes, though few are rich, hardly any are in actual want."[95] But these observations are undoubtedly more applicable to the working class, artisans, and other strata above the truly marginal population described here, and the situation probably deteriorated even among the former groups in the course of the nineteenth century. The British consul in Tabriz reported in 1897: "[The lower classes'] wants are few, a little 'sangak,' a native bread, and a bit of cheese will satisfy them, but their power to procure these must be decreasing day by day."[96] Olson too believes that the peasantry and urban poor suffered a deterioration in their situations in the 1870s and early 1880s.[97]

Two further important groups in urban society were the ulama and the emerging intelligentsia. The ulama lived, as in the past, by collecting religious taxes and by serving as religious leaders, judges, educators, and notaries of commercial contracts in the bazaar, where they were sometimes guild leaders as well. Vaqf land had shrunk in extent since 1722, but it still existed and supported certain ulama, while others became landowners. Some received stipends from the state. The most learned and respected attained the title of mujtahid and were more independent of the state. Below this religious elite were far vaster numbers of less wealthy or prestigious mullas. The gap in wealth was matched by a gap in status between the widespread authority of the mujtahids and the (sometimes) lack of reverence for the ordinary mulla and sayyid. Bayat argues that the ulama were not a cohesive, unified class, but rather were riven by internal factions, conflicts of interest and divergent religious outlooks.[98] One factor which may have united them was the growing perception of a real decline in their well-being in the course of the nineteenth century. The wealthy and middle ulama lost control of vaqfs and saw their fees from involvement in bazaar affairs contract, and the poor were affected by rising prices and erosion of the urban economic base which supported them. The Qajar state and foreign powers came to be held responsible for most of these ills.

Alongside the ulama, a new urban middle class came into existence in the Qajar era. Like the ulama, the intelligentsia came to be important political actors by virtue of their shaping of ideologies in Iran. Their base was in the at most five percent of the population that was literate, but the sources of their education were quite other than those of the ulama. Few in number, they included those Iranians who had been educated in the West or the new technical college in Iran, the Dar al-Fonun, which was soon admitting 250 students a year. Their occupations included working for the state as teachers, bureaucrats, military officers, or journalists, and in the private sector, primarily in journalism and publishing. In some cases, the line between the ulama and intelligentsia blurred, as many in both groups shared educational profiles and many of the intelligentsia continued to wear religious dress.

Finally, the situations of Iran's minorities and women cut across the class categories adopted above. All of these groups were to some extent, legally or practically, second-class citizens. Iran's Christian minorities included Nestorians and Armenians who were taxed relatively lightly. Many urban Christians managed to get good educations, sometimes in foreign-run missionary schools. Armenians maintained their presence in trade and were often employed in foreign enterprises, but many members of the community lived working-class lives and some joined the migrations to Russia in search of work.[99] Iran's Jewish population was more heavily taxed and persecuted, according to contemporary reports. Curzon judged in 1890 that "As a community, the Persian Jews are sunk in great poverty and ignorance. ... The majority of Jews in Persia are engaged in trade, in jewellery, in wine and opium manufacture, as musicians, dancers, scavengers, peddlars, and in other professions to which is attached no great respect. They rarely attain to a leading mercantile position."[100] But the community also produced small traders and wealthy merchants and in some places attained high degrees of literacy. Like the Jews of Iran, "the Zoroastrians suffered from both great poverty and severe discrimination. ... Most of them seem to have earned a living in silk cultivation and weaving."[101]

Upper-class urban women were in general the most restricted and heavily veiled in Iranian society, kept in their quarters at home. Women—or their female servants—spent much time and effort in the provision and preparation of food and other household labor. Working class women were less restricted and according to Fraser, "in the families of mechanics and villagers, the mysteries of the veil almost disappear,"[102] but of course their material well-being was less than that of their European counterparts or Iranian upper-class sisters. Urban women sometimes received an education, had their own religious services (and female mullas), and on occasion led urban bread riots. Yet in terms of the institutions of polygamy, temporary marriage, and the divorce laws, they were second-class people. Sheean argues they were oppressed as a whole, even by Islamic standards, writing in 1926: "The position of women is lower than in almost any other Mohammedan country; there is a tremendous gulf between the women of Cairo and Constantinople and the women of Teheran, even those of the very highest position."[103]

A key question that arises is how did the secular trends in the Iranian economy affect the living standards of the urban population? Data on the relative movement of prices and wages, while scanty, suggests increasing hardship by the turn of the century. Food prices rose 5.5 times in Tehran between 1880 and 1900 (though they then declined through 1908), a trend replicated in Tabriz and Rasht. Cities less central to the international trade saw slower price rises, or none at all.[104] The overissue and consequent devaluation of the copper currency caused the main money used by artisans, workers, and the urban poor to become worth less and less; Rabino wrote in 1891, "As this currency constitutes the whole fortune of the poor, the sufferings caused by the maladministration of the mint may be imagined."[105] Available evidence shows wage rises of 50-100 percent from the 1890s to 1910, but this was less than inflation. Other evidence from Mashhad suggests that unskilled laborers' and carpenters' wages lagged behind inflation; more skilled masons and blacksmiths roughly kept up. Seyf has made an ingenious argument to the effect that urban unemployment and the loss of the handicraft sector depressed wages, while the shift to cash crops raised prices for food. The result would be an increasing gap in the urban population's ability to pay for food. Issawi, too, although admitting that "To draw a general conclusion is almost impossible," feels that craftspeople saw some deterioration in their standard of living, while for the unskilled, wages rose less prices.[106] A final, telling statistic is that average life expectancy in Iran as a whole in 1900 was less than thirty years. We may tentatively conclude, then, that the urban population in general and artisans, workers, and the urban poor in increasing order, suffered significant material decline in their standards of living at the end of the nineteenth century, in the period leading up to the Constitutional revolution.

The Tribal Sector

Demographic data on Iran's tribespeople in the Qajar period is incomplete and difficult to present with confidence. Population seems to have increased to about 1870 (the time of the Great Famine), followed by a sudden decline in the famine years and a gradual, perhaps accelerating recovery through 1914. Gilbar points to tribes such as the Guklan Turkomans who migrated to Russian Central Asia in the 1880s and 1890s due to closer border controls, and to a tendency to sedentarization among other tribes.[107] The issue of the proportion of the population that was "tribal" is just as vexed. While there is wide agreement on the figure of 25 percent for 1900-1914, the starting point—1800—has widely varying estimates of 25 to 50 percent and Gilbar's 33 percent for mid-century presents us with a dilemma. A downward progression seems most plausible because the eighteenth-century dislocation of the economy probably increased the proportion of people living from pastoralism and in the course of the nineteenth, with its Great Famine and the start of a trend toward greater sedentarization the primarily nomadic segment of the population probably decreased. The starting point may well have been below 50 percent however. The logic of a sedentarization process among certain tribes derives from the restoration of central authority early in the century, followed much later by the impact of the famine combined with the new incentives to produce cash crops. Recall too that combinations of agriculture and pastoralism had long been a viable (indeed common) intermediate way of life.[108]

The primary labor process for most of Iran's tribespeople continued to be pastoral production, however. Extensive areas—Lambton sees no decline in their size during the nineteenth century—remained tribal grazing lands, "notably Fars, the Bakhtiari, Khuzistan, the frontier areas of

Khurasan, and parts of Azarbayjan and Baluchistan."[109] Tribal output continued to consist of a variety of pastoral products: meat, milk, and ghee (clarified butter), sheep and camel wool, skins and hides, carpets, and live animals themselves. Animal husbandry was very heavily hit by the 1869-72 famine, especially in the south. An 1871 British estimate was that two-thirds of southern pack animals had died. In the 1880s and 1890s the situation improved. Tribespeople had contacts with local, regional and foreign merchants and markets. Wool was in great demand for the carpet industry. It was purchased directly from nomads for cash, according to an 1891 report from Mashhad, and exports increased fifteen times between 1889 and 1906/7.[110] Skins and hides were also exported in increasing numbers in the course of the century, while tribal carpets were collected by urban merchants for sale and export, but the bulk of the profits certainly accrued to the urban sector and tribal chiefs, rather then tribal craftspeople. So pastoralists too were drawn into contact with the world and national markets; though this probably had a less decisive impact on their way of life than it did on peasants and artisans, it didn't benefit them greatly either.

Economic relations with the state impinged in the form of taxes and military service. Various reports on the tax on flocks suggest surprisingly that it was paid in cash at a fixed rate per animal, such as three krans per camel, one per sheep or goat, with other rates for asses, horses, and cows. Though this reflects increasing tribal participation in a cash economy, undoubtedly there continued to be considerable payment in kind as well as, or in lieu of, such taxes. Tribal leaders collected these taxes and the khans would take fairly stiff amounts from their followers, to keep for themselves what was not forwarded to the state. Military skills remained a tribal monopoly in the Qajar period: "The tribemen's mastery over the horse and their marksmanship, the relatively good tribal organization, and the spirit of tribal solidarity could make a tribal confederacy, under a dynamic leadership, a formidable military unit."[111] Various tribes served in the Qajar armies of the early nineteenth century and from the 1880s on, the Cossack Brigade was composed of Shahsavan, Kurds, and others. But the army career in general stagnated and far more tribesmen remained outside it, in a more adversarial relationship with the government, putting their skills to use in raiding caravans and settlements and resisting local authorities, with the purchase of arms proving a major point of contact with the market economy. On balance the tribes were circumscribed at the level of state power, but fairly autonomous in their own areas. No longer capable of seizing central control, as had the Safavids' qizilbash followers, as well as the Afghans, Afshars, Zands, and Qajars from 1500 to 1800, their sights had to be set lower, and in terms of remaining unmolested locally they did have considerable success through the 1920s. The Qajar state employed several mechanisms to divide and rule them, and its task was made easier by the "constitutional inability" of tribal leaders to combine.[112] One effective method was to incorporate tribal chiefs into the ruling class. Certain chiefs became extensive landholders, had mercantile connections, and served as provincial governors. This naturally encouraged identification with the state and dominant classes, and furthered internal stratification within tribes as patronage and favoritism extended downward. The Qajar tribe itself declined even as it furnished part of Iran's elite. Tribes such as the Qashqa'i, Bakhtiari, and the newly-formed Khamseh were reined in by royal appointment of their head as an *ilkhan* (tribal leader). The first ilkhan of the Bakhtiari—Husayn Quli Khan Ilkhani—possessed large landholdings and held government offices, which gave him the means to assert his power over the whole tribe but also bound him to the state. As he wrote to Nasir al-Din Shah in 1878: "It is now thirty years that I have served and labored dutifully night and day, and I have transformed the unruly Bakhtiyari into the likes of the peasants of Linjan."[113] Tribes who did not develop or accept the institution of ilkhan or its equivalent—Kurds, Arabs, and above all Turkomans—were less effectively ruled by the Qajars, with the Turkomans in particular moving quite freely in their area.[114] Tribes also entered into political relationships with foreigners—Russians, British, and Germans—as well as the Qajar state. British payments of gifts and arms to tribes who would support their aims, especially the Bakhtiari who were paid road taxes to let British goods pass through their territory, are typical of such relationships.[115]

Women continued to be far more active economically in the tribal sector than elsewhere in Iranian society. Afshari discerns "intensive use of woman power in the process of production, both in tending the animals and in sideline production."[116] Such sidelines included handicraft production, particularly of carpets, a valuable commodity. Tribal women went unveiled more often than their urban and village sisters. They were thus in most respects more equal to men in status and activity. Lambton writes of their "far higher degree of liberty than the townswomen"; Keddie of their relative freedom.[117]

The well-being of tribespeople, particularly the pastoralists, as a whole can be generally considered to have been greater and more secure than for the Iranian peasantry, although the degree to which this was true varied from place to place and over time. Many tribespeople were very poor, as in Kurdistan, where Lambton deciphers a vicious cycle of "poverty, disorder, frequent rebellions, and insecurity."[118] The Great Famine period certainly exacted a heavy toll on the pastoral groups too. Taken all in all, however, the material circumstances of those who survived, already better than the peasants', were most likely better maintained and less eroded, if not actually improving within the limits of the demographic decline, during the Qajar period. This may be ascribed to their lesser contact with the state and the international economy, reinforcing the dependency thesis in a contrastive sense. As tribal khans enhanced their position materially, this may have created stresses for the ordinary tribesperson who continued to live in the same way as before, fairly close to the margin of subsistence. But formation of class consciousness, either within tribes (directed against grasping khans), or across tribes (overcoming their feuds and mutual suspicions to unite against the central government), was precluded by the isolated, familial nature of the labor process and the deep roots of tribal custom, which instilled respect for the elders and chief and defiance of the outsider.

Conclusions: The Changing Qajar Social Formation

Between 1630 and 1800, virtually no changes had taken place in either the fundamental modes of production, or their constituent classes, within the Iranian social formation. Diagram 4.1 depicts this with the same figure utilized in chapter two. The *size* of the economy had contracted considerably in the eighteenth century and the proportion of the population involved in each of the three modes of production had shifted

DIAGRAM 4.1 The Iranian Social Formation circa 1800

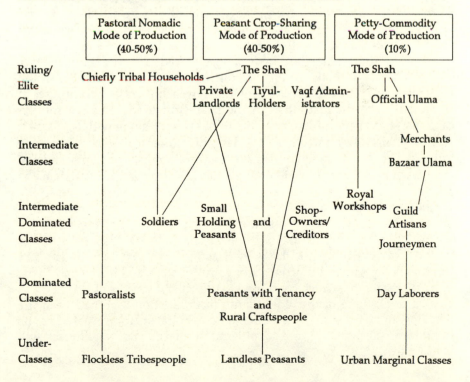

TABLE 4.4 Percentage of Population in Each Mode of Production, 1630-1914

Year	Pastoral	Peasant Crop-Sharing	Petty-Commodity	Capitalist
1630	33-40	45-55	10-15	0
1800	30-50	40-50	10	0
1914	25	50-55	17-22	3-4

somewhat—compare 1630 to 1800 in Table 4.4. By 1914, both quantitative and qualitative changes had occurred in the Iranian social formation. Quantitatively, the proportion of pastoralists had dropped quite significantly, the urban sector (petty-commodity plus capitalist modes of production) had almost doubled its share of the population, and the peasantry had become an even clearer majority (since the pastoral mode declined in size). Qualitatively, a small capitalist sector had emerged, with a more prominent native working class than capitalist class, due to the presence of rival foreign capitalists and the additional Iranian workers in Russia. Diagram 4.2 suggests the contours of Iran's new class structure circa 1914. Other changes since 1800 included the growing hegemony of private landlords in the peasant crop-sharing mode of production at the expense of the state and small peasants, and the decline of the royal workshops in the urban sector (now in parentheses to indicate a decline), replaced in part by the shah/state as a small-scale capitalist running munitions factories and the like in the capitalist mode. The tribal sector provided fewer soldiers (in parentheses to suggest this) to the state than in the past. British and Russian foreign capitalists have been added to the dominant classes, along with Iran's own small capitalist class, and a working class, still quite small in size, has come into existence as a dominated class alongside pastoralists, peasants, and day laborers in the bazaar. A small intelligentsia has also come into existence as an intermediate dominated class, apposite to the bazaar ulama, but in the capitalist mode of production. Taken all in all, the nineteenth century had witnessed a major transition from the period 1500 to 1800, changing the shape of Iran's class structure and altering somewhat the balance of forces within it. Artisans in particular were hard hit by the Western impact and merchants experienced a mixed set of gains for some and losses for others. The Qajar state too, which continued to tap several sources of surplus, was weaker in all three of the older modes of production than had been the Safavids, and hardly active at all in the new capitalist mode. Analysis of its organizational structure and ideological strengths and weaknesses will confirm this.

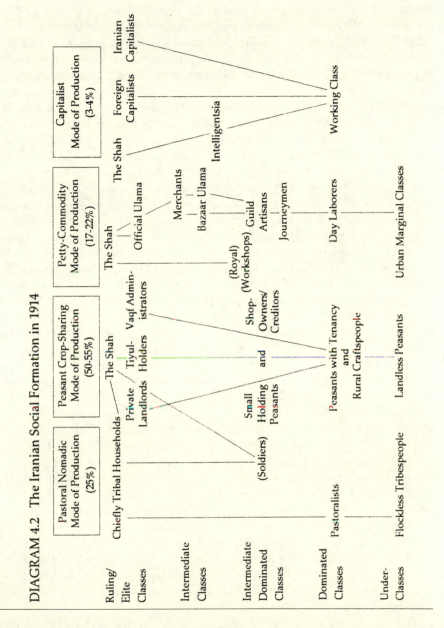

DIAGRAM 4.2 The Iranian Social Formation in 1914

The State

The shah's powers remained, as in the past, far-reaching and wide-ranging in principle: He declared war and peace, made treaties, granted tiyuls and offices, determined and collected taxes, was the seat of last recourse in the legal system, and had the power of life and death over all subjects, as well as the final claim on virtually anyone's property. This led to an imperious and absolute style of government, which was to some degree transmitted downward to all levels of the state. The bureaucracy of circa 1800 was quite rudimentary and small, but in the course of the nineteenth century, the administration both grew and modernized itself, until by the 1890s there were ten ministries. Examples of modernized areas of the state include the postal service, the official newspaper, telegraphs, and education. On the traditional side of the state, both Fath 'Ali Shah (r. 1797-1834) and Nasir al-Din Shah (r. 1848-96) maintained huge harems (the latter had 200 "wives," each with her own servants, carriage, and establishment). The shah's wives had considerable influence at court and his daughters would extend this by marrying leading governors, bureaucrats, religious, and other dignitaries. At the top of the bureaucracy, offices tended to become the private property of their holders and to concentrate in the hands of a few families constantly engaged in rivalries. Early governors were drawn from among the leading families and tribes, and included a large number of Qajar princes. This revision to earlier (pre-1600) Safavid practices "meant that in each provincial capital there was a copy (on a smaller scale) of the court at Tehran with all the burden which that imposed on the local population."[119] Governors enjoyed considerable local autonomy and kept much of their jurisdictions' surplus. To stanch their various fiscal crises the Qajar shahs began to auction off governorships, the mint, and customs. By the second half of the century governorships were systematically sold to the highest bidder—the one who promised to remit the most in taxes. The new governor then sub-farmed districts and offices in the same way, until the peasantry at the base of the social order paid for it all. In 1893 the prime minister Amin al-Sultan told the British minister Lascelles: "Do not expect any patriotism from us. It does not exist in the country. Self-interest, greed and avarice abound. Beyond that no one cares what happens."[120] In the provinces, as in the central bureaucracy, the practice of tax-farming and sale of offices cost both the state a loss of revenue and the lower classes in higher taxes. Urban administration was conducted in a less spectacular or extortionate manner, with top officials named by the shah, who had to be mindful of public opinion. The legal system remained dual: The *darugha* (police prefect) handled urban criminal affairs, the religious qazis handled personal law.[121]

The Qajar army went through many changes in the course of the nineteenth century, none of which solved its problems sufficiently to make it a useful instrument of state externally or internally. The troops used by Aqa Muhammad to capture the throne in the 1790s were little different in nature from those of 'Abbas the Great; numbering 60-70,000, paid for 6-7 months a

TABLE 4.5 Revenues of the Iranian State, 1800-1907

Year	Estimator	Revenues in Tumans	Revenues in Pounds Sterling
1807	Gardane	2,000,000+	2,000,000+
1810/11	Malcolm	—	3,000,000
1820	Fraser	2,500,000	2,200,000
1836	Issawi	2,461,000	—
1839/40	Rabino	3,402,615	1,835,994
1853/54	Rabino	3,368,558	1,153,163
1868	Thomson	5,012,500	1,965,000
1876/77	Rabino	5,070,000	1,950,800
1888/89	Curzon	5,531,000	1,653,000
1907	Jamalzadeh	8,000,000	1,538,000

Sources: Nashat, "From Bazaar to Market," 54; Rabino, "Banking in Persia," in Issawi, *EHI*, 352; Issawi, "Population and Resources," 389 note 46.

year, "Their principal arms were bows and arrows, clubs, lances, swords, and daggers. The cavalry wore coats of mail and some used small shields. Fire-arms consisted of long muskets, mostly matchlocks. Artillery was seldom employed."[122] 'Abbas Mirza, the crown prince, made efforts to modernize training and armaments after 1800, but the latter were of poor quality and the Russians (after some early setbacks) prevailed decisively in the wars of 1810-13 and 1826-28. For a brief time under Amir Kabir around 1850 the army was systematically recruited, better trained, and regularly paid. Its theoretical strength of 100,000 infantry and 30,000 cavalry remained far above its actual size of perhaps 20,000 men. This force quelled revolts in 1850 but degenerated again soon after Amir Kabir's downfall and had to back down under English pressure over Afghanistan in 1853-56. The dilapidated military institution ate up some 41 percent of the state's budget in 1868 and abuses increased here as elsewhere in the government in the 1890s. These funds were lent out in profit schemes in the bazaar at high rates, while soldiers went half-starved and had to engage in manual labor to survive. By 1900 the army—apart from the Russian-trained Cossack Brigade of about 10,000 fairly efficient troops—was reduced to a 2,000-man personal bodyguard. As one shah said, "I have neither an army nor the ammunition to supply an army." The military preparedness and discipline of the soldiers were slight or non-existent.[123]

Abrahamian has argued that the Qajars relied on a weak, fragmented society, carefully kept in equilibrium by a policy of "divide and rule," and that this obviated the need for either a standing army or a well-developed bureaucracy.[124] The Qajar state, nevertheless—or as a result—was clearly smaller, less in control and far more venal than its Safavid predecessor, though institutionally it was more solid in 1900 than in 1800. Its underlying lack of strength reposed in large measure on its nearly permanent situation of fiscal crisis. This in turn derived in part from its weakness within the world-system and led to legitimation problems vis-à-vis civil society.

Fiscal crises occurred with some regularity in Qajar Iran, especially in two waves, from the 1820s to 1850 and from the 1880s onward. Table 4.5 gives an overview of some estimates on the size of Iran's revenues from 1800 to 1907. Significantly, due to the depreciation of the Iranian currency, the state revenues expressed in pounds sterling reached their peak of three million in 1810, declined to 2.2 million in 1820, and never surpassed two million for the rest of the century, reaching in fact their second *lowest* level in 1907 of just over 1.5 million pounds sterling. As the Iranian state and economy became enmeshed in the world system over this period, presumably the weight of this decline was felt fiscally despite the gains in terms of tumans. The sources of this state income were above all the land tax, 78 percent of total revenues according to Thomson in 1868, and the customs at about 11 percent; by 1911 the customs were up to over 40 percent of the total.[125]

The first reports of a fiscal crisis of the state go back to the 1820s, when Fraser spoke of "the deficiency in revenue."[126] This shortfall developed into a full-blown crisis in the early 1830s due to the wars with Russia which both removed some of the revenue base by taking Iranian territories and saddled Iran with a large war indemnity to pay. Lambton judges that "From the reign of Muhammad Shah (1834-48) onwards there were repeated financial crises."[127] Amir Kabir instituted financial reforms from 1848 to 1851, reducing pensions and civil service salaries, and perhaps balancing the budget before his fall from grace (partly due to disgruntled officials and pensioners).[128] The situation unraveled definitively in the 1880s and 1890s, leading to a state of more or less permanent fiscal crisis. External pressures played a role in this: Compensation for the cancelled tobacco concession led to the first large foreign loan in 1892, the depreciation and debasement of the tuman meant that increased tax rates still brought in less revenues; the collapse of silk production reduced the land revenue. Total public debt reached 7,650,000 pounds sterling in 1913, requiring annual servicing of 400-500,000 pounds, which ate up one quarter of all government revenues.[129] Internal factors included the shah's lavish spending on his harem and trips, both locally and to Europe; abuses in the customs and from tax-farming and sale of offices generally; the cut-rate sale of crown lands; and the wasted military expenditures for a paper army. The state seems to have gone into chronic fiscal crisis in the 1890s, acquiring a permanent deficit of about 300,000 tumans (60,000 pounds sterling). In the fifteen years before the Constitutional revolution broke out in 1905, the deficit climbed by ten times to three million tumans, or 600,000 pounds sterling.[130]

The fiscal crises and the desperate measures to which they gave rise— foreign borrowing and concessions, debasement of the currency, and the abuses and corruption attending the sale of offices—fueled political discontent and as such contributed to the growing de-legitimation of the Qajar state. An 1838 letter from Mirza 'Ali, deputy minister for foreign affairs, to the British minister expresses the absolutist claims of the Qajar dynasty:

> the Monarchs of Persia, as far back as memory reaches, or is preserved in history, have always been despotic over Persian subjects, in like manner over their lives, and property, and families, and reputations, and lands, and goods: so that even if they should order a thousand innocent persons to be put to death, it would be in no one's power to call them to account.[131]

By century's end, the reality of Qajar power fell far short of its projected ideal. As Abrahamian notes: "The Qajars . . . were despots without the instruments of despotism; Shadows of God on Earth whose writ did not extend far beyond the capital; Kings of Kings who trembled before armed demonstrators; and absolutists ruling with the kind permission of the provincial magnates, the religious dignitaries, and the local officials."[132] The state's centralizing project was circumscribed, not just by the economic power of the West, but by serious inroads into its prestige internally in Iranian society. A key step in the erosion of the Qajars' absolutist ideal was taken with the separation of religious and political sources of legitimation in the first part of the nineteenth century. The ruler was recognized by eminent mujtahids as "the Shadow of God on earth," but not held to possess any divine attributes, nor to be the deputy of the Hidden Imam. Herein lies an incipient differentiation of political and religious functions: "kings were needed for the preservation of order, the '*ulama*' for the protection of religion."[133] The shah was legitimized as the "Shadow of God on Earth" in the temporal realm, while the court acknowledged that the most eminent of the mujtahids was the "viceregent of the Imam."[134] The shah was technically subordinate, like any other believer, to the guidance of a leading mujtahid as his *marja'-i taqlid* (source of imitation). Yet he was also considered the "King of Islam and of the Shi'ite nation," responsible for protecting Islam against encroachment by infidels.[135] Thus, there is as usual a degree of ambiguity in Shi'ism's political implications: Separation of politics and religion, or state and ulama, made confrontation as well as cooperation possible.

In the course of the nineteenth century, state and ulama relations oscillated between these poles, gradually crystallizing into fairly widespread ulama criticism of and disenchantment with the Qajar state. Fath 'Ali Shah was generally considered very pious and even respected as a religious scholar of sorts, but tensions mounted in Muhammad Shah's reign from 1834 to 1848. From the 1850s to the 1880s Arjomand discerns a lull in which the state was dominant and the ulama cooperative, with little conflict. Many ulama developed close ties with the Qajar political elite. But a counter-trend was at work as well: The Qajars were perceived as progressively associating themselves with non-Muslim powers who wanted to destroy the Islamic community of Iran. In 1902, leading ulama told the British minister in Tehran that they were "very much disappointed with the subserviency of the Shah and Grand Vizier to Russia, and especially with the second Russian loan, and talk openly of excommunicating (which means practically deposing) the Shah," unless the policy was changed.[136] Thus by the turn of the twentieth century, the earlier separation of legitimate religious and political domination in Iranian society had evolved into increasing interventions by the ulama into politics as a result of perceptions that the state was faltering in its leadership by not confronting foreign powers in defense of the Shi'i nation.

The Qajars had moved from a situation of unpopularity within Iran to one of spreading belief in their patent illegitimacy. According to Fraser they were already unpopular rulers in the 1820s and 1830s, seen as unconcerned with the people, unwilling to finance public works, and seeking only to tax the provinces for all they were worth: "The very name of the Kujurs is detested throughout the Kingdom."[137] They never overcame this sentiment, which by the last quarter of the century was linked to the resentment of significant sectors of the urban population—merchants, artisans, ulama—against foreign domination of Iran's economy, polity, and culture. Parallel to the dominant critique of the Qajars as failing to safeguard Islam against infidels was the intelligentsia's contention that arbitrary rule should be checked by the rule of law and eventually a constitution. Tribal autonomy too was a factor precluding successful imposition of the state's absolutist project on Iranian society. These diverse currents undermined Qajar legitimacy and provided rationales for action in the social movements of the late Qajar period.

Conclusions: The Nature of Dependency

Throughout this chapter I have tried to make a case for the concept of dependent development as a heuristic device for answering the questions posed at the beginning: How much and what type of development occurred in Qajar Iran? This period has found a number of good historians but has been plagued by problems of conceptualization and interpretation. Two very different judgments have arisen: On the one hand, Nowshirvani, Gilbar, and Nashat have advanced analyses highlighting *progress*, in terms of "commercialization of agriculture," "modernization of institutions," "rise in per capita incomes," and so forth. On the other hand, Issawi, Bharier and Keddie have painted more sober portraits emphasizing "relative economic stagnation and very slow development," especially compared with Egypt and the Ottoman empire. A third group of scholars, including Seyf, Ashraf, Anna Enayat, and Amanat, have come closer, but never fully or explicitly enough, to the perspective employed in this chapter. Namely, as the term "dependent development" suggests, Iran experienced both growth and limits to growth, economic "development" and dependency on external forces, absolute *increases* in numerous key indicators—population, gross domestic product, foreign trade—but entailing significant negative repercussions on standards of living, balance of payments, inflation, the state budget, employment in the crafts, and so on.

Theoretically we saw Iran's transition from an external arena largely outside the ambit of the world-economy to an increasingly integrated peripheral role in the capitalist world-economy, as supplier of raw materials—silk, opium, cotton, fruits and nuts, and so on—and one "traditional" manufacture—carpets—and consumer of manufactured imports—textiles, hardware, and processed agricultural products such as sugar and tea. This produced differential internal impacts on various groups and social classes. The three modes of production that combined in the period from 1500 to 1800 were preserved, although the petty-commodity mode of craft production was heavily undermined by the Western imports, and agriculture turned increasingly to the cultivation of crops for export. Relations of exchange rather than production were most affected. Meanwhile, a small new capitalist mode of production emerged, with certain unique historical features: Foreign capital was prevalent at the top and an Iranian working class formed partly outside the country in Russia. The growing weakness of the Qajar state vis-à-vis Western states and their more powerful armies and economies was linked to processes of fiscal crisis and delegitimation internally. While contact with the world economy did create pressure for reforms and the elaboration of some new institutions, it did not result in any successful centralization of the Qajar polity. The Qajars' misfortune was that they were neither too strong (unlike the Safavids) nor too remote (as the eighteenth-century "dynasties" had been) to be directly dominated. Instead, capitalism came to them from the outside in the guise of two strong rivals, Great Britain and Russia, who completely disaggregated their dreams of strong central control internally.

We have seen that dependence has political, economic, and ideological aspects. It was imposed by military power, channelled into economic domination, and ended in substantial political and strategic control of two Western powers, Russia and Great Britain, over Iran. But the story does not in fact end here. In chapter five we shall reassess the period in terms of the social movements that occurred, largely as *responses to dependency*, directed against the twin forces of domination in late nineteenth-century Iran: the Qajar state and foreign encroachment.

Notes

1. Ann Lambton, "Persian Society under the Qajars," pp. 123-139 in *Journal of the Royal Central Asian Society*, volume XLVIII, part II (April 1961), 124, citing G. H. Hunt, *Outram and Havelock's Persian Campaign* (London, 1858), 127.

2. Cited by Shaul Bakhash, *Iran: Monarchy, Bureaucracy and Reform under the Qajars: 1858-1896* (London: Ithaca Press, 1978), 205, 244 note 4.

3. A version of the central argument of this chapter has been published as "The Concept of Dependent Development as a Key to the Political Economy of Qajar Iran (1800-1925)," pp. 5-56 in *Iranian Studies*, volume XXII, numbers 2-3 (1989).

4. Julian Bharier, *Economic Development in Iran 1900-1970* (London: Oxford University Press, 1971), 19-20. Nikki Keddie feels "There was little economic development before 1925": *Roots of Revolution*, 92.

5. This is the more or less implicit thrust of three important researchers on Qajar Iran, Gad Gilbar, Guity Nashat, and V. F. Nowshirvani, whose specific works will be analyzed (and drawn on) below.

6. On these early contacts, see R. M. Savory, "British and French Diplomacy in Persia, 1800-1810," pp. 31-44 in *Iran* (Journal of the British Institute of Persian Studies), volume X (1972), 35-36; and Hurewitz, *Diplomacy*, I, 68-70.

7. On these events, see David Gillard, *The Struggle for Asia 1828-1914. A Study in British and Russian Imperialism* (London: Methuen & Co Ltd., 1977); Hurewitz, *Diplomacy*, I, 86-88, 141-43, 161-63; and Lambton, "Persia," 454-55.

8. For early British trade with Iran, see Roger T. Olson, "Persian Gulf Trade and the Agricultural Economy of Southern Iran in the Nineteenth Century," pp. 173-189 in Michael E. Bonine and Nikki R. Keddie, *Modern Iran. The Dialectics of Continuity and Change* (Albany: State University of New York Press, 1981); Ahmad Seyf, "Commercialization of Agriculture: Production and Trade of Opium in Persia, 1850-1906," pp. 233-250 in *International Journal of Middle East Studies*, volume 16, number 2 (May 1984); Ann K. S. Lambton, "Persian Trade under the Early Qajars," pp. 215-244 in D. S. Richards, editor, *Islam and the Trade of Asia*; Guity Nashat, "From Bazaar to Market: Foreign Trade and Economic Development in Nineteenth-Century Iran," pp. 53-85 in *Iranian Studies*, volume XIV, numbers 1-2 (Winter-Spring 1981); Issawi, *EHI*, 71-72; and Charles Issawi, "Iranian Trade, 1800-1914," pp. 229-241 in *Iranian Studies*, volume XVI, numbers 3-4 (Summer-Autumn 1983), 235.

9. For a list of some twenty-one major concessions to Britain or its subjects see Wilhelm Litten, *Persien von der 'pénétration pacifique' zum Protektorat. Urkunden und Tatsachen zur Geschichte der europäischen 'pénétration pacifique' in Persien 1860-1919* (Berlin, 1920), extracts translated pp. 358-361 in Issawi, *EHI*.

10. Curzon, *Persia and the Persian Question*, I, 480.

11. Ram Nandan Kumar, "Economic Background of British Diplomacy in Persia, 1858-1907," pp. 229-236 in *Islamic Culture* (Hyderabad), volume L, number 4 (October 1976)," 233; Hurewitz, *Diplomacy*, I, 205.

12. "William Knox D'Arcy Oil Concession in Persia," May 29, 1901, pp. 249-251 in Hurewitz, *Diplomacy*, I.

13. Chris Paine, "Iranian Nationalism and the Great Powers: 1872-1954," pp. 3-28 in *MERIP (Middle East Research and Information Project) Reports*, number 37 (1975), 9; Hurewitz, *Diplomacy*, I, 272, 278-79; Issawi, *EHI*, 261.

14. For these and other trade data, see Litten, *Persien*, in Issawi, *EHI*, 359; Ahmad Ashraf, *Mavane'-i Tarikhi-yi Rushd-i Sarmayehdari dar Iran: Daureh-i Qajariyyeh* [Historical Obstacles to the Development of Capitalism in the Qajar Era] (Tehran: Payam Press, 1359/1980); A. Ashraf and H. Hekmat, "Merchants and Artisans and the Developmental Processes of Nineteenth-Century Iran," pp. 725-750 in A. L. Udovitch, editor, *The Islamic Middle East, 700-1900: Studies in Economic and Social History* (Princeton: The Darwin Press, Inc., 1981), 734; Ahmad Ashraf, "Historical Obstacles to the Development of a Bourgeoisie in Iran," pp. 308-324 in M. A. Cook, editor, *Studies in the Economic History of the Middle East: from the rise of Islam to the present day* (London and New York: Oxford University Press, 1970), 325; H. W. MacLean, "Report on the Conditions and Prospects of British Trade in Persia," pp. 136-142 in Issawi, *EHI*, 137; and Issawi, "Iranian Trade," 235-36.

15. On these events, see Hurewitz, *Diplomacy*, I, 84-86, 96-102; Lambton, "Persia," 443-45; Lambton, "Persian Trade," 226-27, 232; Ervand Abrahamian, "Oriental Despotism: The Case of Qajar Iran," pp. 3-31 in *International Journal of Middle East Studies*, volume 5, number 1 (1974), 21; Keddie, "The Impact of the West," 47, 54; and Gillard, *The Struggle for Asia*, 22-23.

16. See data in Ter-Gukasov, *Politicheskie*, in Issawi, *EHI*, 145-46; Issawi, *EHI*, 108-9; Marvin L. Entner, *Russo-Persian Commercial Relations, 1828-1914*, University of Florida Monographs, Social Sciences, number 28 (Gainesville: University of Florida Press, 1965), 8-9; Issawi, "Iranian Trade," 235; and Malcolm, *The Melville Papers*, in Issawi, *EHI*, 264.

17. See V. F. Nowshirvani, "The Beginnings of Commercialized Agriculture in Iran," pp. 547-591 in A. L. Udovitch, editor, *The Islamic Middle East, 700-1900*, 563; Gillard, *The Struggle for Asia*, 154; Issawi, *EHI*, 143; and Entner, *Russo-Persian Commercial Relations*, for developments generally.

18. Entner, *Russo-Persian Commercial Relations*, 77.

19. Cited in ibid., 41-42.

20. Donald N. Wilber, *Riza Shah Pahlavi: The Resurrection and Reconstruction of Iran* (Hicksville, New York: Exposition Press, 1975), 7.

21. The treaty can be found in Hurewitz, *Diplomacy*, I, 265-267.

22. Malcolm, *The Melville Papers*, in Issawi, *EHI*, 262-67, calculations mine.

23. Issawi, "Iranian Trade, 1800-1914," 231; Issawi, *EHI*, 132; Nowshirvani, "The Beginnings of Commercialized Agriculture," 564, on the increase in "real" trade.

24. Issawi, *EHI*, 70. Per capita foreign trade in 1906, expressed in British pounds sterling puts Iran at 1.2 pounds, behind Turkey's 1.8, Egypt's 5.1, and Brazil's 6.0: see Ahmad Seyf, "Some Aspects of Economic Development in Iran, 1800-1901," Ph.D. dissertation, Department of Agricultural Economics and Management, University of Reading (1982), 592.

25. For 1857, Blau, *Commerzielle Zustände Persiens*, analyzed by Gilbar, "The Persian Economy in the mid-19th Century," 210 table 1; for 1903, MacLean, "Report on the Conditions and Prospects," 136; for 1913, see Issawi, *EHI*, 135-36, based on trade returns.

26. A. C. Kia, *Essai sur l'histoire industrielle de l'Iran* (Paris, 1939), 87-88, cited by Nikki R. Keddie (with the research help of Wells H. Keddie) *Historical Obstacles to Agrarian Change in Iran*, Claremont Asian Studies, number 8 (Claremont, California: September 1960), 6.

27. Issawi, *EHI*, 18, 70; Robert A. McDaniel, "Economic Change and Economic Resiliency in 19th Century Persia," pp. 36-49 in *Iranian Studies*, volume IV, number 1 (Winter 1971), 39.

28. For wheat, McDaniel, "Economic Change and Economic Resiliency," 37; for opium, Seyf, "Commercialization of Agriculture," 247 table 8; for silk, Gilbar, "Persian Agriculture," 349; for rice, Seyf, "Some Aspects," 592.

29. Nowshirvani, "The Beginnings of Commercialized Agriculture," 555 table III.

30. Wallerstein, *The Modern World-System I*, 301-302.

31. Bausani, *The Persians*, 172. See also Halliday, *Iran. Dictatorship and Development*, 33, and Anna Enayat, "The Problem of Imperialism in Nineteenth-Century Iran," pp. 48-72 in *RIPEH*, volume II, number 1 (December 1977), 56-57.

32. Gad G. Gilbar, "The Persian Economy in the mid-19th Century," pp. 177-211 in *Die Welt des Islams*, volume 19, numbers 1-4 (1979), 178, 180-81; Gavin Hambly, "An introduction to the economic organization of Qajar Iran," pp. 69-81 in *Iran* (Journal of the British Institute of Persian Studies), volume 2 (1964), 70. Other population data I have consulted are found in Homa Katouzian, *The Political Economy of Modern Iran. Despotism and Pseudo-Modernism, 1926-1979* (New York and London: New York University Press, 1981); Gad G. Gilbar, "Demographic developments in late Qajar Persia, 1870-1906," pp. 125-156 in *Asian and African Studies*, volume 11, number 2 (Autumn 1976), 144; Robert Hill, cited by Issawi, "Population and Resources," 162; Helfgott, "The Rise of the Qajar Dynasty," 78, 85, 86; Malcolm, *History of Persia* (1815), II, 519; Curzon, *Persia and the Persian Question*, II, 493-94; Bharier, *Economic Development in Iran*, 3; Issawi, *EHI*, 20 note 2, 28, 33; Floor, *Industrialization in Iran*, 3; Nowshirvani, "The Beginnings of Commercialized Agriculture," 563; Nashat, "From Bazaar to Market," 61; and M. S. Ivanov, *Tarikh-i Nuvin-i Iran* [Modern History of Iran], translated from the Russian by Hushang Tizabi and Hasan Qa'im Paneh (Stockholm: Tuden Publishing Centre, 1356/1977), 9.

33. On epidemics and famines see Gilbar, "Demographic developments," 139-43; Gilbar, "The Persian Economy in the mid-19th Century," 179, 208; Issawi, *EHI*, 21-22; Hassan Hakimian, "Wage Labor and Migration: Persian Workers in Southern Russia, 1880-1914," pp. 443-462 in *International Journal of Middle East Studies*, volume 17, number 4 (November 1985), 453; Nowshirvani, "The Beginnings of Commercialized Agriculture," 556; Lambton, "Persian Trade," 237; and Ahmad Seyf, "Silk Production and Trade in Iran in the Nineteenth Century," pp. 51-71 in *Iranian Studies*, volume 16, numbers 1-2 (Winter-Spring 1983), 71 note 55.

34. Gad G. Gilbar, "Persian Agriculture in the Late Qajar Period, 1860-1906: Some Economic and Social Aspects," pp. 312-365 in *Asian and African Studies*, volume 12, number 3 (1978), 315; Gilbar, "The Persian Economy," 186; McDaniel, "Economic Change," 37, 39, 46-47 note 2; Issawi, *EHI*, 211.

35. Gilbar, "The Persian Economy," 187; Gilbar, "Persian Agriculture," 34-496; Abbas Amanat, editor and introduction, *Cities & Trade: Consul Abbott on the Economy and Society of Iran 1847-1866*, Oxford Oriental Monographs No. 5 (London: Ithaca Press, 1983), xvii; Seyf, "Silk Production and Trade," 60-64.

36. Robert A. McDaniel, *The Shuster Mission and the Persian Constitutional Revolution* (Minneapolis: Biblioteca Islamica, 1974), 37; Gilbar, "Persian Agriculture," 325, 329-30, 337, 339, 346; Olson, "Persian Gulf Trade," 187-88, 418 note 36; Seyf, "Commercialization of Agriculture," 242-48; Issawi, *EHI*, 238.

37. Issawi, *EHI*, 238, quoting the British consul at Bushire; Seyf, "Commercialization of Agriculture," 244, citing an 1893 report by Consul Thomson; Nikki Keddie, "The Economic History of Iran, 1800-1914, and its Political Impact," pp. 119-136 in her *Iran: Religion, Politics and Society* (London: Frank Cass, 1980), 128.

38. Issawi, "Iranian Trade, 1800-1914," 233-34; Issawi, *EHI*, 76, 209, 245-46; Seyf, "Commercialization of Agriculture," 237; Nowshirvani, "The Beginnings of Commercialized Agriculture," 573; Ter-Gukasov, *Politicheskie*, in Issawi, *EHI*, 146; Gilbar, "Persian Agriculture," 320-23, 355-56; McDaniel, *The Shuster Mission*, 37; McDaniel, "Economic Change and Economic Resiliency," 42-43; Entner, *Russo-Persian Commercial Relations*, 75.

39. This is my own rough estimate based on Gilbar's observation that Gilan's 216,000 pounds sterling in taxes represented 11 percent of the total state revenue. Since the land tax was roughly ten percent of the crops' market value, total agricultural GDP was (very) roughly 216,000 X 9 X 10 = 19,440,000 pounds sterling. See also Katouzian's rather lower estimate of 24.8 million tumans (about 12 million pounds sterling) for 1867: *The Political Economy*, 44 table 3.9.

40. Gilbar, "Persian Agriculture," 360.

41. Nowshirvani, "The Beginnings of Commercialized Agriculture," 579. See further ibid., and Issawi, *EHI*, 17.

42. Seyf, "Commercialization of Agriculture," 234, 238-40.

43. Lambton, *Landlord and Peasant*, 152. Eastwick is cited by Gilbar, "The Persian Economy," 189.

44. Minorsky, "Tiyul," 801.

45. Michel Pavlovitch, "La situation agraire en Perse à la veille de la révolution," pp. 616-625 in *Revue du Monde Musulman*, volume XII, number 12 (December 1910), 618. For hints of this process, see Lambton, *Landlord and Peasant*, 152; Minorsky, "Tiyul," 801; and Issawi, *EHI*, 210.

46. On these trends, see Ann K. S. Lambton, "Rural Development and Land Reform in Iran," pp. 52-54 in Issawi, *EHI*, 53; Ann K. S. Lambton, "The Case of Hajji Nur al-Din, 1823-47: A Study in Land Tenure," pp. 54-72 in *Bulletin of the School of Oriental and African Studies*, volume XXX, part 1 (1967), 71-72; Lambton, *Landlord and Peasant*, 142-43, 156; Lambton, "Persian Society," 130-31; and Mary-Jo DelVecchio Good, "Social Hierarchy in Provincial Iran: The Case of Qajar Maragheh," pp. 129-163 in *Iranian Studies*, volume X, number 3 (Summer 1977), 133, 149.

47. On the new landed classes, see Amanat, "Introduction" to *Cities & Trade*, xx; Floor, "The Merchants (*tujjar*) in Qajar Iran," pp. 101-136 in *Zeitschrift der Deutschen Morgenländischen Gesellschaft*, volume 126, number 1 (1976); Mehrain, "Emergence of Capitalist Authoritarian States," 80-82; Nowshirvani, "The Beginnings of Commercialized Agriculture," 578; Lambton, *Landlord and Peasant*, 140, 173; and Keddie, "Iran, 1797-1941," 146.

48. Lambton, *Landlord and Peasant*, 140. On land taxes, see Katouzian, *The Political Economy*, 33.

49. Gilbar, "The Persian Economy," 189; Pavlovitch, "La situation agraire," 620.

50. Olson, "Persian Gulf Trade," 185; F. Lafont and H.-L. Rabino, *L'industrie séricole en Perse* (Montpellier, 1910), extracts translated pp. 235-238 in Issawi, *EHI*, 236; Keddie, "Iran, 1797-1941," 148-49; Nowshirvani, "The Beginnings of Commercialized Agriculture," 579.

51. Eric J. Hooglund, "Rural Socioeconomic Organization in Transition: The Case of Iran's Bonehs," pp. 191-207 in Michael E. Bonine and Nikki R. Keddie, editors, *Modern Iran. The Dialectics of Continuity and Change* (Albany: State University of New York Press, 1981), 195-96, 198-201.

52. See Lambton, *Landlord and Peasant*, 157, on village sizes. The text should read "10-20" and not "10-50," as corrected by personal correspondence with Ann Lambton, February 16, 1987. See also Good, "Social Hierarchy in Provincial Iran," 157; Bausani, *The Persians*, 174-75; Nowshirvani, "The Beginnings of Commercialized Agriculture," 576; Issawi, *EHI*, 40-41; Gilbar, "Persian Agriculture," 339; and Keddie, "Iran, 1797-1941," 148-49.

53. Pavlovitch, "La situation agraire," 621.

54. James B. Fraser, *Historical and Descriptive Account of Persia, from the Earliest Ages to the Present Time* (New York: Harper & Brothers, 1833), 260.

55. Gilbar, "Persian Agriculture," 361-62.

56. See Nowshirvani, "The Beginnings of Commercialized Agriculture," 575, and Seyf, "Silk Production and Trade," 57.

57. I present more accounts in my article, "The Concept of Dependent Development," 31-34.

58. Malcolm, *History of Persia* (1829 edition), II, 353, cited by Lambton, *Landlord and Peasant*, 137.

59. Fraser, *Historical and Descriptive Account of Persia*, 258.

60. Edward B. Eastwick, *Journal of a Diplomat's Three Years' Residence in Persia* (London: Smith, Elder and Co., 1864), 3 volumes: II, 86, cited by Gilbar, "The Persian Economy," 191.

61. Jenner is cited by Gilbar, "Demographic developments," 140.

62. The British consul is cited by Issawi, *EHI*, 40.

63. Lascelles's report of January 13, 1893 is cited by Hakimian, "Wage Labor and Migration," 453.

64. Sir Thomas E. Gordon, *Persia Revisited* (London, 1896), 39-40, cited by Gilbar, "Persian Agriculture," 365. Similarly favorable comments were made by Sheil in 1856 and Benjamin in 1887, both quoted by Abrahamian, *Iran Between Two Revolutions*, 70.

65. Gilbar, "The Persian Economy," 192-95.

66. Gilbar, "Persian Agriculture," 363. For his more sober assessment of the period from 1800 to 1850, see "The Persian Economy," 188, 195.

67. Nowshirvani, "The Beginnings of Commercialized Agriculture," 576-77, though he himself cites an 1893 British report from Sistan: "The people are so wretchedly poor that there is no demand for these things. They make their own clothes and don't drink tea."

68. Keddie, "Introduction" to *Iran: Religion, Politics and Society*, 5. For further arguments advanced here, see Olson, "Persian Gulf Trade," 185, 187-88, 418 note 36; Seyf, "Commercialization of Agriculture," 238; Nasser Pakdaman, "Preface," pp. 125-135 in *Iranian Studies*, volume XVI, numbers 3-4 (Summer-Autumn 1983), 126; Abdullaev, *Promyshlennost*, in Issawi, *EHI*, 49; and Nowshirvani, "The Beginnings of Commercialized Agriculture," 576.

69. Keddie, "The Economic History of Iran," 125; Keddie, *Historical Obstacles*, 2, 4. Eric Hooglund, too, an authority on twentieth-century agriculture, feels that by 1900 peasant living standards had worsened compared with earlier in the nineteenth century: Eric J. Hooglund, *Land and Revolution in Iran, 1960-1980* (Austin: University of Texas Press, 1982), 11.

70. Issawi, *EHI*, 22. Cf. Lambton on the peasantry in mid-century: "There was no security of life or property, and peasants in particular were subjected to grinding tyranny": "Persia," 454.

71. Atrpet, *Mamed Ali Shah* (Alexandropol, 1909), 141, cited by Abdullaev, *Promyshlennost*, in Issawi, *EHI*, 43. See also Gad G. Gilbar, "The Big Merchants (*tujjar*) and the Persian Constitutional Revolution of 1906," pp. 275-303 in *Asian and African Studies*, volume 11, number 3 (1977), 288.

72. Abdullaev, *Promyshlennost*, in Issawi, *EHI*, 44-45; Ashraf and Hekmat, "Merchants and Artisans," 735-36; Floor, "The Merchants," 128.

73. For data on these merchants, see Ashraf, *Mavane'-i Tarikhi*, 24; Issawi, *EHI*, 67; Curzon, *Persia and the Persian Question*, I, 167-68; and Gilbar, "Persian Agriculture," 344.

74. Muhammad Reza Afshari, "The *Pishivaran* and Merchants in Precapitalist Iranian Society: An Essay on the Background and Causes of the Constitutional Revolution," pp. 133-155 in *International Journal of Middle East Studies*, volume 15, number 2 (May 1983), 137, 142; Gilbar, "The Persian Economy," 203, 205; Ashraf and Hekmat, "Merchants and Artisans," 730.

75. On changing relations with foreigners, see Floor, "The Merchants," 120, 122, 133; Amanat, "Introduction" to *Cities & Trade*, xx; Issawi, *EHI*, 68; and Nashat, "From Bazaar to Market," 70, 75.

76. Issawi, *EHI*, 17, 259.

77. Olson, "Persian Gulf Trade," 416 note 23; Guity Nashat, *The Origins of Modern Reform in Iran, 1870-80* (Urbana: University of Illinois Press, 1982), 6.

78. Ashraf, "Historical Obstacles," 325.

79. Curzon, *Persia and the Persian Question*, II, 41, cited by Ashraf, "Historical Obstacles," 325.

80. Mirza Husayn, *Jughrafiya-yi Isfahan* [Geography of Isfahan] (Tehran, 1342/1963), extracts translated pp. 279-282 in Issawi, *EHI*, 279-81.

81. Willem Floor, *Industrialization in Iran 1900-1941*, Occasional Paper Series, number 23 (University of Durham, England: Centre for Middle Eastern and Islamic Studies, 1984), 5 table 3, 8 table 4; Issawi, *EHI*, 259 note 6.

82. On carpets, see sources in Issawi, *EHI*, 68, 297-300, 302-3; Dillon, "Carpet Capitalism," 285-91, 468-75; Nowshirvani, "The Beginnings of Commercialized Agriculture," 590 note 87; McDaniel, "Economic Change and Economic Resiliency," 41; Ashraf, *Mavane'-i Tarikhi*, 55; Pakdaman, "Preface," 130; and Floor, *Industrialization*, 7.

83. For details, see Willem Floor, *Labour Unions, Law and Conditions in Iran (1900-1941)*, Occasional Papers Series number 26 (University of Durham, England: Centre for Middle Eastern and Islamic Studies, 1985), 11, 88-91, 101-2.

84. Bausani, *The Persians*, 169; John H. Lorentz, "Iran's Great Reformer of the Nineteenth Century: An Analysis of Amir Kabir's Reforms," pp. 85-103 in *Iranian Studies*, volume III, number 2 (Spring-Summer 1971), 91; Gilbar, "The Persian Economy," 199-200; Faridun Adamiyat, *Amir Kabir va Iran* [Amir Kabir and Iran], third edition (Tehran: Khwarazmi, 1348/1969), extracts translated pp. 292-297 in Issawi, *EHI*; Sayyid Muhammad 'Ali Jamalzadeh, *Ganj-i Shayagan ya Auza'-yi Iqtisadi-yi Iran* [Abundant Treasure, or, the Economic Situation of Iran] (Berlin: Kaveh, 1335 Q./1916).

85. Cited by Floor, "The Merchants," 131.

86. See Ashraf, *Mavane'-i Tarikhi*, 98 table 2, based on Abdullaev; Jamalzadeh, *Ganj-i Shayagan*, 93-96; Ashraf and Hekmat, "Merchants and Artisans," 737; and Floor, *Industrialization*, 9 table 5.

87. Issawi, *EHI*, 67. On the problems involved, see ibid., 260, and Floor, *Industrialization*, 9.

88. See Ashraf, *Mavane'-i Tarikhi*, 65-66, 99 table 3, based on Abdullaev; Jamalzadeh, *Ganj-i Shayagan*, 93-96; and Floor, *Industrialization*, 9 table 5.

89. Abdullaev, *Promyshlennost*, in Issawi, *EHI*, 49, 50; Nowshirvani, "The Beginnings of Commercialized Agriculture," 576.

90. This paragraph draws on Hakimian, "Wage Labor and Migration"; Gilbar, "Demographic developments," 152-53; and Abdullaev, *Promyshlennost*, in Issawi, *EHI*, 52.

91. Floor, *Labour Unions*, 99-100.

92. On wages, see Issawi, *EHI*, 41-42, and Floor, *Labour Unions*, 104, 112.

93. Abdullaev, *Promyshlennost*, in Issawi, *EHI*, 50.

94. Lambton, *Islamic Society in Persia*, 18-19; Keddie, "Iran, 1797-1941," 148.

95. Malcolm, *History of Persia* (1829 edition), II, 353, cited by Lambton, *Landlord and Peasant*, 137; Amanat, "Introduction" to *Cities & Trade*, xv.

96. Cited in Issawi, *EHI*, 41.

97. Olson, "Persian Gulf Trade," 187.

98. Mangol Bayat, *Mysticism and Dissent. Socioreligious Thought in Qajar Iran* (Syracuse: Syracuse University Press, 1982), 22. On the ulama, see ibid., 24-25; Lambton, "Persian Society," 135; Lambton, "Persia," 438; Arjomand, *The Shadow of God and the Hidden Imam*, 230, 232-33, 242, 247; Floor, "The Merchants," 103-4; Keddie, "Iran, 1797-1941," 146; and Hamid Algar, *Religion and State in Iran, 1785-1906. The Role of the Ulama in the Qajar Period* (Berkeley and Los Angeles: University of California Press, 1969), 60-61.

99. On the Christian community, see Thomson, "Report on Persia," in Issawi, *EHI*, 30-31; and Issawi, *EHI*, 24, 58-59.

100. Curzon, *Persia and the Persian Question*, I, 510. See also Issawi, *EHI*, 24, 62; and Arjomand, *The Shadow of God and the Hidden Imam*, 250.

101. Issawi, *EHI*, 63. See also ibid., 64; Keddie, "Iran, 1797-1941," 150-51; and Arjomand, *The Shadow of God and the Hidden Imam*, 250.

102. Fraser, *Historical and Descriptive Account of Persia*, 260.

103. Vincent Sheean, *The New Persia* (New York and London: The Century Co., 1927), 232. See too Keddie, "Iran, 1797-1941," 150.

104. On the currency and inflation, see Katouzian, *The Political Economy*, 36, 38, Bakhash, *Iran*, 270-72; Lambton, "Persian Trade," 238; Rabino di Borgomale, *Coins, Medals and Seals*, table IV between pages 18-19; and Gad G. Gilbar, "Trends in the Development of Prices in Late Qajar

Iran, 1870-1906," pp. 177-198 in *Iranian Studies*, volume XVI, numbers 3-4 (Summer-Autumn 1983).

105. Rabino, "An Economist's Notes on Persia," 278. See also Bakhash, *Iran*, 271.

106. Issawi, *EHI*, 42. See also ibid., 40-42; Seyf, "Commercialization of Agriculture," 238; and, on life expectancy, Roger M. Savory, "Social Development in Iran during the Pahlavi Era," pp. 85-128 in George Lenczowski, editor, *Iran Under the Pahlavis* (Stanford: Hoover Institution Press, 1978), 86.

107. Gilbar, "Demographic developments," 145-46; Helfgott, "The Rise of the Qajar Dynasty," 91, 101; Thomson, "Report on Persia," in Issawi, *EHI*, 28; McDaniel, "Economic Change and Economic Resiliency," 40.

108. For examples, see Gilbar, "Demographic developments," 146-47; Lambton, *Landlord and Peasant*, 159, on the Khamseh; Helfgott, "The Rise of the Qajar Dynasty," 97-98, on the Kurds; Bausani, *The Persians*, 173, on "semi-sedentarization." For conflicting estimates of the tribal population, see Helfgott, "The Rise of the Qajar Dynasty," 85-86; Nowshirvani, "The Beginnings of Commercialized Agriculture," 563; and Malcolm, letter of April 10, 1801, cited by Hambly, "An introduction to the economic organization," 70.

109. Lambton, *Landlord and Peasant*, 140, 157.

110. Cited by Gilbar, "Persian Agriculture," 359-60. Data in this paragraph is also drawn from Gilbar, "The Persian Economy," 188, and Olson, "Persian Gulf Trade," 181, 417 note 25.

111. Afshari, "The *Pishivaran*," 138. Other data here are drawn from McDaniel, *The Shuster Mission*, 24; Lambton, *Landlord and Peasant*, 142, 158, 169; and Pavlovitch, "La situation agraire," 624.

112. Lambton, "Persian Society," 130.

113. Gene R. Garthwaite, "Khans and Kings: The Dialectics of Power in Bakhtiari History," pp. 159-172 in Bonine and Keddie, editors, *Modern Iran*, 170. On the Qajars, see Helfgott, "Tribalism as a Socio-Economic Formation," 60-61 note 40.

114. Lambton, *Landlord and Peasant*, 159-61; Lambton, "Persia," 434; Garthwaite, "Khans and Kings," 169; Gilbar, "The Persian Economy," 201; Lois Beck, "Tribes and the State in Nineteenth and Twentieth Century Iran," lecture at the University of California, Berkeley, November 13, 1985.

115. Mehrain, "The Emergence of Capitalist Authoritarian States," 118-20; Beck, "Tribes and the State."

116. Afshari, "The *Pishivaran*," 138.

117. Lambton, "Persian Society," 139; Keddie, "Iran, 1797-1941," 140-42, 150.

118. Lambton, *Landlord and Peasant*, 162.

119. Lambton, "Persian Society," 127. On the Qajar state, see Lambton, "Persia," 434-435, 451; Keddie, "The Economic History," 125; Rabino, "An Economist's Notes"; Abrahamian, "Oriental Despotism," 11, 19-20; Nashat, "From Bazaar to Market," 55; Floor, *Industrialization*, 13 note 3, 41 note 67; Nowshirvani, "The Beginnings of Commercialized Agriculture," 568; Lorentz, "Iran's Great Reformer," 95-96; Bausani, *The Persians*, 167; and Bakhash, *Iran*, 263, 268-71, 277, 278.

120. Cited in Bakhash, *Iran*, 264. See also Keddie, "Iran, 1797-1941," 138; and Olson, "Persian Gulf Trade," 176-77, on southern Iran.

121. On urban government, see Lambton, "Persia," 438; Dillon, "Carpet Capitalism," 119; Mehrain, "The Emergence of Capitalist Authoritarian States," 70.

122. Abrahamian, "Oriental Despotism," 436. See also Lambton, "Persian Society," 131.

123. See Abrahamian, "Oriental Despotism," 11 (for the quote); Bakhash, *Iran*, 269, 275-76; Ivanov, *Tarikh-i Nuvin-i Iran*, 15; Lorentz, "Iran's Great Reformer," 94-95; and Thomson, "Report on Persia," in Issawi, *EHI*, 32.

124. Abrahamian, "Oriental Despotism," 31.

125. Thomson, "Report on Persia," in Issawi, *EHI*, 29-30; Nowshirvani, "The Beginnings of Commercialized Agriculture," 571. As with earlier figures on revenues, it is quite difficult to judge the accuracy of the estimates involved here.

126. Fraser is cited by Lambton, *Landlord and Peasant*, 145-46 note 7.

127. Lambton, "Persian Trade," 237.

128. Thomson, "Report on Persia," in Issawi, *EHI*, 31-32. See also Lambton, "Persia," 453-54; Lorentz, "Iran's Great Reformer," 92-93; and Amanat, "Introduction" to *Cities & Trade*, xxii.

129. Issawi, *EHI*, 128, 339. He points out that this was a lesser debt-to-revenue ratio than Egypt (1/2) or Turkey (1/3) but Iran had almost no productive investments to show for its debt.

130. Bakhash, *Iran*, 279; Edward G. Browne, *The Persian Revolution of 1905-1909* (Cambridge: At the University Press, 1910), 240.

131. Mirza 'Ali to Mr. McNeill, January 8, 1838, cited by Lambton, "Persian Society," 128.

132. Abrahamian, "Oriental Despotism," 13.

133. Arjomand, *The Shadow of God and the Hidden Imam*, 223.

134. Ibid., 225, 229. See also Lambton, "Quis Custodiet Custodes?" part 2, 143, and Cole, "Shi'i Clerics," 26-27.

135. Arjomand, *The Shadow of God and the Hidden Imam*, 234, 251-52; Hamid Algar, "The Oppositional Role of the Ulama in Twentieth-Century Iran," pp. 231-255 in Nikki Keddie, editor, *Scholars, Saints and Sufis: Muslim Religious Institutions since 1500* (Berkeley and Los Angeles: University of California Press, 1972), 235.

136. Denis Wright, *The Persians Amongst the English. Episodes in Anglo-Persian History* (London: I. B. Tauris, 1985), xvii, citing a letter in the Public Record Office of August 27, 1902. This paragraph is based on accounts of Arjomand, *The Shadow of God and the Hidden Imam*, 218, 248, 252, 265; and Algar, "The Oppositional Role," 233, 236.

137. Fraser, *Historical and Descriptive Account of Persia*, 204, 226.

5

Reform, Rebellion, Revolution, Coup: Social Movements in Qajar Iran

There appear to be two distinct and opposing causes for these disturbances.

On the one hand the partisans of Malkom Khan who share his "liberal" and "reforming" views, chiefly perhaps for the purpose of attacking the Shah's Chief Minister, are trying to open the eyes of the nation to the tyrannical and corrupt form of Govt under which they are living, and to imbue the people with an idea of democratic power; on the other, the fanatical Mollahs, taking advantage of Ramazan, are preaching everywhere against the surrender of the Faithful into the hands of the Infidels. Trade of all kinds, Mines, Banks, Tobacco, Roads, are, it is said, sold to Europeans, who will gradually obtain corn land and even Mussulman women.

—Report by the British minister R. J. Kennedy, April 29, 1891,
cited in Keddie, *Religion and Rebellion*

This chapter gives an analytic account of the main movements for social change in Iran in the period from 1800 to 1925, focusing in particular on the events of 1890 to 1925—the Tobacco rebellion, the Constitutional revolution, the radical local movements during and after World War I, and Reza Khan's coup. The title "Reform, Rebellion, Revolution, Coup" hints at the progression of steadily more dramatic events. The failure of the state's reform efforts to cope with growing grievances from below and increasing foreign penetration led to the first nationwide mass movement, the Tobacco rebellion of 1890-92. This proved to be the dress rehearsal for a more prolonged conflict, the Constitutional movement or revolution, from 1905 to 1911, which began with the grant of a national assembly and constitution but ended when Russian troops moved into Iran to disband the one and abrogate the other, propping up a weakened Qajar monarchy. The collapse of this attempted revolution was followed by military occupation, crop failures and famine during World War I, and the ensuing local rebellions, aggrandizing maneuvers of Great Britain, and weakness of the Qajar state created the environment for a centralizing military coup in 1921 and its leader's establishment of a new, Pahlavi dynasty in 1925.

For each of these major social movements the center of attention will be the underlying causes, principal social actors, and reasons for the outcome. The complexity of Iranian social structure, with its division into three (and then four) modes of production and some sixteen or more constituent social classes or groups, dictated the necessity of alliances on both sides of all social movements. Different groups and classes articulated a range of grievances against the state, internal, and foreign domination and these common targets led to a pattern in most social movements of broad, multi-class "populist" alliances to get them under way. Initial successes however were often followed by the emergence of internal differences in the revolutionary coalition and external interference from threatened foreign powers, which together limited the outcome as in the case of the Tobacco rebellion, or reversed it altogether as in the Constitutional revolution.

The approach of this chapter to social movements thus relies on the groundwork laid in chapter four on social class formation in the nineteenth century to clarify who was benefitting and who suffering as Iran became more closely integrated into the capitalist world system and dependent on Russia and Great Britain. The tentative classes-for-themselves that formed and coalesced, or ultimately failed to do so in these struggles for the hearts and minds of key groups—the ulama, artisans, merchants, and marginal urban classes—also indicate the importance of the subjective factors of political consciousness and culture in shaping the fragility of the very real resistance they could mount.

Succession Struggles and Uprisings, 1800-1850: From Traditional to Transitional Forms of Protest

The succession struggles of 1797, 1834, and 1848, as well as the later one of 1896, were brief moments of concern that the designated heir might be displaced by a brother or uncle upon the death of the reigning shah. They were basically a traditional and rather limited form of "change" and were each time decided in favor of the heir, although interestingly, in 1834 and 1896 this required some Russian and British help. What was "traditional" in each of these four succession crises were the inter- and intra-tribal conflicts surrounding the issue of which member of the royal family would succeed. What was transitional to the modern epoch was the growing foreign role evidenced by the weight of foreign diplomatic pressure and, by 1896, a

Russian-trained Iranian military unit. The increased involvement of the West in 1834 prefigures the Qajars' shrinking scope of action and early stages of the dependence which would become so marked by the end of the century.[1]

Instances of small-scale, local social struggles and political conflicts continued to be quite common in the Qajar period, just as they had been in the long Safavid era from 1500 to 1800. Ashraf and Hekmat note that "According to one account, there were 169 incidents of rebellion, unrest, sedition, and local war during the first forty years of Nasir al-Din Shah's reign,"[2] i.e. from 1848 to 1888. Though difficult to quantify, such events would seem to have been fully as numerous in the first half of the nineteenth century as well. The record of tribal unrest, including local rebellions, raids on towns and villages, and inter- and intra-tribal feuds and struggles, is a long one. To a certain degree the Qajar state coped by gaining the loyalty of tribal khans, particularly in the northwest, south, and center, with appointments to local office and land grants; in other areas, such as the northeast and southeast, the tribes remained rather autonomous and outside effective central control. No tribal rebellion led to full local independence or the successful establishment of a new dynasty, however, reflecting less on the forcefulness of the Qajar state than on the diminished aspirations of tribal leaders and their integration into the national elite, underpinned by the declining demographic and economic centrality of the tribal population in the overall Iranian social formation.

Even more common (or perhaps merely better documented) were the numerous outbreaks of urban disturbances of several sorts. Serious challenges to the political order itself occurred at Kirman and Yazd in 1830-31, Isfahan in 1835, Shiraz in 1840, Kirman in 1842, a half dozen or more cities in 1848, Tabriz in 1855-57, and Shiraz again from 1865 to 1867. These were most often expressions of public dissatisfaction with provincial authorities over such issues as excessive tax burdens, high food prices and shortages of bread, unpopular governors, and so on. To judge by the Shiraz revolt of 1840, about which relatively more data is available, protests against unjust governors were initiated and carried through by the artisans, shopkeepers, and urban poor, who had to enlist the support of higher-ranking classes such as the ulama, merchants, and local notables (the last often engaged in personal rivalries with the authorities). Their goals were generally limited to the correction of specific abuses, but if these were not met, participants might arm themselves, close the bazaar, escalate their demands to the removal of the governor, and create a situation of ungovernability until the shah replaced the governor. Such "limited objective movements," even when successful, thus stopped short of becoming fully revolutionary in scope and were always confined to their urban or regional setting.[3]

One urban incident which acquires heightened interest in light of subsequent social movements was the murder of the Russian envoy Griboyedov by a Tehrani crowd in 1829. Griboyedov was believed to be holding two Georgian women from the harem of a Qajar prince against their will. The significance of this event has at least two dimensions. For Hamid Algar, it was "the first clear confrontation between the government and the people. . . . The government became increasingly suspected of treason and cooperation with foreign, non-Muslim powers; the ulama were the natural leaders of opposition to it."[4] The second and perhaps central significance of the incident itself was clearly Iranian popular resistance to foreign (in this case Russian) domination and power. These sentiments would resurface sixty years later in the Tobacco rebellion and mark the Griboyedov affair as a *transitional* (partly traditional, partly new) type of social movement.

The most serious challenge to the Qajar state in the first half of the nineteenth century came during the first five years of Nasir al-Din Shah's reign in the form of the Babi revolts. A series of armed uprisings against provincial and royal authority occurred in the widely separated areas of Mazandaran (1848-49), Zanjan (1850), and Nairiz (1850 and 1853), in addition to an unsuccessful attempt on the shah's life in Tehran in 1852. In each case poorly armed but highly motivated fighters for the new faith of Babism held out against stronger governmental forces until they met final defeat due to starvation, attrition, or deception. Debates have arisen over the traditional/religious or modern social and economic causes and significance of these revolts, as well as the composition of the social forces that followed the Babi leaders. While most writers agree that artisans and ulama participated, some see evidence of peasant mobilization as well, while others argue that *all* classes, including merchants and upper class groups, were attracted to Babism. The concept of a *transitional* social movement will help adjudicate the first of these disputes and a critical look at the available evidence will aid in clarifying the controversy on the classes and groups involved. Consideration of the ideological content of Babism and the political culture of the movement further substantiates its mixed (but not indiscriminate) social bases and transitional nature.

The founder of Babism, Mirza 'Ali Muhammad, was born into a merchant family at Shiraz in 1819. After working as a trader in Bushire, he went to Karbala in Iraq for further religious studies, becoming a disciple of Sayyid Kazim Rashti. Rashti was the leader of Shaikhism, a recent trend within Shi'ism based on the idea that there must always be an intermediary—the "Perfect Shi'i"—between the Hidden Imam and believers. After Rashti died in 1844, Mirza 'Ali Muhammad, back in Shiraz, proclaimed himself the Bab ("Gate") through whom the Hidden Imam would communicate, thus distancing his mission from orthodox Shi'ism and the Iranian ulama. He subsequently went even further, intimating that he was the expected Imam, the Mahdi, and eventually, by 1847, that he was a new prophet who superseded Muhammad and that his book, the *Bayan* (Declaration) replaced the Quran. He was at first dismissed by the ulama in Shiraz as "a lunatic of no further consequence," but as he attracted patrons and followers including leading religious and political figures, he was harassed by the ulama and finally ordered imprisoned by the shah. Rather than quelling the excitement his movement had generated, his execution in 1850 led to further uprisings which did not fully end until 1853.[5]

Of particular relevance from a social movement point of view are the social and economic doctrines of the Bab and his revolutionary lieutenants. The Bab called for the realization of a utopia of believers in the provinces of Azarbaijan, Mazandaran, Khurasan, Fars, and 'Iraq-i 'Ajam, in which only Babis (along with socially beneficial foreign merchants) would be allowed to live. He called specifically for the legalization of interest on loans, fixing of a unified money standard in the Babi lands, and inviolability of commercial correspondence. The need for good commercial roads, freedom of trade, and security for one's property were further points on which the Bab favored merchants. Tax and welfare pronouncements on the other hand advocated significant redistribution of income. Moreover, "All lands of great value and all palaces must 'return to God,' for God is the sole owner of such properties. The Bab also declared it lawful to expropriate the land of unbelievers, who could reclaim their property only if and when they convert."[6] The poor, orphans, and widows were to be properly provided for and women's status was made less unequal to that of men with respect to marriage and association. Though she denies that the Bab promised a wholly new economic order or social policy, Bayat characterizes his message as a "populist" one, which "implied a commitment to change in the poor's favor."[7]

While these reformist notions were themselves virtually unheard of in the context of mid-nineteenth century Iran, several of the Bab's disciples radicalized them still further in mobilizing the uprisings of 1848 to 1853. Various among them promoted "the abolition of all taxes, obligations, and private property and the introduction of common ownership and equality of woman and men."[8] At the 1848 pre-insurrectionary congress in Badasht, the charismatic Qurrat al-'Ain threw off her veil and spoke of the necessity of freeing women from such restrictions, declaring "the coming of resurrection and the abeyance of the sacred law" and encouraging the audience to distinguish good from evil for themselves.[9] At the same meeting the equal sharing of the community's wealth was discussed and thereafter practiced during the several uprisings. The leader of the Zanjan revolt "commanded his followers that they should all be as one family and one household; and that all things, from eatables to clothing, whatever there was, should be divided for use; and his followers did even as he commanded so that they even opened their houses to one another, and passed in and out in unity and concord."[10] The differences between the moderate reformist doctrines of the Bab and the more revolutionary ones of these leading disciples who took charge of the movement while he was in prison, may in part account for the eclectic appeal of Babism among various social strata and the widely varying analyses of its "principal" social bases.

The standard position on the social bases of the revolts is that of Minorsky, who notes that "the new preaching was addressed definitely to the middle classes, to the petty bourgeoisie, the lesser clergy, and the traders."[11] Arjomand, Amanat, and Algar all concur in the importance of the ulama in the movement (though Amanat emphasizes "the young seminarians, overwhelmingly from humble social origins," while Algar observes that the vast majority of the ulama rejected the Bab's claims).[12] Two variants on this analysis extend it in different directions to the point of contradicting each other, however. The Soviet historians Kuznetsova and Ivanov make the significant addition of the *peasantry* to the middle strata of the bazaar (ulama, artisans, merchants), while Bausani and Bayat note the presence of *upper-class* landlords, high officials, and "aristocrats" in the movement.[13] Moojan Momen caps this argument by explicitly discounting the participation of peasants (the few he finds having been manipulated by their landlords), concluding that otherwise "Those converted to Babism were drawn from all social classes with a preponderance from the ulama, who also provided the leadership of the movement."[14]

A careful look at the excellent data compiled by Momen on the participants in the three major uprisings raises some problems with his interpretation however. Table 5.1 aggregates Momen's data reclassifying unidentified rural participants as peasants, and further grouping the movement into its upper, middle, and lower class components. Fragmentary as this data is, it suggests that not only did peasants participate in the Babi revolts, they did so in great numbers. These peasants may have been led in some cases by their local landlord or mulla into the revolts, they may have been coerced to a certain extent, and they probably came overwhelmingly from agricultural districts in the vicinity of the urban centers of revolt, but rebel in large numbers they did. The next largest group of participants came, as most historians have noted, from the minor ulama (27.1 percent of the total sample), followed by artisans and small-scale ("guilded") merchants (12.3 percent). The numbers of landowners, urban officials, and high-ranking ulama were much smaller, and the large merchants (supposedly favored by the Bab's pronouncements) accounted for less than one percent of the total. The level of upper-class participation (8.8 percent) comes close to reflecting the proportion of these groups in the total population, but they were far from being preponderant within the movement, as the radical views of the Bab's lieutenants after 1848 undoubtedly alienated the

TABLE 5.1 Social Bases of the Babi Revolts

Class	Shaikh Tabarsi	Nairiz	Zanjan	Total	Percent
Nobility, Landowners, Officials	12	11	5	28	4.1
Major Ulama	14	6	7	27	3.9
Large Merchants	5	0	1	6	.9
Upper Class Totals	31	17	13	61	8.8
Minor Ulama	122	60	5	187	27.1
Artisans and Traders	48	25	12	85	12.3
Middle Class Totals	170	85	17	272	39.4
Unskilled Workers	6	3	3	12	1.7
Peasants	78	232	35	345	49.9
Tribespeople	1	0	0	1	.1
Lower Class Totals	85	235	38	358	51.8

Source: Momen, "The Social Basis of the Babi Upheavals," 162, 168, 170, recoded by the author.

wealthy. A history written by a survivor of the Zanjan uprising notes that the poor were more active than the wealthy:

> And as for the Babis, whichever of them were of the poorer classes of the town, or the traders or the sayyids or the *tullab* [religious students] or others resisted the enemy with complete constancy, and began to build fortifications. Some who were of the rich, and wealth had become a veil for them, went over to the side of the Muslims.[15]

Women were active participants at Zanjan and Nairiz, dressing as men and fighting alongside them. Indeed, at the second Nairiz uprising in 1853, they appear to have outnumbered the men, who had died in great numbers in the first revolt there.[16]

This hypothesis that the Babi movement tended to be a fairly broad populist coalition of middle and lower class strata is bolstered by the available evidence on its popular culture and the political consciousness of participants. Bayat suggests three reasons for conversion: Many saw the Bab as the long-awaited Imam, Sufis and Shaikhis saw him as a new spiritual master, reformers and revolutionaries were attracted by the prospect of social change.[17] The first two of these appealed to certain members of the ulama and bazaar classes, and the third to radical intellectuals and domi-nated classes, while peasants (and others) may have adhered for both religious and political reasons. Difficult as it is to know what the mass of followers actually thought and felt, Afshari notes that "What impressed the people were the Babis' down-to-earth sense of justice, their uncompromis-ing stands against the authorities, and their indomitable courage and fortitude."[18] The "this-worldliness" of Babism, as opposed to an emphasis on the past or the future, was "supremely attractive to many converts."[19] Bayat also discerns a degree of religious nationalism: Iranian centers of pilgrimage replaced Arab ones, the Persian *Bayan* became the new holy book, Iranian New Year's (the spring equinox) would be the first day of the Babi calendar. Despite the hierarchical tendencies implicit in Babi religious doctrine—the tripartite division into leader, elite, and a mass of ordinary followers—there were strong anti-authoritarian and egalitarian impulses in the Babis' actual social practices. Sidney Churchill, the British diplomat in Tehran, wrote in 1889: "when [the Persian] finds in [a creed] as one of its fundamental principles the liberty of thought and expression thereof, with the ultimate possibility as a result that he may shake off the oppression he suffers at the hands of the local authorities . . ., he readily affiliates himself with those holding such doctrines with the object of combating existing evils."[20] Afshari notes such terminology in their literature of 1848 as *mujahid* (fighter) and *shahid* (martyr), the opposition of *zalimin* and *mazluman* (op-pressors and oppressed), and references to the late Muhammad Shah as *Sultan-i batil* ("the false king").[21] These attitudes, taken as a whole, found resonance on several levels of Iranian political-religious subcultures: Is-lamic welfare ideals and struggles for the faith, radical millenarian hopes, artisanal solidarity and opposition politics, and peasant egalitarianism.

Yet the Babi religion and revolts did not attract a majority of the popu-lation and ultimately failed.[22] Curzon's estimate of nearly one million followers, at ten percent of the total population, is most likely far too high. Momen concludes that "In most places, only a handful of persons would be converted to the new religion"; as for the uprisings themselves he estimates there were 540 to 600 participants at Shaikh Tabarsi, one thousand in the two revolts at Nairiz, and two to three thousand at Zanjan.[23] Initial suc-cesses at each place were countered by the expeditions of increasingly strong contingents of government troops, who in each case ultimately prevailed and often followed victory with selective executions or a general massacre of the participants. The movement's aims united two powerful and usually antagonistic forces against it—its extremist religious claims alien-ated the majority of the ulama and its political ambitions spurred the Qajar state into action. The army, fortuitously reorganized by the reforming prime minister Amir Kabir in 1848, proved equal to the task of subduing the rebels at Zanjan and Nairiz in 1850.

While most scholars see Babism primarily as a religious movement activating one of the traditional Iranian political-religious orientations, that of messianic, millenarian regeneration,[24] Ivanov considers the revolts "popular uprisings . . . against the feudal system, and objectively, against the incipient enslavement of the country by foreign capital."[25] This judgment seems too forward-looking in that evidence of its "anti-foreign" content is conspicuously lacking (the Bab, it will be remembered, allowed foreign merchants in the Babi utopia and the areas of revolt were not those of heaviest foreign economic penetration by mid-century). However, the increasingly negative consequences of growing trade relations with the West in the case of artisans and the generally exploited condition of the Iranian peasantry were undoubtedly partially responsible for the presence of numerous members of these two classes in the movement. A more encompassing perspective would entail recognition of the movement's significance on several levels—as a religious challenge to Shi'a orthodoxy, a political threat to the monarchical state, and a radical egalitarian questioning of the socioeconomic order. Accepting then that the religious content of the movement resonated with traditional millenarian expectations and that its class basis was populist and social doctrines very progressive in content, the Babi revolts may be classified as an important instance of a transitional type of social movement in Qajar Iran, simultaneously sharing traits of social movements going back to the Safavid era and serving as a precursor of the Tobacco rebellion and Constitutional revolution to come. The new factor in the Iranian political economy—its crossing the threshold of dependence on the West—can be increasingly discerned in the causal background of both the Griboyedov attack and the Babi revolts.

Reform Efforts from 1800 to the 1880s: The Inadequacy of the State's Response

Partly in response to the growing intensity of internal unrest which climaxed in the Babi revolts and partly out of a complex encounter with the West, which had followed military victories with increasing political and economic pressure, Qajar bureaucrats made two comprehensive efforts to strengthen the state and develop the economy, from 1848 to 1851, and 1870 to 1880. These found an earlier, abandoned precursor in crown prince 'Abbas Mirza's attempt to modernize the army in Azarbaijan in the first part of the century. These individuals had an increasingly acute awareness of the need for reforms in Iran, but in each case their efforts ultimately came to naught, due partly to the inherent difficulties encountered and largely to the internal resistance of vested interests within the state itself, the dominant class, and the ulama. The resulting lack of change led by the state only made it more vulnerable to change initiated from below in the subsequent period from 1890 to 1910.

The first realization of a need for reform originated in the military threat posed by Russia from 1805 to 1828. Early reformers such as 'Abbas Mirza, Qa'im Maqam, and Amir Kabir all came from Azarbaijan, the "front-line" province bordering Russia. 'Abbas Mirza, in Bausani's view "the only person who might have saved Persia," died in 1833 before he could come to the throne.[26] His minister, Qa'im Maqam, served briefly as prime minister of Iran until 1835, when he was disgraced and murdered. The year 1833 then may be seen as an early political turning point, as 'Abbas Mirza's untimely death sealed off a path not taken in Iran's battle against dependency. The next, more far-reaching aim at a comprehensive reform of Iranian institutions was undertaken by Amir Kabir, prime minister from 1848 to 1851. Specific policies included the establishment of state-run factories and a college, auditing and balancing the budget, and universal conscription for the army; all aimed at strengthening the Qajar state to meet both internal social movements and external pressures. Even more damaging than the lack of personnel and technical knowledge, a powerful elite coalition of those affected by his reforms emerged to oppose him. Among them were landowners, bureaucratic officials, ulama (angry at losing pensions, the establishment of a secular institute for higher learning and other measures), and disgruntled courtiers organized in a faction around the queen mother. The latter's favorite, Mirza Aqa Khan Nuri, convinced the shah that Amir Kabir was plotting against him: "[Amir Kabir's] dismissal was soon followed by his exile, and in January, 1852, his death at the hands of royally appointed assassins."[27] This episode represents a second turning point in efforts to respond to the European challenge on a basis of equality. The next two decades saw the collapse of virtually all of Amir Kabir's projects: The army deteriorated, factories were abandoned, budget deficits reappeared. Royal inaction and conservative repression were capped by the famine of 1869-70.[28]

Reform reappeared on the agenda again in the 1870s under the auspices of prime minister Mirza Husain Khan Mushir al-Daula. He had spent the previous twenty-two years outside the country, in France, India, Tiflis, and Istanbul, where he had had the opportunity to observe both Western societies and reform efforts by and in Muslim areas. Late in 1871 he embarked on the most comprehensive set of reforms since Amir Kabir, ranging from immediate famine relief to ambitious economic development plans, governmental reorganization and military modernization. Government officials, from the most powerful princes down to lower-level bureaucrats, had their salaries reduced. These policies generated much resentment, which simmered until it found a powerful outlet in the opposition to the Reuter Concession. The concession, for railroads, telegraphs, irrigation, mining, and river navigation, was seen by modernizers as a rapid shortcut to industrialization and development after the failure of Amir Kabir's program two decades earlier. There is little doubt that Mirza Husain Khan was sincere in his advocacy of the concession, but the influential enemies he had made took this opportunity to mobilize public and royal opinion against him and it. These included factions at court who either disliked him personally, or had suffered from his reduction of salaries and stipends, or were sympathetic to the Russians who naturally opposed the concession. Certain ulama too joined out of similar motives. A few, such as the leading Tehran mujtahid Hajji Mulla 'Ali Kani, made cogent Islamic and nationalistic arguments that the concession would allow Europeans to overrun the country, turning Iran into a colony like India. The British government decided to remain neutral in the affair, preferring not to jeopardize relations with Russia and its whole position in Iran by any aggressive backing of Reuter, a private capitalist. The resulting agitation forced the prime minister's resignation and Nasir al-Din's abrupt change from an interest in liberal reforms to a more traditionally-inclined conservatism.[29] No further concessions were offered the Europeans between 1873 and the mid-1880s. We thus reach a third turning point in the fortunes of state-initiated reforms in Iran. The Reuter Concession agitation presents the paradoxical spectacle of courtiers and ulama seeking personal and corporate goals preventing a foreigner from gaining control of much of Iran's economy, while a modernizing prime minister looked to the West from inside the state to industrialize the country. In this case a mixed elite and popular movement both resisted foreign encroachment and blocked the state from modernizing, setting the stage for later popular movements, especially the Constitutional revolution, that *would* force it to modernize. In 1873 the tangled issues of reform, modernization, centralization, industrialization, and national independence were but dimly understood, and the popular movement was tinged with personal interests. In the Tobacco rebellion eighteen years later the line-up of forces would change and Iran's first truly mass nationwide social movement would clarify the underlying issues a great deal further.

The Tobacco Rebellion, 1890-1892: A Turning Point

The Tobacco rebellion was the first national mass movement directed against both the state and foreign domination. Though it might have gone further in protesting *all* concessions, as ultimately articulated it was limited to the cancellation of the unpopular tobacco monopoly granted to an English company, in which it was successful. The social forces involved were truly broad and populist—what Keddie called a "strange and unstable coalition" included participants from among the ulama, merchants, artisans, shopkeepers, intelligentsia, and the urban poor. The nature of the leadership, which was largely composed of the ulama with a leavening of other intellectuals and merchants, will be seen as the key to the limiting of the movement's demands and indicative of the sometimes conflicting, sometimes congruent goals of elements of Iran's multi-class populist alliance, a phenomenon that would emerge more clearly in the Constitutional revolution. Before exploring these central analytic issues, an overview of the sequence of the events themselves is in order.[30]

On March 8, 1890, after large bribes had been given to Iranian officials and apparently without the knowledge of the English government, the shah granted a monopoly concession on Iran's tobacco crop to Major G. F. Talbot. In exchange for 15,000 pounds sterling a year and one-quarter of the net profits paid to the shah, Talbot would be allowed to purchase all the tobacco produced in Iran for export or internal consumption. Cultivators were to register with him and the guilds of tobacco sellers had to obtain permits from him. The concession was to last for fifty years. More than any previous concession granted to a foreigner, this one directly impinged on a segment of Iran's merchants, shopkeepers, and guildspeople (as well as peasant cultivators); it also affected many hundreds of thousands of consumers (in 1890 an estimated 4,000,000 kilograms of tobacco were consumed in Iran, and 5,400,000 kilograms exported, with the 1891 crop valued at 335,900 pounds sterling). While the Iranian government tried to keep the agreement secret, Talbot sold his concession to the newly formed Imperial Tobacco Corporation of Persia (also known as the Régie), which projected 500,000 pounds sterling in net annual profits, pointing out that it would pay only 15,000 pounds rent to Iran, compared with the Turkish Régie's 630,000.

The first complaints against the concession were formally registered by the Russian minister Bützov in September 1890; he told both England and Iran that it overlooked the freedom of commerce clause in the 1828 Treaty of Turkmanchai, an argument which both parties rejected. The secret gradually became more widely known: In November 1890 the Istanbul Persian-language paper *Akhtar* wrote an article criticizing the government for allowing tobacco exports to be included (they were not in the Ottomans' monopoly) and warning that cultivators would be forced to sell to the company. In February 1891 Talbot arrived to help set up the company and the shah publicly announced the concession. Protests began almost immediately. Sixty tobacco merchants petitioned the shah in March, offering to pay a tax which would generate more revenue than the concession. On

March 6 all the Tehran tobacco merchants took bast (asylum) at 'Abd al-'Azim shrine and wrote a petition promising non-compliance with the Régie. The shah was already having doubts about the concession, but the British advised him not to cancel it, while his council was divided on the matter, with those ministers who had benefitted from the concession wanting to continue it. In March it seemed to the British diplomat Kennedy that the Russian legation and Russian tobacco merchants would acquiesce to the concession, and in May the British consul at Tabriz reported favorably on the attitude of Iranian merchants there. But a serious opposition had already begun with protests at Shiraz in April 1891, during Ramazan. Crowds gathered at the telegraph office and a shrine to protest the arrival of the company's agents, and the governor's tribal troops opened fire, killing several people, including a woman and a little girl, and wounding many more. The deported cleric Sayyid 'Ali Akbar went to Bushire where he met Jamal al-Din al-Afghani, the pan-Islamic critic of the shah. Afghani wrote a letter castigating the shah for his concessions to Europeans, which the sayyid took to the leading Shi'a mujtahid Hajji Mirza Hasan Shirazi in Samarra (Iraq), who would later play a crucial role in the movement.

In August and September the movement exploded in Azarbaijan, Iran's major tobacco-producing area. The ulama of Tabriz preached against the concession and telegrams and petitions were sent to the shah. The shah again wanted to cancel but both Amin al-Sultan and the British chargé d'affaires Kennedy argued that he must stand firm as his authority was being attacked. On September 4 a large crowd assembled; only a telegram from the shah promising cancellation of the concession defused the situation. In Mashhad, meanwhile, in early October the shah combined the threat of military force with an offer to postpone the concession in Khurasan province for six months, and after five days the protests subsided. These struggles were paralleled and then surpassed by the movement in Isfahan. In September merchants had petitioned the powerful pro-English governor Zil al-Sultan, while the leading mujtahid Aqa Najafi preached against the concession. The governor's threat of reprisals quieted the situation for a time. On November 21 Aqa Najafi and his brother called a demonstration during which they declared tobacco unclean. A boycott was announced and the people of Isfahan ceased smoking.

In late November protests and unrest resumed in Tehran and Tabriz. On about December 2 a nationwide boycott of tobacco started when a fatva attributed to the spiritual leader Shirazi in Samarra was made public. It said: "In the name of God, the Merciful, the Forgiving. Today the use of *tanbaku* and tobacco in any form is reckoned as war against the Imam of the Age (may God hasten his glad Advent!)."[31] The boycott was extremely successful, extending even to the shah's wives and servants, and to Christians and

Jews among the non-Muslim population. More desperate than ever, the shah oscillated between heavy-handed actions and negotiations with the movement. The government sought at first to cancel only the internal monopoly (this was offered on December 18), but on December 25 placards appeared in the bazaar threatening declaration of a holy war. Events reached their climax early in January 1892. On January 3 the government ordered Tehran's leading mujtahid, Mirza Hasan Ashtiani, to either end the boycott by smoking in public, or to leave the city. When he prepared to leave the next day, crowds gathered at his house after closing the bazaar, to prevent the army from forcing him to depart. Some 4,000 men and women, led by sayyids, marched towards the royal palaces. After first ignoring orders to do so, troops fired on the crowd, killing seven or more people. The crowd calmed down only when the shah sent a message saying Ashtiani could stay and reaffirming that the concession was cancelled. Ashtiani urged the people to disperse, promising they would reconvene if the matter wasn't settled within two days. On January 5 the Régie agreed to the cancellation of its concession, realizing that not to do so would lead to an untenable situation in which further bloodshed and perhaps revolution would be inevitable. The atmosphere remained tense until January 26, when the town crier announced the end of the ban on tobacco. The Tobacco rebellion had ended.

The social forces that made the rebellion comprised the first very broad, fully mass movement in Iranian social history. Keddie writes of "The strange and unstable coalition of ulama, nationalists, discontented merchants and city populations, and powerful domestic and foreign interests who were opposed to the government."[32] These "city populations" should be disaggregated a bit further: The urban crowds that engaged in the decisive confrontations included, in addition to merchants and ulama, artisans, small shopkeepers, and some of the urban poor, both women and men. The tobacco merchants who were most obviously affected by the concession comprised several groups: small-scale retail tobacco dealers, large wholesale merchants and exporters, those with investments in cultivation and those engaged in processing tobacco.[33] According to its prospectus, the Régie intended to satisfy both consumers and cultivators, apparently at the expense of the merchant middle-men. Urban consumers were not convinced of this claim, as they supported the boycott in overwhelming numbers. Nor were the cultivators won over as allies to the company; according to Keddie, "In the tobacco growing areas the peasants were also made to believe that they would suffer great losses."[34] The widespread participation of the urban lower classes is suggested by the British consul Paton in Tabriz: "the agitation ... has evidently been taken up strongly by the whole population, high and low."[35] Finally, the mass movement involved women as well as men. The crowds that faced royal troops in Shiraz and Tehran included a number of women: A woman and a girl were killed at Shiraz, while women were active in the determining events of January 1892 in Tehran.

The political culture of the Tobacco rebellion affirms its populist social bases. The mosques were generally the place where artisans and merchants would congregate whenever they closed their shops in protest. There they would listen to stories of the life and deaths of 'Ali and Husain in an emotionally charged atmosphere. Bodies of dead demonstrators would be carried to the mosques, further agitating the crowds. Public attitudes toward the shah evinced a humorous, deeply-rooted anti-authoritarian strain. On the day an envoy was scheduled to enter Tabriz with a message from Nasir al-Din Shah, a crowd of people paraded a dog through the streets with a letter attached to its neck bearing the shah's autograph. Satire of the court and ruling class was expressed through various popular acts; Afshari notes that "a very imaginative and deriding poetry circulated in Tehran and women and children took an active part in spreading it around."[36] Such actions are telling indicators of the growth in political consciousness of the urban population as a result of their struggle against the concession.

The Tobacco rebellion was led by the ulama, now in an emergent alliance with members of the radical, secular nationalist intelligentsia. Some individuals from the bureaucratic elite also played a role, but this was out of rivalry with other ministers or due to pro-Russian sentiments.[37] It was the ulama who provided the principal leadership of the movement, often at the request of aggrieved merchants and guildspeople.[38] Though there were some exceptions and limits to their unity and demands (to be treated below) and though their motives may have been mixed, their role was generally one of decisive intervention on the side of the rebellion. The British minister Lascelles reported on December 22, 1891: "I have been informed by persons long resident in Persia that they have been astonished at this assertion of power on the part of the Mollahs, both as regards their opposition to the Government and the implicit obedience which the people have yielded to their commands."[39] A network of ulama extended downward from the most eminent mujtahid, Mirza Hasan Shirazi in Iraq, who had become the sole marja'-i taqlid (source of imitation) in the 1870s, to the clerical leaders in each of the cities. Use of the telegraph facilitated communications among them and word then spread in each city through them to the neighborhood mullas and general population. The religious feelings animating the movement had several bases. Keddie suggests "there was bound to be opposition to the handling of an item of intimate use by unbelievers. According to stricter Shi'is, close contact with an article handled by unbelievers was defiling."[40] A more solid legal argument against the concession saw it as an unlawful monopoly which restricted the freedom of Muslim merchants.

Shirazi telegraphed the shah in September 1891 that the concessions "are the cause of the ruin of order in the country, and they oppress the subjects."[41] There was a general concern that Islam was endangered, as the Shiraz mujtahid Mirza Muhammad 'Ali told the British diplomat there: "Doubtless the corporation would flood the country with Europeans who would have constant intercourse with the people to undermine their religion."[42] This analysis reached its logical conclusion in underground calls for jihad. Though armed confrontations ultimately did not take place, the disciplined observance of Shirazi's fatva prohibiting the use of tobacco signalled the symbolic, inner aspect of jihad in the movement: a striving against evil with all one's being. Much of the population was doubtless inspired by the general position of the ulama that Islam itself was being attacked by foreigners and that the shah was doing nothing to defend the faith.

A key mediator between the religious opposition of the ulama and the incipient nationalism of the intelligentsia was Sayyid Jamal al-Din al-Afghani. At various intervals between 1886 and 1890 he had spoken both to the shah and to "all classes" of people in Iran of the urgent need for legal and human rights, safeguards of life and property, freedoms of thought and the press.[43] In January 1891 he was expelled from the country after an anonymous letter reached the shah upbraiding him for selling the resources of Iran to foreigners and failing to protect religion. Before leaving he formed a secret society for the twin purposes of bringing about internal reforms and reducing foreign control.[44] His May letter to Shirazi castigates the shah in religious terms for his concessions to Russia and Britain: "In short this criminal has offered the provinces of the Persian land to auction amongst the Powers, and is selling the realms of Islam and the abodes of Muhammad and his household (on whom be greeting and salutation) to foreigners."[45] Shirazi's telegram to the shah in September made arguments along similar lines. Since Shirazi's leadership was decisive in the boycott of tobacco, Afghani as well can be seen to have played a pivotal role in the rebellion.

The secondary leadership of the movement came from a new group, the intelligentsia, some of whom were followers of Afghani. They included journalists, writers, diplomats, and bureaucrats, members of the middle class who had received a secular education or travelled abroad. One group was composed of Azari-speaking Russian subjects living in the Caucasus. Two newspapers, the Istanbul-based *Akhtar* and Malkam Khan's *Qanun* from England, helped expose the concession and generate opposition to it. *Qanun's* first issues, appearing in 1890, voiced a range of criticisms of state and society in Iran. On July 18 it addressed the prime minister, "By what law do you sell these rights and privileges of our State to foreign adventurers? . . . How do you dare to sell to unbelievers the means of livelihood of the Muslims?"[46] Another relevant document is "A Petition from Iranian Reformers to the Foreign Representatives in Tehran," which calls for "the establishment of the organic laws of the land" which should be based on "the just and human application of our Shariat [Islamic law]."[47] Behind these fervent words (with their implicit wish for an alliance between intellectuals and the ulama) loomed the wider range of reforms sought by the intelligentsia: an end to foreign economic and political hegemony in Iran, legal limits on the autocratic powers of the shah, and development of educational, judicial, and other institutions along somewhat ambiguous "modern" lines. The nature of the intelligentsia's alliance with the ulama and the less than total congruence of their demands played a role in limiting the outcome of the movement.

What accounts for the more limited outcome of the Tobacco rebellion then, given these larger demands and the opinions of observers regarding its revolutionary potential?[48] One element was the emergence of splits and wavering among certain members of the ulama at the last moment. There had not, of course, been total unanimity to begin with: In December 1891 Sayyid 'Abdullah Bihbihani, opposed to the activism of Shirazi and possibly bribed by the Régie, had gone so far as to actually smoke in the mosque while preaching.[49] The Imam Jum'a of Tehran, a relative of the shah, as well as the key ulama in Mashhad, refused to back the protest. But beyond these scattered non-participants, Ashtiani himself moderated his demands on January 5, 1892, when the government and Régie agreed to cancel the concession. This may have been a prudent political compromise on his part, or it may have been due to money or threats (or both) coming from the government. Whatever the exact reason, Ashtiani wrote to Shirazi urging him not to bring up the issue of other foreign concessions.[50] Shortly afterwards greater pensions were paid to certain members of the ulama, while others were newly added to the government's list. A second element in the end of the movement was that the Russians ceased their encouragement of it as soon as the tobacco concession was cancelled, naturally not wanting to see any larger steps taken against foreign power in Iran generally.[51] Finally, it should be noted that the intelligentsia, bound in some cases to a strategy of "using" the ulama and Islamically-couched appeals to further their aims while remaining in the background of events, had less influence in pushing a broader agenda for change (on which they themselves were far from in agreement) when leading ulama brought the movement to a close.

The outcome then was a victory within firm limits. By focusing on a single concession which affected much of the population, the movement became widespread and determined. But by not pushing beyond this for an end to all foreign concessions in Iran and dismissal of the ministers responsible for them, the victory was largely symbolic, as Keddie has pointed out. Likewise Afshari considers it a "limited-objective" type of revolt, and Lambton "not a revolutionary movement."[52] These observations are retrospectively true, but the Tobacco rebellion was also a victory for the populist coalition that made it, demonstrating a newly-found capacity to resist both the shah and a foreign power. Political consciousness clarified itself and advanced considerably in the course of the struggle, and issues were articulated which would resurface in the Constitutional revolution.

The consequences and aftermath of the rebellion provide evidence of the difficulties of bringing about change within the restricted parameters of dependency. Total compensation was finally fixed in April 1892 at 500,000 pounds; since the company was to give its assets in Iran, allegedly worth 139,000 pounds, to the government, it would appear that Iran's net loss was 346,000 pounds sterling, for which it got nothing of value, a grossly unfair settlement in view of Talbot's original investment of a mere 15,000 pounds. The shah had to borrow the 500,000 pounds from the British bank, Iran's first major foreign debt, a significant milestone in its dependence on the West. In 1892 the Iranian government quietly granted an export monopoly on tobacco to a French company discretely located in Istanbul. The clergy were consulted on this and in some cases given pensions. Merchants seem to have contented themselves with control over the internal markets. Nor did the Russians this time object. This strange afterlife of the concession underlines the *symbolic* content of the movement.

A second consequence highlighting change within continuity was the reversal of the British and Russian positions in Iran. There was a marked shift from British influence in the 1880s to Russian in the 1890s at the Qajar court, as the prime minister Amin al-Sultan adopted pro-Russian policies in place of his earlier pro-British ones. While it is certainly true that the British had lost much of their political position in Iran, the result was not a gain in the state's freedom to maneuver, but rather a closer dependence politically and economically on an even more reactionary Western power, Russia. This would have important repercussions on the balance of social forces in the Constitutional revolution fifteen years later, as the Russians would now be the targets rather than the (self-interested) supporters of a popular social movement in Iran. Internally, meanwhile, the shah's "popularity" plunged and the state's fiscal problems were exacerbated. Peasants suffered as taxes went up generally to pay for the loan and to address the budget deficits. Finally, on May 1, 1896 Nasir al-Din Shah, after forty-eight years of rule, was assassinated by Mirza Muhammad Reza of Kirman, a follower of Afghani. Thus was Afghani's 1891 call for the cutting off of the shah's head carried out. This, too, represented change within continuity, as the new shah Muzaffar al-Din inherited a host of problems with no effective policy instruments to meet them, while a huge popular movement loomed on the horizon.

The Constitutional Revolution, 1905-1911: An Opportunity Missed

The centerpiece of social change in the Qajar period was the massive upheaval fought between 1905 and 1911 known as the Constitutional revolution or movement. After reviewing the course of events, the present analysis focuses on assessing the degree and nature of participation by various groups and classes on both sides as the key to understanding the causes and outcome of the revolution. This will enable us to see it as an urban, multi-class, *populist* social movement, in which the key factors at work were the differential Western impact on social groups and classes, the internal complexity of the Iranian social structure and state, and the external pressures brought to bear by Britain and especially Russia.

The Course of Events[53]

After a brief liberal phase, the reign of Muzaffar al-Din Shah from 1898 on witnessed a replay of the recurrent problems of late Qajar society: a state burdened by the shah's need for European loans to finance extravagant trips abroad, combined with continued urban unrest generated by high bread prices and the arbitrary rule of grasping and inflexible provincial governors, and in the capital the new government of 'Ain al-Daula which took over from Amin al-Sultan in 1903-4. Though inflation fluctuated, the major northern cities experienced high rates in the 1890s; a sudden deflation in the years 1900-1905 only led to worse unemployment and an economic downturn.[54] Merchants were upset by the customs revision of 1903 that favored Russian goods and the use of Belgian customs administrators under Joseph Naus since 1899. By 1905, the pensions of certain ulama were three years in arrears and the government proposed tightening its control over vaqfs. Meanwhile inspiration was drawn from the Japanese victory over Russia in their 1904-5 war: It seemed to some intellectuals significant that the only Asian constitutional state had defeated the major Western non-constitutional one, and that segment of the Iranian population aware of the news undoubtedly enjoyed the reverses of their overbearing northern neighbor, which continued with the 1905 Russian revolution. Secret societies of secular intellectual and clerical leaders formed in the capital and elsewhere to discuss these developments.

The existence of these grievances and the abuses that caused them meant that a large portion of the urban population was prepared for the confrontation with the government that came in 1905. A series of initially minor incidents touched off three increasingly serious protests in Tehran beginning in April 1905 and culminating in the grant of a national assembly and constitution in August 1906. On April 26, 1905 two hundred moneylenders and merchants of Tehran closed their shops and demanded a range of reforms, including repayment of their loans to the state and dismissal of the unpopular Naus. The shah defused the situation with promises, but no action was taken for the rest of the year. On December 11, 1905 two prominent sugar merchants were beaten for charging high prices. Some two thousand ulama, students, tradespeople, and merchants took bast at 'Abd al-'Azim on December 13, and before this ended a month later, their demands had escalated to dismissal of the prime minister and the establishment of an *'adalatkhana* (House of Justice). The shah gave in, but again followed through only on the lesser demands. The third and gravest set of protests came in the summer of 1906. On July 11 the prime minister tried to expel a popular preacher; a crowd formed and troops fired, killing a sayyid. Further confrontations the next day led to fifteen or more deaths. This massacre sharpened the demand for a House of Justice. In the next week two enormous basts were started: Some one thousand of the ulama, led by Sayyid Muhammad Tabatabai and Sayyid 'Abdullah Bihbihani, left Tehran for Qum, ninety miles away, taking their religious and legal services on strike with them. Meanwhile, with the permission of the British chargé d'affaires Grant Duff, merchants, artisans, ulama, and students occupied the gardens and grounds of the British Legation in Tehran. By August 1 this group numbered 14,000 people. They demanded the removal of 'Ain al-Daula, the promulgation of a code of laws, and the recall of the ulama from Qum. With the army starting to show sympathy for the bastis, the shah dismissed his prime minister on July 30 and agreed to invite the ulama back, but the protestors now demanded a constitution and a representative national assembly (*majlis*). In early August the shah issued the order granting an assembly.

A provisional body was set up to draft the electoral code and organize the establishment of a majlis. Over 2,000 people took part. The electoral code provided for a majlis chosen by six categories of electors: "(i) Princes and the Qájár tribe: (ii) Doctors of Divinity and Students: (iii) Nobles and Notables: (iv) Merchants: (v) Landed proprietors and peasants: (vi) Tradeguilds."[55] "Landed proprietors and peasants" had to possess property worth 1,000 tumans (200 pounds sterling), effectively disenfranchising the peasantry. Merchants and artisans were required to have established businesses, which ruled out workers and the urban poor. Women could not vote. The majlis opened on October 7 with the Tehran delegates present. The Fundamental Law (the first part of the constitution) was ready by late October, but Muzaffar al-Din Shah signed it only on his deathbed, on December 30, 1906. He died January 8, 1907.

From January 1907 to June 1908 a sharp conflict developed between the new, more autocratic Muhammad 'Ali Shah and the increasingly self-confident and politically aware majlis. In February the assembly forced the dismissal of Naus from his posts and detained him until he gave an account of his actions in office. The shah scored a victory in April by bringing back the conservative Amin al-Sultan as prime minister. In July a serious split developed among the ulama when Shaikh Fazlullah Nuri began an agitation against the constitutionalist leaders as "atheists, freethinkers, Bábís and the like"; other leading ulama opposed him. Matters came to a dramatic head on August 31, when the Anglo-Russian agreement dividing Iran into "spheres of influence" (while formally promising to guarantee its sovereignty) was signed at St. Petersburg. The same day (yet before news of the agreement had circulated) a young radical member of a secret society assassinated the prime minister Amin al-Sultan. Iranian public opinion was generally outraged at the agreement between Russia and England. The shah meanwhile had to take note of public opposition to his reactionary policies; this climate permitted the majlis to force his signing of the Supplementary Fundamental Laws (the second part of the constitution) on October 7, which gave it wide legislative powers at the expense of the monarchy. Later that month it passed its first budget, with greatly reduced pensions for the court and its favorites, and abolition of the abuses of tax-farming and tiyuls in land tenure. The shah then took more desperate action, dismissing the cabinet on December 14-15 and inciting a royalist crowd to threaten the majlis building, while he demanded the assembly's dissolution. The majlis was defended by armed volunteers however, and the bazaars went on strike. The shah was forced to back down, taking an oath before the assembly to observe the constitution.

Tension mounted between Muhammad 'Ali Shah and the constitutional movement in 1908. In June the shah moved to just outside Tehran and rallied his tribal and urban lower-class supporters. The Russian ambassador, endorsed by the British chargé d'affaires, issued warnings that anti-shah actions would not be tolerated. On June 11 Muhammad 'Ali declared martial law. The bazaar went on strike and constitutionalist volunteers occupied the Baharistan (the majlis building). On June 23 1,000 Iranian Cossacks under the command of their Russian officers surrounded the Baharistan and the adjacent Sipahsalar mosque. Heavy guns bombarded the majlis and its defenders, who were under orders not to shoot at the Russian officers opposing them for fear of touching off a full-scale Russian intervention. Several hundred volunteers were killed before the shah's forces carried the day; leading constitutionalists were arrested, exiled, executed, or fled. The Russian Colonel Liakhov of the Cossack Brigade was made military governor of Tehran (though an Iranian later nominally replaced him). Despite demands from the provinces, by November the shah had reneged on his promises to England and Russia to reconvene the majlis and declared that the constitution would not be restored. In this he was assisted by the anti-constitutionalist mujtahid Nuri.

Meanwhile the locus of resistance to the shah had shifted to Tabriz. Soon after the June coup the tribal leader Rahim Khan entered the city to assert authority in the shah's name. Local constitutionalists—artisans, merchants, and others—began to oppose this immediately, forming units of *mujahidin* (fighters). The shah's forces were expelled by October, after which they attempted to blockade the city. By November 1908 constitutionalist forces were in control of other cities in Azarbaijan province, while the local *anjuman* (popular assembly) governed Tabriz. In February 1909 however the royalists' blockade became complete. By April people were dying of starvation. England finally agreed that Russian troops should end the siege of Tabriz, and on April 29 they marched into the city to protect Russian and foreign citizens, dispersing the shah's tribal blockaders. Though they no longer faced starvation, the residents soon were unhappy with their Russian occupiers.

Despite its ultimate failure the resistance of Tabriz bought time for other provincial cities to revive the constitutionalist opposition, especially at Rasht and Isfahan. In early 1909 the Bakhtiari tribe revolted when the shah tried to change their il-khan. They soon gained control of Isfahan and declared for the constitutionalist side. At Rasht on the Caspian, social democrats from Russian Azarbaijan together with local Armenian and Muslim radicals launched an attack against the governor. When they succeeded, they invited a wealthy landowner known as the Sipahdar ("Commander")—who had recently abandoned the shah's forces at Tabriz—to assume control of their movement. In May the constitutionalist army of Rasht reached Qazvin, and the shah agreed to English and Russian "recommendations" to re-establish constitutional government. But the Sipahdar also wanted foreign troops to evacuate, the shah's own irregulars to disarm and dismissal of certain reactionary ministers. When these demands were not met, the northern constitutionalists and southern Bakhtiaris began to converge on the capital in early July, despite dire British and Russian warnings and the landing of more Russian troops at Anzali. On July 13 the Bakhtiari and Rasht volunteers entered Tehran with minimal initial resistance and set up headquarters symbolically in the ruins of the Baharistan. After two days of fighting in which 500 men were killed or wounded, Muhammad 'Ali took refuge at the Russian legation, while the Cossack Brigade surrendered to the new minister of war, the Sipahdar. On July 18 the eleven-year-old son of Muhammad 'Ali was crowned Ahmad Shah and a regent was appointed by an extraordinary grand council of constitutionalist deputies and military leaders, ulama, princes, and notables, thus bringing Muhammad 'Ali's counterrevolutionary reign to a close.

In August 1909 elections were held in Tehran for the second majlis. The new electoral law lowered the voting age and the wealth qualifications, but paradoxically this led to a more elite body. The representation of the provinces in the majlis was also increased and seats were reserved for each of five tribes, and for one representative each from the Armenian, Nestorian, Zoroastrian, and Jewish communities. 1910 provided a lull in the dramatic events that had transpired in each of the five previous years, but ominous tensions arose both within the constitutionalist ranks and between the majlis and foreign powers. On July 15 Sayyid 'Abdullah Bihbihani, the cleric who had played a conspicuous role in touching off the revolution in 1905-6, was assassinated, and in retaliation two secular radicals were murdered on August 2. These events exacerbated a growing split between radicals and moderates in the majlis, and alienated certain ulama from the movement. Russia kept 3,000 troops in the north while the British created controversy with an ultimatum (later toned down) that they would organize a security force in the south if order wasn't restored. Tribal unrest also plagued the provinces into the fall, in part stirred up by ex-shah Muhammad 'Ali, who left Russia surreptitiously for Rome.

In early 1911 Iran reached agreement on bringing in sixteen American financial experts under W. Morgan Shuster to organize the tax administration. Shuster arrived in May and quickly gained the trust of progressives in the majlis with his independent stance toward Russia and Britain. By June he had been granted extensive powers over the budget, tax collection, and customs as treasurer-general of Iran. Russia soon objected however to his proposal to place a new treasury gendarmerie for the collection of taxes under British command. In July internal stability was shaken when Salar al-Daula seized Hamadan and proclaimed his brother Muhammad 'Ali as shah. Several days later the ex-shah himself appeared in Iran with tribal supporters and tacit Russian backing.[56] When the government protested this violation of its 1909 protocol with England and Russia, the two powers replied that it was an internal Iranian affair. In August, however, Muhammad 'Ali's forces were defeated by Bakhtiari and Armenian fighters. The next month Muhammad 'Ali took refuge on a Russian ship on the Caspian and went to Russian soil. Salar al-Daula continued to capture cities in September with an army of Kurds and Lurs, but was defeated twice at the end of the month and again in November, definitively ending the restoration attempt.

A new crisis exploded in the fall however, this one caused by continued tensions between the reformer Shuster and the Russian government. Clashes occurred in October between Shuster's treasury gendarmes and Cossacks answering to the Russian consul. Shuster's efforts to enforce tax collection against the elite also earned him the enmity of powerful Iranian statesmen, including the Sipahdar and 'Ala al-Daula. At the end of November the prime minister Samsam al-Saltana approached both the British and Russian legations with a proposal to use Bakhtiari forces to disband the majlis; both promised not to intervene if he did. The Russians then took the initiative, issuing a second ultimatum demanding the dismissal of Shuster, assurances that foreigners would not be hired without Anglo-Russian approval, and an indemnity for the costs of maintaining Russian troops in the north. This was unanimously rejected by the majlis which voted instead to extend its two-year session then ending until the resolution of the crisis. Huge anti-Russian demonstrations took place in Tehran as Russian troops advanced toward the city. As the crisis deepened the Russians softened their terms slightly, though continuing to insist on Shuster's dismissal, while the majlis appointed a five-member commission to work with the cabinet, which wanted to accept the ultimatum. On December 22 this committee and the cabinet accepted the Russian demands. In the next three days the regent dissolved the majlis and sent a force to clear its buildings, while Shuster was informed of his dismissal.

Resistance to Russian coercion was initially widespread, but it was met with brutal repression. At Tabriz, forty-four leading constitutionalists were executed. Executions also occurred at Rasht. Up to 20,000 Russian troops remained in northern Iran to disband anjumans, establish press censorship and restore landlord control over rural areas. The Sipahdar worked closely with them for which he was rewarded in his home area on the Caspian. The British did nothing to soften these measures, garrisoning the south and finding their own collaborators among the Bakhtiari in the central government. Abrahamian notes that "National opposition to foreign intervention was transformed from overt resistance to covert resentment."[57] After six tumultuous years, the Constitutional revolution was finally checkmated.

The Causes of the Revolution

The Constitutional revolution, like other revolutions, had multiple, complex causes. As chapter one argued generally, and chapter three showed with respect to the fall of the Safavids, these consisted of an instance of *intertwined* economic, political, and ideological crises in the Iranian social formation. But now we may see these crises as caused largely by the effects of *dependence*, unlike in earlier periods of Iranian social change. Most classes and groups in the Iranian social formation—and all of those in the constitutionalist alliance—had grievances as a result of a century of increasingly intense contact with the West. Thus, merchants had watched while their control of the export trade and some internal markets fell into Western hands; though a few large ones had enriched themselves through profitable collaboration with foreign companies or internal monopoly of a product, the vast majority of medium and small traders had lost much of their standing. Artisans had suffered the collapse of their livelihood in many sectors, especially the formerly central handicraft textile one, under a flood of European imports. The lower urban classes and working class labored (when they could find work) in a setting characterized by high food prices and unemployment. Peasants saw their standard of living inexorably decline as cultivation shifted from food staples to export crops and rising land values enmeshed them in a cash-based relation to their landlords that increased their indebtedness. Tribespeople witnessed the circumscribing of their economic activity by the new value placed on urban and agricultural production, compounded by diminishing political-military roles in the nineteenth century and the ravages of natural disasters such as drought-induced famines. Two key groups—the ulama and the nascent intelligentsia—increasingly conceptualized these disasters as signs that Islam itself was in danger or that Iran was falling prey to a more economically powerful, industrialized West; in either case the Qajar state and foreign powers were perceived as the responsible parties. Dependence *was* an economic process but one that had far-reaching political consequences, and was experienced and filtered through the value systems and cultural beliefs present in Iranian society.

So many groups and classes had particular grievances that it was fairly easy to magnify a series of incidental confrontations in 1905-6 into a large mass movement opposed to the state. This was because the state was so clearly identifiable with the hated Qajar monarchy, whose legitimacy had steadily eroded over the course of a century, from the defeats to Russia that provoked the Griboyedov massacre, to the failure of reform efforts from the 1830s to the 1880s, to the concession-mongering that touched off the Reuter concession agitation and the Tobacco rebellion. The emperor retained only the barest shreds of legitimating cloth by the turn of the twentieth century. The crisis of the state was certainly political (weakness versus the West, repression and autocracy internally), economic (dependence on loans and foreign trade, loss of control over the customs, etc.), and finally ideological (the mass perception that the state had failed to protect either the nation's interests or its Islamic identity).

Crucially, too, the world-system situation in 1905 was one of special opportunity for the embryonic revolutionary alliance. Russia, which had gained the upper hand in the long struggle with Britain for pre-eminent control in Iran's affairs, was just at that moment weakened and distracted by its own internal and external crises (the 1905 revolution, the war with Japan). Britain, which had played the opposite role in 1890-92, could now side with the groups that might erode the Russians' supremacy—the merchants and oppositional ulama—and moreover, possessed the added ideological cachet of being a constitutional state itself. Thus, while top British foreign policy makers such as Grey may have been nearly as imperialistic in Iran as Russia (though admittedly with an eye more on India than Iran's value to them per se), the man on the spot in Tehran, Grant Duff, offered the bastis asylum and support at the British Legation in the critical months of July and August 1906. At that point, with the whole capital paralyzed by a general economic strike and the exodus of the religious authorities to Qum, the tiny Iranian intelligentsia scored one of its greatest victories by raising the stakes of the movement to demand a constitution and a national assembly. With 14,000 merchants and artisans opposed to it, with the ulama in symbolic defiance withdrawn from the scene, and with its own small army wavering in its support, the Qajar state caved in precipitously and the revolution marked moments of triumph: the August 5, 1906 grant of an assembly and the December 30, 1906 signing of the Fundamental Law which the assembly produced in the fall. Iran was in transition from despotic state to constitutional monarchy. These elements of an explanation, then, refer back to the broad framework of social change adumbrated in diagram 1.3 of chapter one:[58] Dependent development results from the interplay of external world pressures with internal modes of production, altering social structure. The actions of a repressive state that anchor this new structure may be challenged by political cultures of opposition to the process. The result under favorable circumstances such as the distraction of Russia in 1905 and the extra hardship caused by further economic dislocation after 1900 was a broad-based movement for social change.

Social Forces in the Constitutional Revolution

Quite interesting and complex debates exist regarding the nature of the Constitutional revolution and the social forces that contended in it. The standard interpretations for many years in both the basic works of Iranian historians such as Kasravi, Kirmani, and Malikzadeh, and Western accounts from Sykes onward stressed the role of ideas, especially Western concepts of constitutionalism and nationalism. This view highlights the role of intellectuals in the revolution. Orthodox Marxists, both Iranian and Soviet, by contrast, have generally interpreted the events as a bourgeois revolution led by a merchant class blocked in its aspirations for democracy by landed classes and imperial powers. These positions, paradoxically, are not incompatible if one considers the intelligentsia's ideas as representing the Iranian bourgeoisie.[59]

More recently historians of several perspectives have constructed more complex explanations. The works of Keddie and Lambton, outside the Marxist tradition, correctly identify the several classes in alliance in the revolution, though more in empirical fashion than with an underlying theoretical model. Closer to the Marxist perspective, Abrahamian argues that the key social forces were two "middle classes"—a traditional bazaar-centered one which he terms "the propertied middle class" including merchants, artisans, and ulama, and a modern intelligentsia, with the former far more powerful. Afshari radicalizes this position by stressing that the core of the movement was made up of the pishivaran—artisans, traders, small shopkeepers.[60] This is an advance in that it breaks down Abrahamian's "propertied middle class" into its constituent elements, not all of whom had similar interests or outlooks. Recent important revisionist work has highlighted the ambiguous role played by the ulama in shaping public opinion.[61]

If we examine the actions of each class or group in the Constitutional revolution we find that it was fought above all by the artisans and intelligentsia, against the court, foreign powers and landlords, and that the merchants were divided and ultimately wavered, as did the ulama, many of whom gradually went into opposition to the movement. The tribal chiefs fought on both sides, as did probably the urban marginal classes. Peasants and tribespeople were largely not involved, although some peasants were and some tribal armies were engaged on either side. The working class gave its support to the revolution but was numerically limited in impact. So, rather than a bourgeois revolution, it was more of a popular, democratic, mass urban movement fought by a pre-capitalist class in decline (the artisans) and two small capitalist classes in formation (the intelligentsia and working class), and *led* by two classes or groups that were divided (ulama and merchants). Notable also is the substantial participation of women and the regional location and ethnic identity of particularly radical currents in the Azari Turkish-speaking northwestern province of Azarbaijan, as well as the local Persian dialect areas of the Caspian. The revolution thus reposed on a *mixed* alliance in terms of classes and their constituent modes of production. This coalition may be termed an urban, multi-class, populist alliance. The line-up of social forces then consists of a constitutionalist alliance (artisans, intelligentsia, and workers, and some merchants, ulama, and marginalized urban classes), the royalist social base (the court and its retainers and some of the ulama, tribes, and marginalized urban classes), the less involved peasant and tribal masses, and foreign powers.

Iran's merchants played an important role in launching the Constitutional revolution—they were prominent at the three basts of 1905-6 and in the first majlis. Dissatisfied with the bankruptcy of the Qajar state, desirous of security of property, many of them also had grievances with foreign capital's advantageous tariff rates and domination of banking, though some (the "comprador" fraction in the import/export business) had profitable relations with foreign trading firms. Merchants were particularly active at Tabriz, helping organize and fund the Tabriz resistance, while those abroad, especially at Istanbul, also supported the movement. Their political non-representation propelled them into the movement, but their elite economic status ultimately caused many to feel threatened by it, both as landowners and as businessmen. Smaller-scale merchants probably tended to support the revolution longer, though some must have followed the ulama out of the movement and others were alienated by the continued political and economic instability. Larger merchants and those tied to foreign capital probably went into opposition sooner and more forcefully. On the eve of the coup in 1911 the German ambassador in Tehran wrote: "At the bottom of their hearts the great landowners of the country, the clergy, the wealthier businessmen, are all sick and tired of the ruling parliamentary demagogy."[62] Iran's merchants, then, should be seen as a class divided in its sympathies, which ultimately withdrew much of its early support for the revolution.

Artisans, craftspersons, apprentices, small shopkeepers—all known as the pishivaran—and the nascent urban working class provided the mass backbone of the revolution. From the huge Tehran bast of 1906 to the futile resistance to the Russians at Tabriz in 1911, artisans were in the forefront of the movement. They closed their shops, joined anjumans, faced armed troops, and composed constitutionalist crowds. The reasons for their participation are not far to seek: the massive erosion of craft jobs under the flood of European imports. Kirmani in fact judges the textile guild "the most revolutionary group" after religious students in the July 1906 confrontations with the army;[63] textile workers had been the most decimated craft in the nineteenth century. At the Legation bast, each guild, "even the cobblers, walnut sellers, and tinkers," had a tent.[64] Tehran's 105 guilds were given thirty-two seats in the first majlis, to the merchants' ten. Sellers of books, lamps, rubble, and watchmakers made many speeches in the first majlis, ranging themselves with the progressives. Sattar Khan, a horse-dealer, and Baqir Khan, a stone mason, led the Tabriz armed resistance which relied on the artisans and shopkeepers for its mass base in the mujahidin units. After the 1909 restoration of the constitution, however, the guilds were effectively barred from representation as such in the assembly and this undoubtedly undermined the militancy of the second majlis. Nevertheless, in the repression at Tabriz in 1911-12, eighteen out of thirty-five Tabrizis executed were artisans and shopkeepers.[65] For the most part then, the artisans did not waver, but rather were cut out of the new coalition of tribal leaders and other elite elements that gained the upper hand in the movement's last stages.

Iran's small working class also embraced the revolution enthusiastically, engaging in a vast number of strike activities from 1906 to 1910 and organizing in Iran's first trade unions. Fishermen in the Russian-owned Caspian fisheries, dockers and boatmen at Anzali, Tehran's printers and telegraphers, and Tabriz tannery workers conducted vigorous strikes. The first two groups were exposed to social-democratic ideas emanating from the Russian Caucasus, while the printers shared the radical intellectuals' milieu at the newspapers.[66] The early labor movement rose and fell with the Constitutional revolution and was crushed in 1911 by the Russian intervention. It may be concluded that the working class itself, still quite small numerically in this period, largely supported the revolution but was limited by its size from playing as decisive a role as the artisans, ulama, and merchants.

Abrahamian has made a strong case that the lower classes were generally monarchist, easily manipulated against the revolution by the upper classes. Their presence has been documented at the attempted anti-majlis coup of December 1907, where lutis, "hired ruffians," and "unskilled workers and the poorest of the poor from the Tehran bazaar" were mobilized for several days, and likewise in the shah's successful coup of June 1908.[67] In the civil war at Tabriz in 1908, the royalists came from the poorer districts of Davachi and Sarkhab, "crowded with dyers, weavers, coolies, laborers, muleteers, and the unemployed."[68] The high price of bread was an issue whether the government was constitutional or despotic, as far as the poor were concerned. It is also plausible that the urban marginal classes accorded traditional respect both to the monarch and to their local ulama, who could mobilize them when necessary. In the July 1906 events however Browne records the actions of "tradesmen, artisans, and people of yet humbler rank," while "humble trades-folk," presumably just above the poorest of the poor, defended as well as attacked the majlis in December 1907.[69] Sattar Khan, the hero of the Tabriz resistance, was himself a luti as well as a horse-dealer, and his second-in-command, Baqir Khan, was also a luti; though both served as kadkhudas in their districts, they were certainly not well-to-do.[70] The urban underclass, then, had a variety of reactions to the constitutional movement: Passive support, active participation, and indifference were all possible in addition to the counter-revolutionary role that Abrahamian ascribes to what well may have been a minority, albeit a significant one. They could be mobilized out of religious convictions to support either side and their economic plight gave them both some cause to support the popular forces and yet made them susceptible to offers of food and money from the direction of the court.

Women engaged in a remarkable array of activities, nearly all in favor of the constitutional movement. Their presence has been recorded at most of the key events, including the Tehran basts of 1905-6, the Tabriz demonstrations that secured the constitution, and the December 1911 resistance. Exclusion from the vote did not deter their participation in political and other forms of education such as the establishment of schools and newspapers. Women formed their own anjumans, by the dozens, according to Shuster, "with a central organization by which they were controlled." Pro-constitutional actions ranged from selling their jewelry to raise money for the proposed national bank, to giving fiery speeches, to actual fighting in the ranks of the national volunteers. One source records a battle fought in Azarbaijan after which it was found that twenty of the dead were women dressed as men. A woman also assassinated a royalist mulla speaking to the crowd at Tupkhana Square just before the 1908 coup and was "immediately arrested and put to death on the spot."[71] Three hundred women, some of them armed, descended on the majlis during the December 1911 crisis and urged resistance against the Russians. All the evidence adds up to a picture of dynamic activism by urban women, presumably cutting across class lines but concentrated especially in the bazaar, the middle, and upper-middle classes.

Iran's intelligentsia and ulama were active in leading the movement. A nascent intelligentsia of newspaper editors and journalists, poets and translators, educators and professionals, and some bureaucrats, made numerous contributions. The bulk of this group wholeheartedly backed the constitutional movement, providing most of its leading ideas and staffing its institutions. Intellectuals like Sani' al-Daula and his brothers were instrumental in drawing up the regulations for the majlis and serving in the assembly and to a lesser extent, in some of the first constitutional cabinets. Others participated in the anjumans and early political parties, providing leadership and knowledge about constitutional, nationalist, and social-democratic ideas. It was "certain more or less Europeanized Persians of the educated official class" who fatefully changed the demand at the Legation bast from a House of Justice to a Constituent National Assembly.[72] Others were organizers of the Tabriz resistance, including 'Ali "Monsieur," so-named for his knowledge of French and study of the French revolution. The only part of the intelligentsia in the royalist ranks were some of the high civil servants tied by family, culture, and service to the court. Even here, while some worked in the conservative party of the majlis and served in the cabinet, others supported the constitutional movement. The intelligentsia, taken as a whole, threw its weight behind the revolution, standing to gain from the constitutional freedoms of assembly, press, education, and participation in the institutions thereby won—the majlis, anjumans, schools, and newspapers.

The role played by the ulama was complex, contradictory, and shifting, which has led to conflicting interpretations. According to Browne they were constitutionalist and to Algar they were anti-shah, while Arjomand argues that though they may have started with these orientations, many ended up anti-constitutional and pro-shah. The best way to reconcile these positions is to note the different factions, periods, and salient issues (the shah, foreigners) within the ulama. Many—perhaps most—of the ulama, from the leading mujtahids to lesser clerics to the young seminary students—were at some point on the side of the revolution. Ulama had both ideological and material motivations to support the movement, especially in its early stages. It will be recalled that pensions had gone unpaid for three years by 1905-6. As Algar has shown the ulama of Qajar Iran had for several generations opposed the state on a variety of popular issues, especially the threat posed by foreign penetration of society; Arjomand notes that many constitutionalist ulama felt the majlis and constitution would further this cause.[73] The somewhat opportunistic 'Abdullah Bihbihani and the more sincerely populist Muhammad Tabatabai took leading roles in the three basts of 1905-6. Popular preachers, often Babi sympathizers such as Malik al-Mutakallimin and Sayyid Jamal al-Din Isfahani, were active in anjumans and very adept at mobilizing crowds into action; Sayyid Jamal al-Din in particular "had an enormous influence with the *'kulâh-namadîs,'* or felt-capped artisans and humble folk of the *bázárs*, to whom he spoke in graphic and forceful language which they could understand, and who loved him accordingly."[74] Both he and Malik al-Mutakallimin were executed by the shah after the 1908 coup. In the provinces, two constitutionalist mujtahids were tortured and killed by the brutal royalist governor of Maragheh in 1906, ulama led protests in Mashhad and Isfahan in late 1908, and some joined in the actual fighting in the Tabriz resistance. In Najaf, three of the four leading mujtahids were constitutionalist; in 1908 they effectively excommunicated the shah in a telegram, charging "that his 'conduct wounds the heart of the believer and is an offense against the absent Imám'."[75] These top-ranking ulama would remain in the constitutionalist ranks through 1911.

By 1907 however an anti-constitutional current led by Shaikh Fazlullah Nuri had launched a traditionalist, anti-parliamentary movement to defend Islam. Three hundred Tehran ulama took bast to protest provisions of the constitution and its supplement such as the equality of all religious groups and the extensive jurisdiction of the secular courts (even the constitutionalist ulama were uneasy at these provisions, and became somewhat more passive in their support). They formed their own anjuman and joined with Muhammad 'Ali against the majlis. Some, such as the Friday prayer leader of Tehran, had ties of wealth and family to the court; some could be bribed. Others wanted to protect their judicial prerogatives, while still others had material interests as landlords to make common cause with the shah. Nuri himself seems to have been motivated largely out of jealousy for Bihbihani and Tabatabai to whom he considered himself superior in learning. The defense of Islam endangered by "reprehensible innovation" (the following of Western constitutional ideas) provided an ideological motivation as well. A number of mujtahids and clerics—Arjomand says "the great majority of the middle- and high-ranking *'ulama'*"[76]—were won over to Nuri's position in 1908, and they in turn caused some members of the bazaar to waver in their support, providing the shah a base for his June coup. Nuri thus became openly pro-monarchy in 1908, excommunicating all journalists and the constitutionalist *maraja'* of Najaf. As the revolution's forces regathered strength in 1909 however, many of Nuri's followers began to distance themselves from him, and after the deposition of the shah in July, most quietly withdrew from politics, while Nuri himself was hanged. The ulama as a whole seemed discouraged from participating to as great an extent as before and the constitutionalist ones who did tended to the conservative side in the majlis, especially after a secular radical assassinated Bihbihani in August 1910. Thus the ulama, who had been instrumental in winning the battles of 1905-6, thereafter split, aligning on both sides from 1907 to 1909 and becoming less of a factor on either side in the last two years of the struggle.

The two dominated classes of tribespeople and peasants had at best auxiliary parts in the revolution, isolated geographically and by their modes of production, while their corresponding elites—landlords and tribal chiefs—were far more active. Iran's tribes and their chiefly khans played a variety of roles in the period 1905-11: Many of them were uninvolved, while others used the revolution to make local inroads through pillage or to take a larger share in the local surplus, and a few of them vied for real power, either on a provincial or even the national level. The first two of these possible roles were not political in any real sense; those who pillaged and raided merely took advantage of the unsettled conditions provided by the revolution. This type of activity was prevalent in Baluchistan, Kurdistan, and Luristan, among other places. Even on the provincial and national level the tribes were basically following their chiefs in a quest for the political power and enhanced prestige that might accrue from backing one side or the other. Sometimes they claimed to support the revolution while seeking local independence, sometimes they were manipulated by royalist governors.[77] The central government was often powerless to restore order in these areas. On the national level, Muhammad 'Ali used Turkomans, Kurds, Shahsavans, and others against the constitutionalists at Tabriz and after his fall from power relied on tribal forces for his attempted restoration. These tribal armies were traditionally motivated by the promise of booty and plunder; Liakhov told the troops departing for the siege of Tabriz in October, 1908, "Whatever wealth is contained within the walls of Tabríz, all shall be yours."[78] On the other side the Bakhtiari of the Isfahan area achieved national prominence in 1909 by fighting to restore the constitution. Their leaders were motivated in a few cases by genuine liberal views, but also by alliances with the British seeking to weaken Russian influence, and materially by the loss of revenues from the disrupted trade in their areas. The confused images that inspired the ordinary tribesman to participate in this undertaking have been suggested by Bausani: "It is even said that, in order to persuade the Bakhtiari to fight for the constitution (*Mashrutè*), they were told that this mysterious *Mashrutè* was a venerable old man, who was a saint and a close friend of the *shah*."[79] Meanwhile the dominance of the Bakhtiari chiefs in the government after 1909 activated the opposition of other tribes in the provinces, especially Fars. Once again tribal rivalries and struggles for power took precedence over abstract issues such as constitutionalism versus despotism. The British used the resulting insecurity to intervene in southern politics in 1910-11.[80] To sum up, the tribes, while not deeply motivated to fight on one side more than the other, played a destabilizing role overall in the events of 1905-11, contributing to the internal problems that created the climate for intervention and counter-revolution.

Peasants are generally held to have been uninvolved in the Constitutional revolution.[81] Certain radical actions were however carried out by peasants in the course of the conflict. These included expulsion of overseers and tax collectors from several villages in 1905, the organization of a few rural anjumans which levied their own taxes, and the refusal to pay rents and seizing of landlords' storehouses in certain northern districts.[82] Peasants around Tabriz sometimes resisted the royalist tribes that were ravaging the countryside in 1908. Only in Gilan was there an actual peasant movement. Some peasants attacked and drove off their landlords and burned their houses. Concerned landlords telegraphed the majlis that the peasants thought "Mashrutiyat" (constitutional rule) meant complete freedom. Peasant rebels were sometimes aided by social democrats and radical artisans, but the local anjumans and national majlis put the brakes on the movement and insisted that taxes be paid.[83] The abolition of tiyuls in 1907 benefitted some peasants, but in reality it meant only that the state now collected taxes, rather than tiyuldars. Abrahamian, in fact, has gathered evidence that some peasants, especially near cities, were persuaded by the ulama to oppose the revolution, while others may also, as in the past, have been coerced by their landlords with the same result.[84] Overall, the lack of articulation of peasants' interests on the national level and the difficulties of organizing peasants across isolated villages in most parts of the country did keep the role of the peasantry as a class from escalating beyond the scattered actions mentioned here. Thus the accepted interpretation of "peasant noninvolvement," while it must be emphatically qualified to include the radical local events that did occur, is sustainable on the level of national politics.

The backbone of the anti-constitutionalist alliance came, naturally enough, from the Qajar royal family, courtiers, ministers, and key institutions, notably the army. The very existence of a constitution, with its limits on the legislative power of the monarch, materially and ideologically undermined the position of the Qajars. Muhammad 'Ali at first refused to sign the Supplementary Fundamental Laws in 1907, expressing his preference for a German-type constitution. When this failed he organized an armed opposition to the majlis, mobilizing royalist crowds at Tupkhana Square in December 1907, whose base was among his owns retainers and the remnants of the state-controlled royal workshops—"the thousands employed in the royal palace with its extensive gardens, stables, kitchens, storehouses, armories, and workshops."[85] At the apex of the state were the governors, often Qajar princes, and all those who lived from its pensions, some 2,000 courtiers who saw their means of livelihood circumscribed by the majlis's budget cutting. The shah also drew support from conservative ulama such as Nuri and the urban classes they could mobilize. And finally, standing behind the shah was the Russian-officered Cossack Brigade and indeed, formal Russian diplomatic and military "aid": "Muhammad 'Alí Sháh . . . was commonly reported to have declared that he would rather be a Russian vassal with autocratic powers over his own people than the constitutional ruler of a free and independent nation."[86]

The state's greatest allies in the Constitutional revolution were the landed class and "notables" generally. When the majlis abolished the tiyul land-revenue grant in 1907, it alienated completely the landed elite of Iran by legally undermining its right to a portion of the agricultural surplus. Individual members of this class staffed the court's high bureaucracy and its cabinets. Qajars and government officials, many of whom were landowners, constituted 27 to 40 percent of the first majlis.[87] After 1909 landlords even appeared among the constitutionalist leadership, most notably in the person of the Sipahdar, who served as minister of war and then prime minister, severely diluting the radical potential of the movement. The proportion of landowners, tribal leaders, and the Qajar landed bureaucracy in the second majlis may have been as high as 83 percent.[88] The replacement of the guild artisans and oppositional ulama by these groups further sapped the momentum of the constitutionalist cause. Finally, Qajars and other landed magnates retained most of the provincial governorships throughout the 1905-11 period. In more isolated provincial settings the revolution penetrated only obscurely and conservative elites were able to run things much as before by ignoring the constitution and majlis and dampening the spread of institutions such as anjumans and independent newspapers.

There were two powerful external actors in the Iranian Constitutional revolution. Of these, England played the subordinate role. Its support of the movement was at best ambiguous and at worst veered into outright hostility. Its most positive actions came early, as in its facilitation of the 1906 general strike that led to the grant of the constitution.[89] Whenever the revolution turned in a more radical direction British support and "neutrality" melted away and no objections were registered to aggressive Russian interventions. Browne suggests that many Iranians felt "that Great Britain's real object was to prevent the spread of constitutional ideas in Asia, for fear of the influence they might exert on India and Egypt; to keep Persia weak and distracted; and to maintain in their present deserted and depopulated condition those provinces of Persia (Kirmán and Sístán) which lay nearest to her Indian frontier."[90] The material interests of Britain in Iran itself—its trade relations, the valuable (after 1908) southern oil fields, the loans—were definitively protected by the 1907 Agreement, a sort of "historic compromise" in Asia, in which Britain sought to safeguard its imperial possessions in India in exchange for allowing Russia a freer hand in northern Iran, the main locus of the revolution. With this document England signalled the end of serious support for the constitutional movement or opposition to Russia's counter-revolutionary plans.

Russia was plainly hostile throughout the constitutional movement, although its hands were tied during the crucial 1905-6 events by its problems internally and with Japan, and this contributed to the early success of the revolution, just as its massive intervention in 1911 basically sealed the failure of the movement. Russia's impact on the course of events rose with the 1907 coronation of Muhammad 'Ali, who owed its bank some 300,000 pounds sterling. Its diplomats supported his 1908 coup and tried to save him a year later, while Russian officers under Liakhov commanded the Iranian Cossack Brigade on which his rule depended. Browne produces possible evidence of official Russian planning and support in the shah's 1908 disbanding of the majlis. The Russian government formally denied that Liakhov acted with its "orders, knowledge or approval."[91] In April 1909 Russian troops intervened directly in the siege of Tabriz and while their presence ended the starvation there and prevented the shah's tribal forces from sacking the bazaar, its occupation was generally to the advantage of Muhammad 'Ali. The 1909 restoration of the constitution was as much an anti-Russian as an anti-shah movement, since Muhammad 'Ali was correctly perceived as a virtual Russian puppet and Russian troops were occupying Azarbaijan. After this the Russians quietly supported Muhammad 'Ali's military campaign to return to the throne in 1911; there was allegedly an agreement whereby in case of success he would have ceded the rich territories of Azarbaijan and the Caspian coast to Russia.[92] When this failed, as well as the Bakhtiari-led coup that was rumored to be planned for late November, the Russians used diplomacy and armed forces to bring about the dismissal of the reformer Shuster, the dissolution of the majlis, and the end of the revolution.

Organizations, Ideologies, Popular Culture

Keys to the tentative alliances that formed and coalesced, or ultimately failed to do so during the Constitutional revolution can be found in the organizations that emerged, the ideologies articulated and the popular cultures that flourished in the course of the struggle. This period witnessed the proliferation of a variety of organizations which had not existed before in Iranian society, including the trade unions already discussed, the anjumans, the first political parties, and the armed units known as mujahidin. The term "anjuman," meaning association or society, has three referents: pre-revolutionary secret societies whose purpose was to discuss the political and social problems of Iran, the municipal and provincial councils provided for in the 1906 constitution to supervise local affairs, and the unofficial societies that formed all over the country with various political orientations and purposes.[93] The Tehran Secret Society (Anjuman-i Makhfi), with its traditional religious and bazaari members, was influential early in the revolution through its contacts with Bihbihani and Tabatabai, the two clerical leaders. The Tabriz Secret Center (Markaz-i Ghaybi) was formed by twelve "young radicals" among whom were merchants, artisans, and intellectuals. It had close ties with the Social Democratic Party of Iran whose program it distributed. The Secret Center constituted the radical wing of the larger Tabriz provincial or "national" anjuman, which administered the city during the resistance to the 1908 coup and the ensuing blockade. Consisting of merchants, artisans, ulama, and intellectuals, this anjuman assumed responsibility for defense and internal security, ran the schools, put out a newspaper, repaired the bazaar, established contact with the foreign consulates, and operated bakeries that provided bread for the armed volunteers and their families.[94]

A second type of organization related in some cases to the anjuman movement was the armed volunteer units known as the mujahidin (literally, "those who strive for jihad"). Their first major action was the defense of the majlis building in December 1907 which was conducted by armed members of the Tehran anjumans. When the resistance shifted to Tabriz after the June coup, the ranks of the mujahidin, led by Sattar Khan and Baqir Khan, swelled with "the poorest and most downtrodden elements of the *pishevaran* population."[95] These artisans and small tradesfolk were organized under a commander in units of twenty to twenty-five and expressly ordered not to extort a penny from anyone. Social democrats in the Caucasus also sent one hundred volunteers to Tabriz. These units fought with considerable élan and achieved conspicuous successes against the shah's forces before succumbing to the starvation induced by the long blockade of the city. Mujahidin forces then spearheaded the nationalist army that took Rasht, placed itself under the Sipahdar, and together with the Bakhtiari restored the constitution in July 1909. Unfortunately, in one of the more confusing episodes of the revolution, disaffected units of Sattar Khan's Tabriz Revolutionary Army refused to disband thereafter, and had to be forcibly disarmed in August 1910 by the Tehran police, now headed by Yifrim Khan, a former officer in the Rasht volunteers. Thereafter the defense of the revo-

lution fell largely to the government's own troops, some of whom undoubtedly had been incorporated from the mujahidin units, and while these
successfully contained the ex-shah's tribal forces in 1911 they were not able
to withstand the Russian occupation. Without the efforts of the mujahidin
and *fida'is* ("those who sacrifice themselves") however, the revolution
would have ended in 1908 with Muhammad 'Ali as shah.

The final set of new institutions that appeared in Iran in this period were
its first political parties, in most cases loose associations of individuals in
the second majlis, but also somewhat more organized extra-parliamentary
groups such as the social democrats. The Tabriz Social Democrats, starting
with thirty members, organized in the bazaar districts, among the Armenians (who had their own socialist Dashnak party), and in the tannery there.
Eventually there were said to be social democratic branches in Tabriz,
Mashhad, Tehran, Khui, Isfahan, and Anzali/Rasht. Meanwhile repression
in Russia in 1907 prompted a number of Iranian and Russian Azarbaijanis
to move to northern Iran and work for the Constitutional revolution. After
1909 the Social Democrats of Baku ordered their members to dissolve their
branches in Iran and join the new Democrat Party. It is difficult to judge the
overall impact of these early socialists on the Constitutional revolution; as
Lambton and Floor argue, it was not major, but neither was it insignificant
in that they inaugurated the propagation of socialist ideas and groups in
Iran. An American consular report states: "Members of these [socialist and
anarchist] clubs were the backbone of the July [1909] revolution and they
are spreading their ideas and their system among the Persians."[96]

Other parties eventually emerged from within the majlis. As it defined
the major issues facing it, royalist, moderate, and progressive wings took
shape in the first majlis, mostly personalized associations with loose organization and no real ideology. In 1907 and 1908 there was a great deal of
cooperation: The progressives knew they needed the influence of the ulama
and bazaar classes, while the latter were compelled to follow the popular
movement. By early 1908 however the three factions were mutually hostile
and the effectiveness of the majlis ground to a halt as Muhammad 'Ali
prepared his coup and the popular initiative was taken by the anjumans.
The second majlis (1909-11) was more conservative in social composition:
Mehrain has it as 83 percent landowners, Qajar landed bureaucrats, and
tribal chiefs, 12 percent ulama and bazaar classes, and 5 percent intelligentsia.[97] This time two parties emerged, more formally than in the first majlis.
The Moderate Party (Firqah-i 'Itidal) generally got two-thirds of the votes
or more, while the Democrat Party (Firqah-i Dimukrat) was the minority.
The smaller Democrat Party had twenty-seven delegates and these included
eight civil servants, five journalists, five ulama, one doctor, and one landowner. Their program emphasized equality before the law, separation of

religion and politics, free education with emphasis on women, progressive taxation, land distribution, industrialization, and a ten hour limit on the working day. Articles in their paper *Iran-i Nau* (New Iran) identified the enemies as oriental despotism, the feudal ruling class, and Western imperialism. The Moderate Party was led by Bihbihani, Tabatabai, the Sipahdar, and a constitutionalist Qajar prince, and its fifty-three deputies included thirteen ulama, ten landlords, ten civil servants, nine merchants, and three tribal chiefs. Its program reflected these more conservative social bases, calling for strengthening constitutional monarchy, upholding the shari'a, protecting family life and private property, assisting the middle class in the bazaar, "instilling 'a cooperative attitude' among the masses through religious education . . . and defending society against the 'terrorism' of the anarchists, the 'atheism' of the Democrats, and the 'materialism' of the Marxists."[98] It acquired to some extent a popular base in the bazaar, a fact which portended a key shift in the political sympathies of the bazaar merchants and artisans. The fact that the Moderates had a clear majority in the second majlis undoubtedly slowed down the momentum of the revolution and ultimately limited the resistance of the majlis to the Russian ultimatum of 1911.

Ideological developments took two primary forms in the Constitutional revolution—secular and religious, with some overlap in themes, but in the end rather more serious divergences in conception and aims. The intelligentsia, as we have defined it, was the natural originator of secular ideas, including those of a majlis and constitution. Milani, who has tried to characterize the core principles of the new ideologies, lists the need for law, a call for equality, the rights of the individual, freedom of trade and commerce, and a modern, critical education based on scientific, religious, and literary enlightenment. These ideas were worked out in the late nineteenth century by writers and journalists such as Akhundzadeh, Mirza Aqa Khan Kirmani, Taliboff, Maragha'i, Malkam Khan, Muntashar al-Daula, and others.[99] By 1905 these aspirations had grown into the demand for a House of Justice and then in 1906 a National Assembly and a Constitution, the two great demands of the intelligentsia that were achieved in the early part of the revolution. Egalitarianism was logically an element of this, taking several forms—equality among all subjects (and the equality this implied among the religious communities), and in some cases calls for equality between the sexes. Other core values addressed the need to extricate Iran from its political and economic dependence on the West (though somewhat paradoxically by making use of Western *ideas*). Thus Akhundzadeh stated that the central concern of his work was "the protection of *vatan* [the fatherland] from foreign encroachment."[100] In January 1906 after the second bast, the cry "Long Live the Iranian Nation!" was heard for the first time.[101]

Nationalism meant the simultaneous assertion of Iran's rights vis-à-vis the West and the people's rights vis-à-vis the state. Another area where nationalism connected foreign and internal problems was in the demand for "free trade" in Iran, associated with ideas of equality and progress. The development of Iran's own productive forces would strike a blow against foreign domination and provide opportunities for its merchants, craftspeople, and workers. This linked a progressive section of the merchant class with the aspirations of those below it in the bazaar, albeit with somewhat blurred political implications. Finally, modern, secular education was espoused as a way to meet the challenge of the West. Malkam Khan wrote, "Our hopes are entirely upon science," while Maragha'i criticized Iran's lack of technical schools.[102] In some writers a corollary to the enlightenment ideal was criticism of "superstition," verging on anti-clericalism in Akhundzadeh, Mirza Aqa Khan Kirmani, and Dihkhuda. Even Afghani, who tried to reconcile Islam and modern science, blamed the ulama for "The ruin and corruption we have experienced."[103] This suggests one line of tension between secular and religious ideologies in the period.

Ideological development within a religious framework was split on the issues raised by the revolution, just as the ulama themselves were. The constitutionalist mujtahids of Iran and the shrine cities in Iraq agitated against the tyranny of the shah as well as his reliance on outside powers. There was a different emphasis here than with the secular ideologists who opposed the same evils, for they were filtered through fundamentally different views of the world: "Arbitrary rule" was seen in terms of the shah's authority versus that of the mujtahids and the state's law versus the shari'a, while foreign interference was a question of infidels in the abode of Islam rather than imperialism per se. In the early stages of the revolution however there was a marked congruence between secular and religious ideologies in support of constitutionalism. Most of the ulama saw the events of 1905-6 as an attempt to enforce the Islamic shari'a. The second article of the Supplementary Fundamental Laws stated that legislation must be in accord with Islam and a committee of at least five mujtahids was to determine whether it was, a clause which though never implemented, was more or less satisfactory to the pro-constitutional ulama. These ulama felt that constitutionalism was permitted by Islam, issuing a circular letter in 1909 or 1910 calling on the people to defend the majlis and the ideas of freedom and justice.[104] Opposed to these conceptions were those ulama Arjomand has termed the "traditionalist," anti-parliamentary ulama, led by Nuri in Tehran and Sayyid Kazim Yazdi in Iraq. Nuri considered the proposed constitution *bid'at*—a "reprehensible innovation," actually opposed to Islam. Nuri's objections to the meaning and content of constitutionalism as it emerged in the revolution were several:

'the inauguration of the customs and practices of the realms of infidelity', the
intention to tamper with the Sacred Law which is said to belong to 1300 years
ago and not to be in accordance with the requirements of the modern age, the
ridiculing of the Moslems and insults directed at the *'ulama*, the equal rights
of nationalities *and* religions, spread of prostitution, and the freedom of the
press which is 'contrary to our Sacred Law'.[105]

He ultimately considered the constitution a direct threat to Islamic law and
the privileged position of the Muslim community in Iran. The majlis, accused of being led by atheists, freethinkers, and Babis, was deemed by Nuri
a group of supporters of the West, beguiling "the masses who are more
benighted than cattle."[106] Nuri's alternative was variously a *mashruteh-i
mashru'a*—a constitution in accordance with the shari'a—or, once Muhammad 'Ali had successfully disbanded the majlis, the position that the government should be *mashru'a* and that constitutionalism itself was contrary
to Islam. Nevertheless he had no specific, comprehensive blueprint for an
Islamic political system. By 1907-8 he was explicitly supporting the reactionary Muhammad 'Ali and what was in effect traditional despotic monarchy
with some imprecise checks and balances imposed by ulama who agreed
with him. After Nuri's death the ulama moved toward a more centrist
position from both sides of the ideological divide. Nuri's positions had
failed to pull the ulama as a whole into the opposition but they had
undercut their strongly constitutionalist sentiments of 1905-6. They also
had an impact on the religiously-minded masses of the bazaar, causing a
muting of the mobilization of some key groups—merchants, artisans, and
lesser ulama.

The available evidence on the political consciousness and cultures of the
participants in the Constitutional revolution strengthens our theses on its
mass, popular social bases. Religious imagery played a definite role in
mobilizing the masses. Browne's eyewitness at the Legation bast wrote him:

> Perhaps the scene was most picturesque at night. Nearly every tent used to
> have a *rawza-khwan*, and it was really an admirable tableau, these tents with
> their circles of listeners and the *rawza-khwan* at one end, relating the old, old
> stories of Hasan and Husayn.[107]

Shi'i appeals to martyrdom and revolt were effective in inspiring the
mujahidin to fight the shah's armies and the fida'is to assassinate leading
conservative figures, meeting a sure death in the process. It is true that these
motivations were somewhat undermined later in the revolution by the
work of the ulama; Malikzadeh noted "the clergy . . . fooled the public,
especially craftsmen and tradesmen, into believing that the Democrats were
the sworn enemies of Islam."[108] Katouzian describes one large street pro-

cession in which the slogan was "We support the Prophet's religion, *Mashruteh* we do not want."[109]

Anti-authoritarian attitudes and resistance to state power thrived in their own right. By May 1907 the British minister Sir Cecil Spring-Rice was reporting

> One after another, unpopular Governors have been expelled. . . . A spirit of resistance to oppression and even to all authority is spreading throughout the country. . . . The sentiment of independence in the widest sense, of nationality, of the right to resist oppression and to manage their own affairs is rapidly growing among the people. It is strongest in Azerbaijan. It is very strong in the capital.[110]

Popular attitudes toward the elite underwent a change too, as an Iranian correspondent told Browne:

> A certain builder came to the house of a Minister to repair an iron fire-place. On entering, he saluted the Minister. The Minister's servant bade him do obeisance. He replied, 'Knave, do you not know that we now have a Constitution, and that under a Constitution obeisances no longer exist?' A strange independence and freedom are observable in the people, and it is impossible to say how this change in their character has been so suddenly effected.[111]

The shah himself was taken down off his pedestal in the popular imagination, as a revolutionary proclamation of late 1907 warned him not to forget

> that he was not born by his mother possessed of crown and signet-ring, nor does he hold in his hand a warrant of absolute sovereignty from the Unseen World of Spirits. Assuredly if he had but reflected for a moment that this sovereignty depends only in the acceptance or rejection of the People, and that those who have elected him to this high position and acknowledged him [as King] are able also to elect another [in his place], he would never have swerved aside to this extent from the straight Path of Justice and the requirements of constitutional monarchy.[112]

These attitudes found media of expression in the innumerable *shabnamehs* ("night letters") that were posted anonymously, the proliferation of newspapers during this period (often read aloud in coffeehouses), and the ballads and verses of nationalist poets.[113]

The Outcome of the Revolution

Ultimately, the Constitutional revolution failed due to a double determination of the internal instability of its shifting alliances and the force

TABLE 5.2   Coalition Changes, 1906-1911

Populist Alliance	
1906	1911
Most merchants	Some medium and small merchants
Intelligentsia	Intelligentsia
Ulama	Fewer ulama
Artisans	Fewer artisans
Workers	Workers
Urban marginals	Fewer urban marginals
British slightly supportive	

Royalist Alliance	
1906	1911
Wavering shah	Figurehead with Russian support
Landed elite	Landed elite
Russians preoccupied at home	Large merchants
	Some ulama
	Some marginals who could be "bought"
	Russian tsar and army
	British acquiescent

brought to bear on it from external intervention. At work here was the articulation of the complexities of the Iranian social formation and the dependence imposed on it within the world-system. The foregoing analysis of the social forces involved indicated the importance of the attempt to build a viable oppositional coalition and the shifting vicissitudes of the struggle for the hearts and minds of the most active social classes. Splits in the alliance and key turning points in the revolution underline this process (see table 5.2).[114] From 1905 to early 1907 a working, if uneasy, coalition of intelligentsia, artisans, merchants, and ulama united to confront the state. The urban poor and working class were broadly supportive, and Britain proved helpful on the spot. During the course of 1907 the drafting of the supplementary laws of the constitution and the exact definition of the relations between secular and religious laws and their respective spheres, breached this unity and led to Nuri's split within the ulama. The year of Muhammad 'Ali Shah's restoration of autocracy during which the majlis was disbanded from June 1908 to July 1909 really set back the revolution. Although the resistance of Tabriz was courageous and new social forces with more radical ideas entered the fray, the restoration stalled all legislation passed from 1906 to 1908 from budget reforms to land and tax measures, and broke their momentum, forcing the second majlis to reconstitute itself and begin anew. The post-1909 period saw a sharpening of class conflict in some respects but a muting of it in others. The state was now "constitutional" but conservative in its social bases, reflecting the tribal and landed elements that had combined to depose Muhammad 'Ali. In the provinces, old elites remained in place and tribal disruptions continued apace. The majlis was now controlled by a conservative majority of landowners, large merchants and ulama terrified by the possibility of a more radical turn of events, while the continued support of the constitutionalist ulama and the bazaar classes outside the majlis weakened somewhat due to all of these developments. This provided an opening for the Russians to step in and quash the attempted reforms that were still being proposed by the radical Democrats and Shuster. Crucially, the Russian state had regained its equilibrium after the repression of its own internal opposition by 1907, coupled with its 1907 Agreement with England and the 1910 Potsdam Convention with Germany. The Russian army found willing collaborators in counterrevolution and repression in the Iranian cabinet, court, conservatives in the majlis, and landlords, large merchants, and some ulama in the population at large.

The Constitutional revolution ended then in a defeat, but it stands out as a revolutionary movement that attempted to change the balance of power and nature of Iranian society. Rather than a bourgeois revolution led by the merchant class, we have seen it as an urban multi-class populist revolution of artisans, oppositional ulama, merchants, workers, and lower classes. The institutions they created—majlis, constitution, anjumans, trade unions— were new in the history of Iran. The means they found to struggle for them—general strikes, mass demonstrations, basts, and when necessary armed defense of one's rights—were Iranian adaptations of the methods of modern social movements and were conducted with determination, vigor, and imagination. Failure came because the coalition that carried the revolution was a shifting and fragile one that could not hold itself together politically or ideologically, rooted in a complex class structure which had experienced the Western impact in divergent and not fully congruent ways. Key middle-class and elite groups wavered in the alliance, threatened by the prospect (which never materialized) of lower-class hegemony. After both the constitutional alliance and the monarchy it opposed had exhausted themselves, the ultimate (external) guarantors of Iran's dependence stepped in to preserve the system and suppress the popular movement.

"Resolution from Above":
World War I and Reza Khan's Rise to Power, 1914-1925

The roots of the 1921 coup that eventually brought the Pahlavi dynasty to power in 1925 lie in the devastation caused by World War I and the unsettled state of the world-system, compounded by the demoralization of the Iranian opposition due to the reversal of the Constitutional revolution. From 1911 to 1914 the northern portion of the country was dominated by Russia, the south by England. Russia had the most influence over the cabinet, while it vastly increased its trade until it was three times higher in 1914 than in 1900. Gillard considers that "By 1914, northern Persia had for all practical purposes become part of the Russian Empire, occupied by Russian troops and with Russian consuls assuming governmental functions."[115] In the south the British worked with Shaikh Khaz'al, the Arab ruler of Khuzistan, to ensure their control over the newly producing oilfields. In May 1914 the British government attained controlling interest in the Anglo-Persian Oil Company and sent troops which policed almost all of the "neutral zone" specified in the 1907 Agreement. The Iranian state itself was severely weakened in this situation (though it did not have to face the constitutional movement anymore); tribal leaders and large landlords became autonomous in their local jurisdictions.

Despite its declaration of neutrality, Iran became a battlefield for Turkish, Russian, and British troops throughout World War I. The general economic impact of the war on Iran was devastating. In the agricultural sector, livestock and crops were appropriated by the contending armies, irrigation works fell into disarray, peasants were pressed into road-building and other military projects, villages were deserted. The pre-war level of agricultural production was still not regained by 1925. Industrial development came to a standstill, though local trade and craft production survived. Inflation gripped the cities, imports outstripped exports (and both fell considerably in volume), and the trade dislocation led to depressed conditions in the north. The height of suffering was reached in the winter of 1918-19 when severe famine struck due to the war's exhaustion of the surplus, compounded by problems of distribution and local hoarding. Estimates of death by starvation range from at least 100,000 to two million; the British financial adviser Balfour found that in the Tehran area "approximately a quarter of the agricultural population had died during the famine."[116] Thus did the Iranian people pay dearly for a war they had played no part in, waged by the European powers that dominated their country. The central government under Ahmad Shah meanwhile looked on helplessly, running through some fifty cabinets between 1909 and 1921.

By 1916 the British and Russians were regrouping themselves for the reassertion of their power in Iran. In March 1915 the two powers had signed a secret treaty which made no mention of Iranian independence, allowing for British control of the neutral zone (with its oilfields) in exchange for granting Russia "full liberty of action" in its sphere and postwar control of Istanbul and the Turkish straits. This seemingly implied the right for the Russians to annex northern Iran and for England to directly administer the south.[117] The government-in-exile at Kirmanshah (consisting of delegates to the third majlis who had refused to disband under Russian threats in 1915) collapsed when the British took that city in 1916. The February and October 1917 revolutions in Russia dramatically altered the political landscape in Iran, leading to the evacuation of Russian troops from the north and the denunciation in 1918 by the new Soviet government of all Tsarist treaties and concessions concerning Iran. Though this removed at a single stroke the vise-like grip of the Russians on Iran's economy and polity that had been so relentlessly tightened from the mid-nineteenth century till World War I, its immediate effect was to leave all of Iran to the British, who sent their troops into the north and began paying subsidies to the powerless Iranian government.[118]

The period between the disaster of World War I and the coup of 1921 was one of increasing conflict between the state, internal social movements, and foreign powers. No one of these forces could gain hegemony in Iran but each could thwart the others from reaching their goals, and this fundamental stalemate among the contenders prepared the ground for Reza Khan's assumption of power. Powerful resistance movements to foreign occupation and the Qajar state emerged in Gilan, Azarbaijan, Khurasan, and elsewhere. The Jangali ("Forest") movement in the Caspian region was by far the most serious of these. Its origins have been traced back to anti-British and anti-Russian actions as early as 1913, but its real impetus came in the early years of the World War under the leadership of Mirza Kuchik Khan, a radical preacher and minor landlord who had fought in the Constitutional revolution and had been affiliated with the Moderate party. Fleeing to Gilan in 1915, he organized a guerrilla force called the Committee of Islamic Unity to harass the Russians in the north and oppose the corruption and weakness rampant in the central government. Support came from diverse sources: merchants, ulama, and landowners on the one hand, few of whom sought fundamental social change, and a large rank and file of Gilani peasants and mountaineers with a more radical bent, who fought for the abolishment of labor services, reform of the sharecropping arrangement, and confiscation of the property of hostile landlords. These differences led to an ebb in the movement by mid-1919, due to splits and the occupation of northern Iran by the British and White Russians. Activity revived in the spring and summer of 1920 with an infusion of support from the Communist

Party of Iran (CPI), newly formed in the wake of the arrival of Soviet forces at Anzali to clear out the remnants of British and Tsarist forces. The CPI under Haidar Khan and the Jangalis of Kuchik Khan joined in establishing the Soviet Socialist Republic of Iran, sending Lenin a message asking for "help in liberating us and all weak and oppressed nations from the yoke of Persian and English oppressors," and declaring the abolition of the monarchy in a note to Tehran.[119] The program of the new republic, with its emphasis on radical land reform and calls by left-wing and communist Jangalis for the unveiling of women, soon alienated Kuchik Khan who held to the Islamic sanctity of private property and more conservative views. In late 1920 however negotiations resumed between Kuchik Khan and Haidar Khan and despite a stalling of Soviet support, preparations were being made for a march on Tehran.

Several other regions and social sectors also posed threats to the central government. Autonomy movements occurred in Azarbaijan under Shaikh Muhammad Khiabani, Khurasan under Colonel Muhammad Taqi Khan Pesian and local Democrats, in Kirmanshah under Amir Afshar, a Democrat in alliance with local landed interests, and in several southern provinces, especially Khuzistan, ruled by Shaikh Khaz'al of Muhammareh.[120] There were also urban and tribal rebellions in Kurdistan in the 1920s; tribal autonomy was in fact widespread everywhere. In the urban centers moreover the union movement revived in 1917-18, with strikes and demonstrations by bakers and printers. A Central Union Council, with informal ties to the new CPI and the Soviet Union met in late 1921, encompassing sixteen unions and supported by the paper *Haqiqat* (Truth).[121] Taken together, by 1921 all these movements—the Jangalis, Azarbaijan, Khurasan, the tribal areas, and the unions—posed a considerable threat to the survival of the central government.

The counterweight to these social movements came less from the Iranian state than from the British, who made a bid for hegemony with the change of government to the Soviets in Russia.[122] British policy in Iran after 1918 was of two minds. The government wanted to reduce its military commitments in the Middle East, but Lord Curzon, the acting foreign secretary with great knowledge of Iran, "dreamt," in Nicholson's words, "of creating a chain of vassal states stretching from the Mediterranean to the Pamirs and protecting, not the Indian frontiers merely, but our communications with our further Empire. . . . In this chain of buffer states . . . Persia was to him at once the weakest and most vital link."[123] The instrument for integrating Iran into this chain was the 1919 Agreement, by which Britain would provide, at Iran's expense "expert advisers . . . for the several departments of the Persian Administration," especially officers and equipment to Iran's military. The Agreement went on to provide for a two million pound loan to Iran with the southern customs and if necessary, *all* the customs, as a guarantee.[124] Secretly negotiated with Iranian cabinet ministers, who re-ceived an "advance" on the loan (in effect, a bribe), the Agreement was instantly unpopular in Iran. Despite the protests of the Iranian press and public demonstrations against it as well as French, American, and Soviet objections, the British did not wait for its ratification (by the as yet unelected fourth majlis), but sent a mission to take over the Iranian administration, finances, and military. The British forced a new tariff treaty on Iran in 1920, which made their imports even cheaper and brought Iran less revenue, while Russian imports were made more expensive. Vussuq al-Daula, the prime minister who had negotiated the 1919 Agreement, was forced to step down in June 1920; his successor Mushir al-Daula declared the Agreement suspended until all British and Russian troops had left the country, but he was forced out in the fall of 1920 in favor of the more pro-British Sipahdar. The Sipahdar put British officers in charge of the Cossack Brigade, but though he wanted to, he could not bring the Agreement up for ratification in the majlis. The British continued to support the Iranian state with a subsidy of 225,000 pounds sterling a month, but had given up hopes of ratifying the Agreement and were considering withdrawing their forces from Iran, though they were at a loss as to how to contain the Bolshevik threat and protect their valuable southern oilfields.

By late 1920 and early 1921 then a situation of stalemate and crisis existed. The Gilan movement was seen as a possible military threat to Tehran, the shah was unable to form a cabinet, the British could not secure their Agreement, there was still no majlis, tribes were autonomous everywhere, the Cossack Brigade was in retreat from the Caspian, the economy was suffering from indebtedness, a balance of trade deficit, and assorted other ills. The stalemate between the Iranian state, the British (and to a lesser extent, Soviets and Americans), and the several internal opposition move-ments, was by this point a highly unstable one. It was in these unsettled circumstances that a hitherto rather obscure military officer named Reza Khan marched the Cossack Brigade from Qazvin to Tehran in February 1921 to seize the reins of power. The most interesting question (and the most difficult to answer) about the coup d'état is the exact extent of the British role in it. On balance, a plausible case can be made that there was *significant* British involvement in the coup.[125] The available evidence suggests that while the Foreign Office in England had little or indeed nothing to do with the coup (it was in fact rather unclear about its policy toward Iran at this crucial juncture), leading British military and diplomatic personnel in Iran were instrumental in bringing it about.

Let us consider the following known facts. Reza Khan had risen through the ranks from second lieutenant in 1912 to full general by 1920, when the Cossack Brigade's Russian officers were dismissed and replaced by British officers, headed by General Edmund Ironside. Between November 1920 and

February 1921 Ironside brought Reza Khan into the position of commander of the Cossack Brigade. Over the winter, Ironside and Lieutenant-Colonel Henry Smyth provided ammunition, supplies, and pay to the Brigade, restoring its morale. In January, Ironside wrote in his diary, "a military dictatorship would solve our troubles and let us out of the country without any trouble at all."[126] On February 14, 1921, recalled to Baghdad, Ironside released Reza Khan from his command and gave him the go-ahead to do as he saw fit, with the simple promise not to depose the shah.[127] Smyth meanwhile was in touch with two of Reza's officers, as well as Sayyid Zia al-Din Tabatabai, a thirty-four year-old French-educated Tehran journalist who was reform-minded and fairly pro-British. Smyth gave Reza advice on how to carry out the coup.[128] The British minister Herman Norman seems to have been informed by Ironside a week before the coup (February 14 or 15), and was fearful for the shah. Walter Smart, the Oriental Secretary at the British legation, definitely knew what Smyth and Ironside were doing. On the evening that the coup occurred, Lieutenant-Colonel Haig from the legation advised the Swedish commander of the Tehran gendarmerie that resistance to the Cossacks would be futile, while the next day Norman counselled the shah to acquiesce in the demands of the coup-makers. After the coup Norman urged his government to support the new regime, which he characterized as being "the most favourable to British interests which could possibly have arisen."[129] *Why* would the British officials on the spot have favored the coup? At this point they saw it as the best alternative to the unobtainable 1919 Agreement, one which would bring to power a strong government capable of meeting the challenges posed by the radical social movements and a possible Soviet advance once British troops left Iran. As Ironside noted in his diary: "Better a coup d'etat for us than anything else."[130] Reza himself would say in 1924: "England brought me to power, only she did not know with whom she was dealing."[131]

Thus, on February 18, 1921 some two thousand Cossacks set out from Qazvin under Reza Khan's command for the capital 140 kilometers away, entering Tehran on February 21. Reza told Haig and another British officer on February 20 that he was "marching to the capital to establish a Government which would set its house in order instead of prating about the *Majlis*, the Constitution, and such irrelevant matters."[132] By February 23 Ahmad Shah had agreed that Sayyid Zia al-Din would be the prime minister, with Reza Khan his minister of war. The new government of Zia al-Din pledged internal order, social reforms, and national independence. An early proclamation promised to renounce the 1919 Anglo-Persian Agreement, strengthen the army, and distribute crown lands among the peasants. These and other proposals soon alienated merchants and landlords from Zia's regime and a showdown occurred with Reza Khan over the retention of British officers in charge of the army, which the new minister of war staunchly refused. Reza Khan, the shah, and some of the imprisoned conservative politicians arranged the departure of Zia in May 1921, and three other prime ministers (one twice) came and went in the next two years.[133]

The post-coup government moved decisively to improve its relations with the two new powers, the United States and the Soviet Union, to offset Iran's dependence on Great Britain in the 1918-21 period. Reza Khan himself had little affection for any of the foreign powers, including Britain which had done so much to establish him.[134] Britain did support the Zia government, providing 80,000 tumans for the army *one day* after the coup. In a general way they were pleased at the prospect of a central government strong enough to maintain a modicum of social order, as they were withdrawing their own forces from Iran. But they were far from certain they could deal with Reza Khan and until 1924 they also supported the autonomous tribal chief Shaikh Khaz'al in Khuzistan where their oilfields lay. The United States increased its political and economic ties with Iran, seeking oil concessions for American companies in the north (unsuccessfully, due to British and Soviet opposition), and sending Dr. A. C. Millspaugh in August 1921 as a financial adviser to the Iranian government. Millspaugh brought about budgetary reforms and raised taxes, but was unable to secure a loan or capital investments from American sources—the U.S. was still far from being aware of Iran's strategic value. Soviet support for the new regime was quick in coming: On February 26, 1921, just a few days after the coup, relations were normalized by the signing of a treaty of friendship, as both governments were in need of mutual recognition. This laid the groundwork for the withdrawal of Soviet forces from Gilan later in the year. The Soviets seemed almost as eager for stability in Iran as the British, given the threat of foreign intervention against their revolution.

This last development contributed to the defeat of the postwar social movements by Reza's armed forces, the next step in his bid for power. Rapprochement between the U.S.S.R. and the Iranian government undercut the former's support for the Jangal rebellion in Gilan; Blumkin, the Bolshevik intelligence officer among the Jangalis, is said to have claimed that "the Gilan movement was called off from Moscow."[135] In any case, the movement split, with the communist leadership becoming less militant and Kuchik Khan remaining in opposition to the central government. The end came late in 1921, after Kuchik murdered his former partner, Haidar Khan, and himself fled before Reza's advancing army, dying on the frozen slopes of the northern mountains. The less threatening movements in Azarbaijan and Khurasan soon came to an end as well, due to a combination of internal conflicts, lessened Soviet support, and military actions by the central government. Thus, by early 1922, in a dramatic reversal of fortunes, the central government had bested the most radical of the postwar social movements. A second series of campaigns, sewing of internal dissension, and cooptation restored order to the tribal areas within Iran's territory. The most significant of these victories was against the British-backed tribal coalition of Shaikh Khaz'al, for this proved the turning point in Britain's relations with the government, with whom they thereafter "shared" the southern oilfields.[136]

How was Reza Khan able to bring about this restoration of internal order? The answer lies to a certain extent in the changes he effected in the nature of the Iranian state. With little interest in social reforms, he moved quickly instead to strengthen and centralize the key institutions of finance and the army. He approved Millspaugh's introduction of indirect taxes on tobacco and matches, and a government monopoly on tea and sugar, which generated sufficient income to balance the budget (at the expense of the urban poor and other consumers of these necessities). The army took up to 40 percent of expenditures by 1922, and was expanded from less than 10,000 to some 40,000 men. Reza saw to it that the troops got paid and that their needs were attended to before any other government employees', thereby binding the loyalty of the troops to himself. He was aided in this by the beginnings of a recovery in Iranian agriculture and the growth of oil production and revenues. Though the government's share of 1.4 million pounds sterling represented a scandalously low five to ten percent of the value of the oil exported, it made possible the balancing of the budget, increased imports, and public spending which consolidated the new position of the Iranian state.[137]

Reza used these military successes and increments of state power to consolidate his own rise to the monarchy after 1923, in a series of adroit political maneuvers and manipulation of social forces. In October 1923 he moved from the ministry of war into the prime minister's office, while Ahmad Shah left the country for Europe on a trip of indefinite duration (he would in fact never return to Iran). In 1924 Reza made a single misstep from which he deftly recovered—the proposal that the majlis abolish the Qajar monarchy in favor of a republic with himself as president. He backed down from this when the ulama registered strong objections, concerned by the recent abolishing of the Ottoman Caliphate in the new Turkish republic.[138] A few months later Reza rebounded politically by manipulating events surrounding the murder of the American counsel Robert Imbrie in the midst of a religiously-agitated crowd. Despite incriminating evidence of army involvement in this incident, Reza turned the occasion completely to his purpose by using it as a pretext for declaring martial law, arresting political opponents and putting the press and the ulama on the defensive. He emerged from it as the conspicuous alternative to weak Qajar government, preferable to either a left-wing democratic or ulama-led political option in the eyes both of many Iranians and foreign governments, especially the British and Americans.[139]

The final elements to consider in this process are the composition of the internal and external social forces that backed Reza in his bid for power and his skillful manipulation of these groups—the ulama and conservative party, Western-educated liberal democrats and more authoritarian-minded nationalist modernizers, and the socialist and communist parties and trade union movement—all of whom he would attack later in his reign. In essence he managed, if not to be "all things to all people," at least to offer something to nearly everyone, while, on their side, his erstwhile "partners" were rather easily deceived, at least in retrospect. Internally, he commanded diffuse support from key classes and groups within society at large. Merchants and landlords recognized that Reza was not a radical reformer and would safeguard their property against left-wing social movements. He also made conspicuous gestures toward the ulama, on the republican issue, by pilgrimages to the holy cities of Iraq, with receptions at his house in Tehran, and organization of religious processions. His leading religious opponent Mudarris was temporarily neutralized in 1924-25 by a conciliatory peace-offering. Part of the intelligentsia, including some poets and writers, civil servants, politicians, and professionals, was even more impressed by Reza, especially the veneer of nationalism he acquired in lessening British power in Iran and strengthening the state. There was a fairly widespread expectation that he would modernize and industrialize the country along lines that would benefit this class. Individuals who opposed him or saw the undemocratic future he was constructing were murdered, intimidated, or bought off. The extra-parliamentary left, notably the trade unions and communists, also offered some support, first for the republican proposal in 1924, and in general approved what they perceived as his nationalist and secular tendencies, again with the consequence of ignoring his authoritarian and anti-progressive views. They realized their mistake only at the last moment, in 1925, when Reza suppressed the unions and communists thoroughly.[140]

The three principal sources of Reza's assumption of the monarchy were the army, the majority parties in the fifth majlis, and the major foreign powers. Reza's use of patronage brought the army as an institution back into the power structure for the first time since the eighteenth century. Martial law allowed him to offer governorships to loyal officers, create regional divisions and staff them with his own men, and send inspectors to public works projects and all governmental departments. The army thus gave him total support and its material defeat of the radical and tribal movements was an important legitimating mechanism.[141] The fifth majlis, opening in 1924, was a second pillar in Reza's rise. The elections were manipulated to a certain degree in the provinces and tribal areas by Reza's handpicked martial law governors. He himself "took the position that the successful man in each district would be one who came from the leading family and who would support his policies."[142] The conservative, clerical Reformers Party (*Hizb-i Islahtalaban*), which had held the majority in the fourth majlis, gave way to the young, Western-educated reformers of the Revival Party (*Hizb-i Tajadud*), whose program emphasized a well-run state and army, expansion of education, development of Iran's industry, and other modernizing reforms. Reza shifted his own support from the Reformers to the Revival Party as the balance of power between the two shifted. In May 1924 a new journal supporting the Revival Party called for a "revolutionary dictator."[143] Though the party also contained prominent Democrats from the constitutional movement and worked in a loose alliance with Iskandari's Socialist Party, it became on the whole the vehicle of Reza Khan in his bid for total power, seeing in him the answer to the problems of national disunity, dependence, and backwardness.

Finally, the world-system provided favorable conditions in this period. By 1924, with Reza's defeat of Shaikh Khaz'al and the definitive integration of the oil-producing provinces into Iranian national territory, the British came to see in him the strong man who would protect "their" oil and contain any Bolshevik threats. Thus, the British minister saw "benevolent inaction" as "the last choice left" and their policy turned to one of support for him.[144] The Soviets meanwhile had pressing internal problems of their own and chose to support a non-revolutionary government in Iran as a factor of stability that would ward off *Western* intervention. In 1923 the Comintern praised prime minister Reza Khan for "his progressive and anti-imperialist orientation."[145] The newest world power on the scene, the United States, followed Britain's foreign policy, accepting Reza's conduct of the hasty investigation into the murder of Imbrie because it saw in him the only man capable of maintaining order in Iran and able to recognize American "strength and majesty."[146] Thus did Reza perform the amazing feat of satisfying the major capitalist *and* socialist world powers while still appearing to be a nationalist within his own country.

There was opposition to Reza's rise to power, but it was circumscribed in a number of ways. Artisans had marched and demonstrated against Reza's proposed republic in 1924, but less out a democratic egalitarian ideal than because they feared his secularism. Individual journalists and editors had criticized him in their papers, for which more than one was threatened with violence, beaten, or murdered. And likewise individual politicians of diverse views had sensed and opposed his increasingly despotic tendencies. These included the popular conservative preacher Mudarris, and nationalists and democrats such as Taqizadeh and a young man of the landed elite, Muhammad Mussadiq. But these individuals found themselves boxed into a corner and isolated by Reza's astute maneuvering, left with the non-viable options of defending the discredited Qajar monarchy or the stillborn democratic republic.[147] At the end of October 1925 the majlis voted to depose

Ahmad Shah Qajar. On December 12, 1925 a constituent assembly voted by a wide margin that Reza Khan assume the title Reza Shah Pahlavi. Though "The change of dynasty . . . was not marked by any spontaneous enthusiasm,"[148] Iran had turned a historical corner, propelled not by a mass movement for social change, as this was checked with the defeat of the Constitutional revolution in 1911, but by a 1921 coup d'état favored by the main external power of the time, Britain, and pushed through to a change of dynasty in 1925 by a skillful military centralizer with significant, if misplaced, urban support from the ulama, left, and nationalist middle classes.

Notes

1. For accounts, see Hasan-i Fasa'i, *History of Persia under Qajar Rule*, translated from the Persian by Heribert Busse (New York and London: Columbia University Press, 1972), 72-81; Lambton, "Persia," 446-48; 451-52; Lorentz, "Iran's Great Reformer," 88-90; and Keddie, *Roots of Revolution*, 69.

2. Ashraf and Hekmat, "Merchants and Artisans," 730, based on I'timad al-Sultanah, *Al-Ma'athir va al-Athar* (Tehran, 1307 Hijri/1890), 37-52.

3. These events are mentioned or discussed in Lambton, "Persia," 446, 448, 450, 452, 455; Fasa'i, *History of Persia*, 262-67, 283-87, 356-57; Algar, *Religion and State*, 111-112; and Muhammad Reza Afshari, "A Study of the Constitutional Revolution within the Framework of Iranian History," Ph.D. dissertation, Department of History, Temple University (1981), 143-45, 148, 151, who provides the term "limited objective movements."

4. Algar, *Religion and State*, 95. Accounts of the episode and the events leading up to it vary somewhat in their details. Two of the more detailed discussions are given by Fasa'i, *History of Persia*, 187-89, and especially, Algar, *Religion and State*, 95-99, who discusses the various alternate versions. See also Arjomand, *The Shadow of God and the Hidden Imam*, 251, and Keddie, *Roots of Revolution*, 46.

5. This paragraph is based on Bayat, *Mysticism and Dissent*, 87ff., and Afshari, "A Study of the Constitutional Revolution," 147ff. A major study now exists: Abbas Amanat, *Resurrection and Renewal. The Making of the Babi Movement in Iran, 1844-1850* (Ithaca and London: Cornell University Press, 1989).

6. Bayat, *Mysticism and Dissent*, 106. Other data in this paragraph are drawn from V. Minorsky, "Persia: Religion and History," pp. 242-259 in V. Minorsky, *Iranica. Twenty Articles* (Tehran: University of Tehran Publication, volume 775, 1965), 254; and Afshari, "The Pishivaran," 146.

7. Bayat, *Mysticism and Dissent*, 108.

8. M. S. Ivanov, articles on "Babism" and "Babi Uprisings" in *The Great Soviet Encyclopedia*, volume 2 (New York and London: Macmillan, 1973), 521.

9. Arjomand, *The Shadow of God and the Hidden Imam*, 255; Bayat, *Mysticism and Dissent*, 113-14, 116; Afshari, "A Study of the Constitutional Revolution," 151 note 1. See also V. Minorsky, "Review Essay on *The Babi Risings in Iran in 1848-1852* (M. S. Ivanov, 1939)," pp. 875-883 in *Bulletin of the School of Oriental and African Studies*, volume 11 (1943-1946), 880.

10. E. G. Browne, "Personal Reminiscences of the Babi Insurrection at Zanjan in 1850," pp. 761-827 in *Journal of the Royal Asiatic Society*, volume 19 (or 29?) (1897), 793, quoted in Moojan

Momen, "The Social Basis of the Babi Upheavals in Iran (1848-53): A Preliminary Analysis," pp. 157-183 in *International Journal of Middle East Studies*, volume 15, number 2 (May 1983), 178.

11. Minorsky, "Persia: Religion and History," 254. See also Afshari, "The *Pishivaran*," 146.

12. Arjomand, *The Shadow of God and the Hidden Imam*, 254, referring to Abbas Amanat, "The Early Years of the Babi Movement: Background and Development," Ph.D. dissertation, Oxford University (1981); Algar, *Religion and State*, 147-48.

13. N. A. Kuznetsova, *Auza'-i Siyasi va Ijtima'i-yi Iqtisadi-yi Iran dar Payan-i Sadeh-i Hijdahum ta Nimeh-i Nakhustin-i Sadeh-i Nuzdahum-i Miladi* [The Political and Socioeconomic Condition of Iran from the End of the Eighteenth Century till the Middle of the Nineteenth Century], translated from the Russian by S. Yazdani (Tehran: n.p., 1980), 143, cited by Afshari, "A Study of the Constitutional Revolution," 162; Ivanov, "Babi Uprisings," 521; Bausani, *The Persians*, 166; Bayat, *Mysticism and Dissent*, 125.

14. Momen, "The Social Basis of the Babi Upheavals," 179, 177.

15. Ibid., 170, citing a manuscript of Mirza Husain Zanjani.

16. Ibid., 175-76, 167; Bayat, *Mysticism and Dissent*, 123.

17. Bayat, *Mysticism and Dissent*, 109.

18. Afshari, "A Study of the Constitutional Revolution," 158.

19. Bayat, *Mysticism and Dissent*, 107. See also 108, 120.

20. Sidney Churchill, letter of December 12, 1889, quoted by E. G. Browne, *Materials for the Study of the Bábí Religion* (Cambridge: At the University Press, 1918), 293, and cited by Afshari, "A Study of the Constitutional Revolution," 161 note 3.

21. Afshari, "A Study of the Constitutional Revolution," 152-53.

22. In 1866 the majority of the surviving Babis accepted the new dispensation of Bahaullah, leading to the moderate, depoliticized universal religion of Bahaism. The minority who continued to embrace Babism became known as Azalis and a generation later a number of them played progressive roles as individuals in the constitutional movement. See Bayat, *Mysticism and Dissent*, 128-131, and Afshari, "A Study of the Constitutional Revolution," 163-64.

23. Momen, "The Social Basis of the Babi Upheavals," 179, 164, 169, 170. See also Curzon, *Persia and the Persian Question*, I, 449, considered exaggerated by Afshari, "A Study of the Constitutional Revolution," 149.

24. Lambton, "Persian Society," 136; Arjomand, *The Shadow of God and the Hidden Imam*, 256; Momen, "The Social Basis of the Babi Upheavals," 176-77, 180. Algar, in a disagreement from within this point of view, sees it as a failure since it went outside what he takes as the orthodox, oppositional attitude of the ulama toward the state: *Religion and State*, 141 note 20.

25. Ivanov, "Babi Uprisings," 521. Variants of this more materialist interpretation have found favor with Afshari, "A Study of the Constitutional Revolution," 149-50, and Minorsky, "Review Essay on *The Babi Uprisings in Iran in 1848-1852*," 879.

26. Bausani, *The Persians*, 165.

27. Lorentz, "Iran's Great Reformer," 86, 92-94, 97-98; Nashat, *The Origins of Modern Reform*, 16-17, 21; Amanat, "Introduction" to *Cities & Trade*, xxiii-xxv; and Adamiyat, *Amir Kabir va Iran*, 227ff.

28. Lambton, "Persian Society," 133; Bakhash, *Iran*, 4; Nashat, *The Origins of Modern Reform*, 21-24; Abrahamian, *Iran Between Two Revolutions*, 66.

29. On the opposition to the Reuter Concession, see Keddie, *Religion and Rebellion*, 6-7, and Nashat, *The Origins of Modern Reform*, 91-94.

30. For accounts of the events, see Keddie, *Religion and Rebellion*; Ann K. S. Lambton, "The Tobacco Régie: Prelude to Revolution," pp. 119-157 in *Studia Islamica*, volume XXII (1965), and pp. 71-90 in volume XXIII (1965), 121, 127; Browne, *The Persian Revolution*; and Afshari, "A Study of the Constitutional Revolution." For the terms of the concession, see "Concession of the Tobacco Régie in Persia" (March 8, 1890), in Hurewitz, *Diplomacy*, II, 205-6.

31. Quoted by Keddie, *Religion and Rebellion*, 95-96. Doubts surrounding authorship of this fatva have been documented by Lambton, "The Tobacco Régie," 145 note 4, but as Algar has noted, Shirazi's opposition to the concession was known and he never rejected the attribution of the fatva to him: *Religion and Rebellion*, 211-12.

32. Keddie, *Religion and Rebellion*, 131.

33. Gilbar, "The Big Merchants," 290-92. Deteriorating economic conditions in key areas may have made other merchants join the protests as well. Tabriz had witnessed a certain decline in importance since mid-century, while Shiraz suffered a temporary slump in 1889-91 due to bad harvests and the depreciation of Iran's silver currency: see chapter four and McDaniel, *The Shuster Mission*, 42, who notes that in relatively prosperous Khurasan, the ulama refused to back the merchants against the concession.

34. Keddie, *Religion and Rebellion*, 65. See the remarks of Antoine Kitabji in the prospectus, dated August 2, 1890, cited by Browne, *The Persian Revolution*, 34-35.

35. Paton to Kennedy, August 15, 1891, cited by Keddie, *Religion and Rebellion*, 76. See also ibid., 104; and Afshari, "A Study of the Constitutional Revolution," 170, 182-83.

36. Afshari, "A Study of the Constitutional Revolution," 185. This paragraph draws on ibid., 181-82; and Keddie, *Religion and Rebellion*, 80.

37. The Russians were involved in organizing the opposition, though Keddie concludes that "the exact extent and nature of Russian activity is difficult to determine": *Religion and Rebellion*, 66.

38. There is a growing debate on the precise nature of the ulama's role in these events, in part due to the revising of Iranian history in light of the 1979 revolution. Thus Faridun Adamiyat downplays their role in his *Shurash bar Imtiaznameh-yi Rizhi* [Rebellion Against the Régie Concession] (Tehran: Payam, 1360/1981), while Shaikh Hasan Karbala'i conversely exaggerates their role in *Qaradad-i Rizhi-yi 1890 M.* [The Régie Agreement of 1890] (Tehran: Mubarizan Publishers, 1361/1982). Mansoor Moaddel discusses these interpretations, generally favoring the first and stressing ulama opposition to the movement in Tabriz, Mashhad and Kirman in "Shi'i Political Discourse and Class Mobilization in the Tobacco Movement of 1890-92," in *Sociological Forum* (1992).

39. Lascelles's report is quoted by Keddie, *Religion and Rebellion*, 99. Data in this paragraph is also drawn from Algar, *Religion and State*, 207, 209, 213.

40. Keddie, *Religion and Rebellion*, 50.

41. This telegram is quoted by Keddie, *Religion and Rebellion*, 89.

42. Keddie, *Religion and Rebellion*, 131, citing a consular report of June 2, 1891.

43. Ibid., 19-26. Also Browne, *The Persian Revolution*, 44.

44. Keddie, *Religion and Rebellion*, 49, 46-47. By autumn 1891 he told E. G. Browne that there was no hope of reform until the shah's and Amin al-Sultan's heads had been cut off: *The Persian Revolution*, 45.

45. Browne, *The Persian Revolution*, 19. The letter is translated and quoted in full in ibid., 15-21.

46. *Qanun*, issue number 6 (July 18, 1890), quoted in Browne, *The Persian Revolution*, 41. See also ibid., 36ff, and on the Azari-speaking opposition, Lambton, "The Tobacco Régie," 142.

47. Quoted in Keddie, *Religion and Rebellion*, 152-53.

48. In an echo of the revolution in France a century earlier, the French diplomat de Balloy felt the events of January 4, 1892 were "not an uprising but a revolution," while the shah's French physician Feuvrier judged it "a serious affair which has deeply stirred the country, driving it to the verge of rebellion": quoted respectively in Keddie, *Religion and Rebellion*, 106-7, and Browne, *The Persian Revolution*, 57.

49. Algar, *Religion and State*, 213, and idem, lecture on the Tobacco rebellion at the University of California, Berkeley, February 8, 1982.

50. Ashtiani to Shirazi, quoted in Lambton, "The Tobacco Régie," 156-57. See also Keddie, *Religion and Rebellion*, 105-6, 116.

51. Keddie, *Religion and Rebellion*, 117-19; Algar, *Religion and State*, 219.

52. Keddie, *Religion and Rebellion*, 114, 131; Afshari, "A Study of the Constitutional Revolution," 166; Ann K. S. Lambton, "The Persian Constitutional Revolution of 1905-6," pp. 173-182 in P. J. Vatikiotis, editor, *Revolution in the Middle East and Other Case Studies* (Totowa, New Jersey: Rowman and Littlefield, 1972), 175.

53. In addition to the sources cited on specific points, this section draws on Browne, *The Persian Revolution*; E. G. Browne, "Chronology of the Persian Revolution," pp. 310-336 in his *The Press and Poetry of Modern Persia* (Los Angeles: Kalamát Press, 1983 [London: Cambridge University Press, 1914]); idem, *The Persian Crisis of December, 1911; How it Arose and Whither it May Lead Us* (Cambridge: Cambridge University Press, 1912); Abrahamian, *Iran Between Two Revolutions*; Ahmad Kasravi, *Tarikh-i Mashruteh-i Iran* [History of the Constitutional Revolution of Iran] (Tehran: Amir Kabir, 1344/1965); Afshari, "A Study of the Constitutional Revolution;" Nikki Keddie, "Popular Participation in the Persian Revolution of 1905-1911," pp. 66-79 in Keddie, *Iran: Religion, Politics and Society* (London: Frank Cass, 1980); and McDaniel, *The Shuster Mission*. The best recent account of events is that of Mangol Bayat, *Iran's First Revolution. Shi'ism in the Constitutional Revolution of 1905-1909* (Oxford: Oxford University Press, 1991).

54. Gilbar, "Trends in the Development of Prices," 197; idem, "Demographic developments," 156.

55. The Electoral Law of September 9, 1906 is found in Browne, *The Persian Revolution*, 355-359.

56. In a meeting in Vienna in July 1911 with Russian diplomat N. H. de Hartwig, Muhammad 'Ali was told "that the Russian government could give him no direct support, but that Russia would not stand in his way. He was free to return to Russia if he thought he could succeed. If he failed, Russia would deny all responsibility": McDaniel, *The Shuster Mission*, 135, citing Viennese police records. Muhammad 'Ali passed through Russia and reached Iran on July 19.

57. Abrahamian, *Iran Between Two Revolutions*, 110.

58. I am also foreshadowing here a theory of revolution more fully elaborated in diagram 9.1 of chapter nine.

59. This line of reasoning is suggested by the work of Abbas M. Milani, "Ideology and the Iranian Constitutional Revolution. The Political Economy of the Ideological Currents of the Constitutional Revolution," Ph.D. dissertation, Department of Political Science, University of Hawaii (1975).

60. Abrahamian, *Iran Between Two Revolutions*, 80; idem, "The Causes of the Constitutional Revolution in Iran," pp. 381-414 in *International Journal of Middle East Studies*, volume 10 (1979), 403, 412-13; and Afshari, "A Study of the Constitutional Revolution," 187.

61. See Vanessa Martin, *Islam and Modernism. The Iranian Revolution of 1906* (London: I. B. Tauris, 1989), and Bayat, *Iran's First Revolution*. Bayat makes a strong case for the relevance of personal networks over class or institutional approaches. A network, however, in many cases can be seen as a "cross-class" alliance.

62. McDaniel, *The Shuster Mission*, 190 note 1, citing German archives. This paragraph draws on Ashraf, *Mavane'-i Tarikhi*, 120-21; Nashat, "From Bazaar to Market," 71; Browne, *The Persian Revolution*, 137; Afshari, "The *Pishivaran*," 137; and idem, "A Study of the Constitutional Revolution," 199.

63. Nazim al-Islam Kirmani, *Tarikh-i Bidari-yi Iranian* [History of the Awakening of the Iranians], three volumes (Tehran: Bunyad-i Farhang-i Iran, 1346/1967), III, 242. Volume three of this basic history has been translated by Seyed Taghi Barakchian, "An Annotated Translation of Nazim al-Islam Kirmani's *Tarikh-i Bidari-i Iranian* (History of Iranian Awakening), Vol. III," Ph.D. dissertation, Department of History, State University of New York at Binghamton (1983). The present reference is found in the Barakchian translation, 69.

64. Abrahamian, *Iran Between Two Revolutions*, 84, quoting Kasravi, *Tarikh-i Mashruteh*, 110.

65. Ashraf and Hekmat, "Merchants and Artisans," 743. See also Abrahamian, *Iran Between Two Revolutions*, 98 note 110; and Ashraf, *Mavane'-i Tarikhi*, 120.

66. Floor, *Labour Unions*, 9-11. On the June 1910 printers' strike, which included Armenians, Jews and Muslims, see National Archives, 891.00/533, despatch 51, Russell to Secretary of State, June 24, 1910.

67. See Abrahamian, *Iran Between Two Revolutions*, 94-96; Browne, *The Persian Revolution*, 163, 166.

68. Ervand Abrahamian, "The Crowd in the Persian Revolution I," pp. 128-150 in *Iranian Studies*, volume II, number 4 (Autumn 1969), 143.

69. Browne, *The Persian Revolution*, 118, 164, citing an eyewitness correspondent.

70. Afshari, "A Study of the Constitutional Revolution," 233-35; Abrahamian, *Iran Between Two Revolutions*, 97-98. Sattar Khan's father was a "wandering cloth-dealer." Abrahamian himself notes that lutis "were to be found on both sides during the Civil War": Ervand Abrahamian, "The Crowd in Iranian Politics 1905-1953," pp. 184-210 in *Past & Present*, number 41 (December 1968), 195 note 37.

71. Mangol Bayat-Philipp, "Women and Revolution in Iran, 1905-1911," pp. 295-308 in Lois Beck and Nikki Keddie, editors, *Women in the Muslim World* (Cambridge, Mass.: Harvard University Press, 1978), 302. On women, see also Kasravi, *Tarikh-i Mashruteh*, 69, 97, 159, 181-82; Daughter of Aga Shaykh Hadi, "Il faut prendre exemple sur les femmes," pp. 282-284 in *Revue du Monde Musulman*, volume XII, number 10 (October 1910); and W. Morgan Shuster, *The Strangling of Persia* (New York: The Century Co., 1912), 198.

72. This was related to Browne by Taqizadeh: *The Persian Revolution*, 122 note 1. Bayat has good biographical profiles of individual leaders in *Iran's First Revolution*, 38-44. It should be noted that her "religious dissidents" cuts across my categories of intelligentsia and popular ulama—some were secular radicals, others genuinely devout.

73. Algar, *Religion and State*, passim; Said Amir Arjomand, "The Ulama's Traditionalist Opposition to Parliamentarianism: 1907-1909," pp. 174-190 in *Middle Eastern Studies*, volume 17, number 2 (April 1981), 185.

74. Browne, *The Persian Revolution*, 116. On Bihbihani and Tabatabai see Kasravi, *Tarikh-i Mashruteh*, 48-51, and Faridun Adamiyat, *Fikr-i Dimukrasi-yi Ijtima'i dar Nahzat-i Mashrutiyat-i Iran* [Social Democratic Thought in the Iranian Constitutional Movement] (Tehran: Payam Press, 1354/1975), 4.

75. Browne, *The Persian Revolution*, 262. See also ibid., 219, 271; Katouzian, *The Political Economy*, 64, 70 note 11; Good, "Social Hierarchy in Provincial Iran," 139-40; and McDaniel, *The Shuster Mission*, 85.

76. Arjomand, "The Ulama's Traditionalist Opposition," 174. On royalist ulama, see ibid.; McDaniel, *The Shuster Mission*, 67, 73; Browne, *The Persian Revolution*, 113, 148 note 1, 262; and Katouzian, *The Political Economy*, 62. The key works on this whole topic now are Martin, *Islam and Modernism*, and Bayat, *Iran's First Revolution*.

77. Afshari provides evidence on these cases, "A Study of the Constitutional Revolution," 247-75, as does McDaniel, *The Shuster Mission*, 100-107.

78. Quoted by Browne, *The Persian Revolution*, 258. On these royalist forces, see McDaniel, *The Shuster Mission*, 142, 156-57; Afshari, "A Study of the Constitutionalist Revolution," 235-39; and Tapper, "Black Sheep, White Sheep and Red-Heads," 70.

79. Bausani, *The Persians*, 171.

80. Abrahamian, *Iran Between Two Revolutions*, 107-8; Afshari, "A Study of the Constitutional Revolution," 281-90.

81. Kazemi and Abrahamian, "The Nonrevolutionary Peasantry"; Good, "Social Hierarchy in Provincial Iran," 157; Afshari, "A Study of the Constitutional Revolution," 299.

82. Pavlovitch, "La situation agraire," 622; Keddie, *Historical Obstacles to Agrarian Change*, 8, based on a British report of 1909; Milani, "Ideology and the Iranian Constitutional Revolution,"

135. For an interesting effort to revise the standard accounts of peasant non-involvement, on which I have drawn, see Janet Afary, "Peasant Rebellions of the Caspian Region during the Iranian Constitutional Revolution, 1906-1909," pp. 137-161 in *International Journal of Middle East Studies*, volume 23, number 2 (May 1991).

83. See the account of events in Gilan by Adamiyat, *Fikr-i Dimukrasi-yi Ijtima'i*, 66-74.

84. Abrahamian, *Iran Between Two Revolutions*, 99, 99 note 111.

85. Ibid., 94, 89-91.

86. Browne, *The Persian Revolution*, 251.

87. Ashraf, *Mavane'-i Tarikhi*, 119 table 4; Ashraf and Hekmat, "Merchants and Artisans," 742; Abrahamian, "The Crowd in the Persian Revolution I," 142.

88. This is Mehrain's calculation: "The Emergence of Capitalist Authoritarian States," 192.

89. This decision seems to have been taken unilaterally by the British chargé d'affaires at Tehran, as Wright notes that Sir Edward Grey, the foreign secretary, disapproved of it: *The Persians Amongst the English*, xviii.

90. Browne, *The Persian Revolution*, 195. On England, see also ibid., 201, 294-95, 307, 309; Ann K. S. Lambton, "Persian Political Societies 1906-11," pp. 41-89 in *St Antony's Papers*, Middle Eastern Affairs, number 16 (Carbondale: Southern Illinois University Press, 1963), 65, 86-87; and McDaniel, *The Shuster Mission*, 196 (but see 191 for less helpful action in 1911).

91. Browne, *The Persian Revolution*, 221-25. Browne speculates that owing to the various factions in the Russian government, it is possible that Liakhov acted without the knowledge of the foreign minister Izvolsky (who denied knowing) but with "incitements and encouragements" "from high quarters": ibid., 227. On these factions, see ibid., 263, 341.

92. Browne, "Chronology," 330. The data on which this paragraph is based generally are found in McDaniel, *The Shuster Mission*, 135-196; Browne, *The Persian Revolution*, 149, 170 note 1, 201, 209-10, 251, 258, 272-87, 294, 297, 306-9, 319-22, 325, 341, 349; and idem, *The Persian Crisis of December, 1911*. Further evidence of anti-Russian sentiment can be found in U.S. consular documents of 1910: see, inter alia, National Archives, 891.00/505, despatch 234, Mr. Frederic de Biller to Secretary of State, March 19, 1910, and the letter of U.S. Minister Charles W. Russell of March 31, 1910, 891.00/508.

93. See Browne, *The Persian Revolution*, 245, 383; Lambton, "Persian Political Societies," 47-51, 88; Abrahamian, *Iran Between Two Revolutions*, 87; Afshari, "A Study of the Constitutional Revolution," 218-19; and Mehrain, "The Emergence of Capitalist Authoritarian States," 177-78.

94. Afshari, "A Study of the Constitutional Revolution," 214, 231-33; Abrahamian, *Iran Between Two Revolutions*, 75-76, 97.

95. Afshari, "A Study of the Constitutional Revolution," 235-36. On the mujahidin, see Lambton, "Persian Political Societies," 60-70; McDaniel, *The Shuster Mission*, 78, 111-12; and Abrahamian, *Iran Between Two Revolutions*, 97, 107.

96. National Archives, 891.00/505, despatch 234, Frederic de Billier to Secretary of State, March 19, 1910. See also Abrahamian, *Iran Between Two Revolutions*, 87, 97 note 105, 99-100, 105; Abrahamian, "The Causes of the Constitutional Revolution," 402; Tadeusz Swietochowski, *Russian Azerbaijan, 1905-1920. The Shaping of National Identity in a Muslim Community* (Cambridge: Cambridge University Press, 1985), 53, 68; Floor, *Labour Unions*, 4, 5, 9; Kasravi, *Tarikh-i Mashruteh*, 194-95; Lambton, "The Persian Constitutional Revolution," 177; and Bayat, *Iran's First Revolution*, 98-105.

97. Mehrain, "The Emergence of Capitalist Authoritarian States," 192.

98. Abrahamian, *Iran Between Two Revolutions*, 106, 105, citing the program of the Moderate Party. On the Democrat Party, see ibid., 103-5; Floor, *Industrialization in Iran*, 10; and McDaniel, *The Shuster Mission*, 173.

99. Milani, "Ideology and the Iranian Constitutional Revolution," 142-72; also Kasravi, *Tarikh-i Mashruteh*, 45-47; Keddie, *Roots of Revolution*, 71-72. The works of Faridun Adamiyat in Persian are rich sources for this whole topic.

100. Milani, "Ideology and the Iranian Constitutional Revolution," 144, citing Adamiyat, *Akhundzadeh* (Tehran, 1961), 117.

101. Kirmani, *Tarikh-i Bidari-yi Iranian*, I, 364.

102. Milani, "Ideology and the Iranian Constitutional Revolution," 166 cites Malkam Khan, *Majmu-i Asar-i Malkam Khan* [Collected Works of Malkam Khan] (Tehran, 1948), 79-90, and Maraga'i, *Siyahatnama-yi Ibrahim Beg*, 87, 104.

103. See Milani, "Ideology and the Iranian Constitutional Revolution," 170, 169. This was a common theme among many of the "religious dissidents" discussed by Bayat, although others took care to hide their views: *Iran's First Revolution*, passim.

104. F. Adamiyat, *Idiolozhi-yi Nahzat-i Mashrutiyyat-i Iran* [The Ideology of the Iranian Constitutional Movement] (Tehran: Payam Press, 1976), 3, quoted by Said Amir Arjomand, "Review Essay: Religion and Ideology in the Constitutional Revolution," pp. 282-291 in *Iranian Studies*, volume XII, numbers 3-4 (Summer-Autumn 1979), 284.

105. Said Amir Arjomand, "Traditionalism in Twentieth-century Iran," pp. 195-232 in Said Amir Arjomand, editor, *From Nationalism to Revolutionary Islam* (Albany: State University of New York Press, 1984), 201, quoting Nuri's published open letters known as his journal (*ruznama*).

106. Ibid. See further ibid., 202; idem, "The Ulama's Traditionalist Opposition," 183, 186; Martin, *Islam and Modernism*; and Abrahamian, *Iran Between Two Revolutions*, 106.

107. Quoted by Browne, *The Persian Revolution*, 120.

108. M. Malikzadeh, *Tarikh-i Inqilab-i Mashrutiyat-i Iran* [History of the Iranian Constitutional Revolution], 5 volumes (Tehran: Suqrat Press, 1949), IV, 212, translated in Abrahamian, *Iran Between Two Revolutions*, 106.

109. Katouzian, *The Political Economy*, 59.

110. Quoted by Lambton, "Persian Political Societies," 54-55.

111. Letter from Browne's correspondent, December 29, 1906, in *The Persian Revolution*, 127.

112. Browne, *The Persian Revolution*, 169, quoting a revolutionary proclamation from one of the anjumans.

113. On the shabnamehs, see Milani, "Ideology and the Iranian Constitutional Revolution," 149-50; on the press, Browne, *The Press and Poetry* and *The Persian Revolution*, 143; on poetry and satire, Swietochowski, *Russian Azerbaijan*, 67.

114. On the thrust of this analysis and for table 5.2, see John Foran, "The Strengths and Weaknesses of Iran's Populist Alliance: A Class Analysis of the Constitutional Revolution of 1905-1911," pp. 795-823 in *Theory and Society*, volume 20, number 6 (1991).

115. Gillard, *The Struggle for Asia*, 178. See also Keddie, "The Impact of the West," 136.

116. J. M. Balfour, *Recent Happenings in Persia* (Edinburgh and London: William Blackwood and Sons, 1922), 23. See also Keddie, *Roots of Revolution*, 81; idem, *Historical Obstacles*, 10; Floor, *Industrialization in Iran*, 11; Issawi, *EHI*, 129; and Wilber, *Riza Shah Pahlavi*, 17.

117. Keddie, *Roots of Revolution*, 79.

118. This paragraph is based on Denis Wright, *The English Amongst the Persians During the Qajar Period 1787-1921* (London: Heinemann, 1977), 175-76; Wilber, *Riza Shah Pahlavi*, 33; and J. C. Hurewitz, *Diplomacy in the Near and Middle East*, volume II, *A Documentary Record: 1914-56* (Princeton: D. Van Nostrand Company, Inc., 1956), 34-36.

119. Quoted in Richard H. Ullman, *Anglo-Soviet Relations, 1917-1921*, volume three, *The Anglo-Soviet Accord* (Princeton: Princeton University Press, 1972), 369. See further, ibid., 171-73; Keddie, *Roots of Revolution*, 85; Alexandre A. Bennigsen and S. Enders Wimbush, *Muslim National Communism in the Soviet Union. A Revolutionary Strategy for the Colonial World* (Chicago and London: The University of Chicago Press, 1979), 79; Kazemi and Abrahamian, "The Non-revolutionary Peasantry," 285-86; Abrahamian, *Iran Between Two Revolutions*, 112-16; and Eric Hooglund, "The Effects of the Land Reform Program on Rural Iran, 1962-1972," Ph.D. dissertation, Department of Political Science, Johns Hopkins University (1975), 67-68.

120. On these movements, see Abrahamian, *Iran Between Two Revolutions*, 119; Mehrain, "The Emergence of Capitalist Authoritarian States," 235; Bennigsen and Wimbush, *Muslim National Communism*, 80-81.

121. Floor, *Labour Unions*, 12-16.

122. The civil war in Russia changed the situation somewhat, as the Soviets became alarmed by the White Russian military threat from across the Caspian. Thus in May 1920 they landed at Anzali to seize the British- and Iranian-held former White Russian Caspian fleet, an act which involved them in the affairs of the Jangali movement.

123. H. Nicholson, *Curzon, the Last Phase* (London, 1934), 121-27, quoted in Hurewitz, *Diplomacy*, II, 64.

124. "Agreements: Great Britain and Persia" (August 9, 1919), pp. 64-66 in Hurewitz, *Diplomacy*, II. Iran's indebtedness to Britain stood at 5,590,000 pounds sterling by 1922: Issawi, *EHI*, 371.

125. Arguing for no real British involvement are Lt.-Col. Sir Wolseley Haig, "The Rise of Riza Khan Pahlavi," pp. 624-632 in *The National Review* (London), volume 86 (December 1925), 626; Balfour, *Recent Happenings in Persia*, 218; and Peter Avery, *Modern Iran* (London: Ernest Benn Limited, 1965), 228. Evidence of some British role is provided by Wilber, *Riza Shah Pahlavi*, 39ff; Katouzian, *The Political Economy*, 80; Keddie, *Roots of Revolution*, 87; Wright, *The English Amongst the Persians*, 180; and Lieutenant-Colonel W. G. Grey, "Recent Persian History," pp. 29-42 in *Journal of the Central Asian Society*, volume XIII, part I (1926), 35. Arguments similar to mine are made by Ullman, *The Anglo-Soviet Accord*, 385, and Michael P. Zirinsky, "Blood, Power, and Hypocrisy: The Murder of Robert Imbrie and American Relations with Pahlavi Iran, 1924," pp. 275-292 in *International Journal of Middle East Studies*, volume 18, number 3 (August 1986), 280-81.

126. Ironside's diary for January 14, 1921, quoted by Wright, *The English Amongst the Persians*, 181 note. See also Ullman, *The Anglo-Soviet Accord*, 386, and Wilber, *Riza Shah Pahlavi*, 9-15.

127. Wright, *The English Amongst the Persians*, 182. Ironside's diary for February 23, 1921 reads: "Reza Khan has carried out a coup d'etat in Tehran, but true to his promise to me he has declared his loyalty to the Shah.... I fancy that all the people think I engineered the coup d'etat. I suppose I did strictly speaking": ibid., 183.

128. When Lieutenant-Colonel W. G. Grey asked Smyth about this later, Smyth replied: "I was asked for military advice, and as Instructor I had to give it." Grey seems to have found this reasonable: "It is certain that if a thing like this is going to take place, it is better that it should be carried out in an orderly manner, as it was": "Recent Persian History," 35.

129. Zirinsky, "Blood, Power, and Hypocrisy," 280, citing Foreign Office records. See also Wright, *The English Amongst the Persians*, 183, 184 note; Wilber, *Riza Shah Pahlavi*, 48 note 9; and Haig, "The Rise of Riza Khan Pahlavi," 629-30.

130. Diary entry of February 14, 1921, quoted by Wright, *The English Amongst the Persians*, 184 note.

131. See Farhad Diba, *Mohammad Mossadegh. A Political Biography* (London: Croom Helm, 1986), 41, citing *Donya Annual* (Tehran: 1331/1952), viii, 90. The story is also found in Katouzian, *The Political Economy*, 136 note 12.

132. Quoted by Haig, "The Rise of Riza Khan Pahlavi," 629. See further Wilber, *Riza Shah Pahlavi*, 43-47, and Balfour, *Recent Happenings in Persia*, 225.

133. See Abrahamian, *Iran Between Two Revolutions*, 118-19; Balfour, *Recent Happenings in Persia*, 228, 233; Grey, "Recent Persian History," 35-39; and Avery, *Modern Iran*, 253-54.

134. Just before the coup itself he is said to have told an Iranian officer: "All the Cossack officers at Qazvin and Tehran must unite to get the foreigners out of Iran, and to annihilate the foreigner-lovers": Wilber, *Riza Shah Pahlavi*, 42, quoting Husain Makki, *Tarikh-i Bist Saleh-yi Iran* [Twenty-Year History of Iran] (Tehran: 'Ilmi, 1944), I, 108. This paragraph draws on Mehrain, "The Emergence of Capitalist Authoritarian States," 244; Keddie, "The Impact of the West,"

165-70; and idem, *Roots of Revolution*, 89-91. The "Treaty of Friendship: Persia and Russia" (February 26, 1921), is contained in Hurewitz, *Diplomacy*, II, 90-94.

135. See Katouzian, *The Political Economy*, 96 note 6. This paragraph draws on ibid., 77; Kazemi and Abrahamian, "The Nonrevolutionary Peasantry," 386-87; Rey, "Persia in Perspective," 54; Bennigsen and Wimbush, *Muslim National Communism*, 80-81; Ullman, *The Anglo-Soviet Accord*, 371; Abrahamian, *Iran Between Two Revolutions*, 119; and Keddie, *Roots of Revolution*, 89.

136. Abrahamian, *Iran Between Two Revolutions*, 120; Keddie, *Roots of Revolution*, 91; and Gene R. Garthwaite, *Khans and shahs. A documentary analysis of the Bakhtiyaris in Iran* (Cambridge: Cambridge University Press, 1983), 139. The circumstances surrounding the murder of Haidar Khan and Kuchik Khan's precise role in this event remain somewhat unclear.

137. Data in this paragraph are drawn from Katouzian, *The Political Economy*, 93 table 5.1, 100 note 3; Keddie, *Roots of Revolution*, 90; Avery, *Modern Iran*, 262; Abrahamian, *Iran Between Two Revolutions*, 120; and Grey, "Recent Persian History," 35-36.

138. On the republic issue, see Wilber, *Riza Shah Pahlavi*, 79-79; Abrahamian, *Iran Between Two Revolutions*, 134; Zirinsky, "Blood, Power, and Hypocrisy," 280-81; Grey, "Recent Persian History," 39; and Avery, *Modern Iran*, 267.

139. On the various aspects of the murder of Imbrie, see Zirinsky, "Blood, Power and Hypocrisy," passim, and Avery, *Modern Iran*, 263-64.

140. On merchant and landlord support, see Avery, *Modern Iran*, 265, and Keddie, *Roots of Revolution*, 87, 91-92. On Reza Khan and the ulama in this period, see Zirinsky, "Blood, Power, and Hypocrisy," 284; Avery, *Modern Iran*, 264; and Katouzian, *The Political Economy*, 90-91. On Reza and the intelligentsia, see Floor, *Industrialization*, 17-18, and Katouzian, *The Political Economy*, 89. On Reza's relations with, and the nature of the unions and left in general, see Floor, *Labour Unions*, 22-23, 70-71 note 102; Abrahamian, *Iran Between Two Revolutions*, 127-33; and Kazemi and Abrahamian, "The Nonrevolutionary Peasantry," 286.

141. Avery, *Modern Iran*, 259.

142. Wilber, *Riza Shah Pahlavi*, 75. See too Avery, *Modern Iran*, 265, and Abrahamian, *Iran Between Two Revolutions*, 132, on the elections.

143. From the opening editorial of *Farangistan* (Europe [!]), May 1924, quoted by Abrahamian, *Iran Between Two Revolutions*, 124. On the Reformers' and Revival parties, see ibid., 120-24.

144. Avery, *Modern Iran*, 260. Evidence of typical official views of Reza as the required strong man can be found in the remarks of Sir Louis Dane, Major-General Sir George MacMunn, and Lieutenant-Colonel W. G. Grey in Grey's "Recent Persian History," 40, 42. Diba suggests that Ahmad Shah's refusal to sign the 1919 agreement surprised the British and cost him his throne: *Mohammad Mossadegh*, 51.

145. Bennigsen and Wimbush, *Muslim National Communism*, 81. See also Cottam, *Nationalism in Iran*, 190.

146. Zirinsky, "Blood, Power, and Hypocrisy," 285, quoting U.S. Chargé Murray's words.

147. On artisans, see Floor, "The Big Merchants," 135, and Abrahamian, *Iran Between Two Revolutions*, 134; on journalists, Avery, *Modern Iran*, 261; on Mudarris see Katouzian, *The Political Economy*, 86-88; on Mussadiq and other progressives in the fifth majlis, Avery, *Modern Iran*, 265-66.

148. "Recent Developments in Persia," pp. 130-132 in *Journal of the Central Asian Society*, volume XIII, part II (1926), 132.

The Theoretical Significance of the Qajar Period

Virtually all of the conceptual apparatus elaborated in chapter one has been brought into play in part two of this study and all of it has been found useful. Dependent development and world-system considerations provided the keys to the articulation of modes of production in the Iranian social formation. Chapter four analyzed the degree of stasis and change in the nineteenth century as the three modes of production that combined in the period from 1500 to 1800—the peasant crop-sharing, pastoral nomadic, and petty-commodity craft modes—were preserved but undermined under the Western impact and internal logic of development. Alongside them meanwhile emerged a small new capitalist mode of production with particular features, including the dominance of foreign capital and the partial formation of the Iranian working class outside the country as migrant labor in adjacent Russia. The world-system also impinged on this process of class formation and dependency, making the Qajar social formation dependent on *two* world core powers—Britain and (in this context at least) Russia—whose rivalry blocked the hegemonic situation of colonialism found elsewhere, as in India, *and* limited development within the dependent context. When the world-system shifted radically after 1917 a whole new situation was created in Iran and Reza Khan's coup was made possible partly as a result of this (see the concept of *stalemate* below).

The complexity of the Iranian class structure as it formed in these conditions set the parameters of the social movements which occurred in the Qajar period. The historical-comparative analysis of these in chapter five led to the elaboration of a key new concept—the urban multi-class populist alliance. We saw that when a wide range of dominated and intermediate classes has grievances *and* external circumstances are favorable, that explosive anti-state, anti-foreign social movements can emerge and make initial gains. By the same token, however, the differences among the principal classes involved in both the leadership and social bases of these movements rendered ultimate success elusive. The discussion of these internal and external causes of the Constitutional revolution also contributes in a preliminary way to the elaboration of a *theory* of Third World social revolutions developed more explicitly later on the 1977-79 events in chapter nine.

Class alliances and conflicts reposed on the socio-economic structure but were expressed in political and ideological terms, highlighting the importance of *political cultures* of opposition and legitimation. Thus, at the level of the leadership of the Constitutional revolution the ulama split between constitutionalism, royal absolutism, and revolutionary Islam, while the intelligentsia elaborated new ideologies of nationalism, democracy, and socialism. The classes composing the mass movement likewise exhibited complex and sometimes contradictory value orientations: the artisans' devotion to both Islam and a communal, egalitarian social order; workers' blend of Islam, trade unionism and nationalism; tribespeople's mix of tribal loyalty, Islamic fervor, respect for the monarchy and instinctive egalitarianism. Opposed to these was the elite value system of landlords, bureaucrats, tribal chiefs, and the Qajar family itself, based on hierarchy and domination. The ways in which these ideologies and their carriers coalesced or contended, trying to forge alliances or mobilize against their opponents, helped account for both the basic line-ups of social forces (the pro- and anti-constitutional coalitions), as well as the splits within such key classes as the ulama, artisans, and merchants. No united front could be maintained against the main enemies, the Qajar state and foreign powers, and this crucial failure led to the defeat of the constitutional movement.

The notion of an intertwined political, economic, and ideological crisis (what Althusser has called *overdetermination*) proved useful again for understanding the periods of 1906-11 and 1918-25, as it had for the 1722 change of dynasty in part one. The difference is that in the Qajar period this crisis owed its roots to dependency, itself a concept which chapter four showed had economic, political, and ideological dimensions. Methodologically this was discerned by a framework sensitive to the dialectical relationships posited between culture, politics, and economy; external structures of control and internal responses of resistance to them; and on a greater level of abstraction, the general interplay between structure and history. Chapters four and five each tried to capture one side of this dialectic, which is seen fully only in considering the two types of analysis together.

The state ultimately emerged in the period from 1800 to 1925 as a key actor in the Iranian social formation. This is seen in the comparison between the weakness of the Qajars, caused by the world-system's pressures and internal challenges, and the eventual stability of Reza Khan's new state, which found its source of strength after 1921 in a new component in the

Iranian state, an efficiently-administered army. In between these weak and strong states there existed from 1906 to 1921 a transitional state with its own new institutions—the majlis, and in civil society, the political parties, trade unions, and free press—which would eventually come into conflict with Reza Khan's vision of the state.

Finally, the concept of a stalemate of social forces—the state and internal elites/foreign capital/social movements—proved an illuminating notion for understanding the conjuncture that led to the coup. By 1920, so many forces had pulled Iran in different directions for so long that something had to give. The temporary withdrawal of the Soviets and the uncertainty of the British (i.e., the new conjuncture in the world-system), the weakness of the Qajar state, and the fragmentation of the social movements gave Reza Khan his chance. The new order would be different from the old, as will be seen in part three of this study. A stronger state would clamp down its hold on civil society and face a changing world-system in which the United States and Soviet Union began to contend for power in Iran, as well as a slowly declining Great Britain, which still had the strongest position in 1925.

Social Structure and Social Change in Pahlavi Iran and After, 1925-1991

We have now arrived at the threshold of the contemporary period. Part three of this study deals with the tremendous changes in social structure associated with the emergence of the capitalist mode of production in Iran under the aegis of dependent development, and the series of dramatic social upheavals that punctuated this process, either fostering or challenging it—the abdication of Reza Shah, the Allied invasion and occupation during World War II, Soviet-inspired secession movements in Kurdistan and Azarbaijan after the war, the oil nationalization struggle led by Dr. Muhammad Mussadiq, the CIA-backed coup that established Muhammad Reza Pahlavi's domination in 1953, and the massively popular but loosely united revolution that brought the shah down in 1978-79. The period covered is the sixty-odd years from 1925 to the early 1990s, corresponding to the entire reign of the Pahlavi dynasty and the first dozen years of the Islamic Republic.

Full use will be made in part three of the central concepts derived from our synthesis of perspectives on development and social change—dependency, world-system, modes of production, state autonomy, and political cultures of opposition—and a case will be made for the basic relevance of this framework to shed light on the making of the Iranian revolution. Briefly put, we will observe a protracted struggle for national independence in a world-system dominated after World War II by a new core power, the United States. The Pahlavis' ambitious attempt to bring Iran out of the periphery of this system and raise the country to semiperipheral status was accomplished within the limits of dependent development, fueled by an oil-enclave economy and guaranteed by a strong military-autocratic state ultimately backed with American support. In modes of production terms the spread of capitalist relations and growth of the Iranian working class will be traced, but equally significant is the perseverance of classes located in other modes of production—ulama, artisans, and merchants in the petty-commodity mode; peasants and landlords in the crop-sharing mode; tribes-people and khans in the pastoral-nomadic mode—and the appearance of a large marginalized underclass with diverse origins in the urban sector. In the course of half a century, these dominated groups and classes elaborated and forged several political cultures of opposition to the process of dependent capitalist development stamped on Iran by the Pahlavis and the United States. These political currents included varieties of Islam, liberal nationalism, and socialism, and in the long run would together prove capable of mobilizing a powerful populist mass movement against the state and foreign domination. All of these threads of analysis will be specified and brought into mutual contact in the four chapters that follow.

Chapters six and eight chronicle the transformations of social structure by taking "snapshots" of Iran in 1925, 1941, 1953, and 1978. Chapters seven and nine follow the vicissitudes of social movements, focussing on two principal periods—1951-53 and 1978-79—but attending to several other key moments (1941, 1946, 1963) as well. A continuing dialectic of objective economic transformations and subjective opposition movements will be pursued: The two chapters on social structure explore a new concept—"the compression of social forces"—referring to periods in which social classes are fettered from expressing themselves by a hegemonic state; in each case however this led to an explosion of opposition to dependent development, and the chapters on social movements will thus continue our earlier analysis of Iran's "populist alliance." The analysis culminates in a theory of social revolution to account for the tumultuous upheaval of 1978-79 and its fateful outcome in the 1980s.

6

State, Society, and Economy in the Reza Shah Period, 1925-1941: The Compression of Social Forces

[W]ithout falling into unnecessary eulogizing and mythologizing . . . [consider] . . . the concrete facts of putting the entire country under the control of a newly created central administration, of modernizing its institutions, maintaining the integrity of its frontiers, establishing a new code of common law, creating a national bank as a firm basis for the national currency and business, designing a modern pattern for the national education, founding universities and schools of all grades and levels, building a railway that is one of the greatest feats of modern times, erecting factories for the production of common goods, developing modern industries, socially reforming the country from its roots, repressing if not totally obliterating secular abuses and corruption, liberating womenfolk from the veil and making them eligible for every degree of instruction and advancement, and putting an end to the foreign exploitation of the natural richness of Iranian soil.
  —Pio Filipanni Ronconi, "The Tradition of Sacred Kingship in Iran"

*   *   *

Altogether he thoroughly milked the country, grinding down the peasants, tribesmen, and laborers, and taking heavy toll from the landlords. While his activities enriched a new class of "capitalists"—merchants, monopolists, contractors, and politician-favorites—inflation, heavy taxation, and other measures lowered the standard of living of the masses.
  —A. Millspaugh, *Americans in Persia*

The reign of Reza Shah Pahlavi from 1925 to 1941 has engendered rather contradictory assessments, as these paired epigraphs alone would suggest. Among other reasons this may be because a hitherto unprecedented constellation of state, society, and economy was forged in the hothouse of dependent, increasingly capitalist, development in the changing world-systemic conjuncture of the 1930s. During this period Reza Shah's newly consolidated autocratic state took advantage of lessened *direct* domination by Great Britain to initiate industrial and infrastructural development by clamping down on society and reasserting central control in a way unseen since the Safavids at their zenith. This process was riven with political, economic, and ideological contradictions, some of which assumed their full stature only after Reza's abdication in 1941 before the advancing allied armies. Here we will attempt to adjudicate the polarity of judgments of this period by exploring, in sequence, Iran's state, class structure, relations with the West, and frustrated social movements within the context of dependent development and a compression of social forces, largely orchestrated by the new Pahlavi state.

Reza Shah's State:
Military Autocracy, Modernization, and Westernization

The Iranian state assumed extensive political and economic powers during the reign of Reza Shah by comparison with the dismal standards of the Qajar dynasty. Authority reposed ultimately in the hands of the shah, whose key institutional base was the army, and hence we may term the regime a *military autocracy*. Strong internal domination in turn underpinned considerable *state intervention* in the economic activity of the country, both in infrastructure and in industry. The ideological justifications for the extensive reforms of the judiciary, educational, and other institutions that this "modernization" project required included a contradictory blend of secular nationalism and Westernization and further intruded the state's new bureaucratic apparatus into the lives of the population, urban, tribal, and peasant alike.

Reza Shah's fundamental reform was the creation of a strong army capable of enforcing state authority. Upton points out that most of his other reforms, large and small, centered around this, or contributed to it in some way.[1] These included raising state revenues through taxation, banking, and customs measures; improving the communication system by building Iran's first significant railway and adding to the existing road, telegraph, and telephone networks; making military service compulsory through conscription, which required provincial reorganization generally; creation of secular judicial and educational systems which seriously undermined clerical power; the participation of women in education, the economy, and public life (though not in elections); the extension of health and sanitation services; and a prototype of urban renewal to enhance law and order by cutting wide boulevards through the crowded districts of the major cities. We might term this process "state-led military modernization"; it is the congruence and underlying direction of these measures as well as the manner of their devising and implementation that justify characterization of the regime as a military autocracy.

The army, the bureaucracy, and the government proper (cabinet and majlis) constituted the three institutional pillars of the regime. The army was enormously expanded from the several thousand members of the Cossack Brigade in the early 1920s to some 126,000 men under arms and a total mobilizable force of 400,000 by 1941, a huge number given a national population of less than five million economically active males. This was made possible by requiring two years of compulsory military service from every male (plus many more years on active or nominal reserve). Recruits, reluctantly taken from their villages, were exposed to urban life and perhaps a bit of literacy education and instruction in trades. Official budgetary figures indicate an average of 33.5 percent of total revenues spent for military purposes from 1926 to 1941; in addition, a large proportion of the oil revenues (which did not figure in the budget) was devoted to purchasing expensive weaponry and establishing a few armaments industries in Tehran and elsewhere. High-ranking officers, though kept out of the civil bureaucracy and cabinet, became wealthy and powerful members of the ruling class, often acquiring landed estates. As will be seen, this vast military apparatus was used primarily to crush internal social movements and opposition in the 1920s and 1930s (aided by the regular police and a newly established secret police), but proved powerless against greater external forces when the Allies occupied Iran in 1941.

The second pillar of Reza Shah's state was the civil bureaucracy, which like the army was greatly expanded, reorganized, and far better trained than under the Qajars. The new bureaucracy comprised some 90,000 civilian employees. Formerly the province of the Qajar elite and the old administrative families, its ranks were now increasingly open to the educated middle classes. Salaries however were low and bribery and graft continued to plague the system at all levels, with those at the highest echelons becoming part of the elite, while the middle and lower ranks occupied corresponding rungs in urban society, often finding it difficult to make ends meet. Inefficiency too remained a problem as the machinery of government became more complex; both unwieldiness of size and the total control of the shah at the top hindered the smooth working of the various departments. In the provinces the state spread its control through a territorial reorganization of the country from the Qajar system of four huge provinces into eleven provinces with further county and district subdivisions. Little local initiative was allowed as the ministry of the interior at Tehran appointed municipal officials, although a 1930 law did empower city governments to spend their own revenues locally.[2]

This expansion of government was made possible by the state's entry into the field of education. While the ulama-run schools which had predominated in the Qajar era lost tremendous ground, the Iranian elite and middle classes increasingly pursued state-provided education at the upper levels, in the newly founded University of Tehran, technical schools run by the various ministries, or universities abroad. Keddie underlines the class bias of the system, pointing out that "Less than 10 percent of the population received any elementary education, and, for secondary education, the figure was under one percent."[3] Such as it was, this expansion of education not only helped staff the growing bureaucracy, but also contributed to the emergence and growth of a new professional and intellectual class. Furthermore, the state made use of the system to stifle free political inquiry and impose conformity on this intelligentsia, channelling curricula to inculcate "servile adulation, propaganda support, and ideological justification."[4]

Reza Shah was not, of course, the sole architect of the reforms of his period. Particularly in the first half of his reign he was ably assisted by accomplished administrators within his cabinet, which together with the more docile majlis formed a third pillar of his regime. Chief among these top advisors were 'Ali Akbar Davar, Abdal Husain Khan Taimurtash, Sardar As'ad, and Firuz Mirza. The last of these served as finance minister until his fall from grace in 1929, when he was arrested, accused of bribery, and murdered. Taimurtash acted as minister of court from 1926 to 1932 at which time Reza Shah decided he was too powerful and had him imprisoned for taking bribes. He died in 1933, officially of heart failure and pneumonia. Sardar As'ad, the Bakhtiari chief who served as minister of war was likewise arrested in 1933 and though never charged with a crime, died in prison the next year. Finally, in 1937, Davar, the architect of Iran's Civil Code and then minister of finance, committed suicide after falling out with the shah over economic policy. All of these men, having literally outlived their usefulness, were precipitously discarded by Reza Shah, suspicious of their independence and potential popularity. The figures chosen to head ministries after the mid-1930s were less strong-willed, which suited Reza's purpose of autocratic control but undermined his access to critical information and astute administration. These factors would play a role in his own fall in 1941.[5]

A similar pattern of increasing royal control over the majlis and public political life is readily discerned. The most outspoken figures of the mid-1920s were soon removed from the scene: An unsuccessful attempt on the life of the cleric Sayyid Hasan Mudarris in 1926 was followed by his imprisonment and banishment to a remote village in 1928-29 and his murder in 1938, while the voice of the liberal nationalist Muhammad Mussadiq was silenced in 1928 when he was not "re-elected" to the majlis, after which he retired to his estate and was put under house arrest in 1940-41. Other opposition personalities were arrested, exiled or retired from public life; in all Upton estimates several hundred state-sponsored political murders during Reza Shah's reign. The majlis degenerated into a totally compliant rubber stamp quite early on. The four political parties that had seats in the late 1920s were all essentially pro-regime, but Reza abruptly dissolved them, again fearing the emergence of articulate rivals. Majlis deputies continued to be elected every two years, but as private individuals rather than as members of parties. Landlords, non-bazaar businessmen, and senior civil servants constituted up to 84 percent of all deputies in the Reza Shah period, while the number of ulama dropped from twenty-four in 1925 to virtually none by 1940. Elections from the sixth majlis (1926) to the thirteenth (1940) were carefully controlled through the ministry of the interior with the aid of the provincial governors. Thus Reza kept up constitutional appearances but in reality acted as a "constitutional dictator" who brooked no organized dissent within the state and ruthlessly crushed any outside it.[6]

A final, non-institutional pillar of the new state was its economic resources, on a scale and scope far outstripping the Qajar dynasty's and indeed harking back to the Safavids' position of economic hegemony under Shah 'Abbas, with his silk monopoly. Total state revenues grew over fifteen times between 1924 and 1941, from 237 million rials to 3.61 billion rials.[7] Oil revenues rose tenfold from 469,000 pounds sterling in 1919/20 to 4,271,000 pounds in 1939/40. Since this represented as little as 10 percent (and possibly up to 25 percent) of state income, the vast majority must have come from other sources, with significant contributions from the state trade and industrial monopolies (28 percent), the land tax (10-20 percent), customs (about 10 percent), the new income taxes (about 7 percent), and government monopoly taxes on tea and sugar (over 5 percent), these last being items of mass consumption.[8] Expenditures rose enormously in this period as well, from 276 million rials in 1928 to 4.17 billion rials by 1941. As spending rose however, priorities shifted: State investment in industries and trade leaped from 1.1 percent of budget allocations in 1928 to 24.1 percent in 1941, while direct defense spending fell from 40.4 to 14.2 percent (though still growing fourfold in absolute terms). The only other large allocation in 1941 went to "communications" (26.2 percent, some of which was indirect military spending), while health accounted for only 2.0 percent of the budget and agriculture a mere 2.9 percent (up from nothing in 1928). The budget, which had been balanced in 1925, went into a deficit of 710 million rials by 1941 (about $39 million), the result of massive spending on the military, the railroad, and industries.

Largely in order to finance construction of the Trans-Iranian Railway—Reza Shah's gigantic symbol of state power, national independence, and economic development—the state moved to gain control of Iran's foreign trade, exchange rates, and currency. When Iran's balance of payments and the value of its currency deteriorated at the end of the 1920s, a state monopoly on foreign trade was declared in 1930. The government was less interested in direct control of trade than in avoiding deficits and capturing some of the foreign exchange earned by exports so it could import goods for the railroad. Monopolies on specific items of trade were awarded to government agencies or private companies. By the mid-1930s the state had direct or indirect control of about one-third of imports and one-half of exports and Iran managed a slight surplus in its trade generally in that decade. In 1936 multiple exchange rates for various categories of exports were tried, with negative consequences for Iran's trade relations, forcing the country into extensive barter arrangements with Germany and the USSR. The long-awaited dream of a national bank was finally realized in 1927/28 when the Bank Melli was established and empowered to issue currency and regulate fiscal policy. These measures went part of the way toward addressing Iran's unequal relationship with the core powers of the world-economy, as well as helping cushion the impact of the great depression, but their limits will become apparent in discussing the domestic and international sides of the political economy below.[9]

The new power of the state was not without an effect on its autocratic head's personal wealth. Despite a pious pronouncement in 1926 that the desire for wealth "causes considerable mental annoyance and prevents one from devoting his attention to the public interests," by the end of his reign Reza Shah had become the wealthiest man in Iran. His account at the National Bank rose from one million rials in 1930 to 680 million by 1941 (worth seven million pounds sterling). He had in addition acquired enormous estates covering three million acres and owned shares in "numerous local factories, companies and monopolies that yielded excellent returns."[10] His land-grabbing habits were notorious. Landlords offered him "gifts" of their land, either out of terror or under duress. Some were compensated with lands elsewhere in the country. Nearly all of Reza's home province of Mazandaran and large areas of nearby Gilan and Gurgan—the rice baskets of Iran—became his private property. In this way he came to possess an estimated two thousand villages with over 235,000 inhabitants. Though Wilber questions whether Reza was "aware of all the methods used [by zealous agents] in his name," he admits that "Finally, as one of his associates remarked, he owned so much land that he was happiest on rainy days because they were the best for the crops."[11]

At the heart of the regime's legitimation project lay a contradictory and ambivalent mixture of nationalism and Westernization. Nationalism was of course very much in the air in the international system of the 1930s, not just in its fascist variants but also in such Third World cases as the Mexican state

after the 1910-20 revolution and in Atatürk's Turkey. In the case of Iran
Banani notes the paradox presented by this period, simultaneously one of
"intense Westernization" and on the other hand, xenophobia, "suspicion
and resentment" towards the West.[12] In order to strengthen Iran against
the West—particularly the long-standing encroachments of Great Britain
and "Russia"—Reza borrowed heavily from the West a host of economic,
political, and judicial concepts and realities, from dress codes to urban
architecture, judicial statutes to the educational system, secular ideologies
glorifying the state and nation to modern industry and technology.

Reza's own attitudes toward the West suggest a complex love-hate
relationship. In a speech to students departing for European universities in
1930 he revealed a strange admiration for the West's "morals":

> Our chief aim in sending you to Europe is that you should receive a moral
> education, for we note that Western countries have acquired a high standing
> as a result of their thorough moral education. Were it merely for scientific
> instruction it would not have been necessary to send you abroad. We could
> have engaged foreign instructors.[13]

He went on to express a peculiar hope for the effect exposure to the West
might have on Iranians:

> I don't want to turn the Persian into a bad copy of a European. That is not
> necessary, for he has mighty traditions behind him. I mean to make out of my
> countrymen the best possible Persians. They need not be particularly Western
> or particularly Eastern. Each country has a mold of its own, which should be
> developed and improved until it turns out a citizen who is not a replica of
> anyone else, but an individual sure of himself and proud of his nationality.[14]

At the same time he felt that "Persia must learn to do without foreigners."[15]
He thus wanted to emulate the West in order to become independent and
strong, a contradiction-ridden aspiration. Katouzian coins the term
"pseudo-modernism" to capture the superficiality of this effort to appropriate the achievements of the West.[16]

Reza Shah's nationalism, too, differed from much earlier Iranian nationalism in that it was cast in secular rather than Islamic terms and focused on
the might and glory of the state and shah. The only variety of nationalism
permitted was what Keddie designates as "official nationalism stressing
national homogeneity, anticlericalism, and a modernity and strength that
were read into the pre-Islamic past."[17] Tellingly, at the instigation of the
Iranian embassy in Nazi Germany, the shah decreed in 1934 that the name
of the country in the West should be "Iran" and not "Persia"; the new name
"invoked ancient glory and signified the birthplace of the Aryan race."[18]

The pre-Islamic ideal was also used as a wedge in the drive for secularism: "Although no frontal attacks were ever made on Islam, the new generation was taught to regard it as an alien faith imposed on Iran by an inferior civilization."[19] Thus the notion of royal glory was reinvoked to place the shah at the top of society as "king of kings," the undisputed ruler of his country.

In order to assert this autocratic self-conception, Reza Shah's state made various efforts to legitimize itself before the Iranian people and was certainly more self-confident in this regard than the Qajars had been. The regime's ideology can be discerned as it was propagated by the "Department of Public Enlightenment," formed within the ministry of education in the late 1930s: "This organization sponsored public lectures by well-known authorities and professional men on a wide range of topics, including ethics, history, hygiene, literature, social sciences, education, and 'modernism, patriotism and loyalty to the sovereign and the remarkable improvements achieved in the country in recent years'."[20] Wilber notes: "Apparently modelled after the examples of the Nazi and Fascist propaganda machines, the organization was designed to channel public thinking along desired lines, to acquaint the public with the activities of the government, to enlist popular support for the government, and to arose national consciousness and pride."[21] As mentioned above, the educational system as a whole was geared to inculcate secularism, as well as nationalism and the glories of the Iranian imperial state.

How deeply did the regime's attempt to secure its own legitimation touch Iranian society? The reforms of Reza Shah and the claims of his state were aimed primarily at winning the hearts and minds of the urban population, whose several components were at best split in their approval of him. Peasant society was largely unaffected in this period, while the tribes were brutally and forcibly made to settle. Reza Shah's state ultimately reposed on force and in this respect, while his centralization and economic development policies evoked the Safavid period, the lack of deep legitimation and the military underpinning of the new Pahlavi state also hearkened back to the harsh reign of Nadir Shah.[22] The question of civil society's reaction to the legitimation claims of Reza's state can only be fully answered after considering the economic shape of society and the crushing of all social movements in this period.

Economy and Class Structure

The 1930s were the key transitional era between the pre-capitalist dependent development of the Qajar period and the capitalist dependent development of the post-World War II period. The nature and extent of the economic and class changes in Iran's social structure is thus a matter of considerable importance, on which various observers have taken rather different positions.[23] This chapter addresses these issues and debates through the prism of our concept of dependent development: The present section will sketch in one side of this by analyzing the class structure empirically and in modes of production terms, while the next will document the world-systemic constraints placed on Iran's growth—the two sections taken together indicate the parameters of a transitional phase of dependent development by exploring its internal and external possibilities and limits. Despite the problem of finding wholly reliable data for this period, there yet exist enough good historiographic materials for our purpose here, namely, the mapping of Iranian class structure in the interwar period.

Population data indicate steady overall growth with some significant internal shifts as well. The total population of Iran, estimated at around ten million people between 1900 and 1914, grew by almost 50 percent, to 14.6 million in 1940. The compound rate of population growth, which due to war and famine had been only 0.08 percent a year for 1900-1926, increased considerably to 1.50 percent annually for 1926-1940. By sector there were some dramatic shifts. In 1900 the population was 20.9 percent urban (2.07 million people), 25.1 percent tribal (2.47 million), and 54.0 percent peasant (5.32 million). 1940 estimates suggest 22.0 percent urban (3.20 million), only 6.9 percent tribal (about one million), and some 71.1 percent peasant (10.35 million). This reflects the devastating degree of sedentarization and semi-settlement of the tribal sector. Other data on the labor force suggest a fall for the agricultural sector from 90 percent of the total population in 1906 to 85 percent in 1926 to 75 percent in 1946, though the number of agricultural workers grew in absolute terms from 3,431,000 to 3,828,000.[24] Stimulated by military conscription, factory production, and the huge railroad projects, the urban population grew at 2.30 percent a year from 1935 to 1940, compared with only 1.30 percent in the rural sector. Six cities boasted populations of 100,000 or more by 1940, according to various estimates: Tehran (540,000), Isfahan (250,000), Tabriz (200-300,000), Mashhad (200,000), Shiraz (200,000), and the new oil terminus at Abadan (100,000). Iran was thus becoming somewhat more urban and industrial at the end of this period, but still retained a vast majority of its population on the land.

Rural Modes of Production

The two long-standing modes of production in rural Iran—the peasant crop-sharing and the pastoral-nomadic—continued to operate, with the former largely intact, but the latter entering a serious crisis due to state policy.

The principal types of landholding identified for the sixteenth to nineteenth centuries in chapters two and four persisted in the 1925-1941 period, but their relative importance shifted decisively in favor of large privately-owned estates. A survey of various estimates from the 1930s and 1940s suggests the following rough proportions: 10 percent state lands, 10 to 25 percent vaqfs, 5 to 15 percent small-holdings, and 50 to 80 percent large estates.[25] The key development in this period was the consolidation and growth of large, absentee-owned estates. Reza Shah set the precedent for this by his massive acquisitions through confiscation and purchase. Landlords used their power in the courts to register much land to which they held dubious title. Mahdi claims that just thirty-seven families owned 20,000 villages in 1941. A 1949 survey of 1,300 villages in the Tehran area showed that five percent of the landlords owned 83 percent of the land, while 85 percent of the rural population was either landless (60 percent) or owned less than one hectare (25 percent).[26]

The predominant mode of production in agriculture continued to be the peasant crop-sharing mode theorized in chapter two. Lambton found sharecropping the most common form of relation between peasant and landlord, as did Sanjabi, whose 1934 study observed its prevalence on the land of large and middle landowners. The 1934 civil code defined sharecropping, but did not stipulate any particular division of shares, and "contracts" were generally of the customary verbal type. The actual share taken by the landlord varied widely by region, local custom, type of crop, and which party provided water, animal power, fertilizer, tools, and seed. On the whole landlords probably took one-third to one-half of the total crop.[27] This does not mean that individual peasants kept one-half to two-thirds of the remainder, for it was often subdivided among several tenants and various other shares were given to people who provided services in the village. Sharecropping peasants had certain customary rights to cultivate but in practice often lacked true security of tenure. Though evictions might not be common due to the strength of tradition and the relative scarcity of labor in many places, around large cities the opposite prevailed, with very few openings for peasants to become sharecroppers.

Export and commercialized agriculture likewise continued to exist, but there is little sign that these forms deepened significantly beyond the levels of Qajar times. The drive to produce locally some of the vast quantities of sugar consumed in Iran led to a switch to beet crops around the refineries, but peasants seem to have found this a questionable improvement in their lot as it led to increased supervision and the indebtedness a money economy usually brought. Between 1925 and 1939 annual production of wheat grew 67 percent, barley 36 percent, rice 44 percent, cotton 90 percent, and tobacco

114 percent. Silk, cotton, tea, and tobacco were sold on the world market; of the major subsistence crops one estimate for the late 1940s is that two percent of production was exported. One major cash crop—opium—which had accounted for 10-15 percent of Iran's visible exports in the 1920s and 30 percent of the world's opium, declined by two-thirds after the state prohibited or restricted its cultivation.[28] Other cash crops were supposed to replace it, but as the government paid minimal attention to agriculture, no real export boom occurred. We may thus conclude that while there were a few signs of capitalist agriculture at the level of the world-market and of the middlemen domestically, Iran's settled agriculture remained dominated by the peasant crop-sharing mode of production.

In terms of overall performance, Iranian agriculture in the 1930s basically seems to have kept up with population growth, but did not register any conspicuous qualitative improvements. Relative to the industrial and oil sectors its share in the gross national product declined steadily from about 80-90 percent in 1900 to about 50 percent in the 1930s. Since the agricultural work force accounted for 75 percent or more of Iran's total labor force, productivity lagged compared with the more dynamically expanding urban sector. Still, output of the basic grains rose 52.5 percent for 1925-39, as against 25 percent for land under cultivation and 22 percent in population, so some improvement did occur, and most importantly, output exceeded population growth by a factor of two or more. Iran in 1940 was still fundamentally self-sufficient in food (leaving aside sugar and tea, which were imported in great quantities even as domestic production rose): Rice and grain were actually exported in certain years, although wheat was sometimes imported from abroad in the 1930s.[29]

Three main reasons can be adduced for the limited development of agriculture in this period. First, agricultural techniques did not change at all. There was virtually no mechanization of agriculture, drilling of deep wells, or systematic introduction of new seed varieties, except for a few scattered experiments on Reza Shah's properties or by the minority of progressively-minded landowners. Reaping and threshing continued to be done by hand. Secondly, the government paid little attention to the development of agriculture. There was no land reform outside of a mismanaged and corrupt attempt on crown lands in distant Sistan. In fact the opposite of a land reform occurred to the extent that the power and security of large landlords was stabilized and enhanced. Agricultural policy in general was virtually ignored and the budget allocated to this vast sector of the national economy was miniscule. Government pricing policies actually worked against agricultural expansion. The failure to address the problem of land reform points to a third factor—the stagnationist tendencies within the crop-sharing mode of production itself. The mechanics of sharecropping discouraged production or productivity increases on all sides. Peasants feared that bringing in a larger crop would only lead to greater demands on them; a larger than normal output went mostly to the landlord in any case who took the greater share of the crop. By the same token, the landlord already received such a large share that there was little incentive to invest in land improvements. The result of these tendencies in technique, state policy, and extraction of surplus was to leave the existing system more or less intact, which meant a building pressure on the agrarian sector as population began to grow steadily.[30] The continuation of these trends after the war would have major consequences for Iran's social structure.

Iran's landlord class suffered some changes in its composition and power vis-à-vis the state, but on the whole remained intact in the 1930s and continued in its strong position vis-à-vis the peasantry. Certain older landed families and tribal khans lost estates, while merchants, contractors, military officers, and bureaucrats, as well as Reza Shah himself, all acquired land. This partial circulation of incumbents was not in itself an unusual development after the rise of a new dynasty and operated within set limits. Abrahamian observes that thirty-seven of the fifty cabinet members from 1925 to 1941 "had been born into titled and aristocratic families."[31] Landlords also made up a large portion of the majlis deputies. What *was* new was the relative diminution of landlord political authority generally, as bemoaned by a landlord in the Maragheh area: "Before Reza Shah, everybody was a king. But after Reza Shah came to power, he controlled all of us."[32] Abolishing their aristocratic titles, Reza Shah brought the landed elite clearly to a level below himself in terms of political authority. Though much landed resentment of Reza Shah undoubtedly remained, accommodation and adaptation were the order of the day. If their political power was somewhat circumscribed, their wealth was left largely intact, with no land reform or shift in the tax burden. Many landlords in fact expanded their holdings and influence in their regions. While the profits to be made in agriculture started to lag behind those possible in the urban sector they continued to run at 10-15 percent a year. In the late 1940s Hadary made the rough estimate of an annual income of $2,300 per landlord family, some ten times that of his estimate for peasant incomes and undoubtedly many times lower than the income of the larger landlords.[33] Finally, on their own estates landlord power and authority may have undergone some alteration, but remained great. Though Lambton judges that since the Constitutional revolution, "the status of the large landed proprietor [had been altered] from that of a petty territorial prince to that of an ordinary landowner," Lyle Hayden's sketch of a typical village on the central plateau suggests that this still entailed great power: "The owner has absolute control of the business affairs of the land, and to a large extent controls the personal destiny of each inhabitant."[34]

What was the situation of Iran's three and a half million peasants and their families? The typical village, if it was large enough, was somewhat differentiated internally. While the majority of the work force would be landless sharecropping tenants there would also be a group of crafts and service people, including one or more blacksmiths, carpenters, bathkeepers, barbers, and ulama, all of whom received a share of the crop for their services or were paid by the occasion. There would likely also be a group of poor peasants who were not only landless but also without the right to share-crop, who had to hire themselves out in times of peak work, or migrate to nearby towns in search of part-time employment. Peasant women made significant contributions to meager family incomes by weaving, collecting the chaff in the fields after the harvest, and in some places working in the fields, such as on the rice plantations of the Caspian and as hired labor at harvest time, as, for example in Kirman where they received one-half the already low pay of casual male labor.[35] Peasant incomes were at the subsistence level or below in the 1930s. The state turned the terms of trade against the rural population by keeping grain prices low for the urban sector.[36] Data on sharecropping incomes suggests they were as low as $100-200 a year or less and certainly these varied from region to region and even within villages.[37] In one estimate from the Tehran area, four cultivators in a work team produced 100 loads of wheat, and after distribution of shares to the landowner (47.5 loads), for seed (7.5-10 loads), for the blacksmith, bathkeeper, ulama, and field guard (8 loads in all), and to the owner of the oxen (17-18.5 loads) each peasant was left with about 4.5 loads of wheat (1300 kilograms). This share was "clearly insufficient to support him and his family unless supplemented from other sources."[38] Other sources of income and consumption were the weaving done by women, tending of small garden plots, or ownership of a few animals. Even the small-holder who owned a bit of property could slip below the margin of self-sufficiency unless income was derived from other activities. The state moreover could now seriously undermine one's source of livelihood by requiring military service at inopportune times. In the end, inevitable shortfalls had to be made good by recourse to moneylenders.[39]

The overall standard of living of Iran's peasantry was not very satisfactory, to say the least. Many observers held it to have deteriorated by the end of Reza Shah's reign.[40] Even if the standard of living remained stationary, this meant great hardship. Diet in a typical peasant household might be "breakfast: bread and tea; lunch: bread and *mawst* (yoghurt); dinner: bread, mawst, and tea."[41] As Keddie concludes, "peasants were usually hungry."[42] A 1950s survey by the United Nations found daily caloric intake in Iran at under 1800 calories per adult, "the lowest in the entire impoverished Middle East."[43] Health conditions were equally abysmal: In the late 1940s one study found "Infant mortality is estimated at 50 percent; rural life expectancy is about 27 years; diseases affect the majority of the people; and most villages are without any kind of health facilities."[44] Obviously, to become sick was a serious affair. Schools were rarely found in villages in this period, nor could children be easily spared from agricultural and household labor. In general landlords made little or no improvements in the educational, housing, or health situation of peasants.[45]

Iran's tribal sector was severely affected by state policy in the Reza Shah period. His experience of tribal pacification campaigns after 1921 had imbued him with the attitude that tribespeople were "uncouth, unproductive, unruly, and uneducated savages who have been left behind in the primitive state of nature."[46] Lambton feels that such attitudes, or at least state policy based on them, had "the general support of the non-tribal element of the population of the country."[47] Given this climate of opinion, the full weight of the state was thrown into the battle against the tribal population, first to establish central authority once and for all in a continuation of the military campaigns of the 1920s, then to "civilize" the tribes and bring them into the modern world by a program of forced sedentarization. Qashqa'i, Arab, Lur, and other revolts were quelled between 1927 and 1932. After disarming the tribes, their migration routes were blockaded in an effort to compel them to settle and become cultivating peasants rather than pastoralists. Sometimes they were given or sold state land and seed as inducements, often in areas far from their migration routes and of limited agricultural value. Military governors were installed in tribal areas, conscription was applied to the tribesmen, and the authorities fined, imprisoned, or shot those who resisted, sometimes on such pretexts as failure to observe the 1928 uniform dress code. The building of roads and railways enhanced the government's powers of surveillance and control, while settlement was accompanied by stricter collection of taxes.

The impact of these policies on the tribes varied, but was generally devastating. There was naturally resistance, but the struggle against the growing military, economic, and administrative resources of the Pahlavi state was increasingly unequal. Tribal population and production declined dramatically, on the whole. Enormous loss of life is suggested by Bharier's staggering statistic that there were 2,470,000 nomads in 1900, but that by 1932, this had fallen to about one million (the difference covers both those who settled and those who died).[48] Such great human losses seriously undermined the pastoral economy and supply of livestock products in the country. Production of meat, leather, hides, and dairy goods all must have declined, as well as the provision of animals for transport.[49] Forced settlement meant that the same numbers of animals could no longer be maintained, while the poor quality of the lands the tribes received and the lack of support in making what would have been under any circumstances an inconceivably difficult transition to a new mode of life, condemned the new tribal "peasantry" to the most marginal settled existence.

The two main constituent classes of the pastoral nomadic mode, khans and ordinary tribespeople, both felt the effects of the devastation of their ways of life, but naturally continued to be far separated in their relationship to the surplus produced and in their life chances generally. Qashqa'i, Bakhtiari, Boir Ahmadi, and Mamassani khans paid dearly for resisting the state's authority, by banishment, house arrest in Tehran, confiscation of property, imprisonment, or ultimately, with their lives. Other leaders fared better and were brought into line with more conciliatory approaches or outright cooptation. The Qavam family of Shiraz received state lands in distant Khurasan and Mazandaran in exchange for the local lands it forfeited. They and many others retained considerable wealth, though now as much under the heading of large landlords as under that of tribal khans. Those who were kept hostage at Tehran could live fairly comfortably and their metamorphosis into part of the settled elite was cemented by the education of their children in Tehran or even in Europe.[50]

At the opposite end of this class relation were the members of the tribes, the (till then) migrating pastoralist population. Their condition without doubt deteriorated during the Reza Shah period. Forced to settle, or at best with their migration routes disrupted and more tightly controlled, their standard of living suffered enormously. Impoverishment was the natural and obvious result of this experience. In settled communities their diet, housing, and health conditions could not have been better than those of the peasantry discussed already, and, given the radical break with their previous way of life, must often have been not only worse than they had enjoyed under pastoralism, but worse than the conditions of the long-standing peasant population. Conscription, disarming, increased taxes, systematic and arbitrary harassment by the military authorities in their areas all took a toll. Once settled, tribespeople tended to be more exploited by their khans and the government than other peasants—a cruel loss of livelihood, status, and well-being was the result. Tribal women continued to perform more labor and (as a result) possessed more personal freedom than women in the urban or agricultural sectors, though as migration gave way to farming, they may have come somewhat closer to the norms of peasant society.[51]

The hard experience of the coercive might of the state undoubtedly made its mark on tribal attitudes and political consciousness. The Pahlavi state did not rule the tribes with strong legitimation claims but rather by armed force or its threat. Repression politicized many tribes to see their own identities in terms of their migration routes, costumes and culture generally, and language. In a sense strong ethnic minorities really coalesced in this period in the resistance to "Persianization."[52] Exposure to industrial and urban settings (such as that of the Bakhtiari who worked in the oil fields) also led in some cases to the spread of new political ideas of freedom and equality which played a role in certain uprisings examined below. The thin veneer of the success of the government's policy was exposed after 1941 when many tribespeople resumed their migrations in the new political space opened by the abdication of the shah, a development that belongs to chapter seven. But the toll that had been exacted in the 1930s was, unfortunately, extremely high.

Urban Modes of Production

Iran's urban modes of production remained two—the petty-commodity in the craft sector and the capitalist in the industrial sector—but the capitalist mode now began to expand greatly both in absolute terms and relative to artisanal production. In the 1930s the state took the lead in extending the development of capitalism in Iran (though the private sector played more than a small part in this process). A major portion of the state's development resources went into infrastructural projects of which the most spectacular was the railroad. While a major coup for the state's image, the 850-mile long Trans-Iranian Railroad was a wasteful, costly project with numerous drawbacks—it proved inflationary, served minimal economic purposes, bypassed most important cities and lowered the living standard as it was paid for by a regressive tax on tea and sugar. At 35,000 pounds sterling per mile, to build its equivalent in motor vehicle roads would have cost about 1-1.5 percent as much. Its main practical function seems to have been to improve internal security south of Tehran by making the military more mobile, while to the north it facilitated trade toward the Soviet Union, not coincidentally making Reza's properties in Mazandaran more valuable. Other infrastructural developments occurred as well, including 20,000 kilometers of roads, the inauguration of air transport, installation of electric power in all major cities (though water systems remained unimproved), and in communications.[53] The result of these investments was that Iran's infrastructure for capitalist and industrial development was markedly enhanced between 1925 and 1941, though still remaining at a low level with respect to other Middle Eastern countries and with much capital used unwisely to build the railroad.

While chapter four documented the inauguration of factory production in Iran in the pre-World War I period, it is fair to say that *industrialization* really began on a significant scale only in the 1920s and was further consolidated in the 1930s. The government played a major role in initiating this process, but private capital participated in sizable amounts too, as did mixed private-state ventures. Though the Iranian state does not seem to

have consciously carried out a strategy of import-substitution industrialization (ISI), seeking to create industries that would meet domestic consumption needs and reduce imports, to a great extent this *is* the type of
industrialization that occurred, with textiles, food-processing, and auxiliary
industries all fitting this pattern. Actual state policies did not or could not
however include such measures as protective tariffs for Iran's fledgling
factories, while distorted and incorrect foreign exchange rates actually
made certain imports more attractive than local products after 1936.[54] There
is no doubt that the government meant to promote industrialization generally and that a great amount was accomplished in this regard, planned or
not, by 1941. The number of factories grew from less than twenty in 1925
(only five larger than fifty workers) to something over 300 small and large
factories (twenty-eight had more than 500 workers) by 1941. By that date
some $260 million had been invested, about one-third by the state and over
one-half from private capital.[55] Korby's list of 105 enterprises in 1941 suggests that 21 percent were state-owned, 55 percent private (but these employed only 13.5 percent of the work force), 24 percent jointly managed by
the two sectors and 1 percent foreign-owned (the oil industry, which
employed 40 percent of the workers).[56] The state's largest sector was in
textiles; it was the only employer in sugar refining, tobacco, and cement,
the major employer in food-processing, and accounted for nearly all of the
metalwork industry. The private sector's biggest roles were in textiles,
food-processing, and chemicals, with the key area of joint state-private
ventures being textiles. Cotton, wool, and silk textiles were the largest
sector, with 50-60 percent of the industrial work force and thirty-four of the
fifty-seven factories with over 200 workers. The second leading area was in
processing agricultural products, involving eight sugar refineries, one large
tobacco plant, facilities for tea, beverages, rice, preserves, meat, and other
food products. Other industries included a highly successful cement sector,
matches, soap, paper, glass, and chemicals. A small military sector was also
developed, with munitions and armaments factories and equipment repair
facilities. Plans were made for heavy industries in iron and steel and blast
furnaces were imported from Germany but World War II interrupted the
project.[57]

For all these accomplishments, Reza Shah's industrialization program
had several drawbacks and limitations. First, it was both highly specialized
and overconcentrated in a few places, notably Tehran, Tabriz, Isfahan, and
a few sites in Reza's privileged area of the Caspian. Secondly, as argued
already, it was not conducted according to any well-conceived plan. A third
area of problems had to do with costs, profits, and investment. The $260
million invested in all industries combined only equalled the amount spent
on the railroad, proving that the latter project cut into Iran's developmental
potential. The state sector in particular was notorious for its high produc-

tion costs and low profits; indeed, practically all state factories seem to have lost money. Finally, though Iran did make great strides compared with the Qajar period, it continued to lag well behind other Middle Eastern industrializers such as Turkey and Egypt throughout the 1930s.[58]

The capitalist class in Iran continued to be split among state, foreign, and local capital, all of which grew in this period. The state sector encompassed the managers of the state-owned industries and Reza Shah himself who owned shares in a number of companies. Foreign capital, consisting mainly of the British-run oil operations and the Soviet fisheries, will be dealt with below. Within Iran's private sector two main components can be discerned: owners and managers of the new industries on the one hand, and large-scale merchants and contractors on the other. Two schools of thought exist on this new industrial bourgeoisie. One argues that it was small and insignificant vis-à-vis the state and not particularly forthcoming in starting up new factories; the other sees this group as growing by leaps and bounds.[59] Both positions have merit: While it is true that Iran's capitalists were more attracted to commerce than industry and that the state had to capitalize some of the largest industrial concerns, it is also the case that by 1941 the vast majority of industrial enterprises were in the private sector. Iran's new factory owners seem to have come from among the large merchants, state bureaucrats, and perhaps some landed families. The profits to be made were quite attractive, largely because of the captive character of the domestic market, whose consumers were forced to pay high prices for low quality. By one estimate dividends in industry averaged over 22 percent a year between 1931 and 1937. After 1935 industrial profits swelled with inflation which redistributed income upwards. Profits from trade and government contracts may have been even greater than from industry and this spawned the second component of Iran's private sector capitalist class—the "merchants, monopolists, contractors and politician-favorites" mentioned in Millspaugh's epigraph to this chapter, to which may be added speculators, smugglers, and profiteers. The foreign trade and exchange monopolies discriminated against Iran's traditional merchant class in the bazaar in favor of a few large trading firms, mostly in Tehran, which enjoyed government connections. Small traders were forced out of business, unable to obtain import and export licenses, especially in the provinces. Windfall profits were made in foreign trade throughout the 1930s. Contractors in construction and building materials also profited from the creation of the railroad, state factories, and other infrastructure. Another group consisted of individuals involved in smuggling and black market operations. This sector as a whole depended not only on the state (as did the industrial capitalists to a large degree), but also had ties to the foreign markets in which they bought and sold, making them a dependent, or comprador-type bourgeoisie.[60]

Iran's (non-craft) working class grew considerably in the 1930s, reaching, according to various estimates, from 170,000 to 260,000 people in all.[61] The largest sector consisted of the 60,000 construction laborers, followed by 20-30,000 each in textile factories, the oil industry, wool and rice cleaning, and transportation. Other sizable categories included railwaymen, food-processing workers, dockers, and fishery workers. There were perhaps 45,000 factory workers in all.[62] Working conditions naturally varied by sector, but the long hours, low wages, and exploitation of women and children discerned for the 1920s in chapter four persisted: Conditions were likened to "slavery" by both British and American observers. Wages in textile mills were about 1.5-2 rials (8-11 cents) for a ten-hour day in 1934-37; this rose to 3-6 rials a day for men and 1-2 for girls in 1941. (Textile wages of six pence a day in Iran compared with 63 pence in Britain, 23 in India and 14 in Japan in 1936.) Construction labor made 2-3 rials for a twelve-hour day around 1930. A decline in real wages is quite probable: Pay raises lagged behind inflation by 30-50 percent between 1920 and 1940, according to a 1941 U.S. embassy report. Floor's data on wages and food prices suggests a subsistence-level standard of living for the working class in Fars and Azarbaijan. In these circumstances it is not surprising that working-class consciousness developed to some degree, especially in the large industrial settings of the oil fields, railroads, textiles, and other factories. Though strikes were banned and the trade union movement was outlawed, labor was still not inactive as will be evident in assessing social movements below. But both the political and economic pressures on Iran's growing working class were very great and survival must have taken precedence over militancy under these conditions.

In the petty-commodity mode of production, artisans, craftspeople, and small traders suffered political and economic losses relative to the state and capitalist sector during this period. Economically the hardest impact came not from the state but from industrial production and imported manufactures. The state abolished taxes on over 230 guilds and income taxes were very low. Urban development, however, laid out straight, broad streets which sometimes cut through part of the bazaar, creating opportunities for new shops to open outside of the bazaar, accessible to automobile traffic. And insofar as the state promoted industrialization, artisanal production declined. The expansion of textiles, metalwork, and other machine-produced factory articles, in conjunction with the dramatic reduction of transport costs after 1930, was the main source of craft decline. Estimates of the total craft sector vary enormously, from Abdullaev's very low 10,000 to Floor's 250,000, which seems closer to the mark. Artisans' wages were estimated at five to ten krans a day circa 1928, some two to three times higher than factory labor. A slightly more varied and nutritious diet than for the rural population may be inferred as well.[63]

A second class associated with the petty-commodity mode of production, as in the past, were merchants. A number of the largest merchants left the bazaar to participate in the large trade monopolies and industries, propelling them fully into the capitalist mode of production. The many who were left behind continued to operate on a smaller scale and were undoubtedly harmed by the general trends in the petty-commodity mode during this period. Some merchants were forced out of business. All who travelled from city to city required an official permit, so the state's hand was never far from this sector. The numbers of these small and medium merchants remained great however and it should be kept in mind that in class terms they continued to exploit the artisans, journeymen, and day laborers in descending order below themselves.

On the political plane, guilds were more closely supervised by the state than at any time in the past, having to report their meetings to the local police, who could send someone to observe. In terms of political culture, the bazaar remained a bastion of support for Islam and presumably of growing resentment against the state, tempered slightly perhaps by appreciation for the provision of security. Small traders seem to have had little affection for the shah, and collective memories of heroic participation in the Constitutional revolution lingered as well. Again it is hard to accept Upton's view that "such things as the novelties and superficial improvements around [the artisan] gave him a sense of satisfaction and pride which at least counterbalanced his resentments."[64]

The intelligentsia, ulama, and urban marginal classes can be considered urban groups or classes that in the 1930s were no longer strictly speaking *constituent* classes of either urban mode of production but rather had members in both the capitalist and petty-commodity modes. The situations of these three classes did vary a great deal however: The intelligentsia was primarily a capitalist class and the ulama a bazaar-based (petty-commodity) one, and both were intermediate groups or classes in the urban social structure, while the marginal classes were truly split between the two modes of production and were at the bottom of urban society as an underclass. The situations of Iran's religious minorities and urban women generally also cut across Iran's class structure.

The intelligentsia, consisting of teachers, students, doctors, lawyers, artists, writers, publishers, and some civil servants, grew along with the state in the 1930s. The social prestige of intellectuals, particularly those educated abroad, rose greatly. Abrahamian, who must be counting most of the civil service, puts the intelligentsia at a high seven percent of Iran's labor force. Whatever their precise numbers, they were close to the capitalist mode of production, paid salaries by state and private institutions, though not all members were yet within this mode, some doctors, teachers, writers, and others remaining close to the bazaar.[65] Banani feels that Reza Shah was "inspired, encouraged and supported by an articulate majority of the intel-ligentsia."[66] This is probably true of those who entered the ranks of the civil service and army. Cottam discerns a more basic dilemma facing intellectuals: Many felt affinities with Reza's secularism, industrialization program, and some type of nationalism, but not his authoritarianism and proto-fascist tendencies.[67] The intelligentsia then were split in political terms, with minorities supporting the regime (and benefitting from it) and opposing it (and suffering repression), and a middle group which was indeed neutral, noncommittal, or alienated, who benefitted generally from expansion of the bureaucracy, education, and industry.

The ulama had a very different experience in the 1930s, at least materially. They lost most of their positions in the judicial and educational systems which now required secular credentials and thus were cut off from key sources of income and power. Islamic educational institutions in particular were undermined by the state through legislation of their required courses, conscription of young men, imprisonment and harassment of teachers and students. Compulsory religious education in the schools was abolished, dervish orders were banned, passion plays and other religious ceremonies were suppressed. Vaqf properties were more tightly administered by the government, further reducing some ulama incomes. The ulama retained material and political support in the bazaars, however, continuing to collect religious taxes there and perform some notarizing and other services. This bound them more closely to the petty-commodity mode of production and the decline of this mode vis-à-vis the capitalist corresponds to the rise of the secular intelligentsia at the expense of the ulama. Some leading clerics did retain considerable amounts of wealth of course, others diligently tried to preserve their educational traditions, and many were undoubtedly im-poverished in this period. As will be seen below, some opposition to the state was expressed, but it was generally ruthlessly repressed in what was a dark period for the ulama as a whole.[68]

The most destitute class in the urban sector was the marginal population living as servants, watchmen, part-time manual labor, beggars, prostitutes, and thieves. Already the poorest people in the cities, their income declined further or at best did not increase in the 1930s, as day labor made very low wages and inflation and unemployment grew. Estimates of unemployment vary widely from 50 percent among unskilled labor in the 1920s to 2-4 percent of the urban population in the 1930s; the figure of 30,000 has been suggested for 1940. Reverend R. J. Thompson noted in the 1940s that "a great proportion are poor, ill-fed and in rags."[69] Reza Shah is said to have broken the hold of the lutis (popular armed toughs involved in "protection" and prostitution rackets, along with more legal activities) in the various neigh-borhoods of Tehran in the 1920s, but undoubtedly this element continued to exist. They and the other urban marginal groups lived precariously in the interstices of the capitalist and petty-commodity modes of production.

The role of women in urban society is a large topic about which a few points may be suggested here. Women began to get educations and entered the labor force in increased numbers in this period. About 450 graduated from high school in 1940 (compared with 645 boys) and the first women university graduates went on to distinguished professional careers. At the working-class end of the social structure, as many as 80,000 women worked in industry and unknown numbers of others in shops and offices. They were paid extremely poorly, worse than male labor, and worked long hours in bad conditions, especially in carpets and textiles. Despite the shah's general image as the emancipator of women, the civil code restated most of the Islamic shari'a's discriminations against women in family law, and even the celebrated "unveiling" of women in 1936 has found its critics on the grounds that it confined traditional, particularly older, women to their houses, while the younger generation had independently made consider-able progress toward taking part in public life without the legislation. Women did not get the vote and the women's movement was generally less active and autonomous than it had been from 1905 to 1925. So overall much progress was made in terms of participation but within a limited set of opportunities and life chances, both compared to men and in class terms.[70] Evidence on the religious minorities suggests that the 1930s were a better time than the Qajar reign in that they afforded a modicum of security and opportunity, again within real limits.[71]

Modes of Production and the Limits to Development

To return to the debate with which this section opened, we can now conclude that neither was Iran's class structure static and unchanged, nor did economic development amount to a thorough-going "breakthrough." Diagrams 6.1 and 6.2 make the first of these points by providing a basis for comparison of the constituent modes of production and their relative proportions of the population in 1914 and 1941.[72] Internal shifts in the relative strength of each mode of production are quite significant. As tribal nomads declined from 25 to 7 percent of the population, peasants rose as a result from 50-55 percent to almost 70 percent; and the working class rose from 3-4 to 10 percent of the population at the expense of artisans who fell from 17-22 to 13.5 percent of the work force (recall that in absolute terms all but the tribes increased in numbers since population grew by 50 percent from 10 to 14.55 million). Measuring the contribution of each sector to Iran's gross national product, a very rough estimate would be that the crop-sharing mode contributed 50 percent, pastoralism 10 percent, capitalism 20

DIAGRAM 6.1 The Iranian Social Formation in 1914

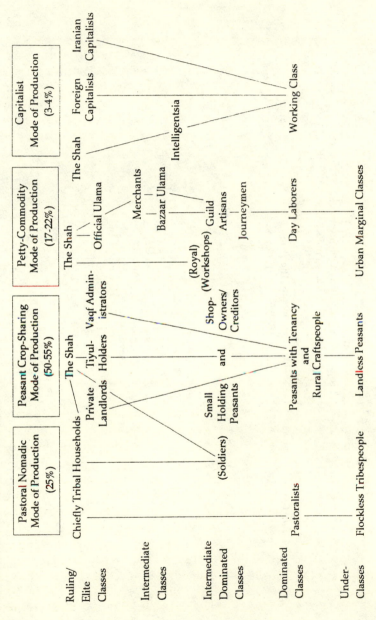

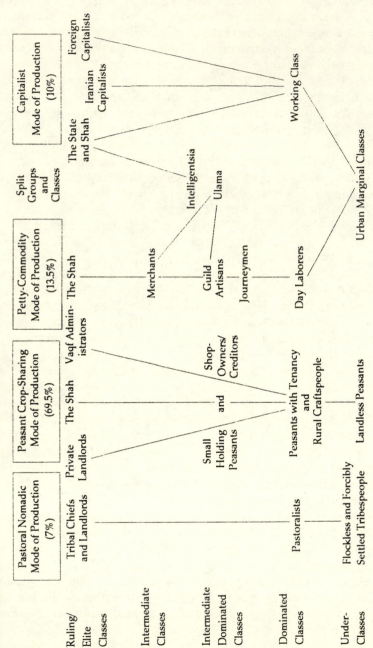

DIAGRAM 6.2 The Iranian Social Formation in 1941

percent and the petty-commodity mode 20 percent.[73] Thus the capitalist, and to a lesser degree the petty-commodity and pastoral sectors, contributed more than their share of the population, the peasantry much less.

In terms of the class structure itself, further changes occurred within and between each mode of production. In the tribal sector khans became landlords to a greater extent than formerly, while some tribespeople, forced to settle, became peasants in such desperate circumstances as to constitute an underclass. Soldiers were no longer provided to the state by the tribal levy system and have dropped out of the picture, even though tribespeople, like all others, were now conscripted. The crop-sharing mode of production remained virtually intact: Private landlords consolidated and perhaps raised their position and the shah no longer controlled as many state lands (though he became the largest private landlord). More changes occurred in the urban sectors. In the petty-commodity mode there were no longer the royal workshops of Safavid and Qajar times, and the category of state-appointed "official ulama" no longer makes much sense given the reduced role played by the ulama. Instead, the ulama, along with the intelligentsia and especially the urban marginal classes, have been conceptualized as split between the petty-commodity and capitalist modes of production, and to signify the rise of the intelligentsia at the ulama's expense they have been placed in different intermediate levels in the class structure. The ulama retained their links with artisans and bazaar merchants, and the intelligentsia was tied to the state to some degree. In the capitalist mode the state has emerged as a dominant actor and Iranian capitalists have been joined by the large merchants of the import-export trade. There is perhaps the embryo of a "triple alliance" forming in the capitalist mode, but foreign capital was really quite distinct from state and private, and state capital predominated qualitatively if not quantitatively over private. As before, Iran's class structure remained extremely complex, with multiple elite, intermediate, dominated, and underclass groups, and these divisions and their potential alliances will come into play in analyzing social movements later in this chapter and in chapter seven generally.

In terms of economic development a considerable amount of industrialization did occur and while this was on a scale unprecedented in Iranian perspective, severe limits on this process have been exposed as well. In agriculture there was no land reform, increase in productivity or change in techniques. Production kept up with population but the peasantry remained at a very low standard of living. The tribal sector was severely dislocated by state efforts to sedentarize nomads, with great loss of livelihood and a decrease in pastoral production. Nor in the urban sector where the state concentrated its developmentalist efforts did daily life improve for the majority of the population. The standard of living, as measured by income and diet, housing, health, and education, did not rise significantly.

Industrialization, along with state interference in foreign trade to build the railroad, contributed to a long bout of inflation after 1933 that caused prices to double or more by 1941. Wages could not keep pace. While gross national product doubled between 1925 and 1940, income inequality worsened. The rural sector paid for the cities' cheap food and the urban masses paid through heavy taxes for capitalists' and merchants' profits.[74] The benefits of industrialization were spread unevenly, touching only a few cities and making Tehran far too central relative to the provinces. Iran, moreover, continued to lag behind such other Middle Eastern industrializers as Egypt and Turkey.

This picture of growth with its uneven benefits across classes, sectors, and regions is the pattern we have conceptualized as a *dependent development*. To understand the world-systemic parameters of this process, Iran's relations with other countries, particularly in the West, should be taken into account.

Iran in the World-System of the 1930s

Reza Shah and his government made various attempts to establish Iran's independence in the world-system of the 1930s. The system of "capitulations" was unilaterally cancelled in 1928, thus rescinding the extraterritorial privileges granted to a series of countries by the Qajars. A number of other rights were subsequently denied foreigners—to own land in Iran, to operate schools, to marry Iranians, to take administrative positions in the state, and even to travel freely. As we have seen the state took control of Iran's foreign trade, directly participating in part of it and regulating the rest. The state also took over the customs and telegraph network from foreign administrators. Though loans and capital were sought abroad until the early 1930s, when these were not forthcoming, Iran raised its own capital for investments such as the railroad, thereby turning a necessity into a virtue.[75] The national debt was similarly reduced. Reza Shah was in general deeply suspicious of foreign influences (though he sought to remake his country in the image of the West) and did little to cultivate friendships abroad.

Despite these attitudes and measures, the realities were ones of continued dependence. The loss of capitulations, for example, had a limited effect, as the new legal codes gave foreigners the security to operate in Iran, while tariff rates were guaranteed through 1936. More seriously, the depression caused prices for Iran's export commodities to fall on the world market, a trend exacerbated by the depreciation of the rial. Foreign investment was limited mainly to two areas—the British-operated oil fields and Soviet-operated Caspian fisheries—but it continued to grow, and British control of Iran's most valuable resource was consolidated by renegotiation of the oil concession in 1933. Finally, the geo-political balance of power also seriously circumscribed Iran's freedom to maneuver after world war broke out in 1939. The West continued to impinge fairly heavily on Iran in the 1930s. This time, instead of the Anglo-Russian rivalry of the pre-1917 period or sole British hegemony from 1918 till the 1921 coup, there was a shifting, three-way struggle for influence in Iran among imperial England, the Soviet Union, and Nazi Germany.

Great Britain remained on the whole the most powerful Western country in Iran. The intense political pressure which had been exerted throughout the Qajar period and had almost culminated in the 1919 Agreement subsided to a great degree, and outright interference in domestic politics and national sovereignty virtually ceased. Reza Shah, for his part, as had the Qajar shahs before him, looked to Great Britain as a possible friend and ally against the more tangible possibility of a threat from his north (the Soviet Union). British policy too remained one of grudging acceptance of Reza as the strong ruler needed to vouchsafe stability in Iran, both against domestic opposition and the spread of Soviet influence.[76] Economic relations were the most prominent aspect of British influence in Iran. In the 1920s Britain became Iran's leading trading partner, providing (with British India) 67 percent of Iran's imports from 1920 to 1924, a figure which fell however to 46 percent for 1925-29 and 29 percent for 1930-34. Iran's exports to England and India declined from a lower plateau: 37 percent in 1920-24, 20 percent in 1925-29, 23 percent in 1930-34. By the late 1930s Britain ranked a distant third in Iran's trade after Germany and the Soviet Union, at about 17 percent. The balance of this trade was in England's favor throughout the decade although Iran's deficit diminished somewhat. In July 1941, on the eve of Reza's fall, a commercial agreement was signed between the two countries "that could so operate as to give the British a virtual monopoly over Iran's trade."[77] The war prevented this from coming to pass.

The key to the British position in Iran was neither politics nor trade. The simple possession of the D'Arcy oil concession guaranteed the British the lion's share of the profits on Iran's most valuable resource and made the Anglo-Iranian Oil Company (AIOC, formerly APOC) the largest capitalist employer in the country. After Iran's royalties proved very erratic from 1924 to 1931 (during which period Iran received 7,348,000 pounds sterling to the company's 31,501,000), Reza Shah tried to unilaterally cancel the concession. Britain appealed to the League of Nations and in 1933 a new contract was negotiated which changed the basis of the royalty from 16 percent of net profits to four shillings (about $1) a ton, with a minimum annual payment of about one million pounds sterling. The area covered was reduced by four-fifths but included all the known oil fields, and a key clause extended the duration of the concession by twenty-eight years till 1993. Thus did Reza Shah act hastily to abolish the concession and irrationally end up by extending it. In the 1930s Iran averaged about 2.5 million pounds sterling a year in royalties and taxes, up from less than one million pounds annually in the 1920s. The company continued to make five times what Iran received and by 1932 was worth 50 million pounds. Production levels were geared to meet the needs of the industrialized European economies. Through the institution of the AIOC the English retained a preeminent position in the Iranian economy.[78]

The Soviet Union, too, exercised less political control than the Tsarist government had in the past but exerted vigorous commercial pressure on Iran in the 1930s. Politically, on balance the Soviets accepted the Reza Shah regime as a factor working for stability in the region, one which would at least prevent encroachment on the U.S.S.R. by hostile forces and at best might actually oppose British imperialism. A 1927 treaty guaranteed neutrality and non-intervention between the two countries.[79] Trade was initially interrupted after 1917 but by 1927 the Soviet Union was again Iran's principal market for the rice, tobacco, dried fruit, cotton, and wool of the northern provinces and trade had regained its high pre-1914 levels. The Soviet state monopoly on trade prompted Iran's own trade monopoly in 1931, driving trade increasingly into a bilateral, barter-type pattern. Imports from Iran were curtailed when the Soviets undertook heavy industrialization in the 1930s. The new Soviet trade surplus was another factor which depressed the economy of northern Iran. Trade fluctuated in the 1930s: About 28 percent of Iran's imports and 24 percent of exports were with the Soviet Union, reaching as high as 38 percent of Iran's foreign trade in 1938. This placed the U.S.S.R. ahead of Britain. Trade dropped abruptly however due to a dispute in 1938/39 and virtually ceased in the next year. In 1940 a new commercial treaty was signed which Iran hoped would facilitate transit of German goods through the U.S.S.R. Again the war intervened to dash this plan. The main Soviet investment in Iran was the concession to operate the Caspian fisheries, renewed in 1927/28 for twenty-five years as a Soviet monopoly with most of the profits accruing to Moscow. The overall economic relationship continued to be one between vastly unequal partners, with the requirements and rhythms of the Soviet economy setting the tone for commerce and investment.[80]

The main beneficiary of the relaxation of British and Soviet pressure on Iran was Nazi Germany. If Reza Shah sought a counterbalance to British and Soviet strength, his relationship with Hitlerian Germany was also one of a more general affinity. Iran was accorded "the honor of Aryan status." Katouzian considers Reza "both pro-German and pro-Nazi. For he was an *étatiste*, a militarist, a despot, a racist and pan-Iranist."[81] On the German side, a 1934 report to Hitler recommended:

When in the future we shall be staking out an adequate living space [*Lebens-raum*] for our nation, among the lands between Asia and Africa, it will be imperative that we work towards the creation of a block of nations in which the predomination of the strongest Teutonic races would be ensured. It would be necessary first of all to incorporate into this sphere the states of the Danube basin, Turkey and Persia.[82]

Even more ominously, a 1937 agreement between Italy and Germany accorded Iran and Iraq to a German sphere of influence, Egypt and Syria to an Italian sphere. Inside Iran there was much diffuse support for Germany, especially among bureaucrats, intellectuals, and army officers, motivated above all by anti-British and anti-"Russian" sentiment.[83] These relations spilled over into the trade domain, where by the late 1930s Germany was Iran's largest partner, surpassing first Britain and then the Soviet Union. Imports from Germany rose from two percent (1920-24) to five percent (1925-29) to eight percent (1930-34) and then leaped to 25 percent from 1935 to 1939. Exports in the same periods climbed from nothing to 32 percent. In 1940-41 Germany accounted for 42.6 percent of Iran's imports and 47.9 percent of exports. As German industrialization quickened in the 1930s demand for food and raw materials grew, while as Iran industrialized it required machinery and spare parts. A 1939 agreement promised that Iran would export cotton, wool, wheat, rice, barley, and other agricultural products in sizable quantities. Bilateral barter-type trade expanded. This was primarily to Germany's advantage since Iran required German products more than the reverse and terms of trade and exchange rates favored Germany's finished and capital goods. The trade became imbalanced in 1939 with Iran's exports exceeding imports by 40 million marks (about $15 million), which the barter system made a form of "involuntary lending" to Germany. In addition to the commerce, German firms played large roles in the building of the railroad and other industrial projects, including an order for a steel mill. By the eve of the Allied invasion of Iran, the Germans had fashioned a very strong relationship with Reza Shah's state and the Iranian economy. Only the invasion would bring this to a halt.[84]

Compared with Britain, Germany, and the Soviet Union, the United States in the 1930s was a distant power as far as Iran was concerned. The Millspaugh financial mission left Iran in 1927 with Reza Shah disappointed at its failure to generate foreign loans, coupled with mistrust of the American advisor's authority. A diplomatic flap occurred in 1936 when Iran withdrew its personnel from Washington to protest the 1935 arrest of its ambassador for speeding and subsequent negative newspaper articles on the shah. Ties improved in 1938 when Reza wrote to Roosevelt: "We personally, as well as the Iranian people, value . . . the maintenance and strengthening of the friendship which for long years has existed between the two countries."[85] When world war broke out Reza made requests for loans and military equipment but little came of them. On the economic front, the United States ranked fourth in Iran's trade in the 1930s providing 7-8 percent of imports, mostly motor vehicles and agricultural machinery, and taking 12-13 percent of exports, mainly carpets from Kirman, which were badly hit by the depression. These fairly modest measures did give the United States a solid foothold in Iran, but this would grow into a dominant presence only with World War II and its aftermath.[86]

Iran's relations with its neighbors in Asia and the Middle East were certainly important in some cases but were not factors in establishing the shape of Iranian social structure through any mechanism approaching dependence. The most significant regional undertaking in which Iran played a part was the 1937 Sa'adabad Pact with Afghanistan, Iraq, and Turkey. Formally called a "Treaty of Nonaggression," a careful reading of its contents suggests that it was aimed less at meeting any external threats posed by each to the others, or by third parties to any of them, than at containing internal threats from revolutionary movements within each country, as article seven makes clear:

> Each of the High Contracting Parties undertakes to prevent, within his respective frontiers, the formation or activities of armed bands, associations or organisations to subvert the established institutions, or disturb the order or security of any part, whether situated on the frontier or elsewhere, of the territory of another Party, or to change the constitutional system of such other Party.[87]

This interpretation is reinforced by the fact that the treaty did not prevent the British from intervening in Iraq in 1940 or the British and Soviets from invading Iran in 1941. For that matter it was not invoked on the security dimension either, but it did constitute an effort to conduct regional diplomacy by a group of non-Western nations without resorting to dealings with core world powers. Individually, there were strained relations with Iraq over boundaries on the Shatt al-Arab waterway and warm ones with Turkey based on Reza's admiration for Atatürk's industrialization and secularization projects.

The political climate of the 1930s was conducive to contact with one Asian power—Japan. Large orders were placed for Iranian cotton in 1933, so that Japan could export goods of its own to Iran (this was necessary due to the trade monopoly). This worked to the point where Japan supplied nine percent of Iran's imports from 1930-34 and seven percent from 1935-39, though it accounted for only 2-3 percent of Iranian exports.[88] Japan, the one great Asian power of this period, ultimately was too far from Iran and too little concerned to play a larger role within the country. The Asian and Middle Eastern world thus did not approach the capacity of the European core in influencing the Iranian economy and polity between the world wars.

The 1930s can be seen as a transitional period in Iran's place within the world-economy. For Ashraf, the Reza Shah era represents a transition from "the semi-colonialism of the 19th century and early 20th century to the neo-colonialism of the cold war era."[89] In terms of the perspectives adopted in this study, the period was more a temporary interlude between the dependence on rival imperialisms—Great Britain and Russia—of the Qajar period and the new dependence on America that would emerge after World War II. No Western power re-shaped the economy to the degree that Britain and Russia had during the Qajar era, yet Iran remained dependent despite Reza Shah's avowed nationalism, self-reliance, and strong state, due chiefly to three inter-related mechanisms: control of oil by the British, unequal trade with the Soviet Union and Germany, and the vicissitudes of trade as a peripheral supplier of raw materials.

The emergence of oil as a key commodity in the world-economy and of Iran as the fifth-largest producer in the 1920s and 1930s confirmed Iran's peripheral role in the world-system. Iran's exports consisted almost entirely of oil, agricultural produce, and carpets. Iran's major trading partners—Germany, the Soviet Union, Great Britain, and the United States—supplied finished manufactures and capital goods. During the world depression this pattern of trade worked against Iran as the value in rials of its raw material exports fell by two or three times while the cost of its imports rose in the stronger currencies of the core. When Iran introduced its trade monopoly, this shifted its trade to Germany and the Soviet Union who benefitted from bilateral arrangements which naturally favored the larger, more industrialized (read "core") economy. Thus Iran was exploited by the terms of trade for the products it bought and sold, the strength of the various core economies with which it traded, and the debilitating commercial consequences of being a peripheral economy during a world-wide depression.

Finally, the 1930s were transitional in the sense that Iran's economy moved closer to dependence on a single commodity to finance state projects and balance trade. Without oil royalties the trade balance would have continued to be negative as it had been since before the turn of the twentieth century. With oil, Iran began to run positive overall trade balances after 1931, obviating the need for foreign loans. Nevertheless, the bulk of the profits from possession of this valuable resource accrued to the Anglo-Iranian Oil Company owned by the British government, which took about an 80 percent share to Iran's 20 percent. And the oil sector became an isolated enclave with minimal industrial, technological, or employment links to the domestic economy, geared instead to the demands and cycles of the advanced industrial nations of the core.

Thus the 1930s solidified Iran's place as a periphery of the world-economy. Trade dependence vis-à-vis Germany, Great Britain, and the Soviet Union remained as great as it had been on Tsarist Russia and Great Britain in Qajar times. Instabilities in the world geo-political situation would show the political extent of this dependence on external powers in 1941.

Social Movements and External Intervention in the Reza Shah Period

The period from 1925 to 1941 can be seen as one of a *compression of social forces*, that is, a period in which social forces were fettered from expressing themselves by a strong state. In a sense this evokes the classic Marxist tension between forces and relations of production, the idea being that over a period of time classes develop to the maximum point permitted by the technological level of production and the balance of power between exploiters and exploited. When that point is reached, pressures build up which can only be resolved through class conflict. In Iran during the 1930s Reza Shah clamped down on all forms of dissent in society through legislative, institutional, and military measures. This was made possible by a certain division of labor in dependency and exploitation effected during his reign: Foreign domination became more solely economic rather than political and economic as in the past, while internal domination shifted to the state as sole political power and a growing economic actor. When Reza was removed by external forces in 1941 this led to an explosion of social movements in the period from 1941 to 1953 and then, interestingly, another period of compression from 1953 to 1977, followed by a second explosion in 1978-79. In both periods of compression we find a combination of economic expansion and political repression.

A brief consideration of the balance of social forces in the 1930s substantiates this thesis. Reza Shah's main sources of support came from the incumbents of the institutions he created—army officers, bureaucrats, monopoly traders, industrialists, and a segment of the intelligentsia. Groups and classes which opposed him—the ulama, tribes, progressive intellectuals, and working class—were ruthlessly repressed. Others were either closely watched (the guilds), coopted or indifferent (landlords), or struggling too hard for daily survival to resist the state (peasants, urban marginals, day laborers, and, to an extent, the working class). Though Reza's state lacked deep legitimation in civil society it was able to rule by this combination of extending material advantages to new groups, repressing longstanding opponents and the losers in the developmental process, and keeping much of the population either apathetic, apolitical, or frightened. Reliance on the army successfully underpinned this approach to power for most of his reign and though social movements did occur they were defeated. Eventually Reza was forced to abdicate by the application of irresistible force from outside the country, which in turn allowed expression to pent-up internal forces once again.

The typical pattern followed by a few revolts early in Reza's reign was a spontaneous uprising over local grievances by tribespeople, peasants, army garrisons, or urban lower classes, followed by swift military reprisal.[90] From 1927 to 1932 there occurred the rebellions of Arab, Qashqa'i, Bakhtiari, Kurdish, Baluchi, and other tribes already noted. These ended in military defeat, cooptation or execution of khans and settlement or strict military rule over tribespeople. One further intriguing episode was recorded by the British consul in Isfahan in 1928:

> A few of the landowning khans have had difficulties with their peasant tribesmen who have rebelled and claimed that the land and water belong to God and those working on the land, namely themselves. In one village, a committee composed of ex-servants, who had been dismissed by the khans and had visited Tehran and Isfahan, adopted a program of an unmistakably Bolshevik complexion. They propagated among the villagers new ideas of freedom and equality. The government, therefore, has authorized the military to use force if necessary to get the peasants to pay the local khans.[91]

The complexity of Iranian social structure is well illustrated by this image of peasant tribespeople being instigated to rebel by urbanized tribal servants against tribal landlords. The severity of government reprisals is also suggested by the estimate that in the period from July to December 1932 more than 150 peasants were shot by the army. All of these revolts were isolated and effectively repressed, eventually discouraging further attempts by the early 1930s.

Relations between the state and ulama broke down soon after Reza's 1926 coronation at which he had professed his support for Islam. Protests erupted when universal conscription was put into effect in 1927 with strict conditions on exemptions for the ulama that included passing a government-sponsored exam. The bazaars were closed at Shiraz and Isfahan, and the government resorted to a combination of threats and concessions to stop the agitation, making promises it later broke concerning exemptions and other measures demanded by the ulama. In Tabriz in 1928 further protests were put down by troops and the leaders were banished. Another blow was struck in 1928 with the arrest of Sayyid Hasan Mudarris, Reza's most vocal clerical critic in the majlis. At Qum in 1928 a female member of the shah's family entered the shrine of Fatima and was admonished by a local mulla for improper veiling; Reza is said to have rushed from Tehran to Qum, strode into the shrine with his boots on and beaten the offending mulla.[92]

In 1935 a far greater offense was perpetrated by the shah when he ordered force to be used against a large crowd gathered at the shrine of Imam Reza in Mashhad who had been listening to a preacher attack the European dress code and the unveiling of women. Between four hundred and five hundred people were killed, while others were arrested, banished, or executed afterwards. Reza's harsh treatment of religious opposition to his reforms and authority generally compelled the majority of the ulama to remain out of politics in the 1930s, either practicing dissimulation of their attitudes in the face of persecution, or in a few cases going underground, often by retiring to villages where their stands against the government were more popular. Leading ayatullahs, however, remained aloof from taking political positions and government repression was successful in eliminating active opposition from the clergy.

A similar sequence of protests, repression, and muting of opposition can be discerned among left-wing opponents of the regime. The trade union movement at first maintained its momentum, celebrating May Day in Tehran in 1927 and 1929, and engaging in a series of strikes between 1928 and 1932. The two most well-known labor actions occurred in the oil industry in 1929 and at the Vatan textile factory at Isfahan in 1931. Abrahamian maintains that 11,000 workers participated in the Abadan refinery strike, winning wage hikes despite the arrests of 500 strikers by the government, while Floor plays it down as "a storm in a tea-cup, with no lasting influence on labour relations."[93] Floor's own account, which is the fullest discussion, belies his interpretation however. There were organized cells of workers, well-articulated demands, a series of confrontations ending in hundreds of arrests, and a great deal of anxious concern for their position on the part of the Anglo-Persian Oil Company. It is true that the repression which followed kept the industry relatively quiet for a decade afterwards, but this does not minimize the place of the strike in Iranian labor history. Two years later five hundred textile workers struck at the Vatan mill in Isfahan, gaining total support from the work force, including children, and winning reduction of the working day from twelve to nine hours, a pay raise of 20 percent, improved treatment by management, and better working conditions. Several dozen workers were arrested however and some spent ten years in prison. This kind of response by the state discouraged unions and strike activities, although strikes have been recorded among dockers on the Caspian in 1928, at the Tabriz match factory in 1930, at a Shiraz factory in 1936, several times among railway workers between 1929 and 1937, as well as by students on several occasions between 1934 and 1939. Some of these resulted in concessions but others ended with arrests and defeat. The workers movement was on the whole severely repressed in the 1930s, with Reza Shah banning unions, arresting organizers, and strictly monitoring meetings of groups larger than three persons by the secret police. Floor ends his study with the judgment that "unionism as a political and social force played no role whatsoever during the 1930s."[94]

Left-wing groups met a similar fate. Anti-communist legislation in 1931 made it a crime to organize a party or association "having for its aim the establishment by force of the power of one social class over the other classes, or to overthrow by violence the political, social and economic order of the country."[95] The socialist party of Sulaiman Iskandari was dissolved and its clubs were burned down. The fledgling communist party resisted the regime, which its 1927 congress denounced as one of "feudalists, semi-colonialists, and comprador capitalists."[96] The Soviet Union ordered its embassy to break off contacts with Iranian communists in 1929 in order to maintain good relations with Reza Shah. There followed the arrests of some two thousand members or suspected supporters of the Iranian communist party. Some were imprisoned until 1941. Others went to the Soviet Union where several leading Iranian communists died in Stalin's purges. In the mid-1930s a group of left-wing intellectuals led by Dr. Taqi Arani, a physics professor educated in Germany, managed to put out a theoretical journal called *Dunya* (World) which published articles on historical materialism in an academic vein. In 1938 however Arani and a group of others who have become known as "the fifty-three" were tried on charges of being members of a communist party, receiving funds from the Soviet Union, conducting propaganda, and advocating strikes. Arani died in prison in 1940; others of the fifty-three emerged after 1941 as leaders of the Tudeh Party, Iran's first mass-based left-wing party.[97] In the Reza Shah period, however, the left was tightly controlled by arrests and censorship. Like the ulama and trade unions it constituted another social force kept under control by a strong, autocratic state.

The Abdication of Reza Shah

The sudden fall from power of Reza Shah in September 1941 was brought about by the strong application of irresistible world-systemic pressure on his position, coupled with secondary contradictions in his autocratic style of rule. When World War II broke out in 1939 Iran immediately declared its neutrality.[98] Iran's dependence on German trade required it to protest Britain's decision to prevent trade between Germany and neutral countries. The period of the German-Soviet pact allowed Iran some breathing space in 1940 and the first part of 1941, as it facilitated a certain amount of trade with Germany across the Soviet Union. German influence in Iran grew with the appointment of the pro-German 'Ali Mansur as prime minister in June 1940 and the presence of a considerable pro-German faction in the Iranian army.

The international equation changed suddenly to Iran's disadvantage when Germany invaded the Soviet Union on June 22, 1941. Iran reaffirmed a somewhat disingenuous neutrality in this conflict on June 26 (insincere because there was widespread sympathy for a German victory that would remove the threat of Soviet power in Iran and perhaps even result in the return of parts of the Caucasus lost in 1813 and 1828). The Soviets and the British were now formidably allied and this put a great deal of pressure on Iran to expel the several hundred Germans in the country who were probable Nazi agents. This demand was formally made by the Allies on July 19 and rejected by Iran ten days later with a note proclaiming the country's need for German technicians in industry while promising to keep a watchful eye on all German nationals in Iran. Already however there were plans in both England and the Soviet Union for unilateral military intervention in Iran to secure their own interests—British oil in Khuzistan and the Soviet oil fields at Baku—against the Germans. There was in addition the need for the Soviets and British to maintain a secure, year-round line of communications and supplies, and in late July this prompted the formulation of joint planning to invade Iran. By mid-August the decision had been taken.

At this point Iran was in an impossible bind, being asked by England and the Soviet Union to take actions against a Germany that appeared on the verge of crushing the Soviet army and reaching the Iranian border, and by Germany to lend it support and not expel its citizens as the Allies, who for the moment had the strongest position in Iran, were asking. The knot grew tighter when a second Allied note asking for expulsion of most of the Germans was issued on August 16 at the same time as Hitler wrote to Reza to resist this claiming Germany would occupy the southern Soviet Union by autumn. On August 22 Reza finally ordered the prime minister to expedite removal of non-essential Germans but it was far too late and too little to deter the Anglo-Soviet invasion, which came on the 25th. The Iranian army offered minimal resistance that was quickly overcome.[99] Fighting stopped within a day or two; by September 1 the army had completely disintegrated. Reza Shah was incredulous and his actions indicated the bind he was still caught in: He asked why the Allies had not simply requested what he would have granted (the supply route) and yet when he heard of German broadcasts that Iran stand firm he instructed the newspapers to deny the reports, but not in such a way as to displease the Germans. The reason why England and the Soviets had not stated more clearly their need for a supply route through Iran was because if it had been rejected they would have had to invade anyway, and if accepted, they would have had to contend with an intact, largely pro-German Iranian army.

On September 7, as their armies advanced toward Tehran, Britain and the U.S.S.R. demanded immediate expulsion of all Axis personnel from Iran. The next day the majlis considered a bill to strip Reza Shah of his title as commander of the armed forces, a serious blow to his legitimacy. The shah fought back in an editorial in *Ittila'at* "that deplored the closing down of all Axis Legations and the severance of diplomatic relations with the Axis governments," stating "our missions in the capitals of those countries will remain as before, and our political relations with them will continue."[100] This determined the Allies on the necessity of Reza's removal. On September 14 the BBC Persian-language broadcast attacks on the shah claiming he was a tyrant and a robber. His legitimacy fell beyond repair. Majlis deputies refused to denounce the broadcasts, stating that "the radios had said nothing but the truth and that there was no democracy in Iran."[101] This was accompanied by the threat of the Soviet army advancing to occupy Tehran. Reza Shah now found the moment right to abdicate in favor of his son, Muhammad Reza, with the transfer of power taking place on September 16-17. British and Soviet troops entered the capital on the 17th and Reza departed, going abroad into exile. His reign—but not his dynasty—had come to an abrupt end.

The Allied invasion put a seal on Iran's continued dependence in the Reza Shah period, which had already been tellingly signalled by the outcome of the 1932-33 oil dispute extending British control an extra twenty-eight years. Reza Shah, so strong internally, was still easily overthrown by external powers. Reza miscalculated the German-Soviet-British equation rather badly and his inability to disentangle himself and his state from an uneasy attraction to the Germans made his downfall inevitable. This was compounded by the autocratic style that made his advisors reluctant to contradict him or provide critically-formulated information. As he told his cabinet at his last meeting with them: "With regard to my plans and ideas, the secret of my success was that I never consulted anyone."[102] This was also a reason for his fall in 1941. Reza Shah could *arguably* have remained in power if he had possessed a real social base or measure of legitimacy internally. In their absence, however, the tensions in the world-system which had given him an opportunity to rise to power in 1921-25, proved his undoing in 1941. With Reza's abdication, the social forces that he had so assiduously compressed were released, eventually unleashing the social movements of the post-1945 period.

Notes

1. Joseph Upton, *The History of Modern Iran: An Interpretation* (Cambridge: Harvard University Press, 1968), 53-54. The reforms are covered in detail in Amin Banani, *The Modernization of Iran, 1921-1941* (Stanford: Stanford University Press, 1961); Wilber, *Riza Shah Pahlavi*; and Lester A. Lee, "The Reforms of Reza Shah: 1925-1941," M.A. thesis, Department of History, Stanford University (1950).

2. Abrahamian, *Iran Between Two Revolutions*, 136-37; Floor, *Industrialization in Iran*, 32; Wilber, *Riza Shah Pahlavi*, 250; and Banani, *The Modernization of Iran*, 60-61, 118.

3. Keddie, *Roots of Revolution*, 108. Other data in this paragraph are drawn from Banani, *The Modernization of Iran*, 91, 105, 108, 116; Wilber, *Riza Shah Pahlavi*, 260-61; Ivanov, *Tarikh-i Nuvin-i Iran*, 87; and Abrahamian, *Iran Between Two Revolutions*, 145.

4. Banani, *The Modernization of Iran*, 101; also 92-93, 110-111.

5. On these figures see Miron Rezun, "Reza Shah's Court Minister: Teymourtash," pp. 119-137 in *International Journal of Middle East Studies*, volume 12, number 2 (September 1980); "The Rise and Fall of Teymourtache," p. 93 in *Journal of the Royal Central Asian Society*, volume XXI, part 1 (January 1934); Wilber, *Riza Shah Pahlavi*, 113, 121, 154-57, 253; Keddie, *Roots of Revolution*, 94; Katouzian, *The Political Economy* , 119; and Upton, *The History of Modern Iran*, 59.

6. On the majlis see Abrahamian, *Iran Between Two Revolutions*, 138-140, 150; Keddie, *Roots of Revolution*, 94; Wilber, *Riza Shah Pahlavi*, 122-23, 147, 164, 254, 255, 263; and Shahrough Akhavi, *Religion and Politics in Contemporary Iran. Clergy-State Relations in the Pahlavi Period* (Albany: State University of New York Press, 1980), 59. On Mudarris and Mussadiq, see Katouzian, *The Political Economy*, 122, 123, 125, 135 note 2; Wilber, *Riza Shah Pahlavi*, 130, 145; and Keddie, *Roots of Revolution*, 94. Upton's estimate of political murders is found in *The History of Modern Iran*, 59.

7. Banani, *The Modernization of Iran*, 169 note 26. Keddie notes that this represents only a tenfold increase measured in terms of the pound sterling: *Roots of Revolution*, 102. Two very rough benchmarks to use are eighteen rials to the dollar and five dollars (thus ninety rials) to the pound sterling, for the 1930s.

8. On oil revenues, see Banani, *The Modernization of Iran*, 142; Bharier, *Economic Development in Iran*, 159; and Gholam Reza Moghadam, "Iran's Foreign Trade Policy and Economic Development in the Interwar Period," Ph.D. dissertation, Department of Economics, Stanford University (1956), 223. On other sources of income, see Abrahamian, *Iran Between Two Revolutions*, 148; Bharier, *Economic Development in Iran*, 77; and Moghadam, "Iran's Foreign Trade Policy," 112 table 24. Further data in this paragraph are drawn from Katouzian, *The Political Economy*, 113 table 6.1, 114 table 6.2, 130 tables 7.1 and 7.2; "Recent Developments in Persia," 131; and Wilber, *Riza Shah Pahlavi*, 200.

9. On trade, foreign exchange, and banking developments, see Banani, *The Modernization of Iran*, 118, 130-32; Bharier, *Economic Development in Iran*, 123, 126, 242-44; Moghadam, "Iran's Foreign Trade Policy," 62-169 passim; Wilber, *Riza Shah Pahlavi*, 143, 195, 265; and Ashraf, "Historical Obstacles," 328.

10. Wilber, *Riza Shah Pahlavi*, 244-45. The 1926 quote is from ibid., 118.

11. Ibid., 244. Wilber also lends credence to the ridiculous claim of Reza's son, Muhammad Reza Shah, that his father "bought land in the north in order to protect the country from Communism": ibid., 245. Cf. by contrast Taqizadeh's dismissal as ambassador to France in 1935, in part caused by his reference to the shah as a "land-eating wolf": Katouzian, *The Political Economy*, 121 note 17. On Reza's land holdings, see Robert Graham, *Iran: The Illusion of Power* (New York: St. Martin's Press, 1979), 55; and Lambton, *Landlord and Peasant*, 256-258.

12. Banani, *The Modernization of Iran*, 3.

13. Quoted in Wilber, *Riza Shah Pahlavi*, 135.

14. Ibid., 135-36.

15. Ibid., 136. He told a newly appointed ambassador to France: "You are to report from Europe on other things that will be useful to Iran. But I want you to know that we are in no sense inferior to them": ibid., 176.

16. Katouzian, *The Political Economy*, 101ff.

17. Keddie, *Roots of Revolution*, 94.

18. Abrahamian, *Iran Between Two Revolutions*, 143.

19. Banani, *The Modernization of Iran*, 47. Though Elwell-Sutton euphemistically refers to Reza as "a Moslem of average piety," it is abundantly clear that he lacked any real personal piety

or belief in Islam: see L. P. Elwell-Sutton, "Reza Shah the Great: Founder of the Pahlavi Dynasty," pp. 1-50 in Lenczowski, editor, *Iran Under the Pahlavis*, 39, as against Wilber, *Riza Shah Pahlavi*, 246.

20. Banani, *The Modernization of Iran*, 106.

21. Wilber, *Riza Shah Pahlavi*, 189. Katouzian refers to this society as "led by spineless and demoralised intellectuals": *The Political Economy of Modern Iran*, 123.

22. Wilber quotes approvingly the shah's statement that "Force makes right." Reza's coming to power through a coup, his reliance on the army as an instrument of state power, the emphasis on the glory of "Iran" at the expense of the population, and his anti-ulama campaigns all remind one of Nadir Shah's reign from 1736 to 1747. This despite Reza's reaction when someone suggested the comparison to Nadir: "What? That bandit...": Wilber, *Riza Shah Pahlavi*, 237, and 249 for the quote that "Force makes right."

23. For example, the Marxist Fred Halliday, after tracing the contours of the socioeconomic system up to 1900, claims that "This pattern changed little up to the 1940s," while Keddie judges that "A breakthrough had been made toward economic growth," and Upton writes of "rapid and extensive development": see Halliday, *Iran*, 14; Keddie, *Roots of Revolution*, 111; and Upton, *The History of Modern Iran*, 60.

24. Bharier, *Economic Development in Iran*, 25-28, 31, 34. See also Floor, *Industrialization in Iran*, 26.

25. See the estimates in Gideon Hadary, "The Agrarian Reform Problem in Iran," pp. 181-196 in *Middle East Journal*, volume 5, number 2 (Spring 1951), 185; Mahdi, "The Iranian Social Formation," 361; Nikki Keddie, "Stratification, Social Control, and Capitalism in Iranian Villages: Before and After Land Reform," pp. 158-205 in Keddie, *Iran: Religion, Politics and Society*, 169, citing Karim Sanjabi, *Essai sur l'économie rural et le régime agraire de la Perse* (Paris: Domant-Montchrestien, 1934), 138; Keddie, *Historical Obstacles*, 1-2; Keddie, *Roots of Revolution*, 103; and "Agricultural and Industrial Activity and Manpower in Iran," pp. 550-562 in *International Labour Review*, volume LIX (January-June 1949), 551.

26. Mahdi, "The Iranian Social Formation," 359, 357 citing M. Agah, "Some Aspects of Economic Development in Modern Iran," Ph.D. dissertation, Oxford University (1958), 171; Hadary, "The Agrarian Reform Problem," 185. For trends on the various types of landownership, see Banani, *The Modernization of Iran*, 114, 121, 168-69 note 4, 169 note 7, 170 note 35; Wilber, *Riza Shah Pahlavi*, 200; Keddie, "Stratification, Social Control and Capitalism," 167-69; "Agricultural and Industrial Activity," 552; and Lambton, *Landlord and Peasant*, 232-78 passim.

27. Based on Lambton, *Landlord and Peasant*, 308-18; Banani, *The Modernization of Iran*, 123; Keddie, *Roots of Revolution*, 104; and Hadary, "The Agrarian Reform Problem," 188.

28. On agricultural output, see Wilber, *Riza Shah Pahlavi*, 265-66; Bharier, *Economic Development in Iran*, 132, 134 table 1; Banani, *The Modernization of Iran*, 140; and Hadary, "The Agrarian Reform Problem," 183.

29. On these trends see Wilfred Korby, *Probleme der industriellen Entwicklung und Konzentration in Iran* (Wiesbaden: Dr. Ludwig Reichert Verlag, 1977), 3; Bharier, *Economic Development in Iran*, 59-60, 131, 134-36; "The Borderlands of Soviet Central Asia. Persia. Part II," pp. 382-431 in *Central Asian Review*, volume IV, number 4 (1956), 409; and Wilber, *Riza Shah Pahlavi*, 265.

30. Keddie argues that "The growth of landlordism and declining agricultural standards were the clay feet of the whole modernization program of Reza Shah": "Stratification, Social Control and Capitalism," 172.

31. Abrahamian, *Iran Between Two Revolutions*, 150. For these changes in landlord composition, political power, and status I have drawn on Wilber, *Riza Shah Pahlavi*, 252-53; Ashraf, "Historical Obstacles," 330; Abrahamian, *Iran Between Two Revolutions*, 149-50; Upton, *The History of Modern Iran*, 55-56; and Lambton, *Landlord and Peasant*, 259.

32. Quoted in Mary-Jo DelVecchio Good, "The Changing Status and Composition of an Iranian Provincial Elite," pp. 269-288 in Michael E. Bonine and Nikki R. Keddie, editors, *Modern*

Iran. The Dialectics of Continuity and Change (Albany: State University of New York Press, 1981), 271; see also 281, 284.

33. Hadary, "The Agrarian Reform Problem," 187. On profits see Lambton, *Landlord and Peasant*, 263-64. Katouzian feels that the land tax was increased and notes that the state paid low prices for its monopoly on agricultural products, hurting landowners: *The Political Economy*, 297. Agriculture was in general squeezed somewhat to pay for industrialization: Halliday, *Iran*, 133.

34. Lambton, *Landlord and Peasant*, 260, and Lyle J. Hayden, "Living Standards in Rural Iran," pp. 140-150 in *Middle East Journal*, volume 3, number 2 (1949), 145.

35. Lambton, *Landlord and Peasant*, 277, 344-48, 361-62, 374-84; Hayden, "Living Standards in Rural Iran," 144; and Upton, *The History of Modern Iran*, 66.

36. Katouzian, *The Political Economy*, 132. There is some debate on this point. Issawi holds that "farmers did benefit from price support and credit," but Keddie notes that in the depression prices for agricultural goods fell more than for manufactured goods: Charles Issawi, "The Iranian Economy 1925-1975: Fifty Years of Economic Development," pp. 129-166 in Lenczowski, editor, *Iran Under the Pahlavis*, 132; Keddie, "Stratification, Social Control and Capitalism," 171, based on Bank Melli, *Bulletin* (March 1934), 2-4.

37. For some estimates see Hayden, "Living Standards in Rural Iran," 187; and Lambton, *Landlord and Peasant*, 374.

38. Lambton, *Landlord and Peasant*, 374-75.

39. Ibid., 277, 330-36, 350-58, 368, 380-83. One (admittedly extreme!) example of an agricultural loan is recorded of a merchant from Kashan who lent 130 rials (15 shillings, 3 pence) to a peasant, and after ten years of compound interest the total due was 70,000 rials (412 pounds sterling).

40. See Keddie, "Iran, 1797-1941," 154; Banani, *The Modernization of Iran*, 123-24; Wilber, *Riza Shah Pahlavi*, 266; and Lambton, *Landlord and Peasant*, 394.

41. Hayden, "Living Standards in Rural Iran," 142. See also Upton, *The History of Modern Iran*, 66, and Lambton, *Landlord and Peasant*, 388-89.

42. Keddie, "Stratification, Social Control, and Capitalism," 170.

43. Cited by Keddie, *Historical Obstacles*, 2. The minimum intake required to function in Iran was calculated at something over 2000 calories by Hadary, "The Agrarian Reform Problem," 183.

44. Cited by Keddie, *Historical Obstacles*, 2. Life expectancy gradually increased from twenty-five years in 1900 to thirty years in 1950: Bharier, *Economic Development in Iran*, 39.

45. Hayden, "Living Standards in Rural Iran," 144-46; Lambton, *Landlord and Peasant*, 263, 303, 387, 390-91.

46. These are Abrahamian's words: *Iran Between Two Revolutions*, 141.

47. Lambton, *Landlord and Peasant*, 285. On wars, settlement, and government policy, see Banani, *The Modernization of Iran*, 128-29; Wilber, *Riza Shah Pahlavi*, 146; Lois Beck, *The Qashqa'i of Iran* (New Haven and London: Yale University Press, 1986), 129-142; Beck, "Tribes and the State"; and Paul Barker, "Tent Schools of the Qashqa'i: A Paradox of Local Initiative and State Control," pp. 139-157 in Bonine and Keddie, editors, *Modern Iran*, 143.

48. Bharier, *Economic Development in Iran*, 31; Lambton, *Landlord and Peasant*, 286.

49. Keddie, *Roots of Revolution*, 97; Bharier, *Economic Development In Iran*, 135 table 2; "The Borderlands of Soviet Central Asia, II," 409; "Agricultural and Industrial Activity," 550 note 3.

50. On the khans see Richard W. Cottam, *Nationalism in Iran* (Pittsburgh: University of Pittsburgh Press, 1964), 61; Wilber, *Riza Shah Pahlavi*, 146, 162, 171 note 11; Garthwaite, *Khans and shahs*, 139; Barker, "Tent Schools of the Qashqa'i," 143; Abrahamian, *Iran Between Two Revolutions*, 150-51; Keddie, "Iran, 1797-1941," 152; and Banani, *The Modernization of Iran*, 128.

51. On tribespeople's conditions of life, see Keddie, "Iran, 1797-1941," 154; Banani, *The Modernization of Iran*, 67; Cottam, *Nationalism in Iran*, 61-62; Keddie, "Stratification, Social Control, and Capitalism," 170; and Keddie, *Roots of Revolution*, 97. Lambton provides specific

examples of exploitation by their khans among Qashqa'is, Kurds and Baluchis: *Landlord and Peasant*, 286-94.

52. This point is suggested by Beck's lecture on "Tribes and the State."

53. On the railroad and other infrastructural projects, see Banani, *The Modernization of Iran*, 134-36, 171 note 83; Wilber, *Riza Shah Pahlavi*, 125, 185, 265; Keddie, *Roots of Revolution*, 99-100; Katouzian, *The Political Economy*, 115-16, 132; Issawi, "The Iranian Economy 1925-1975," 131-32; Bharier, *Economic Development in Iran*, 87, 195-98, 203, 214-17, 226-27, 233, 235; and Moghadam, "Iran's Foreign Trade Policy," 217.

54. Evidence against an ISI strategy is found in Banani, *The Modernization of Iran*, 117; Bharier, *Economic Development in Iran*, 176; and Moghadam, "Iran's Foreign Trade Policy," 137, 139, 174. Keddie feels there *were* high tariffs: *Roots of Revolution*, 101.

55. Abrahamian, *Iran Between Two Revolutions*, 146-47; Bharier, *Economic Development in Iran*, 179 table 3, 181 table 4; Floor, *Industrialization in Iran*, 30-31, 33; Ehsan Tabari, *Jam'eh-i Iran dar Dauran-i Riza Shah* [Iranian Society in the Reza Shah Period] (Stockholm: Tudeh Publishing Center, 1356/1977), 79. For the sizes of factories, see Floor, *Labour Unions*, 59 table 4; Bharier, *Economic Development in Iran*, 181 table 4; and Ashraf, "Historical Obstacles," 329.

56. Korby, *Probleme der industriellen Entwicklung*, 60 table 6.

57. These data draw on Bharier, *Economic Development in Iran*, 151, 176-80, 224; Banani, *The Modernization of Iran*, 139, 141; Floor, *Industrialization in Iran*, 130-31; "Affairs in Persia," pp. 84-88 in *Journal of the Royal Central Asian Society*, volume XV, part 1 (1928), 88; Moghadam, "Iran's Foreign Trade Policy," 218 table 43; "The Borderlands of Soviet Central Asia, II," 411; and "Agricultural and Industrial Activity," 553.

58. Korby, *Probleme der industriellen Entwicklung*, illustrations 4 and 5 at the end of the book; Bharier, *Economic Development in Iran*, 87, 180, 182 table 5; and Issawi, "The Iranian Economy, 1925-1975," 130-33.

59. For the first position, see Banani, *The Modernization of Iran*, 138; Wilber, *Riza Shah Pahlavi*, 244, 264-65; Ahmad Ashraf, "Iran: Imperialism, Class and Modernization from Above," Ph.D. dissertation, Faculty of Political and Social Science, New School for Social Research (1971), 79; Bharier, *Economic Development in Iran*, 53; and for the latter point of view, Floor, *Industrialization in Iran*, 24. This paragraph relies on Floor, *Industrialization in Iran*, 24, 25, 40, 40 note 55; idem, *Labour Unions*, 61-62, 79-80 note 237; and Bharier, *Economic Development in Iran*, 176-77.

60. On this group see Wilber, *Riza Shah Pahlavi*, 266; Moghadam, "Iran's Foreign Trade Policy," 176-77; Keddie, *Roots of Revolution*, 102, 107; Floor, *Industrialization in Iran*, 34 table 13; and Ashraf, "Iran," 68, 75.

61. Abrahamian, *Iran Between Two Revolutions*, 147; Floor, *Industrialization in Iran*, 27-28.

62. Data on these occupations can be found in Floor, *Industrialization in Iran*, 27-28 tables 8, 9 and 9a, 30-31, 41 note 67; Korby, *Probleme der industriellen Entwicklung*, 60 table 6; Abrahamian, *Iran Between Two Revolutions*, 147; "Agricultural and Industrial Activity," 554-56; and Tabari, *Jam'eh-i Iran dar Dauran-i Riza Shah*, 79.

63. For data on artisans and small shopkeepers, see Floor, "The Guilds in Iran," 109-10; Michael E. Bonine, "Shops and Shopkeepers: Dynamics of an Iranian Provincial Bazaar," pp. 233-258 in Bonine and Keddie, editors, *Modern Iran*, 235-36; Bharier, *Economic Development in Iran*, 143, 171-74; Floor, *Industrialization in Iran*, 27 table 8, 28 table 9a, citing Z. Z. Abdullaev, *Formirovanie rabochego klassa Irana* (Baku, 1968), 84; "Agricultural and Industrial Activity," 556; on wages, Floor, *Labour Unions*, 103; on diet, Upton, *The History of Modern Iran*, 73.

64. Upton, *The History of Modern Iran*, 77; also 76. On political power and class consciousness, see Lambton, *Islamic Society in Persia*, 30 note 1; Bonine, "Shops and Shopkeepers," 235; Ashraf, "Iran," 73-74; Nikki R. Keddie, "Religion, Society, and Revolution in Modern Iran," pp. 21-36 in Bonine and Keddie, editors, *Modern Iran*, 29; Floor, *Industrialization in Iran*, 43-44 note 104; and Abrahamian, *Iran Between Two Revolutions*, 151-52.

65. Keddie, "Iran, 1797-1941," 155; Banani, *The Modernization of Iran*, 29, 102-3, 108; Abrahamian, *Iran Between Two Revolutions*, 145-46; Byron. J. Good, "The Transformation of Health Care in Modern Iranian History," pp. 59-92 in Bonine and Keddie, editors, *Modern Iran*, 74.

66. Banani, *The Modernization of Iran*, 47. See further Cottam, *Nationalism in Iran*, 41-42.

67. Abrahamian, *Iran Between Two Revolutions*, 152-55; Keddie, "Religion, Society and Revolution," 29; Cottam, *Nationalism in Iran*, 254-55; and Ashraf, "Iran," 81.

68. For this overview I have drawn on Arjomand, "Traditionalism in Twentieth-century Iran," 203-4; Akhavi, *Religion and Politics*, 54-59; Algar, 1982 lectures on "Islam in Iran"; Keddie, "Iran, 1797-1941," 52; Banani, *The Modernization of Iran*, 18 note, 71-81, 172 note 120; Wilber, *Riza Shah Pahlavi*, 263; Abrahamian, *Iran Between Two Revolutions*, 145; and Ivanov, *Tarikh-i Nuvin-i Iran*, 87.

69. Reverend R. J. Thompson, "Conditions of Daily Life in Iran, 1947," pp. 199-208 in *Journal of the Royal Central Asian Society*, volume XXXV, parts III-IV (July-October 1948), 205. For this paragraph generally I have drawn on Wilber, *Riza Shah Pahlavi*, 238-39; Willem M. Floor, "The Political Role of the Lutis in Iran," pp. 83-95 in Bonine and Keddie, *Roots of Revolution*, 102; Floor, *Labour Unions*, 79 note 223, 103; Ashraf, "Iran," 81-81; Elwell-Sutton, "Reza Shah the Great," 43; Floor, *Industrialization in Iran*, 28 table 9; and Bharier, *Economic Development in Iran*, 35.

70. On women see Banani, *The Modernization of Iran*, 108; Wilber, *Riza Shah Pahlavi*, 173-74, 262; Keddie, *Roots of Revolution*, 97-98, 101, 108-9; Katouzian, *The Political Economy*, 126-27; Abrahamian, *Iran Between Two Revolutions*, 144; Floor, *Industrialization in Iran*, 26, and *Labour Unions*, 104; Kumari Jayawardena, *Feminism and Nationalism in the Third World* (London: Zed Press, 1987), 67-70; and Elwell-Sutton, "Reza Shah the Great," 34.

71. On Iranian Jews, see Cottam, *Nationalism in Iran*, 84; Laurence D. Loeb, "The Religious Dimension of Modernization Among the Jews of Shiraz," pp. 301-322 in Bonine and Keddie, editors, *Modern Iran*, 308; Floor, *Labour Unions*, 80 note 237; Abrahamian, *Iran Between Two Revolutions*, 163. On Armenians, Abrahamian, *Iran Between Two Revolutions*, 142; Floor, *Labour Unions*, 80 note 237; Lambton, *Landlord and Peasant*, 275. On Zoroastrians, Wilber, *Riza Shah Pahlavi*, 198; Cottam, *Nationalism in Iran*, 86-87.

72. The calculation of the population involved in each mode of production in 1941 is a complicated one and only a very rough estimate is possible. Starting with Floor's figures of 3.75 million workers in agriculture and 1.2 million in urban areas, we can give the two agrarian modes of production 76.5 percent and the two urban modes 23.5 percent of the total. For the crop-sharing and nomadic modes, I have then worked from Bharier's figures of 10.35 million peasants and 1 million nomads out of a 14.55 million total population, giving the pastoralists 7 percent of the population and the peasantry 69.5 percent to make the total rural sector correspond to 76.5 percent. To divide the urban share between capitalist and petty-commodity modes I took Floor's highest estimate of the working class—525,000 people—giving the capitalist mode 43 percent of the urban sector's 1.2 million workers: 43 percent of 23.5 percent gives us 10 percent. By default the petty-commodity mode is left with 13.5 percent. See Floor, *Industrialization in Iran*, 26, 28 tables 9 and 9a; and Bharier, *Economic Development in Iran*, 27 table 2, 31.

73. This is based on crude calculations from scattered data in Korby, *Probleme der industriellen Entwicklung*, 3 diagram; Floor, *Industrialization in Iran*, 1; Ivanov, *Tarikh-i Nuvin-i Iran*, 76; Bharier, *Economic Development in Iran*, 131; and Tabari, *Jam'eh-i Iran dar Dauran-i Riza Shah*, 78.

74. On inflation see Bharier, *Economic Development in Iran*, 46-47 table 3, 48-49 table 4; Kamran M. Dadkhah, "The Inflationary Process of the Iranian Economy: A Rejoinder," pp. 388-391 in *International Journal of Middle East Studies*, volume 19, number 3 (August 1987), 389 table 1; and Abrahamian, *Iran Between Two Revolutions*, 148. On GNP and income inequality, see Korby, *Probleme der industriellen Entwicklung*, 3 diagram; Floor, *Industrialization in Iran*, 2; Bharier, *Economic Development in Iran*, 59; Keddie, *Roots of Revolution*, 102; Katouzian, *The Political Economy*, 132; and Moghadam, "Iran's Foreign Trade Policy," 175-76.

75. Wilber, *Riza Shah Pahlavi*, 141, 142, 199, 243, 257.

76. Ibid., 256; Banani, *The Modernization of Iran*, 13; Katouzian, *The Political Economy*, 111.

77. Wilber, *Riza Shah Pahlavi*, 202. Data on trade and banking may be found in Bharier, *Economic Development in Iran*, 108 table 3, 111-12 table 4, 238; Moghadam, "Iran's Foreign Trade Policy," 46 table 5, 67, 68 table 15, 69 table 16, 70; and "The Borderlands of Soviet Central Asia, II," 406.

78. The data in this paragraph are drawn from Bharier, *Economic Development in Iran*, 157-58 table 3; Robert B. Stobaugh, "The Evolution of Iranian Oil Policy, 1925-1975," pp. 201-252 in Lenczowski, editor, *Iran Under the Pahlavis*, 203-5; Moghadam, "Iran's Foreign Trade Policy," 56, 58, 74-82; Banani, *The Modernization of Iran*, 142; and "Revised Agreement: Persia and the Anglo-Persian Oil Company," pp. 188-196 in Hurewitz, *Diplomacy*, II.

79. "Russo-German Negotiations for a Projected Soviet Sphere of Influence in the Near and Middle East," pp. 228-230 in Hurewitz, *Diplomacy*, II, 230; Wilber, *Riza Shah Pahlavi*, 136-37, 256; "The Borderlands of Soviet Central Asia, II," 317; Ashraf, "Iran," 55-56, 59.

80. Data in this paragraph are drawn from Banani, *The Modernization of Iran*, 130, 132; Wilber, *Riza Shah Pahlavi*, 121, 145, 194-95, 199; "A Letter from Teheran," 91; Keddie, *Roots of Revolution*, 105-6; Bharier, *Economic Development in Iran*, 108 table 3, 113 table 5, 148, 253; Hurewitz, *Diplomacy*, II, 150-54; Ivanov, *Tarikh-i Nuvin-i Iran*, 90; Moghadam, "Iran's Foreign Trade Policy," 66, 89, 99, 135-36, 191-202; and "The Borderlands of Soviet Central Asia, II," 407, 410.

81. Katouzian, *The Political Economy*, 134.

82. Report of Alfred Rosenberg, chief of the Nazi Foreign Policy Office, quoted in Miron Rezun, *The Iranian Crisis of 1941. The Actors: Britain, Germany and The Soviet Union* (Cologne and Vienna: Böhlau Verlag, 1982), 90 note 72.

83. On Germany and Iran in the 1930s, see ibid., 7-30, 33; Elwell-Sutton, "Reza Shah the Great," 44; Wilber, *Riza Shah Pahlavi*, 177, 201; Rezun, *The Iranian Crisis of 1941*, 95-96 note 150; Ashraf, "Iran," 59; and Ivanov, *Tarikh-i Nuvin-i Iran*, 93.

84. For these economic ties see Bharier, *Economic Development in Iran*, 108 table 3, 113 table 5; Moghadam, "Iran's Foreign Trade Policy," 203-212; Wilber, *Riza Shah Pahlavi*, 162-64, 199; and Ivanov, *Tarikh-i Nuvin-i Iran*, 90-91.

85. Quoted by Wilber, *Riza Shah Pahlavi*, 187-88 note 5.

86. On the United States and Iran see ibid, 123, 175, 192, 194; Banani, *The Modernization of Iran*, 96; Hurewitz, *Diplomacy*, II, 160-61; Bharier, *Economic Development in Iran*, 108 table 3, 113 table 5, 156; Moghadam, "Iran's Foreign Trade Policy," 47; and Dillon, "Carpet Capitalism," 294.

87. "Treaty of Nonaggression (Sa'adabad Pact)," pp. 214-216 in Hurewitz, *Diplomacy*, II, 215. See also Sepehr Zabih, *The Left in Contemporary Iran. Ideology, Organisation and the Soviet Connection* (London and Sydney: Croom Helm, and Stanford: Hoover Institution Press, 1986), 3.

88. On Iran's relations with Japan, see "A Letter from Teheran," 91-91; Bharier, *Economic Development in Iran*, 108 table 3, 113 table 5; and Upton, *The History of Modern Iran*, 62.

89. Ashraf, "Iran," 60-61.

90. Revolts of peasant conscripts with local support occurred in Salmas, Dilman, Fuman, and Turkoman Sahra in 1926: Ivanov gives the fullest description in *Tarikh-i Nuvin-i Iran*, 82-83. Wilber, *Riza Shah Pahlavi*, 117-18, mentions all but Fuman.

91. "Report on the Bakhtiari Tribes" (1928), quoted by Abrahamian, *Iran Between Two Revolutions*, 142. See also Ivanov, *Tarikh-i Nuvin-i Iran*, 84.

92. Different versions of this story are found in Akhavi, *Religion and Politics*, 42, and Wilber, *Riza Shah Pahlavi*, 127. Events discussed in this paragraph are based on Wilber, *Riza Shah Pahlavi*, 126, 129, 166-67; Abrahamian, *Iran Between Two Revolutions*, 152; and Mohammad H. Faghfoory, "The Ulama-State Relations in Iran: 1921-1941," pp. 413-432 in *International Journal of Middle East Studies*, volume 19, number 4 (November 1987), 424-28.

93. See Abrahamian, "The Strengths and Weaknesses of the Labor Movement in Iran, 1941-1953," pp. 211-232 in Bonine and Keddie, editors, *Modern Iran*, 214, and Floor, *Labour Unions*, 44-53.

94. Floor, *Labour Unions*, 58. On the strikes, see ibid., 40-42, 53-58; Ivanov, *Tarikh-i Nuvin-i Iran*, 81-82; Wilber, *Riza Shah Pahlavi*, 193; Abrahamian, *Iran Between Two Revolutions*, 154-155; and Abrahamian, "The Strengths and Weaknesses," 214.

95. This bill is quoted in Wilber, *Riza Shah Pahlavi*, 151 note 1.

96. Abrahamian, *Iran Between Two Revolutions*, 139.

97. On these individuals and events see ibid., 139-40, 155-62; Wilber, *Riza Shah Pahlavi*, 187-88; Zabih, *The Left in Contemporary Iran*, 2; and Floor, *Labour Unions*, 58. The total number of political prisoners in 1941 is estimated at 15,000 by Reza Shahshani, "The Background of Iranian Affairs," pp. 113-131 in *Science & Society*, volume X, number 2 (Spring 1946), 117.

98. For the account of this section generally I have drawn on Wilber, *Riza Shah Pahlavi*, 192-227, and Rezun, *The Iranian Crisis of 1941*, 46-80.

99. On the army's collapse see the ironic formulations of Katouzian, *The Political Economy*, 135, and Lucien Rey, "Persia in Perspective—2," pp. 69-98 in *New Left Review*, number 20 (Summer 1963), 78.

100. Rezun, *The Iranian Crisis of 1941*, 78.

101. Ibid., 104 note 259, quoting Hassan Arfa, *Under Five Shahs* (New York: William Morrow & Company, 1964), 301. For further evidence on popular attitudes toward the fall of the shah, see Abrahamian, *Iran Between Two Revolutions*, 164, 165, 165 note 138.

102. Quoted by Wilber, *Riza Shah Pahlavi*, 208.

7

Democratization, Separatism, Nationalization, Coup: Social Movements from 1941 to 1953

. . . neither the native government nor the native inhabitants are capable of pursuing a prolonged and formidable policy of hostility toward us.
> —Winston Churchill, in the British parliament on June 17, 1914, on why Iran was a particularly suitable source for oil, quoted in Platt, *Finance, Trade and Politics*

*   *   *

The Government is bound to dispossess at once the former Anglo-Iranian Oil Company under the supervision of the mixed board.
> —Article 2 of the bill for the Nationalization of the Oil Industry in Iran (May 1, 1951), in Hurewitz, *Diplomacy*, II

*   *   *

The United States will avoid any unwanted interference in the oil dispute.
> —U.S. Secretary of State John Foster Dulles, "Report on the Near and Middle East" (June 1, 1953), in Hurewitz, *Diplomacy*, II

*   *   *

The night of the coup, General Zahedi's son, Ardeshir (who later became something of a Washington celebrity as the Shah's ambassador), went up to [CIA officer Howard] Stone at a victory party and said, "We're in. . . . We're in. . . . What do we do now?" The Shah

*himself, after his return, told [CIA agent Kermit] Roosevelt, "I owe my throne to God, my
people, my army—and to you!"*

—Powers, "A Book Held Hostage"

The period from 1941 to 1953 brought a second whirlwind of social
change to Iran, equal in scope and significance to the earlier events of 1905
to 1925. The Allied occupation undermined the autocratic system of Reza
Shah, releasing Iran's pent-up social forces who responded by reviving the
press and political organizations and engaging in vigorous social movements after World War II. This chapter first assesses Iran's experience in the
war and then turns to the attempts of Kurdistan and Azarbaijan to assert
their regional and ethnic rights in 1945-46. These events ushered in a new
situation of competition for influence in Iran among England, the Soviet
Union, and the United States, which thus added a built-in international
dimension to the explosion of Iran's social forces.

The struggle for control of the state culminated in the 1951-53 oil nationalization movement led by prime minister Muhammad Mussadiq, which
activated the second full-scale twentieth-century version of Iran's urban
multi-class populist alliance. The complex dynamic of domestic and external
forces, and competing ideological orientations and their social bases, once
again touched off a massive movement for social change, this time aimed at
breaking Iran's dependence on the British in the world-system. These
dramatic events afford another case for analyzing the interplay of the
factors involved in social change in Iran—internal class structure, dependent position in the world-economy, the nature of state power, and political
cultures of opposition—one which can be compared and contrasted with
the Constitutional revolution of 1905-11 and the Iranian revolution yet to
come.

Iran in World War II

The period of World War II in Iran brought growing economic problems,
a revival of political debate and activity, and renewed foreign pressures. As
in World War I Iranians experienced severe economic hardships and dislocation of everyday life. Politically, the new young shah Muhammad Reza
Pahlavi was only one of several major actors, joined now by a proliferation
of parties, newspapers, and a new trade union organization. All of this
occurred in the context of the Allied occupation, with Soviet troops in the
north, British forces in the south, and American personnel advising the
Iranian government and army in Tehran, as well as transporting supplies
to the Soviet Union. These changes in the internal and international situa-

tion of Iran during World War II formed the background for the subsequent social movements of 1945-46 and 1951-53.

Iran's fifteen million people had a difficult time during World War II as their country became a staging area for Allied troops supplying equipment and provisions to the Soviet Union. Despite the Allies' pledge to disturb the population as little as possible, all key economic sectors—agriculture, industry, services, foreign trade, state budget, and living standards—were drastically impacted by the occupation. Agriculture, the backbone of the economy employing 75 percent of the labor force and accounting for about 50 percent of GDP, saw significant declines in production of the basic crops and livestock levels during the war years, with wheat and barley down by 25 percent, cotton 39 percent, rice ten percent, cattle nine percent, and tobacco seven percent.[1] Only a few sectors such as sheep and horses made gains, a slight countervailing trend due to the relaxation of Reza Shah's disastrous sedentarization campaigns against the tribes, which permitted demographic expansion of pastoralists from the 1930s' low of one million to about two million in the 1940s. In other sectors fruit production dropped 25-30 percent and the Caspian fisheries' output was down due to overfishing. The shortfall in production was compounded by the great demands for food from the occupying armies, resulting in serious famine in most regions outside Azarbaijan and the Caspian.[2]

Industry likewise felt the pinch of war, contributing its share to the overall drop in Iran's GNP from perhaps 180 billion rials to 150 billion between 1941 and 1945. While Floor's data show an increase in industrial companies from 460 to 635 and of industrial capital from 527 million rials to 1.505 billion between 1939/40 and 1944/45 (which in real terms represented an increase from only $28.7 million to $46 million in capital, due to rapid depreciation of the currency), most other data on industry point to a decline, relatively if not absolutely. The establishment of "large" (more than ten workers) modern factories fell to two per year during the war, after averaging eight a year in the 1930s. The leading sector—textiles—slowed due to difficulties in procuring replacements for spare parts and new machinery. Heavily dependent on German-supplied equipment in the 1930s, many factories fell into disrepair. State industries were ignored, partly on the recommendation of American economic adviser Arthur Millspaugh.[3] One urban activity which tended to prosper during the war was the commercial sector of merchants and speculators. While small and medium merchants suffered in many cases from the general dislocation of the economy, some large merchants were well-placed to capture windfall profits. One field where speculators thrived was in diverting the carpet market from the provinces to Tehran. More generally, as middlemen between the local markets and Allied wartime needs the merchant community found a lucrative niche in an otherwise deteriorating economy.[4]

These activities formed part of the larger pattern of Iran's foreign trade and its related service sector. Allied demand for workers on the railroad, in the oil industry, in construction, and in all manner of service activities increased. The British alone employed 75,000 Iranians during the war. The consequences were however far from solely beneficial. The key item—use of the railroad—was valued by Mussadiq (then a majlis representative) at $140 million during this period, but the Allies offered Iran only $5.2 million for its use. They provided $21 million worth of repairs, maintenance, equipment, and services, but Iran still lost over $100 million by this arrangement. Oil production burgeoned from 6.6 million tons in 1941 to 16.8 million in 1945, while British payments remained at four million pounds sterling for 1940-43 and increased to only 5.62 million pounds by 1945. Foreign trade was another area in which the Allies exploited Iran, acquiring their supplies at rock-bottom rates by devaluing Iran's currency, printing money, and granting themselves credits. The devaluations alone gave the Allies double value for their purchases. Iran's ability to import dropped precipitously, undermining industry's demands for capital goods and consumers' for finished products, which simply were no longer available on the world market. Exports, especially of oil, remained high, to meet Allied needs. Iran thus accumulated a huge trade surplus during the war of about $50 million a year, but much of it wasn't paid to Iran, remaining instead in England and the Soviet Union. By war's end, Iran's reserves in Moscow came to $12 million in gold and $8 million in currency, which were kept frozen there, out of reach.[5] The state's budget deficit therefore grew, from $38 million in 1941/42 to $50 million in June 1943, after having been balanced throughout the 1930s. Customs revenues declined as trade fell, and taxes, particularly from large landlords, proved difficult to collect, as always, though greater sums were generated than in the past. Iran meanwhile obtained no loans during the war period.[6]

These economic developments had a harsh impact on the population, especially in the cities. The most ready measure of this is the hyperinflation experienced in the first years of the war due to the distortions caused by Allied consumption, shortages of basic goods, and forced devaluations of the currency. Data show a sevenfold increase in prices between 1940 and 1944, when an American-devised stabilization plan took effect and halted the rise (though prices remained at a high level after the war).[7] The consequences of the inflation were shortages of staple items on the official government-regulated markets and the creation of a thriving black market which became equal in scope and importance to the regular economy. Thus sugar was rationed at 8 rials ($0.25) a kilogram in mid-1944, but could be bought in any amount for 133 rials ($4.12) on the black market, while tea was sold officially at 40 rials ($1.24) a kilogram but at 400 rials ($12.40) in the underground economy. Tires were the most valuable item, fetching $2,000 each in Tehran in 1942. Aspirin could not be found on the official market but glutted the black market.[8]

The most serious wartime shortage was in the bread supply. In Tehran bread prices skyrocketed on the open market from six cents to one dollar in the first half of 1942. When Ahmad Qavam became prime minister in August 1942 he held up a piece of bread at his news conference and said simply, "This is my program. If I can put bread of good quality in the hand of all Iranians, other problems will be easy to solve."[9] Shortages became acute in the autumn, however, and the quality of bread declined as bakers sifted out flour for good bread to sell the rich and mixed cinders, pebbles, dirt, and sawdust into the bread of the poor. The crisis culminated on December 8-9, 1942 when bread rations were lowered, prompting thousands of demonstrators, many of them students and women with small children, to converge on the majlis, crying, "You may kill us, but we must have bread." Troops were called out to contain the looting that followed and 20 people were killed, 700 wounded, and 156 arrested, with $150,000 damage done to the bazaar. There were disturbances elsewhere over bread prices and shortages in 1942 and 1943 before Allied shipments and government measures brought the food supply situation under control.[10] The result was a perceptible deterioration in the standard of living for the urban lower and middle classes during World War II. Income inequality grew as merchants, speculators, and the urban upper classes found ways to profit from the crisis, while the rest of the population was hard hit by the inflation and shortages.

If the Allied occupation had primarily negative consequences for Iran's economy, its impact on the political system produced more positive effects. In fact, in releasing the social forces which Reza Shah had compressed (by forcing the latter's abdication), the Allies opened up the political arena to new groups and actors over whom they had less than full control and who proceeded to engage in political struggles and lay the groundwork for significant social movements in the postwar period. The political process expanded well beyond the shah to include a range of independent institutions and social actors—including the cabinet, majlis, parties, labor movement, ulama, and tribes. Muhammad Reza Shah's power base was in the army (and to a lesser extent the conservative and royalist parliamentary factions and their press). Dealt a crushing blow by the Allied invasion, the Iranian army was slowly rebuilt from its low of 65,000 men (down from 124,000 under Reza Shah) back to 80,000 by mid-1943. The shah continued to propose prime ministers, but these were now subject to votes of confidence in the majlis, and the 1941-53 period saw twelve prime ministers come and go, nine of whom were titled members of the old Qajar elite, two bureaucrats under Reza Shah and one a member of Reza's military elite. The old elite also remained fairly entrenched at the cabinet level, somewhat to the shah's advantage.[11]

The majlis emerged for the first time since the pre-1925 period as an independent power center. Though elections remained subject in large measure to the control of the shah, army, large landlords, and the foreign embassies, there was a gradual democratization of the system in the 1940s. The thirteenth majlis (1941-43) had been "prepared" by Reza Shah before his abdication and so proved willing to compromise with the new shah, letting him control the army if he did not dictate in politics. The line-up of social forces in the majlis became broader and the conflicts more acute during the fourteenth majlis from 1944 to 1946. While the elections were still manipulated by vested interests, Abrahamian has called them "the most prolonged, the most competitive, and hence the most meaningful of all elections in modern Iran, particularly in the urban areas where landlords could not control the results."[12] The body that resulted was similar in its conservative landed social composition to previous ones, but with sixty new deputies out of 126 elected. It divided itself into seven major factions: the royalist National Union Caucus, with about thirty deputies, of whom thirteen had been in Reza Shah's majlises; the conservative, pro-British Patriotic Caucus, with twenty-six deputies, including Sayyid Zia al-Din Tabataba'i, the journalist who had helped organize Reza Khan's 1921 coup and then spent twenty years in exile; the conservative, pro-tribal Democrat Caucus, allied with the Patriots, numbering eleven deputies led by two Bakhtiari chiefs; the Liberal Caucus of anti-court liberals from the Soviet-occupied zone, with twenty deputies favoring closer ties with the U.S.S.R.; the Tudeh (Masses) Party—a major new left of center grouping that worked with the Liberals, with eight deputies; the Independent Caucus, with fifteen members, stressing independence from the shah and landed class internally, and from Britain and the Soviet Union externally; and the Individuals Caucus—sixteen deputies, five of them moderate professionals associated with the Iran Party, and two intellectuals of the Comrades Party, and including Muhammad Mussadiq, the Qajar landowner who had opposed Reza Shah's rise to the throne in 1925 and now stood for an independent foreign policy, civil control of the army, and fair elections. These parties differed on the major issues facing Iran, with the Patriots and Democrats pro-British, the Tudeh and Liberals pro-Soviet, the Independents and National Unionists pro-U.S., and the Individuals non-aligned in foreign policy; the Tudeh, Individuals, and sometimes the Independents working for social reforms domestically; and all but the National Unionists pressing for civilian control of the army.[13]

The most well-organized and numerous of these organizations was the Tudeh, founded just thirteen days after Reza Shah abdicated in September 1941 by twenty-seven younger members of the famous "fifty-three" imprisoned Marxists in the late 1930s. Most commentators agree that the Tudeh in the 1941-47 period was a broad-based organization of progressives and radicals, some of whom were Marxists and communists, but that the party itself was neither the direct descendant of the original Iranian Communist Party of the 1920s, nor organizationally and ideologically a true communist party.[14] In the war years, the Tudeh's leadership was three-fourths intellectuals, one-fourth working class; its social base was the reverse (one-fourth intellectuals, three-fourths workers, artisans, and craftspeople, with perhaps two percent peasants). The party grew rapidly in size from 6,000 members in 1942 to 25,000 in 1944 to 50,000 core members and 100,000 active supporters by 1946, making it by far Iran's largest political force and indeed its only large, well-organized party. The 1943 party program made appeals to workers with labor reforms, peasants with land reform, and artisans, intellectuals, women, and students with calls for political rights and job security. It also advocated national independence from foreign domination and constitutional rule internally. A related progressive force that developed close ties with the Tudeh was the revivified labor movement, as strikes involving more than fifty workers grew from three in 1941 to fifty-seven in 1944 and a peak of 183 in 1946. On May 1, 1944 four labor confederations merged to form the Central Council of Federated Trade Unions of Iranian Workers and Toilers (C.C.F.T.U), led by veteran labor organizers mostly from the working class and members of "the fifty-three." The C.C.F.T.U. grew by 1946 to claim a membership of 335,000 workers, including industrial labor, craftspeople, artisans, professionals, unskilled wage earners, and service sector employees. Its organizing issues were primarily economic but it represented a formidable political force as well, demanding the right to form unions, bargain collectively, and to strike.[15]

Other groups and classes which returned to political activity in the war years included the ulama, lutis, and tribes. Though the most prominent cleric, Sayyid Abu'l-Hasan Isfahani (died 1945) "held aloof from politics," many ulama joined political parties and prepared the ground for a more active role in postwar politics. Religious expression in the form of the celebration of the Muharram passion plays was allowed to revive and prime minister Sohaili in 1943 brought ulama into higher profiles in the judiciary and educational systems which Reza Shah had so thoroughly secularized.[16] As ulama power grew, the status of women accordingly regressed in terms of the secular legislation of the 1930s. There was a general return on the part of urban middle and lower class women to the veil, although this was less so in Tehran.[17] In the absence of more data on other aspects of women's lives in this period, one may infer that the gains of the Reza Shah legislation were not fully reversed, and that in particular, women continued to participate in the educational system in increasing numbers at all levels. Another urban group which may be briefly mentioned is the lutis (sometimes called the *chaqukashan*, "knife-wielders")—the young lower-class urban toughs who had participated in street demonstrations in the Qajar period but who were more tightly controlled by the state in the Reza Shah era. Active in the 1942 bread riots, they became mainstays of the urban political scene, retaining some of their Islamic sentiments and neighborhood patron-client affiliations, but now more strictly payable in cash.[18] Finally, the tribes too resumed their former economic and political activities in a general resurgence of independence after 1941. Demographic renewal, resumption of migration patterns (by some, not all), widespread re-arming, and in some cases reorganization under their former chiefs were the order of the day. Tribal revolts against the government, sometimes with German support, peaked in 1942-43, after which certain khans were appeased with appointments as local governors, election to the majlis, or financial arrangements with the British. The Kurds (both sedentary and nomadic) would play a major role in their region in 1945-46, however, as would southern tribes like the Bakhtiari and Qashqa'i in postwar political events.[19]

Taken together, these trends and organizations allowed hitherto unimaginable expression to Iran's underlying social forces, which would be articulated in several explosive social movements between 1945 and 1953, borne by new variants of the multi-class populist alliance. The final factor in the political-economic equation was, of course, the external forces acting on Iran in this period. Iran's strategic importance to the Allies had prompted the joint British-Soviet invasion in August 1941, and concern with winning the war against Germany forced Britain, the Soviet Union, and the United States to cooperate closely in Iran through 1944, after which tensions began to arise among the powers that continued into the postwar period and ultimately played a major role in determining the form and outcome of the social movements that occurred. The role of the foreign powers, then, was instrumental in effecting the transition from world war to cold war, and Iran would play a key part in the larger global context.

Britain remained the preeminent foreign economic actor in Iran by virtue of its control of the oil industry, which pumped large amounts of oil and profits out of Iran into the war effort. Britain and British India provided 32 percent of Iran's imports for 1940-44 and took 19 percent of non-oil exports. Politically too the British possessed great influence among conservative tribal leaders, newspaper editors, certain of the ulama, and other monarchist and anti-communist groups, especially Zia al-Din's misnamed National Will party. As Sir Reader Bullard, Britain's ambassador, reported candidly in 1942: "we were obliged to interfere frequently and radically in the local administration . . . there was a time when we used to wonder whether in the end we might not have to take over the country . . . we have succeeded in establishing a number of Persian governments."[20]

The Soviet Union likewise used its occupation of northern Iran to rebuild its influence in the country to new levels after the loss of much ground in the 1930s to Germany and Britain. Trade reached 21 percent of Iran's non-oil exports and 17 percent of imports for 1940-44. The Soviet trade deficit with Iran totalled $20 million by the end of the war and was not repaid, leading to strained relations between the two countries and damaging Iran's economy well into the Mussadiq period. A second problem was Soviet appropriation of Azarbaijan's grain surplus in 1942, contributing to the famine conditions in Tehran. This was belatedly made up by release of 25,000 tons of grain in 1943; the Soviets also built hospitals, roads, and wells in Iran during the war.[21]

World War II was the turning point for the American presence in Iran. Thirty thousand troops arrived in December 1942 to assure transport of massive amounts of lend-lease supplies to the Soviet Union. In 1943 the U.S. sent a military mission under Colonel Norman Schwartzkopf and an economic team under Dr. Arthur A. Millspaugh to restructure Iran's military and finances at the request of prime minister Qavam. Under Schwartzkopf's wide powers the Iranian army and Imperial Gendarmerie were fashioned into a 90,000-man force, with a marked improvement in esprit de corps. Meanwhile, U.S. trade with Iran doubled from eight percent of non-oil exports in 1935-39 to 17 percent in 1940-44 and from ten to 20 percent of exports. The context for this growing involvement was an emerging American policy goal of achieving a new international economic order to avert a relapse into the 1930s' depression by taking measures to ensure the free international movement of capital—both raw materials and finished manufactures—rather than returning to the exclusive trading blocks that had existed prior to the war. In January 1944 Millspaugh outlined a twenty-year program for the use of American aid, arguing: "Iran, because of its situation, its problems, and its friendly feelings toward the United States, is (or can be made) something in the nature of a clinic—an experiment station—for the President's post-war policies—his aim to develop and stabilize backward areas."[22] President Roosevelt responded to the suggestion (made by General Patrick Hurley) that the United States urge Iran to develop "a pattern of self-government and free enterprise," by saying he was "rather thrilled with the idea of using Iran as an example of what we could do by an unselfish American policy."[23] There was mutual interest on the side of the Iranian state in nurturing closer ties with the U.S. to offset British and Russian interference and to control domestic social movements. Prime minister Sohaili sought American governmental and business contacts with Iran, while the shah confidentially told the American minister in 1943 that "he would prefer that Allied forces remain in Iran to prevent a revolution against the monarchy, at least until he could rebuild his army and gain an upper hand in the domestic power struggle."[24]

Iran's growing closeness to the United States created problems for both the British and the Soviet Union in the latter stages of the war, touching off an initially delicate but increasingly acrimonious three-way competition for hegemony in Iran. In July 1943 the British formally complained to the U.S. State Department about "an impression, however false, that there may be some desire on the American side to supplant British traders in the established and traditional markets, not only for the war period, but permanently thereafter."[25] A wider conflict came out into the open over the issue of new oil concessions. In early 1944 British and American companies opened talks with Iran regarding concessions in the southeast. After word of this was leaked by a majlis member the Soviets began to insist on their "rights" to a northern oil concession. In late 1944, the majlis, on Mussadiq's initiative, passed a bill prohibiting cabinet ministers from discussing or negotiating any petroleum concession with a foreign country, and this forced the Iranian government to suspend all talks on oil until after the war.[26]

Confrontation among the United States and Great Britain on one side and the Soviets on the other now became acute. Throughout 1945 the Soviets conducted propaganda castigating their Western allies; while U.S. troops left Iran in December 1945 and the British withdrew in February 1946 in compliance with treaty obligations to evacuate within six months of the war's end, the Soviets retained their forces in the north. In conjunction with movements for autonomy in Azarbaijan and Kurdistan declared in December 1945, this action touched off the round of postwar social movements in Iran and led to the first battle of the Cold War.

Social Movements in Azarbaijan and Kurdistan, 1945-1946

The postwar movements for autonomy in Azarbaijan and Kurdistan were the first tests of the potential for new social movements in the changing domestic and international environments of post-Reza Shah Iran. As such they present challenging cases for theories of social change, not only with respect to the roles played by internal and external factors, but, insofar as they were provincial rather than national in scope, to see how well an analysis focussed primarily on class coalitions can deal with instances of social movements motivated by important ethnic, nationalist, and regional grievances.

On December 12, 1945 a locally-chosen provincial assembly led by the Democratic Party of Azarbaijan under Jafar Pishivari declared the establishment of the "Autonomous Government of Azarbaijan" at Tabriz. The local dialect of Azari Turkish was proclaimed the official language and equality of rights for all the peoples inhabiting Azarbaijan—Azaris, Kurds, Armenians, and Assyrians—was demanded. Then on December 17 a crowd marched on the department of justice at the town of Mahabad in Kurdistan, shot the Iranian coat of arms off its façade, and raised the Kurdish flag on the roof. On January 22, 1946, Qazi Muhammad, a local notable from a family of landlords and judges, declared the "Autonomous Republic of Kurdistan" at Mahabad. In both cases Iranian forces were powerless to intervene because the 30,000 Soviet soldiers still occupying Azarbaijan made it impossible for them to enter the area.[27]

Meanwhile in Tehran Ahmad Qavam again became prime minister, in February 1946, despite the shah's objections, chosen as the person most capable of getting the Soviets to withdraw. Qavam went to Moscow to negotiate, returning only on the last day of the fourteenth majlis in mid-March, which Tudeh-organized demonstrators prevented from reaching a quorum and possibly extending its session. The majlis thus dissolved, and as no new assembly was convened until mid-1947, it played no role in the key events of 1946.[28]

Rather than their agreed-upon evacuation, Soviet armored troops *advanced* into Azarbaijan in early March. This touched off an international crisis, although the extent of these maneuvers was certainly exaggerated by the American consul at Tabriz and the Iranian government. The United States protested vigorously, Iran lodged a complaint at the newly established United Nations, and by early April Qavam successfully negotiated an agreement whereby the troops would be withdrawn and the Soviet Union would be granted an oil concession in the north (subject however to ratification by the as yet unelected majlis). Tehran agreed to withdraw its grievance at the U.N. and to negotiate with the Pishivari government in Azarbaijan. Soviet troops began to evacuate Iran on April 22 and had left altogether by May 10.[29]

In June 1946 Qavam reached an agreement with the Azarbaijan Democrats granting most of the province's demands regarding use of the local language, retention of tax revenues, and progressive social reforms administered by the provincial assembly, while the latter acknowledged that Azarbaijan was part of Iran. Kurdistan was mentioned only in passing and implicitly assumed to be linked with the Azarbaijan dispute. A temporary truce was thus in effect between Tehran and its rebellious northwestern provinces.[30]

The Nature of the Autonomous "Republics"

Azarbaijan, it will be recalled, provided much of the radical impetus behind the Constitutional revolution and had declared a short-lived separatist state named Azadistan ("Land of Freedom") after World War I under Shaikh Khiabani. During the 1930s this populous commercial and agricultural province continued to stagnate as Tehran grew at its expense. Local grievances included the right to use Azari Turkish in schools, government, and the press; to retain its own tax revenues (the 1944-45 budget allocated Tehran twenty times more funds than Azarbaijan, despite the latter having three times the population); to elect its own local and provincial governing bodies; and to carry out progressive reforms in such areas as compulsory education and land distribution. Fuel was added to the fire during the 1943-44 majlis elections when the supreme electoral council refused to accept Tabriz's winning candidates, Jafar Pishivari (a Communist from the post-1918 era imprisoned between 1930 and 1941) and a Tudeh member, because they advocated autonomy for the province.[31]

In September 1945 Pishivari formed the Democratic Party of Azarbaijan (DPA) with veterans of the early communist movement and the Khiabani revolt. Shortly thereafter the local branches of the Tudeh and the C.C.F.T.U. trade union movement voted independently of their organizations in Tehran to join the DPA. In mid-October a "nearly bloodless revolt" began as DPA-armed volunteers known as *fida'is* seized local governments throughout Azarbaijan under cover of the Soviet occupying forces. In November the DPA convened a National Congress of Azarbaijan and on December 12, 1945 the National Majlis met at Tabriz with 100 members, almost all from the DPA, electing Pishivari as "prime minister" and declaring the formation of the Autonomous Government of Azarbaijan.[32]

The program of the DPA called for freedom and autonomy in Azarbaijan within the national territory of Iran; support for democracy, constitutional government, and local self-rule; use of Azari in schools and administration; protection of minorities' and women's rights; and economic measures aimed at reducing unemployment, distributing land, and retaining provincial tax revenues. Though some historians have stressed its separatist dimension, the main thrust of the DPA program, statements, and actions was for local autonomy and cultural self-determination inside the Iranian state. Thus, it never used the term "Democratic Republic of Azarbaijan" as some historians later did, and indeed "dropped the terms National Majles, Autonomous Government, cabinet minister, and prime minister in favor of Provincial Assembly, Provincial Council, department head, and governor-general," nor did it ever appoint a minister of war or foreign affairs as a separatist regime would have.[33] What the DPA and Pishivari stood firm on and chose to emphasize over class issues and social reforms was the right to use their own language and communal solidarity generally against the encroachments of Tehran.

Though one or the other might be emphasized depending on the situation, the time or the organization in question, the admixture of class and ethnic issues is clear not only in the DPA program, but in its social base, accomplishments, and problems. Membership in the DPA reached 75,000, according to the newspaper *Azarbaijan* in January 1946, of which 56,000 were peasants, 6,000 intellectuals, 3,000 artisans and shopkeepers, 2,000 merchants, 500 landowners, and 100 ulama. Peasants adhered in great numbers, though they later developed grievances with the DPA. Many large landlords did flee Azarbaijan, but others participated in the government. Labor was enthusiastic, with 50,000 members of the C.C.F.T.U. supporting the DPA. U.S. diplomat Robert Rossow stated that "The bulk of the party members are illiterate peasants and city rabble."[34] Another commented on "the 'new,' 'independent' attitude of domestic servants, gardeners, and artisans, who no longer display the same respect and deference which was accorded to their employers only a few years ago."[35] Women were permitted to vote for the first time in Iranian history.[36] The movement was thus a *local* variant of the populist alliance, with the unique addition of a sizable peasant contingent and the influential presence of a few landlords, in addition to the predictable urban classes of workers, intellectuals, artisans, merchants, and a few ulama. This broader alliance is in part attributable to the ethnic solidarity emphasized by the DPA to appeal to landlords and large merchants as well as peasants and workers, and to unite Muslims and Christians, Kurds, Azaris, and Armenians against the exploitative central government in Tehran.

In the area of social and economic reforms the DPA regime showed its sensitivity to class grievances and made great attempts to shore up its populist social base. On the economic front it

> decreed a comprehensive labor law; tried to stabilize prices by opening government food stores; and shifted the tax burden from food and other necessities to business profits, landed wealth, professional incomes, and luxury goods. It also changed the face of Tabriz by asphalting the main roads; opening clinics and literacy classes; founding a university, a radio station, and a publishing house; and renaming streets after Sattar Khan, Baqer Khan, and other heroes of the Constitutional Revolution.[37]

Other measures included nationalization of banks, building of orphanages, houses for the aged, and hospitals, and in the cultural arena, creation of a theater and publishing houses for works in Azari, including poetry and folklore collections. Cottam judges that the DPA accomplished more reforms in one year in Tabriz than Reza Shah had in twenty.[38]

The most historically significant of the reforms was in agriculture, where the DPA tried to enact Iran's first land reform. This was effected by distributing to peasants lands belonging to the state or landlords who opposed the regime or had fled Azerbaijan. In this way an estimated 257,066 hectares were given to 209,096 peasants. On other lands still in landlord hands, the share of the crop for the peasants was raised (estimates vary, from 30 to as high as 85 percent for the peasant). Land distribution efforts were somewhat attenuated by the continued landlord presence in the DPA regime and by the poor harvest of 1946, but the reforms of the government won it much popular support: "The British consul in Tabriz reported that the land reform gained many friends, the work projects alleviated unemployment, the administrative reforms brought more efficiency, and the changes, on the whole, found considerable popular support."[39]

Despite these accomplishments, the Autonomous Government of Azerbaijan found itself increasingly beset by problems in the second half of 1946. External relations with both enemies and ostensible allies grew increasingly strained. Most obviously there were difficulties with the central government in Tehran, despite the June accord which provided a temporary lull. As will be seen, Azerbaijan's fate was largely tied to the balance of forces in Iran as a whole, and this changed drastically in the autumn. Support from the Soviet Union was also far weaker than is imagined by those who have called the DPA regime a Russian puppet.[40] Although Mir Jafar Baqirov, the party chief of Soviet Azerbaijan, seems to have had Stalin's blessing to try to attach Iranian Azerbaijan to the Soviet Union, it is extremely doubtful that this could have been popular among Iranian Azerbaijanis, who wanted autonomy from outside control.[41] The withdrawal of Soviet troops in May left the province on its own militarily, and Soviet promises of heavy artillery and tanks were never kept, leaving Tehran with a huge military advantage over Tabriz. Relations with the Tudeh Party were also less than ones of complete encouragement and support. In essence, Tudeh policy was to keep a fair distance from the DPA but not to openly criticize it, thereby undermining effective solidarity with the movement. Finally, relations with the Kurdish Republic were also based on an uneasy half-cooperation, as Azerbaijan's formal alliance with Kurdistan won only suspicion in Tehran, while the Kurds felt considerable resentment at their subordinate status vis-à-vis Tabriz and over territorial disputes in mixed Kurdish-Azari areas such as Urumiyah, as well as general doubts on the part of Kurdish tribal khans about the more radical social reformers in Azerbaijan.

Serious internal contradictions were experienced as well. Economic problems cut into popular support for the DPA. These included capital flight as land reform frightened urban merchants and industrialists, who feared they might be next to be expropriated. Workers suffered layoffs, cuts in benefits and greater industrial discipline as the regime sought to increase factory productivity and profits. The urban population in general was alienated by new taxes and compulsory military service. Peasants saw new exactions (as did landlords) on top of a bad harvest, plus the imposition of price controls. Pro-Soviet rhetoric, compounded by a harsh internal security force which some commentators consider engaged in a "reign of terror," further disenchanted the population, which retained strong Islamic sensibilities. Tribal revolts by Afshars, Shahsavans, and Zulfaqaris were encouraged by Tehran and disturbed the social order while wearing down the local militia.[42] Thus, while regional, linguistic, and ethnic aims united the populist alliance, social reforms first split off landlords and capitalists, and then the DPA's economic problems weakened the mass base of the movement. The situation was therefore a highly fragile one by autumn of 1946.

In neighboring Kurdistan, the roots of nationalism lay in a centuries-old sense of a distinct history, coupled with Sunni rather than Shi'i religious beliefs. More recently, there had been several tribal revolts and an urban nationalist movement between 1919 and 1930. In the 1930s power shifted to settled urban Kurds as Reza Shah weakened the tribal chiefs, although social organization remained predominantly tribal, whether nomadic or settled agricultural at the economic base (there were numerous sedentary tribal peasants). During World War II much of Kurdistan, including the key city of Mahabad, lay just south of the Soviet zone of occupation and north of the British zone, nominally closer to the Soviet forces. The major tribes re-armed, leading chiefs and urban dignitaries visited Baku to discuss national aspirations with the Soviet authorities, and in May 1943 a raid on the Iranian police station at Mahabad drove the Iranian gendarmerie out of the town for the duration of the war. Mahabad and much of the surrounding countryside were thereafter de facto independent.[43]

Meanwhile a small group of middle class men met at Mahabad in September 1942 to organize a Kurdish political party called the Komala (Komala-i Zhian-i Kurdistan, "Committee of the Life (or Resurrection) of Kurdistan"). By 1945 the Komala had attracted most of the tribal chiefs and urban notables to its banner, and its leader by general consensus was Qazi Muhammad, a respected religious judge of Mahabad with a forceful personality. A delegation travelled to Baku in September 1945 to reiterate desires for a separate Kurdish state and request Soviet financial and military assistance. Later in the autumn some 10,000 Barzani Kurds from Iraq under Mulla Mustafa Barzani fled into Iran and pledged their support to the cause. The Komala changed its name to the Democratic Party of Kurdistan (DPK) on Soviet advice. Its program called for self-government of the Kurdish people in local affairs, use of Kurdish as the official language and for education, a provincial council, Kurdish government officials only, retention of tax revenues for local use, fraternity with the people of Azarbaijan, and improvement of the moral standards, health, and economic conditions of the Kurdish people. Events culminated with Qazi Muhammad's declaration of an autonomous Kurdish *republic*, thereby going beyond both the DPK's earlier program and the government in Azarbaijan.[44]

The tiny sixty by 120-mile Kurdish Republic of Mahabad reposed on a mixed urban and tribal social base. The state consisted of urban merchants, officials, and landlords from Mahabad in the cabinet, and a mostly tribal army of 12,750 men from twenty-eight different groups, skilled in ambush and mountain siege warfare but also relying on outmoded cavalry charges. The movement was genuinely popular among a broad section of the urban population in Mahabad, where both women's and youth sections of the DPK were formed. Tribal support was wide but perhaps not too deep— many chiefs affiliated with the DPK, some participated in the army, others were content to enjoy autonomy in their localities with only loose ties to Mahabad. There was a marked drop in tribal support as the situation became more precarious later in 1946, and there was naturally some tension between urban and tribal elements and among the tribal chiefs themselves.[45] Discernable here is yet another variation of the multi-class populist alliance, notable for the participation of tribal chiefs and their followers alongside urban members of most classes. This was of course made possible by the movement's emotional appeal to *all* Kurds, but it would set distinct limits on how radical the changes attempted could be.

On the positive side, contemporary reports noted the more open political atmosphere than in the past under Iranian control. People could carry arms, there was no secret police, and indeed no real internal opposition to the republic to be feared. Culturally, publications in Kurdish became available, including textbooks for the primary grades, a newspaper and a monthly journal both called *Kurdistan*, two literary magazines, a children's magazine, and *Nishtman*, the organ of the Komala. Radio broadcasts from Ankara and London were freely listened to (this reportedly carried the death penalty in DPA-run Tabriz). Thus the regime was widely popular, "at least among the citizens of Mahabad, who enjoyed their respite from the exactions and repression they considered to be characteristic of the central Iranian government."[46] Economically, taxes were coming in, both from tribal chiefs who wanted to be associated with the regime and as a result of levies on some of the wealthier families of Mahabad, who were less enthusiastic. Merchants thrived on goods smuggled in more easily from Iraq for sale in Mahabad, or further afield in Tabriz and Tehran. The 1945 harvest was a good one and the entire tobacco crop was sold to the Soviet Union for $800,000 in Iranian currency and Soviet goods (even though the Iranian government had already made a ten percent payment on it).[47]

As in the case of Azarbaijan however, there were both internal and external limits and problems faced by the Kurdish Republic. Internally, there was no move toward land distribution and no hint of a socialist dimension to the DPK program as there were in Azarbaijan. Roosevelt notes that "The villages were run by their old landlords and tribal leaders with the aid of a gendarmerie locally recruited and dressed in Kurdish costume, but commanded by officers from Mahabad with Soviet uniforms"—a subtle improvement at best from the point of view of the Kurdish peasant. Tribal support gradually dropped off too; khans were generally wary of the urban leadership and suspicious of the possibility of a leftward turn as in neighboring Azarbaijan. Rivalries existed between the Barzanis of Iraq, who remained supporters of the DPK, and Iranian tribal groups, partly due to the pressures on the food supply. By autumn 1946 key tribes, concerned for their own future under Iranian control, were promising their loyalty to the central government's plan to retake Azarbaijan. The main armed defenders of the republic thus became increasingly unreliable.[48]

Mirroring this lack of internal unity, external relations were not particularly favorable either. Kurdistan was locked into a tense conflict with the central government, and in May and June 1946 small-scale skirmishes were frequent in the border zones. When Qazi Muhammad went to Tehran in August to negotiate with Qavam, the latter slyly offered to make Kurdistan a province with Qazi as probable governor, knowing full well that Qazi could not accept this since the Soviets and Azarbaijan would oppose it. The Soviet position in Kurdistan was one of general encouragement but limited material or diplomatic aid. The two sides collaborated more out of mutual need versus the Iranian state than from any genuine affinity, as the movement was primarily nationalist and partly conservative in thrust. There was a minimal Soviet presence in Kurdistan compared with Azarbaijan and while some 6,200 light weapons were supplied, no tanks or artillery were ever sent. The Soviets thus had some influence because they could withdraw support, but little positive control over the direction taken by the DPK. Relations with the DPA regime in Tabriz were formally friendly but in reality somewhat strained by territorial disputes and the larger issue of Kurdish autonomy from Azarbaijan, which considered most of Kurdistan part of its jurisdiction. Overtures to the United States and the British led to no alternative support as the British were concerned not to arouse Arab resentment in Iraq and the United States stood behind Tehran in seeing in the movement a Soviet-sponsored threat to the shah.[49]

The contradictions faced by the Kurdish Republic thus sharpened in the course of 1946. The stresses of a Soviet-encouraged regional movement had been symbolically embodied in the dress of Qazi Muhammad when he had declared the republic in January, attired in "a Soviet-style uniform and the white turban of a religious dignitary."[50] When the time came to face the Iranian army nine months later, Qazi had to reckon with enmities to the north with Azarbaijan, limited tribal support internally, and little Soviet aid externally.

Dénouement

The fate of the rebellions in Kurdistan and Azarbaijan was inextricably bound up with the larger context of the balance of social forces in Iran as a whole (which in turn included the even larger international dimension). In the spring and summer of 1946 this context was quite favorable for progressive social movements. The C.C.F.T.U. was at the peak of its power, claiming 335,000 unionized workers. An equal number of peasants may have been organized in their own unions, especially concentrated throughout the north, but also forcing landlords to relinquish a greater share of the crop in such southern and central locations as Isfahan, Yazd, and Kirman.[51] Between May and July one of the largest (if not the largest) industrial strikes in Middle Eastern history till then was waged and won by the oil workers. On May Day 1946, 80,000 workers paraded at Abadan, the site of the oil refinery: "A woman orator described oil as the 'jewel' of Iran, and, accusing the British of spending more on dog food than on workers' wages, demanded nationalization of the AIOC. This was probably the first time that the call for oil nationalization had been heard in the streets of Abadan."[52] On May 10, more than two thousand workers struck at Agha Jari oilfield for higher wages. The company cut off water to the area but gave in three weeks later when the C.C.F.T.U. threatened a general strike in Abadan. By mid-June the Tudeh was effectively governing much of the province, setting food prices, controlling communications and transport, patrolling the streets, and guarding the oil installations. On July 10 the Anglo-Iranian Oil Company struck back with wage cuts and the provincial government declared martial law. This prompted a four-day general strike of up to 100,000 workers both inside and outside the oil industry, and despite armed clashes between the strikers and British-incited Arab tribesmen, the outcome was a cancellation of the wage cuts and a raise in the minimum wage.

These events pushed the Qavam government in what appeared to be a leftward direction during the summer of 1946. A progressive labor law was enacted and landlords were directed to give 15 percent of the harvest back to peasants, although neither measure was seriously enforced. Restrictions on the Tudeh were relaxed and there was a crackdown on conservative newspapers and organizations instead. On August 1 Qavam took the unprecedented step of naming three Tudeh members to his cabinet as ministers of commerce, health, and education, while liberals or progressives also received the ministries of justice (Allahyar Saleh) and labor (Muzaffar Firuz).[53] The Tudeh was at the apogee of its power and popularity, de facto administrators of such industrial cities as Abadan, Ahwaz, Isfahan, Sari, Rasht, and Anzali. The *New York Times* estimated the Tudeh would take 40 percent of the vote in a fair election, a huge plurality given the number of political parties.[54] This was the high watermark of the national social movement however. The beginning of the end occurred in late September with a revolt of southern tribes led by the Qashqa'i under their chief Nasir Khan. At first motivated by military repression of small-scale Bakhtiari disturbances at Isfahan, by September 23 a coalition of Qashqa'i, Bakhtiari, Khamseh, Arabs, and Boir Ahmadis had captured Bushire, Kirman, and other small cities. Their major demands were for southern autonomy equal to that of Kurdistan and Azarbaijan, local development, removal of certain oppressive army officers, and, most significantly, dismissal of the Tudeh cabinet ministers on the grounds that "communism, atheism, and anarchism endangered democracy, Iran, and Islam." This provided an opening for conservative social forces in Tehran: Chief of staff Razmara refused to attack the Qashqa'i unless he could also go into Kurdistan and Azarbaijan.[55]

Prime minister Qavam now came under considerable pressure from another source to address these crises. The shah, Razmara, and leading conservative politicians plotted a coup to oust him. They approached American ambassador George Allen on October 14, who at first refused to either support or dissuade them, but then promised that the United States would keep the gendarmerie from interfering in Qavam's removal. On October 16-17, Qavam acted first by dismissing the Tudeh governors of Tehran, Isfahan, and Kirmanshah and then the Tudeh ministers. He next announced an agreement with the southern tribal rebels granting most of their demands, and resigned. On October 19 he was re-appointed and his new cabinet had no Tudeh or pro-Soviet members, with Firuz being sent off as ambassador to Moscow.[56] In the next several weeks he completed his rightward turn, arresting Tudeh members and trade unionists, banning leftwing publications, declaring martial law in key provinces, and appointing anti-communist governors. He also announced that the elections for the next majlis would begin in December and indicated his intention to send troops into Azarbaijan and Kurdistan to "supervise" them.

Changing circumstances in the international balance of forces contributed to Qavam's political *volte-face*. Though the Truman doctrine of containing the Soviet Union was first announced only in a March 1947 speech before Congress, the United States made a quieter decision to take a more activist role in Iran during the course of 1946 "not only by words but by appropriate acts." This involved something of a shift from traditional non-interventionism (at least in the Middle East) and avowed support for democratic forces to a decision impelled by anti-communism as a guiding principle to support the shah and Iran's armed forces in their efforts to retake the autonomous provinces. Bolstered by promises of American economic and military aid, the shah was able to force Qavam's rightward tilt, thereby laying the groundwork for the invasions of Azarbaijan and Kurdistan. The Soviet Union did little to oppose these moves, acquiescing in the decision to send Iranian troops to Tabriz to supervise elections for a majlis that it hoped would ratify its northern oil concession. It had little leverage with Iran anymore and could not react to Qavam's moves with any real effectiveness. It could only hope that a minimal force would enter Tabriz for the elections and then leave.[57]

Such was not the case. Both the Autonomous Government of Azarbaijan and the Kurdish Republic came to a quick end when Iranian troops approached in December 1946. The DPA in Tabriz was split on whether to surrender or resist, but after two days of uncertainty, quietly gave up. There were violent reprisals against DPA members both before and after the Iranian army arrived, in which anywhere from 500 people (according to British and American sources) to as high as 14-15,000 (according to Soviet and Kurdish sources) perished. Many others either fled to the Soviet Union or were arrested. Of the latter, the leftwing press reported 860 people hung or shot by July 1947.[58] After Tabriz collapsed, Qazi Muhammad in Kurdistan ruled out flight or resistance, and submitted to the Iranian forces before they reached Mahabad. While most of the tribes other than the Barzanis cooperated with the army, the people of Mahabad showed no enthusiasm for the arrival of Iranian troops, as had been the case in Tabriz. After a military trial, Qazi, two of his relatives, and five Kurdish officers were hanged. Mulla Mustafa Barzani and his tribesmen eventually made a daring move through Iraq and Iran to the Soviet Union in June 1947, eluding the Iranian army.[59]

The social movements in Azarbaijan and Kurdistan in 1945-46 departed in some significant respects from both earlier and later struggles in Iran and present a somewhat unusual mix of the factors involved. They were, first of all, not national in scope, but regional, and thus ethnic as well as class issues were raised. Like all primarily local movements from those of the Safavid period to the short-lived governments in Gilan, Khurasan, and Azarbaijan after World War I, they were effectively isolated and eventually crushed by the central state. Halliday's judgement that they posed the most serious twentieth-century threat to the government[60] is plausible only because of yet another unusual factor—the two autonomous regions rose and fell with reliance on an outside power, the Soviet Union. Local grievances and issues of cultural identity touched them off, but the Soviet occupation made them viable. Similarly, when a combination of international pressure, Iranian diplomatic skill, and wishful thinking or plain miscalculation on the Soviet side removed Soviet troops and limited Soviet aid to the two rebellious areas, they were quickly retaken by Iran.

This points to the limits of these regional variants of the populist alliance. Far more broadly based than the typically urban form of the populist alliance in the Constitutional revolution, the movement in Azarbaijan involved both peasants and landlords, and in Kurdistan tribal chiefs, peasants, and tribespeople, as well as urban elements. The mobilization of the populace was made possible by appeals to ethnic solidarity to face the hostile central government, but ultimately foundered due to internal conflicts of interest between peasants, landlords, and the DPA in Azarbaijan, and tribal and urban interests in Kurdistan. Economic contradictions undermined cross-class ethnic solidarity, especially in Azarbaijan, and the lack of genuine social reforms probably reduced the DPK's mass base in Kurdistan. United by ethnicity, fragmented by class, paradoxically tied to the shifting policies of an external power to oppose the internal domination of the Iranian state, and regionally strong but nationally weak, the movements of 1945-46 were brief flourishings of oppressed ethnic and national minorities within Iran.

The defeat of the Kurdish and Azarbaijani movements marked a general checkmate for the left in Iran and for the Soviet Union as an external actor. Throughout 1947 the trade union movement suffered mass arrests, as did the peasant organizations and Tudeh Party. The fifteenth majlis (1947-49) consisted largely of landlords and large merchants, and was divided into three major factions, all conservative—Qavam's Democrat Party (which soon disintegrated), a royalist bloc, and a pro-British grouping. The Soviets' oil concession was overwhelmingly rejected by the majlis in October 1947 by a vote of 102 to two, signalling the complete defeat of postwar Soviet policy in Iran. The bill refusing the concession also directed the Iranian government to enter negotiations and take action to reestablish the rights of Iran to all its resources, especially the southern oil concession with the British.[61] The end of one wave of regional social movements thus faintly signalled the beginning of another, nationwide struggle to come.

The Oil Nationalization Movement, 1951-1953

Between 1951 and 1953 the second mass social movement to take place in the twentieth century swept Iran. Like its predecessor the Constitutional revolution, the oil nationalization struggle led by Muhammad Mussadiq confronted both the monarchy and foreign powers in Iran, mobilized a vast urban multi-class populist alliance, and after initial successes, suffered internal fragmentation and external intervention, to end in failure. Judgments on the thrust of this movement have yielded interpretations ranging from "a liberal constitutional reformist movement" to "a revolutionary episode."[62] The point of view adopted here enables us to see it as a revolutionary attempt to break Iran's external dependence on the West, and in particular, on Great Britain, and internally, a far-reaching reform-oriented attempt to make Iran a functioning democratic constitutional monarchy. The keys to this interpretation lie in the nature of the oil nationalization issue and the struggle to construct a solid populist alliance capable of confronting Britain and the shah.

Though there was a return to state repression after December 1946, the situation was far from one of order and tranquility, either economically or politically. Inflation resumed in the late 1940s. In 1949 an assassination attempt on the shah failed, but provided a pretext for a ban on the Tudeh and renewed crackdowns on the left and labor movements. It also allowed the shah to gain new constitutional powers to dissolve the majlis and set up a senate with one-half of its members royally appointed. The 1949-50 elections were stormy, with charges of fraud, the assassination of prime minister Hazhir, and eventually the election of a small eight-member nationalist group led by Mussadiq in an otherwise fairly conservative body. Unemployment surged, as did business bankruptcies, in 1950. In the summer of that year, General 'Ali Razmara became the first non-civilian prime minister since Reza Shah. He soon alienated conservatives by relaxing controls on the Tudeh, and progressives by not pressing for oil nationalization. In early March of 1951 Razmara was assassinated by an assailant variously presumed to have been a religious extremist or a communist.[63]

Concurrently, since 1949, the oil issue had been assuming a greater profile in national politics. Recognition was growing of the fundamental injustice of keeping royalties fixed while prices and profits increased. From 1933 to 1949 the AIOC had a net income of 895 million pounds sterling. Of this amount, 500 million pounds were profits retained for capital investment, 175 million pounds were paid in taxes to the British government, 115 million pounds went as dividends to non-Iranian (mainly British) shareholders, and only 105 million pounds were paid to the Iranian government, some 11.9 percent of net income, or 14.6 percent of net profits.[64] Other aggregate figures for the whole existence of the AIOC from 1908 to 1950 put its total profits as three to five billion dollars and Iran's share of these at ten to twenty percent.[65] In 1947, with Iran's royalties at seven million pounds, the AIOC had customs exemptions on imports into Iran worth six million pounds, and exempting oil from export taxes cost Iran 20 million pounds.

After World War II the importance of Middle Eastern oil became increasingly apparent. Having hitherto produced only 3.8 percent of the world's petroleum, the Middle East was estimated in 1945 to contain 42.1 percent of proven oil reserves, and by 1954 this had jumped to 64 percent. In 1945 Iran produced more oil than all Arab countries combined and circa 1950-51 was accounting for 30 million of the world's 637 million tons produced, but was receiving only 18 cents per 42-gallon barrel, compared with 35 cents in Bahrain, 56 cents in Saudi Arabia, and 60 cents in Iraq. In the late 1940s U.S. oil companies agreed to 50-50 profit-sharing arrangements with Saudi Arabia and Venezuela. When Iran demanded revisions of its royalties, the AIOC proposed only a "Supplemental Agreement" that would have given Iran a royalty of six rather than four shillings per ton in 1949. Mussadiq led a filibuster against this in July 1949 and it was never ratified by the majlis.[66]

Events moved quickly in 1951 to prove Churchill's 1914 prognosis wrong (see the first epigraph to this chapter). In January mass meetings were held both by Mussadiq's National Front and in mosques demanding nationalization of oil. The majlis oil committee recommended nationalization on March 8 (the day after Razmara's assassination); the majlis endorsed the resolution on March 15 and the senate on March 20. In April oil workers struck for two weeks to protest wage cuts and to demand nationalization. On April 28 Mussadiq became prime minister by a vote of 79 to 12; on April 30 both chambers of the assembly passed the oil nationalization bill; and on May 1 the shah promulgated the law formally dispossessing the AIOC and authorizing creation of the National Iranian Oil Company (NIOC).[67] These events touched off a British economic blockade and signalled the start of the two-year oil nationalization struggle, a tumultuous period in the history of Iranian social change.

Mussadiq, the National Front, and the New Populist Alliance

The National Front had its origins in a dual protest by various critics of government manipulation of the 1949 elections and the proposed supplementary oil agreement. The group eventually elected eight representatives from Tehran, including Mussadiq, Husain Makki, Dr. Muzaffar Baqa'i, and Abulhassan Hairizadeh, as well as Allahyar Saleh, elected from Kashan. In the next two years, a larger group of parties representing various middle and lower classes joined the National Front, while other progressive elements, including the Tudeh and part of the ulama, generally supported its main issue—the nationalization of oil. The main constituent parties in the National Front included: the Iran Party, a left-of-center non-communist grouping of intellectuals, technocrats, professionals, and students; the Toilers Party, divided into a group of intellectuals and workers under Khalil Maliki which had left the Tudeh and a group of artisans, traders, and more centrist intellectuals around Baqa'i; the bazaar-rooted Mujahidin-i Islam of traders, guild leaders, religious students and ulama led by the clerics Shams al-Din Qunatabadi and Ayatullah Kashani; and the small Pan-Iran Party of Dariush Furuhar, appealing with a right-wing nationalism to secondary students and marginal classes, including some lutis.[68] The acknowledged leader of the National Front coalition was the extremely popular prime minister Muhammad Mussadiq. Mussadiq's main political platform centered around three somewhat related issues—the nationalization of Iran's resources, parliamentary democracy, and internal reforms to ensure economic improvement. Mussadiq's populist appeal shows through in an October 1951 speech in which he said: "Wherever the people are, the *majless* is in the same place."[69]

The movement also included organizations and classes outside those represented in the National Front itself. The Tudeh Party retained great popular support among progressive intellectuals and the working class.

Although its membership was down (due to repression and the adoption of a more cell-like underground structure), it was capable of calling large demonstrations, and on at least one occasion (in July 1952) its crowds (if not its leadership) helped keep Mussadiq in power. Relations between the Tudeh and Mussadiq were generally not harmonious however. Mussadiq was tolerant of Tudeh activities, permitting much freedom to organize and publicize its views, but he was restrained in his political dealings with the party. The Tudeh leadership, for its part, was split on how to deal with the oil nationalization movement; the more experienced members saw Mussadiq as progressive and anti-British, but the newer cadres tended to set the overall policy, opposing him "as the puppet of the comprador bourgeoisie attached to American imperialism" and as a feudal landlord.[70] Despite the wishes of many activists and ordinary citizens at the base, the two sides never worked effectively together throughout most of this period. To the extent that the Tudeh had more working-class support, especially in the trade union movement, this tended to mute somewhat the participation of a crucial force in the populist alliance.

Another important social group that forged a more fluid relationship with the movement was the ulama, and beyond them, the bazaar classes generally. The ulama in this period split into various groups: High-ranking ulama were for the most part inactive or neutral, as the leading mujtahid, Ayatullah Burujirdi, had in 1949 prohibited ulama from joining parties and instead urged them to attend primarily to rebuilding the religious institutions of Iran. Many younger, lower-ranking ulama enthusiastically supported the movement however, as did other high- and middle-rank ulama, including Ayatullah Zanjani, Sayyid Mahmud (later Ayatullah) Taliqani, Mirza Muhammad Taqi Khwansari, Ayatullah 'Ali Akbar Burqa'i (known as the "Red Ayatullah"), and others. As many as one-third of the majlis members were ulama, many in the Mujahidin-i Islam. Other religious elements were not so supportive. The less eminent but very popular Ayatullah Kashani was in the early part of the struggle an active advocate for the movement, but later broke with Mussadiq at a crucial juncture. The Fada'ian-i Islam, a small, radical, fervently Islamic group that carried out political assassinations (including Razmara's in 1951) gave some support to Kashani but was resolutely opposed to the National Front and Mussadiq, because of the generally secular thrust of the movement. It came to support the shah in the final showdown of 1953, as did Kashani, not to mention a number of long-standing royalist ulama, such as Ayatullah Muhammad Bihbihani. The various trends within the ulama influenced the other elements of the bazaar social structure, which was on the whole a source of pro-Mussadiq forces among the artisans, small traders, and merchants. The marginal class luti toughs, it may be added, participated on both sides of the movement (though more decisively for the royalists) and could be mobilized by the ulama and some elements in the Tudeh and National Front.[71]

Two final classes to take note of are the peasants and the tribes. Mussadiq found a somewhat unlikely ally in the Qashqa'i tribe, which had remained a locally powerful force since the 1946 rebellion and which remembered him as a popular governor of Fars in the 1920s. Mussadiq was seen as a symbol of nationalism opposed to the British (and by extension to the British-backed Bakhtiari tribe, the Qashqa'is' regional rival) and as an alternative to the return of the oppressive monarchic dictatorship of the 1930s. Other tribal groups were not very active in the movement on either side. Nor were the peasants on the whole; as in the Constitutional revolution they were difficult to mobilize for reasons of geography, landlord domination, and the government's lack of interest in any substantial land reform project.[72]

We are now in a position to make a preliminary assessment of the class composition of the oil nationalization movement. Ivanov's generalization that the National Front was limited to "nationalistically inclined land-owner-bourgeois politicians and representatives of the intelligentsia," that it was a "national bourgeois organization,"[73] will not do for characterizing the movement as a whole. Diba, Abrahamian, and Katouzian rightly point to the participation of students, industrial workers, artisans, traders, merchants, ulama, urban women, and the Qashqa'i—what Abrahamian refers to as "two divergent forces: the traditional middle class . . . and the modern middle class."[74] I would conceptualize these social forces as a multi-class alliance of dominated and middle classes from the petty-commodity, capitalist, and a section of the pastoral-nomadic modes of production. Both conceptions point to the *mixed* bases of this populist alliance and the material and ideological strains that were forming within it. Abrahamian notes that in terms of political culture, of its two components, "one was conservative, religious, theocratic, and mercantile; the other was modernistic, secular, technocratic, and socialistic."[75] There was also, in my view, a centrist, democratic, and liberal outlook embodied in the person of Mussadiq. Only the broadest aims could hold this coalition together—opposition to British imperialism and to the claims of the monarchy and military on state and society. Both internal political economic developments and external forces put severe pressures on the populist alliance, ultimately causing it to fragment.

The Political Economy of the Mussadiq Period

The drama of Iran's economy in the 1951-53 period centered around the question of oil. Mussadiq had nationalized oil for both economic and moral-political reasons. Economically, he felt, "With the oil revenues we

could meet our entire budget and combat poverty, disease, and backwardness among our people."[76] In the event that nationalization led to a short-
term fall in production he felt that the new terms would still equal past
receipts and leave Iran's oil in the ground for the benefit of coming generations. In fact, almost *all* of Iran's oil remained in the ground after April 1951
due to a British-organized international boycott and military blockade,
which was widely observed by the world's oil companies. This forced the
elaboration of a new economic policy around the concept of an "oil-less
economy" predicated on doing without oil revenues (which it could be
argued were used unproductively by the state anyway in the past and had
benefited only an elite of top bureaucrats, army officers, the court, and
indirectly, landowners and merchants who paid little or no income tax as a
result).

The keys to the success of an oil-less economy lay in readjusting foreign
trade and expanding domestic production. In 1952, the only full year of the
Mussadiq administration, Iran's oil exports were reduced to negligible
levels, yet a positive balance of trade without oil was achieved for the first
time, a result repeated in 1953. This was accomplished by cutting imports
by almost 25 percent in 1952. Non-oil exports such as carpets, Caspian fish
and caviar, live sheep, rice, tobacco, and cotton were increased to meet the
reduced import demands. The favorable balance of trade moreover obtained despite a fall in the terms of trade from a level of 100 in 1948 to 90 in
1949 and 69 in 1952. The total surplus however was less than in the pre-1951
period when large oil exports made the picture more favorable. The effect
of these new trade patterns on merchants was mixed: Large import-export
businessmen in the chamber of commerce were alienated, but traders in
carpets, dried fruits, and other products did well and the bazaar merchants
remained pro-Mussadiq.[77]

In terms of overall production there was a slowing but not a decline in
the growth of GNP. There is some debate on the main trends in industry;
Graham and others feel industrialization was impeded. Certainly, the import of capital goods was down, as was capital formation generally.[78]
Keddie however argues that there was industrial expansion in the direction
of increased import-substitution and self-sufficiency, due to the limits on
imports. Thus sugar-refining, textiles, cement, and mining increased their
output. The construction industry in housing and commercial building
continued to expand though there was less government building undertaken. On balance it would seem that there was a reactivation of domestic
industry compared with the immediate pre-1951 years. There was a business
recession in 1952, but there had been many bankruptcies in 1950 as well, so
the Mussadiq policies were not entirely to blame. Strike data show a great
increase in incidents, from 4-5 per year in the 1948-50 period to 42 in 1951,
55 in 1952, and 71 in the first eight months of 1953; this can be read as a sign

of health both in terms of the political atmosphere and the bargaining position of labor. Finally, it is difficult to gauge developments in the artisanal sector which accounted for so much of Iran's small-scale production; one may hazard the guess that it too benefited from the drop in imported goods, and bazaar support for the government is another possible sign of improved conditions.[79] Agriculture maintained or increased production levels as well. As late as May 1953 the U.S. commercial attaché reported that agriculture was doing well. In the absence of any land reform other than an unenforced decree in 1952 that landlords return a ten percent share back to the peasant, living standards however remained poor and inadequate in the countryside. The first signs of a burgeoning rural-to-urban migration underline this point. The tribes seem to have continued their post-1941 recovery, and the pro-Mussadiq Qashqa'i in particular "enjoyed unprecedented peace and prosperity."[80]

One sector which was hard hit by the oil crisis was the state itself. The lack of oil revenues was compounded by reduced customs receipts as trade fell, the difficulties of collecting income taxes, and the unpopularity of such new taxes as the one on cigarettes and tobacco. Britain froze Iran's sterling funds, worth $26 million. The government issued $25 million worth of bonds in February 1952, called "Popular Debt"; the bazaar and lower classes bought them but the wealthy held back. Nevertheless the state deficit grew even larger than in the past, rising sixfold between 1951 and 1954, as the obligation to pay the oil labor force was taken on even as exports were cut. The state thus faced severely straitened circumstances.[81]

The overall economic situation during the Mussadiq period was neither "desperate" nor, on the other hand, "thriving." There was a reduction in foreign trade which altered consumption patterns but also encouraged steps toward import-substitution (or at least expansion of existing capacity) and greater self-sufficiency. The standard of living in the cities and especially in the countryside was certainly not high, but it does not seem to have worsened appreciably nor were all the economic problems of the period unique in that most of them predated the Mussadiq administration. Nevertheless the state had more or less severe fiscal problems, and the urban population did suffer from inflation of seven to 16 percent a year, low factory wages, and a degree of unemployment.[82] Thus, while some real achievements were registered, notably in proving that Iran could subsist without oil revenues, there was an underlying reality of widespread, if not deep, economic discontent.

If the domestic economy was not completely in a shambles, political happenings were often on a crisis plane, and Iran's external relations were decidedly unfavorable during 1952-53. Mussadiq's general program internally aimed at greater democratization of society. A number of gains were made: Some political prisoners were released, the Tudeh's front organizations operated more freely, numerous publications opposed to the govern-ment circulated. Mussadiq himself was personally incorruptible and lived a widely-admired austere lifestyle. Reforms of the judicial, electoral, and educational bureaucracies were mandated, and their performance was gen-erally impressive.[83] The overall limits to this program lay in the lack of economically-oriented reforms—especially in agriculture, but also with respect to labor—and the fact that the democratic transformation of society was constrained by a larger struggle for control of the state, which led Mussadiq into political contradictions.

In the complex struggle over the nature of the state Mussadiq had to battle both long-standing conservative elements and the disparate forces within and without his own populist alliance, a most difficult balancing act to sustain. Basically he aimed to shift the locus of power away from the shah, senate, and army to the majlis and the cabinet, including his own office of prime minister. The 1952 majlis elections were a revealing setback for the government. Mussadiq wanted them to be free (i.e. unmanipulated by his government), but this left the field open to control by the army, shah, and conservative elite in the provinces. The National Front did well in the freer atmosphere of the major cities, winning all twelve seats for Tehran. Mussadiq was compelled however to stop the voting due to the coercive situation in the provinces as soon as a quorum of seventy-nine deputies was elected. Of these, only thirty were members of or close to the National Front, while another bloc of 25-30 were fence-sitters who would vote with the prevailing side, and at least a dozen were solidly pro-shah.[84]

A serious political crisis arose in July 1952 when Mussadiq resigned over the issue of whether he or the shah would control the army. The shah's appointment of Qavam as prime minister provoked the National Front to call a general strike for July 21, on which day Tudeh-, religious-, and nationalist-led crowds fought the police and army in the streets. Shouts of "Down with the Shah! We want a people's republic!" were heard and at least sixty-nine people were killed and 750 wounded, most of them workers and artisans. The shah finally ordered Qavam's resignation in order to restore order, and the majlis unanimously renominated Mussadiq as prime minis-ter. The brief mobilization of Tudeh supporters for Mussadiq both showed the Tudeh's mass following as nearly equal to and critical for the success of the National Front's, and alienated conservative and religious groups within the oil nationalization movement, without firmly attaching the Tudeh to the alliance in their place.[85]

Mussadiq used his return to power to press his struggle for control of the state more aggressively against the court. In August 1952 he was granted "emergency powers" by the majlis to implement legislation in connection with his reform program without majlis approval for six months. In January 1953 these special powers were extended for twelve more months. His majlis supporters then forced the dissolution of the royalist-dominated senate, and Mussadiq promised elections in the near future with a term limited to two years. The court's budget was cut, the shah had to transfer the royal estates back to the government, and a critical battle for control of the army was begun. Senior officers were purged, some on charges of embezzlement, and nationalist officers were promoted. At the same time the defence budget was cut 15 percent. By the spring of 1953 Mussadiq was in nominal control of the military and police, but the retired officers and others still active were plotting against him in a situation where the balance of power was rather unclear.[86] Mussadiq's assumption of plenary powers also alienated some members of the populist alliance itself, notably speaker of the majlis Ayatullah Kashani and Dr. Muzaffar Baqa'i of the Toilers Party. Both acted as much from personal jealousy as political or religious principles. These splits took from the oil nationalization movement some of its ability to mobilize street crowds at crucial moments. At the very least the defectors from the populist alliance indirectly aided the anti-Mussadiq coalition consisting of the court, retired and active army officers, conservative ulama such as Ayatullah Bihbihani, pro-British conservative landlords, large merchants, and the majlis opposition.[87]

The stage for a coup was further set in 1953 by the evolution of Iran's foreign relations with the major outside powers—Great Britain, the United States, and the Soviet Union. Mussadiq's foreign policy was predicated on the concept of "negative equilibrium," in effect a neutral, non-aligned pursuit of national independence which would deny concessions and influence to all outside powers rather than balance them off against one another as had been the case since Qajar times. Such straightforward rejection of all demands would have been difficult in the best of world-systemic conjunctures. In the context of the oil nationalization and the cold war it brought sharp conflict with Great Britain, growing involvement of the United States in Iran's affairs, and the inactive hostility of the Soviet Union—all of which contributed greatly to the coming coup.

The consequences of failure to resolve the oil dispute with the British were grave for Iran. Unsuccessful negotiations in 1951 and 1952 foundered on British unwillingness to accept the principle of nationalization as well as excessive concern with their own prestige (and beyond that, of course, with profits). The British began a production slowdown immediately in April 1951 and after being expelled from Abadan in the summer undertook a full naval blockade and international boycott to prevent Iran from exporting oil on its own. This cut exports from 241.4 million barrels in 1951 to 10.6 million in 1952. The AIOC meanwhile suffered no great economic inconvenience because it simply stepped up production in Iraq. There is evidence that Mussadiq personally wanted to settle the dispute in 1952, either with

World Bank mediation or directly with Britain, but that he feared the unpopularity of this measure at home, and his advisers talked him out of it. Katouzian argues persuasively that this was a decisive turning point in the movement, for getting the best terms possible could have reversed the internal and external pressures building toward a coup and given the government breathing space and the revenues to carry out reforms. On the other hand, it is difficult to see how the issue could have been resolved in the eyes of the Iranian people short of nationalization and how the British would have accepted anything less than non-nationalization. Instead of a resolution, the advent of a conservative government in Britain by 1952 put active plans to carry out a coup in Iran on the agenda.[88]

In this the British were ultimately aided by the United States. If the 1946 crisis over Azarbaijan had been the turning point in American-Iranian relations, the 1951-53 period marked the point of no return, during which the United States eventually committed itself to bolster the shah on his throne and took over from Great Britain the role of hegemonic power in Iran. The United States at first looked like a possible source of support for Mussadiq in his struggle with the British, promising continued aid and delivery of a previously discussed $25 million Export-Import Bank loan in May 1951. In November 1951 Mussadiq asked Truman for a $120 million loan; the new Eisenhower administration refused this in 1952 on the grounds that Iran "had access to plentiful revenues from its oil reserves."[89] In November 1952 Mussadiq and Kashani asked again for a $100 million loan and that U.S. companies buy Iranian oil, a policy favored by the smaller independent American oil companies. Eisenhower however informed Mussadiq in June 1953 that "the Government of the United States was not presently in a position to extend more aid to Iran or to purchase Iranian oil."[90] The only American aid that continued to flow to Iran in this period took the form of advisers and equipment to the army and police. Mussadiq in fact halted this briefly because it was conditional on a commitment to Western defence, but the United States, eager to retain influence with the military, backed down and stated that Iran could follow a non-aligned policy.[91]

Meanwhile, since 1948, the newly established CIA had operated a propaganda and political action program in Iran called BEDAMN, directed against Tudeh and Soviet influence. Two Iranians codenamed Nerren and Cilley were given one million dollars a year to get anti-communist articles, books, and cartoons published, to distribute leaflets, start rumors, and hire street gangs (especially from the SUMKA (Nazi) and Pan-Iran parties) to fight with Tudeh crowds, to infiltrate Tudeh demonstrations, to pay ulama to attack the Tudeh in sermons, and to organize attacks on mosques and public figures which could then be blamed on the Tudeh. The CIA, seemingly independently of the Truman administration and the state department, also used BEDAMN against Mussadiq's National Front, making efforts to provoke splits and approaching Kashani, Baqa'i, and others through intermediaries with incentives to break from Mussadiq.[92] U.S. policy was increasingly dictated by a reflex anti-communism which failed to distinguish Third World nationalists from pro-Soviet forces; in the context of the Truman doctrine aimed at containing revolutionary movements in the Third World, Mussadiq was a somewhat ambivalent phenomenon—a non-communist nationalist. In January 1952 the U.S. state department described American aims in Iran: "Our primary objective is the maintenance of Iran as an independent country aligned with the free world. A secondary objective is to assure access of the Western world to Iran's petroleum, and as a corollary to deny access to the Soviet bloc."[93] As late as the end of 1952 state department analysts concluded that Mussadiq should be accorded support and understanding. The newly-installed Eisenhower administration however came increasingly to see Mussadiq as a direct or indirect threat to the status quo. In April 1953 secretary of state John Foster Dulles noted: "there has developed a spirit of nationalism (in the Middle East) which has at times grown fanatical in its opposition to the Western powers."[94] Whereas the Truman administration had generally favored the independent American oil companies, the Eisenhower regime listened more attentively to the international oil cartel. Dulles and his brother Allen (head of the CIA) were senior partners in the law firm of Sullivan and Cromwell which had long represented the Anglo-Iranian Oil Company. Though John Foster Dulles was stating in June 1953 that "The United States will avoid any unwanted interference in the oil dispute," the truth is that serious planning for a coup had begun in late 1952 in joint consultations with the British.[95]

The Soviet Union, meanwhile, did not return to a position of real influence in Iran after the 1946 débâcle. In fact, it did almost nothing to support Mussadiq, but nevertheless was perceived as a serious threat to Iranian independence by the United States, thereby dealing a double blow to the National Front's cause. Economically, it obstinately refused to repatriate the $20 million it still owed the Iranian state from World War II. This exacerbated considerably the regime's fiscal crisis. Barter and trade with the Soviet Union did increase in the 1952-53 period and contributed to the balancing of Iran's trade, but when the Caspian fisheries concession finally expired in January 1953 Iran was in no mood for a renewal. Politically, the U.S.S.R. maintained formal relations with the Mussadiq government, but in Diba's judgment, "the Soviet attitude . . . vacillated between a 'hands-off' policy and the maintenance of correct but politically distant relations."[96] This reserve and the underlying lack of clarity in its assessment of the National Front was a factor in Tudeh policy, which also hurt the movement a great deal. When Stalin died in March 1953 Soviet diplomatic initiatives became even more tentative and further removed the country from the international arena. There was thus little credible Soviet geo-political threat to Iran, but Mussadiq's resolute non-alignment unfortunately appeared all too pro-Soviet to a West accustomed to thinking of Iran as a country which must be in a subordinate relation to one or another "greater" power.[97]

The sum of these vectors of external relations was the isolation of the Mussadiq government from effective support internationally in its struggle with Great Britain, and moreover to align against it the considerable resources of American foreign policy by 1953, the critical year for the nationalist movement. Iran was once again enmeshed in a geo-political battle not of its own making, but which would affect it with irresistible force, tipping the scales in an internal social struggle.

The Coup of August 19, 1953

What were the causes of the coup d'état of August 19, 1953? Social scientists and historians have emphasized varying factors. Zabih and Abrahamian stress internal reasons, such as the importance of the mistakes made by Mussadiq or the growing strength of a conservative opposition. Kermit Roosevelt (one of the CIA operatives involved) and Gasiorowski highlight the role played by outside forces, arguing that the coup would never have succeeded without American involvement. A few writers, notably Keddie, Katouzian, and to a lesser extent Cottam, have noted the importance of both internal and external factors, a more judicious judgment in my view.[98] Each of these factors, internal and external, played a role and must be carefully appraised. Ultimately, they are inter-related in a fashion such that no one could have succeeded without the others, a conclusion which emerges from careful analysis of the general background, actors involved, and the flow of events during and after the coup itself.

From January to August 1953 both domestic and international developments buffeted the Mussadiq administration, finally building to a tense height on the eve of the coup. In January the National Front suffered the defections of Kashani, Baqa'i, and other leaders, as already mentioned. In February, General Fazlullah Zahidi was arrested for plotting with foreigners to overthrow the government; in retrospect his release can be seen as an error. On February 28 came an abortive coup attempt through royalist rioting possibly directed at the assassination of Mussadiq. On March 20 the latest Western proposals on the oil problem were rejected. The end of April brought the kidnap and murder of police chief General Muhammad Afshartus, a man loyal to Mussadiq. This was followed by street clashes which continued into June between groups of royalists, nationalists, and factions inside and outside the movement. In late May Mussadiq requested help in marketing oil from the Eisenhower administration; the negative American response came on June 29, 1953.[99]

In the meantime a constitutional crisis was brewing. The opposition deputies boycotted sessions, refusing to allow a quorum to vote on the extent of the shah's powers. In late June Dr. 'Abdullah Muazimi, the National Front's candidate for speaker of the majlis, narrowly defeated Kashani, 41 to 32. Mussadiq began to seriously consider dissolving the majlis, something which only the shah could do, although the prime minister could request it. In late July the National Front deputies prepared the way for this by resigning en masse, followed by most of the independents who thought it prudent to emulate them in hopes of being re-elected. This was followed by a national referendum on whether the majlis should be dissolved—an extraordinary event—between August 3 and 10. The opposition boycotted the vote; the National Front was supported in it by the Tudeh, tribes, and peasants. In non-secret (i.e. rather coercive) balloting the results were a landslide for Mussadiq: 2,043,389 votes for, only 1,207 against. On August 12 Mussadiq demanded the shah's farman to dissolve the majlis, setting the scene for the crucial events of August 16-19.[100]

On the side of the coup-makers, the British, the United States, and a variety of conservative Iranian elements collaborated in planning and carrying out the series of moves that resulted in the overthrow of Mussadiq. The first plans were drawn up by British intelligence and the foreign office as early as June 1951. The British had contemplated an invasion of Abadan in autumn 1951 but called it off when Truman withheld American support and pushed for negotiations instead. Serious Anglo-American coup planning began in late 1952 after the British embassy staff was forced to leave Iran and the Eisenhower administration had come into office. Two weeks after the latter's inauguration, on February 3, 1953, the two sides met and agreed to a plan for the overthrow of Mussadiq and his replacement as prime minister by General Zahidi, a plan codenamed AJAX, suggesting the "cleansing" action they had in mind. Besides the oil boycott and economic blockade, the British contribution was its network of Iranian intelligence operatives inside the country—"Majlis members, royal court officials, newsmen, bank officials, both active and retired military officers and even the bazaaris and some of the clerics."[101]

The CIA already had its ongoing anti-Tudeh operation BEDAMN in place. The focus was simply changed to a direct attack on Mussadiq. Indeed the anti-communist mentality of the highest levels of the CIA and the state department seems to have been such that there was no problem in blurring the distinction between Mussadiq and the communist "threat" to Iran. Money was spent on anti-Mussadiq newspaper articles, radio broadcasts, and the "purchase" of demonstrators at the crucial moment. Contacts with opposition members of the majlis, retired and active army officers, and the shah himself were made. On August 10 CIA director Allen Dulles, American ambassador to Iran Loy Henderson and the shah's twin sister Ashraf met at a Swiss resort, while Brigadier General Norman Schwartzkopf conferred with the shah at his summer palace on the Caspian. Thus was set in motion "the first peacetime use of covert action by the United States to overthrow a foreign government."[102]

These foreign plotters worked with a variety of internal elements to plan and carry out their coup. The most important of these were Zahidi as the man designated to replace Mussadiq, agents such as Nerren, Cilley, and the Rashidian brothers who made contacts and mobilized crowds, and the shah himself who played a reluctant but significant role if only as a figurehead and rallying point. Zahidi, a landowner from Rasht whose career had spanned high military, police, and government posts, coordinated a group of retired officers in the secret Committee to Save the Nation, and key active personnel including commander of the Imperial Guards Colonel Nasiri, air force chief General Gilanshah, tank commanders in Tehran and the heads of the secret police and gendarmerie. The shah was at first noncommittal and hesitant when Schwartzkopf broached the suggestion that he dismiss Mussadiq at the height of his popularity and try to put Zahidi in his place, but finally agreed to it after he was radioed assurances of official American and British involvement. Not a part of the actual plotting but ready to play supporting roles were certain ulama such as Ayatullah Bihbihani, large merchants, tribal chiefs, and landlords, disaffected majlis deputies, the religious extremists of the Fada'ian-i Islam, luti elements led by Sha'ban "Bimokh" (the Brainless), and the social forces associated with each of these, many encouraged by the anti-National Front slogan, "Better Shah than the Tudeh."[103]

With the majlis dissolved (or almost) after the referendum, it was unclear, from a constitutional point of view, whether the shah could dismiss the prime minister. Nevertheless, this is the form the first coup attempt took, on the night of August 15-16. The shah sent Colonel Nasiri of the Imperial Guards late at night to Mussadiq's house with a decree dismissing him and appointing Zahidi in his place. Prepared for such a move, Mussadiq ordered his own guards to arrest Nasiri and the Imperial Guards unit at Shemiran outside Tehran, where foreign minister Husain Fatemi and other National Front members had been detained, thus completely forestalling the shah's attempted constitutional coup.[104]

Having failed to oust Mussadiq, the shah flew out of the country on Sunday, August 16, first to Baghdad and then to Rome. Zahidi went into hiding at a CIA safe-house in Tehran. That morning Mussadiq addressed the country over the radio, stating that he was taking full control of the government, dissolving the majlis. His position was that the decree dismissing him was a forgery or illegal, since only the majlis could dismiss a prime minister. The shah claimed that only he could dissolve the majlis, while CIA operatives made copies of the shah's decree available to the press to bolster Zahidi's claim. Meanwhile, foreign minister Fatemi made a fiery speech calling for the abolition of the monarchy. The flight of the shah was greeted by widespread demonstrations of popular approval: Statues of Reza Shah and Muhammad Reza Shah were toppled in Tehran and Hamadan, portraits were taken down in restaurants, offices, homes, and even public buildings.[105]

On Monday and Tuesday, August 17-18, demonstrations occurred during which crowds clashed with the police, stoned American cars, and ransacked U.S. information centers in Tehran and the provinces. Slogans included the call for a republic. Gasiorowski documents that CIA agents Nerren and Cilley hired some participants in these anti-shah demonstrations, while others were right-wing Pan-Iran Party members, with real Tudeh members naturally joining in. U.S. ambassador Henderson asked Mussadiq to break them up with the police, and in a fateful decision, Mussadiq agreed, responding to the public's fears of disorder. The Tudeh then called its cadres off the streets. In part the Tudeh may have done this because it realized the crowds were organized by provocateurs. Other explanations include miscalculation and confusion on its part, or the adoption of a wait-and-see attitude toward events not of its own making. The next day, as the coup unfolded, Mussadiq (perhaps fearing a civil war) did not call on the population to resist, and his own National Front supporters also stayed off the streets as he had asked them to do on the 18th, to restore order.[106]

These events prepared the way for the easy success of the second coup on Wednesday August 19. On this day, under cover of a pro-shah demonstration, army units took the radio station, moved tanks into central Tehran, and fought a pitched battle around Mussadiq's house, from which he was convinced to flee by his associates. Zahidi announced the success of the coup on the radio, imposed a curfew, and pledged to prepare for the shah's return. By nightfall the city was calm and in the army's hands. The coupmakers had played the decisive role in all of these events. The several thousand people in the royalist crowd consisted of lutis and urban marginals mobilized by Sha'ban Bimokh and Ayatullah Bihbihani, peasants trucked in from the countryside and some onlookers either angered or worried by the "Tudeh" demonstrations or disillusioned with Mussadiq. They were paid with CIA funds provided to Iranian operatives. The exact role played by Kashani is unclear: At the least he is alleged to have stayed on the sidelines, as did the Tudeh and National Front (who had been so directed by their leaders); at the most he seems to have led one crowd and may have received money through intermediaries whom he didn't know were paid by the CIA. Cottam's account uses the term "Bihbihani dollars" for the CIA money used to mobilize the crowd; so much American money flooded the market that the value of the dollar fell precipitously.[107]

The coup itself claimed 300 lives. In the next few days there was passive resistance in the bazaar and provinces, met by hundreds of arrests under martial law. National Front leaders received jail terms of up to ten years; foreign minister Fatemi was executed. The Tudeh Party was even more ruthlessly repressed: Between 1953 and 1957, forty officials were executed, fourteen tortured to death, 200 imprisoned for life and 3,000 rank and file members arrested. The leading Qashqa'i chiefs were exiled from Iran, their property confiscated. Mussadiq defended himself eloquently at his court martial; the court was unable to sentence him to death. He spent three years in prison followed by strict house arrest in his village, unable to communicate with his country, until his death in 1967.[108] The new Zahidi regime restored the monarchy, soon benefited from massive American aid, and in 1954 made a deal with the international oil cartel to resolve the oil dispute on terms short of a thorough-going nationalization.

Conclusions: A Second Opportunity Missed

Important similarities and contrasts exist between the Constitutional revolution of 1905-1911 and the oil nationalization movement of 1951-53. Both saw multi-class, urban popular alliances respond to situations of dependency by initiating massive social movements aimed in part against the state and in part against foreign control of Iran. Both went through a course characterized by initial successes, followed by splits in the populist alliance which provided an opening for massive external intervention. Both were followed by a period of stronger central control under the shah and compression of Iran's underlying social forces by the state.

The 1951-53 oil nationalization movement differed from the earlier revolution in that it emphasized the struggle against external dependency more than the internal conflict with the shah. Mussadiq was in many ways a pioneering figure in the efforts of small Third World nations to break through situations of dependency on the West. He popularized the principle of using national wealth, linking "oil, political power, sovereignty."[109] He wanted Iran not only to own, but to run, its oil industry, without British interference. In this he was the contemporary of Gandhi and Nehru in India, Nasser in Egypt, Sukarno in Indonesia, Nkrumah in Ghana, Arbenz and Arévalo in Guatemala, Ben Bellah in Algeria—leaders of movements of national liberation against colonial power.

The significance of this project of overcoming dependency is also measured by the difficulties encountered along the way. Internally, the populist alliance proved impossible to hold together. The National Front itself was very popular, but weakly organized. The Tudeh Party, which represented much of the working class and intelligentsia, remained somewhat outside the movement. The predominantly secular political culture of the movement could not appeal to all the ulama, some of whom opposed it all along while others, notably Kashani, who left it at the critical moment, siphoned off part of its social base in the bazaar and among urban marginals. Mussadiq himself was a brilliant and charismatic leader, but he also made mistakes or was forced into irresolvable contradictions, such as his inability to end the oil dispute and the assumption of plenary powers which also split off some of his original supporters among them Baqa'i, Makki, and Kashani.

Nor did Mussadiq ever get full control over the institutions of the Iranian state, despite an understanding of the importance of this and valiant efforts to do so. He transformed the small eight-person National Front delegation of 1950 into a legislative force capable of guiding the whole majlis on occasion, and when this failed he managed to have himself granted extraordinary powers to rule by a form of provisional decrees. He reduced the power of the conservative senate by adroit maneuvering and used the referendum to dissolve the majlis when it obstructed the government. But for all his strenuous attempts he was unable to secure the loyalty of the shah's key power base in the army, which was the internal instrument of his overthrow in the end.

The army and shah were guided largely by plans originating from outside the country. In the three-way struggle among the great powers that began during World War II, first the Soviet Union dropped out of the picture with the defeat of the separatist movements in 1946, and then Britain was effectively checkmated in 1951-52 by the nationalization of the AIOC and severance of diplomatic relations. Unable to confront Iran alone, Britain brought the United States into the conflict, literally handing over the plans for a coup, and ultimately losing its hegemonic position in Iran to the American government and oil companies. Iran was in the balance in 1952-53, with a real chance for independence and non-dependence, but a fateful combination of internal problems encountered by the populist alliance and the intervention of powerful external forces caused Mussadiq's bid to fall short. Our argument has been that internal and external factors were inter-related in such a way that no one could have succeeded without the presence of all the others, and the parameters of both were set by the nature of the populist alliance on the one hand and the situation of dependency on the other.[110]

Iran was thus sentenced to another cycle of dependent development and compression of social forces by a repressive state before a third great revolution would bring together in powerful fashion the twin struggles against the state embodied in the Constitutional revolution and against external domination as articulated in the Mussadiq period. The events of 1951-53 therefore stand as a second historical opportunity for development that was missed.

Notes

1. Bharier, *Economic Development in Iran*, 134 table 1, 135 table 2, calculations mine.

2. Stephen Lee McFarland, "The Crises in Iran, 1941-1947: A Society in Change and the Peripheral Origins of the Cold War," Ph.D. dissertation, Department of History, University of Texas at Austin (1981), 142-43; Bharier, *Economic Development in Iran*, 31, 59-60, 131; and "The Borderlands of Soviet Central Asia, II," 409.

3. See Korby, *Probleme der industriellen Entwicklung*, 3 chart (for the very rough estimates of GNP); Floor, *Industrialization in Iran*, 34 table 13; Bharier, *Economic Development in Iran*, 173 table 1, 175 table 2, 219 table 1; Keddie, *Roots of Revolution*, 115-17; Rey, "Persia in Perspective—2," 80; and McFarland, "The Crises in Iran," 148-49, 152-53.

4. See Floor, *Industrialization in Iran*, 34 table 13; Bharier, *Economic Development in Iran*, 235 table 8; and Dillon, "Carpet Capitalism," 296ff.

5. Stephen L. McFarland, "Anatomy of an Iranian Political Crowd: the Tehran Bread Riot of December 1942," pp. 51-65 in *International Journal of Middle East Studies*, volume 17, number 1 (February 1985), 55; Katouzian, *The Political Economy*, 142-43; Bharier, *Economic Development in Iran*, 54 table 6, 105 table 1, 107 table 2, 115 table 6, 157 table 3, 158 table 4; McFarland, "The Crises in Iran," 135, 137.

6. Wilber, *Riza Shah Pahlavi*, 200; Bharier, *Economic Development in Iran*, 66 table 2, 69, 76 table 5; McFarland, "The Crises in Iran," 138.

7. Bharier, *Economic Development in Iran*, 46-47 table 3, 48 table 4, 80-81 table 6, 82 table 7, and Dadkhah, "The Inflationary Process of the Iranian Economy," 389 table 1.

8. McFarland, "The Crises in Iran," 134, 138, 140.

9. Quoted in McFarland, "Anatomy of an Iranian Political Crowd," 54.

10. Ibid., passim; McFarland, "The Crises in Iran," 146-48; and Stephen McFarland, "A Peripheral View of the Origins of the Cold War. The Crises in Iran, 1941-47," pp. 333-351 in *Diplomatic History*, volume 4, number 4 (Fall 1980), 340.

11. Abrahamian, *Iran Between Two Revolutions*, 170, 177-78. For a political overview of the entire period treated here, see Fakhreddin Azimi, *Iran. The Crisis of Democracy 1941-1953* (New York: St. Martin's Press, 1989).

12. Abrahamian, *Iran Between Two Revolutions*, 186-87. For various more negative judgments on the elections see Keddie, *Roots of Revolution*, 117; Ivanov, *Tarikh-i Nuvin-i Iran*, 99; and Farhad Diba, *Mohammad Mossadegh. A Political Biography* (London: Croom Helm, 1986), 78.

13. This line-up of political forces is based on Abrahamian's lucid discussion: *Iran Between Two Revolutions*, 186-203.

14. While Wilber implies that the Tudeh was directed by Soviet-trained Iranian communists as early as 1942 (see *Riza Shah Pahlavi*, 188 note 6), Katouzian, *The Political Economy*, 147, stresses its heterogeneity, and Abrahamian notes that the British ambassador found no real links between the Tudeh and the Soviet Union in 1946 (despite the closeness of their political positions): *Iran Between Two Revolutions*, 304; see also 290, 304 note 48. This paragraph is based

on the account in Abrahamian, *Iran Between Two Revolutions*, 284ff. See also Ivanov, *Tarikh-i Nuvin-i Iran*, 98.

15. Abrahamian, "Strengths and Weaknesses," 215-16, 227; Abrahamian, *Iran Between Two Revolutions*, 292-93, 303-2; McFarland, "The Crises in Iran," 151-53.

16. On the ulama see Arjomand, "Traditionalism in Twentieth-century Iran," 203, 204; Akhavi, *Religion and Politics*, 63; and Abrahamian, *Iran Between Two Revolutions*, 184. I have also drawn on Hamid Algar's 1982 lectures at Berkeley on Islam in Iran.

17. McFarland, "The Crises in Iran," 130.

18. Abrahamian, *Iran Between Two Revolutions*, 183 note 34; McFarland, "Anatomy of an Iranian Political Crowd," 61.

19. On the tribes during World War II, see Thompson, "Conditions of Daily Life in Iran, 1946," 204; Abrahamian, *Iran Between Two Revolutions*, 173-75; Garthwaite, *Khans and shahs*, 139-40; Lois Beck, "Economic Transformations Among Qashqa'i Nomads,1962-1978," pp. 99-122 in Bonine and Keddie, editors, *Modern Iran*, 100; Beck, *The Qashqa'i*, 143-59; Barker, "Tent Schools of the Qashqa'i," 144; Ivanov, *Tarikh-i Nuvin-i Iran*, 95-96; and Keddie, *Roots of Revolution*, 115.

20. Quoted in Diba, *Mohammad Mossadegh*, 79. See also Bharier, *Economic Development in Iran*, 108 table 3, 113 table 5; Amin Saikal, *The Rise and Fall of the Shah* (Princeton: Princeton University Press, 1980), 24ff.; Keddie, *Roots of Revolution*, 115. It is symbolically significant that British foreign secretary Anthony Eden rather insultingly announced that the country was to be referred to—against Iranian wishes—in the West as "Persia," not "Iran": Elwell-Sutton, "Reza Shah the Great," 3.

21. Bharier, *Economic Development in Iran*, 108 table 3, 113 table 5; "The Borderlands of Soviet Central Asia, II," 415; McFarland, "Anatomy of an Iranian Political Crowd," 57, 60; McFarland, "The Crises in Iran," 137.

22. From a letter of Millspaugh to Harry Hopkins, January 11, 1944, quoted in T. H. Vail Motter, *The Persian Corridor and Aid to Russia* (Washington, D.C.: Office of the Chief of Military History, Department of the Army, 1952), 445 note 14. Interestingly, already in late 1942, when Millspaugh was first approached for the post of economic adviser by Iran he was encouraged by the U.S. government to accept: "I was informed . . . that the United States after the war was to play a large role in that region with respect to oil, commerce, and air transport, and that a big program was under way": Millspaugh, *Americans in Persia*, 47.

23. Memo of Franklin Delano Roosevelt to Secretary of State Hull, January 12, 1944, quoted in Motter, *The Persian Corridor*, 445.

24. McFarland, "A Peripheral View," 340. Other data in this paragraph are based on ibid., 337; Paine, "Iranian Nationalism," 15-19; Hurewitz, *Diplomacy*, II, 237-38; Keddie, *Roots of Revolution*, 114-16; Bharier, *Economic Development in Iran*, 108 table 3, 113 table 5; Abrahamian, *Iran Between Two Revolutions*, 184; and Ashraf, "Iran," 109 note 1. For a statement of U.S. policy, see National Archives, 891.00/8-2345, Loy Henderson to Secretary of State/NEA (August 23, 1945), which stresses "the requirements of international secruity."

25. Quoted by Paine, "Iranian Nationalism," 16.

26. See "Iranian Law Prohibiting the Grant of Oil Concessions to Foreigners and its Effect" (December 2, 1944-15 January 1945), pp. 241-245 in Hurewitz, *Diplomacy*, II; McFarland, "A Peripheral View," 341-43; Abrahamian, *Iran Between Two Revolutions*, 210; and Rey, "Persia in Perspective—2," 81.

27. On these events see Paine, "Iranian Nationalism," 20; "The Borderlands of Soviet Central Asia, II," 319-20; William Eagleton, Jr., *The Kurdish Republic of 1946* (London: Oxford University Press, 1963), 61-63; William Roger Louis, *The British Empire in the Middle East 1945-1951. Arab Nationalism, the United States, and Postwar Imperialism* (Oxford: Clarendon Press, 1984), 70; and Abrahamian, *Iran Between Two Revolutions*, 221, who also records a movement of armed rebels in the Caspian area in late 1945 seeking to revive the Jangali rebellion.

28. For two views on these events, see Faramarz S. Fatemi, *The U.S.S.R. in Iran. The Background History of Russian and Anglo-American Conflict in Iran, Its Effects on Iranian Nationalism, and the Fall of the Shah* (South Brunswick and New York: A. S. Barnes and Company, 1980), 108, and Abrahamian, *Iran Between Two Revolutions*, 222-24.

29. McFarland, "A Peripheral View," 345-47; Robert Rossow, Jr., "The Battle of Azerbaijan, 1946," pp. 17-32 in *Middle East Journal*, volume X, number 1 (Winter 1956), 17-26. The amount of American pressure exerted on the Soviet Union in this incident is a matter of debate: McFarland and Abrahamian deny that there was an ultimatum to Stalin or a threat to use nuclear weapons, while later U.S. Senator Henry Jackson recalls that Truman had explicitly threatened to use nuclear weapons to Soviet ambassador Andrei Gromyko. See McFarland, "The Crises in Iran," 436; Abrahamian, *Iran Between Two Revolutions*, 228 note 4, citing J. Thorpe, "Truman's Ultimatum to Stalin in 1946: Fact or Fantasy?" pp. 8-10 in *Newsletter of the Society for Iranian Studies*, volume 4 (October 1972); and Jackson, quoted in *Time* magazine (January 28, 1980), as well as the account in Kuross A. Samii, *Involvement by Invitation. American Strategies of Containment in Iran* (University Park, Pennsylvania and London: The Pennsylvania State University Press, 1987), 84-85. There is no doubt however that major force was brought to bear, at least implicitly, on both the American and Soviet sides.

30. Eagleton, *The Kurdish Republic*, 94; Fatemi, *The U.S.S.R. in Iran*, 138-39; Keddie, *Roots of Revolution*, 120.

31. Abrahamian, *Iran Between Two Revolutions*, 175-76, 198, 208; Katouzian, *The Political Economy*, 150; Wilber, *Riza Shah Pahlavi*, 139-40 note 10; David B. Nissman, *The Soviet Union and Iranian Azerbaijan. The Use of Nationalism for Political Penetration* (Boulder and London: Westview Press, 1987), 16.

32. Abrahamian, *Iran Between Two Revolutions*, 217, 398-401; Ivanov, *Tarikh-i Nuvin-i Iran*, 108; "The Borderlands of Soviet Central Asia, II," 319.

33. The quote is from Abrahamian, *Iran Between Two Revolutions*, 408. See also Katouzian's perceptive distinction between autonomy and separatism (though he also provides evidence of threats by Pishivari to separate from Iran): *The Political Economy*, 150, 151, 161 note 9. Less convincing on the separatist claim are Nissman, *The Soviet Union and Iranian Azerbaijan*, 33, and Rey, "Persia in Perspective—2," 81. See also Abrahamian, *Iran Between Two Revolutions*, 399, 403, 407, 408; and Fatemi, *The U.S.S.R. in Iran*, 85, 91. On the DPA's program and intentions, see also National Archives, 891.00/9-1445, Telegram 3269, unsigned, Moscow, to Secretary of State (September 14, 1945); 891.00/10-1345, Despatch 223 (Secret), Ebling, Tabriz, to Secretary of State (October 13, 1945); and 891.00/11-1745, Despatch 230 (Secret), Ebling, Tabriz, to Secretary of State (November 17, 1945).

34. National Archives, 891.00/2-1946, Despatch 250 (Secret), Rossow, Tabriz, to Secretary of State (February 19, 1946).

35. National Archives, 891.00/1-2745, Despatch 150 (Secret), Ebling, Tabriz, to Secretary of State (January 27, 1945).

36. On the social bases of the movement, see National Archives, 891.00/12-1845, Despatch 192 (Secret), T. Cuyler Young, Tehran, to Secretary of State (December 18, 1945); Ivanov, *Tarikh-i Nuvin-i Iran*, 108, 109; McFarland, "The Crises in Iran," 375; Abrahamian, *Iran Between Two Revolutions*, 396, 399-400; Good, "Social Hierarchy in Provincial Iran," 157; Cottam, *Nationalism in Iran*, 126-27; and Sepehr Zabih, *The Mossadegh Era. Roots of the Iranian Revolution* (Chicago: Lake View Press, 1982), 158 note 11.

37. Abrahamian, *Iran Between Two Revolutions*, 408-9.

38. Cottam, *Nationalism in Iran*, 126-27. See also Paine, "Iranian Nationalism," 20; "The Borderlands of Soviet Central Asia, II," 321; and Nissman, *The Soviet Union and Iranian Azerbaijan*, 41.

39. Abrahamian, *Iran Between Two Revolutions*, 409. The activism of the peasantry and general popularity of reforms is attested to in U.S. diplomatic reports. See, inter alia, National Archives,

891.00/12-2145, Despatch 240 (Secret), Ebling, Tabriz, to Secretary of State (December 21, 1945), and 891.00/1-446, Despatch 242 (Secret), Rossow, Tabriz, to Secretary of State (January 4, 1946). Data on the land reform is from Abrahamian, *Iran Between Two revolutions*, 408; "The Borderlands of Soviet Central Asia, II," 321; Lambton, *Landlord and Peasant*, 312; and Cottam, *Nationalism in Iran*, 127.

40. For the "puppet" thesis, see Rossow, "The Battle of Azerbaijan," 18ff. For measured assessments of the actual Soviet role, see Abrahamian, *Iran Between Two Revolutions*, 218, 411; McFarland, "A Peripheral View," 343; and McFarland, "The Crises in Iran," 433. This paragraph draws on Abrahamian, *Iran Between Two Revolutions*, 402-11; Katouzian, *The Political Economy*, 151-52; Eagleton, *The Kurdish Republic*, 60, 76, 82-83, 94, 106; Archie Roosevelt, Jr., "The Kurdish Republic of Mahabad," pp. 247-269 in the *Middle East Journal*, volume 1, number 3 (July 1947), 259; and the National Archives, inter alia, 891.00/1-2646, Telegram 9, Rossow, Tabriz, to Secretary of State (January 26, 1946).

41. Homa Katouzian has brought my attention to Baqirov, noting that evidence on Soviet-DPA links can be found in Faridun Kishavarz, *Man Muttaham Mikunam* [I Accuse] (Tehran: Ravaq, 1977), and Louise L'Estrange Fawcett, "The Struggle for Persia: The Azerbaijan Crisis of 1946," D. Phil. Thesis, Oxford University (1988).

42. Katouzian, *The Political Economy*, 151-53; Abrahamian, *Iran Between Two Revolutions*, 411-12; Rossow, "The Battle of Azerbaijan," 19; Tapper, "Black Sheep, White Sheep and Red Heads," 75; Rey, "Persia in Perspective—2," 81; National Archives, 891.00/2-1146, Telegram 20 (Secret), unsigned, Tabriz, to Secretary of State (February 11, 1946).

43. Cottam, *Nationalism in Iran*, 66-67, 70-71; Eagleton, *The Kurdish Republic*, 14-37; Abrahamian, *Iran Between Two Revolutions*, 175; Roosevelt, "The Kurdish Republic of Mahabad," 257.

44. Eagleton, *The Kurdish Republic*, 29-63.

45. Ibid., 68, 70-71, 78, 87, 91-92; Cottam, *Nationalism in Iran*, 72-73; Roosevelt, "The Kurdish Republic of Mahabad," 248, 255-56, 257 note 4.

46. Roosevelt, "The Kurdish Republic of Mahabad," 264-65. See also ibid., 262, 262 note 10; and Eagleton, *The Kurdish Republic*, 65, 81, 101.

47. Eagleton, *The Kurdish Republic*, 87-88, 101.

48. Ibid., 64, 103, 109-11; Roosevelt, "The Kurdish Republic of Mahabad," 255, 256, 261 (for quote), 265. For hints of landlord opportunism and concern over possible reforms, as well as "the desire of the less-favored members of the tribes to improve their present unsatisfactory economic condition," see National Archives, 891.00/11-845, Despatch 227 (Secret), Ebling, Tabriz, to Secretary of State (November 8, 1945).

49. Eagleton, *The Kurdish Republic*, 64-66, 74, 90, 95-99, 102-4, 106, 109; Roosevelt, "The Kurdish Republic of Mahabad," 250, 259.

50. Eagleton, *The Kurdish Republic*, 1.

51. Abrahamian, *Iran Between Two Revolutions*, 300, 302, 303; Ivanov, *Tarikh-i Nuvin-i Iran*, 114-15.

52. Abrahamian, "Strengths and Weaknesses," 225, citing a British consular report. On the strike see ibid., 225-29; idem, *Iran Between Two Revolutions*, 303; Ivanov, *Tarikh-i Nuvin-i Iran*, 123; and Rey, "Persia in Perspective—2," 82.

53. Qavam told U.S. ambassador George Allen that his moves were calculated to resolve the Azarbaijan crisis, *limit* the number of Tudeh representatives in the next majlis, and wean the Tudeh away from the Soviet Union: National Archives, 891.00/6-146, Telegram 791 (Secret), Allen, Tehran, to Secretary of State (June 1, 1946).

54. Keddie, *Roots of Revolution*, 121; Ivanov, *Tarikh-i Nuvin-i Iran*, 118-19; Abrahamian, *Iran Between Two Revolutions*, 229, 300 (citing the *New York Times* of June 15, 1946), 301, 304; Katouzian, *The Political Economy*, 155; Fatemi, *The U.S.S.R. in Iran*, 140-41.

55. The quote is from Abrahamian, *Iran Between Two Revolutions*, 235. See also McFarland, "The Crises in Iran," 461-63; Barker, "Tent Schools of the Qashqa'i," 144; and Ivanov, *Tarikh-i Nuvin-i Iran*, 126.

56. It seems that Allen had impressed on the shah the need for Qavam's "pro- Soviet" policy to end; Allen encouraged the coup-makers and shah to threaten Qavam's position; a few days later he expressed U.S. support for Qavam's cabinet. See National Archives, 891.00/12-346, George Allen to Harold Minor (Top Secret), (December 3, 1946); 891.00/10-1446, Telegram 1359 (Top Secret), Allen, Tehran, to Secretary of State (October 14, 1946); 891.00/10-2146, Telegram 1394 (Secret), Allen, Tehran, to Secretary of State (October 21, 1946); and 891.00/10-2446, Telegram A-231, Allen, Tehran, to Secretary of State (October 24, 1946). This paragraph also relies on McFarland, "The Crises in Iran," 465-68; Abrahamian, *Iran Between Two Revolutions*, 237-38; and Abrahamian, "Strengths and Weaknesses," 217.

57. McFarland, "A Peripheral View," 348-49; McFarland, "The Crises in Iran," 465-74, 484; Hurewitz, *Diplomacy*, II, 273-75; Eagleton, *The Kurdish Republic*, 111; Rey, "Persia in Perspective—2," 82. On U.S. determination to resist Soviet encroachment, see National Archives, 891.00/10-846, Office Memorandum, Loy Henderson, NEA, to Dean Acheson (October 8, 1946). British policy meanwhile was extremely opportunistic, contemplating the secession of Azarbaijan rather than letting the DPA control elections and send twenty-one deputies to the majlis, with control over even the "British" areas in the south: National Archives, 891.00/11-746, Telegram A-240 (Secret), Allen, Tehran, to Secretary of State (November 7, 1946).

58. Rossow, "The Battle of Azerbaijan," 29-31; Abrahamian, *Iran Between Two Revolutions*, 239-40, 305; McFarland, "The Crises in Iran," 477-78, 180-81; Ivanov, *Tarikh-i Nuvin-i Iran*, 27, citing *Mardom (The People*, a Tudeh newspaper), July 5, 1947; Halliday, *Iran*, 225.

59. Eagleton, *The Kurdish Republic*, 11-31; Cottam, *Nationalism in Iran*, 73-74.

60. Halliday, *Dictatorship and Development*, 449.

61. Ivanov, *Tarikh-i Nuvin-i Iran*, 127-30; Abrahamian, *Iran Between Two Revolutions*, 242-48, 305-15; Fatemi, *The U.S.S.R. in Iran*, 162; Rossow, "The Battle of Azerbaijan," 31-32; "Iranian Law Rejecting the Draft Oil Agreement with the USSR" (October 22, 1947), p. 280 in Hurewitz, *Diplomacy*, II.

62. For the former, see Zabih, *The Mossadegh Era*, 148, and for the latter, Katouzian, *The Political Economy*, 164. A major recent work on the period is Homa Katouzian, *Musaddiq and the Struggle for Power in Iran* (London: I. B. Tauris, 1990).

63. For the events of these years, see Katouzian, *The Political Economy*, 145, 158-60; Abrahamian, *Iran Between Two Revolutions*, 246-52, 261-66, 305-18; Zabih, *The Mossadegh Era*, 22-26, 42-43, 158 notes 2 and 3; Cottam, *Nationalism in Iran*, 260-61; and Ivanov, *Tarikh-i Nuvin-i Iran*, 138-39.

64. Katouzian, *The Political Economy*, 183 table 9.2.

65. For the higher figures and lower profits see "The Borderlands of Soviet Central Asia, II," 385, and Ivanov, *Tarikh-i Nuvin-i Iran*, 145; for the lower figures and higher profits, William A. Dorman and Mansour Farhang, *The U.S. Press and Iran. Foreign Policy and the Journalism of Deference* (Berkeley: University of California Press, 1987), 39. The British navy also received cheap oil, at 30-40 cents a barrel, when market prices ranged from 90 cents to $2.43. Between 1910 and 1951, they saved some $500 million this way, a sum by itself more than Iran received in taxes and royalties by about 15 percent: Manizheh Zavareei, "Dependent Capitalist Development in Iran and the Mass Uprising of 1979," pp. 139-188 in Paul Zarembka, editor, *Research in Political Economy: A Research Annual* (Greenwich, CT., and London: JAI Press, 1982), 184 note 10.

66. "Supplemental Agreement: Iran and the Anglo-Iranian Oil Company" (July 17, 1949), pp. 305-308 in Hurewitz, *Diplomacy*, II, and "Agreement (Jiddah) for Equal Sharing of the Profits: The Sa'udi Arab Government and Aramco" (December 30, 1950), pp. 314-322 in ibid.; also 249 in ibid; Bruce R. Kuniholm, *The Origins of the Cold War in the Near East. Great Power Conflict and*

Diplomacy in Iran, Turkey, and Greece (Princeton: Princeton University Press, 1980), 180 note 125, 183 note 129; Louis, *The British Empire in the Middle East*, 8-9; Ivanov, *Tarikh-i Nuvin-i Iran*, 146.

67. Paine, "Iranian Nationalism," 22-23; Hurewitz, *Diplomacy*, II, 322-23; Abrahamian, "Strengths and Weaknesses," 218-19.

68. On these parties, see Abrahamian, *Iran Between Two Revolutions*, 253-58; Katouzian, *The Political Economy*, 147-49, 170; Zabih, *The Mossadegh Era*, 49-50; and Cottam, *Nationalism in Iran*, 265-68.

69. Diba, *Mohammad Mossadegh*, 130. As this quote suggests, by "populist" in this study I do not mean authoritarian, but popular in terms of a broad social appeal.

70. Abrahamian, *Iran Between Two Revolutions*, 321-23. On the Tudeh, Mussadiq and the working class, see ibid., 318-24; Zabih, *The Mossadegh Era*, 54, 95; Katouzian, *The Political Economy*, 165-68; Abrahamian, "Strengths and Weaknesses," 220-22; Cottam, *Nationalism in Iran*, 236-37; and "Mosaddeq's Role in the Events of 1951-3 in Persia," pp. 302-306 in *Central Asian Review*, volume IX, number 3 (1961), based on A. K. Lavrent'yev, *Imperialisticheskaya Politika SSHA i Anglii v Irane* [Imperialist Politics of the U.S. and England in Iran] (Moscow, 1960).

71. This paragraph draws on Katouzian, *The Political Economy*, 147, 171, 190; Akhavi, *Religion and Politics*, 62-69; Paine, "Iranian Nationalism," 22; Keddie, *Roots of Revolution*, 139; Floor, "The Guilds in Iran," 110; Abrahamian, "The Crowd in Iranian Politics," 204; Floor, "The Political Role of the Lutis," 92; and Algar's 1982 lectures at Berkeley on Islam in Iran. Evidence of "lower middle-class" support for the movement (i.e. probably artisans and skilled workers) and lack of support among urban marginals and unskilled laborers during the July 1952 events can be found in American diplomatic correspondence: National Archives, 788.00/7-3152, Foreign Service Despatch 82, Melbourne, Tehran, to Department of State (July 31, 1952).

72. On the Qashqa'i, see Rey, "Persia in Perspective—2," 85; Beck, "Economic Transformations Among Qashqa'i Nomads," 100; Beck, *The Qashqa'i*, 152-53; and Barker, "Tent Schools of the Qashqa'i," 144-45. On the peasantry, Rey, "Persia in Perspective—2," 86; Katouzian, *The Political Economy*, 166; Abrahamian, "Strengths and Weaknesses," 223; and Ivanov, *Tarikh-i Nuvin-i Iran*, 169-70.

73. M. S. Ivanov, *Ocherki Istorii Irana* [Outline of Iranian History] (Moscow, 1952), 44, quoted in "The Borderlands of Soviet Central Asia, II," 389; Ivanov, *Tarikh-i Nuvin-i Iran*, 143. Cf. also Lavrent'yev's view that Mussadiq represented the "middle classes of the national bourgeoisie": *Imperialisticheskaya Politika*, cited in "Mossadeq's Role," 302.

74. Abrahamian, *Iran Between Two Revolutions*, 259-60; Diba, *Mohammad Mossadegh*, 96-97; Katouzian, *The Political Economy*, 165.

75. Abrahamian, *Iran Between Two Revolutions*, 260.

76. Mustafa Fateh, *Panjah Sal Naft-i Iran* [Fifty Years of Iranian Oil] (Tehran, 1956), 525, quoted in Paine, "Iranian Nationalism," 39.

77. Bharier, *Economic Development in Iran*, 104-6 table 4, 114-15 table 6, 148 table 5; Katouzian, *The Political Economy*, 184-85; Diba, *Mohammad Mossadegh*, 161, 168; Keddie, *Roots of Revolution*, 137; Zabih, *The Mossadegh Era*, 83; Rey, "Persia in Perspective—2," 85.

78. On these trends, including GNP, see Korby, *Probleme der industriellen Entwicklung*, 3 figure; Bharier, *Economic Development in Iran*, 54 table 6, 59 figure 1, 107 table 2, 175 table 2; and Graham, *Iran*, 46.

79. On these trends and data, see Keddie, *Roots of Revolution*, 128, 136; Zabih, *The Mossadegh Era*, 82; Bharier, *Economic Development in Iran*, 204 table 5, 205 table 6, 209 table 7, 227 table 4, 233 table 7, 235 table 8; Ivanov, *Tarikh-i Nuvin-i Iran*, 138, 170-71; Diba, *Mohammad Mossadegh*, 137-38; and Abrahamian, "Strengths and Weaknesses," 221.

80. Barker, "Tent Schools of the Qashqa'i," 144. Data on agriculture are found in Bharier, *Economic Development in Iran*, 134-35 table 1, 142-42 table 3, 242 table 3; "The Borderlands of Soviet Central Asia, II," 409; Mark J. Gasiorowski, "The 1953 *Coup d'Etat* in Iran," pp. 261-286 in

International Journal of Middle East Studies, volume 19, number 3 (August 1987), 278; Keddie, *Historical Obstacles,* 16-17; and Ivanov, *Tarikh-i Nuvin-i Iran,* 138.

81. Bharier, *Economic Development in Iran,* 71 table 4; Keddie, *Roots of Revolution,* 136; Katouzian, *The Political Economy,* 174; Diba, *Mohammad Mossadegh,* 139; Zabih, *The Mossadegh Era,* 83-84; Ivanov, *Tarikh-i Nuvin-i Iran,* 168.

82. For data on economic conditions, see Diba, *Mohammad Mossadegh,* 162; Dadkhah, "The Inflationary Process," 389 table 1; Bharier, *Economic Development in Iran,* 46-47 table 3, 48-49 table 4; Rey, "Persia in Perspective—2," 83; Abrahamian, "Strengths and Weaknesses," 220; Ivanov, *Tarikh-i Nuvin-i Iran,* 139 (citing *Ittila'at*), 168; "Agricultural and Industrial Activity," 561 table IV; and Keddie, *Roots of Revolution,* 129.

83. Diba, *Mohammad Mossadegh,* 128, 157-58, 168; Katouzian, *The Political Economy,* 187 note 17; Zabih, *The Mossadegh Era,* 28-29; Abrahamian, *Iran Between Two Revolutions,* 272-73.

84. Cottam, *Nationalism in Iran,* 274-76; Katouzian, *The Political Economy,* 174-75; Zabih, *The Mossadegh Era,* 34, 37-38; Abrahamian, *Iran Between Two Revolutions,* 269. The U.S. embassy considered the National Front to have the support of thirty-seven members, the opposition thirty-three, with nine neutral deputies: National Archives, 788.00/8-1652, Foreign Service Despatch 135, Melbourne, Tehran, to Department of State (August 16, 1952). The opposition consisted preponderantly of landlords, the Front of landlords, ulama, and professionals.

85. On the July events see Zabih, *The Mossadegh Era,* 46-64; Katouzian, *The Political Economy,* 176; Gasiorowski, "The 1953 *Coup d'Etat* in Iran," 265-66; and Abrahamian, *Iran Between Two Revolutions,* 271-72.

86. Diba, *Mohammad Mossadegh,* 158-59; Zabih, *The Mossadegh Era,* 78; Ashraf, "Iran," 116; Abrahamian, *Iran Between Two Revolutions,* 272-73.

87. On the splits in the National Front, see Keddie, *Roots of Revolution,* 139; Katouzian, *The Political Economy,* 171, 177; Gasiorowski, "The 1953 *Coup d'Etat* in Iran," 265-66, 281 note 28; Zabih, *The Mossadegh Era,* 94, 97-99, 110; Abrahamian, *Iran Between Two Revolutions,* 254-55 table 6, 274-78; and Cottam, *Nationalism in Iran,* 151-55, 223, 278-79.

88. On Great Britain and Iran, see Diba, *Mohammad Mossadegh,* 108, 118-21, 132-34, 200; Paine, "Iranian Nationalism," 24; Saikal, *The Rise and Fall,* 41; Cottam, *Nationalism in Iran,* 205, 214; Katouzian, *The Political Economy,* 172-76, 181-82; Zabih, *The Mossadegh Era,* 74, 156, 168 note 10; and Gasiorowski, "The 1953 *Coup d'Etat* in Iran," 263-64.

89. Paine, "Iranian Nationalism," 24.

90. Eisenhower to Mussadiq, June 29, 1953, quoted in Zabih, *The Mossadegh Era,* 104.

91. Zabih, *The Mossadegh Era,* 90.

92. Gasiorowski, "The 1953 *Coup d'Etat* in Iran," 267-69.

93. U.S. Department of State, "Steering Group on Preparations for the talks between the President and Prime Minister Churchill: Iran," January 5, 1952, quoted in Dorman and Farhang, *The U.S. Press and Iran,* 36.

94. "The First 90 Days," address by Secretary of State Dulles, April 18, 1953, in *Department of State Bulletin* (April 27, 1953), 605, quoted by Ashraf, "Iran," 98. The State Department, with British prompting, did secretly contemplate offering financial support to a Qavam government during the July 1952 crisis, and after Mussadiq returned to power indicated willingness to work more closely with the British, to the point of taking (unspecified) action in the event Iran appeared in danger of being "lost" to communism: National Archives, 788.00/7-2152, Memo (Secret), Secretary of State (July 21, 1952), and 788.00/7-2252, Henry A. Byroade to Secretary of State (Secret) (July 22, 1952).

95. "Report on the Near and Middle East by Secretary of State John Foster Dulles" (June 1, 1953), pp. 337-342 in Hurewitz, *Diplomacy,* II, 340. For this paragraph, see also Diba, *Mohammad Mossadegh,* 123-24; Thomas Powers, "A Book Held Hostage" (review of Kermit Roosevelt's *Countercoup: The Struggle for Control of Iran*), pp. 437-440 in *The Nation,* volume 230, number 14 (April 12, 1980), 438-39; Ashraf, "Iran," 106-8, 111; and Fatemi, *The U.S.S.R. in Iran,* 183.

96. Diba, *Mohammad Mossadegh*, 138.

97. This paragraph draws on Rey, "Persia in Perspective—2," 86; Hurewitz, *Diplomacy*, II, 150; "The Borderlands of Soviet Central Asia, II," 416, based on D. Beloshapkin, "Economic Relations between the USSR and Persia," in *Vneshnyaya Torgovlya*, number 9 (1954); Abrahamian, "Strengths and Weaknesses," 223; Zabih, *The Left in Contemporary Iran*, 9; and Zabih, *The Mossadegh Era*, 133.

98. See Zabih, *The Mossadegh Era*, 126, 143-45; Abrahamian, *Iran Between Two Revolutions*, 274-75; Powers, "A Book Held Hostage" (on Roosevelt's *Countercoup* account), 437; Gasiorowski, "The 1953 *Coup d'Etat* in Iran," 277, 286 notes 73, 74 and 76; Keddie, *Roots of Revolution*, 140; Katouzian, *The Political Economy*, 178-81; and Cottam, *Nationalism in Iran*, 229-30.

99. Keddie, *Roots of Revolution*, 138-39; Zabih, *The Mossadegh Era*, 98-105.

100. Zabih, *The Mossadegh Era*, 108-13; Katouzian, *The Political Economy*, 178; Abrahamian, *Iran Between Two Revolutions*, 274; Cottam, *Nationalism in Iran*, 282-83; *New York Times*, August 11, 1953.

101. Zabih, *The Mossadegh Era*, 140. See also Gasiorowski, "The 1953 *Coup d'Etat* in Iran," 263-64, 270-72.

102. Gasiorowski, "The 1953 *Coup d'Etat* in Iran," 261. See also ibid., 272, 275-76, 277, 284 notes 58 and 59; Zabih, *The Mossadegh Era*, 124-25, 140-41; Ashraf, "Iran," 117 note 2; and Kermit Roosevelt, *Countercoup. The Struggle for the Control of Iran* (New York: McGraw-Hill, 1979), a first-hand account whose accuracy has been questioned on some points but which is on the whole quite revealing.

103. On these internal actors, see Gasiorowski, "The 1953 *Coup d'Etat* in Iran," 273, 276-77, 286 note 72; *New York Times*, August 20, 1953; Abrahamian, *Iran Between Two Revolutions*, 278-80; Katouzian, *The Political Economy*, 162 note 21, 189; and Zabih, *The Mossadegh Era*, 114-15, 124-25, 128.

104. Katouzian, *The Political Economy*, 178; Zabih, *The Mossadegh Era*, 116-17; Gasiorowski, "The 1953 *Coup d'Etat* in Iran," 273. Press stories on a pending U.S.-backed coup had appeared in *The New York Post* on July 13, in Tass news reports on July 15, and in the Tudeh paper *Shuja'at* since August 13; Eisenhower had hinted broadly at the action in Seattle on August 4. Most importantly, Mussadiq became aware of the precise plot at least six hours before it happened: National Archives, 788.00/8-1653, Telegram 337, Mattison, Tehran, to Secretary of State (August 16, 1953); 788.00/8-553, Telegram 312, Smith, U.S. embassy, to Secretary of State (August 5, 1953); and 788.00/8-1653, Telegram 345 (Secret), Mattison, Tehran, to Secretary of State (August 16, 1953).

105. Gasiorowski, "The 1953 *Coup d'Etat* in Iran," 273; Zabih, *The Mossadegh Era*, 134; *New York Times*, August 18, 1953.

106. Zabih, *The Mossadegh Era*, 120, 135, 137, 167 note 4; Gasiorowski, "The 1953 *Coup d'Etat* in Iran," 274, 285 note 66; Ivanov, *Tarikh-i Nuvin-i Iran*, 176; *New York Times*, August 19 and 20, 1953; Katouzian, *The Political Economy*, 190-92; Abrahamian, *Iran Between Two Revolutions*, 324-25; National Archives, 788.00/8-1453, Telegram 390, Henderson, Tehran, to Secretary of State (August 19, 1953), and 788.00/8-2053, Telegram 419, Henderson, Tehran, to Secretary of State (August 20, 1953). Evidence of a bit of official panic in Washington is provided by CIA director Walter Bedell Smith who wrote in a memo to Eisenhower on the 18th: "we now have to take a whole new look at the Iranian situation and probably have to snuggle up to Mosadeq if we're going to save anything there. I dare say this means a little added difficulty with the British": 788.00/8-1853, W. B. Smith, Memorandum (Top Secret) for the President (August 18, 1953).

107. For the events of August 19 I have drawn on Katouzian, *The Political Economy*, 179; Zabih, *The Mossadegh Era*, 120-23, 138-39; *New York Times*, August 20 and 24, 1953; Abrahamian, "The Crowd in Iranian Politics," 207; Keddie, *Roots of Revolution*, 140; Gasiorowski, "The 1953 *Coup d'Etat* in Iran," 274, 285 note 67; Richard and Gladys Harkness, "The Mysterious Doings of CIA" (Part Two), in the *Saturday Evening Post* (November 6, 1954), 68; Cottam, *Nationalism in*

Iran, 155; National Archives, 788.00/8-1953, Telegram 392, Henderson, Tehran, to Secretary of State (August 19, 1953); and Algar's 1982 lectures at Berkeley on Islam in Iran. For a Tudeh account of the whole period, see F. M. Javanshir, *Tajrubeh-i Bist u Hasht-i Murdad. Nazar beh Tarikh-i Junbish-i Milli-shudan-i Naft-i Iran* [The Experience of the 28th of Mordad (August 19). A Look at Iran's Oil Nationalization Movement] (Tehran: Intisharat-i Hizb-i Tudeh-i Iran, 1359/1980).

108. *New York Times,* August 21-25, 1953; Katouzian, *The Political Economy,* 193-95; Abraham-ian, *Iran Between Two Revolutions,* 280; Barker, "Tent Schools of the Qashqa'i," 145, 151; Keddie, *Roots of Revolution,* 140; Diba, *Mohammad Mossadegh,* 190-95.

109. Diba, *Mohammad Mossadegh,* 202. This paragraph draws on Diba's discussion of Mussadiq's significance generally.

110. The similarities between the 1953 coup in Iran and the 1973 coup in Chile are uncanny. In broad outline they share the combination of governmental problems, internal opposition and external intervention. More specifically, we can note the nationalization of a key raw material (oil, copper), economic blockade by the world power affected, internal popularity but failure of the government to control the army and other elements of the state, and a coup plan designed in the United States by the CIA. There were of course differences in the degree of internal reforms, role of communists in the alliance, opposition of the United States versus Great Britain, proximity of the Soviet Union, strength and class composition of the populist alliance, etc. But even Mussadiq's last speech in public, at his trial after the coup, bears remarkable similarities with Allende's last radio address. Mussadiq said: "Since it is evident, from the way that this tribunal is being run, that I will end my days in the corner of some prison, and since this may be the last time that I am able to address myself to my beloved nation, I beseech every man and woman to continue in the glorious path which they have begun, and not to fear anything" (quoted by Diba, *Mohammad Mossadegh,* 189). Salvador Allende addressed Chile on September 11, 1973: "Probably Radio Magallanes will be silenced and the calm metal of my voice will not reach you. It does not matter. . . . I have faith in Chile and in her destiny. Others will surmount this gray, bitter moment in which treason seeks to impose itself. You must go on, knowing that sooner rather than later the grand avenues will open along which free people will pass to build a better society" (speech in Laurence Birns, editor, *The End of Chilean Democracy* (New York: Seabury Press, 1974), slightly changed translation).

8

The New Situation of Dependency: Dependent Capitalist Development under Muhammad Reza Pahlavi, 1953-1977

Has Riza Khan any sons worthy to succeed him?
> —Lt. Col. Sir Wolseley Haig, "The Rise of Riza Khan Pahlavi"
> (1925)

* * *

A wolf's offspring will always be a wolf (aghabat gurgzadeh gurg shavad).
> —Sa'adi, thirteenth-century verse

The period from the coup of 1953 that restored the shah to the throne until the eve of the revolution that would send him out of the country forever in 1978-79 marked a new chapter in the changing social structure of Iran—one of transformation of pre-capitalist agriculture and rapid industrialization in the urban sector, fueled by enormous oil revenues. These dramatic changes in the Iranian political economy set the stage for the mass upheaval of 1978-79, and the contradictions bound up in this process have been conceptualized in a variety of ways by observers of Iran. For some, the shah attempted to "modernize" Iran too quickly, touching off strains that society could not absorb and thus resisted. For others, he did not achieve results quickly enough, leaving the country underdeveloped, despite promises of creating an industrial power and a "great civilization." Beyond these simple assertions (shared by various members of the Iranian elite and

American policymakers), scholars too have pronounced diverging judgments and posited alternative causes. Ervand Abrahamian argues that much of the oil revenue *was* productively invested and that considerable growth and development occurred, adding up to "a minor industrial revolution." Ahmad Ashraf (as early as 1971) and Homa Katouzian challenged the idea that economic growth alone meant anything like an integrated form of development. Nikki Keddie and Amin Saikal attributed most of Iran's problems and accomplishments to its status as a rentier state dependent on oil revenues for its growth; Marxists such as Patrick Clawson and Assef Bayat saw wider causes in "the internationalization of capital" and "uneven development" in the world economy and in Iran.[1]

These conflicting assessments parallel the earlier debates examined in chapter four about the nature of social structural change during the Qajar period in the nineteenth and early twentieth centuries, and our proposed resolution is again the heuristic concept of *dependent development*, this time of a more decisively capitalist kind, but again as a paradigm embracing both internal modes of production and the external pressures of the world-system. A number of attempts have been made to apply "dependence" in some form to Iran, but these have been either very loose (Keddie, Saikal, Pesaran), simplistic (Motameni), or one-sidedly negative (Zavareei) theoretically.[2] Following Cardoso and Faletto, my use of dependent development is a more wide-ranging, historical-structural method of analysis aimed at discerning both the reality and limits of economic growth in Iran and concerned not just with industrialization, state, and bourgeoisie but with the whole class structure of Iran, and with culture and politics in addition to the economy. The chapter that follows will trace this web of dependent relations through the state, class structure, and foreign relations of Iran. Chapter nine will then take up the effects of this type of development on the groups and classes in the Iranian social formation that came together to make the revolution as a result of the quarter century of dependent development analyzed here.

The Pahlavi State: Monarchic Dictatorship and Oil Rents

M. H. Pesaran has made the useful point that there are two types of political stability—one brought about by increased participation, the other by repression.[3] Of these, the state forged by Muhammad Reza Pahlavi between 1953 and 1978 clearly adhered to the method of repression, seeking to impose a second compression of social forces upon Iranian society as his father had done between 1925 and 1941. Like Reza Shah, his state eventually reposed on the army, oil revenues, and an even more dependent relationship with a leading core economy—the United States. The Pahlavi state developed over a decade into a monarchic dictatorship relying on a repressive army and oil revenues as the twin sources of its hegemony in Iranian society. Before reaching a position of unchallenged supremacy in the polity, the shah had to pass through several moments of trial. In the immediate aftermath of the 1953 coup, General Zahidi served as a strong-man prime minister, overseeing the suppression of the Tudeh Party and National Front with arrests and executions, and initiating a continual harassment and intimidation of opposition in the bazaars, factories, army, tribal areas, and universities. In a first trial, Zahidi was successfully removed from power in April 1955 and sent to Switzerland to treat, in Katouzian's words, a "non-existent illness," and the far more compliant Manuchihr Iqbal, who referred to himself as "the house-born slave of His Majesty," took over as prime minister. Another apparent threat to the state was thwarted in 1958 when a plot to carry out a coup under General Qarani, chief of army intelligence, was uncovered and ended in a secret trial and imprisonment of the general (Katouzian conjectures that there was American support for such a plot, which remains a hazy and bizarre episode for want of further evidence).[4]

A far more serious challenge arose between 1960 and 1963 in the form of mass political movements and outside pressure for reforms. A balance of payments crisis from 1958 to 1960 set the stage for a revival of political activity by the National Front in 1960-61. The shah was forced to annul two patently fraudulent majlis elections, while the Kennedy administration pressed him to appoint the liberal critic 'Ali Amini as prime minister in 1961 and to embark on a program of land reform. The proposed land reform met with the wrath not only of landlords but of leading ulama, some of whom also opposed American influence in Iran, Pahlavi autocracy, and electoral reforms granting women the vote. The National Front failed to respond to overtures from Amini and both were maneuvered back into obscurity by late 1962, but the ulama campaign against the state and foreign influence became stronger. Finally, the government ordered a bloody confrontation in June 1963 that resulted in many hundreds of deaths (some say up to 15,000) and the arrest and eventual exile of a new popular leader, Ayatullah Ruhullah Khumaini. By this combination of coopting secular politicians through claiming the land reform as its own and militarily repressing its religious opponents and their supporters, the regime emerged after 1963 as the overwhelming center of power in Iran, now with more or less unconditional American support as the only viable political option for the country.[5] The shah was thereafter free to fully implement his own vision of state power—a system of militarized, monarchic dictatorship, highly reliant on U.S. backing.

The main institutions of the Pahlavi monarchic dictatorship, in descending order of functional significance, consisted of the oil revenues, the repressive apparatus, the bureaucracy, and the party system. Over all of these presided the main beneficiaries of the system—the shah, royal family, and the court. Though technically part of the economy, the oil sector was both so isolated from it and so instrumental to the rest of the state that it is best analyzed as a state institution. While Mussadiq had managed to run the government largely without oil revenues between 1951 and 1953, the Pahlavi state would have been unthinkable without the vast income generated by the royalties received on the sale of Iran's oil. In 1954 the shah negotiated a new agreement with the West to produce and export oil. Iran was made the nominal owner of its oil (thus preserving the fiction of nationalization) while a consortium of British Petroleum (the new name for the Anglo-Iranian Oil Company, with a 40 percent share), five major American companies (35 percent), Royal Dutch Shell (14 percent), the French CFP (6 percent), and small American independents (5 percent) contracted to extract and market the resource for twenty-five years (renewable for fifteen more). The British AIOC was compensated by a huge 25 million pound payment. Profits were to be shared between Iran and the consortium on a 50-50 basis; Iran's share was raised to 56.25 percent in 1962 and 61.25 percent in 1970. The consortium set prices and production levels, and by one estimate, made a profit of $12.56 on each ton of oil between 1954 and 1963, while Iran received only $1.50.[6]

Despite being exploited vis-à-vis the consortium, the Iranian state received considerable income from oil, especially after the formation of OPEC in 1960 and the threat of oil boycotts following the 1967 and 1973 Arab-Israeli wars led to dramatic price rises. Iran's oil revenues leaped *almost a thousand times* from $22.5 million in 1954 to $20 billion in 1977. Without any increase in production, income rose from $4-5 billion in 1973 to $17-19 billion in 1974, as the price for a barrel of oil jumped from $1.95 to $7. Annual output did rise over this period from 390 million barrels in 1960 and 780 million in 1966 to 1,234 million in 1969 and 1,913 million in 1978 (at this level oil reserves would run dry about the year 2000). Iran also has the world's largest natural gas reserves. The share of oil and gas reserves in financing Iran's development plans increased inexorably from 50 percent in the 1950s to 63 percent between 1962 and 1972 to 80 percent after 1974. In 1977/78 oil accounted for 38 percent of GNP, 77 percent of the state's income, and 87 percent of foreign exchange. In a literal sense the state was dependent on oil income, and the economy would come to depend greatly on the state.[7]

The first beneficiaries of this oil rent were the shah, royal family, and the court. The line between the state and the shah continued to be blurred as it had since Safavid times and earlier. The National Iranian Oil Company secretly channelled a significant portion of its earnings—reportedly at least $1 billion in 1976—to the shah. In 1958 the shah established the Pahlavi Foundation, worth over $3 billion by the late 1970s, to manage funds for royal projects, deliver pensions and grants to clients, and control such key economic sectors as large-scale agriculture, housing and construction materials, insurance, hotels, autos, textiles, food-processing, and publishing, with shares in some 207 companies in all. The royal family numbered some sixty-three princes, princesses, and cousins of the shah, worth a total of $5-20 billion, derived from the largest agribusinesses and industrial enterprises in Iran. The system was rife with officially sanctioned corruption, bribe-taking, and greed, from the shah to his sister Ashraf to the minister of court Assadullah 'Alam on down through the officer corps and economic elite, with each maintaining a mini-court of his or her own, surrounding themselves with clients and attaching a portion of all major contracts in the economy. The lowest estimates of official corruption through the taking of commissions are of $1 billion between 1973 and 1976.[8] This siphoning off of the economic surplus and its disbursement throughout the upper echelons of Iranian society was one material base of the shah's power and secured the allegiance of his associates to the state and to his person.

A second institutional base of power was the repressive apparatus, including the intelligence services and the armed forces. The Iranian military's share of the budget ranged between 25 and 40 percent from the 1950s to the 1970s. When the oil boom occurred, the flood gates opened, with defense expenditures leaping from $1.9 billion in 1973/74 to $9.9 billion in 1978/79, and the size of the armed forces from 191,000 to 413,000 between 1972 and 1977. Some $10 billion in arms was purchased from the United States between 1972 and 1976, requiring the presence of 24,000 American personnel in Iran in 1976 and cementing the dependent relationship of Iran to the United States. Abrahamian notes that "By 1977, Iran had the largest navy in the Persian Gulf, the most up-to-date air force in the Middle East, and the fifth largest military force in the world." The army was twice as numerous and well-equipped as the British army in 1978; the air force was the fourth-largest in the world.[9] After the close call in the 1953 crisis and the subsequent discovery of a Tudeh officer group in the mid-1950s, plus General Qarani's 1958 coup plot, the shah worked to gain complete control of the army, personally scrutinizing promotions and controlling the officer corps by a combination of surveillance and privileges in the form of salaries, housing, and positions in government and industry. By the 1960s the shah clearly controlled the army, and the army controlled society only through the state; for this reason, Iran's was more of a monarchic than a strictly military form of dictatorship. The function of the army was partly to underwrite Iran's claims to regional paramountcy in the Middle East, Persian Gulf, and Asia in the 1970s, and partly to repress domestic forces—"As US Senator Hubert Humphrey put it in 1960: 'Do you know what the head of the Iranian army told one of our people? He said the army was in good shape, thanks to US aid—it was now capable of coping with the civilian population'."[10]

The job of domestic repression and social control was more specifically the domain of SAVAK and the other police and intelligence services (there were up to eight separate organizations in all, partly to keep tabs on each other). SAVAK—the name is a Persian acronym for National Intelligence and Security Organization—was organized in 1957 with help from the CIA, FBI, and Israeli intelligence. Estimates of the number of SAVAK operatives range widely, reflecting the pervasive secrecy and social insecurity engendered by it, from the shah's 2,000 to as high as 200,000, with Eric Rouleau perhaps coming closest in his estimate of 50,000 full-time agents and up to three million part-time informers (one in eleven Iranians). SAVAK was active in censorship, in the government-run trade unions, in screening state employees including teachers, and in directly confronting political critics and opponents of the regime, including liberal politicians, oppositional ulama, and especially left-leaning students and the guerrilla organizations. SAVAK arrested and held suspects at will, without time limits; trials were secret, conducted in the absence of defense witnesses before SAVAK or military judges. Although the true numbers are difficult to verify, Amnesty International estimated there were 25-100,000 political prisoners in 1976 and reported "No country in the world has a worse record in human rights than Iran."[11] Torture was a routine and barbarously inhuman part of the detention and interrogation process from the 1960s on. The effect aimed at by SAVAK was to "spread a deep sense of fear, suspicion, disbelief, and apathy throughout the country," and in so doing it formed an integral part of the state's overall relationship to Iranian society.[12]

A less coercive but equally revealing state institution was the government proper—the cabinet, ministries, civil service, majlis, and political party system. The shah himself delegated little authority, handling all major decisions and many minor ones, often without accurate or sufficient technical input and advice. A handful of his former classmates, confidants, and cronies were recycled among the top posts, wielding tremendous power over all below but totally dependent on the shah for the patronage they dispensed and the authority they enjoyed.[13] Below the ministers labored the vast bureaucracy of the civil services. The civil service grew from twelve ministries and 150,000 civil servants circa 1963 to nineteen ministries and 304,000 employees in the late 1970s. There were in all some 800,000 civilian employees by 1977, reaching well down through the professional middle class into the poorly paid ranks of the service sector of the working class: "In the towns, the state expanded to the point that it hired as many as one out of every two full-time employees."[14]

The majlis and political parties were transformed into part of the state's legitimation mechanism. As such, they cannot have succeeded very well in burnishing the shah's image. In the aftermath of the coup the political parties of the Mussadiq era found themselves banned and a tight censorship imposed. Later in the 1950s two parties loyal to the shah were set up—the ruling Milliyun (Nationalist) Party led by prime minister Iqbal and the "oppositional" Mardom (People's) Party headed by minister of the interior 'Alam. They were popularly known as the "yes" and "yes sir" parties. The majlises of the post-1953 era were filled by landlords and other members from the elite families and as such, if not always aligned with the shah on every issue, they were certainly conservative in nature. Between 1950 and 1970 eighty percent of the members of the senate were landlords. In late 1963 the two party system became a de facto single party when the Milliyun evolved into the Iran-i Nuvin (New Iran) Party under then prime minister 'Ali Mansur and future prime minister Huvaida, and the paper opposition did not contest elections.[15]

In 1961 the shah noted in his autobiography, "If I were a dictator rather than a constitutional monarch, then I might be tempted to sponsor a single dominant party such as Hitler organized or such as you find today in Communist countries."[16] The façade of democracy and constitutionalism came down completely with the formation of just such a single party system in 1975. The new Rastakhiz-i Milli (National Resurgence) Party was set up under prime minister Huvaida and all "loyal Iranians" were ordered to participate. Some of the original members claim to have advocated a party independent of the government and that the 1975 elections featuring a choice among candidates sponsored by the party aroused more voter enthusiasm than in the previous two decades. But the Rastakhiz Party was effectively controlled by the leaders of its predecessor, the Iran-i Nuvin Party. One of its founders, Ahmad Ghoreishi, noted that after the elections, "everyone saw with amazement the same prime minister, the same ministers, 'the same soup and the same bowl' again."[17] Most people entertained no illusions from the start: Ayatullah Khumaini from exile in Iraq counselled all Muslims to avoid the party, and a 1976 survey of university students turned up only 2-4 percent with any faith in the party. The Rastakhiz quickly degenerated into another elite vehicle for personal advancement and lapsed largely into inactivity by 1977. The shah's one-party state had revealed serious underlying problems of legitimacy.

The Pahlavi state had both narrow and broader social bases. At its narrowest, it could be reduced to the shah himself, and there is much evidence to speak for this interpretation—the vast decision-making power wielded by the shah, his extensive wealth and central position among the economic elite, and the general tendency to credit (or conversely, to blame) him for everything that "the state" made happen. Considered as a set of institutions, the practical basis of the Pahlavi state can be broadened to include the heads of the army, cabinet, bureaucracy, and party-system, and it is true that these individuals also exercised enormous power in their capacities as the leading state actors, and were tightly bound up with the shah at the apex of the polity and social structure. Raising the issue of the social bases of the state broadens its definition even further. The state, after all, employed 800,000 civilians and 400,000 military personnel, about 12 percent of the economically active population in 1978. The middle and upper echelons of these extensive organizations benefitted materially from being part of the state, and this represents a considerable number of people. The Rastakhiz Party tried to officially incorporate the political, economic, social, and cultural elites and all legal associations into the Iranian state between 1975 and 1978, though allegiance to it did not run deep in Iranian society.

The shah's own self-conception of this autonomy and the sources of his legitimation claims on Iranian society are revealed in a 1976 text he commissioned on "The Philosophy of Iran's Revolution":

> In making revolution, the leader of the nation plays the crucial role. A strong enlightened leader, fully comprehending existing conditions, nurtures and develops the idea of revolution in his mind, transfers the idea to the people and then moves to implement it. . . . The Shah and the People, according to the 'Philosophy of Iran's Revolution', constitute two superforces and they have allowed 'no intermediary or insulator to intervene in the direct relationship between them.'

> Together they have ensured the survival of the Iranian nation. The Shahanshah moreover stands above class or the interests of special groups in society. He is king of all the people. He is also in a father-son relationship to the nation. . . . The Shahanshah is not just the political leader of the country. He is also in the first instance teacher and spiritual leader, an individual who not only builds his nation roads, bridges, dams and qanats but also guides the spirit, thought and hearts of his people.[18]

The shah's symbolic capital rested on the glories of Iran's pre-Islamic past, the paternalistic rituals of authority and patronage, and the abrogation of functional democracy in favor of a quasi-mystical union directly with the people. These claims, as we shall see, were not embraced by the large segments of the population which developed significant grievances in the course of the shah's twenty-five years in power after 1953.

In class terms, the Pahlavi state was *autonomous* in relation to the dominant classes, in a somewhat different sense than Skocpol has employed this term. I would suggest that this state was conflated rather directly with a part of the ruling class, that is, with the royal family itself. This set it in an uneasy relationship with the rest of the ruling class—industrialists, large landlords, and its own high bureaucrats and military officers. Large landlords, as will be seen, lost political power (though not their economic position) in the land reform of the 1960s. Leading businessmen were dependent on the state and foreign capital, benefitting from the relationship but also chafing under it. Only the high officials that were part of the state itself were unambiguously bound to it. The shah was so closely identified with the state that he (and it) represented the hegemonic part of the ruling class. Autonomous from the rest of this class, he was both the most powerful actor in the polity and economy and the object of resentment by other sectors of the elite and a potential target of social movements from below. The shah and state were thus autonomous within Iranian society, but dangerously so, from the point of view of their own long-term survival.

The Economy and Class Structure

Iran's economy went through three discernible phases between 1953 and 1978, two of which ended in deep recession and social upheaval. From 1953 to about 1960 came a phase of stabilization and normalization of the economy along fairly traditional dependent lines. Oil income and American economic aid were resumed, permitting a reactivation of the development model of the 1930s and 1940s based on long-standing agricultural practices, some light industries and imports of many consumer items. This was followed by a balance of payments crisis due to excessive imports in 1958-60 and then the political instability of the 1960-63 period. The second phase from 1963 to 1973 was a period of transition to a more thoroughly capitalist economy with the land reform doing away with most sharecropping arrangements and steadily growing oil revenues used to initiate a somewhat deeper industrialization process involving infrastructural investments and more complex manufacturing of an assembly type with state and foreign help. Growth rates were steady, inflation was contained, capital from foreign aid and oil was channelled with some care within the limits imposed. After 1973 the oil boom accelerated these processes into a third phase that soon became qualitatively distinct as a full-blown dependent capitalist development going out of control. The attempt to double the goals of the fifth plan in 1975 set off a binge of epic proportions in GNP growth rates, oil revenues, arms purchases, corruption, conspicuous consumption, agribusiness schemes, and heavy industrialization whose flaws will be examined in detail in this section.

Before investigating the four key sectors of the Iranian economy—agriculture, pastoralism, capitalist and petty-commodity manufacturing—the basic aggregate contours of these two and a half decades can be suggested, in terms of trends in population and gross national product. Population grew from 14.6 million in 1940 to 20.4 million in 1956, 27.1 million in 1966 and 33.6 million in 1976, at a high rate that reached 3.2 percent annually in the late 1970s. But this growth was very unevenly distributed by sector, as the proportion of the population living in cities rose from 22 percent in 1940 to 31 percent in 1956, 39 percent in 1966 and 47 percent in 1976. This portended a great underlying shift from agricultural to urban service and industrial occupations and a vast migration of peasants into the cities. The epicenter of this demographic explosion was Tehran, which grew from 2.5 million in 1970 to 5 million in 1977, a sprawling primate city larger than the next dozen cities combined and containing 14 percent of Iran's entire population.[19]

Gross national product meanwhile rose at a significantly faster rate than population. Fueled largely first by increased oil production and then by the much higher oil prices of the post-1973 period, it passed from $3 billion in 1953 to $53 billion in 1977. In per capita terms this represents almost a tenfold increase from $166 a person in 1953 to $1,514 in 1977, raising Iran from the ranks of the lower to the medium income countries in aggregate terms. At current prices, per capita GNP hit $2,160 in 1978 (though without petroleum revenues this figure would be cut in half). Between 1963 and 1978 gross domestic product grew at an average annual rate of 10.8 percent, a figure which only two or three countries in the world surpassed, and only some five to eight did better in terms of per capita growth rate (for 1960-72, in order, these were Libya, Japan, Rumania, Greece, Saudi Arabia, Singapore, Taiwan, and South Korea).[20] These few facts alone demonstrate that rapid change and substantial "development" took place in Iran in this period. To understand the dependent side of this development however requires a closer look at the impact and distribution of these aggregate data among the sectors, classes, and groups that comprised the Iranian economy and social formation.

Agriculture and the Tribal Sector

Iranian agriculture underwent a massive qualitative transformation in the period from 1953 to 1978. This was due to the far-reaching effects (unintended as well as planned) of the 1960s' land reform, the centerpiece of what the shah came to regard as his "White Revolution." The centuries-old cropsharing mode of production rapidly evolved in the course of a decade into a far more capitalist agriculture, whose impact on land tenure arrangements, rural class structure, and agricultural performance was dramatic, and for the most part, decidedly negative.

The system of landlord-dominated villages farmed by share-cropping peasants changed forever with the implementation of land reform in the

1960s. The shah was forced to extend the token sale of a few crown estates to peasants in the 1950s into a fully-fledged land reform by a complex set of pressures emanating from the Kennedy administration, the revival of the National Front, and his own calculations that such a reform could remove landed power as a challenge to the state in the countryside and secure a numerous class of landholding peasants grateful to the regime. The first phase of land reform, proposed and carried out in 1962 under prime minister 'Ali Amini and minister of agriculture Hasan Arsanjani, was rather more progressive than the shah would have liked: It limited landlords to the equivalent of one whole village, compensating them for all land above that at its declared value for tax purposes (a bargain for the state) and then reselling the land to those peasants who sharecropped it (the "landless" non-sharecroppers were left out). Long before this phase was complete landlord protests, peasant mobilizations, and his own jealousy led the shah to dismiss Amini and Arsanjani and water down the reform into a second phase in which landlords' wives and children could own a whole village and mechanized lands and orchards were exempted, giving all landowners the option to rent, sell, or divide the land with the peasants, purchase the latter's cultivating rights, or form joint stock corporations with them. The shah now claimed the reform as his own "White Revolution" (as opposed to a socialist, or "red" revolution), to which various secondary principles were added, the most significant being compensation of landowners with shares of state-owned industries, a move which turned some of them into industrial capitalists. After 1967 a third phase was enacted requiring the conversion of all phase two leases into sales to peasants (thereby promoting small holdings) but on the other hand encouraging large mechanized farms, farm corporations of several villages or more, and large-scale capitalist farming as well.[21]

Was the land reform a success? Table 8.1 summarizes the results based on the work of its leading English-language expert, Eric Hooglund. This suggests that a staggering 93 percent of former sharecroppers received land and became peasant owners by the 1970s. This may be favorably contrasted with the land reforms of Egypt, Syria, and Iraq, each of which affected less than ten percent of villagers. Behind this appearance of relative success however, Hooglund has discerned a far darker reality:

the practical success as measured in terms of actual positive benefits accruing to the peasants as a result of redistribution was virtually nonexistent. . . . the Iranian land reform was actually a very conservative program which in the long term provided most villagers with few positive advantages. . . . by 1971 . . . the overwhelming majority of villagers were in no better economic situation than they had been prior to the implementation of the program.[22]

TABLE 8.1 Land Reform in Iran

Stage of Reform	Number of Peasants Receiving Land
[Sharecroppers, before land reform]	[2,100,000]
Phase 1 of reform	753,000
Phase 2 of reform	213,000
Phase 3 of reform	800,000
Others with long-term vaqf leases	172,000
Total receiving land	1,938,000

Source: Hooglund, *Land and Revolution*, 72 table 4, rounded off.

The reasons for this include the facts that up to a half of village families were unaffected by the reform, as they had no formal sharecropping agreement with the landowner; the vast majority who did receive land received small amounts of fragmented, poor-quality holdings; and up to one-half of the land was not distributed at all, remaining in the hands of large owners. Data on the size of holdings after the land reform underscores its problematic impact on the countryside. In effect large absentee ownership was modified, but survived. Peasant sharecroppers became small peasant proprietors, but remained at subsistence levels, as seven hectares was considered the minimum holding required to support a family. Landless peasants remained landless and very poor. Middlemen and middle peasants consolidated their positions and the latter increased in number. A closer look at each of these classes rounds out this interpretation.

Some 45,000 large, mostly absentee landlords remained after the land reform, and as Table 8.2 indicates, 1,350 of them had substantial holdings of over 200 hectares. The total land held by such absentee owners was as much as 47 percent of all cultivable land, including the most fertile in Iran. Through legal loopholes and subterfuge landlords remained the largest landowners in 90 percent of all villages, though their number was halved and they were no longer the sole possessors or politically as all-powerful. The top 20 percent of the rural population accounted for 43.6 percent of consumption in 1972/73. Those who left the countryside received shares in state-owned factories worth $93 million; some diversified into real estate, trade, banking, and contracting. As capitalist farmers now employing wage labor the rest remained economically powerful on their farms, and varieties of paternalistic attitudes continued to be found among them.[23]

TABLE 8.2 Land Ownership After the Land Reform

Size of Holding	Number of Owners
>200 hectares	1,350
50-200 hectares	44,000
10-50 hectares	150,000-600,000
5-10 hectares	700,000
2-5 hectares	700,000
<2 hectares	1,000,000
0 hectares	700,000-1,400,000

Sources: Hooglund, "The Effects of the Land Reform," 147, 162-63; Abrahamian, "Structural Causes," 23 table IV, and *Iran Between Two Revolutions*, 429-30. There are some discrepancies in the two sets of data, especially at the 10-50 hectare level.

A rural middle class also arose of middle peasants (the 150-600,000 owning 10-50 hectares in Table 8.2) and village merchants. This group emerged out of the former village headmen and production team leaders who received more land than the ordinary sharecropper. They were able to stay out of debt (often acquiring the land of others), consume more, and send children to high school. Another rural middle class group were village shopkeepers, who often doubled as moneylenders, millers, and renters of equipment and draft animals. Along with the landlords, these middle class groups dominated the new rural political institutions such as village councils, cooperative societies, and rural courts, further consolidating their positions as the most well-to-do individuals living in the countryside.[24]

The vast majority of the rural population fell into the two far more destitute categories of small peasants and landless laborers. Table 8.2 shows 2,400,000 peasants with less than ten hectares (71 percent with less then five hectares, i.e. below subsistence-level) and another 700,000 to 1,400,000 completely landless families. Another impoverished group living at subsistence level were village service and craftspeople—the barbers, bath attendants, carpenters, blacksmiths, and shoemakers. Craftspeople saw their living standard deteriorate as inexpensive manufactured goods began to make their way into the villages by the 1970s. Worse off were the landless rural proletariat, up to 1.4 million individuals (and seven million people, counting whole families), who lived by working part-time on others' land or migrating to nearby towns and distant cities, where they became part of the urban marginal classes. After land reform they had fewer employment opportunities as large farms were mechanized and small peasants did their own labor.[25] The standard of living of the rural majority proved almost as bad after the land reform as before (and certainly any gains lagged far behind the more privileged urban sector). Incomes per capita were as low as $131 a year for peasants holding 3-10 hectares, and $70 for those with 0-3 hectares. Rural proletarians made an average of $1.40 a day for men and 74 cents for women in 1972 (for seasonal work of perhaps 100 days a year). Katouzian found 38 percent of the rural population undernourished in 1972/72 (6.6 million people) and another 4 percent (700,000) severely under-nourished. Despite the establishment of rural schools and a Literacy Corps, only 15 percent of the rural population received an education in 1971 and 60 percent of men and 90 percent of women were illiterate in 1975. Ninety-six percent of villages had no electricity in the 1970s.[26]

The main political consequence of the land reform was the effective replacement of the all-powerful landlord in the villages by the obtrusive state. This was accomplished through the Literacy Corps, Health Corps, Extension and Development Corps, government organization of village institutions (cooperative societies, credit unions, rural courts), control of prices, and the coercive power of the rural gendarmerie. One peasant of Kirman province told Ann Lambton in the mid-1960s: "formerly we obeyed the landowners; now we shall obey whoever issues orders to us."[27] Peasants may have obeyed but there was much resentment, directed at both the state and the landed elite. Some felt less than grateful for the land reform, one telling Hooglund in 1967: "Our fathers worked this land for generations; it belongs to us and we should have it free of all burdens."[28] A young Kurdish peasant expressed the carryover of class antagonism from landlord to government authority when he said:

> Yes, we need schools and doctors, but they are just for the rich. I wish I didn't even know doctors existed. Before, we were ignorant, but now we know that pills and shots can help us. But we can't buy them, so we watch our children die from sickness as well as hunger. Before, the elders said that if a child died, it was the will of God (*dast-i khuda*), but now I think that it's the will of the government (*dast-i dowlat*).[29]

Nor did bitter feelings toward landlords or an awareness of class inequalities subside as a result of the reform, as another Kurdish peasant made clear:

> What do I really think? Well, things have changed for the better, that is certain. It was bad here. . . . I'm a poor man, I know, but at least I can feed my family, so I am lucky. Most of the others can't even do that. . . . why didn't [the *khwushnishin*] get any land? These *aghas* [lords] are still here and they own the best land. Some men have no land at all and many others don't have enough on which to grow their families' bread. So what is just about all this? . . . the *aghas*, they just prosper to the end.[30]

Passive resistance and covert resentment on the part of the peasantry was apparently widespread in the 1960s and 1970s, signalling the ultimate failure of the political aim of the regime in creating a large class of loyal supporters in the countryside.

In the absence of any coordinated or comprehensive agricultural development strategy and budget allocations as low as six percent (in 1969), there should be little surprise that overall growth rates in agriculture were extremely disappointing. As the government inflated its production figures by up to 100 percent, it is also not surprising to find disparities among experts' assessments. These cluster in the 2-3 percent range per year in the 1950s, 1960s, and 1970s, according to Graham (2 percent), Keddie (2-2.5 percent), Motameni (circa 2.2 percent), Katouzian (2-3 percent) and Seyfollahi (circa 3 percent), with only Baku's 3.3 percent and Pesaran's 4.4 percent offering a more positive evaluation. When these are measured against a population growth of about 3 percent, one can conclude that agricultural production was virtually stagnant in per capita terms despite land reform, mechanization, the spread of capitalist relations, and other changes. The share of agriculture in the GDP fell from 50 percent in the 1940s to 33 percent in 1959, 23 percent in 1969, and 9.2 percent in 1977/78. Production of wheat, barley, rice, tobacco, cotton, and other key staples and exports grew slowly over the whole period, all suffering declines at some point or other.[31] As agriculture grew at 2-3 percent a year, consumption was rising by as much as 12 percent annually. This meant shortfalls in production of such necessities as wheat and barley, rice, meat, and dairy products. Food imports rose from under $100 million in 1963 (with the agricultural balance of trade still positive as late as 1968), to $211 million in 1972, $1-1.5 billion in 1975, and $2.6 billion in 1977, equal to about 14 percent of Iran's food needs.[32]

One cause of Iran's agricultural problems was the poor performance of the new agribusinesses and farm corporations. Fourteen huge agribusiness ventures of over 5,000 hectares each were established between 1968 and 1978, mostly located near large dam projects. Investors included the government, private capitalists, international banks such as Chase, Citicorp, and Bank of America, and multinationals including Shell, Mitsui, John Deere, and Dow Chemical. Despite massive investments in irrigation, tractors, and fertilizer they proved for the most part to be business failures and indeed were both relatively and absolutely (i.e. regardless of differences in land, water, technology, and capital) less productive than medium-sized peasant holdings. This surprising result may be attributed to mismanagement by foreigners ignorant of Iran's climate, use of inappropriate technologies, inefficiencies of size, high overhead costs, exorbitant infrastructural investments, and the leaving of much land fallow. Meanwhile they displaced peasants and used little labor in the job-starved countryside. Some

100 state-run farm corporations with similarly large capital investments also proved less efficient and productive than peasant-owned villages.[33] Nor could Iran's several million small farmers make up for these failures to feed the whole country. In part this was due to errors in government pricing policy (or a deliberate subsidy to urban consumers) that kept the purchasing price of their crops, especially wheat, below the costs of production. Rather than improving the system of distribution (which accounted for a 30 percent loss of tomatoes and 20 percent in meat), the state paid peasants only about 5.5 percent of the shop price for their products, compared to 44 percent for the wholesalers, 39 percent for the retailers, and 11.5 percent for transportation. This led to disincentives to produce for the market, changes to non-staple, non-price controlled crops, or simple desertion of the land, while Iran's food import bill rose ever higher.[34]

Conceptually, the best way to capture the changes and continuity in Iranian agriculture by the 1970s is as a transition from the peasant cropsharing mode of production to capitalist agriculture. The preservation of millions of small-scale producers (now owners rather than sharecroppers) has led some observers to speak of "the system of family production" or "individual petty production" in the countryside,[35] but Iran's peasants were now increasingly enmeshed in a system stamped by market relations in distribution and the use of landless rural labor in production (on the agribusinesses, farm corporations, middle to large farms, and at certain times on most "family" plots). The nature of the land reform and the inadequacies of the large-scale projects may have preserved the small size of most holdings for a time, but the maintenance and indeed extension of inequalities, creation and release of a huge army of landless agricultural workers, and spread of commercialized production and distribution all made the new system unmistakably capitalist in mode of production terms.

Iran's tribal sector meanwhile continued to shrink in viability throughout the late shah's reign, the victim of conscious state policies and demographic and political trends generally. Official figures for the number of tribespeople actually migrating (as opposed to the much more numerous settled tribal ethnic groups) have ranged wildly: from nearly two million in the 1940s (during the period of tribal "resurgence") down to an improbable 240,000 in 1956 and the same number in 1966, and then, inexplicably, back to 1.87 million in the 1976 census. Even if the 1956-66 estimates are thrown out, the nomadic tribal population fell absolutely from about 2.5 million in 1900 to less than two million in the 1970s, or in the more revealing relative terms, from 25 percent of the population to about six percent.[36] The shah reinstated the sedentarization policies of his father and was possessed of stronger administrative and coercive mechanisms to carry them out. The land reform also eroded tribal holdings by "nationalizing" all pasture land, reducing tribal control, and increasing dependence on the state. The few tribes that resisted—the Boir Ahmadis in 1962, the Qashqa'i in 1963-65, Kurdish guerrillas after 1967—were ruthlessly repressed, "treated with a harshness that, in the view of Nasser Pakdaman (an Iranian political economist), not even the Red Indians in America had suffered."[37]

Tribal social structure and economy were severely impacted by these developments. Tribal chiefs lost political power and social status as a result of sedentarization and land reform, just as large landlords did. But like the landlords some managed to retain economic power, transforming themselves into landowners, businessmen, bureaucrats or military officers. Ordinary tribespeople settled in great numbers due either to government policy or economic hardship. Many became small peasants and landless rural laborers in the countryside, or factory workers, unskilled construction workers or part of the marginal population in the cities. Some, such as the 50-70,000 Shahsavan, managed to remain migratory and continued to produce pastoral products. Life for most became harder, and data on nutritional standards in the countryside showed particularly high levels of malnourishment in Kurdistan, Khuzistan, Kirman, and Bakhtiar, all areas of large tribal settlement. These class and economic changes eroded tribal consciousness to a certain degree: "In short, the horizontal ties of class tended to supplant the vertical sentiments of clan, tribe, sect, and locality."[38]

Sedentarization, land reform, and demographic decline dislocated Iran's production of meat and dairy products in the 1960s. Livestock breeding declined from 40 percent of agricultural production in the 1960s to 26 percent around 1970, before rising back to 33 percent in 1973-78 as a result of government attempts to introduce large, capital-intensive units for poultry products and sheep. In 1966 only 40 percent of goats and sheep were owned by tribespeople. As production of pastoral goods became more capitalist than pastoral-nomadic, Iran's ability to export non-oil products from meat and hides to wool and finished carpets declined. In mode of production terms, despite the inroads made by capitalist livestock production units, the long-standing pastoral nomadic mode of production continued to exist, only in attenuated form, with a far smaller share of the economy and labor force than previously.[39]

The Capitalist Sector

Encompassing manufacturing, construction, services, the state bureaucracy, and middle class professionals, the capitalist mode of production became the largest mode in the urban sector as well by the 1970s. As under Reza Shah in the 1930s, conscious industrial strategy may have been haphazard—Katouzian concludes there was "no strategy worthy of the name," Halliday quotes one expert to the effect that "the only kind of planning in

Iran is what the Shah wants"[40]—but the industrialization *process* nevertheless followed some discernible patterns. The main emphasis in the 1960s was on import substitution industrialization to provide urban consumers with various goods (clothes, food, cars, appliances) and in the 1970s a deepening of this path to undertake production of certain basic and intermediate goods such as chemicals, steel, and machine tools. Assessments of the success of this effort vary from Issawi's conclusion in 1978 that "Iran now provides a significant part of the intermediate and capital goods it requires, and the proportion should rise steeply during the next few years" to the more pessimistic findings of Pesaran and Yaghmaian, with which I am inclined to agree.[41] A look at rates of growth and available data on specific industries will bear out both the achievements and problems of capitalist industrialization in Iran.

Iran's overall industrial growth rate was an impressive 15 percent annually between 1965 and 1975, and registered 14.6 percent in 1976/77 and 9.4 percent in 1977/78, a year of recession. These rates may have been the highest in the Third World over this period, and were twice or more the average of the developing countries generally. Gross domestic fixed capital formation moreover grew at a high 18.4 percent annual rate for 1963-77. These rates were somewhat deceptive however, in at least two respects: Industry's share of GNP at about 18 percent lagged well behind that of services (35 percent) and oil (35 percent) in 1977/78, and manufactured non-oil exports were only 2-3 percent of all exports circa 1975, comparing very poorly with such countries as India (over 50 percent), Singapore (60 percent), and Mexico (33 percent).[42]

Other aggregate industrial data show a rise in small factories (with 10-49 workers) from less than a thousand in 1953 to more than 7,000 in 1977, with corresponding increases in the numbers of medium-size factories (50-100 workers) from 300 to 830, and large factories of over 500 workers from nineteen to 159. (There were, however, over 200,000 small workshops with less than ten workers, showing the persistence of artisanal production.) The number of industrial workers (including those in small shops, construction, transport, and utilities as well as manufacturing) reached almost 2.5 million in 1977. Behind high protective tariffs and licensed monopolies, profits of 30-50 percent were common in the 1970s.[43] Data on output and share of specific industries suggest that textiles remained important, increasing production from 350 million to 533 million meters of cloth between 1965 and 1975, but falling behind motor vehicles in terms of the total value produced. Food processing, led by sugar, vegetable oils, beverages, and tobacco also continued as an important sector carried over from the past. Assembly-type industries such as autos and electrical appliances became increasingly prominent. Dominated by multinational investors, annual production of motor vehicles rose from 7,000 units in 1965 to 109,000 in 1975, of TVs from

12,000 to 31,000, of phones from none to 186,000, and of gas ovens from 87,000 to 220,000. Other high-technology, capital-intensive sectors were in production of steel and aluminum (at great cost and with foreign help) whose output increased ten times but still lagged behind demand; petrochemicals, basic chemicals, and pharmaceuticals (again, all marked by foreign technology and licensing); and machine tools in a plant at Arak. Important non-manufacturing sectors included the huge construction industry, the smallish non-oil mining sector, the overextended transportation sector, and banking, dominated by the key Industrial and Mining Development Bank of Iran, established in 1957 with 40 percent foreign ownership.[44]

Despite the success indicated by the aggregate and sectoral data, Iranian industrialization was plagued by a number of problems. Katouzian notes for example that plants ran at low capacity due to shortages of technicians and managers, crippling bureaucratic restrictions obtained, and production costs were high. Halliday points to the shortage of skilled labor, inefficiency, limits of the internal market, lack of competition due to too-high tariffs, and resulting failure to expand export potential. Pesaran locates the problems of import-substitution industrialization in the pattern of artificially high profits, lack of forward and backward linkages in the economy, discrimination against agriculture due to the overvalued rial, and the brake on employment caused by capital-intensivity. Other difficulties described by Graham include the disastrous overtaxing of infrastructure (ports and roads) during the oil boom which led to great wastage of imports, endemic corruption, and capital flight after 1975 when the state mandated profit-sharing with workers in some industries and initiated an anti-profiteering campaign. These trends resulted in the end of the boom after 1975 and a recession in 1977.[45]

Behind this litany of problems lurked structural weaknesses deriving from the dependent nature of Iran's industrialization process. In this context, and in that of the Third World generally, certain characteristic problems of the import-substitution strategy come to light. The problem of market size has already been mentioned; due to the necessarily limited (even if growing) numbers of the middle and upper classes, there is only a certain amount of production that can be consumed. If, as in Iran, high tariffs and monopoly licensing are used to guarantee profits, then products will not be competitive on the world market, and few manufactured items are exported (high wage bills due to inflation after 1973 compounded this trend). This is a recipe for long-term disaster when oil revenues run out. Furthermore, the modern industrial sector as a whole was grossly dependent on foreign joint ventures, for capital, technology, management, and inputs. Foreign capital was dominant in autos, appliances, chemicals, pharmaceuticals, and plastics, and even made inroads in such traditionally local industries as textiles and construction. The key auto and electrical appliance sectors were essentially "screwdriver" industries, merely assembling imported parts and adding very low amounts to the total value of the finished products. Pharmaceutical companies bought most ingredients abroad, down to the packaging materials: "According to an expatriate manager of a large foreign pharmaceutical firm, his factory in Iran was no more than a 'large drug store'."[46] In 1978 pharmaceuticals were 85-100 percent dependent on imported inputs, chemicals 60-100 percent, textiles 80 percent (for machinery), certain food items 70 percent and certain building materials 57 percent.[47] Multinational companies were willing to help Iran expand into oil refining, petrochemicals, fertilizer, iron, steel, and aluminum, because the West would get some of the finished products and would sell Iran the plants, equipment, technology, management, and some of the inputs, in addition to having some joint ownership. In general, the industrial sector used imported machines to assemble imported parts with imported technology, sometimes in joint ventures, and sold poor quality goods at high, protected prices and repatriated some of the profits out of the country. This was a *dependent* development.

The main urban classes in the capitalist mode of production were the capitalist class (with its state, local, and foreign components), the working class, and the intelligentsia, including professionals and students. The state played the dominant role in industrialization in the 1960s, allocating oil revenues, building infrastructure, and coordinating the Iranian bourgeoisie and foreign capital in joint ventures through the grant of loans, licenses, and contracts. In industry, the state's share of ownership dropped from the 1941 level of 50 percent to 17 percent in 1963 after the transfer of shares in state factories as compensation for the expropriation of landed estates. But as oil revenues grew the state's role in industrial investments increased apace, from 40 percent in the mid-1960s to 60 percent in the 1970s. By virtue of its preponderant role in the highly-capitalized new sectors—steel, petrochemicals, natural gas, machinery—the state proposed to invest $46.2 billion during the Fifth Plan (1973-78), compared with the private sector's $23.4 billion. We can thus agree with Halliday's assessment that industrial development between 1953 and 1978 was generally attributable to the state's dominant role.[48]

The private sector certainly played a supporting part in this process, however. Local capitalists in the Pahlavi period had origins as landowners, longstanding urban notable families, older industrialists of the 1930s and 1940s, some ex-bazaari merchants, top civil servants, and military officers. Almost all enjoyed some contact with the royal family for to succeed one had to be favored by the court. The main lines in which local capital played a role were light industry, construction, and banking. Census data indicate an increase in the number of owners/employers from 68,777 in 1956 to 152,623 in 1966 and 186-220,000 by 1976, but wealth was very concentrated at the top: In 1972 fifty-six families owned shares in 177 of the 364 largest industrial firms, and seventy-two families in a further eighty-eight firms. Halliday reports that in 1974 just forty-five families controlled 85 percent of firms with turnover of more than ten million rials ($133,333), while Abrahamian thinks 1,000 families controlled 85 percent of all firms. Private sector profits ran at 33.2 percent in 1972-74. Bourgeois attitudes toward the state were as often of resentment and insecurity as of loyalty and affection. Toward each other there was considerable factionalism, and toward the workers primarily paternalism, disdain, and condescension.[49]

The third partner in this triple alliance was foreign capital, whose role in this period shaped the Iranian economy on a scale beyond the already significant one we have seen from 1850 to 1950. Ansari, the minister of the economy, estimated total foreign investment in Iran at the beginning of 1977 at $5.2 billion (of which Japan accounted for 30 percent, the United States 28 percent, West Germany 8 percent, Switzerland 8 percent, Great Britain 7 percent and France 6 percent). This capital represented something less than four percent of all capital invested in Iran, which is seemingly fairly small. However, it was concentrated in Iran's most important economic sectors: agribusiness, as we have already seen; three out of five large petrochemical concerns; four out of five large chemical plants; 14 out of 18 pharmaceuticals; all of plastics; all of autos; 37 of 42 producers of electrical and non-electrical machinery; and involvement in the steel and aluminum industries. Even older, established sectors such as food-processing, construction, and textiles were increasingly supplied by multinationals. Banking also had a large foreign presence. By law, foreigners could only own 49 percent of joint ventures, but could repatriate profits freely. The multinationals tended to be the largest companies in Iran, capital- and technology-intensive, and very profitable. Profit rates of anywhere from 50 to 200 percent were possible. Inflow of foreign capital changed from 9.5 billion rials ($126.6 million) in 1962/63 to an outflow of 923.8 billion rials ($12.3 billion) in 1972/73. These considerations indicate that foreign capital was far from a junior partner with state and local capital in Iran.[50]

It is difficult to form a precise idea of the size of Iran's working class, for the definitions vary from "all wage earners" to "workers in large manufacturing establishments" and data sets vary as well. A major problem is the inclusion of large numbers of artisans and rural craft workers in the "manufacturing" statistics. The most sensible estimates are probably in the two to two and a half million range, or 20-25 percent of Iran's ten-million strong labor force. Halliday judges that "In overall terms at least, Iran has one of the larger manufacturing labor forces in the third world."[51] This included 600-900,000 factory workers in plants with over ten workers, 280,000 in transport and communications, up to one million in the construction sector, 88,000 in oil and mining, and 65,000 in utilities. These figures represent a

100-150 percent increase in the twenty years since 1956 (when the total may be estimated at about one million), with the biggest gains in manufacturing and construction. The origins of this working class varied by sector; Bayat found strong rural ties (i.e. recent migrant origins) in the newer and more modern industries (and also in construction), and more second-generation urban labor in the older sectors of textiles and food-processing. Wages also varied by sector, with the more dynamic ones such as pharmaceuticals (at $88 a month in 1972) and autos ($94) higher than textiles ($72) and food-processing ($56). Textile workers had made $25-28 a month in 1960. After the oil boom led to labor shortages and inflation in the 1970s wages rose as much as 300 percent, to over $200 a month by 1976/77, but these are average figures (there were large differentials among unskilled and skilled workers, foremen, and technicians). Some 73 percent of workers were found to be making less than the legal minimum in 1974. Working hours were long, and Bayat has thoroughly documented the appalling conditions of work in all factories—modern, traditional, multinational—problems of fumes, noise, dangerous chemicals, industrial accidents, no enforcement of health and safety standards, lack of insurance benefits, and poor medical treatment. The average worker may have been better off than the average peasant, but life was still very hard for all but some of those in the largest factories, and even there only after the oil boom.[52]

Another sector of the working class not included in the figures above is the "service" category. Again problems of conceptualization and data overlap are attached to this group. Aggregate figures range from 1.5 million to 3.4 million people. The higher figure includes 800,000 in the civil service (and probably the army!), as well as many professionals and students (whom we will classify as urban middle class, below), merchants (whom we consider part of the petty-commodity sector), as well as some of the employees in transport and utilities already counted above. Nevertheless we may note over 150,000 wage earners in banks, offices, and other agencies, 140,000 shop assistants and perhaps several hundred thousand other, non-classified workers. The contribution of the non-state service sector to GNP was as high as 20 percent in 1977 (compared to 16 percent in large-scale manufacturing), but again this includes some bazaar merchants of the petty-commodity mode. When service workers are added to the industrial working class, the working class as a whole rises to over three million individuals, or 30 percent of the economically active population.[53]

Another key class in the capitalist mode was the intelligentsia—teachers, students, writers, artists, and some professionals—all in all, what has been called the educated middle class. The proportion of professionals, technical, and related workers in the labor force more than doubled from 1.6 percent in 1956 to 3.5 percent in 1972. Chief among these were Iran's 208,241 teachers and 6,726 professors in 1977. There were also 61,066 engineers, white-collar workers, and managers, and 21,500 medical personnel. To these may be added the student population at the secondary level and above, which grew enormously in the 1953-77 period from some 138,000 students to over 1,202,000 students (Katouzian puts secondary students alone at 2.3 million in 1978). Wages and salaries for the members of this group varied: In the oil boom a private sector engineer could make $2,000 a month, while teachers were always paid much less. Students and youth moreover faced acute problems; in the 1960s, 13-14 percent of those applying to universities were admitted, while in 1977 60,000 out of 290,000 were accepted. Iran thus sent more students abroad than any other country in the world, with a radicalizing effect on the intelligentsia as a whole. Meanwhile, 75 percent of all suicides were in the 15-30 year-old group, and the rate of heroin addiction was reportedly the second highest in the world, after the United States.[54]

What sort of living standards prevailed in the urban sector? Though relatively better off materially than the countryside, the majority of urban residents suffered from unequal income distribution, inflation, and other problems. Data on income inequality as measured by household expenditures show that the top 20 percent of households increased their share of expenditures from 51.79 percent in 1959/60 to 55.56 percent in 1973/74, while the bottom 40 percent saw their share decline from 13.90 percent to 11.96 percent, and the middle 40 percent also lost ground. Iran's Gini coefficient (a measure of income inequality) in this period worsened from 0.45 to 0.49, and then to 0.51 in 1974/75, and was found by the International Labor Organization in 1969/70 to be "higher than any country in East and Southeast Asia, considerably higher than in Western countries and probably as high or higher than in Latin American countries for which data are available."[55] A survey by Ahmad Ashraf indicates that the top 1.5 percent of the population increased their share of the national income from 29.5 percent in 1960 to 35 percent in 1970. In 1968, the average mean urban income by decile was 95,979 rials ($1,267); for the poorest ten percent, it was 12,466 rials ($165), while for the wealthiest ten percent it was 331,014 rials ($4,370). As Keddie points out, these inequalities undoubtedly grew after 1974 with the dislocations caused by the oil boom.[56]

Inflation likewise took its toll. Spurred in the 1970s by the influx of oil revenues and higher prices for imports (through which the West passed its inflation back to the Middle East), it accelerated after 1972. While for 1963-67 retail prices had risen only an average of 1.5 percent annually, the rate crept upwards to 3.7 percent a year for 1968-72 and then surged to 15.7 percent annually for 1973-77 during the boom.[57] The effect was to erode wage gains and make both housing and food prohibitively expensive in the cities for the working and middle classes. Already in 1972 food expenses consumed 43.6 percent of the average urban income of $122 a month, while rents rose fifteen times between 1960 and 1975, including 200 percent in 1974/75 and

100 percent in 1975/76. The number of urban families living in one room increased from 36 percent in 1967 to 43 percent in 1977.[58]

Other indices of living standards further lay bare the mixed blessings of dependent development. Katouzian found 64 percent of the urban population undernourished in 1972/73 (25 percent severely), a higher rate than in the countryside (at 42 percent). Health statistics record the rises in hospital beds, clinics, doctors, and nurses, but in 1977, "Iran still had one of the worst doctor-patient ratios, one of the highest child mortality rates, and one of the lowest hospital-bed-to-population ratios in the whole of the Middle East."[59] Urban infant mortality in the first year of life was 80 per 1,000 live births in 1974, down from 180 in 1963. Life expectancy had been just forty-one years in 1962; in the 1970s it reached fifty-one (both infant mortality and life expectancy were quite similar to India's). While the rate of illiteracy had officially fallen from 85 percent in 1956 to 65-70 percent in 1977, the number of illiterates rose from 13 million in 1963 to 15 million in 1977 and Iran still had a higher illiteracy rate than India. These data, taken together, show some improvement in urban living standards, but also suggest the widespread deprivation and suffering that existed in 1977.

Neither the working class nor the intelligentsia gave much support to the regime in the 1970s. The state tried to control the former with SAVAK-administered trade unions, of which there were over a thousand in 1978, their organization on a factory-wide basis hinting at their aim of social control at the work place. In a few plants, workers were able to use these company unions to struggle for their own rights. Nor did the 1975 workers' share program in industry affect many workers—only 45,000 were covered in 1976. It was in effect a forced savings plan that held little attraction for the working class, "predominantly [a] symbolic exercise."[60] In terms of religious and political cultures, Kazemi's 1975 survey of workers at several factories suggested that recent migrants had little knowledge of the formal political system, whereas those who had been in the factories longer, both men and women, were more literate and more aware of issues of class. This bears out Ashraf's 1969 survey in which workers located themselves between the middle class and lumpenproletariat. Bayat has argued that class culture is limited by illiteracy among workers, the attendant lack of political education, the non-existence of associations outside the home either at work or in the community. He notes that few factory workers spend time in coffee houses (this is the preserve of new migrants/construction workers and the bazaar classes). This left the mosque and *hayat* circles (groups of friends who gathered on religious occasions) as the main locus of association among workers outside the factory, a circumstance that would facilitate ulama leadership in the 1978 events.[61]

But workers also engaged in militant activities of their own. Strikes, which had declined from seventy-nine in 1953 to seven in 1954 and three from 1955 to 1957, resumed in the 1960s and 1970s despite their illegality. There were twenty from 1957 to 1961, some of which ended in bloodshed. Other strike waves occurred in 1971 and 1974-76, involving textile, bus and pipeline workers, coal miners, chemical, auto, and utility workers. Most were over economic issues, some ending with concessions, many with arrests and police violence. These actions set the stage for the political strikes in 1978-79.[62]

The intelligentsia, too, was not won over to the regime. Pahlavi-style modernization offered new material opportunities to the secular, educated middle classes but constrained intellectuals politically. Independent professional associations were dismantled after 1953 and only government-organized ones were permitted. Workers, actors, and artists nevertheless did organize themselves in such groups as the Writers' Guild of about eighty intellectuals who protested censorship (and were suppressed in 1970). Teachers joined workers in strikes, as in May 1971 when the army killed one and wounded many in Tehran. Students were particularly active. Despite coming from middle and upper class backgrounds at the university level (with more lower-middle and middle class youth making it to high school), students engaged in militant protests in 1960-63, 1969-70, and 1975 for both educational reforms and against the Pahlavi regime generally. Students abroad were often left-wing in view and able to organize more freely. The intelligentsia, then, joined the working class as a major social class with grievances against the state by the 1970s.[63]

The Petty-Commodity Mode of Production and "Mixed" Groups and Classes

As the capitalist mode of production expanded, the bazaar-based petty-commodity mode contracted somewhat, but persisted. Absolute urban growth afforded it a margin of existence, as did its own internal dynamics and ability to find and maintain niches of production and distribution. Small-scale "factories," workshops and handicraft establishments continued to operate in the 1960s and 1970s despite intense competition from local and imported manufactures. Just how numerous this sector was is difficult to discern. Of 2.5 million "industrial workers" in 1977, 68-72 percent, or 1.7-1.8 million, labored in small units employing less than ten workers. Bayat notes the existence of 1.1 million non-agricultural self-employed workers, 602,000 small-scale industrial workers (333,000 urban and 269,000 rural), and 430,000 non-agricultural family workers—a large portion of these were merchants, artisans, and rural craftspeople. Of 250,000 manufacturing establishments, 244,000 employed less than ten workers. Many of these were artisanal urban workshops, and many were rural carpet-weaving sites. Katouzian calculates that this sector accounted for 35 percent of total industrial output and 28 percent of non-oil exports (compared with 57 percent and 21 percent respectively for modern industry). A rough estimate is that 10-20 percent of those employed in the manufacturing sector were "self-employed," meaning there may have been 250-500,000 artisans. Behrang's analysis of census data suggests a substantial rise in the number of "artisans" (seemingly including the 50 percent or more who were rural carpet-makers) from 350,777 in 1956 (6.2 percent of the workforce) to 536,318 in 1966 (8.0 percent) and 1,001,817 (11.5 percent) in 1976.[64]

Against these growth trends there was countervailing pressure from the capitalist mode of production. In 1972, 191,000 small workshops with an average of three workers each employed 65 percent of industrial workers but produced only 35.5 percent of gross value added per worker, a sign of their labor-intensivity and limited application of machinery. Bayat calculates that in 1976 such workshops employed only 36 percent of manufacturing workers, creating 22.8 percent of value added, both suggesting aggregate declines. The labor process remained much as it had been; within workshops, "the guild elders were able to turn the clock back to the 1920s and reassert their power over the many thousand shop assistants, handicraftsmen, workshop employees, and small peddlers working in the urban bazaars."[65] Journeymen and apprentices were poorly paid (one example from Tabriz in 1975 is wages of $1.40 for a fifteen or sixteen hour day). There was little job security, insurance benefits, or chance to organize as paternalistic relations with employers were the norm. Rural craft workers may also be considered part of the petty-commodity sector, especially by virtue of the craft nature of their skills, even if, more than urban artisans, some of them were exploited in capitalist relations as well. In 1966 rural craft workers were enumerated at 1.2 million, 17 percent of Iran's labor force. Many of these were in carpet weaving of a cottage-industry type, and handmade cloth textiles.

These craftspeople were joined in the bazaars by a generally more well-to-do group, the merchant class. If we take the figure 1.1 million "petty-entrepreneurs" as only partly referring to this group, and Abrahamian's 250,000 as too low, the figure of 500-650,000 suggested by Jazani and Moghtader may be about right, representing around eight percent of the labor force. A partial census of 1965 indicated that 75 percent of retail outlets were run by single individuals, acting independently and renting their premises. The bazaar was stratified, as it had been for centuries, into a few large merchants, numerous small and medium shopkeepers, and a great many shop assistants, errand boys, street vendors, and the like. Artisans and shopkeepers who lacked the collateral to get bank loans kept bazaar moneylenders in business at 25-100 percent interest rates. Village shopkeepers and itinerant peddlers also brought the urban bazaar to the countryside, perhaps more than ever before. Moghadam's view that the bazaaris "prospered during the period of capitalist development" can be supported by such facts as their control of three-quarters of wholesaling, two-thirds of retail trade, and important sources of foreign credit, but on the other hand they now handled only 30 percent of all imports and 15 percent of private sector credit. One rough index of their decline due to the rise of banks, chain outlets, and modern shopping areas is the fall in the share of "domestic trade" in the GDP from 9.4 percent in 1963/64 to 5.7 percent in 1977/78. It would be more accurate to say that bazaar merchants continued to exist, rather then prospering, especially relative to the capitalist sector.[66]

Bazaar and state developed definite antagonisms during this whole period. The bazaars had attempted to protest both the 1953 coup and the 1954 oil deal; accordingly, the government tried to regulate their membership, taxes, and representation with legislation in 1957-58 and 1971. After 1975 a new onslaught began when the Rastakhiz Party dissolved the guilds and set up its own guilds under a chamber of commerce in each city often run by a large non-bazaar businessman. The municipal government of Tehran announced plans for an eight-lane highway to pass right through the bazaar, a type of urban "renewal" that was carried out around the bazaar/shrine complex in Mashhad. A vigorous "anti-profiteering campaign" was also launched which resulted in the fining of 200,000 shopkeepers, exile of 23,000, and jailing of 8,000 for two months to five years.[67] Such measures drew the classes of the petty-commodity mode of production together. As one shopkeeper told an American reporter: "if we let him, the Shah will destroy us. The banks are taking over. The big stores are taking away our livelihoods. And the government will flatten our bazaars to make space for state offices."[68] Merchants realized that their common enemy was the state and large-scale capitalist businessmen. SAVAK had difficulty infiltrating the bazaar since merchants, craftspeople, and apprentices were generally known to each other and the family and professional background of newcomers were scrutinized by guild members. Information networks existed through religious circles and the local mosque. Social cohesion was maintained through such practices as bulk purchasing, mutual support, and independent credit systems. Thus, more than sharp resentment between classes in the bazaar, the various groups tended to feel a solidarity with each other. Artisans, merchants, and ulama would form a core constituency of the reemerging populist alliance by the late 1970s.

The concept of mixed (or split) groups and classes has been used in this study to deal with social collectivities that either have more than one class position (such as the ulama) or are locatable in more than one mode of production (the urban underclasses and intelligentsia) or both (women and religious minorities). By the reign of Muhammad Reza Shah the intelligentsia had become solidly entrenched in the capitalist mode of production as an intermediate dominated class. The ulama were still definitely split, in both senses, as were women and minorities. Urban marginals remained a mixed class, but were moving closer to the capitalist mode of production.

The ulama maintained a strong presence as a social group in the changing Iranian social structure despite pressures from the state and economy. Halliday puts the number of ulama—always a subjective, loosely defined category—at 180,000; Abrahamian at 90,000 plus "an unknown number of low-ranking preachers, teachers, prayer leaders, and religious procession leaders."[69] In their upper ranks they included about fifty ayatullahs (a distinction which had evolved in the course of the twentieth century to designate the most widely respected and followed ulama) and below them some 5,000 *hojjat al-islams* (a title meaning "proof of Islam"). The number of religious students aspiring to these ranks grew from a low of 500 in 1946 to 6,000 at the main seminary of Qum in 1962 and to 11,000 in the 1970s. There were an estimated 80,000 mosques throughout Iran, plus countless shrines on which religious devotion was focussed and where ulama offered their services. Despite massive government encroachment on the social services traditionally provided by the ulama, efforts were made by them to staff hospitals, libraries, lecture halls, and welfare institutions that delivered such benefits as rent supplements and health care. Income was generated by assets which included the remaining vaqf properties (some 40,000 in 1965 ranging in size from whole villages to small ploughlands scattered around the country) and the payment of the religious taxes of zakat and khums, in large measure by bazaar merchants who were said to pay more taxes to the ulama than to the state. The U.S. embassy estimated the total annual income of the ulama at $30 million, plus alms, in 1972. It is thus possible to argue, as Moghadam and Abrahamian do, that the expanding economy of the 1960s and 1970s favored the ulama as a whole with a measure of economic prosperity.[70]

Economic advance was not however accompanied by a political opening. State-ulama relations passed from a period of acquiescence and accommodation in the 1950s to the confrontational 1960-63 protests to considerable repression by the 1970s. The royalist ayatullah Bihbihani and the quietist supreme religious authority Burujirdi provided important support for the shah's reassertion of control in the 1953-58 period by condoning unpopular measures on the foreign policy level such as the 1954 oil deal and the 1955 Baghdad Pact alliance in exchange for government support of religious educational institutions and tacit acquiescence in anti-Baha'i campaigns in 1955. Even Burujirdi and Bihbihani however were opposed to land reform in 1959-60, and Burujirdi's death in 1961 and the events culminating in the 1963 uprising projected a new religious leadership onto the national scene ranging from the liberal constitutionalist Ayatullah Kazim Shari'atmadari to the implacable oppositionist Ayatullah Khumaini. A new generation of ulama emerged in the 1970s with fewer ties to the old elites—land reform had cut some links between high ulama and the landed class, while the seminary system modernized itself under the impact of the challenge from state educational institutions. The state struck at ulama power directly and indirectly, promoting the shah as a progressive spiritual leader and denouncing the ulama as medieval reactionaries, scrapping the Islamic and solar Iranian calendars in favor of a monarchic calendar making it the year 2535, sending a "religious corps" into the countryside to teach "true Islam" to the peasantry, closing religious publishing houses, taking control of vaqfs, disbanding religious student organizations, and using the new Family Law to raise the legal age for marriage and give women more rights in marriage, in contravention of the Islamic Shari'a. The state also launched a frontal assault through direct repression, including arrests, exile, and torture. In 1970 the mujtahid Ayatullah Muhammad Reza Sa'idi was tortured to death. In 1975 prominent ayatullahs such as Bihishti, Muntazari, Qumi, Shirazi, Zanjani, and other lesser-rank ulama were arrested. Despite government attempts at repression it was impossible to effectively surveil and control 90,000 ulama (as opposed to only a few hundred left-wing guerrillas).[71]

To the longstanding urban poor and marginal population was added a vast new group of migrants from the countryside in the 1960s and 1970s. The tide of landless peasants pouring into the cities in search of work rose from around 30,000 a year in the 1930s and 130,000 annually from 1941 to 1956, to 250,000 a year for 1957-66 and 330,000 a year between 1967 and 1976. There were some three million migrants in the cities by the late 1970s. About one million of these found unskilled work in the construction sector (and were thus part of the working class), but 900,000 people were unemployed in 1977/78, about ten percent of the working population. Others joined the ongoing urban marginal population as peddlers, street vendors, casual laborers, porters, office tea boys, and domestic servants, or were forced to live on the fringes of marginal society as prostitutes, scavengers, drug dealers (and addicts), thieves, and beggars—Jazani provides some rough estimates suggesting that there were 10,000 professional prostitutes, 30-50,000 part-time prostitutes, 50,000 smugglers (especially of drugs), and 50,000 "professional hooligans, louts and tramps who made a living through extortion, begging, etc."[72]

Once in the city the lives of migrants for the most part paralleled the hard lot of the marginal population as a whole. A high percentage (Hemmasi found it to be 76 percent) remained unemployed. Those who found work were very poorly paid: One 1966 survey of a low-income settlement found average wages of $9 a month for the head of household; in 1969 46 percent of Tehran's employed population earned under $50 a month. Incomes rose during the oil boom, but remained at subsistence levels. Nutrition was very poor: Kazemi describes a typical diet of bread and tea for breakfast, bread and fruit for lunch in the summer and bread and cheese in the winter, and a supper of soup. An Iranian acquaintance once told me of a trip to the poor sections of south Tehran where he saw women outside a slaughterhouse using pails to gather the blood and rejected parts that were running through the gutters. It is true, as Hooglund points out, that migrants were used to living in their villages without such basic services as electricity, sewage, and piped water, and did have some access in cities to education, health, and recreation facilities. They lived, however, in brick kilns, on construction sites, in tents, shacks, or hovels, and descriptions of squatter settlements by Katouzian and Kazemi paint a grim portrait of marginals' living standards.[73] Urban marginals were not generally active in "politics" as they were too busy trying to make ends meet. Young migrants were perhaps more materialistic, worldly, and education-oriented than their parents; they also gravitated toward a more activist, politically-tinged religion. Class-based resentment toward the government, local elite, and foreigners was finding increasing expression in the 1970s: "As early as 1971 a cautious observer of Iran remarked that, on walking through the streets of the southern, poorer part of Tehran, he encountered 'more expressed hatred than I have ever seen before' from 'people who watch the cars of those people who are doing well'."[74] In 1978, on the eve of the revolution, a squatter of Virdabad noted "There is nothing they can do if we are united. As lower classes we must have solidarity. Otherwise, no one will care about our problems. After all, doesn't the Shah's family depend only on the well-to-do?"[75]

Women in general made identifiable advances in this period, as a consequence of Pahlavi modernization. As mentioned above, the 1967 family law gave them more rights in marriage and at work. The number of women receiving higher education rose from 5,000 in 1966 to 74,000 in 1977, with the proportion of women teachers in kindergartens at almost 100 percent, in elementary schools 54 percent and in secondary schools 30 percent. Politically, representation was limited, as independent groups were merged into Princess Ashraf's Iranian Women's Organization. In 1974 there were three women in the cabinet, four in the senate and seventeen in the majlis.[76] In the labor force participation increased as a function of new opportunities and economic necessity. In 1972, 1.4 million women were officially working in Iran—64 percent of them in industry, 22 percent in services, and 11 percent in agriculture. This was 13 percent of all women over age twelve (compared with 68 percent of all men of this age). Indeed many more women than this were actually working in the countryside: 70 percent of all cloth weavers and 72 percent of carpet-weavers were women. For urban women, the Third World average in the early 1970s was about 25 percent in the work force, while for the Middle East it was five percent (3.1 percent in Egypt, two percent in Algeria, less than one percent in Saudi Arabia). In Tehran it was 11 percent in 1971 and rising. Professional women numbered 200,000 in 1971 (45 percent in teaching, 44 percent in clerical and administrative work, 11 percent in the medical field). But the vast majority were in industry and service occupations where they received the lowest wages and had difficult working conditions. In factories there was widespread sexual abuse by foremen; so much so "that the girls deny their working in the factories, since they would be called 'factory girls'."[77] Patriarchy and sexism continued to pervade Iranian society, setting real limits on amelioration of the condition of women as a whole.

Modes of Production and Dependent Development

This whole section on economic development is conceptualized in modes of production terms in Diagram 8.1 (which should be compared with Diagram 6.2 in chapter six on the Iranian social formation in 1941). One of the most striking changes over three decades is the qualitative transformation of the peasant crop-sharing mode of production into a capitalist agricultural sector with the attendant transformation of peasant sharecroppers into small-holding peasants, and landlords into capitalists and agribusiness corporations with state and multinational participation. Secondly, the quantitative shifts among the modes of production are quite dramatic in terms of the proportion of the population involved in each (and behind that, their contribution to GNP). Here we register the decline of the pastoral nomadic mode from 7 to 4 percent and of settled agriculture from 69.5 to just 28.2 percent, with the petty-commodity sector rising somewhat from 13.5 to 19.2 percent and the urban capitalist sector growing enormously from 10 to 48.6 percent.[78] The extent to which the capitalist mode of production had become preponderant by 1977 is seen by the total of 76.8 percent in the agricultural and urban capitalist sectors, versus 23.2 percent in the older pastoral nomadic and petty-commodity modes. The latter figure, primarily representing bazaar-based merchants, artisans, and ulama is not insignificant, however, especially as a proportion of the urban population, the geographical site where most Iranian social movements have occurred.

Finally, analysis of the economy has provided a basis for evaluating the dependent nature of this capitalist development process. We have seen Iran's great dependence on oil revenues to run the state and economy, the key role played by multinationals in both industry and agriculture, the negative aspects of this kind of industrialization (measured by income inequality, inflation, deteriorating living standards, and the like), and its impact on numerous classes, including workers, peasants, tribespeople, merchants, artisans, ulama, and urban marginals. Each of these classes developed grievances against the state, local dominant classes, and foreign

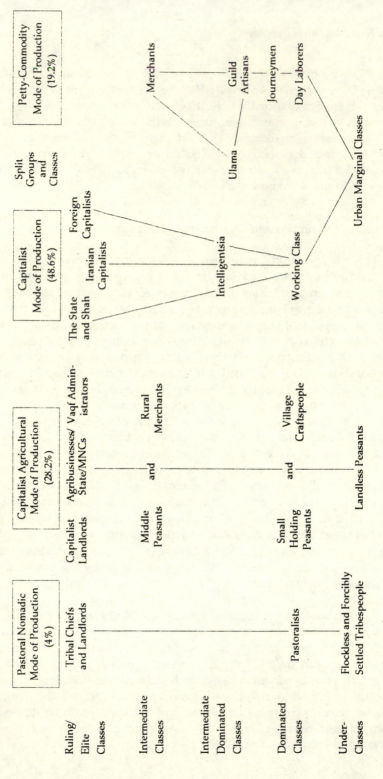

DIAGRAM 8.1 The Iranian Social Formation in 1977

capital in Iran. Our portrait of the new situation of dependency will be completed by an examination of Iran's foreign relations and economic and political place in the world during this period.

Iran in the World-System: Toward the Semiperiphery?

Understanding Iran's place in the world-system of the 1960s and 1970s requires consideration of its economic and political relations with the new core power of the United States, the other advanced industrial nations of Europe and Japan, the socialist countries and especially the Soviet Union, and the Third World, particularly its Middle Eastern and Asian neighbors. Theoretically the most interesting issue is the extent to which Iran was moving from the periphery of the world-economy into what Wallerstein calls the semiperiphery, that middle echelon of states both in terms of economic rewards and political power in the world-system, a group which is simultaneously exploited vis-à-vis the core while itself exploiting the periphery.[79] Secondly, the examination of these relationships contributes to a fuller explanation of the concept of dependency, which after all implies dependency *on* another country or countries. To shed light on these issues, then, we will study both patterns of foreign trade and power-relationships between Iran and the rest of the world.

The key issues in terms of foreign trade are the balance of trade, the nature of imports and exports, and the terms of trade. Table 8.3 reveals the enormous expansion in imports and exports made possible by Iran's oil production, and the corresponding stagnation of non-oil exports between 1953 and 1978. The balance of trade was always negative without oil and only sometimes positive even with it, a serious indication of Iran's absolute dependence on oil income after the promising oil-less experiment of the Mussadiq era was rolled back. When the balance of trade was in deficit, even with oil, this meant reliance on foreign loans, for a total of $2.6 billion between 1963 and 1972.[80] This reliance on oil points to the problematic composition of Iran's export trade. Oil and gas were already 77 percent of all exports by value in 1963, but this rose to 85 percent in 1972 and an incredible 98 percent in 1978 as oil prices rose. Equally discouraging was the performance of manufactured products in the small non-oil export sector. In 1977/78, modern industry accounted for only 21 percent of Iran's non-oil exports ($111 million of $523 million), while agriculture provided $264 million in exports (51 percent) and traditional industry $148 million (28 percent), with carpets alone at $115 million surpassing all modern manufactures.[81] Iran's import-substitution strategy had led to industrial production

TABLE 8.3 Iran's Foreign Trade, 1953-1978
(in millions of dollars)

Year	Imports	Exports (without oil)	Exports (with oil)	Balance (without oil)	Balance (with oil)
1953	66.1	96.7	99.8	+30.6	+33.7
1958	605.9	103.8	402.6	-502.1	-203.3
1963	518.6	127.0	1,015.2	-391.6	+496.6
1968	1,408.9	214.8	2,003.7	-1,194.1	+594.8
1972	3,161.0	440.0	3,040.0	-2,721.0	-121.0
1978	18,400.0	520.0	24,020.0	-17,880.0	+5,620.0

Sources: Bharier, *Economic Development in Iran,* 104-6 table 44; Katouzian, *The Political Economy of Modern Iran,* 325 table 16.2. Exchange rate used: $1 = 87.1 rials (1953), 76.5 rials (1958), 75.75 rials (1963, 1968).

for the domestic market, but had carved out no share of the more competitive world market for itself.

The nature of imports further accentuates the dependent trend of Iran's development. Of $18.4 billion in total imports in 1977/78, $6.1 billion (33 percent) were on machinery and vehicles, $5.3 billion (29 percent) on steel, chemicals, paper, fibres, and so forth, $4.3 billion (24 percent) was "classified" (i.e. mainly on military hardware), and $2.2 billion (12 percent) was on food. If one deducts the import of arms, parts to assemble, and food from total exports, there is about $2.6 billion left over that *might* ideally have been used for real development purposes—only about ten percent of oil income and less than 15 percent of all imports. This was in fact mostly squandered on consumption and corruption. While little data on the terms of trade is available, what is certain is that reliance on oil exports was inherently unstable, as either the West would pass the costs of its own inflation back to Iran or prices for oil would decline, hampering Iran's ability to import. This profile of foreign trade is certainly that of a dependent country.[82]

Iran's foreign trade was oriented largely toward the advanced industrial nations, especially the United States, West Germany, and Japan (in this sense, a member of "the West"), as Table 8.4, on the sources of Iran's imports, suggests. When markets for non-oil exports are considered, the Soviet Union joins this group as an important trading partner. Despite the seeming parity of West Germany, Japan, and the United States as leading commercial

TABLE 8.4 Leading Importers to Iran, 1959-1977
(in millions of dollars, with percent in parentheses)

Country	1959	1965	1970	1974	1977
West Germany	124.3	180.5	347.9	1,185.0	2,747.0
	(22.8)	(20.1)	(20.8)	(17.0)	(19.5)
United States	94.6	170.4	217.4	1,321.5	2,205.0
	(17.4)	(19.0)	(13.0)	(20.0)	(15.6)
Japan	54.7	71.5	201.2	999.4	2,215.0
	(10.1)	(7.9)	(12.0)	(15.1)	(15.7)
Great Britain	78.2	114.7	162.7	529.5	n.a.
	(14.4)	(12.8)	(9.7)	(8.0)	
France	21.2	45.1	77.5	242.1	n.a.
	(3.9)	(5.0)	(4.6)	(3.7)	
Italy	19.5	41.4	67.9	199.4	n.a.
	(3.6)	(4.6)	(4.0)	(3.0)	
Others	151.7	274.8	572.0	2,136.8	6,933.0
	(27.8)	(30.6)	(34.1)	(32.3)	(49.2)
Total	544.2	898.4	1,676.6	6,613.7	14,100.0

Sources: Seyfollahi, "Development of the Dependent Bourgeoisie," 172 table 15; Katouzian, *The Political Economy of Modern Iran*, 322 table 16.1.

allies, one country enjoyed a unique relationship with Iran and the shah, whose significance we must now probe.

The United States took the lead from Great Britain as the undisputed hegemonic core power in Iran after the 1953 coup. Multiple ties—economic, political, and strategic—were established between the two countries. The American attitude was clearly stated in 1957: "Iran is important to the United States for political, economic and military reasons. It has 1200 miles of common border with the U.S.S.R., occupies a strategic location in the Middle East . . . and controls an important part of the world's proven oil reserves."[83] For his part, the shah had stressed as far back as 1954: "the potentialities of friendly and close relations between the people of Iran and the United States are immense. . . . Iran has a great deal in common, in convictions, with the Western world regarding freedom and democracy. The way of life of the Western world fits in with our scheme of Islamic values."[84] In 1976 Harold Saunders, assistant secretary of state for Near Eastern and South Asian affairs, affirmed that American interests in Iran had been constant for a generation because of "Iran's importance to the security of the Gulf region, the future of the Middle East and the production of oil."[85]

A greater American economic interest in Iran was already signalled by Eisenhower in 1953: "of course, it will not be so easy for the Iranian economy to be restored, even if her refineries again begin to operate. . . . However, this is a problem that we should be able to help."[86] The American oil companies' lucrative 40 percent share of the 1954 oil deal—America's major stake in Pahlavi Iran—has already been noted. In the course of the 1960s and 1970s a considerable amount of direct foreign investment by American-based multinationals was added to this, in the agribusiness ventures, in the most advanced industrial sectors, such as petrochemicals, pharmaceuticals, chemicals, and aluminum, and in the growing banking sector, where American banks played a major role. The United States overtook the British as the major foreign investor in the 1950s and held this position until the 1970s when the Japanese surpassed them. Halliday notes that "At the end of 1972 the USA had assets valued at $570 millions in Iran—a large amount, but less than it had in Israel ($600 millions), Libya ($1,145 millions) or Saudi Arabia ($2,000 millions)."[87] In 1978, some 500 American firms had $700 million invested in Iran and twelve large banks had another $2.2 billion in assets in Iran. To the oil interests and direct foreign investment should be added trade between the two countries, in which the United States was a consistent first or second to West Germany or Japan throughout this period. This may be considered a second circuit of capital, for the money paid in royalties and revenues by the West to Iran made possible the purchase of vast quantities of Western goods. There was moreover a massive arms trade in the 1970s which does not figure in the trade data and which was thoroughly dominated by the United States.

Beyond these purely economic ties lurked perhaps even greater political and strategic bonds. Richard Helms, one-time CIA director and ambassador to Iran referred to Iran as "in political terms, the center of the world."[88] Total American economic and military aid to Iran from 1953 to 1960 came to over $1 billion, a sum not surpassed by any other Third World country except Turkey. Aid between 1950 and 1970 totalled $2.3 billion, over $1.3 billion of which was military. A transparent pattern of political influence followed this aid: the first $68.4 million being announced within three weeks after the August 1953 coup, $127 million right after the 1954 oil deal, and other grants after Iran joined the pro-Western Baghdad Pact in 1955 and CENTO in 1958.[89] Though the evidence in the case of the appointment of 'Ali Amini as prime minister in 1961 is not conclusive, it certainly fits within this pattern. Amini's subsequent fall can likewise be attributed in part to the withdrawal of American support; thereafter the United States government settled into a policy of unambiguous support for the shah.[90]

This relationship can be seen in the nexus of strategic alliances entered into by the two countries. After briefly flirting with closer ties to the Soviet Union at the time of the possibly U.S.-condoned Qarani coup plot against him, the shah signed a bilateral military treaty in March 1959 committing the U.S. to take "appropriate action, including the use of armed forces" in case of communist or "communist-inspired" aggression against Iran. This cemented the military relationship going back to World War II. From 1945 to 1970 over 11,000 Iranians received military training in the United States, while American advisers were attached to Iran's police, army, and SAVAK. Tehran became the CIA's Middle Eastern headquarters in 1973, with most of the emphasis on the Soviet Union and China rather than Iranian affairs.[91] After the pullout of British forces from the Persian Gulf kingdoms in 1971, Iran emerged as the dominant military power in the Gulf area. In the midst of the American debacle in Vietnam, this fit well with the Nixon Doctrine of promoting strong regional allies to maintain a favorable economic and political atmosphere in various parts of the Third World. As a 1977 U.S. Senate report acknowledged: "if Iran is called in to intervene in the internal affairs of any Gulf state, it must be recognized in advance by the United States that this is the role for which Iran is being primed and blame cannot be assigned for Iran's carrying out an implied assignment."[92] Iran was the most prominent of a group of pro-American regional powers that included Brazil, Israel, and Indonesia. In a secret agreement of May 1972 Nixon agreed to furnish the shah with any conventional weapons he wanted, bypassing the American departments of state and defence. This blank check was, in Halliday's words, an "unparalleled" step in American relations with a Third World country.[93] It opened the floodgates of weapons sales to Iran in the 1970s, an arms bazaar fully mirroring the scope of the oil boom. Total U.S. military sales to Iran came to $17 billion for 1950-77, $16 billion of this after 1972, a sum which ate up almost 20 percent of Iran's oil revenues and on the American side accounted for over half of all U.S. arms sales to foreign countries by 1977. A bilateral agreement in mid-1976 projected $40 billion in U.S.-Iranian trade between 1976 and 1980. By 1978 there were 37,000 American military and civilian personnel in Iran, most enjoying diplomatic immunity, with military technicians drawing $9,000 a month salaries from the Iranian government. A 1977 U.S. Senate report admitted openly: "The presence of U.S. personnel and the presumed inability of Iranians to utilize all the recent arms purchases could give the U.S. leverage over any Iranian intention that runs counter to U.S. interest."[94] Thus, despite Iran's seemingly independent foreign policy and oil diplomacy, by the eve of the revolution the shah had become increasingly dependent on the United States in a web of economic, military, political, and strategic relations.

No other country came anywhere near the kind of influence exercised by the United States on Iran. Among the European countries Great Britain gradually fell behind West Germany as a leading trade partner, to the position of fourth overall. The Anglo-Iranian Oil Company was well compensated with 25 million pounds sterling and the new British Petroleum had a healthy 40 percent share in the post-1954 consortium, Britain's largest stake in Iran. In the 1970s Britain was a major arms seller, particularly of tanks (accounting for most of the $971 million in exports to Iran in 1977-78), and was active in the auto assembly industry, as well as banking. But all of this was a far cry from Britain's traditional position as a major power in Iran and reflected the United Kingdom's general decline in the world-economy after World War II.[95] By the same token West Germany's economic recovery and eventual "miracle" in the 1960s catapulted it into a strong economic position in Iran, as leading importer from 1959 to 1970 and again in 1977. German investments in Iran fell off in the 1970s (well behind Japan and the United States), but were profitably placed in pharmaceuticals, steel, and agricultural machinery. In 1974 the shah bought a 25 percent share in the Krupp steel industry, Katouzian calling this investment in a declining sector of Western industry "one of His Majesty's greatest follies in the field of foreign investment."[96] The other European countries collectively accounted for about 20 percent of Iran's imports, led by France and Italy, with 3-5 percent each.

Dwarfing all the European countries except West Germany, and generally ranking second in terms of economic relations with Iran to the United States, was the newest core power in the world-economy, Japan. Japan passed Britain by 1970 and the United States by 1977 (excluding arms sales) as a supplier of imports to Iran, especially of electrical equipment. Involved in petrochemicals, electrical appliances, insurance, and the financial markets, Japan was the largest investor in Iran, with 40 percent of the total investments made in 1975/76. This economic power, while significant, fit within the broad pattern of Iran's dependence on the advanced industrial economies, thus not really posing a challenge to American hegemony in Iran.[97]

The socialist and third worlds together loomed relatively insignificant economically for Iran's position in the world-system, though political relations were naturally important both in the case of the Soviet Union, and in that of Iran's neighbors in the Gulf, including Iraq. These countries played no role in Iran's dependent development, but are of some relevance to Iran's claims of acting as a regional military power. As Halliday notes, Iran's overall relations with the Soviet Union have been "relatively tranquil" since 1953, except for the 1959-62 period. The return of Iran's gold reserves in 1954 patched things up as did a 1956 visit to Moscow by the shah. Relations were severely strained by Iran's 1959 bilateral defense treaty with the United

States but relaxed again in 1962-63 when the shah pledged not to allow American missiles to be based in Iran (it was the time of the Cuban missile crisis). Thereafter relations improved and a de facto bargain was struck: The USSR accepted the shah's rule and American hegemony in Iran, while receiving a number of economic agreements of its own and a stable monarchy on its borders. The shah meanwhile used the relationship to neutralize the pro-Soviet Tudeh Party and for certain economic benefits. The relationship therefore was based on mutual trade and political stability. The old pattern of being an important market for Iranian raw materials continued based on the convenience of proximity, but the USSR could not really compete with the United States, Japan, and Europe in world trade. There was also a major joint investment in a steel mill for Iran and a pipeline to transport natural gas to the Soviet Union. This brought 1,500 Soviet technicians to Iran, without a great economic benefit as Iran spent $700 million to construct the pipeline while the steel plant earned only $4 million in 1969-70 instead of a projected $600 million in exports.[98] Other socialist countries also made various economic agreements with the shah's Iran.

It was in the Middle East that the shah sought to make good Iran's claims as a new regional power, politically aggressive and militarily interventionist. The purpose of this policy was to bolster his and the army's image and to weaken any state or movement that could undermine the regime. Military interventions thus included the Yemeni civil war (1962-70), the seizure of three Gulf islands from the newly formed United Arab Emirates in November 1971, the deployment of several thousand troops to aid Sultan Qabus of Oman against rebels in the Dhofar province from December 1973 to late 1976, assistance to Pakistan in 1973 to deal with Baluchi separatists, and support for Iraqi Kurds between 1972 and 1975. In Halliday's 1978 judgment:

> No third-world state has a record of intervention outside its frontiers comparable to Iran's in the period since the mid-1960s. South Korea, Indonesia, Zaire, Israel, Brazil and Saudi Arabia have all intervened, directly or indirectly, in support of counter-revolutionary forces beyond their frontiers, but none have done so on the scale of Iran.[99]

Relations with Iraq were frequently poor due to the Kurdish minority on both sides of the border, occasional involvement in coup plots by both countries, and a border dispute in Khuzistan over the Shatt al-Arab waterway which almost led to war in 1968 (and eventually did in 1980). In March 1975 Iran's military buildup forced an advantageous resolution of the border dispute in exchange for stopping its assistance to Iraq's Kurds.[100] In the mid-1970s Iran tried to improve relations with many of the region's nations from Egypt to India by providing money for joint capital investment projects. Iran's relations with the other American-supported Middle Eastern power, Israel, were even closer, if kept somewhat out of the public eye. Iran had de facto recognized Israel's existence in 1950; the Israelis helped train SAVAK later in the decade. Thereafter, despite the shah's pro-Arab OPEC price maneuvers in 1967 and 1973 the relationship was strengthened, based on large numbers of military officers trained in Israel, arms trade both ways, the common enemy in Iraq, major oil supplies (with Iran financing Israel's pipeline to the Red Sea after 1967 and guaranteeing Israel's oil needs after 1975 as part of the secret clauses of the Sinai disengagement treaty), and growing Israeli exports to Iran (from $22 million in 1970 to $63 million in 1974).[101] The closeness of Iran and Israel well served conservative American policy interests in the Middle East. This pattern of relationships both reinforces the hypothesis of Iran's predominant dependence on the West and buttresses somewhat its claims of constituting a regional sub-power vis-à-vis such neighbors.

Comparisons, Conclusions

We may now bring this chapter to a close by addressing the questions: Was Iran's dependent development of a type and magnitude to pull it out of the periphery into the semiperiphery? How does its experience compare with such countries as Brazil, Mexico, Egypt, Turkey, or India? As we have seen, Iran's GNP and industrial growth rates were among the highest in the Third World. Given the lack of manufactured exports and dependence on oil revenues for its growth, however, these proved rather deceptive indices of development. Like other oil producers—Iraq, Algeria, Venezuela, and Nigeria—Iran suffered from agricultural shortfalls and massive bureaucratic corruption. Iraq and Algeria arguably channelled their wealth into public projects and cooptation of new social classes more astutely than Iran and Nigeria.[102] While pulling ahead of less populous regional competitors and neighbors such as Iraq, Afghanistan, and the Gulf kingdoms, Iran reached a level roughly comparable with such Middle Eastern industrializers as Egypt, Turkey, and Pakistan in many respects.[103] A Hudson Institute report of 1975 concluded however that even if Iran met its own high predicted growth rates, by 1985 "it would have an economy not much more developed than India's and equal to or just behind Mexico's."[104]

Far from becoming a "new Japan" as the shah had boasted, Iran on the eve of the 1980s was not, it would seem, even a solid member of the semiperiphery. Compared with more clear-cut contenders for this rank such as Brazil, South Korea, and Taiwan, Iran was far less industrialized and lacked their financial and monopoly capital sectors, relying instead on its state and oil revenues, and letting both agriculture and industry, the only real long-term guarantees of development, lag far behind. For a brief period in the 1970s Iran had seemed to be moving closer to this group in the semiperiphery but it was an uncertain, *dependent* progress. The failure of this movement would be sealed by a decisive event in world history—the Iranian revolution.

Notes

1. See Abrahamian, *Iran Between Two Revolutions*, 427ff.; Ashraf, "Iran," ix; Katouzian, *The Political Economy*; Saikal, *Rise and Fall*; Nikki Keddie, "The Midas Touch: Black Gold, Economics and Politics in Iran Today," pp. 243-266 in *Iranian Studies*, volume X, number 4 (Autumn 1977); Patrick Clawson, "Capital Accumulation in Iran," pp. 143-171 in Petter Nore and Terisa Turner, editors, *Oil and Class Struggle* (London: Zed, 1980); and Bayat, *Workers and Revolution in Iran*, 19, 53. The "internationalization of capital" approach, as used by Clawson to refer to the outward expansion of capitalism to all areas of the world appears no different from world-system theory to me, while Bayat's and others' use of the term "uneven development" bears a striking resemblance to modes of production analysis, or in some cases, to dependent development. Neither adds precision to the perspectives we are already working with (though as suggested, neither is incompatible with them).

2. See the theoretical disclaimers of Keddie, *Roots of Revolution*, 143-44; Saikal, *Rise and Fall*, 5-6; and M. H. Pesaran, "The System of Dependent Capitalism in Pre- and Post-Revolutionary Iran," pp. 501-522 in *International Journal of Middle East Studies*, volume 14, number 4 (November 1982), 504. I think that Keddie, a historian, and Pesaran, an economist, are reacting to the more one-sided versions of dependency advanced in the early works of André Gunder Frank and would be less uncomfortable with the more sociologically sophisticated version of Cardoso and Faletto that gives due emphasis to both internal aspects of social structure and historical factors generally. Reza Motameni, "An Inquiry Into Iran's Underdevelopment: A Quarter Century of Dependent Development," Ph.D. dissertation, Department of Government, Claremont Graduate School (1981), is simplistic in hypothesizing that "A high level of economic dependency is likely to coincide with low rates of economic growth" (96), but does offer an econometric test of dependence in Iran that is of some interest. Zavareei, "Dependent Capitalist Development in Iran," is not theoretically grounded or historically informed, but provides much useful insight into the period covered in this chapter. As noted in chapter one, Bizhan Jazani, *Capitalism and Revolution* (esp. 73-124), was a pioneer in applying a model of dependent capitalism to Iran, though not in the historical or theoretical manner adopted in the present work.

3. Pesaran, "The System of Dependent Capitalism," 505. A third option — cooptation — was pursued to a slight degree by the shah as well, particularly at the elite level.

4. On the personages and events mentioned in this paragraph, see *New York Times*, August 20, 1953; Ivanov, *Tarikh-i Nuvin-i Iran*, 178; Abrahamian, *Iran Between Two Revolutions*, 421; Katouzian, *The Political Economy*, 195-96, 199; and Dr. 'Ali Amini, in an interview recorded by Habib Ladjevardi, December 6, 1981, Paris, English translation of Persian original, Iranian Oral History Collection, Harvard University, tape 6. Mark Gasiorowski has presented a paper on the Qarani affair at the 1991 meeting of the Middle East Studies Association.

5. A few sources on the 1960-63 period include Akhavi, *Religion and Politics*, 93-111; Keddie, *Roots of Revolution*, 149-59; Abrahamian, *Iran Between Two Revolutions*, 421-26; and Katouzian, *The Political Economy*, 208-32.

6. Ivanov, *Tarikh-i Nuvin-i Iran*, 184. This paragraph draws on Saikal, *Rise and Fall*, 48-51, 97ff.; Günter Barthel, "The Struggle for the Re-establishment of National Rights Over Iranian Oil," pp. 50-71 in Günter Barthel, editor, *Iran: From Monarchy to Republic*, special issue number 12 of *Asia, Africa, Latin America* (East Berlin: Akademie-Verlag, 1983), 66 table 1, 67 table 2; Esmail Baku, "Oil Revenue and Socio-Economic Development in Iran, 1963-78," Ph.D. dissertation, Department of Sociology, University of Wisconsin-Madison (1980), 80-81; and "The Iran-Consortium Agreement" (September 19-20, 1954), pp. 348-383 in Hurewitz, *Diplomacy*, II.

7. Saikal, *Rise and Fall*, 50-51, 104-31; Halliday, *Iran*, 143 table 10; Graham, *Iran*, 15-16, 36-38; Barthel, "The Struggle for the Re-establishment of National Rights," 71 table 6; Clawson, "Capital Accumulation," 143; Hans-Georg Müller, "Remarks on the Role of the State Capital Sector and National Private Capital in the Evolutionary Process of Capitalism in Iran Up to the End of the 1970s," pp. 72-87 in Barthel, editor, *Iran: From Monarchy to Republic*, 73 table; M. H. Pesaran (under the pseudonym of Thomas Walton), "Economic Development and Revolutionary Upheavals in Iran," pp. 271-292 in *Cambridge Journal of Economics*, volume 4, number 3 (September 1980), 279. A wealth of valuable data on oil and the economy is found in Massoud Karshenas, *Oil, State and Industrialization in Iran* (Cambridge: Cambridge University Press, 1990), which reached me too late to be used in this study.

8. On court wealth and corruption, see Graham, *Iran*, 152-63; Abrahamian, *Iran Between Two Revolutions*, 437-38; Ervand Abrahamian, "Structural Causes of the Iranian Revolution," pp. 21-26 in *MERIP Reports*, number 87 (May 1980), 23; Reza Baraheni, *The Crowned Cannibals: Writings on Repression in Iran* (New York: Vintage Books, 1977), 43 note 46; Sir Peter Ramsbotham, in an interview recorded by Habib Ladjevardi, October 15, 1985, London, Iranian Oral History Collection, Harvard University, tape 1: 42, 45; Ali Amini interview, tape 6: 18; Ahmad Ghoreishi, in an interview recorded by Habib Ladjevardi, January 31, 1982, Moraga, California, English translation of Persian original, Iranian Oral History Collection, tape 1: 29, 35.

9. See Abrahamian, *Iran Between Two Revolutions*, 435-36; Graham, *Iran*, 163, 168-83; Halliday, *Iran*, 90-96; and Farhad Kazemi, "The Military and Politics in Iran: The Uneasy Symbiosis," pp. 217-240 in Elie Kedourie and Sylvia G. Haim, *Towards a Modern Iran: Studies in Thought, Politics and Society* (London: Cass, 1980).

10. Humphrey is quoted by Halliday, *Iran*, 75. See also ibid., 52, 68-71, 92, and Abrahamian, *Iran Between Two Revolutions*, 436.

11. Amnesty International, *Annual Report 1974-75* (London: AI Publications, 1975), 8. This report also noted: "The Shah of Iran retains his benevolent image despite the highest rate of death penalties in the world, no valid system of civilian courts and a history of torture which is beyond belief." Chile in this period surely surpassed Iran in human rights violations.

12. The quote is from Zavareei, "Dependent Capitalist Development," 152. This paragraph draws on Paul Balta and Claudine Rulleau, *L'Iran insurgé* (Paris: Sindbad, 1979), who cite Eric Rouleau, "Iran: The Myth and the Reality: Part 1," in *The Guardian*, October 24, 1976; Graham, *Iran*, 140-49; Halliday, *Iran*, 87-88; and Baraheni, *The Crowned Cannibals*, 131-218, with references to articles by Eric Rouleau in *Le Monde*, October 5, 1976 and Philip Jacobson in the *London Sunday Times*, January 19, 1975.

13. Graham, *Iran*, 133-38; Amini interview, tape 6: 1-4; Ghoreishi interview, tape 2: 2-5, 10, 23-28; Ramsbotham interview, tape 2: 18-19; Abolhassan Ebtehaj, in an interview recorded by Habib Ladjevardi, December 1, 1981, Cannes, France, English translation of Persian original, Iranian Oral History Collection, Harvard University, tape 10: 17; Katouzian, *The Political Economy*, 197, 234-35, 241.

14. Abrahamian, *Iran Between Two Revolutions*, 438. Overall, the state employed about 10-12 percent of the work force.

15. On the early party system, see Abrahamian, *Iran Between Two Revolutions*, 419-21, 440; Katouzian, *The Political Economy*, 192-93, 197; Ashraf, "Iran," 172; and Saikal, *Rise and Fall*, 63, 90-91.

16. Muhammad Reza Pahlavi, *Mission for My Country* (New York: McGraw-Hill Book Company, Inc., 1961), 173. Keddie has pointed out that after the Rastakhiz Party was declared the shah recalled his autobiography and reissued it without the passages on one-party regimes as communist or fascist: *Roots of Revolution*, 179.

17. Ghoreishi interview, tape 2: 3. On the Rastakhiz generally, see Katouzian, *The Political Economy*, 242; Graham, *Iran*, 134-35; Abrahamian, *Iran Between Two Revolutions*, 440-42, 445; Saikal, *Rise and Fall*, 190; and Sepehr Zabih, *Iran's Revolutionary Upheaval: An Interpretive Essay* (San Francisco: Alchemy Books, 1979), 6-13.

18. From "The Philosophy of Iran's Revolution," printed in *Kayhan International*, November 11, 1976, and quoted by Graham, *Iran*, 59. Cf. the ironic formulation from a 1975 Ministry of Information decree: "this is a revolution that should always be ahead of the events of the future so that no unexpected event and no social or economic change may catch us unawares": quoted in Hossein Bashiriyeh, *The State and Revolution in Iran 1962-1982* (London and Canberra: Croom Helm, 1984), 91.

19. On population see Halliday, *Iran*, 10; Bharier, *Economic Development in Iran*, 25, 26 table 1, 27 table 2, 28; and Saikal, *Rise and Fall*, 184.

20. For GNP and aggregate income data, see Abrahamian, "Structural Causes," 22; Pesaran, "The System of Dependent Capitalism," 504; Pesaran, "Economic Development," 279 table 3; Issawi, "The Iranian Economy 1925-1975," 162-63; and Ahmad Jabbari, "Economic Factors in Iran's Revolution: Poverty, Inequality, and Inflation," pp. 163-214 in Ahmad Jabbari and Robert Olson, editors, *Iran: Essays on a Revolution in the Making* (Lexington, Kentucky: Mazda Publishers, 1981), 208 Appendix A.

21. Hooglund, "The Effects of the Land Reform," 78-112; Hooglund, *Land and Revolution*, 43-69; Abrahamian, *Iran Between Two Revolutions*, 422-23; Saikal, *Rise and Fall*, 80-82; Katouzian, *The Political Economy*, 225.

22. Hooglund, *Land and Revolution*, xvi, 78, 115. See also ibid., xv, and Eric J. Hooglund, "Rural Participation in the Revolution," pp. 3-6 in *MERIP Reports*, number 87 (May 1980), 3.

23. Hooglund, "The Effects of the Land Reform," 120-23, 188-9, and *Land and Revolution*, 78-83; Baku, "Oil Revenue," 153; Ashraf, "Iran," 182-83. Hooglund quotes at length one absentee agronomist trained in West Germany, who said of the peasants: "They just want to produce enough to stay alive and don't care about improving their lot at all. Why, if all the land had been given to them they wouldn't know what to do.... The peasants are lazy and stupid and it will take one hundred years for them to learn how to farm properly": "The Effects of the Land Reform," 123-24.

24. Hooglund, "The Effects of the Land Reform," 131 table 3, 135 table 4, 137 table 5, 152-54, 193-201, and *Land and Revolution*, 88-89, 124ff.; Eric J. Hooglund, "The Khwushnishin Population of Iran," pp. 229-245 in *Iranian Studies*, volume 6 (Autumn 1973), 233.

25. Hooglund, *Land and Revolution*, 90-97; Abrahamian, *Iran Between Two Revolutions*, 429-30; Katouzian, *The Political Economy*, 260; Halliday, *Iran*, 188.

26. For income data, see Halliday, *Iran*, 132 table 9, 167; Farhad Kazemi, *Poverty and Revolution in Iran. The Migrant Poor, Urban Marginality and Politics* (New York and London: New York University Press, 1980), 42; and Hooglund, "The Effects of the Land Reform," 129-37, 216. On other indices of living standards, see Katouzian, *The Political Economy*, 270-72; Halliday, *Iran*, 120; and Abrahamian, *Iran Between Two Revolutions*, 447.

27. Ann K. S. Lambton, *The Persian Land Reform 1962-1966* (Oxford: Clarendon Press, 1969), 145.

28. A peasant of the Khalkhal district, quoted in Hooglund, *Land and Revolution*, 54.

29. A Kurdish peasant of Kuh-i Sanjabi, in a 1968 interview, quoted in Hooglund, *Land and Revolution*, 137.

30. A Kurdish peasant of the Mahabad area, in a 1968 interview, quoted in Hooglund, "The Effects of the Land Reform," 124-25.

31. On the lack of a plan, see Hooglund, *Land and Revolution*, 112. On the budget and inflated statistics, see Halliday, *Iran*, 129, 157. Growth estimates are found in Graham, *Iran*, 43; Keddie, *Roots of Revolution*, 167; Motameni, "An Inquiry," 155 table 13; Katouzian, *The Political Economy*, 256, 304; Seyfollah Seyfollahi, "Development of the Dependent Bourgeoisie in Iran, 1962-1978," Ph.D. dissertation, Department of Sociology, Michigan State University (1982), 256 table 34; Baku, "Oil Revenue," 141 table 21; and Pesaran, "The System of Dependent Capitalism," 505. Share of GDP is discussed by Bharier, *Economic Development in Iran*, 59-60, and Katouzian, *The Political Economy*, 257 table 13.1. Data on production of specific crops is found in Bharier, *Economic Development in Iran*, 134 table 1; Ivanov, *Tarikh-i Nuvin-i Iran*, 201; Issawi, "The Iranian Economy 1925-1975," 149 table 4.8; and Baku, "Oil Revenue," 143 table 22.

32. Graham, *Iran*, 43; Halliday, *Iran*, 128; Seyfollahi, "Development of the Dependent Bourgeoisie," 195; Behzad Yaghmaian, "Economic Development, Land Reform and Imports Substitution: The Case of Iran," Ph.D. dissertation, Department of Economics, Fordham University (1985), 85 table IV.1, 86 table IV.2; Pesaran, "Economic Development," 281 note; Katouzian, *The Political Economy*, 305; Parviz Asheghian, "American Joint Venture Manufacturing Firms in Iran: Investment Determinants and Comparative Performance," Ph.D. dissertation, Department of Economics, Georgia State University (1980), 59 table 13.

33. On agribusinesses and farm corporations, see Graham, *Iran*, 117-18; Hooglund, *Land and Revolution*, 84-87; Keddie, *Roots of Revolution*, 165-66; Kazemi, *Poverty and Revolution*, 39 tables 3.1 and 3.2; and Katouzian, *The Political Economy*, 309-11.

34. Graham, *Iran*, 117; Hooglund, *Land and Revolution*, 113-14; Edmund Burke, III and Paul Lubeck, "Explaining Social Movements in Two Oil-Exporting States: Divergent Outcomes in Nigeria and Iran," pp. 643-665 in *Comparative Studies in Society and History*, volume 29, number 4 (October 1987), 659 note.

35. Jazani, *Capitalism and Revolution*, 67, 98; Assef Bayat, *Workers and Revolution in Iran: A Third World Experience of Workers' Control* (London and New Jersey: Zed Books, Ltd., 1987), 33; Halliday, *Iran*, 194.

36. For 1900, the 1940s, 1956 and 1966 figures, Bharier, *Economic Development in Iran*, 31-32; for 1976, Hooglund, *Land and Revolution*, 4, 169 note 44. Lois Beck enumerates some 7,455,000 tribal people in the 1970s, but many, indeed most of these, were settled agriculturalists, rather than pastoralists: Lois Beck, "Revolutionary Iran and Its Tribal Peoples," pp. 14-20 in *MERIP (Middle East Research and Information Project) Reports*, number 87 (May, 1980), 16.

37. Pakdaman's remarks are cited in Katouzian, *The Political Economy*, 306. This assessment is clearly written in ignorance of the history of Native Americans, though at the limit the repressions may be somewhat comparable.

38. Abrahamian, *Iran Between Two Revolutions*, 531. This paragraph draws on Garthwaite, *Khans and shahs*, 140-41; Beck, "Economic Transformations," 118; Keddie, *Roots of Revolution*, 167-68; Beck, "Revolutionary Iran and Its Tribal Peoples," 15; and Katouzian, *The Political Economy*, 272.

39. Bharier, *Economic Development in Iran*, 131, 133, 135 table 2, 271-72; Baku, "Oil Revenue," 143 table 22, 145.

40. Katouzian, *The Political Economy*, 277; Halliday, *Iran*, 157.

41. Issawi, "The Iranian Economy 1925-1975," 164; Pesaran, "The System of Dependent Capitalism," 507-10; Yaghmaian, "Economic Development," 147-61.

42. Halliday, *Iran*, 138, 148, 161-62; Saikal, *Rise and Fall*, 184; Pesaran, "Economic Development," 279, 280 table 4; Katouzian, *The Political Economy*, 257 table 13.1.

43. Abrahamian, "Structural Causes," 22; Halliday, *Iran*, 148, 159; Bayat, *Workers and Revolution*, 26 table 3.3; Fred Halliday, "The Iranian Revolution: Uneven Development and Religious Populism," pp. 187-207 in *Journal of International Affairs*, volume 36, number 2 (Fall/Winter 1982-83), 194; Keddie, "The Midas Touch," 249-50; Baku, "Oil Revenue," 138 table 20.

44. Data on these industries is found in Katouzian, *The Political Economy*, 281 table 14.2, table 14.3; Abrahamian, *Iran Between Two Revolutions*, 430-31; Issawi, "The Iranian Economy 1925-1975," 151 table 4.9; Graham, *Iran*, 119-22; and Hushang Moghtader, "The Impact of Increased Oil Revenues on Iran's Economic Development," pp. 241-262 in Kedourie and Haim, editors, *Towards a Modern Iran*, 248 table 7.

45. Katouzian, *The Political Economy*, 279; Halliday, *Iran*, 147, 166; Pesaran, "The System of Dependent Capitalism," 507-10; Graham, *Iran*, 88-94.

46. Zavareei, "Dependent Capitalist Development," 165.

47. Erhard Thiemann, "Iran Under the Shah Regime: Model of Dependent Capitalist Industrialization," pp. 88-102 in Günter Barthel, editor, *Iran: From Monarchy to Republic*, 93.

48. On the state's role, see Ivanov, *Tarikh-i Nuvin-i Iran*, 248-49; Ashraf, "Historical Obstacles," 331-32; Zavareei, "Dependent Capitalist Development," 162; Halliday, *Iran*, 147-55; and Baku, "Oil Revenue," 89 table 10.

49. On private sector capital, see Abrahamian, *Iran Between Two Revolutions*, 432; Seyfollahi, "Development of the Dependent Bourgeoisie," 232 table 25; Behrang [a collective pseudonym for a group of Iranian and French activists], *Iran: Le maillon faible* (Paris: François Maspero, 1979), 174 table; Bayat, *Workers and Revolution*, 26 table 3.3; "Iran: The New Crisis of American Hegemony," pp. 1-24 in *Monthly Review*, volume 30, number 9 (February 1979), 8, citing Behrouz Montazami and Khosrow Naraghi's article in *Le Monde Diplomatique* (December 1978); Baku, "Oil Revenue," 138 table 20, 174-75; Bashiriyeh, *The State and Revolution*, 40-41; and Halliday, *Iran*, 208, quoting the *Tehran Economist* (May 22, 1976).

50. On foreign capital in Iran, see Asheghian, "American Joint Venture Manufacturing Firms," 166-78, 198-99; Keddie, *Roots of Revolution*, 170, 172; Ashraf, "Historical Obstacles," 332; Ali-Akbar Mahdi, "The Iranian Struggle for Liberation: Socio-Historical Roots to the Islamic Revolution," pp. 1-33 in *RIPEH (The Review of Iranian Political Economy and History)*, volume IV, number 1 (Spring 1980), 15; Thiemann, "Iran Under the Shah Regime," 90, 99 note 4; Bayat, *Workers and Revolution*, 23; Katouzian, *The Political Economy*, 262 table 13.5, 293 note 5; and Zavareei, "Dependent Capitalist Development," 162-67.

51. Halliday, *Iran*, 176.

52. On the size of the working class see Abrahamian, "Structural Causes," 22, and *Iran Between Two Revolutions*, 434; Halliday, *Iran*, 176; Bayat, *Workers and Revolution*, 26; Behrang, *Iran*, 174 table; and Moghtader, "The Impact of Increased Oil Revenue," 248 table 7. On wages: "Iran: The New Crisis of American Hegemony," 9; Ivanov, *Tarikh-i Nuvin-i Iran*, 204-5; Halliday, *Iran*, 181 table 18, 189-90; Katouzian, *The Political Economy*, 283 table 14.4, 284-85; Kazemi, *Poverty and Revolution*, 55; Abrahamian, *Iran Between Two Revolutions*, 511; Bashiriyeh, *The State and Revolution*, 88; and Bayat, *Workers and Revolution*, 28 table 3.4, 29, 30 table 3.5. On origins and working conditions, see Bayat, *Workers and Revolution*, 33, 66-75.

53. Data on the service sector are found in Katouzian, *The Political Economy*, 257 table 13.1, 259 table 13.2; Jazani, *Capitalism and Revolution*, 136; Abrahamian, *Iran Between Two Revolutions*, 434; Bayat, *Workers and Revolution*, 26 table 3.3; and Moghtader, "The Impact of Increased Oil Revenue," 250 table 9.

54. This paragraph draws on Halliday, *Iran*, 16, 222-23; Abrahamian, "Structural Causes," 22, and *Iran Between Two Revolutions*, 431, 434; Katouzian, *The Political Economy*, 287; Graham, *Iran*, 90; and Bharier, *Economic Development in Iran*, 37-38 table 4.

55. Pesaran, "Economic Development," 283, quoting the International Labor Organization, *Employment and Income Policies for Iran* (Geneva: International Labour Office, 1973), appendix C, 6. See also Bashiriyeh, *The State and Revolution*, 87, 90, and M. H. Pesaran, "Income Distribution

and Its Major Determinants in Iran," pp. 267-286 in Jane W. Jacqz, editor, *Iran: Past, Present and Future* (New York: Aspen Institute for Humanistic Studies, 1976), 278 table 51.

56. Keddie, "The Midas Touch," 257. Data are in Jabbari, "Economic Factors," 191 table 9. Ashraf's survey is in his "Iran," 242-55.

57. Dadkhah, "The Inflationary Process," 389 table 1.

58. On prices, see Graham, *Iran*, 85-87; Pesaran, "Economic development," 280 table 6; "Iran: The New Crisis of American Hegemony," 9; Halliday, *Iran*, 190; and Abrahamian, *Iran Between Two Revolutions*, 447. Interestingly, *Kayhan* newspaper reported 200 percent inflation for 1973-76, versus official figures of 93.8 percent for 1973-77: Bashiriyeh, *The State and Revolution*, 90.

59. Abrahamian, *Iran Between Two Revolutions*, 446-47. This paragraph also draws on ibid., 431; Katouzian, *The Political Economy*, 271-72; Ivanov, *Tarikh-i Nuvin-i Iran*, 254, 297; Jabbari, "Economic Factors," 208 appendix A; and Halliday, *Iran*, 13, 164.

60. Halliday, *Iran*, 196. See also ibid., 202-4, and Bayat, *Workers and Revolution*, 60-61.

61. Kazemi, *Poverty and Revolution*, 97-102; Ashraf, "Iran," 345; Bayat, *Workers and Revolution*, 48-51.

62. On strikes, see Abrahamian, *Iran Between Two Revolutions*, 420, 422; Ivanov, *Tarikh-i Nuvin-i Iran*, 206-11, 300-305; Baku, "Oil Revenue," 82-84; and Halliday, *Iran*, 206-7.

63. On the intelligentsia, see Halliday, *Iran*, 224-25; Ivanov, *Tarikh-i Nuvin-i Iran*, 208, 211, 305-9; and Katouzian, *The Political Economy*, 289.

64. For data on artisans, see Katouzian, *The Political Economy*, 281, 283, 325; Hooglund, *Land and Revolution*, 118; Halliday, *Iran*, 159, 162 table 15, 182; Bayat, *Workers and Revolution*, 25, 26 table 3.3, 31 table 3.6; and Behrang, *Iran*, 174 table.

65. Abrahamian, *Iran Between Two Revolutions*, 433. This paragraph draws on Baku, "Oil Revenue," 121 table 18, 133-34; Bayat, *Workers and Revolution*, 32, 54-55; Bashiriyeh, *The State and Revolution*, 66; Behrang, *Iran*, 199; Val Moghadam, "Industrial Development, Culture and Working-Class Politics: A Case Study of Tabriz Industrial Workers in the Iranian Revolution," pp. 151-175 in *International Sociology*, volume 2, number 2 (June 1987), 154; and Jazani, *Capitalism and Revolution*, 82.

66. On merchants, see Bayat, *Workers and Revolution*, 31 table 3.6; Abrahamian, "Structural Causes," 24, and *Iran Between Two Revolutions*, 433; Moghtader, "The Impact of Increased Oil Revenue," 250 table 9; Jazani, *Capitalism and Revolution*, 136; Zavareei, "Dependent Capitalist Development," 160; Keddie, "The Midas Touch," 249; Val Moghadam, "Socialism or Anti-Imperialism? The Left and Revolution in Iran," pp. 5-28 in *New Left Review*, number 166 (November/December 1987), 13; Graham, *Iran*, 221; and Pesaran, "The System of Dependent Capitalism," 505.

67. Abrahamian, "Structural Causes," 24-25, and *Iran Between Two Revolutions*, 443; Floor, "The Guilds in Iran," 110-11, 115; Halliday, *Iran*, 220.

68. Quoted by J. Kendell, "Iran's Students and Merchants Form an Unlikely Alliance," *New York Times* (November 7, 1979), as cited by Abrahamian, *Iran Between Two Revolutions*, 444. This paragraph also draws on Davoud Ghandchi-Tehrani, "Bazaaris and Clergy: Socio-Economic Origins of Radicalism and Revolution in Iran," Ph.D. dissertation, Department of Sociology, City University of New York (1982), 103-4, 119-20, 158; and Floor, "The Guilds in Iran," 114.

69. Abrahamian, "Structural Causes," 24; Halliday, *Iran*, 19. Farhad Kazemi, on the other hand, feels the figure is more accurately about 40,000 ulama: personal communication, August 23, 1989, and Farhad Kazemi, *Politics and Culture in Iran* (Ann Arbor: University of Michigan, 1988), 28.

70. Moghadam, "Socialism or Anti-Imperialism?" 13, and Abrahamian, *Iran Between Two Revolutions*, 433. This paragraph also draws on Michael M. J. Fischer, *Iran: From Religious Dispute to Revolution* (Cambridge: Harvard University Press, 1980), 37, 96-97; Algar, 1982 lectures on "Islam in Iran"; Halliday, *Iran*, 19, 218-19; Hooglund, "The Effects of the Land Reform," 127; and

Muslim Students Following the Line of the Imam, *Asnad-i lanah-i jasusi-yi Amrika* [Documents from the Spy Nest of America] (Tehran [?]: n.d.), volume 7: 52.

71. This paragraph draws on Akhavi, *Religion and Politics*, 72-90; Abrahamian, *Iran Between Two Revolutions*, 421, 444-45; Cottam, *Nationalism in Iran*, 156; and Burke and Lubeck, "Explaining Social Movements," 661.

72. Jazani, *Capitalism and Revolution*, 142; Bayat, *Workers and Revolution*, 32, 33 table 3.7; Katouzian, *The Political Economy*, 259; Hooglund, *Land and Revolution*, 118, 168-69 note 44. U.S. embassy estimates put opium addicts at 560,000 and heroin addicts at 20-40,000 in 1977: Muslim Students, *Asnad-i lanah-i jasusi*, volume 7: 219.

73. Kazemi, *Poverty and Revolution*, 44, 48, 49 tables 4.2 and 4.3, 50-51, 54-55, 120-32; Mohammad Hemmasi, *Migration in Iran: A Quantitative Approach* (Tehran: Pahlavi University Publications, 1974), 49; Hooglund, *Land and Revolution*, 115, 169 note 46; Katouzian, *The Political Economy*, 274-75.

74. Halliday, *Iran*, 287, quoting Richard Cottam.

75. Quoted in Chirikha-yi Fada'i-yi Khalq-i Iran, *Guzarishat-i az Mubarizat-i Daliranih-yi Mardum-i Kharij az Mahdudih* [Reports from the Courageous Struggle of the Marginalized Population] (Tehran, 1357/1978), 119, as cited by Kazemi, *Poverty and Revolution*, 89. This paragraph also draws on Abrahamian, *Iran Between Two Revolutions*, 535; Hooglund, "Rural Participation in the Revolution," 5; and Kazemi, *Poverty and Revolution*, 61-93.

76. Abrahamian, *Iran Between Two Revolutions*, 434, 444-45; Keddie, *Roots of Revolution*, 179; Ivanov, *Tarikh-i Nuvin-i Iran*, 256.

77. S. Sanavandi, "Sharayit-i Iqtisadi va Ijtima'i Zanan-i Kargar dar Iran" ["The Socio-Economic Condition of Women Workers in Iran"], B.A. thesis, Tehran University (1974), 63, quoted in Bayat, *Workers and Revolution*, 56. Comparative data in this paragraph are drawn from Halliday, *Iran*, 191-92. For a scathing indictment of patriarchy and sexism in Iranian society, see Baraheni's chapter on "Masculine History," pp. 19-84 in his *The Crowned Cannibals*. Further information on women may be found in Kaveh Mirani, "Social and Economic Change in the Role of Women, 1956-78," in Guity Nashat, editor, *Women and Revolution in Iran* (Boulder: Westview, 1983).

78. These are very rough percentages based on somewhat intractable data. They are arrived at as follows: Katouzian, *The Political Economy*, 259 table 13.2, puts the total agricultural sector at 32.2 percent (3.2 million out of 9.93 million in the labor force). If there were 400,000 nomadic families (a total population of 2 million people) then the pastoral nomadic sector accounted for 4.0 percent and capitalist agriculture for 28.2 percent. This leaves 67.8 percent for the two urban modes, or about 6.8 million people. Giving the petty-commodity sector 500,000 artisans, 400,000 rural craftspeople, 550,000 merchants, 180,000 ulama, and about one-half of urban migrants (circa 300,000 families) this puts its labor force at 1.93 million (or 28.38 percent of 6.8 million) and thus 19.2 percent of the labor force, leaving 48.6 percent in the capitalist mode.

79. On the semiperiphery, see Wallerstein, *The Modern World-System I*, 102-3, 196-97, and "Rise and future demise of the world capitalist system: concepts for comparative analysis," pp. 1-36 in his *The Capitalist World Economy*, 21, 23, 27, 33-34.

80. Pesaran, "Economic Development," 284.

81. See Katouzian, *The Political Economy*, 325 table 16.3, 326, 326 tables 16.4 and 16.5; Halliday, *Iran*, 160-61, 162 table 15; Baku, "Oil Revenue," 96 table 13; and Seyfollahi, "Development of the Dependent Bourgeoisie," 271 table 45.

82. Katouzian, *The Political Economy*, 327 table 16.6; Thiemann, "Iran Under the Shah Regime," 93.

83. *1957 Mutual Security Act*, Hearings Before the Committee on Foreign Relations, House of Representatives, 786, quoted by Ashraf, "Iran," 89. A major new work on all aspects of the U.S.-Iran relationship is Mark J. Gasiorowski, *U.S. Foreign Policy and the Shah. Building a Client*

State in Iran (Ithaca and London: Cornell University Press, 1991), which appeared too late to be used in this study.

84. *New York Times*, December 15, 1954, as quoted by Saikal, *Rise and Fall*, 57-58.

85. U.S. Congress, House Committee on International Organizations: Human Rights in Iran, Hearings, August 3 and September 8, 1976, quoted by Seyfollahi, "Development of the Dependent Bourgeoisie," 180.

86. Quoted by Saikal, *Rise and Fall*, 51.

87. Halliday, *Iran*, 255-56. Data in this paragraph are also drawn from ibid., 153 table 12; Katouzian, *The Political Economy*, 293 note 5; Ivanov, *Tarikh-i Nuvin-i Iran*, 195, 243; Yaghmaian, "Economic Development," 164-5 appendix 1; Asheghian, "American Joint Venture Manufacturing Firms," 85 table 17; Bharier, *Economic Development in Iran*, 193 table 13; Seyfollahi, "Development of the Dependent Bourgeoisie," 231, 234 table 27, 270 table 43; and Mahdi, "The Iranian Struggle for Liberation," 15.

88. See Zavareei, "Dependent Capitalist Development," 174. The quote is not sourced.

89. James A. Bill, *The Eagle and the Lion. The Tragedy of American-Iranian Relations* (New Haven and London: Yale University Press, 1988), 114; Pesaran, "Economic Development," 275; Halliday, *Iran*, 91.

90. Katouzian doubts that the United States actually imposed the choice of Amini: *The Political Economy*, 214, but Abrahamian reports that "As the shah later admitted to an American correspondent, it was the Kennedy administration that had forced him to name Amini as prime minister": *Iran Between Two Revolutions*, 422-23. Hooglund, based on information supplied by William Miller, political officer at the Tehran embassy, notes that the U.S. informed the shah of its support for Amini: *Land and Revolution*, 47-48, 161 note 45. One may also consult Saikal, *Rise and Fall*, who cites *Kayhan International*, October 22 and November 5, 1977, and Halliday, *Iran*, 26.

91. Saikal, *Rise and Fall*, 56-57; Bill, *The Eagle and the Lion*, 116, 119, 402; Katouzian, *The Political Economy*, 200; Halliday, *Iran*, 83, 91-92.

92. U.S. Senate Committee on Energy and Natural Resources, *Access to Oil: The United States' Relationship with Saudi Arabia and Iran* (December 1977), 84, quoted in Zavareei, "Dependent Capitalist Development," 172.

93. On the Nixon Doctrine and Iran's role as a regional power, see Halliday, *Iran*, 93-94, 248, 339 note 1; Ramsbotham interview, tape 1: 8-9, 14-15; Zavareei, "Dependent Capitalist Development," 170; and Saikal, *Rise and Fall*, 205-7.

94. U.S. Senate Committee, *Access to Oil*, 83, quoted by Zavareei, "Dependent Capitalist Development," 171. On the military sales see Halliday, *Iran*, 95; Pesaran, "Economic Development," 285 note, 287 note; Zavareei, "Dependent Capitalist Development," 172; Saikal, *Rise and Fall*, 207; and Graham, *Iran*, 91.

95. "The Borderlands of Soviet Central Asia, II," 393; Katouzian, *The Political Economy*, 321; Yaghmaian, "Economic Development," 166 appendix 1.

96. Katouzian, *The Political Economy*, 321. See also Halliday, *Iran*, 153 table 12, 256; Asheghian, "American Joint Venture Manufacturing Firms," 85 table 17; Ivanov, *Tarikh-i Nuvin-i Iran*, 196-97; and Thiemann, "Iran Under the Shah Regime," 92.

97. Katouzian, *The Political Economy*, 321-22; Asheghian, "American Joint Venture Manufacturing Firms," 85 table 17; Halliday, *Iran*, 153 table 12, 256.

98. On Soviet-Iranian relations see Halliday, *Iran*, 258, 260-61; Jazani, *Capitalism and Revolution*, 43-44; Bill, *The Eagle and the Lion*, 119; Katouzian, *The Political Economy*, 200, 278, 293 note 2, 319-20; Bharier, *Economic Development in Iran*, 108-9 table 3, 113 table 5; and Asheghian, "American Joint Venture Manufacturing Firms," 86 table 18.

99. Halliday, *Iran*, 272. See also ibid., 271-72.

100. On Iraq and Iran see Katouzian, *The Political Economy*, 316; Halliday, *Iran*, 274-76; and Ivanov, *Tarikh-i Nuvin-i Iran*, 270.

101. Halliday, *Iran*, 278-9; Katouzian, *The Political Economy*, 317; Bill, *The Eagle and the Lion*, 403.

102. This is the opinion of Burke and Lubeck, "Explaining Social Movements," 664. The 1991 Gulf War in Iraq and 1992 "autogolpe" and crackdown on Islamist forces in Algeria undermine the cooptation side of this claim rather dramatically.

103. Issawi presents selected indicators of development comparing Iran, Egypt, and Turkey in 1950 and 1972: "The Iranian Economy 1925-1975," 134 table 4.3, 136 table 4.4. See also the comparisons in Peter Evans, *Dependent Development. The Alliance of Multinational, State, and Local Capital in Brazil* (Princeton: Princeton University Press, 1979), 298 table 6.4, which rank Iran well behind Brazil, Mexico, and India in industrial production in the 1970s.

104. Hudson Institute, *Oil Money and the Ambitions of a Nation* (Paris, 1974), as summarized by Halliday, *Iran*, 168.

9

The Making of the Iranian Revolution
and After, 1977-1991

I cannot believe and I do not accept that any prudent individual can believe that the purpose of all these sacrifices was to have less expensive melons, that we sacrificed our young men to have less expensive housing. . . . No one would give his life for better agriculture. Dignity is better than full bellies. Iranian masses have fought only for God not for worldly affairs.[1]
—Ayatullah Ruhullah Khumaini, in September 1979

* * *

The reaction of the workers in the Azmayesh factory to Khomeini's famous statement that 'we have not made revolution for cheap melons, we have made it for Islam' was

they say we have not made revolution for economic betterment! What have we made it for, then? They say, for Islam! What does Islam mean then? We made it for the betterment of the conditions of our lives.

—Bayat, *Workers and Revolution*

These two quotes alone, one from Ayatullah Khumaini, the acknowledged leader of the Iranian revolution, the other by a group of the factory workers whose strikes helped paralyze the shah's regime, hint at some of the wide-ranging debates on the nature and causes of the Iranian revolution of 1977-79. Namely, were economic or religious motivations paramount? Who made the revolution, and why? What causal factors must be considered in giving an adequate account of this social upheaval? What does Iran's recent revolution tell us about theories of revolution, and vice versa?

Theories of Revolution and the Iranian Case

In addition to such common-sense views of revolution as "misery breeds revolt," or the state faces "an unmanageable accumulation of difficulties," or that radical new ideas are somehow crucial to the making of revolutions—all of which may be helpful but raise further questions of why and how—Jack Goldstone has identified three generations of social science theories of revolution.[2] Historians of the first generation, such as Crane Brinton in the 1920s and 1930s, elaborated descriptive "natural histories" of revolution.[3] Goldstone's second generation of theorists dating from the 1950s and 1960s, tried to explain why and when revolutions arise, using explicit, social science theories of several types, mostly derived from the then prevalent modernization paradigm.[4] Since the 1970s a third generation of structural theories focuses analysis on such new dimensions as state structures, international pressures, peasant society, the armed forces, and elite behavior.[5] Though each of these theorists makes important contributions, it is Theda Skocpol's oeuvre which aims at the most comprehensive and potentially generalizable theory of social revolutions, and has attracted the most extensive commentary and debate. Skocpol defines social revolutions as "rapid, basic transformations of a society's state and class structure . . . accompanied and in part carried through by class-based revolts from below."[6] Arguing against the view that revolutions are "made" by mass-mobilizing, ideologically-informed social movements and actors, she stresses the structural reasons for the outbreak of revolutions, especially the weakening of old regimes by outside military pressures, internal splits between elites and the state, and widespread participation by intact peasant communities. In a subsequent article, Skocpol observes that the model used to account for the French, Russian, and Chinese revolutions in *States and Social Revolutions* applies only to certain kinds of states—"established agrarian states facing intensifying pressures from more economically developed competitors within the international states system."[7] She denies it can be generalized to small, dependent Third World states in today's world. In another article she does extend her theory to Third World countries in which "the holders of prerevolutionary state power are either colonial rulers or else indigenous dictators closely dependent upon foreign backing and links to the capitalist world economy."[8] She specifies:

> Social revolutions have happened in such settings when major shifts in world economic and geopolitical conditions have weakened the repressive capacities of colonial or neocolonial regimes, and when peasants have either been able to rebel autonomously through local communal structures, or nationalist guerrilla movements have devised ways to mobilize peasants directly. While

the combinations of causes involved are not "mechanically" the same as in *States and Social Revolutions*, the same theoretical perspective—centered on state structures, international conditions affecting state power, and agrarian class structures—is clearly at work.[9]

As we shall see, when Skocpol turns to the case of the Iranian revolution, she moves further away from her models of social revolution, while trying to remain faithful to her structuralist method. Let us turn now to her and others' explanations of the Iranian case.

Various scholars and commentators have noted the applicability of certain theories of revolution to the Iranian case. Many of the imputed characteristics of all revolutions listed by the Natural History school, and especially Brinton, are broadly found in the Iranian case.[10] The fit of Davies's J-curve (a period of rising expectations followed by a sudden economic downturn) to the situation in the 1970s has also been noted.[11] These observations, however, remain undeveloped in the literature and in any case subject to the criticisms levelled against the first two generations generally—that their "theories" are mainly descriptive and do not tell us what causal factors lie behind the phenomena observed. Theda Skocpol has also tried to explain the Iranian revolution and the difficulties this leads her into are instructive.[12] In the first place, virtually *none* of the structural mechanisms found in the French, Russian, and Chinese cases apply to Iran: There was no external pressure on the Iranian state, no great elite-state conflict, and no mass-based peasant movement in the countryside. Nor does Iran fit the model of Third World revolutions traced by Skocpol: Again, there was no major shift in world economic and geopolitical conditions to weaken the Iranian state, and no mobilized peasantry. She is then forced to turn Iran into a *unique* case and resort to various *ad hoc* mechanisms to explain the revolution, finding these in the rentier nature of the state and the existence of a mobilizing ideology and urban network in Shi'a Islam. She retreats further from the model of *States and Social Revolutions* in concluding that here was one revolution that was "deliberately and coherently made" and that the definition of a social revolution includes transformation of dominant ideologies. While it is to her credit to recognize that the Iranian revolution challenges her previous theories, she uses the case not to revise her model but to claim that Iran is virtually unique. It seems to me that the opposite strategy—of trying to account for the Iranian revolution with other theoretical principles and then reflecting on theories of revolution—might be more fruitful, and I shall elaborate my own perspective below.

First, though, we can approach the case of Iran from a different direction by looking at the rich debates among Iran specialists (rather than theorists of revolution) over the causes and nature of the revolution. These are, after all, the scholars who know the Iranian case most intimately, and if existing theories do not match their accounts, this too raises questions for theories of revolution. Though there are many cross-cutting ways to categorize their views in the literature (and many writers cross the lines adopted here), three basic points of view can be roughly discerned: those who argue for the primacy of political-economic causes, those who insist on the Islamic nature of the revolution, and those who wish to synthesize economic, political and ideological factors.

The Islamic interpretation of the Iranian revolution stresses the role of culture and ideology, insisting on the religious roots of the revolution—that the shah was overthrown for failing to follow Islamic principles, that the revolution's causes were not economic, and that the uniqueness of the Iranian revolution lies in its ideological orientation.[13] This naturally is the view held by the clerical leaders of the revolution, beginning with Ayatullah Khumaini. Thus Khumaini said in October 1979:

> [The left] did not contribute anything. They did not help the revolution at all. . . . They were not decisive for the victory, they were not responsible, they did not contribute anything. . . . [The people who were killed by the tens of thousands died] For Islam. The people fought for Islam.[14]

The degree to which this rewrites history by one involved in the midst of a complex struggle will become obvious below. The view that the revolution was not primarily economic in origin has, however, also found academic proponents. A more developed, social scientifically-informed variant of this position is offered by Arjomand, who argues that revolutions are most meaningfully distinguished by their "value-relevance," thus classifying Iran's as a world-historical revolution on a par with the English, French, Russian, and fascist revolutions. This leads him to focus on the ulama-state relationship as central to the Iranian revolution, and to emphasize its Islamic outcome. He minimizes working-class participation and finds similarities with fascism as a populist, mass-mobilizing ideology, and parallels with Stone's interpretation of the English revolution as driven by Puritanism in its ideas, organization, and leadership: "A parallel assertion can be made regarding the Shi'ite clerics, and with much greater confidence."[15]

Against this interpretation one finds a much larger group of Iran specialists stressing the political-economic origins of the revolution. Perhaps the ideal-typical form of this argument is Ervand Abrahamian's contention that the revolution resulted from a disjuncture of political and economic development:

> the failure of the Pahlavi regime to make political modifications appropriate to the changes taking place in the economy and society inevitably strained the links between the social structure and the political structure, blocked the

channeling of social grievances into the political system, widened the gap between new social forces and the ruling circles, and, most serious of all, cut down the few bridges that had in the past connected traditional social forces, especially the bazaars, with the political establishment.[16]

In this view, Islamic forces simply rushed to fill a void left by the systematic destruction of all other political oppositions available. The triumphant clerical faction then are "radical revolutionaries or reactionary radicals"— radical in ending the Pahlavi dynasty, reactionary or traditional in wanting to replace it with "an early Islamic golden age."[17] Similarly, Pesaran argues that "the February Revolution came about not because of a sudden and dramatic Islamic resurgence, but largely as a result of socio-economic conditions.... Islamic resurgence was not the cause of the February Revolution, it was its effect."[18] The basis of this line of reasoning is to note what the revolution was *against* (the shah's dictatorship) rather than what it turned out to be *for* (an Islamic Republic). Moghadam seconds this approach, observing that the revolution was "a populist, anti-imperialist social revolution," and that Islamization set in *after* the revolutionary takeover, following a year and a half of intense political, ideological, and social struggles.[19]

A third strategy of analysis has been to combine the ideological, political, and economic factors as causes of the revolution, as in Michael Fischer's classic statement: "The causes of the revolution, and its timing, were economic and political; the form of the revolution, and its pacing, owed much to the tradition of religious protest."[20] Moghadam is even more explicit about this multi-causal approach: "The roots of the Iranian Revolution—involving economic, political, and cultural factors, historical and conjunctural causes, internal social processes and external developments—cannot be reduced to any one dimension."[21] The works of Keddie, Halliday, Burke and Lubeck, Bashiriyeh, and Farhi evince this flexibility, with varying degrees of depth and points of emphasis. Thus Keddie notes the combination of economic problems and cultural uprooting, Halliday the conjuncture of "modern" economic development and "traditional" fundamentalist Islam, and Bashiriyeh the coincidence of economic crisis, religious organization, and political mistakes.[22] These analyses, especially Farhi's, come closest to my own analytic strategy. Once we have acknowledged the multi-causal aspects of the revolution, however, the challenge becomes one of explaining *how* economy, politics, and ideology are inter-related, and where the several causes come from.

The heterogeneity of the social forces that made the Iranian revolution has been noted by many observers. In this respect the events of 1977-79 follow the pattern of urban, multi-class populist alliances which we have already discerned in the Constitutional revolution of 1905-11 and Mussadiq's oil nationalization movement in 1951-53. The precise nature of the revolutionary coalition will be explored below. Here we want to specify a theoretical model of how it coalesced. Chapter eight traced out a pattern of dependent development and state repression of society in terms of the combination of world-systemic constraints and internal modes of production. This process resulted in severe economic dislocation and/or political repression of numerous social classes and groups—the ulama, bazaar merchants and artisans, working class, intelligentsia and students, urban marginal classes, peasants, and tribes. The Pahlavi state and its chief supporter, the United States, came to be widely perceived as the cause of Iran's problems. This resulted from the distillation of the experiences of the several groups and classes filtered through the available political cultures—varieties of Islam, secular nationalism, and Marxist analyses. Thus a broad coalition was both possible and ready to emerge when in 1977-78 an internal economic downturn occurred simultaneously with an easing of world-systemic pressure signalled by the Carter administration's ambivalent and conflicted relationship with the shah.[23] Diagram 9.1 illustrates the sequence of factors which touched off the revolution. The result is a complex con-

DIAGRAM 9.1 The Causes of the Iranian Revolution

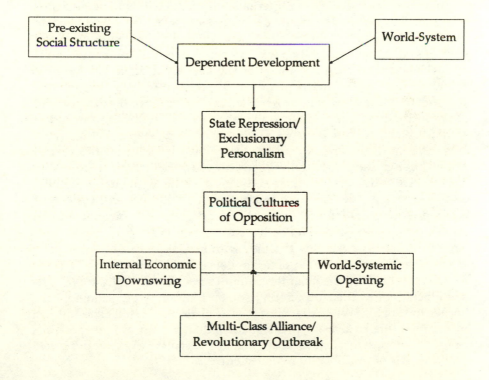

junctural model of revolutionary causation, meaning that a particular constellation of necessary conditions, no one sufficient by itself, lead to the
outbreak of a successful social revolution. These factors, as argued throughout this study, are economic, political, and cultural, and have internal as
well as external determinants.[24]

The 1963 Uprising: A Precursor

The utility of the model proposed can be partly illustrated by considering
a "negative" example: the failed social movements of 1960-63 culminating
in the June 1963 Muharram uprising that was violently repressed by the
shah. Consideration of these events and the positions taken by the participants also provides the necessary baseline for measuring the subsequent
changes that occurred in political culture and class coalitions in the 1960s
and 1970s.

As noted briefly in chapter eight serious economic problems developed
in 1958-60—a budget deficit, foreign borrowing, bad harvests, and rising
inflation. Compounded by an International Monetary Fund stabilization
program, these resulted in a fairly deep recession, which hit domestic trade,
including the bazaar, the hardest.[25] There followed the fraudulent majlis
elections of 1960 which the shah was compelled to cancel and annul, and in
April 1961 the court's appointment of the liberal politician 'Ali Amini as
prime minister in the midst of firm U.S. pressure for reforms. Internal
pressure on the shah was meanwhile accumulating since the August 1960
revival of the remnants of Mussadiq's National Front, led by the Iran Party's
Karim Sanjabi, National Party's Dariush Furuhar, Shapur Bakhtiar, Allahyar Saleh, Baqir Kazemi, and the new Liberation Movement of Iran's
Mehdi Bazargan and Mahmud Taliqani, the progressive cleric. Throughout
1961 and 1962 this loosely organized coalition criticized the shah and Amini
and supported a series of strikes and protests by students, teachers, textile,
oil, and communications workers. The National Front never came to an
agreement with Amini despite both sides' support of land reform, because
Amini wanted to push this through without any majlis to obstruct it,
whereas the National Front's politicians demanded new elections. This lack
of agreement helped the shah force Amini's resignation in July 1962. The
shah then claimed the land reform issue for himself by proclaiming it the
cornerstone of his "White Revolution." The National Front meanwhile lost
momentum due to arrests of its leaders and alienation of both potential
left-wing supporters such as Khalil Maliki's Socialist League and the religious liberals of the Liberation Movement.[26]

The third party to this struggle was the ulama, led by Ayatullah Burujirdi until his death in March 1961. Burujirdi had been apolitical and thus de facto publicly supportive of the shah in the 1950s, averring in 1960 that "I pray day and night for the person of the Shah-in-Shah, for whom I entertain sincere regard."[27] This attitude changed with the state's first land reform proposal in 1960, which was firmly opposed by Ayatullahs Burujirdi and Bihbihani as contrary to Islamic law's sanction of private property. When the issue was revived by the government in 1962 leading ayatullahs such as Gulpaigani, Khwansari, Hakim, Mar'ashi-Najafi, Tunakabuni, and Amuli continued to oppose it. Ayatullah Shari'atmadari, who was favorable to distribution of vaqf land to peasants, and Taliqani, who claimed that the landlord-peasant relationship had no basis in Islamic law, were in a distinct minority.[28]

By early 1963, however, with the receding significance of the National Front and secular opposition, and the emergence of new leadership among the ulama after Burujirdi's death, the ulama were thrust into positions of leadership in a diffuse struggle against the shah. While conservative ulama continued to oppose the land reform, and liberal democratic ulama such as Shari'atmadari and Milani were not against land reform but wanted the shah to rule constitutionally through a majlis, a new radical current led by Khumaini, with support from Taliqani and others broadened the issue by opposing the shah's autocracy and corruption, and ties to foreigners that were exploiting the country. One regressive demand on which many ulama agreed was opposition to women's suffrage. Thus most of the ulama came together to oppose the shah, though for widely varying reasons. The most outspoken of the ulama in late 1962 and early 1963 was the rising figure of Khumaini:

> He denounced the regime for living off corruption, rigging elections, violating the constitutional laws, stifling the press and the political parties, destroying the independence of the university, neglecting the economic needs of merchants, workers, and peasants, undermining the country's Islamic beliefs, encouraging gharbzadegi—indiscriminate borrowing from the West—granting "capitulations" to foreigners, selling oil to Israel, and constantly expanding the size of the central bureaucracies.[29]

Ulama confrontation with the state came to a head in the spring and summer of 1963. The government passed its referendum on the White Revolution reforms decisively in late January, despite National Front calls for a boycott. A month later the vote was granted to women. Around New Year's (March 21), ulama-led demonstrations in several cities, especially Qum where the main seminary is located, resulted in serious clashes with state security forces, with many casualties. Tension rose to a fever pitch as the Islamic

mourning days of Muharram approached in early June. Khumaini continued to denounce the shah's tyranny, collaboration with Israel, and subor-
dination to the United States. On June 4, the tenth of Muharram anniversary
of the seventh-century Shi'i Imam Husain's martyrdom, Khumaini and
Ayatullah Qumi were arrested before dawn, charged with planning disturbances. Their arrest certainly led to demonstrations, which began that day
and affected Tehran, Qum, Tabriz, Shiraz, Isfahan, Mashhad, and Kashan.
Protests were centered in the bazaar areas. According to Katouzian, "small
traders, shopkeepers and artisans, students, workers, the unemployed, and
political activists" participated.[30] Though the shah is said to have wavered,
prime minister 'Alam ordered General Uvaisi to fire on the crowds; total
casualties over several days were estimated at less than ninety by the
government, but several thousand by observers. Martial law, mass arrests,
and a number of executions further quelled the continuation of the movement. Khumaini was released from prison in August, kept under house
arrest from October 1963 to May 1964 for demanding a boycott of elections,
and exiled to Turkey in November 1964 for denouncing the granting of
diplomatic immunity to American military personnel.

In analyzing these events, certain similarities with the 1977-79 revolution
may be noted, as well as some key differences. The similarities lie mainly in
the background to each uprising—an economic downturn preceded each,
and the shah, with American prompting, responded with reforms. After
this, however, patterns diverged. The state controlled events in 1961-63,
reacting to its challengers more adroitly than in 1978. The economic downturn was reversed by 1962, muting the grievances that would be expressed
in 1963. By making the fairly popular notion of a land reform its own, the
state undercut the National Front's demands and made the ulama look more
reactionary. Nor was the United States a strong focus of resentment in 1963,
having encouraged the land reform and not yet received the immunity for
its personnel which came a year later. The state, then, responded with
seemingly effective reform programs, in addition to the massive repression
of June 1963.

By then the populist alliance was no longer strong or united. The
working class had engaged only in scattered strikes in 1961-62 and no
general strike occurred in 1963. Maliki's socialists were spurned by the
National Front, and the Tudeh had been virtually destroyed inside the
country in the 1950s. The National Front and ulama did not work together,
divided on the issues of land reform and votes for women. Nor did they
have a well-articulated political culture of opposition to draw on at this
point, with demands stopping well short of the overthrow of the regime or
structural economic changes. The protest movement was neither sustained
nor widespread as a result; reforms divided and confused the opposition,
repression crushed the leadership and discouraged its social base.

In terms, then, of diagram 9.1, dependent capitalist development was not far advanced, state repression was somewhat mitigated by reforms, and political cultures of opposition were weaker and less articulated. Thus when the world-system opening (U.S. pressure for reforms) and internal economic downturn occurred in 1960-61, the multi-class alliance did not swing into gear. The result was an uprising rather than a revolutionary rupture. These factors would be arrayed rather differently by the mid-1970s, as dependent development sharpened class grievances and made the United States and shah more vulnerable targets. The interim period also witnessed the elaboration of several potent political cultures of opposition, notably radical varieties of Islam and Marxist guerrilla groups. These developments then set the stage for the Iranian revolution.

The New Multi-Class Populist Alliance Emerges

The articulation of new political cultures of opposition to the shah in the 1970s provides a crucial element in the making of the Iranian revolution. The emergence of a new version of the populist multi-class alliance can be discerned through study of the several cultures of opposition, the organizations that espoused them, and the underlying grievances of classes and groups that fed them. My hope is to fashion a truly dialectical account of social change, bringing together economics and culture to explain politics.

Several social scientists have provided useful clues for the study of Iranian Shi'ism. Thus anthropologists Michael Fischer and Henry Munson bid us to look at Islam as a symbolic structure that generates meanings for people, consisting of a language with various inflections (determined by class or social status), an ethos telling people how they should act, and a world view capable of providing answers to human problems.[31] Another general approach is Skocpol's stress on a historically grounded analysis of both organization—the loose but effective network of ulama—and belief— especially symbols of opposition and resistance to domestic tyranny and foreign domination—as resources that were mobilized to make the revolution.[32] Each of these perspectives is consonant with my own, which sees political cultures of opposition as generated by the efforts of numerous actors and groups of actors to interpret their political economic situation in light of the existing cultural elements available to them, and to refashion ideology and culture to bring these into line with their lived experience. This grants considerable autonomy to the domain of culture both as a filter of experience and forum of struggle, and also links it to the political and economic dimensions of society. In the case of Iran, this led to several varieties of Islamic political culture and discourse—Khumaini's militant

Islam, 'Ali Shari'ati's radical Islam, the liberal Islam of Mehdi Bazargan, and the Liberation Movement of Iran—as well as the secular political cultures of liberal-nationalist constitutionalism and Marxism, embodied in the National Front and the guerrilla groups.

Ayatullah Ruhullah Musavi Khumaini (1902-1989) emerged as the undisputed leader of the Iranian revolution in the course of 1978. Though politically aware and critical of the government for much of his adult life, the 1963 events marked a turning point in his opposition to the regime's despotism and American power in Iran. In speeches against the majlis decision to grant American personnel diplomatic immunity in 1964 he stated:

> Until recently, the British enslaved the Moslem nations; now they are under American bondage. . . .
>
> Large capitalists from America are pouring into Iran to enslave our people in the name of the largest foreign investment. . . . This is the result of the political and economic exploitation by the West on the one hand . . . and the submission of the regime to colonialism on the other. . . . The regime is bent on destroying Islam and its sacred laws. Only Islam and the Ulama can prevent the onslaught of colonialism.[33]

Khumaini rose in stature as a result of his opposition in 1963-64 and subsequent exile to Iraq. His 1971 work *Vilayat-i Faqih: Hukumat-i Islami* (Guidance by Religious Experts: Islamic Government) wrought an ideological revolution in that it directly challenged the legitimacy of monarchy and advocated rule by qualified Islamic jurists. Arguing that "Islam knows neither monarchy nor dynastic succession,"[34] Khumaini went on to the justification of Islamic authority:

> The Islamic government we want will be constitutional and not despotic. But it will be constitutional not in the usual sense of the term—that laws will be made by an elected parliament. It will be constitutional in that the state will strictly observe the rules and regulations laid down in the Koran, in the Sunna, and in the Islamic shari'a. . . .
>
> Since the rule of Islam is the rule of law, only the jurists, and no one else, should be in charge of the government. They are the ones who can undertake what the Prophet intended. They are the ones who can govern as God ordered. . . .
>
> The jurist should have authority over the state administration and over the machinery for spreading justice, providing security, and dispensing just social relations. The jurist possesses the knowledge to ensure the people's liberty, independence, and progress.[35]

Abrahamian notes that these views of Khumaini's were not widely known or disseminated outside theological circles in the 1970s. Instead, Khumaini criticized the regime for its corruption, arms expenditures, relations with the West, neglect of agriculture, creation of shantytowns, phony elections, and violations of the constitution. He promised Islamic solutions to all these problems, but in a general and unspecified manner.[36]

The result was a militant oppositional stance toward the shah and Western influence in Iran, which Keddie and Moghadam have characterized as "populist" for its combination of progressive and traditional elements and its appeal to diverse social strata. Though Khumaini's primary social base was among lower-rank ulama, theology students, bazaar merchants, and artisans, his anti-imperialism attracted secular intellectuals, leftists, and workers as well, and his religious idiom was popular among the urban and rural marginal populations whom he extolled as the *mustazafin* (the dispossessed masses).[37] The uncompromising consistency of his opposition while in exile, his personal piety, simplicity, and austere life-style, and the political astuteness of the issues he made his own, further helped Khumaini emerge as the dominant leader of the opposition as the revolution unfolded. He was given crucial organizational support through the existence of a network of his former students inside and outside Iran, including ayatullahs Husain Muntazari, Muhammad Bihishti, Murtaza Mutahhari, Muhammad Javad Bahunar, Sadiq Khalkhali, and Anvari, and hojjat al-islams (a lower theological rank than ayatullah) 'Ali Akbar Hashimi-Rafsanjani and 'Ali Khaminihi. Most of these were members of the Ruhaniyan-i Mubariz (Organization of Militant Ulama), formed by the late 1960s/early 1970s to preach and spread Khumaini's messages. In all, Khumaini had educated hundreds of individuals who rose in the ranks of the ulama over the many years he taught in Iran up to 1965. The resumption of Iranian pilgrimages to the Shi'i shrine cities of Iraq in 1976 facilitated communications and the distribution of resources for the struggle. When the revolution broke out in 1978, then, Khumaini was prepared with a militant ideology and resilient organization to eventually assume the leadership of it.[38]

'Ali Shari'ati (1933-1977) is considered, along with Khumaini, the chief ideologue of the Iranian revolution. Brought up by a politically aware and devout father in the more open atmosphere of 1941-53, he went in 1960 to the Sorbonne on a fellowship, where he studied sociology, history, and literature, and was influenced by Fanon, Sartre, and the Algerian revolution. Returning to Iran in 1964, he taught high school English and then history at the University of Mashhad, but was suspended in 1971 for his politics. He then went permanently to Tehran where he had already been giving vastly popular lectures at the Husainiya-i Irshad, an institution associated with the Liberation Movement of Iran. Between 1972 and 1977 he was harassed, imprisoned for eighteen months and later kept under house arrest. Finally he was allowed to go to England, where he died in June 1977, possibly of a heart attack, or, as was widely believed, the victim of SAVAK foul play.[39] Shari'ati's work as a whole can be characterized as an attempt to construct a radical, activist Islam informed by politics and sociological analysis. He distinguished revolutionary Shi'ism (the religion of Imam 'Ali in the seventh century) from official state Shi'ism (what he called "Safavid Shi'ism"), thereby clearly differentiating the few oppositional clerics from the many quietist ulama who accepted the monarchy. In a similar vein he refashioned the Karbala paradigm of the martyrdom of 'Ali's son Husain into a theology of liberation extolling mass struggle against injustice and heroic sacrifice for an ideal, arguing: "Islam's most basic tradition is martyrdom, and human activity, mixed with a history of struggle against oppression and establishment of justice and protection of human rights."[40] This laid more groundwork for making the already emotionally-charged month of Muharram a period of powerful potential for political expression.

Shari'ati also combatted Western political cultural influence on Iran, including cultural borrowing, bourgeois democracy, and to some degree, Marxism, holding up his revolutionary version of Islam as a comprehensive world view superior to all of these. The responsibility of the intellectual was to identify the ills of his or her society and suggest solutions in keeping with its culture, which in Iran meant Islam. Thus poverty, foreign cultural and economic domination, and internal tyranny are to be condemned.[41] While Marxism too was seen as a product of the West, there is also Shari'ati's admiration for Fanon, Sartre, and Che Guevara while in Paris, and before that, his affiliation along with his father in the Movement of God-Fearing Socialists. He recognized Marxism's utility for understanding society and history, but felt Islam held the answers to the problems thus identified.[42] He placed more faith in critical and independent intellectuals than dogmatic Marxists or status-quo ulama. Western democracy too was criticized as corrupt and unsuited to Iran; more vaguely than Khumaini, Shari'ati called for an Islamic government—a kind of popular, but "directed" democracy. Denying the ulama the exclusive right to rule, he yet foreshadowed Khumaini's leadership by holding that the community should choose a leader and invest him with substantial power.[43]

In terms of a social base for these ideas, Shari'ati served as a bridge from Khumaini and the ulama to university students and intellectuals, and through them to other urban classes such as workers, urban marginals, and migrants. He also inspired the Mujahidin guerrilla group's revolutionary Islam. During the revolutionary year of 1978 his "books" (transcriptions of his many lectures) were sold openly in the university and bazaar, and his portrait appeared on walls and in demonstrations with a frequency second only to Khumaini's. Slogans taken from his writings—"The martyr is the heart of history!", "Every day is 'Ashura; every place is Karbala!"—were inscribed on banners in the street processions.[44] Even more than Khumaini, Shari'ati was the main intellectual force behind the revolution.

Though not as influential within the mass movement as Khumaini and Shari'ati, the liberal ulama and lay thinkers associated with the Liberation (or Freedom) Movement of Iran (Nahzat-i Azadi-yi Iran) did fashion a new political culture in the 1960s and 1970s which had repercussions during the revolution, including the rise of one of its founders, Mehdi Bazargan, to the prime ministership in 1979. This variant of Islam may be characterized as possessing liberal, constitutionalist, and nationalist strains. Born in 1907, Bazargan headed the oil nationalization committee in 1951 and was close to Mussadiq. As early as 1962 Bazargan advocated democratic struggle against corrupt government by an Islamically informed and motivated populace. He is regarded as the founder of Islamic modernism in Iran, based on the compatibility of Islam and scientific rationality, and the continuing relevance of Islam to the problems of contemporary society. He thus admired Western science and certain social ideals such as democracy and humanism but felt that Islam was in accord with these and must guide politics. He also envisioned a role for leadership by the highest-ranking of the ulama:

> The people require of him that he should be like 'Ali, albeit at a lower level; learned and informed; a man ready for the fray, a fighter; a brave and eloquent speaker; a good judge of people; a man who could win the people and carry them with him; an active man who could provide for the needs of his family; a capable administrator; an honest man, wholly committed to God; a leader, well versed in the affairs of religion and the world and in theoretical and practical matters: a man of action as well as words.[45]

We may see in these views of the early 1960s an almost uncanny foreshadowing of Khumaini's later appeal.

The Liberation Movement of Iran was founded in 1961 by Bazargan along with Sayyid Mahmud Taliqani (1910-1979) and Yadullah Sahabi. Taliqani's works included praise for the Constitutional revolution, democracy, and socialism within a devout Islamic framework. On economic systems he wrote that Islam did not justify landownership absolutely and that people's needs should also be met. Politically, he wanted to bring progressive ulama and secular forces together, thereby overcoming the weakness and divisions of the Mussadiq era.[46] Also within the ideological purview of the Liberation Movement (though not formal members) were Ayatullah Kazim Shari'atmadari (born 1905) and the lay economist Abul Hassan Bani Sadr (born 1933/34). Just as Taliqani was to the left of Bazargan, Shari'atmadari was a moderate but staunch constitutionalist to his right, with a major following in his native province of Azarbaijan. Bani Sadr's several books on Islamic government and economics criticize the Pahlavi dynasty as well as quietist ulama, cautioning against personality cults of all kinds, and condemning class inequalities. Politically on the left, he is perhaps classifiable as a right-wing democratic socialist or a left social democrat, within an Islamic framework.[47]

The Liberation Movement was banned in 1963 but continued to exist underground and especially abroad. Its social base was similar to that of its secular counterpart, the National Front—the middle strata of merchants, civil servants, students, professionals. Further left, Taliqani personally inspired the Mujahidin guerrillas and was imprisoned for his support of them in mid-1977. Led by religious lay persons, the Liberation Movement served as a conduit between religious and secular political cultures. Of the exiles who headed its North American branch in the 1970s, several returned to Iran to assume posts in the Bazargan post-revolutionary government: Dr. Ibrahim Yazdi became foreign minister, Mustafa Chamran defence minister, Sadiq Qutbzadeh minister of National Iranian Radio and Television, and 'Abbas Amir Intazam deputy prime minister.[48] Bani Sadr would later become the first president of the Islamic Republic.

Alongside these militant, radical, and liberal variants of Islamic political culture there also grew up secular political cultural trends and opposition forces. Under this disparate heading may be grouped certain intellectuals, writers, and the scattered remnants of the National Front and Tudeh Party. The range of thinking here, from liberal nationalism to forms of Marxism, is well represented in the works of Jalal Al-i Ahmad (1923-1969) and Samad Behrangi (1939-1968). Al-i Ahmad's most important legacy is the 1961 extended essay _Gharbzadigi_ (variously translated as "Westoxication," "Westomania," "West-Struckness" or "Occidentosis"). In this essay he attacked the cultural imperialism and technological superiority of the West and Iranian intellectuals' acquiescence to it: "My main contention is that we have not been able to preserve our own original cultural identity in the face of invasion by the machine, but have in fact given way to it completely."[49] To a certain degree this prefigured Shari'ati's search for an authentic Iranian response to the West, as did Al-i Ahmad's turn to Islam toward the end of his life, ambivalently described in the diary of his 1964 pilgrimage to Mecca. His audience was among committed but politically searching or disaffected intellectuals and university students. Samad Behrangi represented a new generation of committed intellectuals. A village school teacher from Azarbaijan, he too criticized cultural domination by the West but from a fully secular standpoint—Iran's intellectuals were too bourgeois, too subservient to America; the educational system was geared for urban middle class students and entirely inappropriate for village children. His writing was popular, down-to-earth, socially conscious, and critical of the powers that be, urging resistance to the oppressive conditions that he depicted. Using the folktale form to evade the censor, his world-famous short story *The Little Black Fish* is a chronicle of self-discovery, exploration of one's surroundings, resistance to evil and cruel authorities, and solidarity with one's fellow strugglers. Behrangi, who died under somewhat clouded circumstances at age twenty-nine while swimming in the strong Aras River, inspired left-wing students above all, including members of the Iranian Students Association abroad, and the Fada'ian guerrilla organization carried his picture in the revolution's demonstrations and put it on their posters.[50] Other intellectuals opposed the dictatorship in their life and writing, including the playwright Ghulam Husain Sa'idi and the critic Reza Baraheni. Dozens of them were active in the associations of writers, poets, and others that initiated the protests in the fall of 1977.

This brings us to the organizations that loosely drew on these currents to oppose the regime. The National Front was inactive as such between 1963 or so and December 1977 when it announced its re-formation. Already a pale shadow of its 1950-53 peak, it disintegrated further when the 1960-63 movement collapsed. Some members carried on underground.[51] More seriously repressed by the regime were the remnants of the Tudeh Party, which existed primarily in exile from 1953 to 1978, claiming 38,000 members abroad in East and West Europe and North America. Inside Iran, several hundred were arrested between 1964 and the early 1970s, SAVAK managed to infiltrate some cells, and several splits occurred, leading to considerable disillusionment with the party by others on the left. Its networks abroad did however try to organize against the regime, while in 1978, it proved to have some supporters in the factories and particularly in the oil sector. Its political positions included support for the Soviet Union, calls for a democratic republic, a real land reform, rejection of violence, and support for progressive clergy, especially Khumaini.[52]

The repression of the Tudeh and demise of the National Front in the 1960s and 1970s produced something of a vacuum on the left and secular side of the populist alliance, which would be filled by the emergence of guerrilla groups, Islamic and Marxist. From the mid-1960s onwards, a number of small groups operated briefly or for longer periods; towering above them all in numbers of members lost, organizational capacity, and popular stature were the Islamic Mujahidin and the Marxist Fada'ian organizations. The Mujahidin-i Khalq (People's Crusaders) was founded in the mid-1960s by former members of the Liberation Movement dissatisfied with the strategy of peaceful struggle. Almost all were young students or graduates in technical disciplines in Isfahan, Shiraz, and Tabriz, as well as Tehran, who at first met in small groups to study the guerrilla experiences of Algeria, Vietnam, and the Palestinians. Some trained with the PLO in Jordan. In August 1971 they began military operations to coincide with the shah's

2500th anniversary of the monarchy. In the 1970s they assassinated Iranian General Tahiri, six American colonels, and others. Ideologically the Mujahidin began with the Liberation Movement's congruence of Islam and scientific rationality, linking true Islam with revolutionary activity. By 1973 a pamphlet declared their respect for Marxism and argued that imperialism presented a common enemy for Muslims and Marxists. In 1975 an internal split occurred with a Tehran-based faction emerging (later known as Paykar—"Combat") and a provincial Islamic one influenced by Shari'ati retaining the name Mujahidin. The Marxist group sought to work with other left forces and conduct political as well as military actions. In all, the Islamic Mujahidin lost seventy-three members, the Marxists thirty after 1975, including almost all of the original leadership.[53]

The Fada'ian-i Khalq (People's Devotees) also grew out of several study groups in the mid-1960s and were similarly dissatisfied with the Tudeh's lack of armed struggle and cognizant of the difficulties of organizing the working class in conditions of state repression. Most early members were university students in the social sciences and humanities; later a few workers joined. On February 8, 1971, after a member was arrested, they attacked a police outpost in the Gilan forests at Siakhal. Later they assassinated several SAVAK, police, and military personnel, as well as an industrialist involved in a massacre of workers. Like the Mujahidin their strategy was essentially one of guerrilla actions by small groups designed to build momentum for a wider uprising. Also like the Mujahidin, in 1975-77 they split into two groups, one moving closer to the Tudeh and political organizing, the other remaining more guerrilla-oriented. The Iranian Student Association in the United States was pro-Fada'ian and had at least 5,000 members and many more supporters in the 1970s. In Iran, the Fada'ian lost 172 members in the 1970s, seven of whom, including the theorist Bizhan Jazani, were murdered in prison.[54] The overall impact of these two major guerrilla organizations—the Mujahidin and the Fada'ian—was to imbue many students and intellectuals, and some workers, with Marxist and revolutionary ideals, to suggest the vulnerability of the regime to a certain degree, and to create a nucleus of armed members who would be available during the final uprising of February 1979.

These, then were the political cultures of opposition available to the major social classes and groups affected by dependent development in the course of the 1970s. It will be useful here to briefly recapitulate the impact of political-economic processes in shaping the grievances and attitudes of the key actors in the revolution that was brewing. While many—perhaps most—ulama remained quietist and conservative, a new generation that was more progressive and modern in outlook emerged. Moreover, almost all the ulama had some grievance against the government, over the latter's control of education, law, welfare, and vaqf properties, the imposition of urban development at the expense of the bazaar, sending of a religious corps into the countryside, unilateral installation of a monarchic calendar, supervision of theological publications, or changes in the family law. The deep cuts in subsidies to the ulama in 1977 were widely felt and resented. Coupled with this came repression in the form of numerous arrests and a few cases of torture and murder of oppositional ulama. Despite this onslaught, the ulama retained some valuable resources, collecting the religious taxes especially in the bazaar, running mosques and meeting halls, operating seminaries, setting up Islamic societies and libraries in universities and in the provinces. Shocked at the moral decay of society, some went as preachers into the shanty-towns and organized prayer meetings, funeral processions, and passion plays, all of which laid groundwork for further mobilization when the time came.[55]

The educated middle class—the intelligentsia in its broad sense—grew with the processes of urbanization, industrialization, and expansion of the state and education. Intellectuals were needed by the state, but in their capacity as critics they often came to oppose it too. Teachers, technicians, skilled workers, office clerks all grew in number, but received no political rights or responsibilities. Many wanted democratization, greater participation in society, and social reforms. Others, following Al-i Ahmad and Shari'ati, turned to Islam. Students, including those abroad, were particularly likely to be radical in outlook, both from a left-wing and an Islamic point of view. Writers, poets, lawyers, and other professional groups emerged in the mid- to late 1970s and would touch off the revolution in the fall of 1977.[56]

The same processes of dependent development had expanded the size of the working class. Scattered strikes began to occur in the late 1960s and early 1970s. There were at least twenty-five major strikes from 1974 to 1976, ending with a combination of repression and concessions, arrests, and pay raises. Wages rose but grievances remained—difficult working conditions, political repression of the labor movement, a deteriorating urban environment, inflation, and in 1977, growing unemployment as recession set in. Radical ideas were particularly prevalent among northern workers in Gilan and Mazandaran with their history of opposition and organization. Working class culture more commonly was an amalgam of religious beliefs and an intuitive understanding based on the experience of exploitation. Many may have aspired to own their own shop or small business, but the political economy of dependent development ensured that few could realize this ideal.[57]

The merchants and artisans of the bazaar, while distinct classes and stratified internally, shared broad common grievances by the 1970s. Each more than half a million strong, they clung tenaciously to their niches in the new political economy as foreign imports and Iranian manufactures sought alternative distribution outlets and partially replaced them. The state discriminated against them with its credit and oil policies, controlled the guilds, and blamed the bazaar for inflation in the harsh anti-profiteering campaign of 1975-76, which led to thousands of arrests and fines. The shah and foreign capital were thus clearly perceived as threats to their livelihood, and the bazaar classes fought back by retaining their own information networks, banking systems, religious discussion groups, and traditions of social solidarity. They funded the ulama heavily to pursue similar projects. Merchants, by virtue of their higher class position, were not revolutionary in outlook, while artisans often aspired only to become masters of their own shops. But both would furnish the backbone of the pro-Khumaini movement, responding to his populist religious idiom and contributing significant organizational and financial resources to the revolution.[58]

Turning now to the most oppressed classes in Iranian society, the ranks of the urban marginals swelled into the millions in the 1970s, and while wages rose and job opportunities were created, especially in the construction sector, the urban underclasses faced insuperable difficulties of low incomes, abominable housing, malnutrition, slim educational chances, and the like. The construction sector entered a recession in 1976-77, so just when the cost of living took off, jobs became even scarcer. Shanty-town dwellers were often quite religious in outlook, in contact with the local mosque and mulla, organized in their own religious circles, and provided for their own mutual solidarity. Though they might see secular oppositionists as intellectual egg-heads and *kravatis* ("tie-wearers"), their children were sometimes radicalized in the educational system, where some became leftists and others followers of Shari'ati's radical Islam. They themselves were painfully cognizant of the great inequalities in urban social structure, and resentment toward the wealthy, and above all the shah, naturally grew. When the state tried to evict them from their shanties in 1977, slum dwellers fought back in actions that took their place as part of the early signs of the revolution.[59]

Peasants and tribespeople were, as in the past, marginalized economically but faced barriers to political participation—the khans' authority over tribespeople, persistence of landed power and the state's new control in the countryside, the scattered locations of rural communities, coupled with illiteracy, poverty, and other factors worked against both groups. Peasants did develop considerable complaints against the state, however, as the land reform failed to deliver better lives for the majority of tenants and landless families. Hostility and passive resistance to authority permeated many villages. Iran's seven million settled and nomadic tribespeople developed their own grievances in terms of forced settlement policies, military repression, the spread of capitalist production relations, growing poverty, and linguistic and ethnic discrimination. There is some evidence of growing class consciousness within tribes as well. Further, those rural people of both classes who migrated to the cities in such large numbers became part of the urban marginal classes, sharing both their situation and the responses to it. Both in villages and urban slums, the peasantry were religious (but often cynical about the ulama), desirous of education, and bitter at the state and upper classes' monopolization of wealth and power. Such feelings were particularly common among youth.[60]

Out of the complex encounter of the political cultures elaborated above—militant, radical, and liberal Islam, secular liberalism and Marxism—and the classes and social groups just discussed—ulama, intelligentsia, workers, merchants, artisans, urban marginals, and rural classes—emerged a new version of Iran's historic populist alliance. This coalition then touched off a world-historical revolutionary movement in 1977.

The Course of Events

Starting in about 1975 and deepening in the course of 1976-77 came the first major economic downswing of the shah's White Revolution since the early 1960s. Just as the 1973-78 investment plan was being revised upwards by 89 percent after the OPEC price increases of 1973-74, the oil boom burst when world demand contracted in 1975 due to a recession caused in part by the high price of oil itself. In Iran, inflation was fueled by the great amounts of oil revenues that had poured into the economy since 1973. Housing costs reached exorbitant levels as foreigners came to Iran and speculators raised prices while migrants swelled urban populations. Food imports and agricultural failure also pushed up bills. This rise in the cost of living, from 9.9 percent in 1975 to 16.6 percent in 1976 and 25.1 percent in 1977, squeezed any real gains from the wage increases that were being won.[61]

By mid-1977 a recession was in full swing, compounded by prime minister Amuzigar's deflationary policies. Iran was forced to borrow again from Western banks to cover a $2 billion operating deficit. Budgets were cut, contracts were cancelled, building projects were scaled down or deferred. Oil output reached a plateau as Iran refused to sell at Saudi Arabia's lower prices. Imports slowed as well. It should be noted that in some respects this was more a relative slowdown in growth than an absolute decline. Thus Halliday argues that 1977 saw a slowdown or a recession rather than an actual economic crisis. The non-oil industrial growth rate, for example, dropped from 14.1 percent in 1976/77 to 9.4 percent in 1977/78. There was however a real fall in private sector investment in machinery and equipment of 6.8 percent (the first since 1969), and agriculture declined by 0.8 percent.

Meanwhile, inflation took its bite and unemployment became serious at 9.1 percent by 1977-78 (it had been only one percent in 1974), particularly affecting the construction sector's jobs for the working and marginal classes. The closing of some factories and bankruptcies among merchants hurt employment further, with capital flight burgeoning to $2 billion. 1977, too, was the year stipends to the ulama were cut. These negative economic trends would continue on into 1978, as protests grew into revolution.[62]

Simultaneously with this economic recession, the shah's regime was experimenting with a slight liberalization of the political atmosphere. In hopes of relieving middle-class demands for participation, and under pressure from international human rights groups and the new Carter administration, the shah began to tolerate a certain amount of criticism and tone down a few of the most overt excesses of his police state. Some 357 political prisoners were amnestied, torture was "reduced," the Red Cross visited twenty prisons, and new laws restricted military courts somewhat. Society's response soon went further than anticipated, a sign of the degree of compression of social forces from 1953 to 1977. A series of open letters were addressed to the government from prominent individuals and groups of intellectuals calling for implementation of the constitution, extension of human rights and civil liberties, free elections and press freedoms; none were published in Iran, but they circulated from hand to hand. During the spring and summer of 1977, the National Front, Liberation Movement of Iran, Tudeh Party, Fada'ian, and Mujahidin all agitated publicly. In June and August Tehran slum dwellers protested forcible evictions and a number of people were killed in pitched battles with security forces. In the latter month, there were several cases of crowds forming—often high school students—near the Tehran bazaar to protest food prices and shortages. Arson incidents in 130 factories dotted the months from July to October.[63]

SAVAK became more active again in the fall, harassing and beating dissidents (now easier to identify), and resuming secret military tribunals. The death of Khumaini's son Mustafa under mysterious circumstances in Iraq was also attributed to SAVAK. Meanwhile, however, associations of teachers, merchants, writers, lawyers, and theology students were formed. In mid-October a series of "cultural nights" was organized by poets and writers at the Goethe Institute in Tehran. These grew over ten days from 3,000 to 15,000 participants who occupied the surrounding streets to listen to verses in praise of freedom, turning the occasions into demonstrations against censorship. A month later thousands attended poetry nights at Aryamehr University, on the last of which clashes occurred with the police, who killed one student and wounded seventy others. By the beginning of December most of Iran's twenty-two universities were closed or on strike. During the month of Muharram (December) Tehran shopkeepers turned religious gatherings into demonstrations against government economic policy.[64] The year 1977 thus heralded the start of a mass protest, involving students, intellectuals, workers, urban marginals, ulama, and bazaaris at one point or another. Jimmy Carter's celebrated New Year's toast to the shah on January 1, 1978 seems in retrospect a massive misreading of the situation: "Iran is an island of stability in one of the more troubled areas of the world. This is a great tribute to you, Your Majesty, and to your leadership and to the respect, admiration and love which your people give to you."[65] A great tidal wave of revolution was preparing to engulf the island of stability, though few recognized the unmistakable groundswells as 1977 ended.

On January 7, 1978 the regime made a major mistake by publishing an article in the daily newspaper *Ittila'at* which slandered Khumaini as of Indian origins, a "medieval reactionary" with ties to British imperialism, and a writer of youthful love poems with homosexual overtones. Riots broke out at the newspaper's Tehran office; more seriously, at Qum on January 9, the bazaars and religious seminary closed down and a series of political demands were issued. Four to ten thousand people demonstrated in the streets and between ten and seventy were killed by police. The revolution had produced its first martyrs, and the ulama, led by Shari'atmadari, attacked the government as non-Islamic. The regime responded with a series of counter-demonstrations at Qum on January 10, at Tabriz and in cities in Khuzistan on January 18-19, and on the anniversary of the White Revolution on January 26, trucking in peasants, civil servants, and students for these occasions which were duly reported in the press.[66]

The government was unprepared for the cycle of protests which followed at regular forty-day intervals, to commemorate the deaths of martyrs according to Islamic mourning ritual. Thus on February 18 there were large processions in Qum, Tabriz, Mashhad, and nine other cities in honor of those killed on January 9. In Tabriz the police shot a young person, provoking demonstrators to attack banks, liquor stores, pornographic cinemas, and Rastakhiz offices—all symbols of the regime and Western influence. The cry "Death to the shah!" was first heard on this occasion and the army required tanks to regain control of the city two days later with as many as 100 or more people dead as a result.[67]

These protests continued at regular forty-day intervals throughout the spring. On March 28-30 there were demonstrations in as many as fifty-five places, which turned violent in several, especially at Yazd, where thousands of mourners left the mosque to march on the police station and again, up to a hundred were killed in a confrontation that was tape-recorded and distributed throughout Iran. The government in turn mobilized a counter-demonstration on April 9 and claimed 300,000 participated. May 6 brought demonstrations in Tehran, Shiraz, Isfahan, Tabriz, Qum, Kashan, and Jahrum, which continued through May 10, turning violent in some thirty-four cities and resulting in 14-80 deaths (by government and opposition estimates, respectively). Perhaps the most shocking scene occurred when Imperial guards broke into Shari'atmadari's house in Qum mistaking it for that of the more radical Ayatullah Gulpaigani, shooting and killing one of Shari'atmadari's followers, allegedly for refusing to shout "Javid shah!" (Long live the shah). This act undoubtedly turned the cautious, moderate Shari'atmadari more definitely against the regime. The shah responded with apologies to the ayatullah, a media campaign aimed at discrediting the protestors, and various pledges to continue the liberalization process.[68]

For a time in June and July it appeared that this strategy may have worked, as there was a period of relative quiescence. Already in late May the U.S. embassy was reporting hopefully that the number of "incidents" had dropped from one or two daily over the past couple of months to just three or four weekly. There was a one-day general strike on June 5 in Tehran and another in Qum on June 17, but these were peaceful, as was the fortieth-day commemoration a few days later. July too passed relatively calmly with the shah dropping the anti-profiteering campaign, banning pornographic films, replacing the head of SAVAK, and promising "100 percent free" elections in the future. The economy continued to contract however as inflation was brought down and a number of economically motivated strikes occurred. The political peace was shattered later in the month, too, as police fired on a crowd of mourners in Mashhad killing over forty and touching off new mourning ceremonies.[69]

These coincided with the month of Ramazan in August, when dramatic new provocations and confrontations erupted. Demonstrations and clashes resumed in a number of cities, and on August 10 at Isfahan 50,000 marched to protest the arrest of a local religious leader; troops fired on the crowd, killing some one hundred people, and martial law was declared there the next day. The greatest tragedy of the year to date then followed in Abadan on August 19, where over 400 people perished in a fire at the Rex Cinema during the showing of an anti-regime film. Though the perpetrators are shrouded in some mystery (a 1980 trial pointed to religious extremists but both the local police and fire brigades were clearly involved as the former barred crowds from opening the doors and the latter arrived four hours too late), the regime and SAVAK were widely held responsible by all of Iran. Ten thousand mourners shouted "Death to the shah! Burn *him!*" and forced the police from the cemetery. The last ten days of Ramazan saw fifty to 100 people die in confrontations with police in fourteen cities. The shah responded to these events by replacing Amuzigar with the marginally more pious Ja'far Sharif-Imami as prime minister. Sharif-Imami made a series of rapid concessions, mostly with a calculated religious appeal—scrapping the imperial calendar, dismissing some government officials of the Baha'i faith, closing casinos and gambling houses, passing a code to address corruption by members of the royal family, and creating a ministry of religious affairs and abolishing that of women's affairs. The shah meanwhile disowned the Rastakhiz Party, granted more extensive press freedoms, and promised free elections for mid-1979. On August 29 the major papers ran large, front-page pictures of Khumaini as part of a government overture to open a channel to him; the ayatullah refused to respond, as did Shari'atmadari a few days later.[70]

The events of September marked the point of no return for the revolutionary process. The fast of Ramazan ended on September 4 with a large non-violent procession in Tehran of some 250,000 people, calling for Khumaini's return and throwing flowers on watching soldiers. Mass gatherings continued until the seventh, when up to a half million people demanded an end to the Pahlavi dynasty, throwing out of America, and establishment of an Islamic republic. Martial law was declared early the next morning, on Friday, September 8. Large crowds had already gathered at Jaleh square across from the majlis. When ordered to disperse people sat down and bared their chests. Soldiers fired first into the air, then directly into the crowd in a massacre. Shooting continued during the day, including aerial attacks from helicopters on the southern slums. Officially, eighty-six people were killed; bodies in the Tehran morgue were assigned numbers which reached over 3,000. The event came to be known as Bloody Friday, and it marked the declaration of open war between the government and the population. The shah arrested hundreds of political figures and declared martial law in twelve cities on September 17. From the ninth onward, a series of strikes started to spread among the workers in the oil industry. Compromise began to look increasingly unrealistic.[71]

These strikes continued and widened during October, involving oilworkers, government ministries, railway and post office workers, hospital employees, the press, and workers at numerous factories all over Iran. Demands had become political rather than economic in nature—notably for press and political freedoms and the overthrow of the dynasty. Khumaini meanwhile left Iraq for Paris on October 6, where he had at his disposal far more powerful mass media—direct phone links to Iran, cassette tapes, the world print media, and BBC radio coverage—vastly enhancing his capacity to communicate with the Iranian people. The government continued to mix concessions with repression, but met with fewer takers for the former, which were hard to consider seriously with troops continuing to kill unarmed demonstrators. Later in the month Shari'atmadari moved closer to Khumaini's positions, forced by the latter's unwillingness to make a deal with the government. When the academic year began in late October students were able to organize more effectively, closing down classes and planning solidarity actions. Oil production fell from 5.7 million to 1.5 million barrels.[72]

Amidst this atmosphere of growing crisis, both sides intensified pressure in November and December. Two days of violent clashes at Tehran University on November 4 and 5 resulted in more deaths. The evening of November 4, Karim Sanjabi of the National Front read a three point declaration of agreement with Khumaini that the monarchy was no longer legitimate and that the opposition movement demanded a new regime based on principles of Islam, democracy, and independence. As clashes continued in south Tehran and in the oil centers of the south, the shah announced the formation of a military government under General Ghulam Reza Azhari. Schools were closed, newspapers suspended, public gatherings prohibited. Oil workers were forced back to work by the army, but production was sporadic. Other key strikes in government offices, factories, and elsewhere continued, or else similar slowdowns occurred. On November 23 Khumaini issued a call for strikes and demonstrations in Muharram (beginning December 2). On November 29 wildcat strikes resumed in the oil fields and oil production began a permanent decline.[73]

December was the decisive month of 1978 for the opposition. Khumaini's call for action during the emotionally laden mourning month of Muharram was widely heeded. In early December people shouted "Allah-u Akbar!" (God is Great!) from their rooftops at night; thousands marched in the white shrouds of martyrs and over 1,000 were killed in Tehran, Mashhad and Qazvin violating the curfew from December 2 to 4. On the two holiest days of Tasu'a and 'Ashura huge demonstrations were held, involving two to three million people in Tehran, 700,000 (more than the city's population!) in Mashhad, 500,000 in Isfahan. At the end of the second day in Tehran a seventeen-point manifesto was acclaimed by the crowd calling for the abolition of the regime, an end to foreign exploitation, and establishment of a just and democratic Islamic state with full rights for minorities, women, and exiles. On December 12 Carter reaffirmed his support for the shah, but in the next three weeks the government's tenuous hold over society eroded further. Despite army repression and more killing, demonstrations and strikes persisted. Oil production fell to 300,000 barrels a day by late December, less than even Iran's internal needs. As the economy shut down, American support for the shah wavered, as did his own resolve to continue the massacres. When General Azhari suffered a heart attack the shah made his decision to depart the country on a "vacation" and appointed Shapur Bakhtiar of the National Front prime minister. One year to the day from Carter's toast to Iran's stability, a situation of revolutionary dual power was coming into effect.[74]

The period of contestation for power between Bakhtiar and the opposition bore resemblances to the Russian revolution between February and November 1917 but in Iran it was compressed into little more than one month. The son of a tribal chief, the personally ambitious Bakhtiar was disowned by the National Front when he accepted the prime ministership from the shah, and had little popular appeal. He was confirmed by the majlis on January 3 and announced a series of concessions, including the lifting of censorship, release of most political prisoners, disbanding of SAVAK internally, the end of oil sales to South Africa and Israel, and that Iran would no longer police the Persian Gulf or purchase any more arms than necessary. He was greeted by continued work stoppages verging on a nationwide general strike and a series of large demonstrations on the fifth, eighth, and thirteenth, the last involving two million people in thirty cities. Finally, on January 11 it was announced that the shah would soon depart the country on his vacation. After appointing a regency council on the 13th headed by Bakhtiar, Muhammad Reza Shah Pahlavi left Iran for Egypt on January 16 as crowds went wild with joy. The next day Khumaini announced the formation of the Council of the Islamic Revolution from Paris (its members were kept secret for a year, but included Bani Sadr, Bazargan, and other members of the Liberation Movement, and four students of Khumaini—Ayatullahs Bihishti and Mutahhari and Hojjat al-Islams Rafsanjani and Bahunar). On January 19 huge demonstrations of one million in Tehran, 500,000 in Mashhad, and 100,000 in Qum were held. In the Tehran march the crowd adopted a historic resolution by acclamation: "We declare the Shah to be dethroned and remove him from power, which he and his father seized by force. . . . We . . . demand the establishment in Iran of an Islamic order and of a free Islamic Republic."[75] A leftist demonstration drew a far smaller crowd of 10,000 to the technical university on January 21, while Bakhtiar mustered 100,000 the next day, mostly from the army and upper classes. The army occupied the airport on January 24 to prevent Khumaini's return, but after one million people demanded this in Tehran on the 27th, it was decided on January 30 to allow it.

Thus, on February 1, 1979 Khumaini returned triumphantly to Iran after 13 years abroad. Three to four million people, perhaps the largest crowd in world history, lined the streets from the airport to Tehran. On February 5 Khumaini proclaimed the establishment of a provisional government headed by Mehdi Bazargan, to which government employees immediately announced their adherence. Complex negotiations were entered into between Bazargan, the army, and American advisors about a transfer of power from Bakhtiar to the provisional government. On February 8 there were huge demonstrations, including leftist and air force contingents, with the slogan "Khumaini, give us arms." This led to the events culminating in the triumph of the revolution over the weekend of February 9-11. The evening of the ninth, the elite Javidan unit of the Imperial Guards attacked the Farahabad base of the air technicians who had joined the demonstration the day before. The technicians resisted and were soon joined by local civilians and armed members of the Fada'ian and Mujahidin guerrilla groups. Fighting continued all day Saturday the tenth and on into Sunday with the guerrillas on the offensive, attacking and burning police stations, taking a large arsenal, and putting a number of tanks out of commission while suffering several hundred casualties. Evin prison and the main army garrison were taken on Sunday. The army high command then decided to abandon Bakhtiar, who slipped quietly out of the country. At 6 p.m. on Sunday, February 11, the radio announced: "This is the voice of Tehran, the voice of true Iran, the voice of the revolution. The dictatorship has come to an end."[76]

A Theoretical Analysis of the Iranian Revolution

The Populist Alliance in the Revolution

Almost all serious scholars of Iran have noted that a coalition of classes made the Iranian revolution. Abrahamian sees this in terms of an alliance between traditional middle classes (ulama, merchants) and modern middle classes (intelligentsia, students), with workers and lower urban classes acting as "battering rams." Keddie views the mass movement as a mobilization of the urban poor from February to September 1978, with the middle and working classes joining in the fall. Zabih points out that the various components had learned that they could not succeed on their own—the ulama in 1963, students in their demonstrations, workers through strikes. Bashiriyeh observes that the ulama united with Marxists and liberals to overthrow the regime. Ashraf and Banuazizi perceptively break the revolution down into five stages, each with its own actors and modes of struggle: an opening act from June to December 1977 of nonviolent mobilization led by students and intellectuals; a second stage of cyclical riots from January to July 1978 in which the ulama and bazaar classes became involved; followed by a third phase of mass demonstrations in August and September with the above plus urban middle and marginal classes; stage four in the fall of 1978 carried by mass strikes of blue and white collar workers; and a final period of dual sovereignty from December 1978 to February 1979 in which all these classes were united against the shah's regime.[77]

The conceptual framework and empirical results of the present study suggest that the social forces involved in the revolution constitute another instance of Iran's urban, multi-class populist alliance.[78] The revolution witnessed the largest demonstrations against a government in human history and a sustained political general strike that may be considered the most successful in working class history. Its massive rate of participation made possible its triumph through the disciplined use of primarily nonvio-

lent tactics despite the repression directed against it resulting in an estimated 10-12,000 deaths between January 1978 and February 1979.[79] The
analytic strength of the present study rests in not only description of the
multi-class character of the revolution, but also explanations of how each
group and class came to participate, and underlying this, a theoretical model
of how these grievances came about. In the context of Iran's class structure,
ulama, merchants, artisans, intellectuals, workers, and urban marginals
composed the populist alliance. Peasants and tribespeople had small supporting roles. Women and ethnic minorities such as the Kurds, Azaris, and
Turkamans cut across class categories to participate. Let us now turn to the
contributions of each component of this populist alliance during the revolution itself.

Certain ulama, led by Khumaini, and to a lesser extent the bazaar classes
of merchants and artisans upon whom they relied for financial support,
played key roles in the revolution. Khumaini and his circle of former
students, organized in both loose and formal networks, emerged as crucial
leaders during 1978 (but not in the fall 1977 actions leading up to the
revolution). They activated a religious political culture of opposition to
tyranny and foreign domination, organized the funeral processions that
kept the movement in motion at regular forty-day intervals, and led the
largest mass demonstrations of 1978 during Ramazan (August-September)
and Muharram (December). Despite this prominent involvement by
Khumaini's students and the younger ulama generally, there were many
other ulama who took conservative (or neutral) positions during 1978, as
well as significant differences of opinion between the uncompromising
Khumaini and other clerical authorities, such as Shari'atmadari, who called
only for implementation of the constitution and joined in calling for an end
to the monarchy only under some pressure from followers of Khumaini.[80]
Khumaini himself served an indispensable role in providing a clear, firm
alternative to the shah and astutely bringing the heterogeneous social
forces of the populist alliance together under his leadership, including
leftists, workers, and secular middle classes. His most eager followers came
from among the merchants and artisans of the bazaar, who provided financial resources, networks of communication, and participants in many demonstrations. Artisans were active not in their capacity as laborers in small
workshops, but as part of the urban mass movement and in bazaar actions.
They were numerically most significant in the series of fourtieth-day protests in January, February, March, and May 1978, before hundreds of
thousands got involved.[81] The creative organizational embodiment of
ulama and bazaar participation in the revolution was the formation of
Islamic *komitehs* (committees) in neighborhoods throughout the country in
the latter part of 1978. Often headed by pro-Khumaini ulama, these provided strike support, welfare, food, and security in their local areas. By

January and February 1979 the revolutionary komitehs constituted parallel governments with economic, political, and military functions. Though loosely coordinated and locally rather autonomous, virtually all supported Khumaini.[82]

Along with the ulama the other class that aspired to a leadership role in the revolution was the intelligentsia. Writers, poets, journalists, lawyers, and teachers initiated the sequence of events leading up to the revolution with their open letters, formation of associations, and cultural/poetry reading nights in 1977, campaigning for democratic and human rights. Students also were active on their campuses in 1977 and throughout 1978 contributed to both the mass demonstrations and general strike. Likewise, civil servants, professionals, and employees in the government ministries conducted effective white collar strikes parallel to those of the factory and oil workers. Khumaini was accepted by these groups as the leader of the revolution only at a later point (fall 1978), sometimes with considerable reluctance and in a critical spirit, as in the case of the Teachers Union. Students and young members of the intelligentsia moreover suffered the most casualties relative to their size.[83] This class was the social base for both the secular liberals of the National Front and the leftwing guerrilla organizations. The National Front, though small in numbers, played a part in the building of anti-shah momentum in the fall of 1978 by refusing to work with the government for a reform of the system. Instead, on November 4 it allied with Khumaini in Paris behind a program based on Islam, independence, and democracy. This brought many secular intellectuals and the middle classes generally into the movement and thereby assured the alliance of both its secular and religious components, although it is true that the Front's leadership role was vitiated somewhat as well into that of a junior partner.[84] Intellectuals and students were also instrumental in the roles played by the Mujahidin, Fada'ian, and Tudeh during the revolution. All of these groups marched in demonstrations, supported the general strike, and were prepared at the end to confront the regime militarily. All of these groups, and particularly the Tudeh, saw in Khumaini an ardent anti-imperialist and opponent of the regime. Nevertheless they also made their own demands, warning Khumaini not to monopolize the revolution and calling on the population to resist the manipulation of Islam to undermine democracy. Their presence in the December 1978 demonstrations with the slogan "Arms to the people!" radicalized some participants; from this point on they organized openly, distributing pamphlets and newspapers, and recruiting many members, especially among the young. Significantly, in the final uprising of February 9-11, 1979 it was above all members of the Fada'ian, Mujahidin, and Tudeh who did most of the fighting that led to the collapse of the army and the triumph of the revolution.[85]

Iran's working class also played a pivotal role in the mass movement as the initiators of numerous more or less spontaneous strikes which coalesced into a general strike by the end of 1978. Strike activity had picked up in 1977 and the first half of 1978, mostly of an economic nature, contributing to the general ferment during the shah's brief liberalization campaign. In the hot summer of 1978 strikers began to make more political demands. This new trend became apparent in September and October when the oil workers' strike began. They were soon joined by communications, transport, banking, hospital, and industrial workers in the paper, machine tools, tobacco, textile, steel, and other sectors. Despite offers of large wage increases, workers stayed on strike, while frequently voicing support for Khumaini and the growing social movement. The strike by Iran's 30,000 or more oil workers was determinant; forced back to work by the army in November, they went out again in December and stayed out. By then all of Iran was active in what amounted to a massive political general strike. Oil workers said: "We will export oil only when we have exported the shah."[86] Once this had been achieved strikes continued, making it impossible for the Bakhtiar government to function. There is evidence that many of Iran's striking workers admired Khumaini less for religious than political reasons, seeing him as resolutely opposed to the shah. The anti-clerical tendency of some workers is exemplified by the resignation of M. J. Khatami, leader of the oil strikers, in late January 1979 to protest "the dogmatic reactionary clergy," "the new form of repression under the guise of religion" and the "arbitrary interferences" of Khumaini's envoy in the oil strike.[87] The Marxist Fada'i and Tudeh, the Islamic socialists of the Mujahidin, and Shari'ati were all active influences on the strikers among the working class. During the course of the strike movement workers founded their own unique institutions, known as *shuras* ("councils"; cf. "soviets"). These were grass-roots, decentralized strike committees organized at factories, offices, and schools. Their ideological complexion also varied from Islamic to leftist; one activist in a Tabriz shura said "We had all kinds of workers: Left, Right, religious, progressive, reactionary."[88] Shuras took over production and distribution in their factories as the strike came to an end, for managers, particularly in the foreign-owned sector, had often fled the country. The general strike served two purposes: It weakened the shah's regime, delegitimating it internally and making it difficult to repress the movement (for the army needed fuel, the ministries needed communications). And it convinced the West, led by the United States, that the shah could no longer guarantee the flow of Iranian oil, let alone provide a stable outlet for investment capital. It was thus absolutely central to the success of the revolution; Khumaini could not have taken power (or would have had an unimaginably more difficult task doing so) without the working class general strike.

The most important supporting mass role played by the lower classes during the revolution was that of the urban marginals. The marginal classes had fought evictions from shanty town areas in south Tehran in the summer of 1977, thereby showing that the regime could be resisted. Motivated by religious fervor and economic need, and extolled by Khumaini as the *mustazafin* ("oppressed masses," "the disinherited"), the urban marginal classes swelled the ranks of the large demonstrations late in 1978. Here they faced the army's guns, suffering many of the 10,000 casualties of the revolution. Poor urban youth were particularly active, some emerging as leaders of their neighborhoods during the mass marches. Squatters (the poorest of the urban marginals) were less active than settled urban marginals. One squatter told a reporter that to demonstrate "you have to have a full stomach"; another that he had no time to participate but believed "things will get better once the King goes."[89]

The peasants and tribespeople of the countryside were much less active but did participate in the revolution to a certain degree. A few peasants had been mobilized by the regime in early 1978 to attack demonstrations and march in pro-shah processions, but this soon tailed off. On the side of the revolution, those who lived close enough to urban areas to commute, and again, especially young commuters, took an active role in demonstrations from the fall of 1978 onwards, quite similar to nonsquatting urban migrants in the pattern of their involvement. They also brought the revolution home with them to their villages. Rural class struggles intensified near Shiraz in late 1978. The gendarmerie began to abandon its posts in the countryside in mid-December; by early January most villagers were tacitly or openly supporting the winning pro-Khumaini forces. Peasants near Tehran marched in the large Muharram demonstrations of December 1978. Some instances of peasants occupying landlords' properties in early 1979 are recorded, particularly in Kurdistan and Turkaman Sahra (northeastern Iran), where peasants' councils were set up. While Ashraf and Banuazizi claim that peasants "played no significant role in any phase of the revolution," Zavareei feels that peasants eventually provided a base of support for religious fundamentalists. Hooglund however cautions that villagers were in general somewhat ambivalent or superficial in their support for Khumaini because they questioned what he knew about their problems and they could see rural elites ingratiating themselves with the movement and dominating the new village councils.[90] We may conclude that peasants as a class were not instrumental in the populist alliance, but did play a variety of roles in the revolution, somewhat akin to their limited but real participation in the Constitutional revolution.

Tribespeople were even less well placed to be active, although again, there were exceptions. In 1978-79 Kurdistan seized the opportunity to renew its long-standing hostility to the central government. Local Sunni ulama mobilized tribespeople to some degree both there and in Baluchistan. Turkaman Sahra, where police and army posts were attacked, was also an area of tribal revolt. Arabs in Khuzistan were led by their own Ayatullah al-Shabir Khaqani. In some places nomads regained pasture rights. Abrahamian notes that the councils and komitehs in all these areas were demanding a *democratic* Islamic republic, one that would guarantee the rights of the provinces, ethnic minorities, and Sunnis.[91] Tribal youth tended to be more leftist in orientation than their elders. The tribes as a whole were less motivated than others by Islam; indeed, they continued to resist the new government after February 1979 and to suffer repression as a result.

Finally, women also contributed significantly to the revolution, in most respects along their respective class lines. The large demonstrations often featured thousands of chador-clad women in the front ranks in spite of (and to reduce) the danger. Keddie considers these primarily "bazaari women"; the urban lower classes and students could be counted among them as well. Women also participated in the workers' councils in small numbers (presumably proportionate to their fewer numbers in the workforce).[92]

Further insight can be gained into the nature of the 1978-79 version of the populist alliance through an examination of the political cultures at work in the revolution. Here we may usefully distinguish an Islamic populist discourse, a secular nationalist current, and a leftist idiom. Of these the emergent hegemonic political culture was clearly Khumaini's populist Islam. As Khumaini said of his own appeal in late 1978: "The symbol of the struggle is the one who talks with the people. . . . That's why the Iranian people consider me a symbol. I talk their language. I listen to their needs. I cry for them."[93] The terms Khumaini used to address the Iranian public in his speeches included "the aware, combative and courageous people of Iran," "the dear and courageous nation" and "the oppressed of Iran"—all evoking nationalist sentiments. He more frequently employed Islamic terms—"the combative Islamic community," "the Iranian Muslim people." The ulama could virtually command people to participate with such language as "It is expected the entire Muslim community will participate"; "This is an Islamic duty and must be followed"; "This is a Godly duty"; and "It is incumbent upon the Iranian people."[94] For Moghadam the core substantive elements of Khumaini's Islamic populism were "National independence, a more equitable distribution of wealth and resources, and the special place of the poor. . . . Strongly present are also an existential quest for justice (*edalat*) and redress of grievances; these are part of the Shi'i repertoire."[95] Other aspects of the religious populist discourse included the evocation of the theme of martyrdom that inspired the bravery of the crowds in the large demonstrations. The unarmed people faced down a well-equipped army, breaking down its discipline and will to repress them by appeals to a common Islamic identity. As Keddie comments on the peacefulness of the mass movement: "Human life was spared, even of those considered enemies, and except for rare incidents involving a very few persons at the high point of late revolutionary fervor, even American lives were inviolable."[96] Despite much destruction of property, there was little looting. Rather, crowds would remove items from offices, banks, liquor stores, and the like and burn them in the street. The self-perception of this nonviolence was that "a people with empty hands but a great faith, *dast-e khali va iman-e bozorg*, brought down the Pahlavi regime."[97]

Secular political discourses were also articulated during the revolution although in a minor key: "National Front and democratic grouplets tended to use *mardom*, people and *mellat*, nation (as distinct from *dowlat*, the state). Leftist groups such as the Tudeh party, the Feda'i and even the Mujahedin used class-based notions such as *kargaran*, workers; *zahmatkeshan*, toilers; *tudeh*, the masses; *khalq*, people (with ethnic overtones)."[98] The leftist idiom was confined to the educated middle class (especially students and other intelligentsia), some workers, and some urban marginal youth. The National Front's appeals to the nation were broadly congruent with the larger Islamic political culture and easily swallowed up by it. Though Khumaini decried any alliance with the left both early on (May 1978) and after the revolution (August 1979), at the crucial moment—November 1978—his representative in Tehran, Ayatullah Bihishti, called on "the Marxists, materialists and liberals to cooperate for some time and with one voice to continue the valuable struggle against the regime."[99] The left and the National Front for the most part responded to this appeal to unity, submerging differences and taking Islamic populism's themes of national independence, anti-imperialism, overthrow of the monarchy, and social justice as acceptable lowest common denominators.

Another way to enter into the political culture operative in the revolution is to consider the many slogans used in the demonstrations. These too reveal the Islamic and left/secular currents, as well as the ultimate unanimity between them on key demands. Religious slogans—it should be kept in mind that many of these are quite lyrical in Persian—included: "Our movement upholds the Quran, and our country upholds Islam!", "A Muslim's silence is a betrayal of Islam!", and "This filthy government is worse than Yazid!" (the general responsible for the massacre of the Imam Husain and his followers in the seventh century).[100] Khumaini is invoked in the chants "Our party is that of Allah and our leader is Ruhullah!" and "God, the Quran, Khumaini" (used by people overturning a statue of the shah at the university and consciously mocking the regime's version of "God, the shah, the country").[101] Leftwing slogans heard during Muharram 1978 and early 1979 included: "Long live the revolutionary fighters!", "Arms to the people!" and "Glory to the Fada'ian!"[102] The movement could agree on some basic central points: "Death to the shah!" (heard as early as

February 1978 at Tabriz), "The shah is Carter's dog!", "Hang the American puppet!" and "We will kill Iran's dictator, we will destroy Yankee power in Iran!"—each of which single out the shah and foreign domination as the twin opponents of the people.[103] Finally, the themes which the populist alliance ultimately united around are contained in the demand "Independence, Freedom, Islamic republic" (heard from September 4, 1978 on) and the cry "Long live Khumaini, Islam, democracy, freedom and equality!"[104]

State and World-System: Some Considerations

In *States and Social Revolutions*, Skocpol argued that conflict between a potentially autonomous state and elite classes constituted one locus of state breakdowns leading to revolution. In her essay on Iran, she no longer holds to this view, noting the insignificance of elite conflict with the state and instead focussing on the vulnerabilities of the rentier-type state (that it relates to society through expenditures and that it is tied to the "rhythms of the world capitalist economy"). Indeed she rather downplays the role of the state altogether in the Iranian revolution, directing attention instead to the strength of the opposition.[105] The precise role played by the Pahlavi state is best revealed by examining state/elite relations, state/army relations, and the behavior of all of these social forces in the revolution.

As discussed in chapter eight, the Iranian bourgeoisie was essentially dependent on the state as the motor of development and source of capital as well as maker of the rules of the political economic game. The state was thus so "autonomous" (powerful) that elite opposition could not play a part in undermining it; rather, the elite was bound to cooperate with the state and foreign capital in order to take a cut of the surplus on their terms. The "state" moreover in Iran was closely identified with the shah and his family (although in the broad sense it included the key institutions of the army and bureaucracy as well). This made it a solid target for social movements without fully implicating the rest of the dominant classes—landlords, industrialists, large merchants, tribal chiefs, high bureaucrats—who therefore had less of a stake in rushing to defend it.[106] Beyond the upper classes, which were passively connected to it, the state hoped to command the loyalty of other social sectors—peasants through land reform, workers through shares in industry, a few ulama through patronage, civil servants through employment opportunities, middle classes through consumption, and urban marginals through promises and some distribution of money on occasions such as elections and in times of urban unrest. How well these strata responded during the revolution will be considered in a moment, but we already know that Pahlavi claims to legitimation were rather weak even by Iranian standards. Ultimately the shah relied on the security apparatus of police, army, and SAVAK to control society and preserve his position at the head of it. Exorbitant weapons purchases, extravagant perquisites for high officers, and indoctrination of the rank and file with loyalty to God, shah and country were the means used to ensure the support of the army, whose main purpose was one of social control. Thus its response to the revolutionary crisis would prove to be central to the fate of the Pahlavi regime.

The state's reaction to the events of 1978 took the form of a characteristic mix of repression and concessions in an increasingly desperate attempt to buy the support of some sectors and to intimidate the rest of society. Thus elections were promised, censorship, corruption, and torture reduced somewhat, wage increases granted, and so on, at the same time that the army was repeatedly ordered to fire on demonstrators. The shah's mood and policy swings have been attributed by some to his growing cancer; but his woeful ignorance of society—telling a British journalist in September 1978, for example, that there were no slums in Tehran—cannot be so explained and contributed to the poor policy and judgment displayed throughout the year.[107] The loss of trusted advisors like 'Alam and Iqbal hurt the shah, and splits between hard- and soft-liners in his administration only mirrored his own ambivalence. The lack or unwillingness of interlocutors within civil society, be they the National Front, ulama, professional organizations, independent unions or political parties, severely limited the range of options available for dealing with unrest once it got under way. The shah's exacerbation of the economic downswing by following a deflationary policy during 1978 also made matters worse, limiting the patronage resources available to the state and magnifying internal conflict within it.

For all this, the shah did not roll over and quit in 1978. Immediately after the January 1978 demonstration at Qum the state tried to mobilize its social base in counter-demonstrations and the newspapers reported pro-shah crowds of 50,000 at Tabriz on January 18, of 200,000 in Khuzistan a day later, and 300,000 in Tabriz some weeks later on April 9. These crowds included peasants trucked in to the cities for the occasion, schoolchildren, civil servants, and others whom the state could at first coerce into participating. Even when the size of the mass movement removed such fears, the Pahlavi-appointed Bakhtiar government could mobilize 100,000 in January 1979, although by then the opposition demonstrators numbered in the millions. Other efforts included the formation of paramilitary groups such as SAVAK's Underground Committee of Revenge and the Rastakhiz Party's Resistance Corps, to threaten, kidnap, attack, and bomb opposition leaders, organizations, and demonstrations. Such groups paid members of the marginal classes, workers, and some peasants to do their work for them. But the shift from voluntary to coercive forms of "mass support" reflected the deteriorating position of the regime, such that "The Shah himself, in December 1978, summed up the tragicomedy of his sinking regime. When asked by a foreign correspondent where his supporters were, he shrugged his shoulders and replied, 'Search me'."[108]

The regime's last bastion of defense was the army itself. Arjomand has pointed out that the army remained intact for longer than in 1917 Russia (but of course it had not been defeated in a foreign war). It was certainly reliable through the autumn of 1978, killing protestors on numerous occasions and forcing strikers back to work. But by December, appeals from the ulama and demonstrators not to fire on unarmed Muslims began to have an effect and hundreds of rank-and-file soldiers deserted at Qum and Mashhad during Muharram, making it impossible to prevent the huge demonstrations that shook the regime. Defections reached one thousand a day during that month, as devout conscripts abandoned their regiments. Others refused to follow orders, joined demonstrations, distributed weapons to the opposition, shot their officers, or went on hunger strikes. It was left to the officers to do much of the actual firing on demonstrators thereafter. The high command was divided into those who wished to use all the force at their disposal and those who knew it would be useless and even dangerous to do so. Some officers wanted to keep the army out of politics in order to maintain it as an institution, while others were susceptible to religious appeals themselves. Corruption and privilege undermined the actions of the top generals. Eventually, those who remained signed a secret agreement with the opposition to send some of the most abusive officers out of the country and to retain others in their posts. Even this could not prevent the need for the three-day armed uprising in February 1979 to finish off the elite units that remained loyal to the shah to the end. Iran's isolated, untested army could not alone stem the tide of revolution against a regime in economic, political, and ideological crisis, without a strong social base.[109] The "autonomous" Iranian state, despite the absence of elite contenders or military defeat, proved in the end extremely fragile.

These internal weaknesses had an external counterpart as well, though again it did not follow the scenario sketched by Skocpol of intense external pressure in the international system of competing states as a cause of revolutions. Indeed, in her essay on Iran she again downplays what had been a key factor in her book on France, Russia, and China: "By the 1970s, the Shah was far from being a U.S. puppet in any realm of domestic or foreign policy."[110] Here she is in oblique agreement with Halliday's conclusion that world-systemic factors are of much less importance; for Halliday, the regime's collapse

> demonstrated, in the first instance, the relative incapacity of the western powers to control events, even in a country where they had been so influential for decades. As in other apparently secure western allies—Portugal, Ethio-

pia—the events in Iran demonstrated the continuing primacy of the internal class struggle over the influence of imperialism once the opposition movement began to act.[111]

This issue should be looked at more deeply, for the world-systemic conjuncture was such that the revolution succeeded (thus the United States did play a role), and the dependent relation of Iran to the U.S. (*pace* Skocpol) and in the world-economy created the economic and political conditions to which the population was responding (*pace* Halliday).

The United States was indeed a crucial factor in the pre-revolutionary situation of Iran, as demonstrated in chapter eight, having surpassed all other foreign competitors, east and west, in replacing the British as the dominant outside power in the country. From Eisenhower's involvement in the 1953 CIA coup to Kennedy's in the appointment of 'Ali Amini and the land reform of the early 1960s to Nixon's "doctrine" of selling Iran any non-nuclear weapon system it could afford to police the Gulf and contain the Soviets, the United States had forged a strong relationship with the shah.[112] This seemed to be under scrutiny when Jimmy Carter took office in early 1977 with an avowed foreign policy based on respect for human rights. Indeed, the shah expressed serious self-doubt, reportedly remarking to an aide on the eve of Carter's election, "It looks like we are not going to be around much longer."[113] In fact, Carter improbably developed a personal rapport with the shah in the course of visits in 1977 and the strategic relationship was never seriously questioned. Many observers suspected that a deal was made in late 1977: Iran would sell its oil at moderate prices (recall American concerns with inflation and recession at this time), in exchange for less criticism from the U.S. and continued weapons sales. Still, "liberalization" was on the shah's agenda in 1977, and while international opinion may have played the greater role in this, the desire to please the Carter administration was simultaneously served (and throughout the "troubles" of 1978 the United States expressed increasingly unrealistic hopes that liberalization would go forward). So however indirectly, the Carter human rights foreign policy did make the shah waver on the continued use of repression as part of domestic policy in 1977 and encouraged the letters and meetings of the intelligentsia that foreshadowed the revolutionary movement of the next year.[114]

During the revolution itself the United States continued to be a factor in several important ways. On the one hand, Carter's ill-timed public expressions of support for the shah, such as the New Year's Eve toast and the phone call just after the Bloody Friday massacres kept the United States in the popular imagination as a potent symbol of foreign domination tied to the shah ("The shah is Carter's dog!" was a revealing slogan). Further, serious policy splits plagued the effectiveness of the administration's actual support for the shah. While the State Department and later the embassy in Tehran realized that a genuine social revolution was building that could well oust the shah, the National Security Council led by Zbigniew Brzezinski was supported by Secretary of Energy James Schlesinger, Secretary of Defense Harold Brown, and CIA chief Stansfield Turner in seeing the revolution as Soviet-orchestrated and subject to defeat if the army was used resolutely. These two opposed policies effectively cancelled each other out, making neither a workable approach. In either case the seriousness of the situation was not grasped until it was far too late; Ambassador William Sullivan saw matters clearly only in November 1978. Brzezinski meanwhile torpedoed any attempts to establish contact with Khumaini, thus guaranteeing antagonism between the movement and the United States. Carter himself followed no clear policy and neither the opposition nor the shah was really supported. On December 7, for example, Carter simultaneously declared his confidence in the shah and stated that the United States would not interfere in Iran's affairs. The effectiveness of the oil strike may well have tipped the American hand reluctantly against the shah in late December, leading to support for his "vacation" abroad. The January 1979 mission of U.S. General Huyser to Iran with orders to aid the Bakhtiar government and possibly arrange a last minute coup to thwart Khumaini was the final chimera in Brzezinski's cold war scenario. When the National Security Advisor cabled Ambassador Sullivan on February 10 during the final uprising to arrange a coup, the latter's reply was "unprintable."[115]

This *non-action* of the key world power in the equation opened the door to the full play of the internal balance of forces and this did help the revolution succeed, just as the American relationship to the shah from 1953 to 1978 undercut his legitimacy in the first place. The world-systemic conjuncture, then, was favorable to the triumph of the revolution in the sense that its core power did not aggressively intervene to prevent it. One may plausibly contend that the revolution would have succeeded regardless, but the cost would certainly have been higher in human lives and unforeseen historical alternatives could have opened up (coup, intervention, different internal struggles, and so forth).

Iran's Revolution in Comparative Perspective

As we have by now seen, the Iranian upheaval does not fit neatly into Skocpol's model of social revolutions derived from the cases of the French, Chinese, and Russian upheavals. Without entering into the details of these cases here, it may still be suggested that the divergence may be attributable to the differences between large bureaucratic agrarian states and smaller, dependent Third World ones (Skocpol has taken this tack, although Iran does not fit into her Third World model either). It may also have to do with the very different place of each revolution on the continuum of world-historical time—late twentieth-century states face a very different set of political and economic constraints both internally and externally. Indeed, perhaps the Iranian case may lead future researchers to re-examine the cases of Skocpol's "Big Three" to highlight processes which she did not, such as the roles of urban classes in France and Russia, the effects of occupying a dependent place in the world-system (China, or Russia as semiperiphery), and, certainly, the great role played by political cultures of opposition in the making of revolutions.[116]

The most apposite case for comparison with Iran is Nicaragua, which experienced a revolution in the same year of 1979. Both involved multi-class alliances, both succeeded against a military-type dictator, both benefitted from the absence of a strong American intervention. The two differed in the type of struggle that occurred—armed insurrection in Nicaragua cost four times as many lives in a country with one-tenth the population of Iran. But the similarities suggest that the same processes were at work and the model of diagram 9.1 can be applied in large measure to the Nicaraguan case. Thus one observes the consequences of dependent development and state repression, the elaboration of a political culture of opposition in Sandinismo, the economic downswing of the 1972 earthquake that was never overcome, and the same world-systemic opportunity provided by the Carter human rights policy and internal divisions, all leading to a revolutionary outbreak carried by a broad populist alliance against the hated dictator Somoza. These striking similarities suggest that our model may be better suited to the class of twentieth-century Third World revolutions than those of Skocpol and others. Cuba, Chile, and Mexico are further cases worth examining in this light, to name a few.[117]

Comparison of the Iranian revolution with the major earlier instances of social change in twentieth-century Iran is also instructive. In both the 1905 Constitutional revolution and the 1951-53 oil nationalization struggle urban multi-class populist alliances formed, and for essentially the same reasons as in the recent revolution: the ongoing complexity of Iranian social structure, the impact of the West resulting in a situation of dependence, and the elaboration of several political cultures of resistance to this experience. These factors have made the populist alliance a natural social base for movements against the state and foreign domination. But why was the 1978-79 instance more successful than its predecessors? One factor was the strength and solidity of the 1978 populist alliance, especially compared with 1951-53 and 1960-63. Brutal repression did not deter it (as on August 19, 1953 and June 5, 1963); the movement found effective new tactics after Bloody Friday, such as the mass strikes and huge demonstrations. The components of the populist alliance also worked better together—the ulama played their most militant role in 1978 and all secular forces worked with them, compared with the ulama's ambivalence in 1905-11, inactivity in 1951-53, and isolation in 1963. The goal of the movement—to actually change the state radically by abolishing the monarchy and setting up a republic—also distinguished 1978 from earlier movements. In this respect the political cultures of opposition were undoubtedly more effective in articulating grievances and mobilizing the population. Finally, the world-systemic conjuncture was immeasurably more favorable than in 1911 when Russian intervention brought about a counter-revolution or in 1953 when the CIA organized its countercoup. So while the same theoretical factors were present in the outbreak of the three major social movements of twentieth-century Iran, differences in the way these factors played themselves out can account for differences in their outcomes.

Aftermath: 1979-1991

The reflections above raise a final analytic question: How different *has* the outcome of the Iranian revolution been in the context of Iran's history of social change? Ending not in defeat but in the overthrow of the monarchy and the end of the close relationship with the United States, the revolution would seem to have escaped the inevitable failure of the basic pattern of social movements in Iran. On the other hand, it was followed by a bloody foreign war with Iraq and a crumbling of the multi-class alliance that made the revolution. In this concluding section we will not enter into detail on developments in Iran since 1979, but rather make a few analytic remarks in light of the framework adopted in the present study.[118]

The new regime moved swiftly to consolidate its position in society, but typically, this signalled the eventual fragmentation of the diverse coalition that had made the revolution. The initial steps in the institutionalization of the new state were the March 30, 1979 referendum abolishing the monarchy and establishing the Islamic Republic of Iran; the election of a majlis on August 3, 1979; the passing of a new constitution in November 1979; and the election of Bani Sadr as president on January 25, 1980. In the meantime, on November 4, 1979 crowds seized the American embassy in Tehran touching off the 444-day hostage crisis, and a year later, in September 1980, Iraq invaded the oil province of Khuzistan, initiating the bloody Gulf War.

The ulama who supported Khumaini as supreme leader of the revolution moved quickly to gain control of the state during this period. The Islamic Republican Party (IRP), formed in May 1979, gained a majority in the first majlis and controlled the process of drafting the constitution which gave wide powers to Khumaini as the leading Islamic jurist. The hostage crisis provided an occasion for forcing Bazargan to step down as prime minister, seen as tainted by contacts with the United States. The ulama astutely maneuvered the left against secular and Islamic liberals during this period, forcing Bani Sadr to flee Iran in June 1981 over differences with the IRP. The Mujahidin were the next group isolated and defeated when they attempted to mobilize the population against the government in the summer of 1981. Mujahidin bombs killed a president, prime minister, and twenty-seven IRP majlis deputies, but failed to spark an uprising; the organization was subsequently forced completely underground through arrests, torture, and execution of its members. The Tudeh and a section of the Fada'ian continued to support the government as anti-imperialist through all of this, until the time came for arrests and executions of their leaderships beginning in 1983-84.

Of the classes who participated in the revolutionary coalition, only a portion of the ulama, select members of the bazaar classes, and to some degree urban marginals as a class received tangible benefits. It is important to remember that Khumaini's militant form of Islam was enthusiastically embraced by probably only a minority of the tens of thousands of ulama; even among supporters there were numerous conflicts over economic and political policy. In the bazaar, some entrepreneurs emerged to benefit from lessened contact with the world economy and the business opportunities posed by revolution and war, but many others suffered economic losses and political repression. In addition to the defeat of all secular parties, the intelligentsia saw the universities closed for two years as part of an Islamization campaign; at least 200,000 of its members left Iran from 1979 to 1982. The working class's gains in wages and control over production in 1979 were later lost as their independent shuras were replaced by Islamic associations, management returned to run workplaces, and war and recession affected their well-being. While urban marginals were appealed to as a key IRP constituency and a slight shift in their share of income took place, many hardships of housing, food, and jobs remained; Tehran's population swelled from 4.5 million to six million people a year after the revolution. Women were dismissed from schools and offices, and changes in the family law lowered the marriage age from eighteen to thirteen while making divorce easier for men. In the countryside, peasant land seizures were discouraged or reversed by the army, while the Kurds were militarily repressed and Qashqa'is had their chiefs executed in 1980 for plotting against Khumaini.[119] The populist alliance, then, as in 1909-11 and 1953, split soon after power was achieved and only a few of its constituent social classes and political organizations can be said to have obtained what they struggled for in the revolution.

No sooner had Iran's economy begun to restart itself after the strike-interrupted year of the revolution than the war with Iraq again dealt it a severe shock which lasted throughout the 1980s and whose effects would be felt well beyond that. War brought destruction of housing, roads, infrastructure, and oil installations; diversion of funds from development to the military effort; and the closing of factories due to lack of spare parts, drops in consumption capacity, and shortages of labor as workers were ordered to the front. Agriculture has persisted as a major obstacle to better standards of living. Despite a good harvest in 1979, production slowed again after 1980 and food imports continued to run up a large bill. Migration to the cities continued unabated, compounded by the war. The central oil industry benefitted from production cuts in 1979-80 and a doubling of prices in that period, but prices fell drastically again in the 1980s and dependence on oil revenues remained characteristic of the political economy.[120]

Some observers, such as Amirahmadi, felt that revolutionary Iran might follow a "non-capitalist" path of development, while many, such as Samir Amin, thought that "Iran had 'de-linked' from the world system, or at any rate, that its economy had ceased to be a part of the world-capitalist order."[121] But in terms of the theoretical perspectives of the present study, these are dubious claims. Dependency remains a deep structural problem for Iran—dependence on oil revenues, on Western technology, on food imports, and on arms, to name a few significant items. While it may be argued that the hostage crisis had the short-term benefit of keeping American intervention at bay, Iran was soon turning secretly to the United States and Israel for arms to keep the war going against Iraq. And reconstruction of the battered economy will undoubtedly require European and Japanese involvement, if not, in the long run, American participation as well. The declaration of an Islamic Republic does not annul Iran's status as a peripheral country in the world-system with a dependent capitalist form of development.

The task of converting the strength of populist Islam from a revolutionary force to a blueprint for society raised many urgent problems for the economy and polity. In part the dilemma was put off by displacing it to meet the perceived threat of American intervention with the embassy takeover, and the call to export the Islamic revolution that was one cause of the Iran-Iraq war. These episodes allowed the government to consolidate its hold on the population by continuing to pluck the emotional strings of martyrdom and struggle against evil oppressors. Khumaini, for example, tried to lower material expectations as a way of de-linking from the West and encouraging religious sensibilities: "he told President Bani-Sadr that the American embargo during the hostage crisis would not be detrimental to the population: 'In the time of the Prophet, they ate only one date a day'."[122] In the process, the liberating potential of the versions of Islamic political culture espoused by Shari'ati, Taliqani, Bazargan, and Bani Sadr were either distorted or narrowly circumscribed. The political atmosphere and practical results of IRP rule were neither democratic, progressive, liberal or socialist. The clearest evidence of this was the effort by the new regime to distinguish itself from Iran's past social movements. Shaikh Fazlullah Nuri, the monarchist ayatullah hanged by the constitutionalists in 1909, was rehabilitated as a martyr. Conversely, Mussadiq was downgraded as a heroic figure, with Khumaini averring "They say he nationalised [Iranian] oil. So What? We did not want oil, we did not want independence, we wanted Islam."[123] Yet one million Iranians went to Ahmadabad on a pilgrimage to celebrate Mussadiq's memory in March 1979. The narrowing of the new hegemonic political culture after 1979 may have been as predictable as that the populist alliance itself would split into its constituent elements. It likewise suggests the degree to which the triumph of the 1978 revolution has been mitigated by failures to learn the lessons of the past.

The 1989 death of Khumaini, the winding down of the Iran-Iraq war as a costly stalemate, and the 1990-91 Gulf crisis and war between Iraq and the United States marked a new phase in the aftermath of the Iranian revolution. The decline of ideological fervor, diplomatic isolation, and physical exhaustion paved the way for the ascendency of the more Western-oriented, free market clerical rule of the group around President Ali Akbar Hashemi Rafsanjani. The Iranian government is now trying to reenter international economic and political circles, rebuild its war-torn economy, and confront the pent-up demands and expectations of the millions who made the revolution. Doing so in a constructive way will require breaking with the main patterns of dependency and exclusionary rule that have marked the Iranian political economy for almost two centuries. The Iranian people will write the next chapter in this long and conflicted history. The thrust of the present study has been to capture for historical memory and sociological reflection the multiple meanings and strengths—as well as failures—of their countless efforts to do so.

Notes

1. From two speeches on Tehran Radio, September 8, 1979 and September 12, 1979, texts in *Foreign Broadcast Information Service* (FBIS), September 10, 1979 and November 13, 1979, quoted in Hossein Zafarian, "Analytical Approach to Correlation Between Marxism and Iran's Islamic Revolution," Ph.D. dissertation, Department of International Relations, Claremont Graduate School (1984), 162.

2. This section draws on Jack Goldstone's articles, "The Comparative and Historical Study of Revolutions," pp. 187-207 in *Annual Review of Sociology*, volume 8 (1982), and "Theories of Revolution: The Third Generation," pp. 425-453 in *World Politics*, volume XXXII, number 3 (April 1980).

3. Key works include L. P. Edwards, *The Natural History of Revolutions* (Chicago: University of Chicago Press, 1927); G. S. Pettee, *The Process of Revolution* (New York: Harper and Row, 1937); and Crane Brinton, *The Anatomy of Revolution* (New York: Vintage, [1938] 1965).

4. Key works include Neil J. Smelser, *Theory of Collective Behavior* (New York: Free Press, 1963); Chalmers Johnson, *Revolutionary Change* (Boston: Little, Brown, 1966); Ted Robert Gurr, *Why Men Rebel* (Princeton: Princeton University Press, 1970); and J. C. Davies, "Toward a Theory of Revolution," pp. 5-19 in *American Sociological Review*, volume 27 (1962).

5. Their works include S. N. Eisenstadt, *Revolutions and the Transformation of Societies: A Comparative Study of Civilizations* (New York: Free Press, 1978); Jeffery M. Paige, *Agrarian Revolution: Social Movements and Export Agriculture in the Underdeveloped World* (New York: Free Press, 1975); Charles Tilly, *From Mobilization to Revolution* (Reading, Massachusetts: Addison-Wesley, 1978); Ellen Kay Trimberger, *Revolution From Above: Military Bureaucrats and Development in Japan, Turkey, Egypt, and Peru* (New Brunswick: Transaction Books, 1978); and Skocpol's *States and Social Revolutions*.

6. Skocpol, *States and Social Revolutions*, 4.

7. Theda Skocpol, "Analyzing Causal Configurations in History: A Rejoinder to Nichols," pp. 187-194 in *Comparative Social Research. An Annual Publication*, volume 9: *Historical Studies* (Greenwich, Connecticut and London: JAI Press, Inc., 1986), 191.

8. Ibid., referring to her "What Makes Peasants Revolutionary?" pp. 157-179 in Scott Guggenheim and Robert Weller, editors, *Power and Protest in the Countryside* (Durham, North Carolina: Duke University Press, 1982).

9. Skocpol, "Analyzing Causal Configurations," 191-92.

10. This has been noted by James Bill, "Power and Religion in Revolutionary Iran," pp. 22-47 in *Middle East Journal*, volume 36, number 1 (Winter 1982), 30 (although what he takes from Brinton is largely only the view of revolution as "chaos" and violence), and more subtly by Nikki Keddie, "Iranian Revolutions in Comparative Perspective," pp. 579-598 in *American Historical Review*, volume 88, number 3 (June 1983), 589-91.

11. Zabih, *Iran's Revolutionary Upheaval*, 76; Bashiriyeh, *The State and Revolution*, 85, 108 note 84; and Keddie, "Iranian Revolutions in Comparative Perspective," 589-91, who feels that Brinton and the J-curve models fit Iran better than "most existing socioeconomic comparative schemes," i.e. Skocpol, Tilly, Moore, Hobsbawm, Rudé.

12. This paragraph draws on Skocpol's "Analyzing Casual Configurations" and her article on Iran: "Rentier State and Shi'a Islam in the Iranian Revolution." A fuller-scale treatment is offered in Farideh Farhi's comparative study of Iran and Nicaragua, in which Skocpol's general principles of analysis (but not her specific model) are critically applied: Farideh Farhi, *States and Urban-Based Revolutions. Iran and Nicaragua* (Urbana and Chicago: University of Illinois Press, 1990).

13. In addition to the works I shall cite in this paragraph, see the discussions and sources in Pesaran, "The System of Dependent Capitalism," 501-3, and Val Moghadam, "Populist Revolution and the Islamic State in Iran," pp. 147-163 in Terry Boswell, editor, *Revolution in the World-System* (Westport, Connecticut: Greenwood Press, 1989).

14. Oriana Fallaci, "An Interview with Khomeini," pp. 29-31 in *The New York Times Magazine* (October 7, 1979), 30. Recall also the epigraph to this chapter by Khumaini. For further views of the ayatullah on the nature of the revolution, see Zafarian, "Analytical Approach," 162-68, and Imam Khomeini, *Islam and Revolution. Writings and Declarations of Imam Khomeini*, translated and annotated by Hamid Algar (Berkeley: Mizan Press, 1981), 325-27, 338-39.

15. Said Amir Arjomand, "The Causes and Significance of the Iranian Revolution," pp. 41-66 in *State, Culture and Society*, volume 1, number 3 (1985), 60, and passim for his general argument.

16. Abrahamian, "Structural Causes," 21. See also his *Iran Between Two Revolutions*, 427. Another essentially political approach, from within the resource mobilization paradigm, is

found in Misagh Parsa's excellent *Social Origins of the Iranian Revolution* (New Brunswick and London: Rutgers University Press, 1989).

17. Ervand Abrahamian, "Iran's Turbaned Revolution," pp. 83-106 in David H. Partington, editor, *The Middle East Annual. Issues and Events,* volume 1 (Boston: G. K. Hall & Co., 1982), 84. The argument that Islam filled a political vacuum has been advanced by numerous observers, among whom are Zabih, *Iran's Revolutionary Upheaval,* 20, and the perceptive essay by Ahmad Ashraf and Ali Banuazizi, "The State, Classes and Modes of Mobilization in the Iranian Revolution," pp. 3-40 in *State, Culture and Society,* volume 1, number 3 (1985), 9.

18. Pesaran, "Economic Development," 271, 288.

19. Moghadam, "Populist Revolution," 149; Pesaran, "The System of Dependent Capitalism," 501.

20. Fischer, *Iran,* 190.

21. Moghadam, "Populist Revolution," 151.

22. See Keddie, *Roots of Revolution,* 177; Halliday, "The Iranian Revolution," 189-91; Bashiriyeh, *The State and Revolution,* 1, 84, 121-22; and Burke and Lubeck, "Explaining Social Movements," 664.

23. My notion of a world-systemic opening owes much to Goldfrank's concept of a "permissive world context": see Walter L. Goldfrank, "Theories of Revolution and Revolution Without Theory: The Case of Mexico," pp. 135-165 in *Theory and Society,* volume 7 (1979).

24. I have elaborated this model further in two essays: "Theories of Revolution and the Case of Iran," a paper presented to the American Sociological Association, San Francisco (August 1989), and "A Theory of Third World Social Revolutions: Iran, Nicaragua and El Salvador Compared," a paper presented to the International Sociological Association, Madrid, Spain (July 1990).

25. Pesaran, "Economic Development," 275-77; Abrahamian, *Iran Between Two Revolutions,* 421-22.

26. On the events of 1961-62 see Diba, *Mohammad Mossadegh,* 193, 209; Katouzian, *The Political Economy,* 213-18; Abrahamian, *Iran Between Two Revolutions,* 460-61; Ivanov, *Tarikh-i Nuvin-i Iran,* 206-11; Keddie, *Roots of Revolution,* 151-55; and Willem M. Floor, "The Revolutionary Character of the Iranian Ulama: Wishful Thinking or Reality?" pp. 501-524 in *International Journal of Middle East Studies,* volume 12, number 4 (December 1980), 505-508, 510-11.

27. Burujirdi is quoted by Akhavi, *Religion and Politics,* 222 note 7. See also Floor, "The Revolutionary Character," 503-4, with reference to Avery, *Modern Iran,* 481.

28. On the ulama and land reform, see Floor, "The Revolutionary Character," 509-10; Ashraf, "Iran," 218-25; Akhavi, *Religion and Politics,* 93-94, 222 note 9; and Keddie, "Religion, Society and Revolution," 392-93 note 17.

29. Abrahamian, *Iran Between Two Revolutions,* 425. On the disparate currents within the ulama in this period, see Akhavi, *Religion and Politics,* 101; Jazani, *Capitalism and Revolution,* 64; Floor, "The Revolutionary Character," 509-10; and Katouzian, *The Political Economy,* 227, 358-59.

30. Katouzian, *The Political Economy,* 228. On these events, see ibid.; Floor, "The Revolutionary Character," 511-16; Ashraf, "Iran," 222-23, 235; Algar, "Introduction" to Khomeini, *Islam and Revolution,* 16-17, and 1982 lectures on "Islam in Iran"; Fischer, *Iran,* 124, 188; Abrahamian, *Iran Between Two Revolutions,* 426; Ghoreishi interview, tape 2: 27; Keddie, *Roots of Revolution,* 158-59; and Ghandchi-Tehrani, "Bazaaris and Clergy," 148-49.

31. Fischer, *Iran,* 4, 8, 136; and Henry Munson, 1980 lectures on the Iranian Revolution, University of California, Santa Barbara. One may also consult Henry Munson, Jr., *Islam and Revolution in the Middle East* (New Haven and London: Yale University Press, 1988).

32. Skocpol, "Rentier State and Shi'a Islam," 272-75.

33. These passages of Khumaini's are found in Bashiriyeh, *The State and Revolution,* 60-61. To the first ellipsis the text is from the 1964 speech on American immunity (for this whole speech,

see Floor, "The Revolutionary Character," 521-24); the rest of the text comes from a compilation of his letters and speeches published in 1973, so the exact date is unclear.

34. This quote is from the 1971 Najaf edition of *Hukumat-i Islami*, as translated by Richard in Keddie, *Roots of Revolution*, 207.

35. These are composite quotes from the 1976 edition (no publishing information) of *Vilayat-i Faqih: Hukumat-i Islami*, 52-53, 93, 190, as translated by Abrahamian, *Iran Between Two Revolutions*, 478, 477.

36. Abrahamian, *Iran Between Two Revolutions*, 445, 478-79, 532.

37. Keddie, "Iranian Revolutions in Comparative Perspective," 590-91, 596; Moghadam, "Populist Revolution," 150; Abrahamian, *Iran Between Two Revolutions*, 532-33; Keddie, "Religion, Society, and Revolution," 393 note 20; Bill, "Power and Religion," 42-43.

38. On the network of resistance and its constituent personalities, I have drawn on Abrahamian, *Iran Between Two Revolutions*, 475; Algar, 1982 lectures on "Islam in Iran"; Ann K. S. Lambton, "A Reconsideration of the Position of the *Marja' al-Taqlid* and the Religious Institution," pp. 115-135 in *Studia Islamica*, volume 20 (1964), 130; Halliday, *Iran*, 218; Keddie, *Roots of Revolution*, 242; and Bill, *The Eagle and the Lion*, 238.

39. For details of Shari'ati's life I have relied on Algar's 1982 lectures on "Islam in Iran"; Richard, in Keddie, *Roots of Revolution*, 215-16; Abrahamian, *Iran Between Two Revolutions*, 464-66; and Brad Hanson, "The "Westoxication" of Iran: Depictions and Reactions of Behrangi, Al-e Ahmad, and Shari'ati," pp. 1-23 in *International Journal of Middle East Studies*, volume 15, number 1 (February 1983), 13.

40. 'Ali Shari'ati, *From Where Shall We Begin? & The Machine in the Captivity of Machinism*, translated from the Persian by Fatollah Marjani (Houston: Free Islamic Literatures, Inc., 1980), 30. On Shari'ati's ideas generally, in addition to the specific passages cited in this paragraph, I have drawn on Algar's 1982 lectures on "Islam in Iran"; Fischer, *Iran*, 165-70; Richard, in Keddie, *Roots of Revolution*, 216-19; and Abrahamian, *Iran Between Two Revolutions*, 466-67.

41. Shari'ati, *From Where Shall We Begin?*, 20-21, 23-24, 27-28, 34, 44, 47, 51.

42. Ali Shari'ati, *Marxism and Other Western Fallacies. An Islamic Critique*, translated from the Persian by R. Campbell (Berkeley: Mizan Press, 1980), 49 (this title, incidentally, is not Shari'ati's but rather is the coinage of the editor, Hamid Algar); Abrahamian, *Iran Between Two Revolutions*, 464-64, 467-70; Hanson, "The "Westoxication" of Iran," 15-16.

43. See the passages cited by Richard, in Keddie, *Roots of Revolution*, 221, 224; Bashiriyeh, *The State and Revolution*, 71; and Hanson, "The "Westoxication" of Iran," 18.

44. See Algar's "Preface" to Shari'ati, *Marxism and Other Western Fallacies*, 7-9; and Hanson, "The "Westoxication" of Iran," 18.

45. Bazargan's views, as summarized by Lambton, "A Reconsideration," 124. For Bazargan's life and ideas I have drawn on Akhavi, *Religion and Politics*, 111-14; Algar's 1982 lectures on "Islam in Iran"; Richard, in Keddie, *Roots of Revolution*, 213-15; and Abrahamian, *Iran Between Two Revolutions*, 458. The standard work is now H. E. Chehabi, *Iranian Politics and Religious Modernism. The Liberation Movement of Iran Under the Shah and Khomeini* (Ithaca: Cornell University Press, 1990).

46. This sketch of Taliqani relies on Algar's 1982 lectures on "Islam in Iran"; Richard, in Keddie, *Roots of Revolution*, 210-13; and Abrahamian, *Iran Between Two Revolutions*, 458-59.

47. On Shari'atmadari and Bani Sadr, see Richards, in Keddie, *The Roots of Revolution*, 208-9, 225-28.

48. Abrahamian, *Iran Between Two Revolutions*, 462-64.

49. Jalal Al-i Ahmad, *Gharbzadigi*, translated by William G. Millward and Reza Baraheni, in Baraheni's *The Crowned Cannibals*, 82.

50. Samad Behrangi, *The Little Black Fish and Other Modern Persian Stories*, translated from the Persian by Eric and Mary Hooglund (Washington, D.C.: Three Continents Press, 1976); Hanson, "The "Westoxication" of Iran," 2-7.

51. Halliday, *Iran*, 231, 289.

52. Ibid., 233-37, 262, 297; Abrahamian, *Iran Between Two Revolutions*, 451-57.

53. On the Mujahidin, see Halliday, *Iran*, 240, 242; Keddie, *Roots of Revolution*, 238-39; Abrahamian, *Iran Between Two Revolutions*, 480-81, 489-95; and Bashiriyeh, *The State and Revolution*, 74. I have also drawn on Munson's 1980 lectures on the Iranian Revolution and Algar's 1982 lectures on "Islam in Iran." A major recent study is Ervand Abrahamian, *The Iranian Mojahedin* (New Haven: Yale University Press, 1989).

54. Halliday, *Iran*, 241-42, 246-47; Moghadam, "Socialism or Anti-Imperialism?" 10 note 10; Keddie, *Roots of Revolution*, 237, 239; Abrahamian, *Iran Between Two Revolutions*, 480-89.

55. On the ulama in the 1970s, see Richard, in Keddie, *Roots of Revolution*, 213; Abrahamian, *Iran Between Two Revolutions*, 433, 445, 473-75, 535; Halliday, *Iran*, 19, 218-19; Fischer, *Iran*, 109; Bill, "Power and Religion," 24-25; Bill, *The Eagle and the Lion*, 187; Halliday, "The Iranian Revolution," 194; Abrahamian, "Structural Causes," 25-26; Keddie, "Religion, Society, and Revolution," 32; Moghadam, "Socialism or Anti-Imperialism?" 13; Bashiriyeh, *The State and Revolution*, 73-74, 82 note 93; and Muslim Students , *Asnad-i lanah-i jasusi*, volume 12, part 2: 35; volume 7: 52.

56. See Katouzian, *The Political Economy of Modern Iran*, 336-37; Hooglund, "Rural Participation in the Revolution," 6; Zabih, *Iran's Revolutionary Upheaval*, 17; Muslim Students, *Asnad-i lanah-i jasusi*, volume 25: 100; Fischer, *Iran*, 188, 240-41; Syrous Abbasi, "Radicalization of Leftist Youth in Iran," Ph.D. dissertation, Department of Government, Florida State University (1981), 164; Halliday, *Iran*, 224-25; and Bashiriyeh, *The State and Revolution*, 74-75.

57. On the working class, see Fischer, *Iran*, 188; Halliday, *Iran*, 206-8; Ivanov, *Tarikh-i Nuvin-i Iran*, 300-305; Bayat, *Workers and Revolution*, 46-51; and Moghadam, "Industrial Development," 161, 162 table 3.

58. On merchants and artisans in the 1970s, see Abrahamian, *Iran Between Two Revolutions*, 433, 443-44, 498-500, 533; Floor, "The Guilds in Iran," 115; Abrahamian, "Structural Causes," 24-25; Bashiriyeh, *The State and Revolution*, 66-67; Ghandchi-Tehrani, "Bazaaris and Clergy," 103-4, 119-20; Halliday, *Iran*, 219-20; Katouzian, *The Political Economy*, 336-37; Moghadam, "Industrial Development," 161; and Zavareei, "Dependent Capitalist Development," 177.

59. See Abrahamian, *Iran Between Two Revolutions*, 535-36; Kazemi, *Poverty and Revolution*, 61-93, 125-26; and Halliday, *Iran*, 287.

60. On the peasantry, see Hooglund, *Land and Revolution*, 123-37, 171 note 1; Halliday, *Iran*, 213; and Hooglund, "Rural Participation in the Revolution," 5-6. On the tribes, see Beck, lecture on "Tribes and the State"; Garthwaite, *Khans and shahs*, 141; Abrahamian, *Iran Between Two Revolutions*, 531; Halliday, *Iran*, 239-40; Beck, "Economic Transformations," 99; and Beck, "Revolutionary Iran," 15-16.

61. Graham, *Iran*, 88-89; Bashiriyeh, *The State and Revolution*, 89-90; Dadkhah, "The Inflationary Process," 389 table 1, calculations mine; "Iran: The New Crisis of American Hegemony," 9-10.

62. For these recessionary trends see Keddie, "Iranian Revolutions," 588, and *Roots of Revolution*, 234; "Iran: The New Crisis of American Hegemony," 11; Halliday, *Iran*, 145, "The Iranian Revolution," 194, and "The Genesis of the Iranian Revolution," pp. 1-16 in *Third World Quarterly*, volume 1, number 4 (October 1979), 8-9; Bashiriyeh, *The State and Revolution*, 86, 93, 97-98; Saikal, *Rise and Fall*, 184; Pesaran, "Economic Development," 286; Katouzian, *The Political Economy*, 259; Abrahamian, *Iran Between Two Revolutions*, 511; and Bayat, *Workers and Revolution*, 81.

63. Keddie, *Roots of Revolution*, 231-33; Abrahamian, *Iran Between Two Revolutions*, 500-503; Halliday, *Iran*, 289; Katouzian, *The Political Economy*, 342; Muslim Students, *Asnad-i lanah-i jasusi*, volume 24: 7; Fischer, *Iran*, 189-93; Zavareei, "Dependent Capitalist Development," 175-76; Kazemi, *Poverty and Revolution*, 86-89; Bashiriyeh, *State and Revolution*, 112.

64. Fischer, *Iran*, 193; Abrahamian, *Iran Between Two Revolutions*, 503-505; Balta and Rulleau, *L'Iran insurgé*, 22-24; Bashiriyeh, *The State and Revolution*, 112; Zavareei, "Dependent Capitalist Development," 177-78; Ashraf and Banuazizi, "The State, Classes and Modes of Mobilization," 6, 27; Jerrold D. Green, *Revolution in Iran. The Politics of Countermobilization* (New York: Praeger, 1982), 153-54.

65. Algar, "Introduction" to Khomeini, *Islam and Revolution*, 23 note 16, quoting the *New York Times*, January 2, 1978.

66. For the events of January 1978 I have drawn on Algar's 1982 lectures on "Islam in Iran"; Balta and Rulleau, *L'Iran insurgé*, 24; Keddie, *Roots of Revolution*, 242-43; Fischer, *Iran*, 194-95; Abrahamian, *Iran Between Two Revolutions*, 505; Bashiriyeh, *The State and Revolution*, 113; Yadollah Alidoost-Khaybari, "Religious Revolutionaries: An Analysis of the Religious Groups' Victory in the Iranian Revolution of 1978-79," Department of Sociology, University of Michigan (1981), 498-99; and *Kayhan*, passim. For the most detailed account of the events of 1978-79 generally, see Parsa, *Social Origins*.

67. On these events see Balta and Rulleau, *L'Iran insurgé*, 25; Fischer, *Iran*, 195; Keddie, *Roots of Revolution*, 244; Katouzian, *The Political Economy*, 344; Abrahamian, *Iran Between Two Revolutions*, 506-507; and Zavareei, "Dependent Capitalist Development," 179.

68. For March to May 1978, see Fischer, *Iran*, 196; Abrahamian, *Iran Between Two Revolutions*, 507-8; Alidoost-Khaybari, "Religious Revolutionaries," 504-10; Balta and Rulleau, *L'Iran insurgé*, 25-26; Bill, "Power and Religion," 26, 26 note 6; and *Kayhan*, passim.

69. For late May to late July, I have drawn on Algar's 1982 lectures on "Islam in Iran"; Muslim Students, *Asnad-i lanah-i jasusi*, volume 12, part 2: 110; volume 12, part 3: 19; volume 25: 36-37; Fischer, *Iran*, 196; Keddie, *Roots of Revolution*, 248; and Abrahamian, *Iran Between Two Revolutions*, 509-13.

70. For the events of August I have consulted Algar's 1982 lectures on "Islam in Iran"; Balta and Rulleau, *L'Iran insurgé*, 26ff.; Fischer, *Iran*, 197-98; Halliday, *Iran*, 291; Keddie, *Roots of Revolution*, 249-50; Abrahamian, *Iran Between Two Revolutions*, 513-14; Zabih, *Iran's Revolutionary Upheaval*, 51; Zavareei, "Dependent Capitalist Development," 179-80; Ashraf and Banuazizi, "The State, Classes and Modes of Mobilization," 9-10; Alidoost-Khaybari, "Religious Revolutionaries ," 517, 519; and Iranian Students Association in the U.S., *Shah's Inferno: Abadan August 19, 1978* (Berkeley: ISAUS, 1978), 2ff.

71. For the September events I have used Algar's 1982 lectures on "Islam in Iran"; Balta and Rulleau, *L'Iran insurgé*, 29-32; Fischer, *Iran*, 198-200; Munson's 1980 lectures on the Iranian Revolution; *Manchester Guardian*, September 5 and 6, 1978; *Le Monde*, September 6, 1978; Katouzian, *The Political Economy*, 345; Abrahamian, *Iran Between Two Revolutions*, 514-17; and 'Ali Davani, *Nahzat-i Ruhaniyun-i Iran* [Movement of the Clergy of Iran] (Tehran: Bunyad-i Farhangi-yi Imam Reza, 1360/1981), volume 8, 6-105.

72. Fischer, *Iran*, 102-3, 200-201; Graham, *Iran*, 233; Hooglund, *Land and Revolution*, 142; Katouzian, *The Political Economy*, 353 note 14; Muslim Students, *Asnad-i lanah-i jasusi*, volume 12, part 3: 169; volume 25: 95, 103, 113; volume 7: 245; Abrahamian, *Iran Between Two Revolutions*, 517-18; Zabih, *Iran's Revolutionary Upheaval*, 54; Valentine M. Moghadam, "Accumulation Strategy and Class Formation: The Making of an Industrial Labor Force in Iran, 1962-1977," Ph.D. dissertation, Department of Sociology, American University (1985), 309; Bayat, *Workers and Revolution*, 79-80, 85 figure 6.1; Dr. Kamran Kashani, in an interview recorded by Habib Ladjevardi, July 22, 1982, Mykonos, Greece, Iranian Oral History Collection, Harvard University, tape 1: 7.

73. Balta and Rulleau, *L'Iran insurgé*, 43-52; Fischer, *Iran*, 202-204; Keddie, *Roots of Revolution*, 250-52; Katouzian, *The Political Economy*, 520-21; Zabih, *Iran's Revolutionary Upheaval*, 56-57; Terisa Turner, "Iranian Oilworkers in the 1978-79 Revolution," pp. 272-292 in Petter Nore and Terisa Turner, editors, *Oil and Class Struggle* (London: Zed Press, 1980), 281, 283; "How We Organized Strike that Paralyzed Shah's Regime. Firsthand Account by Iranian Oil Worker," pp.

292-301 in Petter Nore and Terisa Turner, editors, *Oil and Class Struggle* (London: Zed Press, 1980), 299-300.

74. For the events of December I have consulted Algar's 1982 lectures on "Islam in Iran"; Balta and Rulleau, *L'Iran insurgé*, 54-79; Fischer, *Iran*, 204-209; Kazemi, *Poverty and Revolution*, 94; Abrahamian, *Iran Between Two Revolutions*, 521-24; Moghadam, "Accumulation Strategy," 310-11; and William H. Sullivan, "Dateline Iran: The Road Not Taken," pp. 175-186 in *Foreign Policy*, number 40 (Fall 1980), 180.

75. Resolution drafted by the Organizational Committee of the Tehran Clergy, quoted in A. B. Reznikov, "The Downfall of the Iranian Monarchy (January-February 1979)," pp. 254-312 in R. Ulyanovsky, editor, *The Revolutionary Process in the East: Past and Present* (Moscow: Progress Publishers, 1985), 270. For the events of January 1979 I have drawn on Balta and Rulleau, *L'Iran insurgé*, 78-85; Fischer, *Iran*, 210-11; Keddie, *Roots of Revolution*, 256; Katouzian, *The Political Economy*, 349-50; Abrahamian, *Iran Between Two Revolutions*, 525-28; Bashiriyeh, *The State and Revolution*, 119; Moghadam, "Accumulation Strategy," 311-12; and Green, *Revolution in Iran*, 164-65.

76. This is a composite quote based on Abrahamian, *Iran Between Two Revolutions*, 529, and Graham, *Iran*, 237. For the events of the final days, I have used Algar's 1982 lectures on "Islam in Iran"; Balta and Rulleau, *L'Iran insurgé*, 86-95; Keddie, *Roots of Revolution*, 257; Abrahamian, *Iran Between Two Revolutions*, 495, 526-29; and Ashraf and Banuazizi, "The State, Classes and Modes of Mobilization," 17.

77. See, respectively, Abrahamian, *Iran Between Two Revolutions*, 532-35; Keddie, *Roots of Revolution*, 250-51, and "The Midas Touch," 261; Zabih, *Iran's Revolutionary Upheaval*, 74; Bashiriyeh, *The State and Revolution*, 116; and Ashraf and Banuazizi, "The State, Classes and Modes of Mobilization."

78. Val Moghadam, while not developing her argument at length, nor extending it back in time to encompass the Constitutional revolution or oil nationalization struggle, has also explicitly stated this: Moghadam, "Populist Revolution," 155-57. See also ibid., and Moghadam, "Industrial Development," 152, 172 note 5, and "Accumulation Strategy," 305, 307.

79. Bill, "Power and Religion," 28, 28 note 9; Abrahamian, "Iran's Turbaned Revolution," 89.

80. On the ulama in the revolution, see Ashraf and Banuazizi, "The State, Classes and Modes of Mobilization," 26; Katouzian, *The Political Economy*, 353 note 14; and Muslim Students, *Asnad-i lanah-i jasusi*, volume 7: 251; volume 25: 95, 103, 113; volume 26: 61.

81. Moghadam, "Accumulation Strategy," 313; Bayat, *Workers and Revolution*, 95.

82. Keddie, *Roots of Revolution*, 257-58; Abrahamian, *Iran Between Two Revolutions*, 526-27; Ashraf and Banuazizi, "The State, Classes and Modes of Mobilization," 16, 34.

83. Muslim Students, *Asnad-i lanah-i jasusi*, volume 26: 31; Ashraf and Banuazizi, "The State, Classes and Modes of Mobilization," 26; Bill, *The Eagle and the Lion*, 225.

84. On the National Front in the revolution, see Balta and Rulleau, *L'Iran insurgé*, 43-44; Fischer, *Iran*, 201; Keddie, *Roots of Revolution*, 252; and Katouzian, *The Political Economy*, 347, 353 note 15.

85. Zafarian, "Analytical Approach," 166; Fischer, *Iran*, 211; Abrahamian, *Iran Between Two Revolutions*, 522; Keddie, *Roots of Revolution*, 251-52.

86. Quoted in *Iran Times*, January 12, 1979, as cited by Abrahamian, "Iran's Turbaned Revolution," 89. On the strike movement, see Fischer, *Iran*, 200-201; Graham, *Iran*, 233; Keddie, *Roots of Revolution*, 251; Muslim Students, *Asnad-i lanah-i jasusi*, volume 12, part 3: 169; volume 7: 245; Abrahamian, *Iran Between Two Revolutions*, 512, 517-18, 522-23, 525; Zabih, *Iran's Revolutionary Upheaval*, 54, 60; "How We Organized Strike," 299-300; Moghadam, "Industrial Development," 167; Moghadam, "Accumulation Strategy," 308-11; and Bayat, *Workers and Revolution*, 85-88.

87. Bayat, *Workers and Revolution*, 94, quoting the newspaper *Ayandigan*, February 2, 1979. See also "Iran: The New Crisis of American Hegemony," 18-19, quoting *New York Times*, November 19, 1978.

88. Quoted by Moghadam, "Industrial Development," 168. On the shura movement, see ibid., 153; Bayat, *Workers and Revolution*, 6, 92-94; Turner, "Iranian Oilworkers," 279-81; "How We Organized Strike," 293-94; and Moghadam, "Accumulation Strategy," 4, 10, 305, 316, 318, 321-28.

89. Kazemi, *Poverty and Revolution*, 95, citing *Washington Post*, January 14, 1979, and *New York Times*, December 4, 1978. This paragraph draws on ibid., 2, 86-89, 95-96; Abrahamian, *Iran Between Two Revolutions*, 535; Hooglund, *Land and Revolution*, 143, 146, 148; and Zavareei, "Dependent Capitalist Development," 175-76.

90. Ashraf and Banuazizi, "The State, Classes and Modes of Mobilization," 25; Zavareei, "Dependent Capitalist Development," 175; Hooglund, *Land and Revolution*, 149-50. On peasants in the revolution, see Hooglund, *Land and Revolution*, ix, 143-51; Abrahamian, *Iran Between Two Revolutions*, 522; Turner, "Iranian Oilworkers," 287; Bashiriyeh, *The State and Revolution*, 114; Moghadam, "Accumulation Strategy," 305-306; Balta and Rulleau, *L'Iran insurgé*, 54; and Val Moghadam (under the pseudonym Shahrzad Azad), "Workers' and Peasants' Councils in Iran," pp. 14-29 in *Monthly Review*, volume 32, number 5 (October 1980), 15-16.

91. Abrahamian, *Iran Between Two Revolutions*, 527. These remarks on the tribes are based on Beck, lecture on "Tribes and the State"; Garthwaite, *Khans and shahs*, 141; Beck, "Revolutionary Iran," 16-17, 19-20; Moghadam, "Workers' and Peasants' Councils," 15-16; and Balta and Rulleau, *L'Iran insurgé*, 54.

92. On women see Keddie, *Roots of Revolution*, 248; Balta and Rulleau, *L'Iran insurgé*, 89; and Moghadam, "Industrial Development," 168.

93. Khumaini, in an interview in *Newsweek* (November 6, 1978), 80, quoted by Bill, "Power and Religion," 92-93.

94. All of these terms are given by Annabelle Sreberny-Mohammadi, "The Power of Tradition: Communication and the Iranian Revolution," Ph.D. dissertation, Department of Communications [?], Columbia University (1985), 221-22, 226.

95. Moghadam, "Populist Revolution," 157.

96. Keddie, *Roots of Revolution*, 244.

97. Sreberny-Mohammadi, "The Power of Tradition," 237. On nonviolence in the revolution, see Ashraf and Banuazizi, "The State, Classes and Modes of Mobilization," 15-16, and *Manchester Guardian*, September 5 and 6, 1978. On acts of street violence, see Abrahamian, *Iran Between Two Revolutions*, 522-23.

98. Sreberny-Mohammadi, "The Power of Tradition," 223-24.

99. Ayatullah Khumaini, Bihishti, et al., *Hukumat-i Jumhuri-yi Islami* [The Government of the Islamic Republic] (Tehran, 1358/1979), 69, as quoted by Bashiriyeh, *The State and Revolution*, 116. For Khumaini's positions in May 1978, see *Le Monde*, May 6, 1978, quoted in Zafarian, "Analytic Approach," 163, and for summer 1979, see ibid., 164.

100. Reznikov, "The Downfall of the Iranian Monarchy," 267, citing *Ittila'at*, January 13, 1979.

101. Balta and Rulleau, *L'Iran insurgé*, 58ff.

102. Ibid.; Abrahamian, *Iran Between Two Revolutions*, 522; Reznikov, "The Downfall of the Iranian Monarchy," 267.

103. Keddie, *Roots of Revolution*, 244; *Manchester Guardian*, September 6, 1978; Abrahamian, *Iran Between Two Revolutions*, 522; Fischer, *Iran*, 190, 205.

104. Halliday, "The Iranian Revolution," 197; Saikal, *Rise and Fall*, 194.

105. Skocpol, "Rentier State and Shi'a Islam," 268-71.

106. There were certainly some tensions between the state and sectors of the elite, which played a role in exacerbating the crisis atmosphere of 1977-78, but these do not add up to a serious split at the top of the social structure: see Bashiriyeh, *The State and Revolution*, 90-97.

107. Halliday, "The Iranian Revolution," 196; Keddie, *Roots of Revolution,* 255-56. For more on the shah, see Marvin Zonis, *Majestic Failure. The Fall of the Shah* (Chicago and London: University of Chicago Press, 1991).

108. Abrahamian, "Structural Causes," 26, quoting *New York Times,* December 17, 1978. On pro-shah social forces, see Alidoost-Khaybari, "Religious Revolutionaries," 498-505; Bashiriyeh, *The State and Revolution,* 115, 119; Abrahamian, *Iran Between Two Revolutions,* 508; Ashraf and Banuazizi, "The State, Classes and Modes of Mobilization," 15, 34; Parsa, *Social Origins,* 224-25; and *Kayhan,* January 11, 14, 15, 16, 18, 19, 1978; April 4, 6, 8, 15, 18, 20, 25, 26, 1978.

109. On the army in the revolution, see Arjomand, "The Causes and Significance," 45; Abrahamian, *Iran Between Two Revolutions,* 523; Bill, *The Eagle and the Lion,* 256; Bashiriyeh, *The State and Revolution,* 119, 123 note 21; Katouzian, *The Political Economy,* 347-48; Reznikov, "The Downfall of the Iranian Monarchy," 269; and Halliday, "The Iranian Revolution," 195-96.

110. Skocpol, "Rentier State and Shi'a Islam," 281 note 4.

111. Halliday, *Iran,* 319.

112. Nixon told the shah on a 1972 visit to Iran: "I envy the way you deal with your [protesting] students. . . . Pay no attention to our liberals' griping." Gerald Ford's assistant secretary for Near Eastern and South Asian affairs testified to congress in 1976 that Iran had made great progress on human rights and that its political prisoners were an internal affair: see Parsa, *Social Origins,* 53, 54.

113. Quoted in Ashraf and Banuazizi, "The State, Classes and Modes of Mobilization," 4.

114. On these issues see Katouzian, *The Political Economy,* 341; Abrahamian, *Iran Between Two Revolutions,* 500; Graham, *Iran,* 210; Keddie, *Roots of Revolution,* 231-32, 234; Bill, *The Eagle and the Lion,* 226-33; and National Security Archive, *Iran 1977-1980. The Making of U.S. Policy,* microfiche collection, documents 1151, 3564.

115. On the United States during the revolution, see Philip Taubman, "Washington Said to Have Weighed Backing Iranian Military in a Coup," in *New York Times,* April 20, 1980; Richard Cottam, "Review of Warren Christopher et al., *American Hostages in Iran: The Conduct of a Crisis,* and Gary Sick, *All Fall Down: America's Tragic Encounter with Iran,*" pp. 251-255 in *International Journal of Middle East Studies,* volume 19, number 2 (May 1987), and the references therein; Sullivan, "Dateline Iran," 177-86; Bill, *The Eagle and the Lion,* 248-60; Ashraf and Banuazizi, "The State, Classes and Modes of Mobilization," 12; Halliday, "The Iranian Revolution," 205; Bashiriyeh, *The State and Revolution,* 120, 122 note 10, 123 note 24, 124 note 29, 124 note 33; Keddie, *Roots of Revolution,* 253-54; Abrahamian, *Iran Between Two Revolutions,* 523-24; Muslim Students, *Asnad-i lanah-i jasusi,* volume 7: 247; and Turner, "Iranian Oilworkers," 273, 281.

116. On this last point see William H. Sewell, Jr., "Ideologies and Social Revolutions: Reflections on the French Case," pp. 57-85 in *Journal of Modern History,* volume 57, number 1 (March 1985), and Theda Skocpol, "Cultural Idioms and Political Ideologies in the Revolutionary Reconstruction of State Power: A Rejoinder to Sewell," pp. 86-96 in *Journal of Modern History,* volume 57, number 1 (March 1985).

117. I begin to extend the application of this model in "A Theory of Third World Social Revolutions," and am working on a book that considers Iran along with Mexico, Cuba, Chile, Nicaragua, Guatemala, El Salvador, and Grenada. A sophisticated comparison of "autocratic modernization" in Iran and tsarist Russia is found in Tim McDaniel, *Autocracy, Modernization, and Revolution in Russia and Iran* (Princeton: Princeton University Press, 1991).

118. A full-length treatment of Iran since 1979 would require a separate study. For informative analyses, see Shaul Bakhash, *The Reign of the Ayatollahs. Iran and the Islamic Revolution* (New York: Basic Books, 1984); Dilip Hiro, *Iran Under the Ayatollahs* (London and Boston: Routledge and Kegan Paul, 1986); Shahrough Akhavi, "Elite Factionalism in the Islamic Republic of Iran," pp. 181-201 in *The Middle East Journal,* volume 41, number 2 (Spring 1987); Said Amir Arjomand, *The Turban for the Crown: The Islamic Revolution in Iran* (New York: Oxford University Press, 1988); Hooshang Amirahmadi, *Revolution and Economic Transition. The Iranian Experience* (Al-

bany: State University of New York Press, 1990); Mansoor Moaddel, "Class Struggles in Post-Revolutionary Iran," pp. 317-343 in *International Journal of Middle East Studies*, volume 23, number 3 (August 1991); John Foran and Jeff Goodwin, "Revolutionary Outcomes in Iran and Nicaragua: Coalition Fragmentation, War, and the Limits of Social Transformation," forthcoming in *Theory and Society*; and Val Moghadam, "Islamic Populism, Class and Gender in Post-Revolutionary Iran," chapter for John Foran, editor, *Social Movements in Iran* (in preparation).

119. On these social classes since the revolution, see Bill, "Power and Religion," 29; Moghadam, "Accumulation Strategy," 330-38; Bayat, *Workers and Revolution*, 100-102; Kazemi, *Poverty and Revolution*, 116-17; Abrahamian, "Iran's Turbaned Revolution," 94-95; Kashani interview, tape 3; Hooglund, *Land and Revolution*, 151; Turner, "Iranian Oilworkers," 287; and Garthwaite, *Khans and shahs*, 141.

120. For some economic data, see Pesaran, "The System of Dependent Capitalism," 514-17.

121. Moghadam, "Populist Revolution," citing Hooshang Amirahmadi, "The Non-Capitalist Way of Development," in *Review of Radical Political Economics*, volume 19, number 1 (1987), and Samir Amin, *La Déconnexion: pour sortir du système mondiale* (Paris: Seuil, 1986).

122. Halliday, "The Iranian Revolution," 188 note 1.

123. Quoted by Katouzian, *The Political Economy*, 362. See also, on Mussadiq's image, Halliday, "The Iranian Revolution," 198; Abrahamian, "Iran's Turbaned Revolution," 97; and Diba, *Mohammad Mossadegh*, 195; and on Nuri, Katouzian, *The Political Economy*, 356-57.

The History of Social Change in Iran: A Theoretical Reprise

Having traversed the history of social change in Iran from 1500 to 1979 in the course of this study, it now falls to us to highlight certain results—empirical, methodological, and theoretical—in terms of their contribution to our knowledge of the topics and approaches involved.

Social Structure and Social Change in Iran: Substantive Results

Let us begin by briefly recalling the empirical findings of chapters two through nine, keeping in mind that certain analytic elements will be added to these points in the sections on method and theory below. The Iranian social formation at its seventeenth-century height under Shah 'Abbas was a hybrid of three partially overlapping modes of production, which may be termed the pastoral-nomadic, the peasant crop-sharing, and the urban petty-commodity modes of production. The Safavid shahs had hegemonic positions in the state and economy, tapping surplus production by tribes-people, peasants, and urban producers, and enjoying military, political, and ideological paramountcy. Other elite groups such as tribal chiefs and urban ulama (clergy) controlled far fewer resources (the former primarily military-political-economic, the latter ideological) in the seventeenth century and could not challenge the shahs' overall control. The economy was predominantly agricultural (nomadic and settled) but there was significant regional and international trade in products such as textiles (carpets and silks), porcelain, and metalware. Profits from this trade were shared by the shah with the local Muslim and Armenian merchant communities. Commercial contacts opened in the early seventeenth century with the Dutch and English East India Companies, who traded in Iran on terms negotiated freely by the shahs. In no sense could seventeenth-century Iran be considered *dependent* on the West; rather it was part of the *external arena* of the emerging capitalist world economy.

In 1722 the Safavid dynasty was abruptly overthrown by rebellious Afghan tribesmen. The causes of its decline, however, were long-term, and were traced to an intertwined set of economic, political, and ideological crises that structurally undermined the state. These included: (1) the results of provincial reforms in the seventeenth century which weakened the military preparedness of the outlying regions by removing tribal chiefs from the administration in favor of centralized control, (2) a fiscal crisis ensuing partly from decreased prosperity in the provinces and rising state expenditures, and partly from inflationary pressures emanating from Europe and the Ottoman Empire, and (3) the attenuation of tribal support due to increasing royal absolutism, and alienation of national and religious minorities (Georgians, Armenians, Sunni Arabs, Kurds, and Afghans) due to growing intolerance on the part of the Shi'i ulama.

The Afghans were in turn routed in 1729 by the adventurer Nadir, who made himself shah in 1736 and ruled till 1747, engaging in wars of territorial reconquest and foreign conquest as far as India. Tribal civil wars continued throughout the eighteenth century, with a period of relative stability in southern Iran under Karim Khan Zand till 1779, and the rise of a new dynasty, the Qajars, in 1795. Throughout this period trade contacts with the West shrank, tribal groups encroached on the sedentary agricultural sector, and wars reduced the population. Royal authority and control decentralized considerably. Social change in the eighteenth century remained almost exclusively *endogenous* in nature; the East India companies were largely passive onlookers as tribal groups struggled for control of their own regions and vied for state power. The significance of the eighteenth century was as a reversal of development of decisive proportions, for it weakened the Iranian state and economy just as a crucial moment in its history was approaching.

During the nineteenth century, the Iranian economy "crossed the threshold of dependency," re-oriented toward England and its colony India in the southern Gulf area, and toward Tsarist Russia in the increasingly more dynamic north (based on Tabriz and the new capital, Tehran). The Qajar armies suffered military defeats at the hands of Russia in 1813 and 1828 and to England in 1857, leading to trade advantages, territory, and political control for the Europeans. This situation can be characterized for the first time as one of dependence on the West, with the presence of two European powers precluding the outcome of colonialism but limiting development through their rivalry. The three modes of production remained in place, with perhaps some slight shifting in their relative importance—beginnings of a decline in the scope of pastoral nomadism, and recoveries in the levels of activity in both the peasant crop-sharing and urban petty-commodity sectors, although by the end of this period foreign manufactures were displacing Iranian handicraft workers to a great extent. Alongside the older modes of production, a small, new capitalist sector emerged, with some unique historical features: Foreign capitalists rather than Iranians tended to predominate and Iran's working class was formed in large measure outside the country, as migrant labor in Russia. Moreover, at the turn of the twentieth century, Iran's principal exports were raw cotton and silk, cereals and fruit, tobacco, opium, and carpets; its principal imports were cotton cloth, sugar, tea, and metal goods—the trading profile of a *peripheral* supplier of mostly raw materials in the world economy (oil would be discovered in 1908 and begin to play a larger role by the 1920s). The Qajar state was independent in name only as its policy options were increasingly determined by the Russian and to a lesser extent, English, governments and banks.

The dissatisfaction of the politically articulate urban classes—merchants, artisans, intellectuals, and ulama—with the internal tyranny of the Qajars and the external domination of the foreigners was signalled first by the Tobacco rebellion in 1891 and then by the Constitutional revolution of 1905-1911. These classes formed a populist alliance with other sectors, including the working class, each interpreting the crisis through its own political cultural filters and economic interests. After the initial granting of a constitution and establishment of a parliament by the popular forces, internal divisions (particularly among the ulama and the large merchants) and external military intervention by the Russians forced the majlis to accede to the restoration of Qajar autocracy. The political stalemate and economic chaos that attended this struggle during and after WWI were among the most important factors in the military coup of 1921 (assisted and supported by the British) which brought a hitherto somewhat obscure military officer, Reza Pahlavi, to the throne in 1925, ending the Qajar dynasty.

Under a centralizing authoritarian state and fueled by a new petroleum-based economy, Iran embarked on a dependent capitalist course in the 1930s. In modes of production terms, the twentieth century has witnessed massive erosion of the pastoral nomadic sector and the gradual "capitalization" of both agriculture and industry. Under Reza Shah the forced settlement of nomads was the most dramatic expression of this, while a more substantial groundwork for the capitalist mode of production was laid by infrastructural projects (railroads, roads, dams) and some light industrial manufacturing. Urban petty-commodity production in the bazaar and peasant crop-sharing continued to predominate otherwise.

From the Allied invasion and abdication of Reza Shah in 1941 until the fall of the popular, nationalist Mussadiq government in 1953 Iran experienced a marked loosening of autocratic monarchic controls and went through a series of intense political conflicts which nevertheless failed to achieve their goals, including the regional autonomy movement in Azarbaijan and the Kurdish Republic in 1945-46 and the oil nationalization struggle led by the National Front and Mussadiq government from 1951 to 1953. Each had important external as well as internal dimensions: Muhammad Reza Pahlavi returned as shah in August 1953 with United States CIA support, some clerical backing, and mobilization of street mobs as the nationalization movement fragmented—certain ulama and secular nationalists left the coalition, while the Tudeh Party never fully supported it on the left. Thus was missed (as in the eighteenth century) another alternative pathway to national independence and development.

After the coup d'état a new period of Iranian dependence on the West was inaugurated, now shaped by a special political, economic, and military relationship with the United States. Significant direct private capital investment by Western multinationals flowed into the country in the 1950s and 1960s, undermining petty-commodity artisanal producers and tradespeople in favor of larger-scale capitalist production and importing/exporting. The shah's land "reform" in the 1960s turned crop-sharing peasants into smallholders and/or landless wage workers as capitalist farms and agribusinesses emerged, unleashing a flood of migrants into the cities. Foreign exchange earnings from oil increased state power in the 1970s, permitting the shah to purchase billions of dollars worth of American weaponry and technology. Iran, which appeared to be making a bid to enter the semiperiphery under the Pahlavi state's grandiose industrial, agricultural, military, and strategic plans, entered into serious economic recession in the middle and later 1970s, triggered by lower oil revenues and overly ambitious and military-oriented development plans, resulting in unemployment, high inflation, a housing crisis, new loans from the West, and deepening forms of social unrest, all of which provided the immediate backdrop to the revolutionary movement of 1978-79.

The opposition drew on several political cultures of resistance to the shah, including the "fundamentalist" Islam of Khumaini, the radical Islam of Dr. 'Ali Shari'ati, the armed struggle approach of the Islamic Mujahidin and the Marxist Fada'ian, the moderate Islamic reformism of the Liberation Movement of Iran (led by Mehdi Bazargan, among others), and the "traditional" secular center and left, the former composed of the remnants of Mussadiq's National Front and the latter represented by the Tudeh Party. These organizations and the heterogeneous social forces which they mobilized forced the shah from power through a powerful movement shaped by huge street demonstrations, a long general strike, and a brief guerrilla uprising in early 1979. The state crumbled in the face of a strengthened populist alliance and uncertain support from the United States. The Islamic

Republic which followed continued to face problems stemming from dependency and the complexity of social structure in Iran, topics briefly touched on in chapter nine.

Comparative Dimensions and Methodological Considerations

In this study, comparisons of several kinds have been made. In the earliest period, from 1500 to 1800, the social structure of Safavid Iran may be compared with the Islamic empires of the Mughals in India and the Ottomans in Turkey. Despite the presence of the same three modes of production in each, the greater proportion of tribespeople in Iran, combined with the greater impact of Europe on India and the Ottomans, explained the endogenous form taken by social change in Iran (the eighteenth century's civil wars) and the exogenous changes in India (conquest by the English) and the Ottomans (military decline vis-à-vis Europe). In the nineteenth century, the differences of Iran with its otherwise most similar neighbors again stand out—the Anglo-Russian rivalry put brakes on development as each sought to block concessions to the other, whereas India and even the fading Ottomans centralized more successfully, the former under colonial control, the latter, under strong European pressure.

In the Pahlavi period since 1925, several brief comparisons were made to highlight certain features of the Iranian case. Rough analogies were observed between the centralizing state of Reza Shah in Iran and Kemal Atatürk's modernization of the new Turkish polity, although Atatürk was more successful in containing the ulama and relied more on political forces in society at large than Reza did, who merely compressed these until they exploded after his abdication in 1941. The striking similarities between the coups in Iran in 1953 and Chile in 1973 were mentioned in chapter seven, suggesting the underlying combination of internal contradictions and external intervention at work in both cases, in addition to a number of secondary similarities (nationalization of a key resource, popularity of Mussadiq and Allende). The dependent capitalist development of Iran in the 1960 and 1970s was found broadly equivalent to that of its Middle Eastern neighbors Egypt, Turkey, and Pakistan, but significantly less than that of Brazil or the East Asian cases of Taiwan and South Korea, making possible the judgment that Iran did not rise to a semiperipheral position in the world-economy. Finally, the model of revolution elaborated in chapter nine permitted us to see similarities between the Iranian and Nicaraguan revolutions of 1979, and hinted at new ways of interpreting social revolutions more generally. For the most part, these comparisons with cases outside Iran confirmed and reinforced the analysis of processes of change in Iran in light of the theories adopted in this study.

A second type of comparison used was of an internal type, and here a historical methodology turned on a single case yielded much of theoretical interest. Again, both similarities and contrastive patterns turned up. For example, a certain parallelism between the rise and fall of the seventeenth-century Safavids and the twentieth-century Pahlavis may be noted: Both dynasties represented peaks of national economic power, dominated very much by the shahs at the top. At a certain point each reached developmental limits and collapsed precipitously. But the differences are equally instructive: The fall of the Safavids was traced to internal processes and conflicts between the state and upper classes, while that of the Pahlavis involved an external dimension (dependence on the United States) that caused the withdrawal of middle and lower class support. The outcome—a social revolution—was thus attributed to a key difference in the two situations—dependent development and its consequences.

Comparative historical reflection on the repeated mass movements of the twentieth century also resulted in fresh conceptual insights. The formation and dynamics of a multi-class urban populist alliance, first noted in the case of the 1905-1911 Constitutional revolution, recurred in the 1951-53, 1960-63, and 1977-79 social movements as well. Behind each of these we found the complexity of Iran's social structure in modes of production terms, the impact of the world-system on that structure, and the elaboration of specific political cultures of opposition to the state and outside powers. In chapter nine the reasons for the apparent success of the latest version of the populist alliance were suggested—unusual unanimity among its constituent classes and groups, combined with a unique opportunity in the world-systemic conjuncture—and the continuing problems faced by the new regime were readily identifiable in terms of Iran's ongoing processes of dependent development, world-systemic pressures, and contending political cultures. Internal comparison, then, has proven a source both of inductively generated new concepts, such as the populist alliance, and a further test of theoretical approaches to social change.

Thus a number of methodological strategies have been simultaneously pursued in the course of this study. One way of seeing this is as a combination of inductive method to form new analytic concepts and deductive work to illustrate theoretical frameworks.[1] Another approach is to contend that this study has been both a way a testing general theories and using concepts to develop a meaningful historical interpretation of a single case. It also suggests for future research (but does not employ) a third strategy—that of analyzing causal regularities in history (one could rigorously investigate the applicability of the framework used here for Iran in a wider context, say, the Middle East and South Asia since 1500).[2] Each of these several strategies flows into the others and the full cycle of them can shed light on a whole range of problems in historical-comparative sociological inquiry.[3]

A second broad methodological contribution of this study has revolved around the utility of a dialectical methodology for empirical social science, that is, one which takes seriously both structural constraints and human agency in the making of social movements. Taking as models the reflections of Marx in "The Eighteenth Brumaire" and Sartre's *Search for a Method*, this approach was used concretely in many ways in the present work: in the notion of intertwined political, economic, and ideological crises used to explain the falls of the Safavids, Qajars, and Pahlavis; in the diptych-configuration that ordered each of the three parts, with chapters on social structural changes—two, four, six, and eight—followed by chapters on social movements—three, five, seven, and nine; and in the model of social revolution arrived at in the last chapter. Each of these studied the interplay among large, seemingly impersonal structures (modes of production, dependent development) and more clearly humanly-created processes (social movements of several types). One proposed link between the two was the role accorded political cultures in mediating "objective" social relations through the "subjective" experiences of groups and classes (in other words, these supposedly separate dimensions mutually constitute each other). The two types of analysis—structural and agentic—must be undertaken together to give a fully satisfying account of social change.[4]

Theories: Findings, Refinements

These considerations debouch onto the final area of inquiry of the present study—the status of the leading theories in the fields of development and social change. This study has argued that five basic approaches are central to understanding these problems—the dependency paradigm, world-system theory, modes of production analysis, the nature of the state, and political cultures of opposition and legitimation. Let us briefly assess each in turn in light of the findings.

Dependency, in the more sophisticated version formulated by Cardoso, Faletto, and Evans, has been found of great value for analysis of a major Middle Eastern case, thus extending the domain of the theory into a new region of the Third World. The concept of dependent development, used in adjudicating rancorous debates on the extent and limits of structural economic change in Qajar Iran (1800-1925), under Reza Shah (1925-41) and under his son (1953-77), proved an illuminating way to reconcile conflicting accounts and specify the content and reality of this mixed type of development. Moreover, the crossing of the threshold of dependency in the nineteenth century decisively marked off the pre-capitalist from the more recent periods of Iranian history and was a key to understanding why social movements since about 1890 took the anti-foreign, anti-state forms they did. The dependency paradigm, overall, proved an adequate guiding thread to the whole range of questions raised in this study.

Iran was likewise put on the map of world-system theory in this study, as we traced the country's halting progress from external arena in the seventeenth century to periphery in the nineteenth. The most interesting empirical finding observed was the stagnation of Iran in the eighteenth century, conceptualized as a decline in the external arena; the Safavids had been too strong to be colonized and dominated by the European core, but were unable (or didn't try) to compete with it in the emerging peripheries of Asia. Trade links with Europe were accorded a secondary role in the fall of the Safavids. Disrupted during the civil wars of the eighteenth century, they were decisively reforged in the nineteenth as Iran *was* converted into a periphery of the British core and Russian semiperiphery. In the twentieth, the shah's ambitious attempts to draw his nation into the semiperiphery fell rather short, and this failure was both cause and consequence of a precarious political economy that foundered onto revolution. Wallerstein's system, then, while undoubtedly an incomplete perspective on development from the point of view of Iran, was nevertheless found conceptually adequate to the task of explaining the relevant aspects of Iran's experience within the larger world economy.

Modes of production analysis, which has not been widely applied empirically, has been found of great utility in rethinking social structure in a Third World country and proven far more nuanced in the result it obtained than trying to fit the Iranian case into some simple conceptual box such as feudalism. It allowed us to construct the diagrams on social structure in 1630, 1800, 1914, 1941, and 1977 that in turn provided the keys to understanding the twists and turns of class alliances in the social movements, and to measure the impact on class structure over time of dependency and world-systemic pressures. These insights are I think a major finding of this study which needs to be tested more widely in other Third World cases, and perhaps even for pre-capitalist Europe, and may someday alter considerably the way we think about pre-capitalist social structure and social change.

With respect to the nature of the state, we were able to account for the strong position of the Safavid shahs in terms of their ability to tap an economic surplus in several modes of production, and the fragmented situation of the upper classes—chiefs, landlords, large merchants. This source of power continued into the twentieth century with the discovery of oil and the establishment of a stronger state based on military coercive force. In Iran the state was very closely associated with the person of the shah and thus conflated rather directly with a part of the ruling class (the royal family).[5] On the one hand, this makes the Iranian case rather unique (strictly comparable only to other monarchies); on the other, the form of dictatorship has been shared widely in the Third World since World War II. Moreover, the close association of the state with foreign powers in sharing responsibility for dependency made it vulnerable to social movements from below in times of crisis. These several findings have made it possible to flesh out Skocpol's and others' insistence on the political signif-icance of the state with economic and cultural considerations as well.

This raises the final conceptual issue of political cultures of opposition and legitimation. These proved to be the major missing link in all the models of development and social change considered above. In this study, close attention was paid to the value orientations of the many social classes and groups active on both sides of movements for change, and proved invalu-able in understanding both the reasons for revolutionary outbreaks and the subsequent splits in the revolutionary coalitions. Political culture was shown to be crucial in mediating structural analysis with historical accounts of social movements. The legitimation problems of the dynasties which followed the Safavids were likewise a factor in their eventual failures to consolidate power in the long run.

The major theoretical contribution of this study has been to effect a synthesis of these partial perspectives on development and social change. The reader will be the best judge of the success of this project. The following features of theoretical synthesis may be noted: (1) the problem of integrating the dependency, world-systems, and modes of production perspectives to solve the puzzle of how internal and external dimensions of development and class formation can be elucidated; (2) the linking of these perspectives on development with considerations on the state and political cultures to construct a comprehensive framework for studying social change; and (3) the model of revolution that this yielded in chapter nine as well as the general approach this suggests as to how social structure is related to social movements.

Finally, mention may be made of a number of new *concepts* which have been constructed, more or less inductively, in the course of doing this work. Part one on the Safavid period generated the notions of intertwined polit-ical, economic, and ideological crises, and sectoral conflicts among elite contenders for power in pre-capitalist social formations. In the study of social movements in Qajar Iran, the concept of a stalemate of social forces (among state, social movements, foreign powers) was introduced to explain the 1921 coup d'état, and a major conceptual innovation, the existence of an urban, multi-class populist alliance, was arrived at to characterize the dy-namics of the Constitutional revolution. This concept was put to work again in part three on the Pahlavi era to shed light on the social movements of

1951-53, 1960-63, and 1977-79. It may prove useful in future research on social movements elsewhere in place and time, reposing as it does in large measure on the greater analytic precision generated by the modes of production approach to social structure. A secondary conceptual line of argument for the 1925-79 period was in terms of successive compressions of social forces under strong centralizing states from 1925 to 1941 and 1953 to 1977, followed by explosions of social forces when the world-system permitted and internal contradictions built up in 1941-53 and 1977-79. All of these concepts served us as middle-range heuristic devices for ordering historical materials, and while they were arrived at for the most part inductively through empirical analysis, they can alternatively be accounted for in terms of the theoretical perspectives employed.

In conclusion, this study has represented an attempt to illuminate Iranian history in sociological perspective as a sequence or series of *fragile* attempts at social change—repeated mass movements which have ended either in foreign intervention, or, in the case of the 1978 revolution, in foreign war and internal repression. Homa Katouzian concluded his 1979 study with the words: "It is to be hoped that for once, after centuries, the dialectic of Iranian history will yield a progressive synthesis."[6] Unfortunately, the promise of those days has not yet come to pass, and remains only a hope. Iran's *history*, we have argued, offers little guarantee of a progressive outcome, only the likelihood of further courageous attempts at change.

Notes

1. See Victoria E. Bonnell, "The Uses of Theory, Concepts and Comparisons in Historical Sociology," pp. 156-173 in *Comparative Studies in Society and History*, volume 22, number 2 (April 1980), 164ff.

2. These three strategies are discussed by Theda Skocpol, "Emerging Agendas and Recurrent Strategies in Historical Sociology," pp. 356-391 in Theda Skocpol, editor, *Vision and Method in Historical Sociology* (Cambridge: Cambridge University Press, 1984). I have begun to test for causal regularities over parts of this period in two essays, "Modes of Production, European Impact and Social Change in the Pre-Capitalist Middle East and South Asia: A Comparative Survey of the Ottoman, Safavid and Mughal Empires from the Sixteenth to the Eighteenth Centuries," a paper presented at the meetings of the Middle East Studies Association, San Francisco (1985), and "Dependency and Resistance in the Middle East: 1800-1925," a paper presented at the meetings of the International Political Science Association, Buenos Aires, Argentina (1991).

3. See Theda Skocpol and Margaret Somers, "The Uses of Comparative History in Macrosocial Inquiry," pp. 174-197 in *Comparative Studies in Society and History*, volume 22, number 2 (April 1980), 196-97.

4. This is the thrust of some of the best recent social theory, notably the work of Anthony Giddens on structuration: see his *The Constitution of Society. Outline of the Theory of Structuration* (Berkeley and Los Angeles: University of California Press, 1984).

5. Though at times of more open democratic struggle, such as 1905-11 and 1951-53, we analyzed the state as consisting of several institutions (royal family, army, bureaucracy, and majlis) whose relationship with other social forces and each other determined in large measure the outcomes of social movements.

6. Katouzian, *The Political Economy*, 182.

References

Abbasi, Syrous. "Radicalization of Leftist Youth in Iran." Ph.D. diss., Department of Government, Florida State University, 1981.

Abdullaev, Z. Z. *Promyshlennost i zarozhdenie rabochego klassa Irana v kontse XIX-nachale XX vv.* Baku, 1963. Extracts translated in *The Economic History of Iran: 1800-1914*, edited by Charles Issawi, 42-52, 297-300. Chicago and London: University of Chicago Press, 1971.

Abrahamian, Ervand. "The Crowd in Iranian Politics 1905-1953." *Past & Present* 41 (December 1968): 184-210.

———. "The Crowd in the Persian Revolution I." *Iranian Studies* 2, no. 4 (Autumn 1969): 128-150.

———. "Oriental Despotism: The Case of Qajar Iran." *International Journal of Middle East Studies* 5, no. 1 (1974): 3-31.

———. "European Feudalism and Middle Eastern Despotisms." *Science & Society* 39, no. 2 (Summer 1975): 129-156.

———. "The Causes of the Constitutional Revolution in Iran." *International Journal of Middle East Studies* 10 (1979): 381-414.

———. "Structural Causes of the Iranian Revolution." *MERIP (Middle East Research and Information Project) Reports*, no. 87 (May 1980): 21-26.

———. "The Strengths and Weaknesses of the Labor Movement in Iran, 1941-1953." In *Modern Iran. The Dialectics of Continuity and Change*, edited by Michael E. Bonine and Nikki R. Keddie, 211-232. Albany: State University of New York Press, 1981.

———. *Iran Between Two Revolutions.* Princeton: Princeton University Press, 1982.

———. "Iran's Turbaned Revolution." In *The Middle East Annual. Issues and Events*, volume 1, edited by David H. Partington, 83-106. Boston: G. K. Hall & Co., 1982.

Adamec, Ludwig W, ed. *Historical Gazeteer of Iran.* Vol. 1: *Tehran and Northwestern Iran.* Vol. 2: *Meshed and Northeastern Iran.* Graz: Akademische Druck-u. Verlagsanstalt, 1976, 1981.

Adamiyat, Feridun. *Amir Kabir va Iran* [Amir Kabir and Iran]. Tehran: Khwarazm, 1334/1955. Extracts also translated in *The Economic History of Iran: 1800-1914*, edited by Charles Issawi, 292-297. Chicago and London: University of Chicago Press, 1971.

———. *Fikr-i Dimukrasi Ijtima'i dar Nazhat-i Mashruyiyat-i Iran* [Social Democratic Thought in the Iranian Constitutional Movement]. Tehran: Payam Press, 1354/1975.

Afary, Janet. "Peasant Rebellions of the Caspian Region during the Iranian Constitutional Revolution, 1906-1909." *International Journal of Middle East Studies* 23, no. 2 (May 1991): 137-161.

"Affairs in Persia." *Journal of the Royal Central Asian Society* 15, part 1 (1928): 84-88.

Afshari, Muhammad Reza. "A Study of the Constitutional Revolution within the Framework of Iranian History." Ph.D. diss., Department of History, Temple University, 1981.

———. "The *Pishivaran* and Merchants in Precapitalist Iranian Society: An Essay on the Background and Causes of the Constitutional Revolution." *International Journal of Middle East Studies* 15, no. 2 (May 1983): 133-155.

"Agricultural and Industrial Activity and Manpower in Iran." *International Labour Review* 59 (January-June 1949): 550-562.

Akhavi, Shahrough. *Religion and Politics in Contemporary Iran. Clergy-State Relations in the Pahlavi Period.* Albany: State University of New York Press, 1980.

Alavi, Hamza. "The State in Post-Colonial Societies." *New Left Review* 74 (July- August 1972): 59-82.

Alexander of Malabar, Friar. "The Story of the Sack of Ispahan by the Afghans in 1722." *Journal of the Royal Central Asian Society* 23, part 4 (October 1936): 643-653.

Algar, Hamid. *Religion and State in Iran, 1785-1906. The Role of the Ulama in the Qajar Period.* Berkeley and Los Angeles: University of California Press, 1969.

———. "The Oppositional Role of the Ulama in Twentieth-Century Iran." In *Scholars, Saints and Sufis: Muslim Religious Institutions since 1500,* edited by Nikki R. Keddie, 231-255. Berkeley and Los Angeles: University of California Press, 1972.

———. *Mirza Malkam Khan. A Study in the History of Persian Modernism.* Berkeley and Los Angeles: University of California Press, 1973.

———. "Shi'ism and Iran in the Eighteenth Century." In *Studies in Eighteenth Century Islamic History,* edited by Thomas Naff and Roger Owen, 288-302. Carbondale and Edwardsville: Southern Illinois University Press, 1977.

———. Lectures on "Islam in Iran." University of California, Berkeley. Winter-Spring 1982.

———. "Imam Khomeini, 1902-1962: The Pre-Revolutionary Years." In *Islam, Politics, and Social Movements,* edited by Ira M. Lapidus and Edmund Burke, III. Berkeley and Los Angeles: University of California Press, 1988.

Alidoost-Khaybari, Yadollah. "Religious Revolutionaries: An Analysis of the Religious Groups' Victory in the Iranian Revolution of 1978-79." Ph.D. diss., Department of Sociology, University of Michigan, 1981.

Amanat, Abbas, ed. *Cities & Trade: Consul Abbott on the Economy and Society of Iran 1847-1866.* Oxford Oriental Monographs, no. 5. London: Ithaca Press, 1983.

———. *Resurrection and Renewal. The Making of the Babi Movement in Iran, 1844-1850.* Ithaca and London: Cornell University Press, 1989.

Amini, Dr. 'Ali. Interview recorded by Habib Ladjevardi, Paris, December 6, 1981. Harvard University, Iranian Oral History Collection.

Amnesty International. *Annual Report 1974-75.* London: AI Publications, 1975.

Anderson, Perry. *Passages from Antiquity to Feudalism.* London: New Left Books, 1974.

———. *Lineages of the Absolutist State.* London: New Left Books, 1974.

Arjomand, Said Amir. "Review Essay: Religion and Ideology in the Constitutional Revolution." *Iranian Studies* 12, nos. 3-4 (Summer-Autumn 1979): 282-291.

———. "The Ulama's Traditionalist Opposition to Parliamentarianism: 1907-1909." *Middle Eastern Studies* 17, no. 2 (April 1981): 174-190.

———. *The Shadow of God and the Hidden Imam. Religion, Political Order, and Societal Change in Shi'ite Iran from the Beginning to 1890.* Chicago and London: University of Chicago Press, 1984.

———. "Traditionalism in Twentieth-century Iran." In *From Nationalism to Revolutionary Islam,* edited by Said Amir Arjomand, 195-232. Albany: State University of New York Press, 1984.

———. "The Causes and Significance of the Iranian Revolution." *State, Culture and Society* 1, no. 3 (1985): 41-66.

Asaf, Muhammad Hashim (Rustam al-Hukama). *Rustam al-tavarikh* [Rustam's History]. Edited by Muhammad Mushiri. Tehran: Shirkat-i Sahami-yi Kitabha-yi Jibi, 1348/1969.

Asheghian, Parviz. "American Joint Venture Manufacturing Firms in Iran: Investment Determinants and Comparative Performance." Ph.D. diss., Department of Economics, Georgia State University, 1980.

Ashraf, Ahmad. "Historical Obstacles to the Development of a Bourgeoisie in Iran." In *Studies in the Economic History of the Middle East: from the rise of Islam to the present day*, edited by M. A. Cook, 308-324. London and New York: Oxford University Press, 1970.

———. "Iran: Imperialism, Class and Modernization from Above." Ph.D. diss., Faculty of Political and Social Science, New School for Social Research, 1971.

———. *Mavane'-i Tarikhi-yi Rushd-i Sarmayehdari dar Iran: Daureh-i Qajariyyeh* [Historical Obstacles to the Development of Capitalism in the Qajar Era]. Tehran: Payam Press, 1359/1980.

Ashraf, Ahmad and Ali Banuazizi. "The State, Classes and Modes of Mobilization in the Iranian Revolution." *State, Culture and Society* 1, no. 3 (1985): 3-40.

Ashraf, Ahmad and H. Hekmat. "Merchants and Artisans and the Developmental Processes of Nineteenth-Century Iran." In *The Islamic Middle East, 700-1900: Studies in Economic and Social History*, edited by A. L. Udovitch, 725-750. Princeton: The Darwin Press, Inc., 1981.

Atkin, Muriel. *Russia and Iran 1780-1828*. Minneapolis: University of Minnesota Press, 1980.

Aubin, Jean. "Etudes Safavides. I. Shah Isma'il et les Notables de l'Iraq Persan." *Journal of the Economic and Social History of the Middle East* 2, part 1 (January 1959): 37-81.

———. "Les Sunnites du Larestan et la chute des safavides." *Revue des études islamiques* 33 (1965): 151-171.

———. "La politique religieuse des safavides." In *Le Shi'isme Imâmite*, Colloque de Strasbourg, 6-9 mai 1968, 235-244. Paris: Presses Universitaires de France, 1970.

Avery, Peter. *Modern Iran*. London: Ernest Benn Limited, 1965.

Bakhash, Shaul. *Iran: Monarchy, Bureaucracy and Reform under the Qajars: 1858-1896*. London: Ithaca Press, 1978.

Baku, Esmail. "Oil Revenue and Socio-Economic Development in Iran, 1963-78." Ph.D. diss., Department of Sociology, University of Wisconsin-Madison, 1980.

Balfour, J. M. *Recent Happenings in Persia*. Edinburgh and London: William Blackwood and Sons, 1922.

Balibar, Etienne. "The Basic Concepts of Historical Materialism." In *Reading Capital*, by Louis Althusser and Etienne Balibar, 201-208. London: New Left Books, 1970.

Balta, Paul, and Claudine Rulleau. *L'Iran insurgé*. Paris: Sindbad, 1979.

Banani, Amin. *The Modernization of Iran, 1921-1941*. Stanford: Stanford University Press, 1961.

———. "Reflections on The Social and Economic Structure of Safavid Persia at Its Zenith." *Iranian Studies* 11 (1978): 83-116.

Baraheni, Reza. *The Crowned Cannibals: Writings on Repression in Iran*. New York: Vintage Books, 1977.

Barakchian, Seyed Taghi. "An Annotated Translation of Nazim al-Islam Kirmani's *Tarikh-i Bidari-i Iranian* (History of Iranian Awakening), Vol. III." Ph.D. diss., Department of History, State University of New York at Binghamton, 1983.

Barker, Paul. "Tent Schools of the Qashqa'i: A Paradox of Local Initiative and State Control." In *Modern Iran. The Dialectics of Continuity and Change*, edited by Michael E. Bonine and Nikki R. Keddie, 139-157. Albany: State University of New York Press, 1981.

Barth, Fredrik. *Nomads of South Persia. The Basseri Tribe of the Khamseh Confederacy*. Boston: Little, Brown and Company, 1961.

Barthel, Günter. "The Struggle for the Re-establishment of National Rights Over Iranian Oil." In *Iran: From Monarchy to Republic*, edited by Günter Barthel, 50-71. Special issue no. 12 of *Asia, Africa, Latin America*. East Berlin: Akademie-Verlag, 1983.

Bashiriyeh, Hossein. *The State and Revolution in Iran 1962-1982*. London and Canberra: Croom Helm, and New York: St. Martin's Press, 1984.

Bastani Parizi, Muhammad Ibrahim. *Siyasat va Iqtisad-i Asr-i Safaviyyeh* [Politics and Economy in the Safavid Period]. Tehran: 1348/1969.

Bausani, Alessandro. *The Persians. From the earliest days to the twentieth century*. Translated from the Italian by J. B. Donne. London: Elek Books, 1971.

Bayani, Khanbaba. *Les Relations de l'Iran avec l'Europe occidentale à l'époque Safavide (Portugal, Espagne, Angleterre, Hollande et France)*. Paris: Les Presses modernes, 1937.

Bayat, Assef. *Workers and Revolution in Iran: A Third World Experience of Workers' Control*. London and New Jersey: Zed Books, Ltd., 1987.

Bayat, Mangol. "Women and Revolution in Iran, 1905-1911." In *Women in the Muslim World*, edited by Lois Beck and Nikki Keddie, 295-308. Cambridge, Mass.: Harvard University Press, 1978.

———. *Mysticism and Dissent. Socioreligious Thought in Qajar Iran*. Syracuse: Syracuse University Press, 1982.

———. *Iran's First Revolution. Shi'ism in the Constitutional Revolution of 1905-1909*. Oxford: Oxford University Press, 1991.

Beck, Lois. "Revolutionary Iran and Its Tribal Peoples." *MERIP (Middle East Research and Information Project) Reports*, no. 87 (May 1980): 14-20.

———. "Economic Transformations Among Qashqa'i Nomads, 1962-1978." In *Modern Iran. The Dialectics of Continuity and Change*, edited by Michael E. Bonine and Nikki R. Keddie, 99-122. Albany: State University of New York Press, 1981.

———. "Tribes and the State in Nineteenth and Twentieth Century Iran." Lecture at the University of California, Berkeley. November 13, 1985.

———. *The Qashqa'i of Iran*. New Haven and London: Yale University Press, 1986.

Behrang. [Collective pseudonym for a group of Iranian and French activists]. *Iran: Le maillon faible*. Paris: François Maspero, 1979.

Behrangi, Samad. *The Little Black Fish and Other Modern Persian Stories*. Translated from the Persian by Eric and Mary Hooglund. Washington, D.C.: Three Continents Press, 1976.

Bennigsen, Alexandre A. and S. Enders Wimbush. *Muslim National Communism in the Soviet Union. A Revolutionary Strategy for the Colonial World*. Chicago and London: The University of Chicago Press, 1979.

Berezin, L. *Puteshestvie po Severnoi Persii*. Kazan, 1852. Extracts translated in *The Economic History of Iran: 1800-1914*, edited by Charles Issawi, 105-108. Chicago and London: University of Chicago Press, 1971.

Bharier, Julian. *Economic Development in Iran 1900-1970*. London: Oxford University Press, 1971.

Bill, James. "Power and Religion in Revolutionary Iran." *Middle East Journal* 36, no. 1 (Winter (1982): 22-47.

———. *The Eagle and the Lion. The Tragedy of American-Iranian Relations*. New Haven and London: Yale University Press, 1988.

Birns, Laurence, ed. *The End of Chilean Democracy*. New York: Seabury Press, 1974.

Blau, Ernst Otto. *Commerzielle Zustände Persiens*. Berlin, 1858. Extracts translated in *The Economic History of Iran: 1800-1914*, edited by Charles Issawi, 132-135. Chicago and London: University of Chicago Press, 1971.

Bloch, Marc. *Feudal Society*. London: Routledge and Kegan Paul, 1961.

Bonine, Michael E. "Shops and Shopkeepers: Dynamics of an Iranian Provincial Bazaar." In *Modern Iran. The Dialectics of Continuity and Change*, edited by Michael E. Bonine and Nikki R. Keddie, 233-258. Albany: State University of New York Press, 1981.

Bonnell, Victoria E. "The Uses of Theory, Concepts and Comparisons in Historical Sociology." *Comparative Studies in Society and History* 22, no. 2 (April 1980): 156-173.

"The Borderlands of Soviet Central Asia. Persia. Part II." *Central Asian Review* 4, no. 4 (1956): 382-431.

Borgomale, Rabino di. *Coins, Medals and Seals of the Shâhs of Irân, 1500-1941*. Hertford, England: S. Austin and Sons, Ltd., 1945.

Boxer, C. R. *Jan Compagnie in War and Peace 1602-1799. A Short History of the Dutch East-India Company.* Hong Kong: Heinemann Asia, 1979.

Braudel, Fernand. *The Mediterranean and the Mediterranean World in the Age of Philip II.* Translated by Siân Reynolds. 2 vols. New York: Harper and Row, 1976.

Brenner, Robert. "The Origins of Capitalist Development: a Critique of Neo-Smithian Marxism." *New Left Review* 104 (July-August 1977): 25-92.

Browne, Edward G. *The Persian Revolution of 1905-1909.* Cambridge: At the University Press, 1910.

———. *The Persian Crisis of December, 1911; How it Arose and Whither it May Lead Us.* Cambridge: University Press, 1912.

———. *The Press and Poetry of Modern Persia.* London: Cambridge University Press, 1914. Reprint. Los Angeles: Kalamát Press, 1983.

———. "Chronology of the Persian Revolution." In *The Press and Poetry of Modern Persia,* 310-336. London: Cambridge University Press, 1914. Reprint. Los Angeles: Kalamát Press, 1983.

Burke, III, Edmund, and Paul Lubeck. "Explaining Social Movements in Two Oil-Exporting States: Divergent Outcomes in Nigeria and Iran." *Comparative Studies in Society and History* 29, no. 4 (October 1987): 643-665.

Calhoun, Craig Jackson. "The Radicalism of Tradition: Community Strength or Venerable Disguise and Borrowed Language?" *American Journal of Sociology* 88, no. 5 (March 1983): 886-914.

Cardoso, Fernando Henrique, and Enzo Faletto. *Dependency and Development in Latin America.* Translated from the Spanish by Marjory Mattingly Urquidi. Berkeley: University of California Press, 1979.

Chardin, Jean [John]. *The Travels of Jean Chardin in Persia, containing a description of Persia in General.* 2 vols. London: J. Smith, 1720.

———. *Voyages du Chevalier Chardin, en Perse, et autres lieux de l'orient.* 12 vols. Paris: Le Normant, 1811.

———. *Sir John Chardin's Travels in Persia.* London: The Argonaut Press, 1927.

Chaudhuri, K. N. "The East India Company and the Export of Treasure in the Early Seventeenth Century." *Economic History Review,* second series, 16 (1963): 23-38.

———. "Treasure and Trade Balances: the East India Company's Export Trade, 1660-1720." *Economic History Review,* second series 21, no. 3 (December 1968): 480-502.

———. *Trade and Civilisation in the Indian Ocean. An Economic History from the Rise of Islam to 1750.* Cambridge: Cambridge University Press, 1985.

Chayanov, A. V. "On the Theory of Non-Capitalist Economic Systems." Translated by Christel Lane. In *A. V. Chayanov on The Theory of Peasant Economy,* edited by Daniel Thorner, Basile Kerblay and R. E. F. Smith, 1-28. Homewood, Illinois: Richard D. Irwin, Inc., 1966.

Chirot, Daniel, and Thomas D. Hall. "World-System Theory." *Annual Review of Sociology* 8 (1982): 81-106.

A Chronicle of the Carmelites in Persia and the Papal Mission of the XVIIth and XVIIIth centuries. 2 vols. London: Eyre and Spottiswoode, 1939.

Clawson, Patrick. "Capital Accumulation in Iran." In *Oil and Class Struggle,* edited by Petter Nore and Terisa Turner, 143-171. London: Zed, 1980.

Cole, Juan. "Shi'i Clerics in Iraq and Iran, 1722-1780: The Akhbari-Usuli Conflict Reconsidered." *Iranian Studies* 18, no. 1 (Winter 1985): 3-34.

Constitution of the Islamic Republic of Iran. Translated from the Persian by Hamid Algar. Berkeley: Mizan Press, 1980.

Cottam, Richard. *Nationalism in Iran.* Pittsburgh: University of Pittsburgh Press, 1964.

————. "Review of Warren Christopher et al., *American Hostages in Iran: The Conduct of a Crisis*, and Gary Sick, *All Fall Down: America's Tragic Encounter with Iran.*" *International Journal of Middle East Studies* 19, no. 2 (May 1987): 251-255.

Curzon, Lord G. *Persia and the Persian Question*. 2 vols. London: Longman, Green and Co., 1892.

Dadkhah, Kamran M. "The Inflationary Process of the Iranian Economy: A Rejoinder." *International Journal of Middle East Studies* 19, no. 3 (August 1987): 388-391.

Davani, 'Ali. *Nahzat-i Ruhaniyun-i Iran* [Movement of the Clergy of Iran]. 10 vols. Tehran: Bunyad-i Farhangi-yi Imam Reza, 1360/1981.

Diba, Farhad. *Mohammad Mossadegh. A Political Biography*. London: Croom Helm, 1986.

Dickson, Martin B. "Sháh Tahmásb and the Uzbeks (The Duel for Khurásán with 'Ubayd Khán: 930-946/1524-1540)." Ph.D. diss., Department of Oriental Studies, Princeton University, 1958.

————. "The Fall of the Safavi Dynasty" (a review of Lockhart, *The Fall of the Safavi Dynasty*). *Journal of the American Oriental Society* 82 (1962): 503-517.

Dillon, Robert. "Carpet Capitalism and craft involution in Kirman, Iran: A study in economic anthropology." Ph.D. diss., Department of Anthropology, Columbia University, 1976.

Dorman, William A. and Mansour Farhang. *The U.S. Press and Iran. Foreign Policy and the Journalism of Deference*. Berkeley: University of California Press, 1987.

Eagleton, Jr., William. *The Kurdish Republic of 1946*. London: Oxford University Press, 1963.

Ebtehaj, Abolhassan. Interview recorded by Habib Ladjevardi, Cannes, France, December 1, 1981. Harvard University, Iranian Oral History Collection.

Elwell-Sutton, L. P. *Persian Oil. A Study in Power Politics*. London: Laurence and Wishart, Ltd., 1955.

————. "Reza Shah the Great: Founder of the Pahlavi Dynasty." In *Iran Under the Pahlavis*, edited by George Lenczowski, 1-50. Stanford: Hoover Institution Press, 1978.

Emerson, John. "Ex Occidente Lux. Some European Sources on the Economic Structure of Persia Between About 1630 and 1690." Ph.D. diss., Department of Oriental Studies, University of Cambridge, 1969.

Enayat, Anna. "The Problem of Imperialism in Nineteenth-Century Iran." *RIPEH (Review of Iranian Political Economy and History)* 2, no. 1 (December 1977): 48-72.

Entner, Marvin L. *Russo-Persian Commercial Relations, 1828-1914*. University of Florida Monographs, no. 28. Gainesville: University of Florida Press, 1965.

Evans, Peter. *Dependent Development. The Alliance of Multinational, State, and Local Capital in Brazil*. Princeton: Princeton University Press, 1979.

Faghfoory, Mohammad H. "The Ulama-State Relations in Iran: 1921-1941." *International Journal of Middle East Studies* 19, no. 4 (November 1987): 413-432.

Fallaci, Oriani. "An Interview with Khomeini." *The New York Times Magazine* (October 7, 1979): 29-31.

Farhi, Farideh. *States and Urban-Based Revolutions: Iran and Nicaragua*. Urbana and Chicago: University of Illinois Press. 1990.

Farmayan, Hafez F. *The Beginnings of Modernization in Iran. The Policies and reforms of Shah Abbas I (1587-1629)*. Middle East Center Research Monograph, no. 1. Salt Lake City: University of Utah, 1969.

Fasa'i, Hasan-i. *History of Persia under Qajar Rule*. Translated from the Persian by Heribert Busse. New York and London: Columbia University Press, 1972.

Fatemi, Faramarz S. *The U.S.S.R. in Iran. The Background History of Russian and Anglo-American Conflict in Iran, Its Effects on Iranian Nationalism, and the Fall of the Shah*. South Brunswick and New York: A. S. Barnes and Company, 1980.

Ferrier, Ronald W. "The Armenians and the East India Company in Persia in the Seventeenth and Early Eighteenth Centuries." *Economic History Review*, second series, 26 number 1 (February 1973): 38-62.

————. "Trade from the mid-14th Century to the End of the Safavid Period." In *The Cambridge History of Iran*. Vol. 6, *The Timurid and Safavid Periods*, edited by Peter Jackson and Laurence Lockhart, 412-490. Cambridge: Cambridge University Press, 1986.

Fischer, Michael M. J. *Iran: From Religious Dispute to Revolution*. Cambridge: Harvard University Press, 1980.

Floor, Willem. "The Guilds in Iran—an Overview from the Earliest Beginnings till 1972." *Zeitschrift der Deutschen Morgenländischen Gesellschaft* 125, no. 1 (1975): 99-116.

————. "The Merchants (*tujjar*) in Qajar Iran." *Zeitschrift der Deutschen Morgenländischen Gesellschaft* 126, no. 1 (1976): 101-135.

————. "The Revolutionary Character of the Iranian Ulama: Wishful Thinking or Reality?" *International Journal of Middle East Studies* 12, no. 4 (December 1980): 501-524.

————. "The Political Role of the Lutis in Iran." In *Modern Iran. The Dialectics of Continuity and Change*, edited by Michael E. Bonine and Nikki R. Keddie, 83-95. Albany: State University of New York Press, 1981.

————. *Industrialization in Iran 1900-1941*. Occasional Paper Series, no. 23. University of Durham, England: Centre for Middle Eastern and Islamic Studies, 1984.

————. *Labour Unions, Law and Conditions in Iran (1900-1941)*. Occasional Paper Series, no. 26. University of Durham, England: Centre for Middle Eastern and Islamic Studies, 1985.

Foran, John. "The Modes of Production Approach to Seventeenth-Century Iran." *International Journal of Middle East Studies* 20, no. 3 (August 1988): 345-363.

————. "Social Structure and Social Change in Iran from 1500 to 1979." Ph.D. diss., Department of Sociology, University of California, Berkeley, 1988.

————. "The Making of an External Arena: Iran's Place in the World-System, 1500-1722." *Review* (Journal of the Fernand Braudel Center for the Study of Economies, Historical Systems, and Civilizations) XII, no. 1 (Winter 1989): 71-119.

————. "The Concept of Dependence as a Key to the Political Economy of Qajar Iran (1800-1925)." *Iranian Studies* XXII, nos. 2-3 (1989): 5-56.

————. "A Theory of Third World Social Revolutions: Iran, Nicaragua and El Salvador Compared." Paper presented at the meetings of the International Sociological Association, Madrid, Spain (1990).

————. "The Strengths and Weaknesses of Iran's Populist Alliance: A Class Analysis of the Constitutional Revolution of 1905-1911." *Theory and Society* 20, no. 6 (December 1991): 795-823.

————. "The Long Fall of the Safavid Dynasty: Moving Beyond the Standard Views." *International Journal of Middle East Studies* 24, no. 2 (May 1992): 281-304.

————. "An Historical-Sociological Framework for the Study of Long-Term Transformations in the Third World." *Humanity and Society* 16, no. 3 (August 1992): 330-349.

Foster-Carter, Aidan. "The Modes of Production Controversy." *New Left Review* 107 (January-February 1978): 47-77.

Fragner, Bert. "Social and Internal Economic Affairs." In *The Cambridge History of Iran*. Vol. 6, *The Timurid and Safavid Periods*, edited by Peter Jackson and Laurence Lockhart, 491-567. Cambridge: Cambridge University Press, 1986.

Fraser, James B. *Historical and Descriptive Account of Persia, from the Earliest Ages to the Present Time*. New York: Harper & Brothers, 1833.

Fryer, John. *A New Account of East India and Persia being Nine Years' Travels*. Vol. 2. London: Hakluyt Society, 1912.

Garst, Daniel. "Wallerstein and his Critics." *Theory and Society* 14 (1985): 469-495.

Garthwaite, Gene R. "Khans and Kings: The Dialectics of Power in Bakhtiari History." In *Modern Iran. The Dialectics of Continuity and Change*, edited by Michael E. Bonine and Nikki R. Keddie, 159-172. Albany: State University of New York Press, 1981.

————. *Khans and shahs. A documentary analysis of the Bakhtiyari in Iran.* Cambridge: Cambridge University Press, 1983.

Gasiorowski, Mark J. "The 1953 *Coup d'Etat* in Iran." *International Journal of Middle East Studies* 19, no. 3 (August 1987): 261-286.

Gay, Peter. *Freud. A Life for Our Time.* New York and London: W. W. Norton & Company, 1988.

Ghandchi-Tehrani, Davoud. "Bazaaris and Clergy: Socio-Economic Origins of Radicalism and Revolution in Iran." Ph.D. diss., Department of Sociology, City University of New York, 1982.

Ghoreishi, Ahmad. Interview recorded by Habib Ladjevardi, Moraga, California, January 31, 1982. Harvard University, Iranian Oral History Collection.

Giddens, Anthony. *The Constitution of Society.* Berkeley and Los Angeles: University of California Press, 1984.

Gilbar, Gad G. "Demographic developments in late Qajar Persia, 1870-1906." *Asian and African Studies* 11, no. 2 (Autumn 1976): 125-156.

————. "The Big Merchants (*tujjar*) and the Persian Constitutional Revolution of 1906." *Asian and African Studies* 11, no. 3 (1977): 275-303.

————. "Persian Agriculture in the Late Qajar Period, 1860-1906: Some Economic and Social Aspects." *Asian and African Studies* 12, no. 3 (1978): 312-365.

————. "The Persian Economy in the mid-19th Century." *Die Welt des Islams* 19, nos. 1-4 (1979): 177-211.

————. "Trends in the Development of Prices in Late Qajar Iran, 1870-1906." *Iranian Studies* 16, nos. 3-4 (Summer-Autumn 1983): 177-198.

Gillard, David. *The Struggle for Asia 1828-1914. A Study in British and Russian Imperialism.* London: Methuen & Co Ltd., 1977.

Glamann, Kristof. *Dutch-Asiatic Trade 1620-1740.* Copenhagen: Danish Science Press, and The Hague: Martinus Nijhoff, 1958.

Gobineau, Arthur de. *Trois ans en Asie.* Paris, 1859. Extracts translated in *The Economic History of Iran: 1800-1914*, edited by Charles Issawi, 36-40. Chicago and London: University of Chicago Press, 1971.

Godelier, Maurice. "The Concept of the 'Asiatic Mode of Production' and Marxist Models of Social Change." In *Relations of Production*, edited by David Seddon, 204-257. London: Frank Cass, 1978.

Gödel, Rudolf. *Über den pontischen Handelsweg und die Verhältnisse des europäisch-persischen Verkehres.* Vienna, 1849. Extracts translated in *The Economic History of Iran: 1800-1914*, edited by Charles Issawi, 99-103. Chicago and London: University of Chicago Press, 1971.

Goldfrank, Walter L. "Theories of Revolution and Revolution Without Theory: The Case of Mexico." *Theory and Society* 7 (1979): 135-165.

Goldstone, Jack A. "Theories of Revolution: The Third Generation." *World Politics* 32, no. 3 (April 1980): 425-453.

————. "The Comparative and Historical Study of Revolutions." *Annual Review of Sociology* 8 (1982): 187-207.

Good, Byron J. "The Transformation of Health Care in Modern Iranian History." In *Modern Iran. The Dialectics of Continuity and Change*, edited by Michael E. Bonine and Nikki R. Keddie, 59-92. Albany: State University of New York Press, 1981.

Good, Mary-Jo DelVecchio. "Social Hierarchy in Provincial Iran: The Case of Qajar Maragheh." *Iranian Studies* 10, no. 3 (Summer 1977): 129-163.

————. "The Changing Status and Composition of an Iranian Provincial Elite." In *Modern Iran. The Dialectics of Continuity and Change*, edited by Michael E. Bonine and Nikki R. Keddie, 269-288. Albany: State University of New York Press, 1981.

Graham, Robert. *Iran: The Illusion of Power.* New York: St. Martin's Press, 1979.

Green, Jerrold D. *Revolution in Iran. The Politics of Countermobilization.* New York: Praeger, 1982.

Gregorian, Vartan. *The Emergence of Modern Afghanistan. Politics of Reform and Modernization, 1880-1946.* Stanford: Stanford University Press, 1969.

————. "Minorities of Isfahan: The Armenian Community of Isfahan, 1587-1722." *Iranian Studies* 7, nos. 3-4 (1974): 652-680.

Grey, Lieutenant-Colonel W. G. "Recent Persian History." *Journal of the Central Asian Society* 13, part 1 (1926): 29-42.

Hadary, Gideon. "The Agrarian Reform Problem in Iran." *Middle East Journal* 5, no. 2 (Spring 1951): 181-196.

Hadi, Daughter of Aga Shaykh. "Il faut prendre exemple sur les femmes." *Revue du Monde Musulman* 12, no. 10 (October 1910): 282-284.

Haig, Lt.-Col. Sir Wolseley. "The Rise of Riza Khan Pahlavi." *The National Review* (London) 86 (December 1925): 624-632.

Hakimian, Hassan. "Wage Labor and Migration: Persian Workers in Southern Russia, 1880-1914." *International Journal of Middle East Studies* 17, no. 4 (November 1985): 443-462.

Halliday, Fred. *Iran: Dictatorship and Development.* New York: Penguin Books, 1979.

————. "The Genesis of the Iranian Revolution." *Third World Quarterly* 1, no. 4 (October 1979): 1-16.

————. "The Iranian Revolution: Uneven Development and Religious Populism." *Journal of International Affairs* 36, no. 2 (Fall/Winter 1982-83): 187-207.

Hambly, Gavin. "An introduction to the economic organization of early Qajar Iran." *Iran* (Journal of the British Institute of Persian Studies) 2 (1964): 69-81.

Haneda, Masashi. "The Evolution of the Safavid Royal Guard." Translated by Rudi Mathee. *Iranian Studies* XXI, nos. 2-3 (1989): 57-86.

Hanson, Brad. "The "Westoxication" of Iran: Depictions and Reactions of Behrangi, Al-e Ahmad, and Shari'ati." *International Journal of Middle East Studies* 15, no. 1 (February 1983): 1-23.

Harkness, Richard and Gladys Harkness. "The Mysterious Doings of CIA." Part Two. *Saturday Evening Post.* November 6, 1954.

Hayden, Lyle J. "Living Standards in Rural Iran." *Middle East Journal* 3, no. 2 (1949): 140-150.

Helfgott, Leonard Michael. "The Rise of the Qajar Dynasty." Ph.D. diss., Department of History, University of Maryland, 1973.

————. "Tribalism as a Socioeconomic Formation in Iranian History." *Iranian Studies* 10, nos. 1-2 (Winter-Spring 1977): 36-61.

Hemmasi, Mohammad. *Migration in Iran: A Quantitative Approach.* Tehran: Pahlavi University Publications, 1974.

Hilton, Rodney, ed. *The Transition from Feudalism to Capitalism.* London: New Left Books, 1978.

Hindess, Barry, and Paul Q. Hirst. *Pre-Capitalist Modes of Production.* London: Routledge and Kegan Paul, 1975.

Hodgson, Marshall G. S. *The Venture of Islam. Conscience and History in a World Civilization.* Vol. 2, *The Expansion of Islam in the Middle Periods,* and Vol. 3, *The Gunpowder Empires and Modern Times.* Chicago: University of Chicago Press, 1974.

Hooglund, Eric J. "The Khwushnishin Population of Iran." *Iranian Studies* 6 (Autumn 1973): 229-245.

————. "The Effects of the Land Reform Program on Rural Iran, 1962-1972." Ph.D. diss., Department of Political Science, Johns Hopkins University, 1975.

————. "Rural Participation in the Revolution." *MERIP (Middle East Research and Information Project) Reports,* no. 87 (May 1980): 3-6.

————. "Rural Socioeconomic Organization in Transition: The Case of Iran's Bonehs." In *Modern Iran. The Dialectics of Continuity and Change,* edited by Michael E. Bonine and Nikki R. Keddie, 191-207. Albany: State University of New York Press, 1981.

————. *Land and Revolution in Iran, 1960-1980.* Austin: University of Texas Press, 1982.

"How We Organized Strike that Paralyzed Shah's Regime. Firsthand Account by Iranian Oil Worker." In *Oil and Class Struggle*, edited by Petter Nore and Terisa Turner, 292-301. London: Zed Press, 1980.

Huart, Cl. "Karim Khan Zand." In *The Encyclopedia of Islam*, edited by M. Th. Houtsma et al., 762. Leyden: E. J. Brill, 1927.

Hurewitz, J. C. *Diplomacy in the Near and Middle East*. Vol. 1: *A Documentary Record: 1535-1914*. Vol. 2: *A Documentary Record: 1914-56*. Princeton: D. van Nostrand Company, Inc., 1956.

Husayn, Mirza. *Jughrafiya-yi Isfahan* [Geography of Isfahan]. Tehran, 1342/1963. Extracts translated in *The Economic History of Iran: 1800-1914*, edited by Charles Issawi, 279-282. Chicago and London: University of Chicago Press, 1971.

Inalcik, Halil. "The Ottoman Economic Mind and Aspects of the Ottoman Economy." In *Studies in the Economic History of the Middle East: from the rise of Islam to the present day*, edited by M. A. Cook, 207-218. London and New York: Oxford University Press, 1970.

Inalcik, Halil, and Niels Steensgaard. "Harir." In *The Encyclopedia of Islam* 3: 209-221. New edition. Leiden: E. J. Brill, and London: Luzac & Co., 1979.

"Iran: The New Crisis of American Hegemony." *Monthly Review* 30, no. 9 (February 1979): 1-24.

Iranian Students Association in the U.S. *Shah's Inferno: Abadan August 19, 1978*. Berkeley: ISAUS, 1978.

Iranian Studies. Special issue on "Iranian Studies in Europe and Japan." Volume 20, nos. 2-4 (1987).

Islam, Riazul. *Indo-Persian Relations. A Study of the Political and Diplomatic Relations between the Mughal Empire and Iran*. Lahore: Ripon Printing Press, 1970.

Issawi, Charles. "Population and Resources in the Ottoman Empire and Iran." In *Studies in Eighteenth Century Islamic History*, edited by Thomas Naff and Roger Owen, 152-164. Carbondale and Edwardsville: Southern Illinois University Press, 1977.

———. "The Iranian Economy 1925-1975: Fifty Years of Economic Development." In *Iran Under the Pahlavis*, edited by George Lenczowski, 129-166. Stanford: Hoover Institution Press, 1978.

———. "Iranian Trade, 1800-1914." *Iranian Studies* 16, nos. 3-4 (Summer-Autumn 1983): 229-241.

Issawi, Charles, ed. *The Economic History of Iran: 1800-1914*. Chicago and London: University of Chicago Press, 1971.

Ivanov, M. S. "Babism" and "Babi Uprisings." In *The Great Soviet Encyclopedia*. Vol. 2, 521. New York and London: Macmillan, 1973.

———. *Tarikh-i Nuvin-i Iran* [Modern History of Iran]. Translated from the Russian by Hushang Tizabi and Hasan Qa'im Paneh. Stockholm: Tudeh Publishing Centre, 1356/1977.

Jabbari, Ahmad. "Economic Factors in Iran's Revolution: Poverty, Inequality, and Inflation." In *Iran: Essays on a Revolution in the Making*, edited by Ahmad Jabbari and Robert Olson, 163-214. Lexington, Kentucky: Mazda Publishers, 1981.

Jamalzadeh, Sayyid Muhammad 'Ali. *Ganj-i Shayagan ya Auza'-yi Iqtisadi-yi Iran* [Abundant Treasure, or, the Economic Situation of Iran]. Berlin: Kaveh, 1335 Q./1916.

Jayawardena, Kumari. *Feminism and Nationalism in the Third World*. London: Zed, 1986.

Jazani, Bizhan. *Iran . . . The Socio-Economic Analysis of a Dependent Capitalist State*. Translated by the Iran Committee. London: The Iran Committee, n.d.

———. *Capitalism and Revolution in Iran. Selected Writings of Bizhan Jazani*. Translated by the Iran Committee. London: Zed Press, 1980.

Jenkinson, Anthony. "Mr. Anthony Jenkinson's Second Voyage from London to Mosco, and thence over the Caspian-Sea into Persia, Anno 1561." In *Navigantium atque Itinerantium Biblioteca . . .*, edited by John Harris, 521-524. Vol. 1. London: Thomas Bennet, 1705.

Jones, Consul-General. "Trade of Tabriz, 1837-71." In *The Economic History of Iran: 1800-1914*, edited by Charles Issawi, 112-116. Chicago and London: University of Chicago Press, 1971.

Kasaba, Resat. "Incorporation of the Ottoman Empire, 1750-1820." *Review* 10, nos. 5-6 (Summer/Fall 1987): 805-847.

Kashani, Dr. Kamran. Interview recorded by Habib Ladjevardi, Mykonos, Greece, July 22, 1982. Harvard University, Iranian Oral History Collection.

Kasravi, Ahmad. *Tarikh-i Mashruteh-i Iran* [History of the Constitutional Revolution of Iran]. Tehran: Amir Kabir, 1344/1965.

Katouzian, Homa. *The Political Economy of Modern Iran. Despotism and Pseudo- Modernism, 1926-1979*. New York and London: New York University Press, 1981.

———. "The Aridisolatic Society: A Model of Long-Term Social and Economic Development in Iran." *International Journal of Middle East Studies* 15, no. 2 (May 1983): 259-282.

Kayhan. January-May 1978.

Kazemi, Farhad. *Poverty and Revolution in Iran. The Migrant Poor, Urban Marginality and Politics*. New York and London: New York University Press, 1980.

———. "The Military and Politics in Iran: The Uneasy Symbiosis." In *Towards a Modern Iran: Studies in Thought, Politics and Society*, edited by Elie Kedourie and Sylvia G. Haim, 217-240. London: Cass, 1980.

———. *Politics and Culture in Iran*. Ann Arbor: University of Michigan, 1988.

Kazemi, Farhad, and Ervand Abrahamian. "The Nonrevolutionary Peasantry of Modern Iran." *Iranian Studies* 11 (1978): 259-304.

Keddie, Nikki. "The Impact of the West on Iranian Social History." Ph.D. diss., Department of History, University of California, Berkeley, 1955.

———. *Historical Obstacles to Agrarian Change in Iran*. Claremont Asian Studies, no. 8. Claremont, California: September 1960.

———. *Religion and Rebellion in Iran. The Tobacco Protest of 1891-1892*. London: Frank Cass & Co., Ltd., 1966.

———. "The Midas Touch: Black Gold, Economics and Politics in Iran Today." *Iranian Studies* 10, no. 4 (Autumn 1977): 243-266.

———. "The Economic History of Iran, 1800-1914, and its Political Impact." In *Iran: Religion, Politics and Society. Collected Essays*, 119-136. London: Frank Cass, 1980.

———. "Iran, 1797-1941." In *Iran: Religion, Politics and Society. Collected Essays*, 137-157. London: Frank Cass, 1980.

———. "Popular Participation in the Persian Revolution of 1905-1911." In *Iran: Religion, Politics and Society. Collected Essays*, 66-79. London: Frank Cass, 1980.

———. "Stratification, Social Control, and Capitalism in Iranian Villages: Before and After Land Reform." In *Iran: Religion, Politics and Society. Collected Essays*, 158-205. London: Frank Cass, 1980.

———. *Roots of Revolution. An Interpretive History of Modern Iran*. With a section by Yann Richard. New Haven: Yale University Press, 1981.

———. "Religion, Society, and Revolution in Modern Iran." In *Modern Iran. The Dialectics of Continuity and Change*, edited by Michael E. Bonine and Nikki R. Keddie, 21-36. Albany: State University of New York Press, 1981.

———. "Iranian Revolutions in Comparative Perspective." *American Historical Review* 88, no. 3 (June 1983): 579-598.

Keyder, Caglar. *The Definition of a Peripheral Economy: Turkey, 1923-1929*. Cambridge: Cambridge University Press, 1981.

Keyvani, Mehdi. *Artisans and Guild Life in the later Safavid period. Contribution to the socio-economic history of Persia*. Islamkundiche Untersuchungen, vol. 65. Berlin: Klaus Schwarz Verlag, 1982.

Khomeini, Imam. *Islam and Revolution. Writings and Declarations of Imam Khomeini*. Translated by Hamid Algar. Berkeley: Mizan Press, 1981.

Kirmani, Nazim al-Islam. *Tarikh-i Bidari-yi Iranian* [History of the Awakening of the Iranians]. 3 vols. Tehran: Bunyad-i Farhang-i Iran, 1346/1967.

Korby, Wilfred. *Probleme der industriellen Entwicklung und Konzentration in Iran.* Wiesbaden: Dr. Ludwig Reichert Verlag, 1977.

Krader, Lawrence. *The Asiatic Mode of Production. Sources, Development and Critique in the Writings of Karl Marx.* Assen, Netherlands: Van Gorcum & Company, 1975.

Krishna, Bal. *Commercial Relations Between India and England (1601-1657).* London: George Routledge & Sons, Ltd., 1924.

Krusinski, Father Judasz Tadeusz. *The History of the Late Revolutions of Persia.* Translated to English with a short History of the Sophies, by Father Du Cerceau. London: J. Osborne, 1740. Reprint. Arno Press, 1973.

Kumar, Ram Nandan. "Economic Background of British Diplomacy in Persia, 1858-1907." *Islamic Culture* (Hyderabad) 50, no. 4 (October 1976): 229-236.

Kuniholm, Bruce. *The Origins of the Cold War in the Near East. Great Power Conflict and Diplomacy in Iran, Turkey, and Greece.* Princeton: Princeton University Press, 1980.

Kuznetsova, N. A. "Urban industry in Persia during the 18th and early 19th centuries." *Central Asian Review* 11, no. 3 (1963): 308-321.

Lachmann, Richard. *From Manor to Market. Structural Change in England, 1536-1640.* Madison: University of Wisconsin Press, 1987.

———. "Elite Conflict and State Formation in Sixteenth and Seventeenth Century England and France." *American Sociological Review* 54, no. 2(April 1989): 141-162.

Laclau, Ernesto. *Politics and Ideology in Marxist Theory.* London: New Left Books, 1977.

Lafont, F. and H.-L. Rabino. *L'industrie séricole en Perse.* Montpellier, 1910. Extracts translated in *The Economic History of Iran: 1800-1914,* edited by Charles Issawi, 235-238. Chicago and London: University of Chicago Press, 1971.

Lambton, Ann K. S. "Two Safavid Soyurghals." *Bulletin of the School of Oriental and African Studies* 14 (1952): 44-54.

———. *Landlord and Peasant in Persia. A Study of Land Tenure and Land Revenue Administration.* London: Oxford University Press, 1953.

———. *Islamic Society in Persia.* An Inaugural Lecture delivered on March 9, 1954 at the University of London School of Oriental and African Studies. Oxford: Oxford University Press, 1954.

———. "Quis Custodiet Custodes? Some Reflections on the Persian Theory of Government (Conclusion)." *Studia Islamica* 6 (1956): 125-146.

———. "Persian Society under the Qajars." *Journal of the Royal Central Asian Society* 48, part 2 (April 1961): 123-139.

———. "Persian Political Societies 1906-11." *St Antony's Papers,* 41-89. Middle Eastern Affairs, no. 16. Carbondale: Southern Illinois University Press, 1963.

———. "A Reconsideration of the Position of the *Marja' al-Taqlid* and the Religious Institution." *Studia Islamica* 20 (1964): 115-135.

———. "The Tobacco Régie: Prelude to Revolution." *Studia Islamica* 22 (1965): 119-157, and 23 (1965): 71-90.

———. "The Case of Hajji Nur al-Din, 1823-47: A Study in Land Tenure." *Bulletin of the School of Oriental and African Studies* 30, part 1 (1967): 54-72.

———. "The Evolution of the *Iqta'* in Medieval Iran." *Iran* (Journal of the British Institute of Persian Studies) 5 (1967): 41-50.

———. *The Persian Land Reform 1962-1966.* Oxford: Clarendon Press, 1969.

———. "Persia: The Breakdown of Society." In *The Cambridge History of Islam.* Vol. 1, *The Central Islamic Lands,* edited by P. M. Holt, Ann K. S. Lambton and Bernard Lewis, 403-467. Cambridge: Cambridge University Press, 1970.

———. "Persian Trade under the Early Qajars." In *Islam and the Trade of Asia. A Colloquium. Papers on Islamic History: II,* edited by D. S. Richards, 215-244. Oxford: Bruno Cassirer, and Pennsylvania: University of Pennsylvania Press, 1970.

————. "The Persian Constitutional Revolution of 1905-6." In *Revolution in the Middle East and Other Case Studies*, edited by P. J. Vatikiotis, 173-182. Totowa, New Jersey: Rowman and Littlefield, 1972.

————. "The Tribal Resurgence and the Decline of the Bureaucracy in the Eighteenth Century." In *Studies in Eighteenth Century Islamic History*, edited by Thomas Naff and Roger Owen, 108-129. Carbondale and Edwardsville: University of Southern Illinois Press, 1977.

————. *State and Government in Medieval Islam. An Introduction to Islamic Political Theory: The Jurists*. London: Oxford University Press, 1981.

Lang, D. M. "Georgia and the Fall of the Safavi Dynasty." *Bulletin of the School of Oriental and African Studies* 14, part 3 (1952): 523-539.

Le Monde. September 6, 1978.

Lee, Lester A. "The Reforms of Reza Shah: 1925-1941." M.A. thesis, Department of History, Stanford University, 1950.

"A Letter from Teheran." *Journal of the Royal Central Asian Society* 21, part 1 (January 1934): 89-92.

Litten, Wilhelm. *Persien von der 'pénétration pacifique' zum Protektorat. Urkunden und Tatsachen zur Geschichte der europäischen 'pénétration pacifique' in Persien 1860-1919*. Berlin, 1920. Extracts translated in *The Economic History of Iran: 1800-1914*, edited by Charles Issawi, 358-361. Chicago and London: University of Chicago Press, 1971.

Lockhart, Laurence. *Nadir Shah. A Critical Study Based Mainly Upon Contemporary Sources*. London: Luzac & Co., 1938.

————. *The Fall of the Safavi Dynasty and the Afghan Occupation of Persia*. Cambridge: At the University Press, 1958.

————. "European Contacts with Persia, 1350-1736." In *The Cambridge History of Iran*. Vol. 6, *The Timurid and Safavid Periods*, edited by Peter Jackson and Laurence Lockhart, 373-409. Cambridge: Cambridge University Press, 1986.

Loeb, Laurence D. "The Religious Dimension of Modernization Among the Jews of Shiraz." In *Modern Iran. The Dialectics of Continuity and Change*, edited by Michael E. Bonine and Nikki R. Keddie, 301-322. Albany: State University of New York Press, 1981.

Lorentz, John H. "Iran's Great Reformer of the Nineteenth Century: An Analysis of Amir Kabir's Reforms." *Iranian Studies* 3, no. 2 (Spring-Summer 1971): 85-103.

Louis, William Roger. *The British Empire in the Middle East 1945-1951. Arab Nationalism, the United States, and Postwar Imperialism*. Oxford: Clarendon Press, 1984.

MacLean, Consul-General. "Report on the Trade of Khorasan for the Year 1889-90." In *The Economic History of Iran: 1800-1914*, edited by Charles Issawi, 122-124. Chicago and London: University of Chicago Press, 1971.

MacLean, H. W. "Report on the Conditions and Prospects of British Trade in Persia." In *The Economic History of Iran: 1800-1914*, edited by Charles Issawi, 136-142. Chicago and London: University of Chicago Press, 1971.

Mahdi, Ali-Akbar. "The Iranian Struggle for Liberation: Socio-Historical Roots to the Islamic Revolution." *RIPEH (The Review of Iranian Political Economy and History)* 4, no. 1 (Spring 1980): 1-33.

Malcolm, Sir John. *The History of Persia from the Most Early Period to the Present Time: Containing an Account of the Religion, Government, Usages and Character of the Inhabitants of that Kingdom*. 2 vols. London: John Murray, 1815, 1829.

————. *The Melville Papers*. In *The Economic History of Iran: 1800-1914*, edited by Charles Issawi, 262-267. Chicago and London: University of Chicago Press, 1971.

Manchester Guardian. September 5 and 6, 1978.

du Mans, Raphaël. *Estat de la Perse en 1660*. Edited by Ch. Schefer. Paris: Ernest Leroux, 1890.

Martin, B. G. "Seven Safawid Documents from Azarbayjan." In *Documents from Islamic Chanceries*, edited by S. M. Stern, 171-206. First series, Oriental Studies, no. 3. Oxford: Bruno Cassirer, 1965.

Martin, Vanessa. *Islam and Modernism. The Iranian Revolution of 1906*. London: I. B. Tauris, 1989.

Marx, Karl. *Pre-Capitalist Economic Formations*. Translated by Jack Cohen. New York: International Publishers, 1964.

———. *Grundrisse. Foundations of the Critique of Political Economy*. Translated by Martin Nicolaus. New York: Vintage Books, 1973.

———. *The Marx-Engels Reader*. Edited by Robert C. Tucker. 2nd ed. New York and London: W. W. Norton & Company, 1978.

———, and Friedrich Engels. *Marx-Engels Selected Correspondence*. London: Lawrence and Wishart, Ltd., 1975.

Matthee, Rudolph P. "Politics and Trade in Late Safavid Iran: Commercial Crisis and Government Reaction under Shah Solayman (1666-1694)." Ph.D. diss., Department of Islamic Studies, University of California, Los Angeles, 1991.

Mazzaoui, Michel M. *The Origins of the Safawids. Shi'ism, Sufism and the Gulat*. Freiburger Islamstudien, vol. 3. Wiesbaden: Franz Steiner Verlag GMBH, 1972.

McChesney, R. D. "Comments on 'The Qajar Uymaq in The Safavid Period, 1500-1722'." *Iranian Studies* 14, nos. 1-2 (Winter-Spring 1981): 87-105.

McDaniel, Robert A. "Economic Change and Economic Resiliency in 19th Century Persia." *Iranian Studies* 4, no. 1 (Winter 1971): 36-49.

———. *The Shuster Mission and the Persian Constitutional Revolution*. Minneapolis: Biblioteca Islamica, 1974.

McFarland, Stephen Lee. "A Peripheral View of the Origins of the Cold War. The Crises in Iran, 1941-47." *Diplomatic History* 4, no. 4 (Fall 1980): 333-351.

———. "The Crises in Iran, 1941-1947: A Society in Change and the Peripheral Origins of the Cold War." Ph.D. diss., Department of History, University of Texas at Austin, 1981.

———. "Anatomy of an Iranian Political Crowd: the Tehran Bread Riot of December 1942." *International Journal of Middle East Studies* 17, no. 1 (February 1985): 51-65.

Medley, Margaret. "Islam, Chinese Porcelain and Ardabil." *Iran* (Journal of the British Institute of Persian Studies) 13 (1975): 31-45.

Mehrain, Fattaneh. "Emergence of Capitalist Authoritarian States in Periphery Formations: A Case Study of Iran." Ph.D. diss., Department of Sociology, University of Wisconsin-Madison, 1979.

Meilink-Roelofsz, M. A. P. "The Earliest Relations between Persia and the Netherlands." *Persica* (Jaarboek van het Genootschap Nederland-Iran Stichting voor Culturele Betrekkingen) 6 (1972-1974): 1-50.

Milani, Abbas M. "Ideology and the Iranian Constitutional Revolution. The Political Economy of the Ideological Currents of the Constitutional Revolution." Ph.D. diss., Department of Political Science, University of Hawaii, 1975.

Millspaugh, Arthur. *Americans in Persia*. Washington, D.C.: The Brookings Institution, 1946.

Minorsky, Vladimir M. "Nadir Shah." In *The Encyclopedia of Islam*, edited by M. Th. Houtsma et al., 810-814. Leyden: E. J. Brill, 1927.

———. "Tiyul." In *The Encyclopedia of Islam*, 799-801. London: Luzac, 1934.

———. "A Soyurghal of Qasim b. Jahangir Aq-qoyunlu (903/1498)." *Bulletin of the School of Oriental and African Studies* 11 (1937-39): 927-960.

———. Ed. and trans. *Tadhkirat al-muluk. A Manual of Safavid Administration (circa 1137/1725)*. London: Luzac, 1943.

———. "Review Essay on *The Babi Uprisings in Iran in 1848-1852* (M. S. Ivanov, 1939)." *Bulletin of the School of Oriental and African Studies* 11 (1943-1944): 875-883.

———. "Persia: Religion and History." In *Iranica. Twenty Articles*, 242-259. University of Tehran Publication, vol. 775. Tehran: University of Tehran, 1965.

Moaddel, Mansoor. "Shi'i Political Discourse and Class Mobilization in the Tobacco Rebellion of 1980-92." *Sociological Forum* (1992).

Moghadam, Gholam Reza. "Iran's Foreign Trade Policy and Economic Development in the Interwar Period." Ph.D. diss., Department of Economics, Stanford University, 1956.

Moghadam, Val. [Sharhzad Azad, pseud.]. "Workers' and Peasants' Councils in Iran." *Monthly Review* 32, no. 5 (October 1980): 14-29.

———. "Acumulation Strategy and Class Formation: The Making of an Industrial Labor Force in Iran, 1962-1977." Ph.D. diss., Department of Sociology, American University, 1985.

———. "Industrial Development, Culture and Working-Class Politics: A Case Study of Tabriz Industrial Workers in the Iranian Revolution." *International Sociology* 2, no. 2 (June 1987): 151-175.

———. "Socialism or Anti-Imperialism? The Left and Revolution in Iran." *New Left Review*, no. 166 (November/December 1987): 5-28.

———. "Populist Revolution and the Islamic State in Iran." In *Revolution in the World-System*, edited by Terry Boswell, 147-163. Westport, Connecticut: Greenwood Press, 1989.

Moghtader, Hushang. "The Impact of Increased Oil Revenues on Iran's Economic Development." In *Towards a Modern Iran. Studies in Thought, Politics and Society*, edited by Elie Kedourie and Sylvia G. Haim, 241-262. London: Cass, 1980.

Momen, Moojan. "The Social Basis of the Babi Upheavals in Iran (1848-53): A Preliminary Analysis." *International Journal of Middle East Studies* 15, no. 2 (May 1983): 157-183.

Monshi, Eskandar Beg. *History of Shah 'Abbas the Great (Tarik-e 'Alam ara-ye 'Abbasi)*. Translated from the Persian by Roger M. Savory. 2 vols. Boulder: Westview Press, 1978.

"Mosaddeq's Role in the Events of 1951-3 in Persia." *Central Asian Review* 9, no. 3 (1961): 302-306.

Motameni, Reza. "An Inquiry into Iran's Underdevelopment: A Quarter Century of Dependent Development." Ph.D. diss., Department of Government, Claremont Graduate School, 1981.

Motter, T. H. Vail. *The Persian Corridor and Aid to Russia*. Washington, D.C.: Office of the Chief of Military History, Department of the Army, 1952.

Müller, Hans-Georg. "Remarks on the Role of the State Capital Sector and National Private Capital in the Evolutionary Process of Capitalism in Iran Up to the End of the 1970s." In *Iran: From Monarchy to Republic*, edited by Günter Barthel, 72-87. Special issue no. 12 of *Asia, Africa, Latin America*. East Berlin: Akademie-Verlag, 1983.

Munson, Henry. Lectures on the Iranian Revolution. University of California, Santa Barbara. 1980.

———. *Islam and Revolution in the Middle East*. New Haven and London: Yale University Press, 1988.

Muslim Students Following the Line of the Imam, *Asnad-i lanah-i jasusi-yi Amrika* [Documents from the Spy Nest of America]. Tehran [?]: n.d.

Nashat, Guity. "From Bazaar to Market: Foreign Trade and Economic Development in Nineteenth-Century Iran." *Iranian Studies* 14, nos. 1-2 (Winter-Spring 1981): 53-85.

———. *The Origins of Modern Reform in Iran, 1870-80*. Urbana: University of Illinois Press, 1982.

Nasr, Hossein. "Religion in Safavid Persia." *Iranian Studies* 7, nos. 1-2 (1974): 271-286.

National Archives. State Department files. Record Group 59. 891.00: 1910, 1945-46. 788.00: 1952-1953.

National Security Archive. *Iran 1977-1980. The Making of U.S. Policy*. Microfiche collection.

New York Times. Various issues.

Nissman, David B. *The Soviet Union and Iranian Azerbaijan. The Use of Nationalism for Political Penetration*. Boulder and London: Westview Press, 1987.

Nomani, Farhad. "The Origin and Development of Feudalism in Iran: 300-1600 A.D." Ph.D. diss., Department of Economics, University of Illinois at Urbana-Champaign, 1972.

Nowshirvani, V. F. "The Beginnings of Commercialized Agriculture in Iran." In *The Islamic Middle East, 700-1900: Studies in Economic and Social History*, edited by A. L. Udovitch, 547-591. Princeton: The Darwin Press, Inc., 1977.

Olearius, Adam. *The Ambassadors from the Duke of Holstein's Travels into Muscovy* . . . In *Navigantium atque Itinerantium Biblioteca,* edited by John Harris, 1-112. Vol. 2. London: Thomas Bennet, 1705.

Olson, Roger T. "Persian Gulf Trade and the Agricultural Economy of Southern Iran in the Nineteenth Century." In *Modern Iran. The Dialectics of Continuity and Change,* edited by Michael E. Bonine and Nikki R. Keddie, 173-189. Albany: State Univerity of New York Press, 1981.

Pahlavi, Muhammad Reza. *Mission for My Country.* New York: McGraw-Hill Book Company, Inc., 1961.

Paige, Jeffery. *Agrarian Revolution: Social Movements and Export Agriculture in the Underdeveloped World.* New York: The Free Press, 1975.

Paine, Chris. "Iranian Nationalism and the Great Powers: 1872-1954." *MERIP (Middle East Research and Information Project) Reports,* no. 37 (1975): 3-28.

Pakdaman, Nasser. "Preface." *Iranian Studies* 16, nos. 3-4 (Summer-Autumn 1983): 125-135.

Parsa, Misagh. *Social Origins of the Iranian Revolution.* New Brunswick and London: Rutgers University Press, 1989.

Pavlovitch, Michel. "La situation agraire en Perse à la veille de la révolution." *Revue du Monde Musulman* 12, no. 12 (December 1910): 616-625.

Perry, John R. "The Last Safavids, 1722-1773." *Iran* (Journal of the British Institute of Persian Studies) 9 (1971): 59-69.

———. "Review of *Iran unter Karim Han* and *Die Zand-Dynastie.*" *Iranian Studies* 5, no. 4 (Autumn 1972): 184-188.

———. *Karim Khan Zand. A History of Iran, 1747-1779.* Chicago: University of Chicago Press, 1979.

Pesaran, M. H. "Income Distribution and Its Major Determinants in Iran." In *Iran: Past, Present and Future,* edited by Jane W. Jacqz, 267-286. New York: Aspen Institute for Humanistic Studies, 1976.

———. [Thomas Walton, pseud.]. "Economic Development and Revolutionary Upheavals in Iran." *Cambridge Journal of Economics* 4, no. 3 (September 1980): 271-292.

———. "The System of Dependent Capitalism in Pre- and Post-Revolutionary Iran." *International Journal of Middle East Studies* 14, no. 4 (November 1982): 501-522.

Petrushevsky, I. P. "The Socio-economic Condition of Iran under the Il-khans," in *The Cambridge History of Iran.* Vol. 3, *The Saljuq and Mongol Periods,* edited by J. A. Boyle, 483-537. Cambridge: Cambridge University Press, 1968.

Pigulevskaya, N. V., A. V. Yakubovsky, I. P. Petrushevsky, A. M. Belenitsky, and L. V. Stroeva. *Tarikh-i Iran az Dauran-i Bastan ta Payan-i Sadeh-i Hijdahumin-i Miladi* [History of Iran from Ancient Times till the End of the Eighteenth Century]. Translated from Russian to Persian by Karim Kishavarz. Tehran: Payam Press, 1354/1975.

Platt, D. C. M. *Finance, Trade, and Politics in British Foreign Policy, 1815-1914.* Oxford: Clarendon Press, 1968.

Pope, Arthur Upham, ed. *A Survey of Persian Art from Prehistoric Times to the Present.* Vol. 6, *Carpets, Metalwork and Minor Arts.* 1938-9. Reprint. London and New York: Oxford University Press, 1964-5.

Poulantzas, Nicos. *Political Power and Social Classes.* Translated from the French by Timothy O'Hagan. London: New Left Books, 1975.

Powers, Thomas. "A Book Held Hostage" (review of Kermit Roosevelt's *Countercoup: The Struggle for the Control of Iran*). *The Nation* 230, number 14 (April 12, 1980): 437-440.

Rabino, Joseph. "An Economist's Notes on Persia." *Journal of the Royal Statistical Society* 64 (June 1901): 265-291.

Ragin, Charles D. *The Comparative Method. Moving Beyond Quantitative and Qualitative Strategies.* Berkeley and Los Angeles: University of California Press, 1987.

Ramazani, Rouhollah K. *The Foreign Policy of Iran. A Developing Nation in World Affairs, 1500-1941.* Charlottesville, Virginia: University Press of Virginia, 1966.

Ramsbotham, Sir Peter. Interview recorded by Habib Ladjevardi, London, October 15, 1985. Harvard University, Iranian Oral History Collection.

Ravandi, Murtaza. *Tarikh-i Ijtima'i-yi Iran* [The Social History of Iran]. Several volumes. Second edition. Tehran, 1977.

"Recent Developments in Persia." *Journal of the Central Asian Society* 13, part 2 (1926): 130-32.

Reid, James J. "The Qajar Uymaq in The Safavid Period, 1500-1722." *Iranian Studies* 11 (1978), 117-143.

————. "Rebellion and Social Change in Astarabad, 1537-1744." *International Journal of Middle East Studies* 13 (1981): 35-53.

————. *Tribalism and Society in Islamic Iran, 1500-1629.* Malibu: Undena Publications, 1983.

Rey, Lucien. "Persia in Perspective." *New Left Review* nos. 19 (March-April 1963): 32-55, and 20 (Summer 1963): 69-98.

Rey, Pierre-Philippe. *Les Alliances de classes: Sur l'articulation des modes de production,* followed by *Materialisme historique et luttes de classes.* Paris: François Maspero, 1973.

Reznikov, A. B. "The Downfall of the Iranian Monarchy (January-February 1979)." In *The Revolutionary Process in the East: Past and Present,* edited by R. Ulyanovsky, 254-312. Moscow: Progress Publishers, 1985.

Rezun, Miron. "Reza Shah's Court Minister: Teymourtash." *International Journal of Middle East Studies* 12, no. 2 (September 1980): 119-137.

————. *The Iranian Crisis of 1941. The Actors: Britain, Germany and The Soviet Union.* Cologne and Vienna: Böhlau Verlag, 1982.

Ricks, Thomas M. "Towards a Social and Economic History of Eighteenth-Century Iran." *Iranian Studies* 6, nos. 2-3 (Spring-Summer 1973): 110-126.

————. "Politics and Trade in Southern Iran and the Gulf, 1745-1765." Ph.D. diss., Department of History, Indiana University, 1975.

"The Rise and Fall of Teymourtache." *Journal of the Royal Central Asian Society* 21, part 1 (January 1934): 93.

Roemer, H. R. "The Safavid Period." In *The Cambridge History of Iran.* Vol. 6, *The Timurid and Safavid Periods,* edited by Peter Jackson and Laurence Lockhart, 189-350. Cambridge: Cambridge University Press, 1986.

Rohrborn, Klaus-Michael. *Provinzen und Zentralgewalt Persiens im 16. und 17. Jahrhundert.* Berlin: Walter de Gruyter & Co., 1966.

Ronconi, Pio Filipanni. "The Tradition of Sacred Kingship in Iran." In *Iran Under the Pahlavis,* edited by George Lenczowski, 51-83. Stanford: Hoover Institution Press, 1978.

Roosevelt, Kermit. *Countercoup. The Struggle for the Control of Iran.* New York: McGraw-Hill, 1979.

Roosevelt, Jr., Archie. "The Kurdish Republic of Mahabad." *Middle East Journal* 1, no. 3 (July 1947): 247-269.

Rossow, Jr., Robert. "The Battle of Azerbaijan, 1946." *Middle East Journal* 10, number 1 (Winter 1956): 17-32.

Rumlu, Hasan. *Ahsan al-tavarikh. A Chronicle of the early Safawis.* Edited and translated by Charles Norman Seddon. 2 vols. Baroda: Gaekwad's Oriental Series, 1931.

Sadrzadeh, Ziya al-Din. *Saderat-i Iran* [Exports of Iran]. Tehran, 1346/1967-68. Extracts translated in *The Economic History of Iran: 1800-1914,* edited by Charles Issawi, 148-151. Chicago and London: University of Chicago Press, 1971.

Saikal, Amin. *The Rise and Fall of the Shah.* Princeton: Princeton University Press, 1980.

Saleh, Jahangir. "Social Formations in Iran, 750-1914." Ph.D. diss., Department of Economics, University of Massachusetts, Amherst, 1978.

Samii, Kuross A. *Involvement by Invitation. American Strategies of Containment in Iran.* University Park, Pennsylvania, and London: The Pennsylvania State University Press, 1987.

Savory, Roger M. "Safavid Persia." In *The Cambridge History of Islam*. Vol. 1, *The Central Islamic Lands*, edited by P. M. Holt, Ann K. S. Lambton and Bernard Lewis, 394-429. Cambridge: Cambridge University Press, 1970.

————. "British and French Diplomacy in Persia, 1800-1810." *Iran* (Journal of the British Institute of Persian Studies) 10 (1972): 31-44.

————. "The Safavid State and Polity." *Iranian Studies* 7, nos. 1-2 (1974): 179-212.

————. "Social Development in Iran during the Pahlavi Era." In *Iran Under the Pahlavis*, edited by George Lenczowski, 85-128. Stanford: Hoover Institution Press, 1978.

————. *Iran under the Safavids*. Cambridge: Cambridge University Press, 1980.

————. "The Safavid Administrative System." In *The Cambridge History of Iran*. Vol. 6, *The Timurid and Safavid Periods*, edited by Peter Jackson and Laurence Lockhart, 351-372. Cambridge: Cambridge University Press, 1986.

Scott, James C. *Domination and the Arts of Resistance. Hidden Transcripts*. New Haven and London: Yale University Press. 1990.

Sewell, William H. Jr. "Ideologies and Social Revolutions: Reflections on the French Case." *Journal of Modern History* 57, no. 1 (March 1985): 57-85.

Seyf, Ahmad. "Some Aspects of Economic Development in Iran, 1800-1906." Ph.D. diss., Department of Agricultural Economics and Management, University of Reading, 1982.

————. "Silk Production and Trade in Iran in the Nineteenth Century." *Iranian Studies* 16, nos. 1-2 (Winter-Spring 1983): 51-71.

————. "Commercialization of Agriculture: Production and Trade of Opium in Persia, 1850-1906." *International Journal of Middle East Studies* 16, no. 2 (May 1984): 233-250.

Seyfollahi, Seyfollah. "Development of the Dependent Bourgeoisie in Iran, 1962-1978." Ph.D. diss., Department of Sociology, Michigan State University, 1982.

Shahshahani, Reza. "The Background of Iranian Affairs." *Science & Society* X, no. 2 (Spring 1946): 113-131.

Shari'ati, 'Ali. *From Where Shall We Begin? & The Machine in the Captivity of Machinism*. Translated from the Persian by Fatollah Marjani. Houston: Free Islamic Literatures, Inc., 1980.

————. *Marxism and Other Western Fallacies. An Islamic Critique*. Translated from the Persian by R. Campbell. Berkeley: Mizan Press, 1980.

Sheean, Vincent. *The New Persia*. New York and London: The Century Co., 1927.

Shuster, W. Morgan. *The Strangling of Persia*. New York: The Century Co., 1912.

Sivanandan, A. "Imperialism in the Silicon Age." *Monthly Review* 32, no. 3 (July-August 1980): 24-42. First published in *Race and Class* (Autumn 1979).

Skocpol, Theda. "Wallerstein's World Capitalist System: A Theoretical and Historical Critique." *American Journal of Sociology* 82, no. 5 (1977): 1075-1090.

————. *States and Social Revolutions. A Comparative Analysis of France, Russia, and China*. Cambridge: Cambridge University Press, 1979.

————. "Rentier State and Shi'a Islam in the Iranian Revolution." *Theory & Society* 11, no. 3 (1982): 265-284.

————. "Emerging Agendas and Recurrent Strategies in Historical Sociology." In *Vision and Method in Historical Sociology*, edited by Theda Skocpol, 356-391. Cambridge: Cambridge University Press, 1984.

————. "Cultural Idioms and Political Ideologies in the Revolutionary Reconstruction of State Power: A Rejoinder to Sewell." *Journal of Modern History* 57, no. 1 (March 1985): 86-96.

————. "Analyzing Causal Configurations in History: A Rejoinder to Nichols." In *Comparative Social Research. An Annual Publication*, volume 9, *Historical Studies*, 187-194. Greenwich, Connecticut and London: JAI Press, Inc., 1986.

Skocpol, Theda and Margaret Somers. "The Uses of Comparative History in Macrosocial Inquiry." *Comparative Studies in Society and History* 22, no. 2 (April 1980): 174-197.

Social Forces. Special issue on "Rethinking Petty Commodity Production." Volume 20 (1986).

Sreberny-Mohammadi, Annabelle. "The Power of Tradition: Communication and the Iranian Revolution." Ph.D. diss., Department of Communications, Columbia University, 1985.

Steensgaard, Niels. *The Asian Trade Revolution of the Seventeenth Century. The East India Companies and the Decline of the Caravan Trade*. Chicago and London: The University of Chicago Press, 1974.

Stobaugh, Robert B. "The Evolution of Iranian Oil Policy, 1925-1975." In *Iran Under the Pahlavis*, edited by George Lenczowski, 201-252. Stanford: Hoover Institution Press, 1978.

le Strange, Guy. Ed. and trans. *Don Juan of Persia, a Shi'ah Catholic (1560-1604)*. London: Broadway Travellers, 1927.

Sullivan, William H. "Dateline Iran: The Road Not Taken." *Foreign Policy* 40 (Fall 1980): 175-186.

Swietochowski, Tadeusz. *Russian Azerbaijan, 1905-1920. The Shaping of National Identity in a Muslim Community*. Cambridge: Cambridge University Press, 1985.

Tabari, Ehsan. *Jam'eh-i Iran dar Dauran-i Riza Shah* [Iranian Society in the Reza Shah Period]. Stockholm: Tudeh Publishing Center, 1356/1977.

Tapper, Richard. "Black Sheep, White Sheep and Red Heads. A Historical Sketch of the Shahsavan of Azerbaijan." *Iran* (Journal of the British Institute of Persian Studies) 4 (1966): 61-84.

Tavernier, Jean Baptiste. *Voyages en Perse*. Paris: Les Libraires Associés, 1964.

Taylor, John G. *From Modernization to Modes of Production. A Critique of the Sociologies of Development and Underdevelopment*. London: Macmillan, 1979.

Ter-Gukasov, G. I. *Politicheskie i ekonomicheskie interesy Rossii v Persii* [Political and Economic Interests of Russia in Persia]. Petrograd, 1916. Extracts translated in *The Economic History of Iran: 1800-1914*, edited by Charles Issawi, 144-146. Chicago and London: University of Chicago Press, 1971.

Ter Yovhaneanc, I. P. Yarutiwn. *Patmutiwm Nor Julayu u Aspahan*. New Julfa, 1881. Extracts translated in *The Economic History of Iran: 1800-1914*, edited by Charles Issawi, 59-62. Chicago and London: University of Chicago Press, 1971.

Thiemann, Erhard. "Iran Under the Shah Regime: Model of Dependent Capitalist Industrialization." In *Iran: From Monarchy to Republic*, edited by Günter Barthel, 88-102. Special issue no. 12 of *Asia, Africa, Latin America*. East Berlin: Akademie-Verlag, 1983.

Thompson, Reverend R. J. "Conditions of Daily Life in Iran, 1947." *Journal of the Royal Central Asian Society* 35, parts 3-4 (July-October 1948): 199-208.

Three Reports of the Select Committee Appointed by the Court of Directors. London: n.d. [ca. 1792]. In *The Economic History of Iran: 1800-1914*, edited by Charles Issawi, 85-89. Chicago and London: University of Chicago Press, 1971.

Trimberger, Ellen K. *Revolution from Above. Military Bureaucrats and Development in Japan, Turkey, Egypt and Peru*. New Brunswick, New Jersey: Transaction Books, 1978.

Turner, Terisa. "Iranian Oilworkers in the 1978-79 Revolution." In *Oil and Class Struggle*, edited by Petter Nore and Terisa Turner, 272-292. London: Zed Press, 1980.

Ullman, Richard H. *Anglo-Soviet Relations, 1917-1921*. Vol. 3: *The Anglo-Soviet Accord*. Princeton: Princeton University Press, 1972.

Upton, Joseph. *The History of Modern Iran: An Interpretation*. Cambridge: Cambridge University Press, 1968.

Wallerstein, Immanuel. *The Modern World-System I. Capitalist Agriculture and the Origins of the European World-Economy in the Sixteenth Century*. New York: Academic Press, 1974.

———. *The Capitalist World Economy. Selected Essays*. Cambridge: Cambridge University Press, 1979.

———. *The Modern World-System II. Mercantilism and the Consolidation of the European World-Economy, 1600-1750*. New York: Academic Press, 1980.

———. *The Modern World-System III. The Second Era of Great Expansion of the Capitalist World-Economy, 1730-1840s*. New York: Academic Press, 1989.

Weber, Max. *Economy and Society. An Outline of Interpretive Sociology.* Edited by Guenther Roth and Claus Wittich. 2 vols. Berkeley, Los Angeles and London: University of California Press, 1978.

Weir, T. H. "The Revolution in Persia at the Beginning of the 18th Century (from a Turkish MS in the University of Glasgow." In *'Ajabnameh. A Volume of Oriental Studies presented to Edward G. Browne,* edited by T. W. Arnold and Reynold A. Nicholson, 480-490. Cambridge: At the University Press, 1922.

Wilber, Donald N. *Riza Shah Pahlavi: The Resurrection and Reconstruction of Iran.* Hicksville, New York: Exposition Press, 1975.

Wilson, Sir Arnold. *The Persian Gulf.* London: Oxford University Press, 1928.

Wolf, Eric R. *Peasant Wars of the Twentieth Century.* New York: Harper & Roe, 1969.

Wolpe, Harold, ed. *The articulation of modes of production. Essays from Economy and Society.* London: Routledge and Kegan Paul, 1980.

Wright, Denis. *The English Amongst the Persians During the Qajar Period 1787-1921.* London: Heinemann, 1977.

————. *The Persians Amongst the English. Episodes in Anglo-Persian History.* London: I. B. Tauris, 1985.

Yaghmaian, Behzad. "Economic Development, Land Reform and Imports Substitution: The Case of Iran." Ph.D. diss., Department of Economics, Fordham University, 1985.

Yar-Shater, Ehsan. "Safavid Literature: Progress or Decline?" *Iranian Studies* 7, no. 2 (1974): 217-270.

Zabih, Sepehr. *Iran's Revolutionary Upheaval: An Interpretive Essay.* San Francisco: Alchemy Books, 1979.

————. *The Mossadegh Era. Roots of the Iranian Revolution.* Chicago: Lake View Press, 1982.

————. *The Left in Contemporary Iran. Ideology, Organisation and the Soviet Connection.* London and Sydney: Croom Helm, and Stanford: Hoover Institution Press, 1986.

Zafarian, Hossein. "Analytical Approach to Correlation Between Marxism and Iran's Islamic Revolution." Ph.D. diss., Department of International Relations, Claremont Graduate School, 1984.

Zavareei, Manizheh. "Dependent Capitalist Development in Iran and the Mass Uprising of 1979." In *Research in Political Economy: A Research Annual,* edited by Paul Zarembka, 139-188. Greenwich, CT., and London: JAI Press, 1982.

Zeitlin, Maurice. *The Civil Wars in Chile (or the bourgeois revolutions that never were).* Princeton: Princeton University Press, 1984.

Zirinsky, Michael P. "Blood, Power, and Hypocrisy: The Murder of Robert Imbrie and American Relations with Pahlavi Iran, 1924." *International Journal of Middle East Studies* 18, no. 3 (August 1986): 275-292.

Index

About the Book and Author

This book traces the transformation of Iran's social structure from the rise of the Safavid dynasty in 1501 to the dramatic social movements of the twentieth century. Rooted in the current debates in the sociology of development, the book offers a new assessment of the encounter of Iran with the West in light of a variety of social science theories including world systems, dependency, and political culture.

John Foran presents a new synthesis of Iranian history, arguing that Iranian social structure is the historical product of both internal and external dynamics and that commercial, political, and military relations with the West shaped social arrangements in ways that activated a series of "populist" movements of resistance. He maintains that these movements have been only partially successful because they rested on fragile social bases and because foreign powers have continued to intervene in the country's affairs. Foran excels in making the 1979 Islamic Revolution intelligible in terms of Iran's history.

John Foran is assistant professor of sociology at the University of California–Santa Barbara.